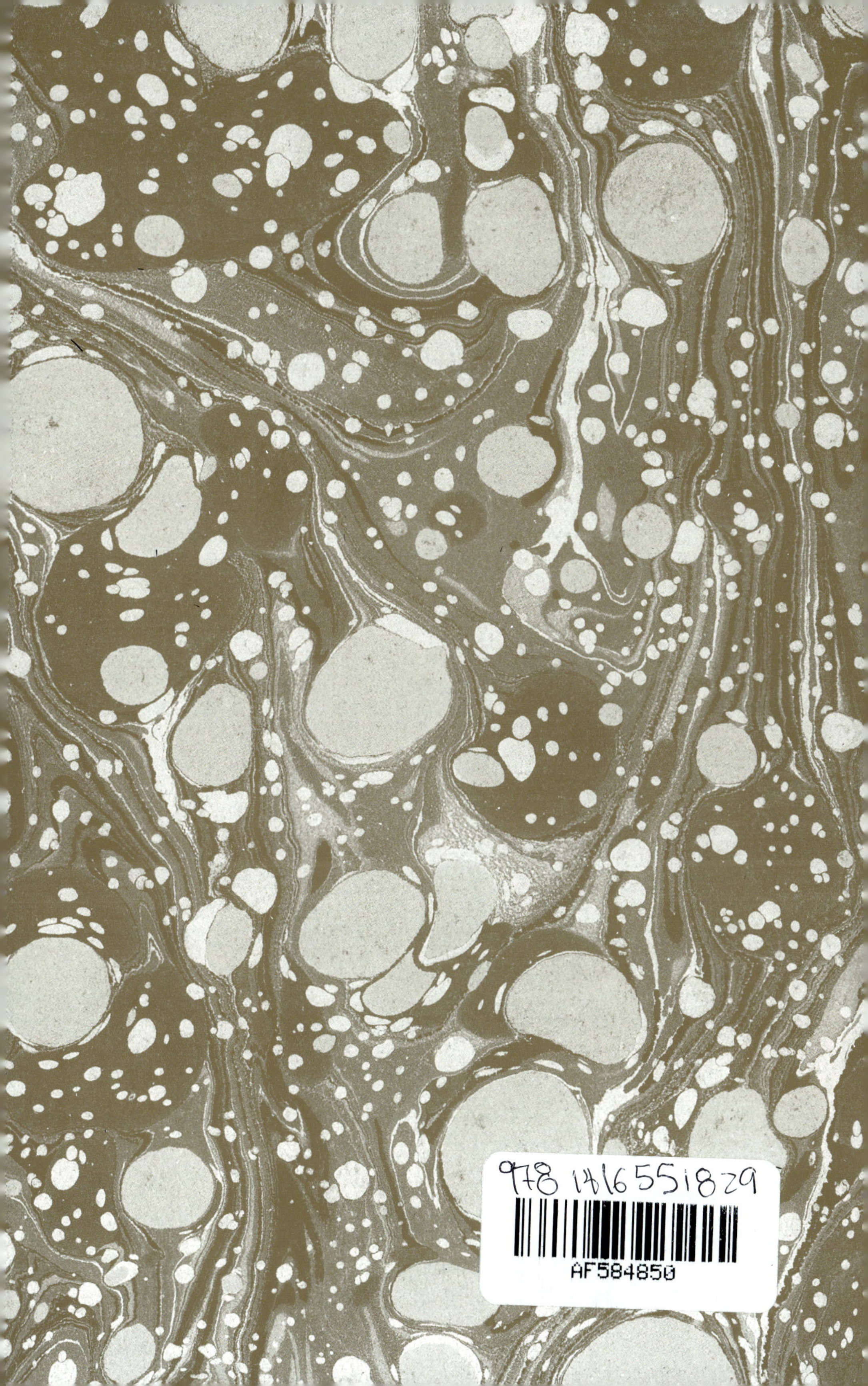
978 1416551829
AF584850

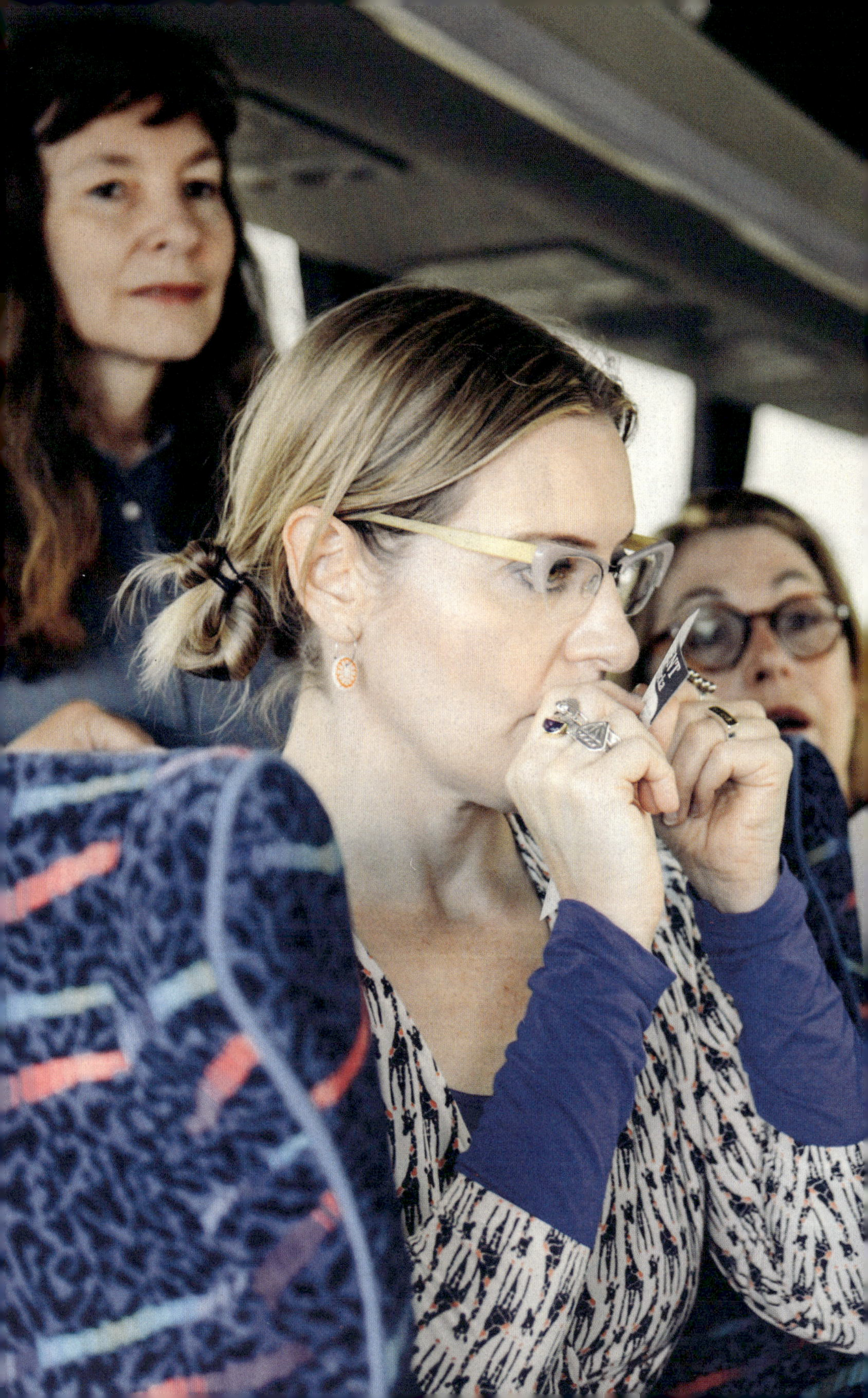

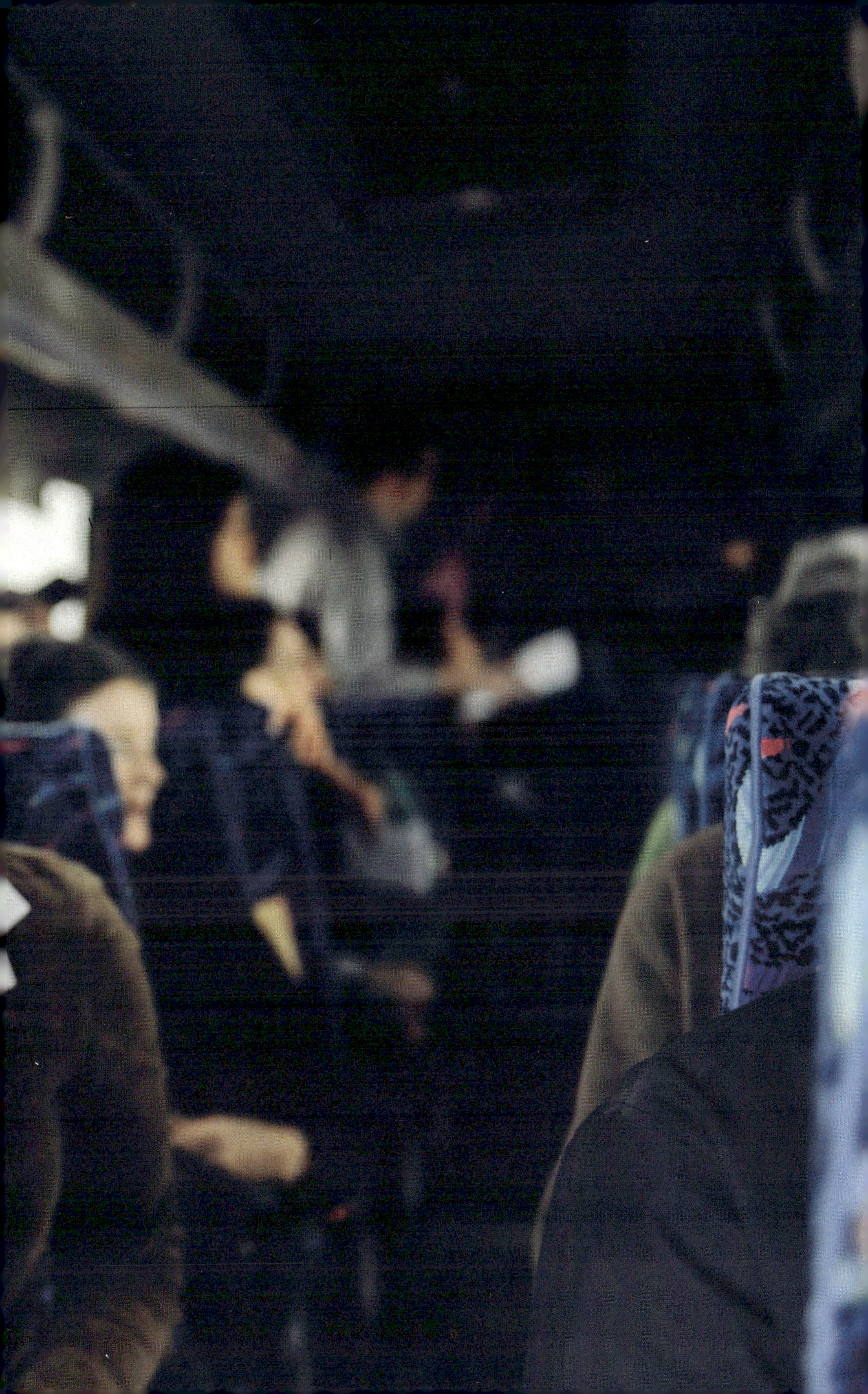

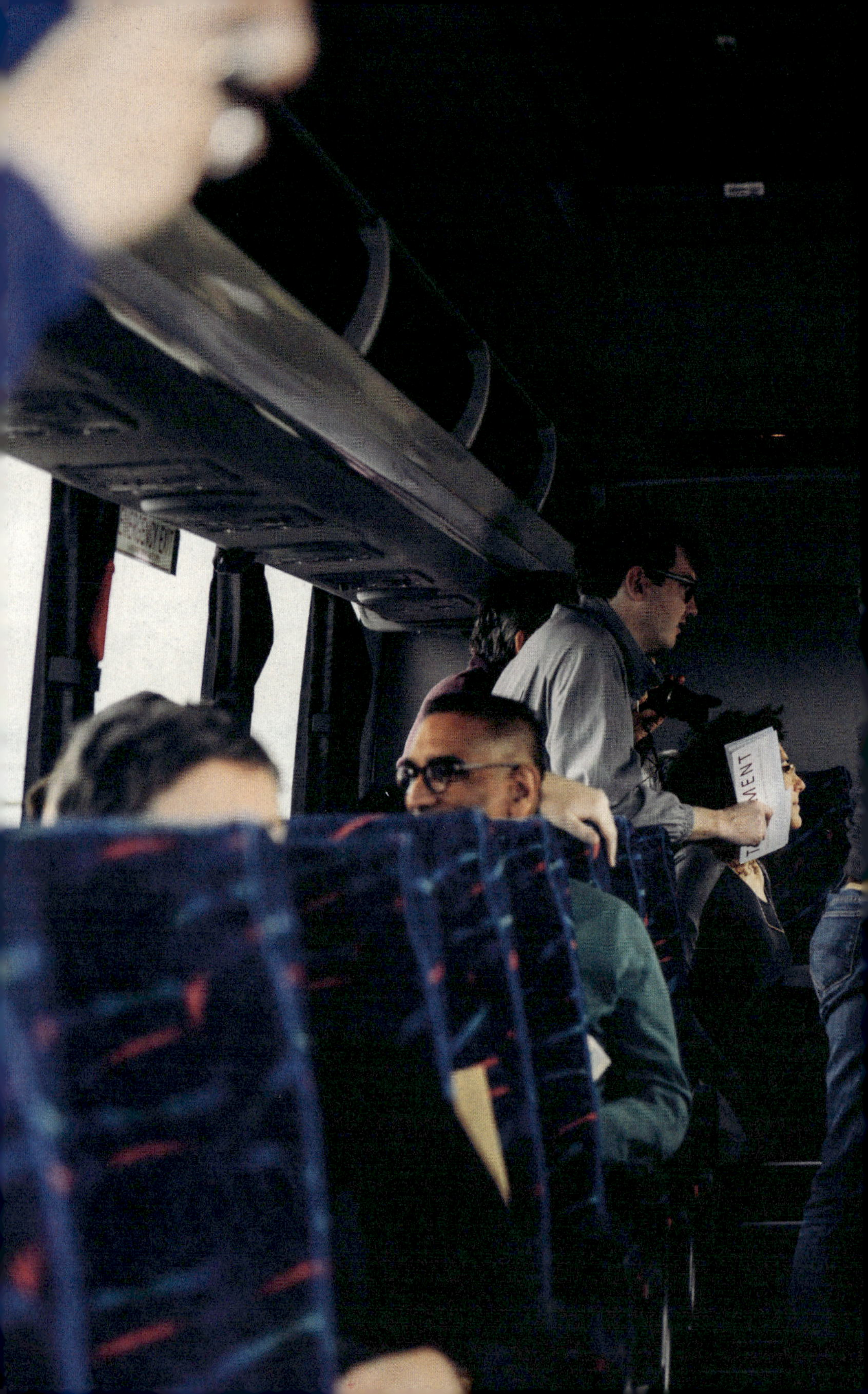
MENT

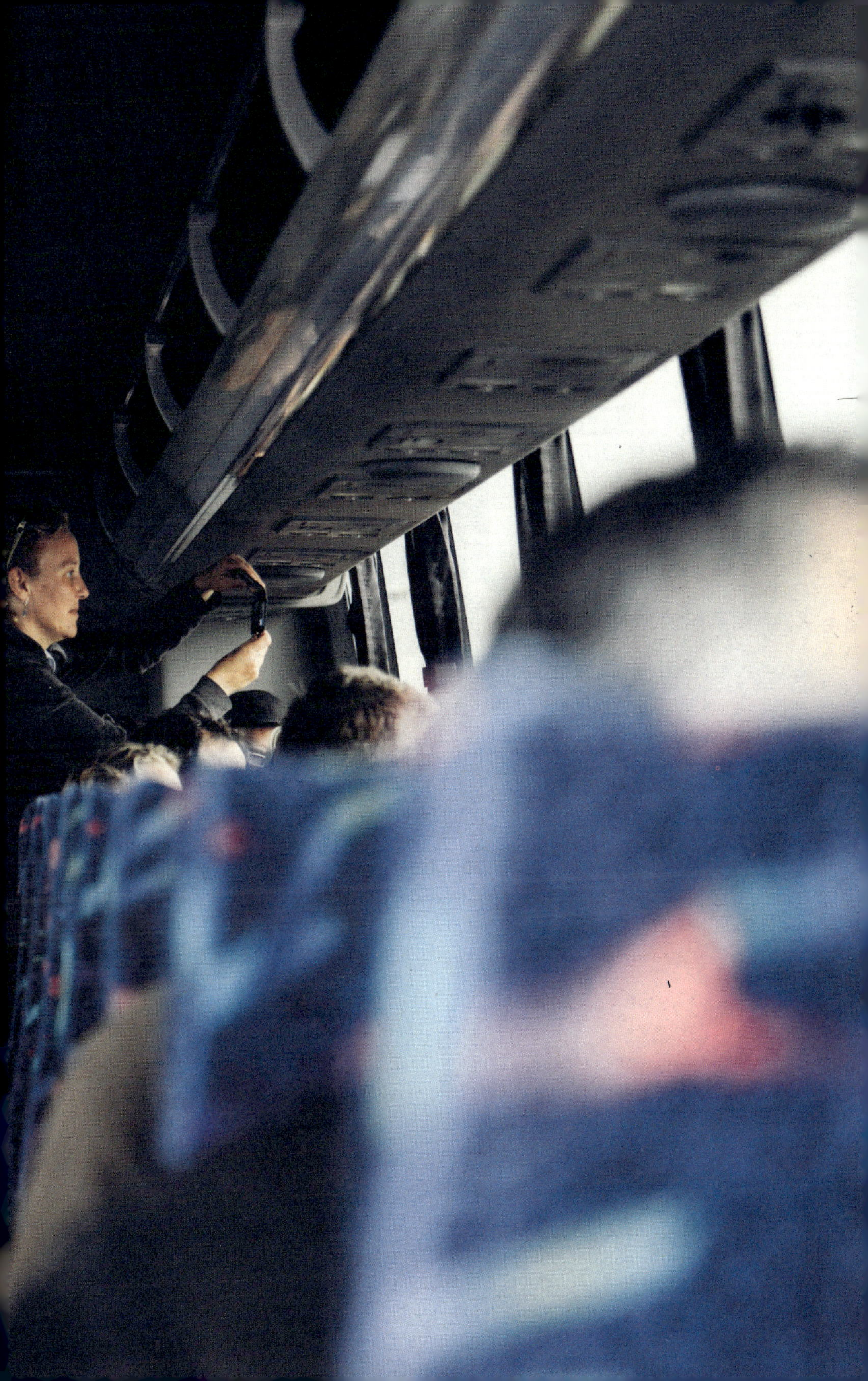

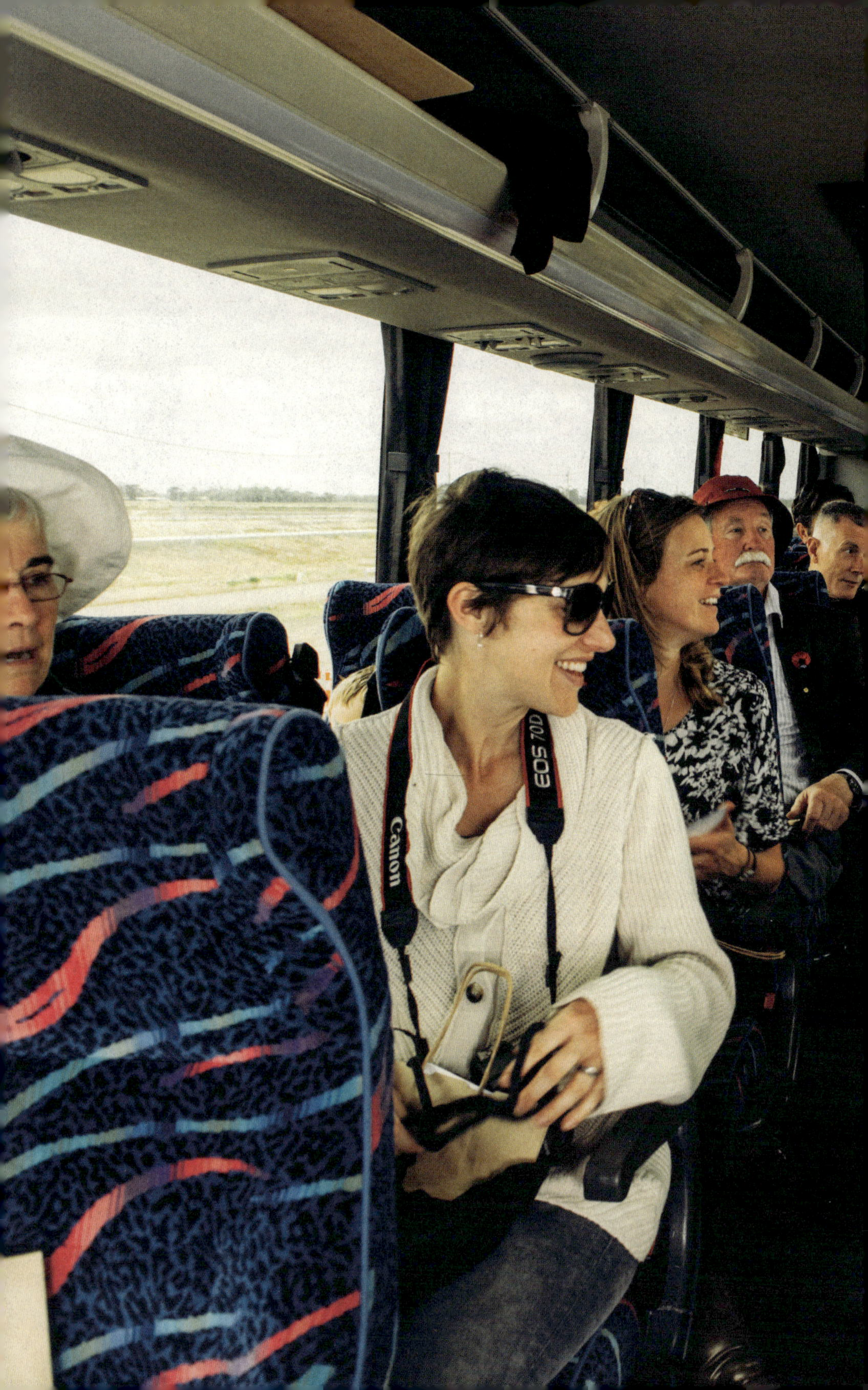
EOS 70D
Canon

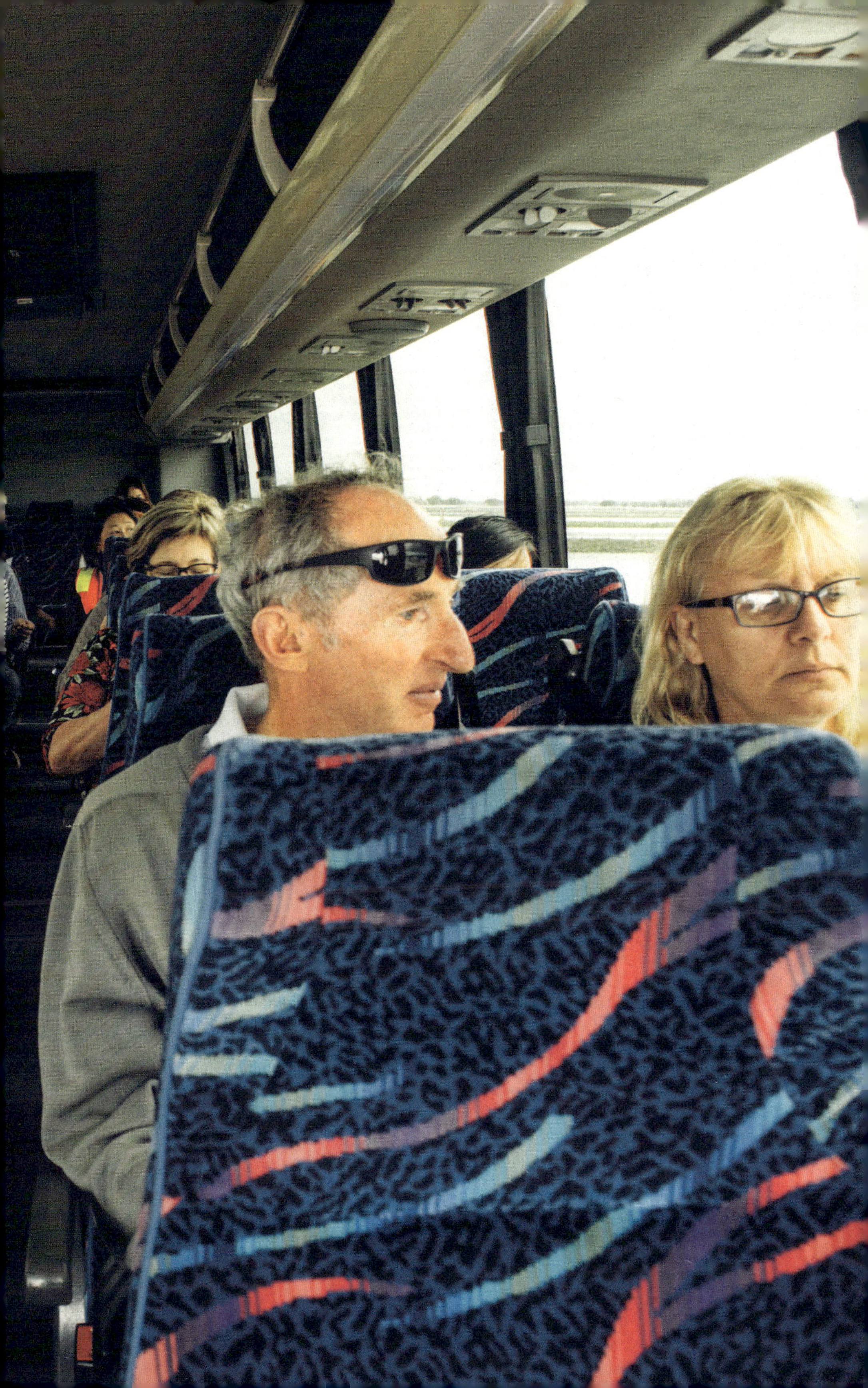

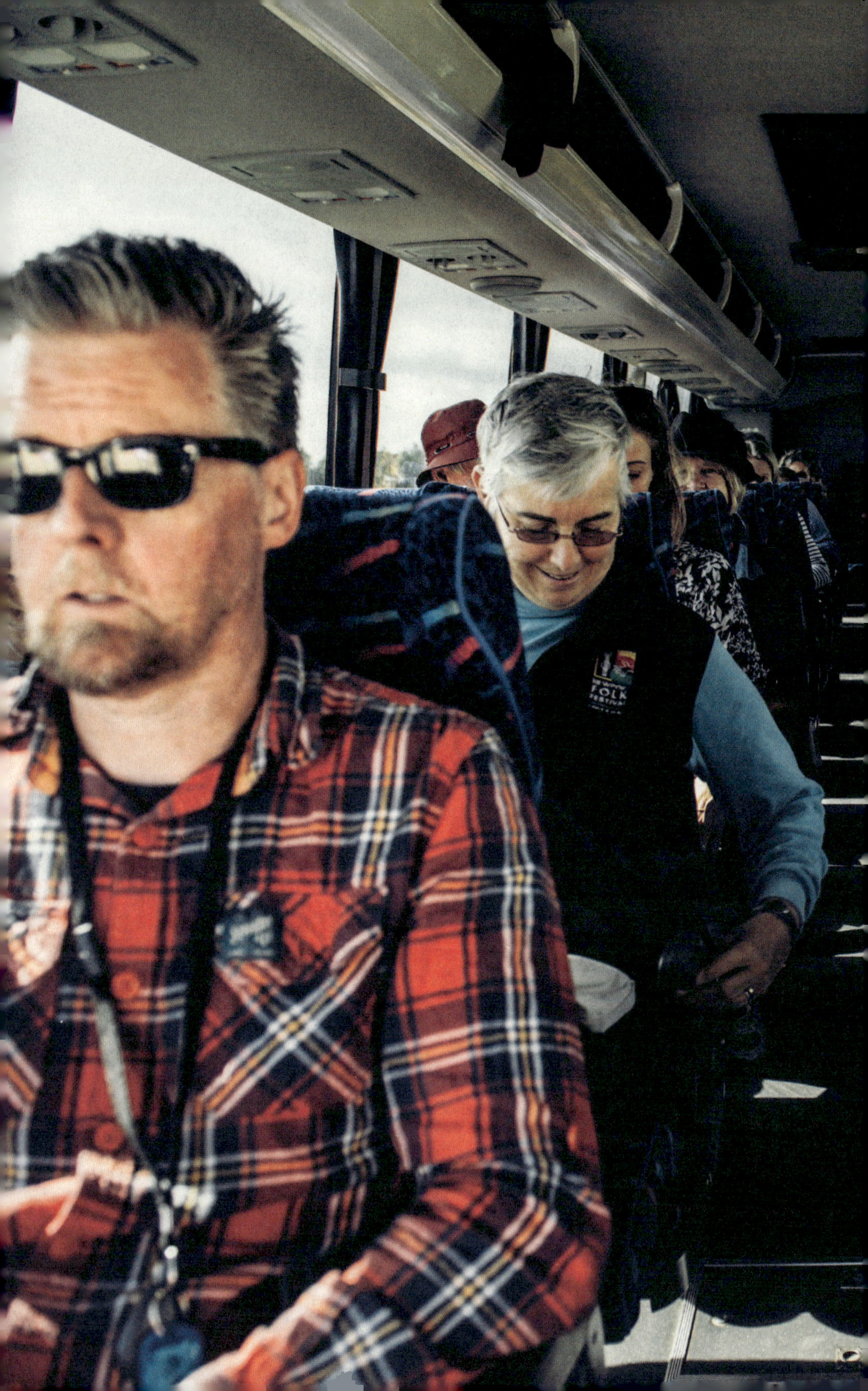
FOLK

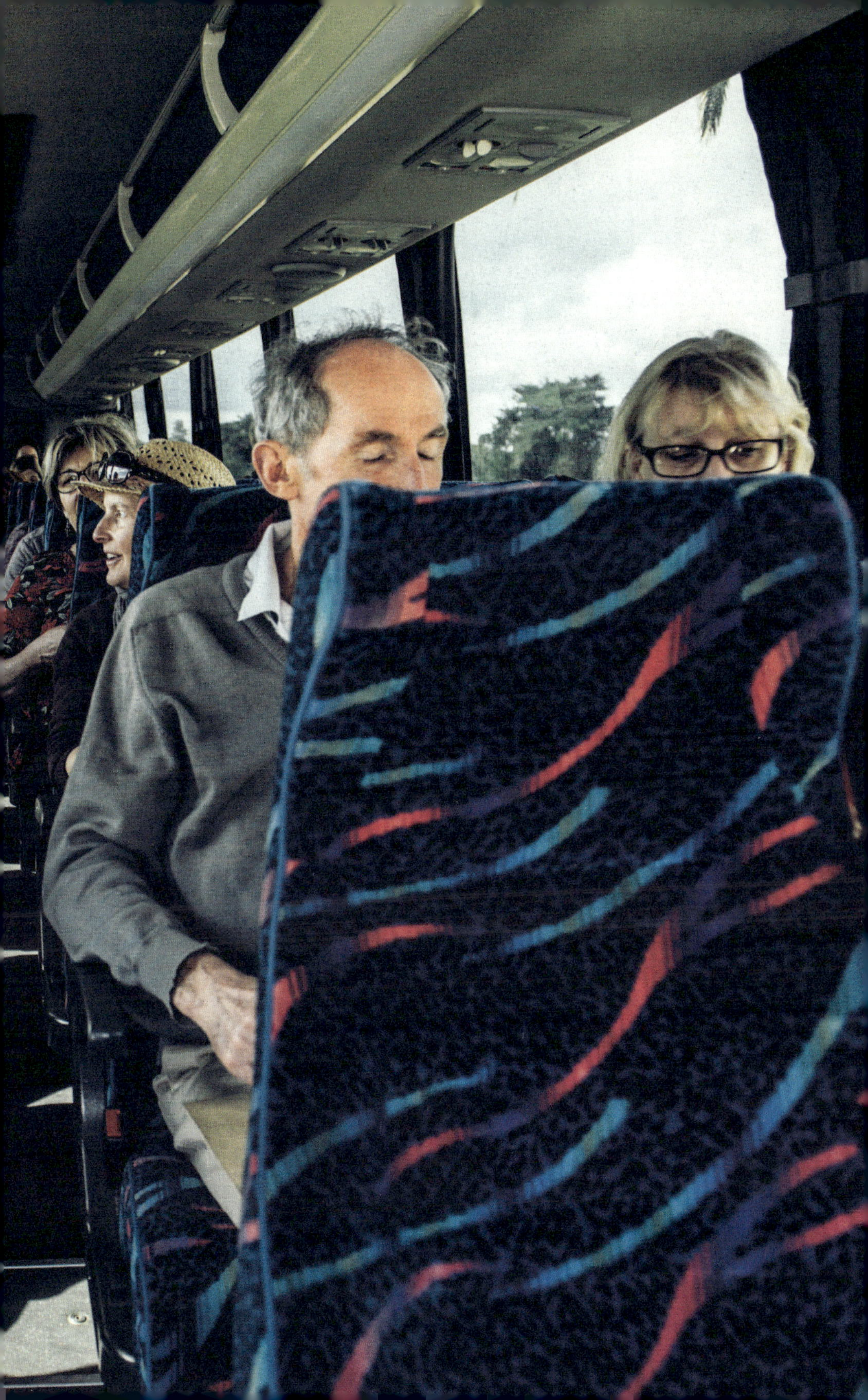

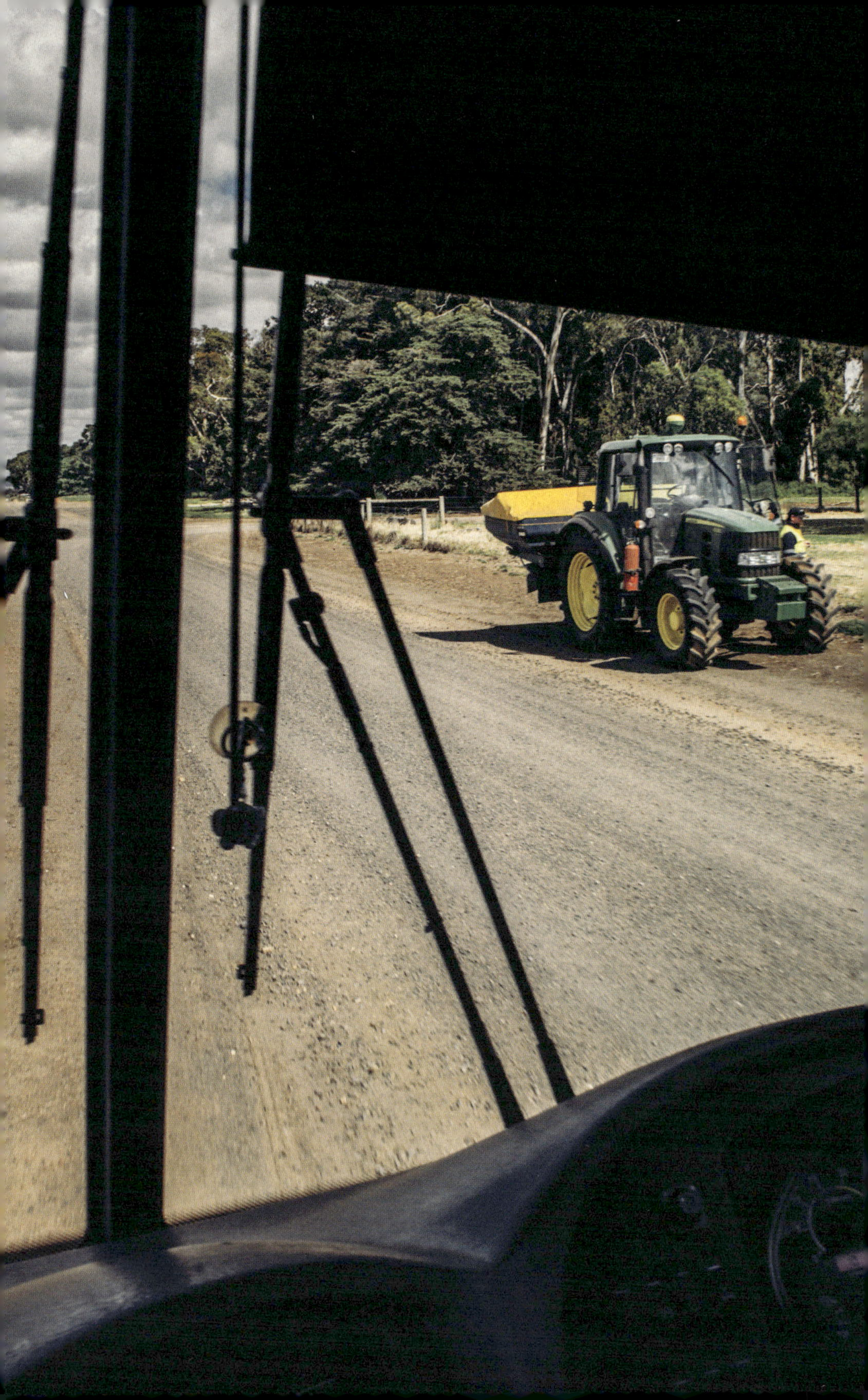

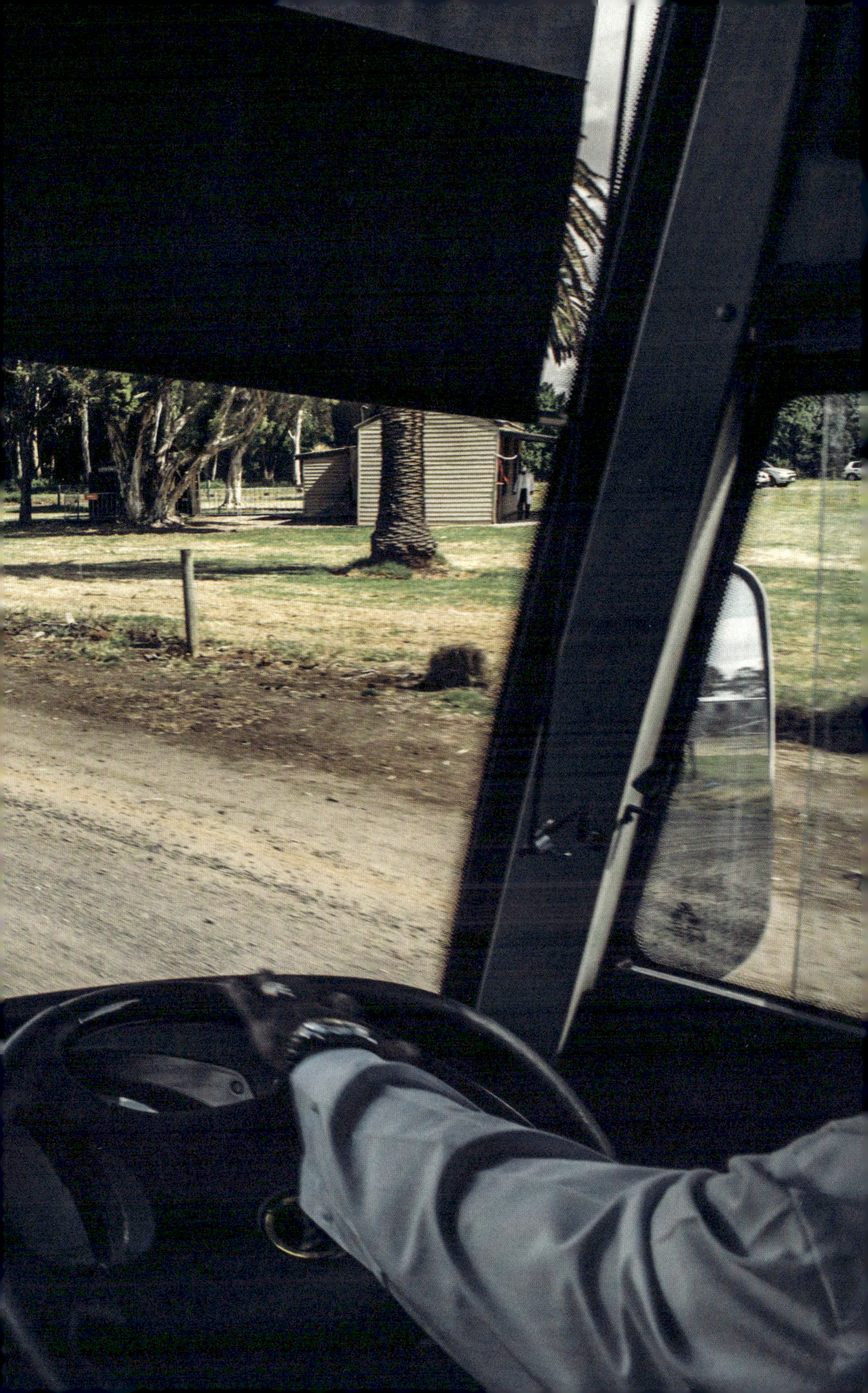

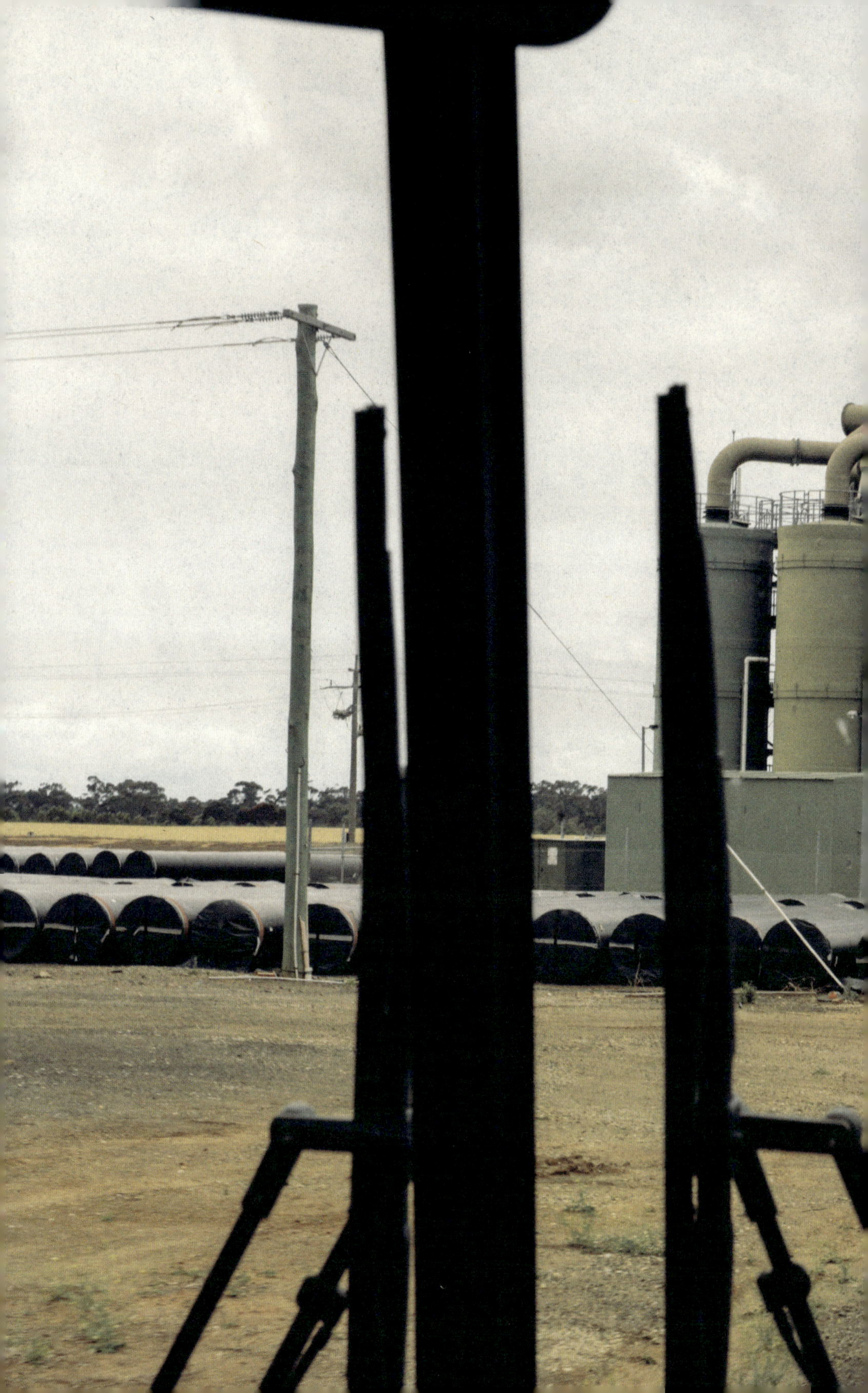

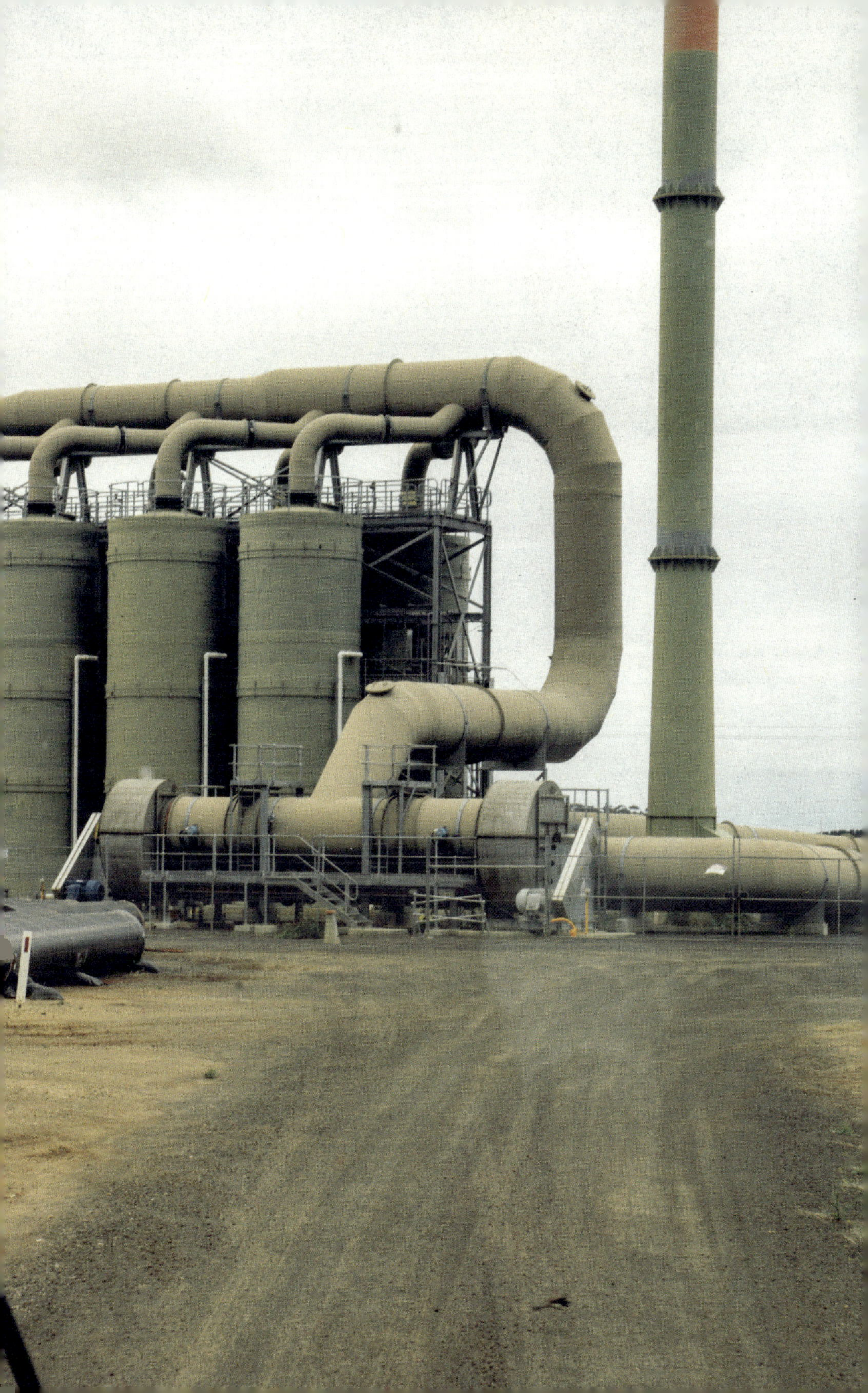

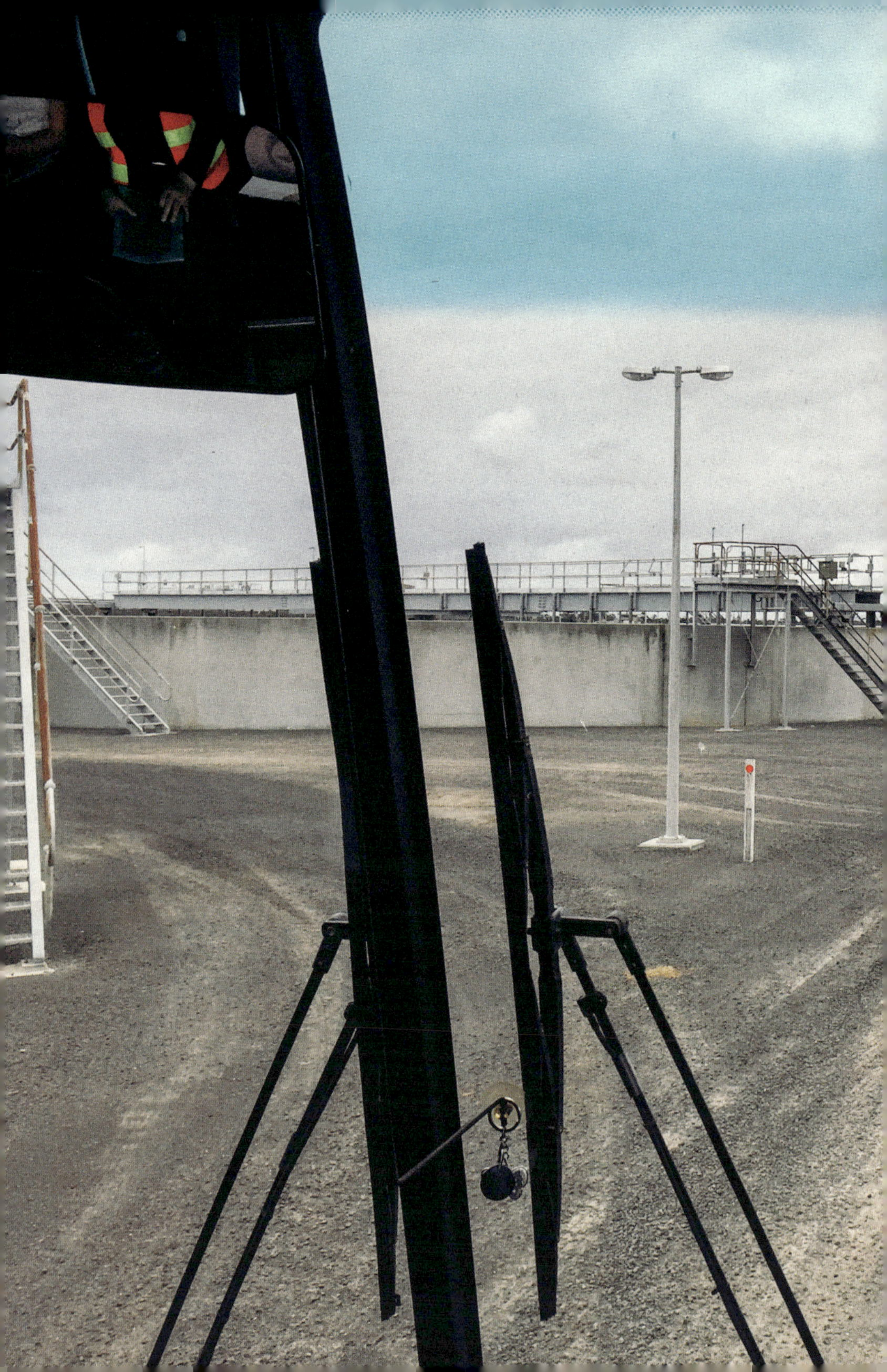

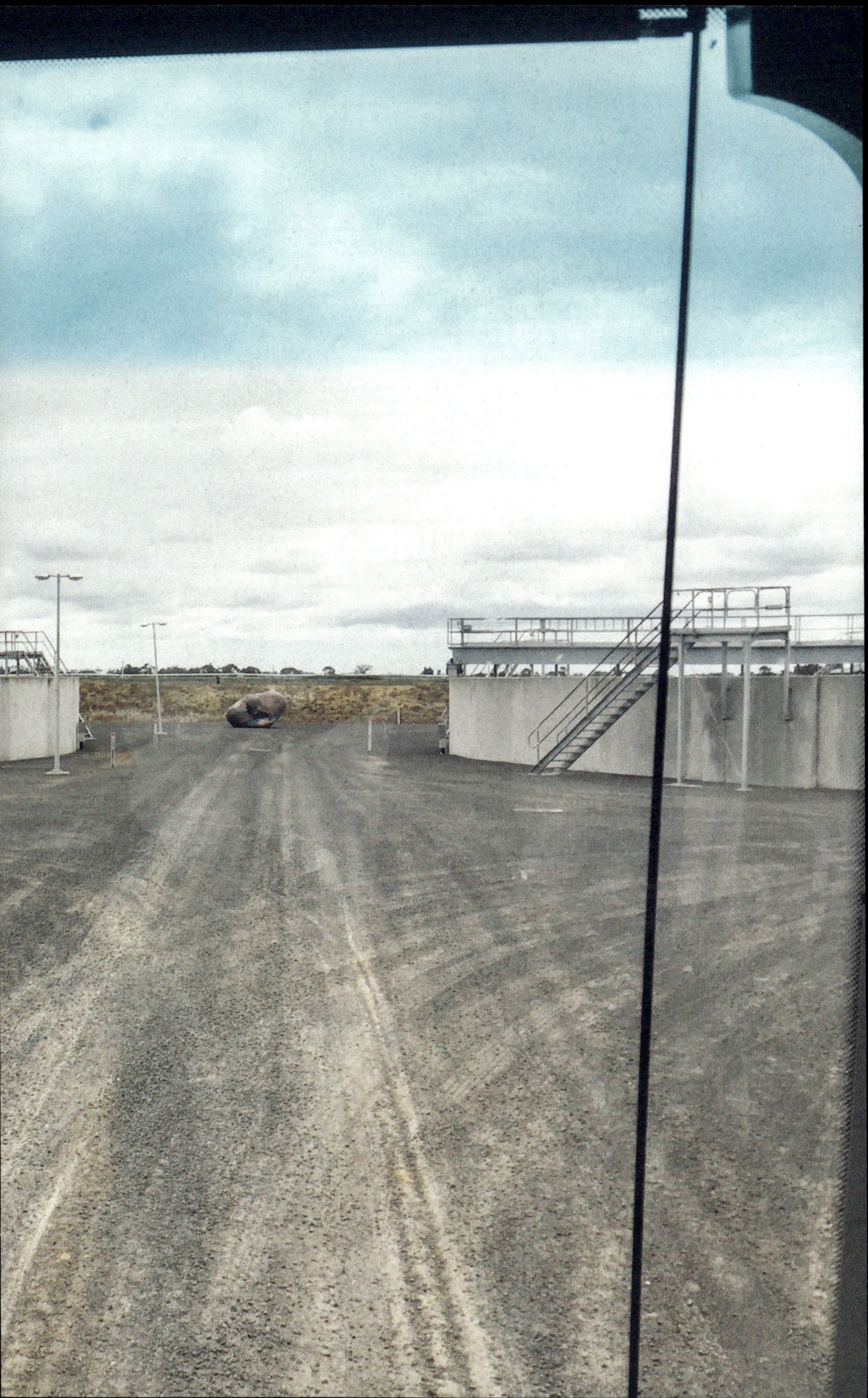

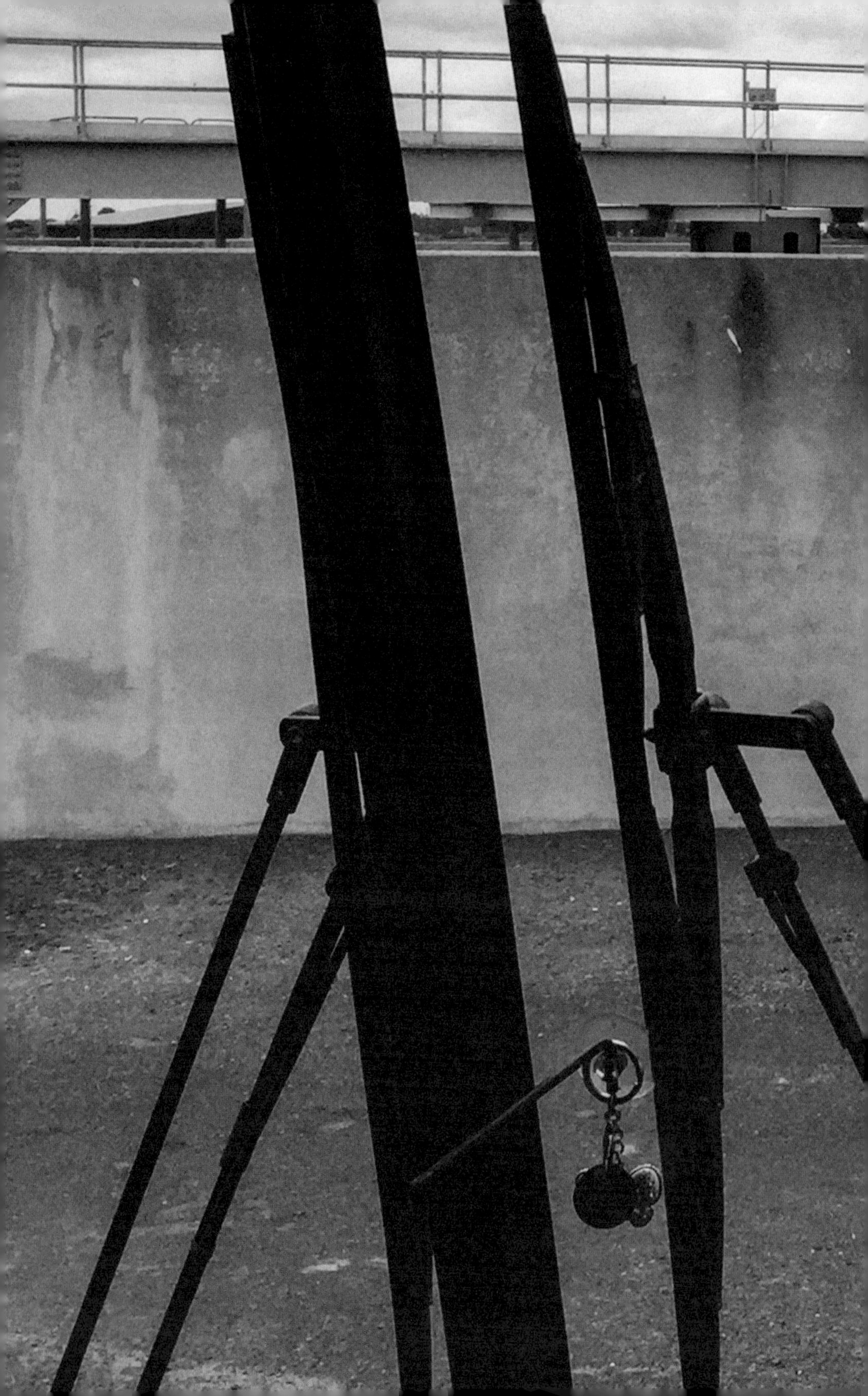

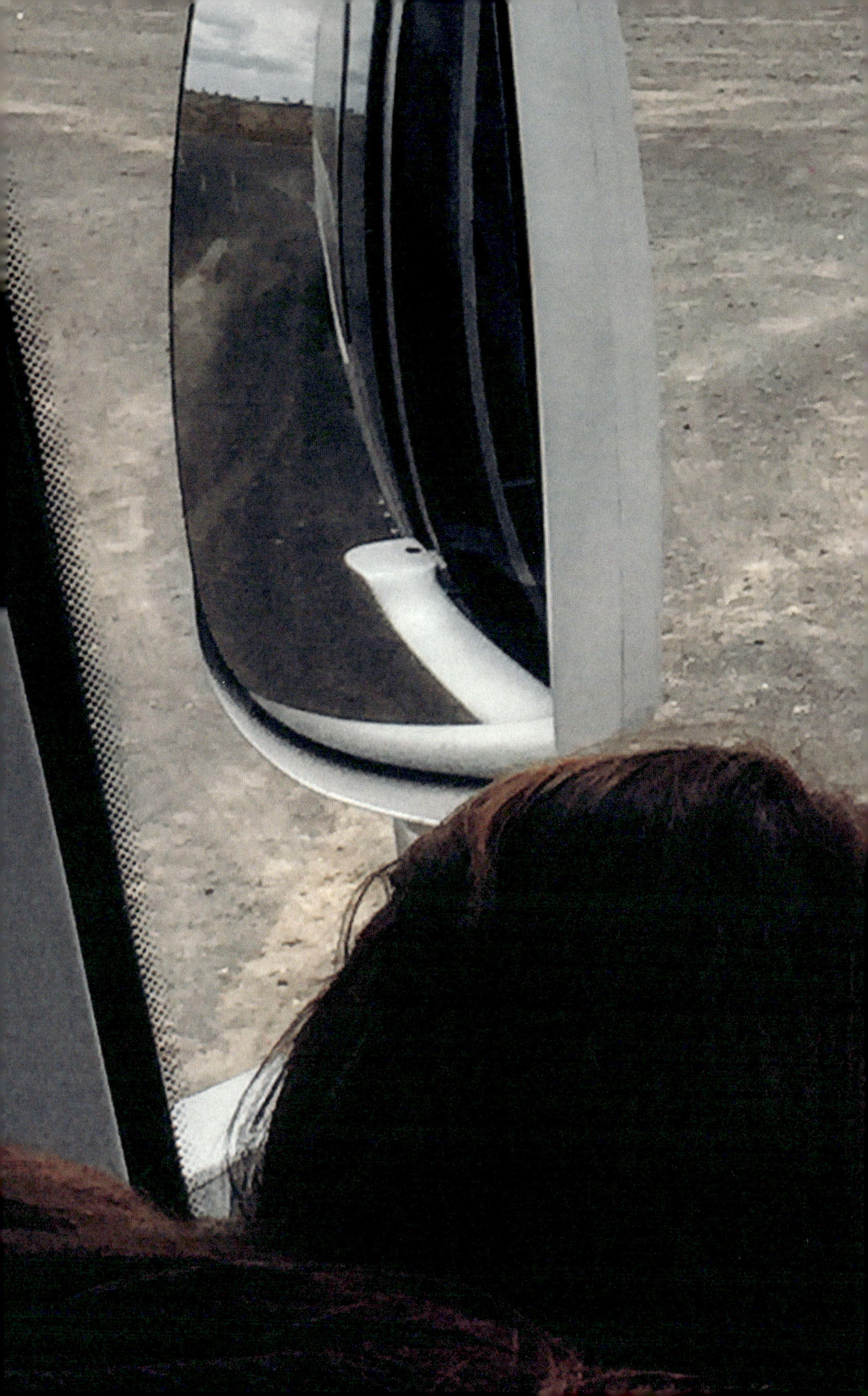

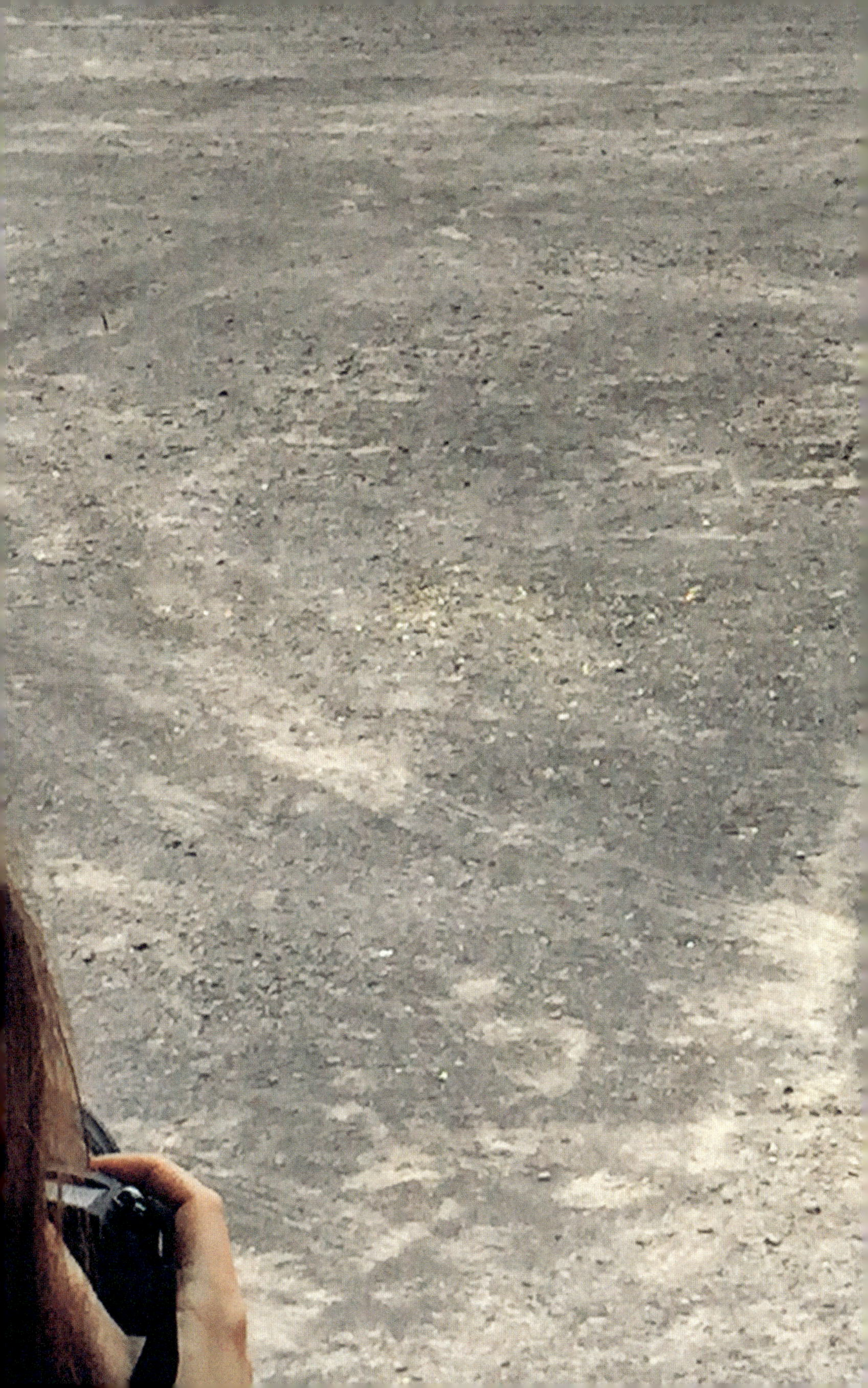

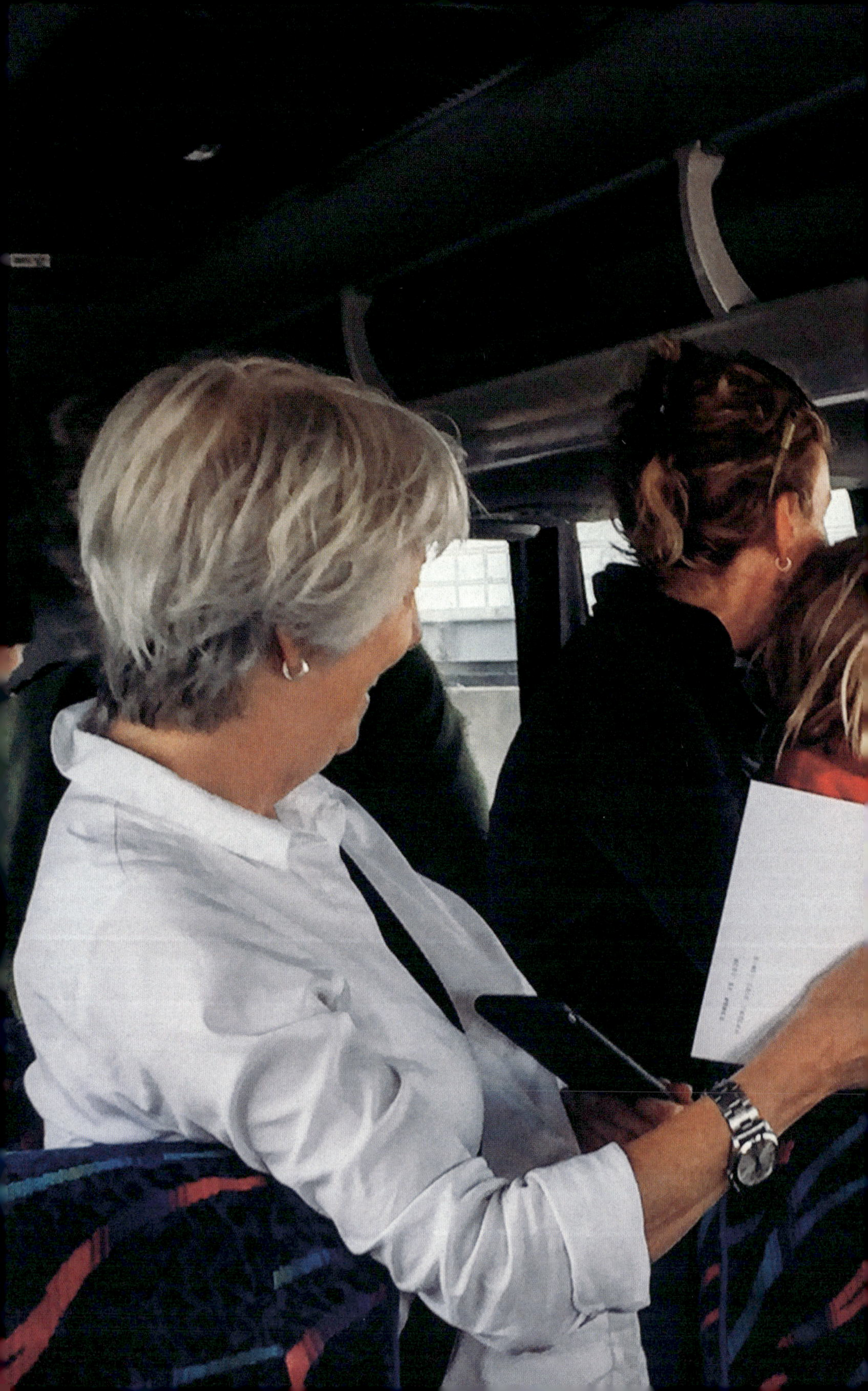

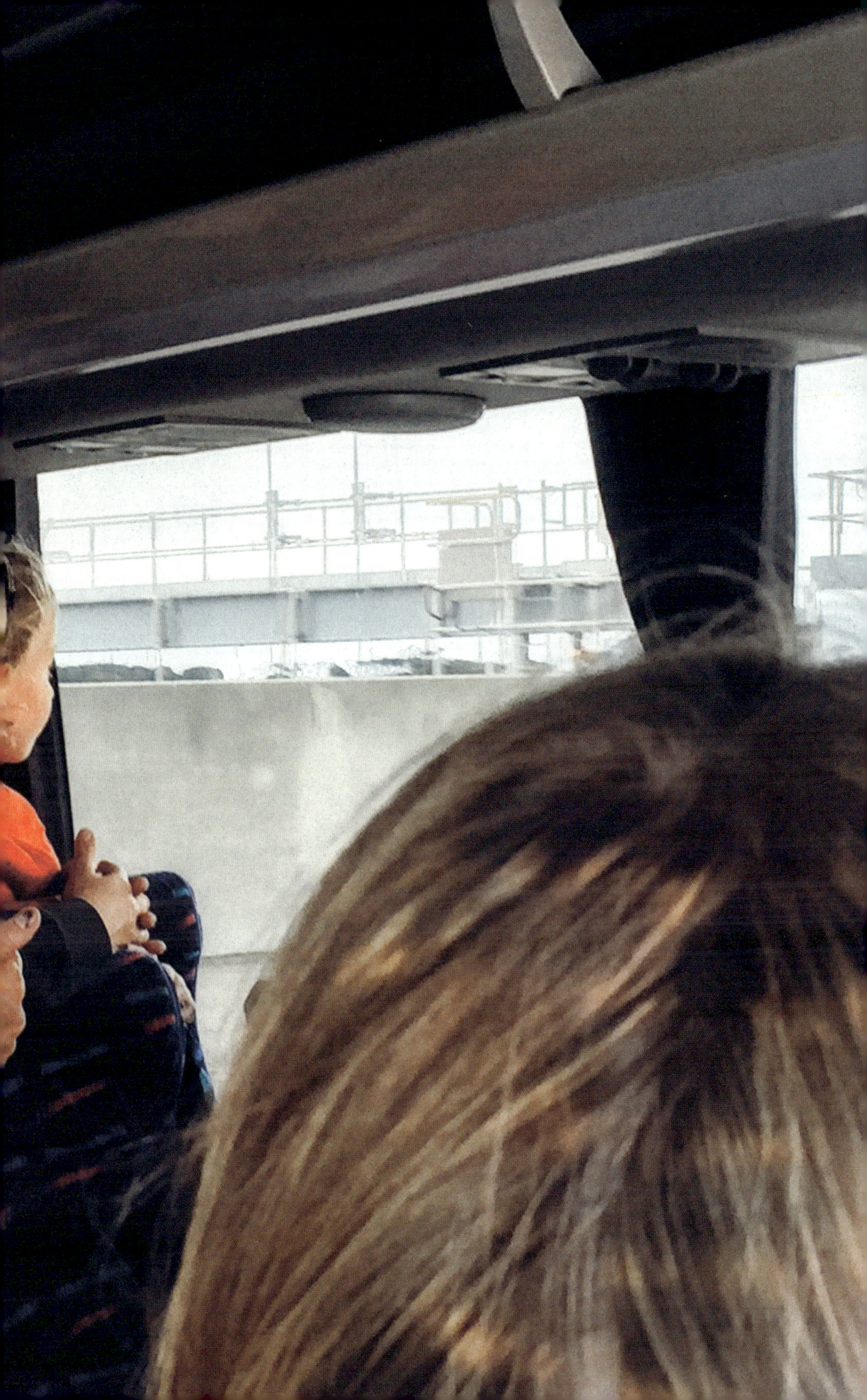

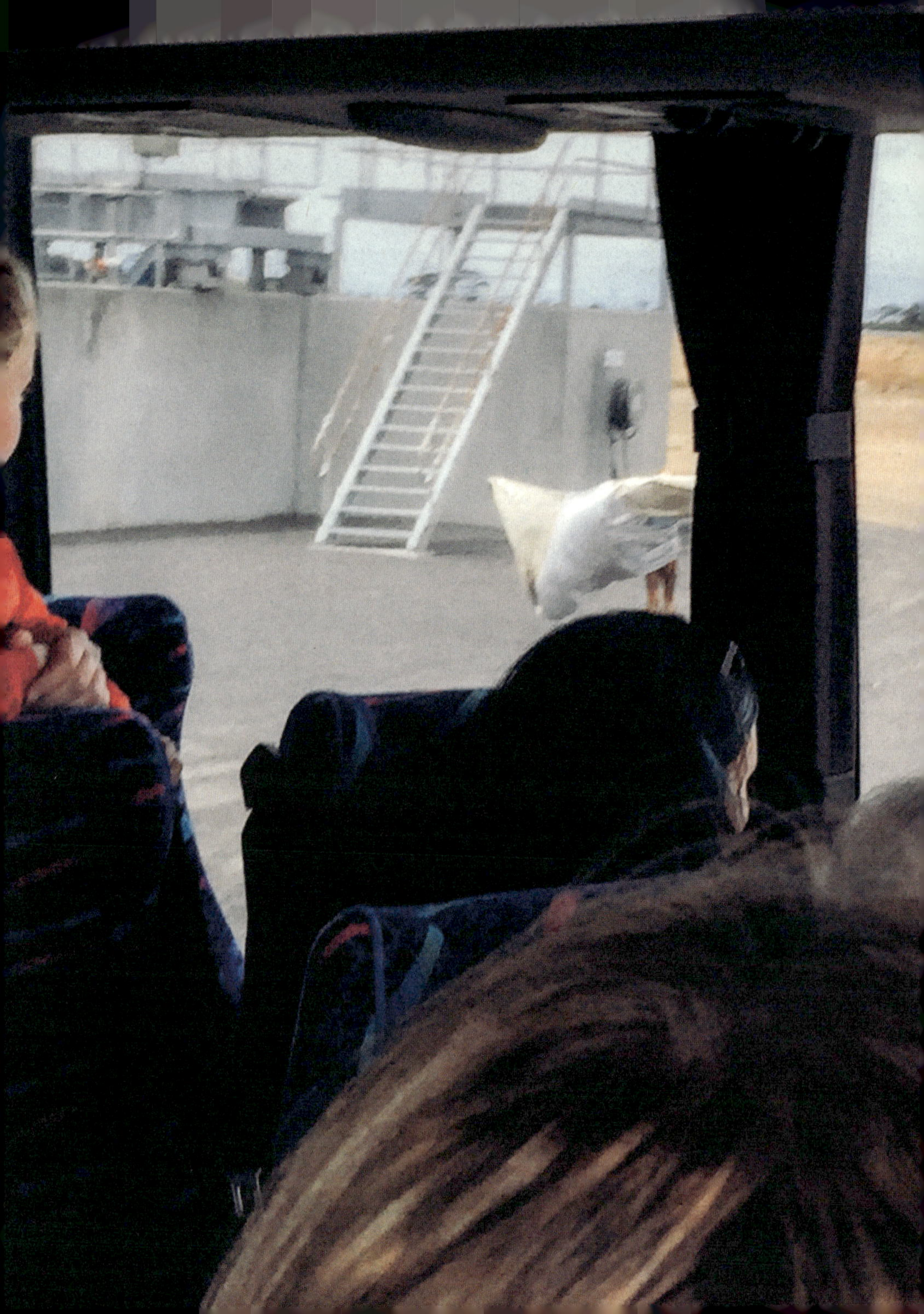

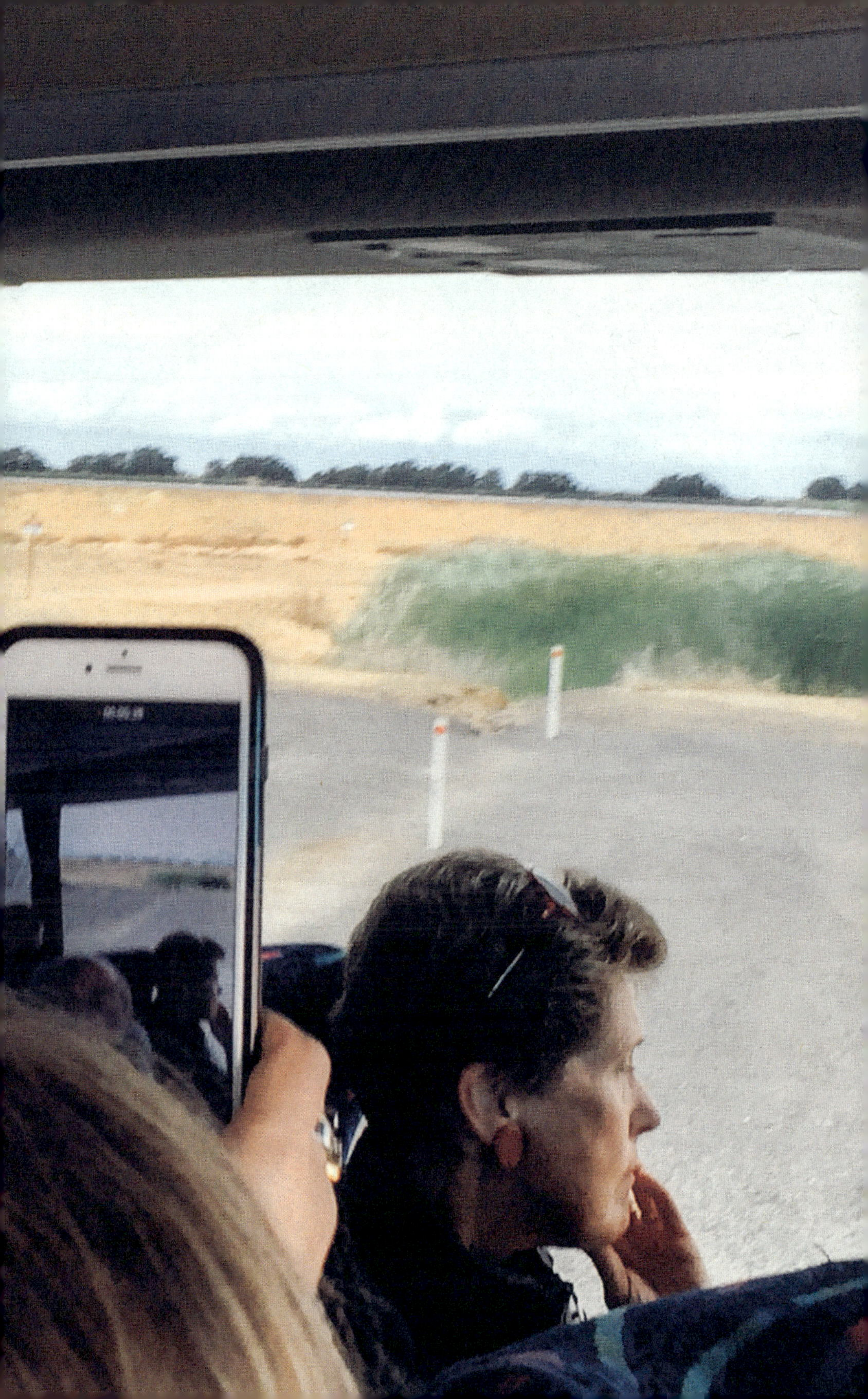

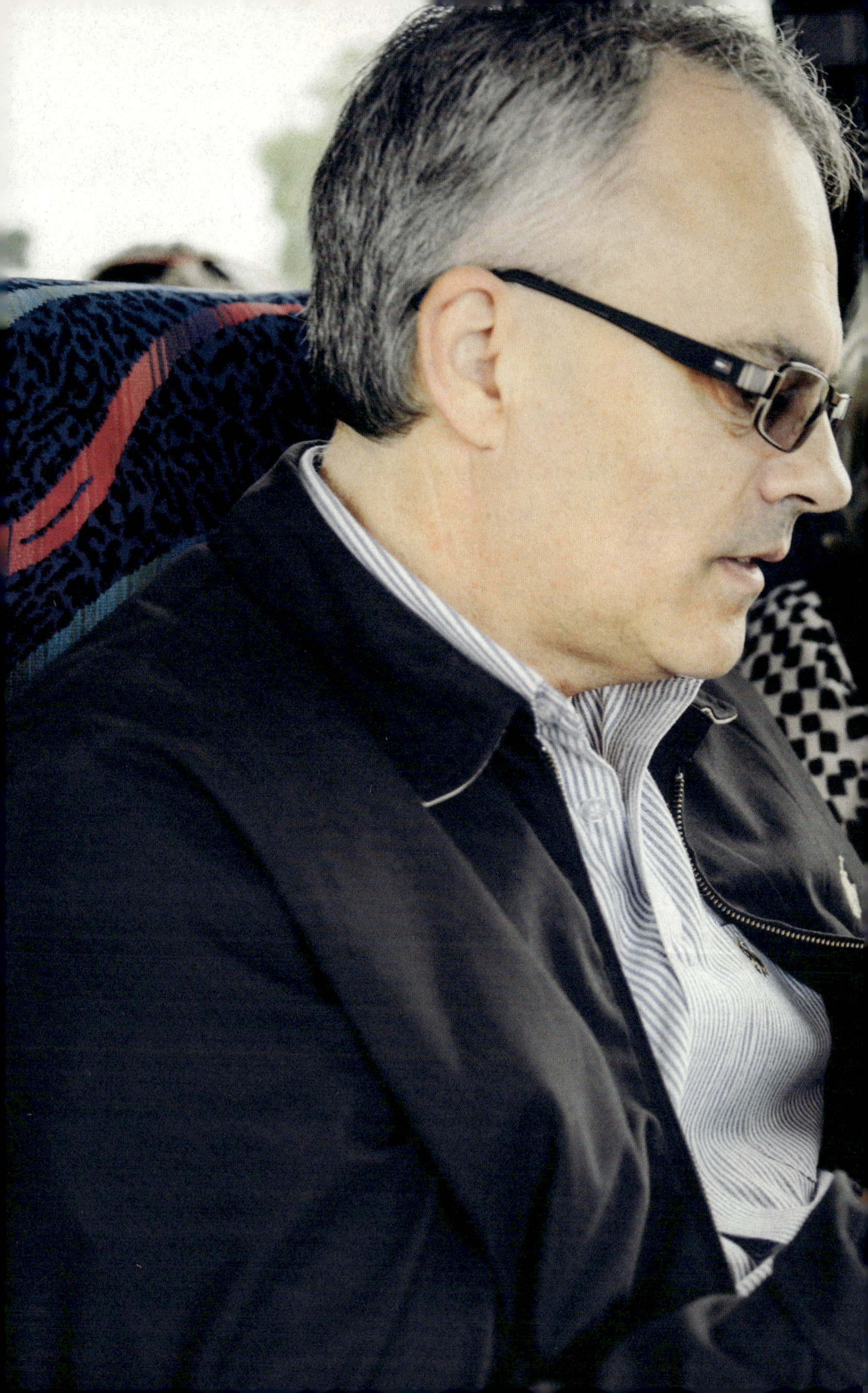

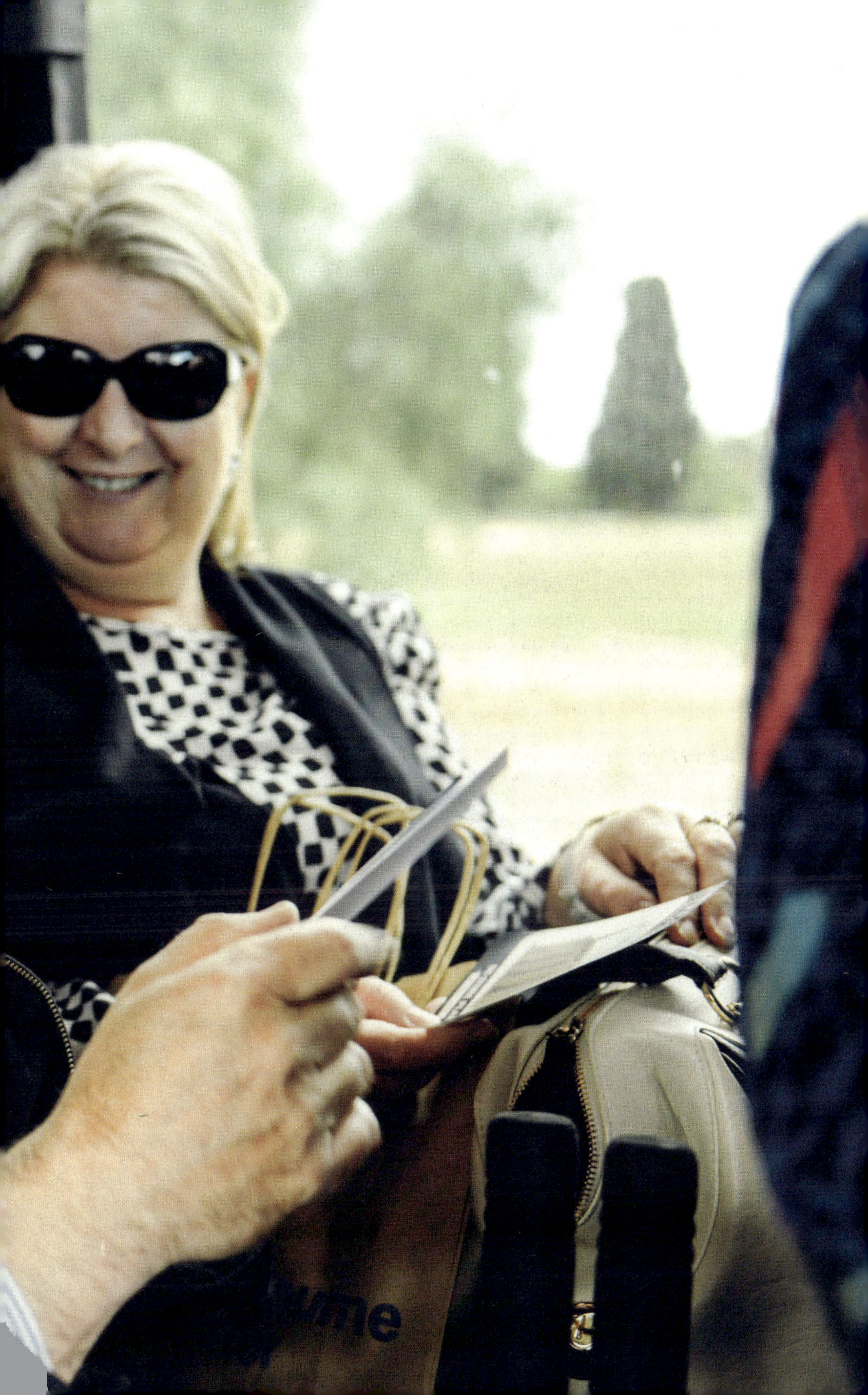

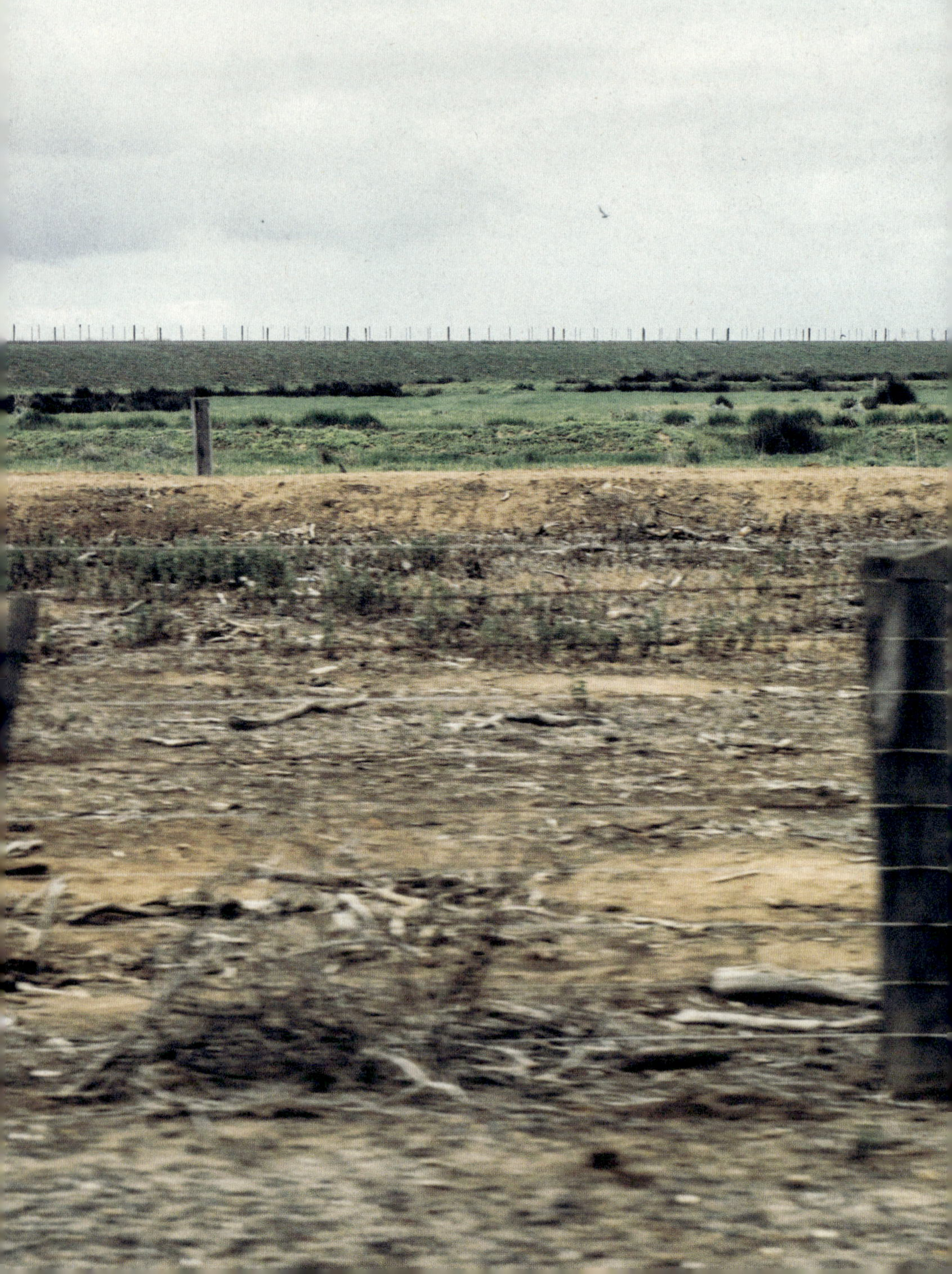

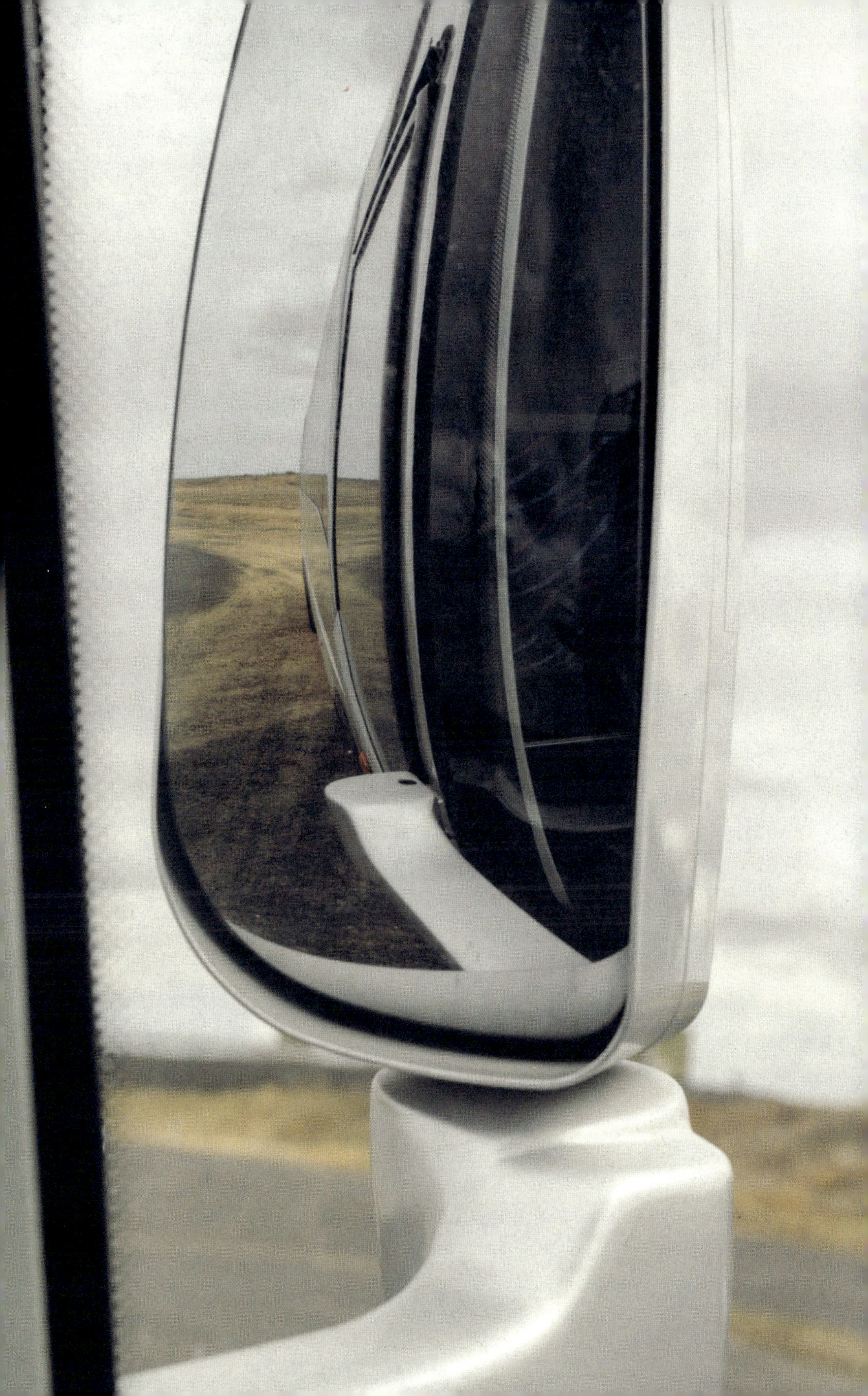

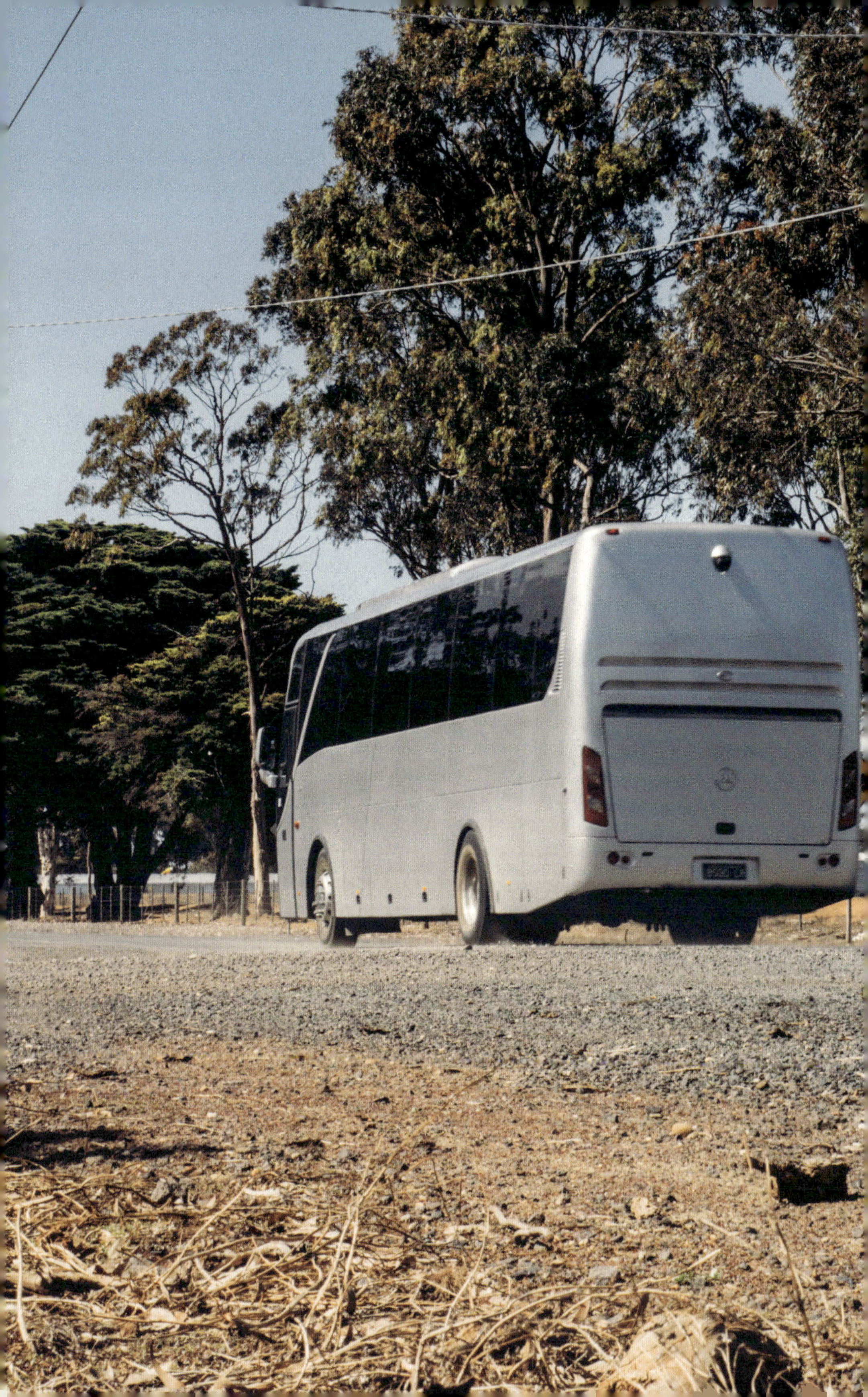

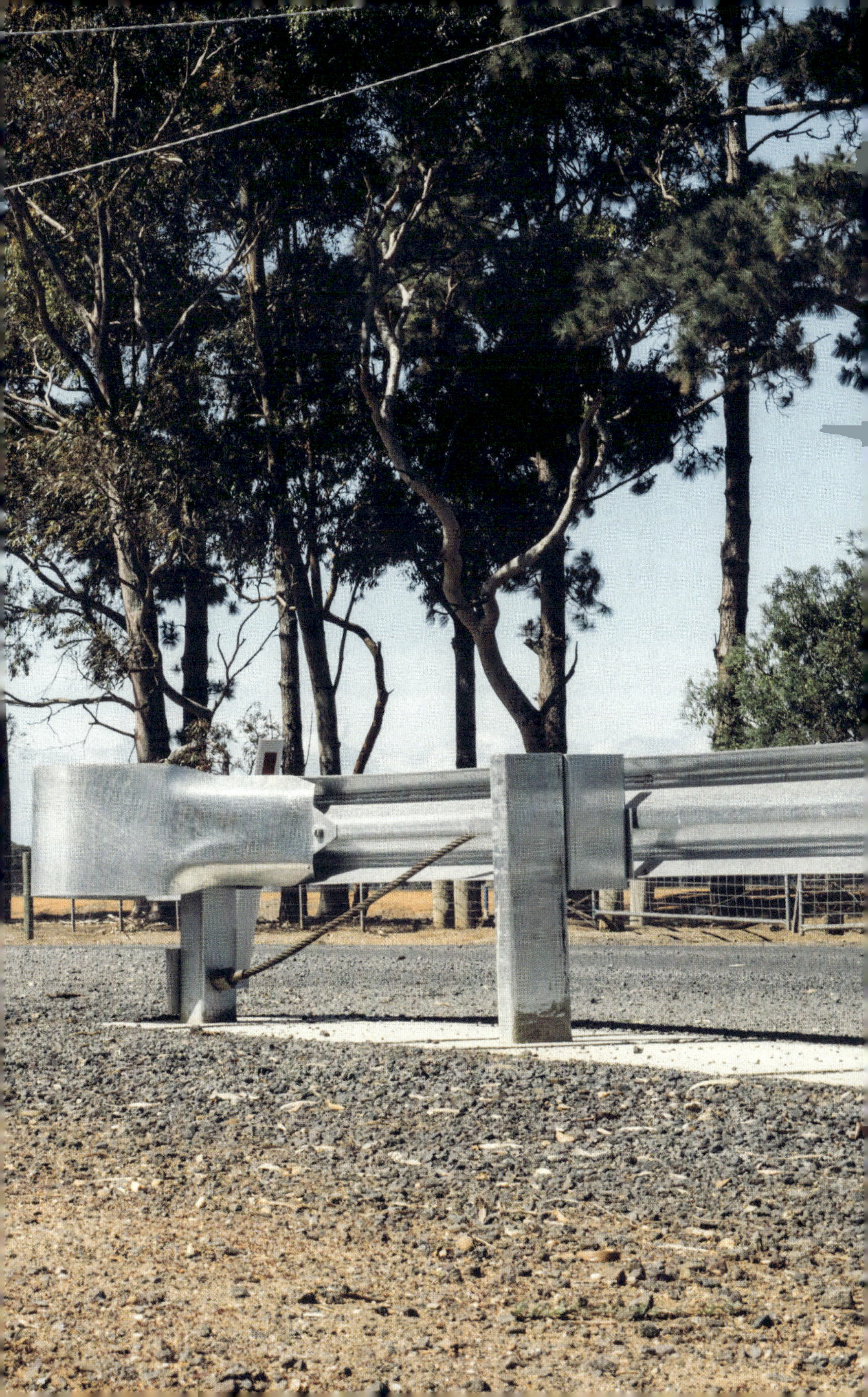

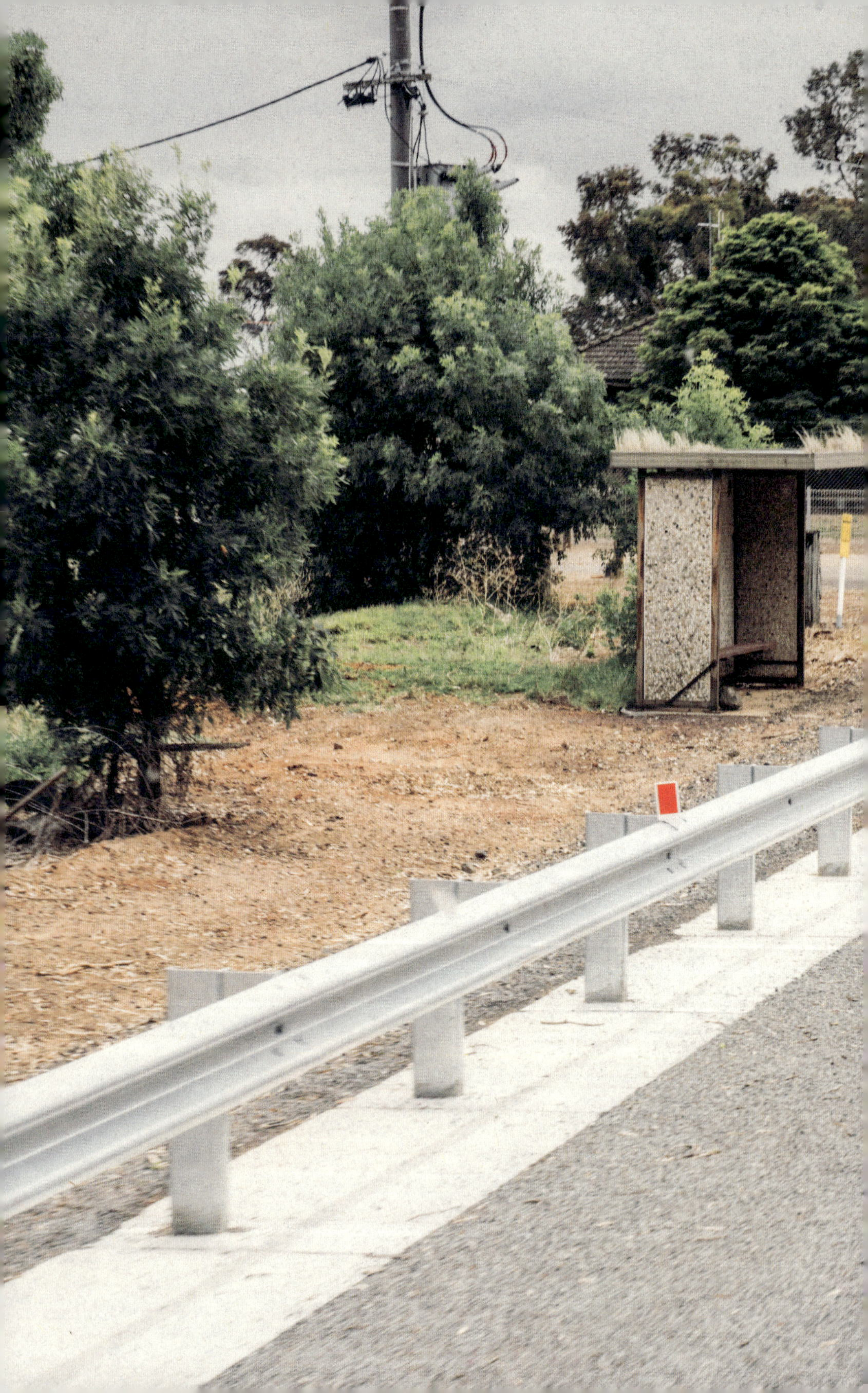

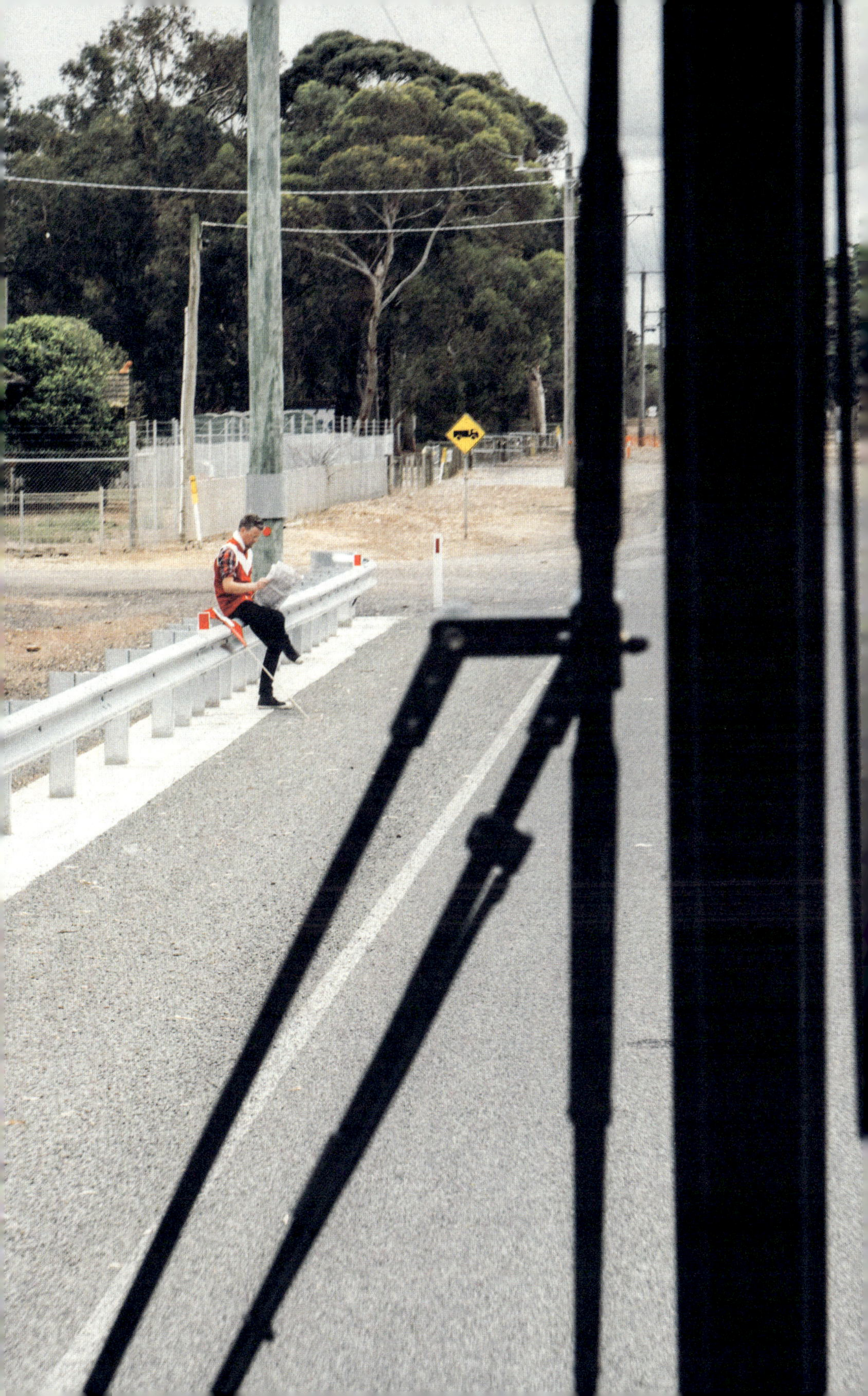

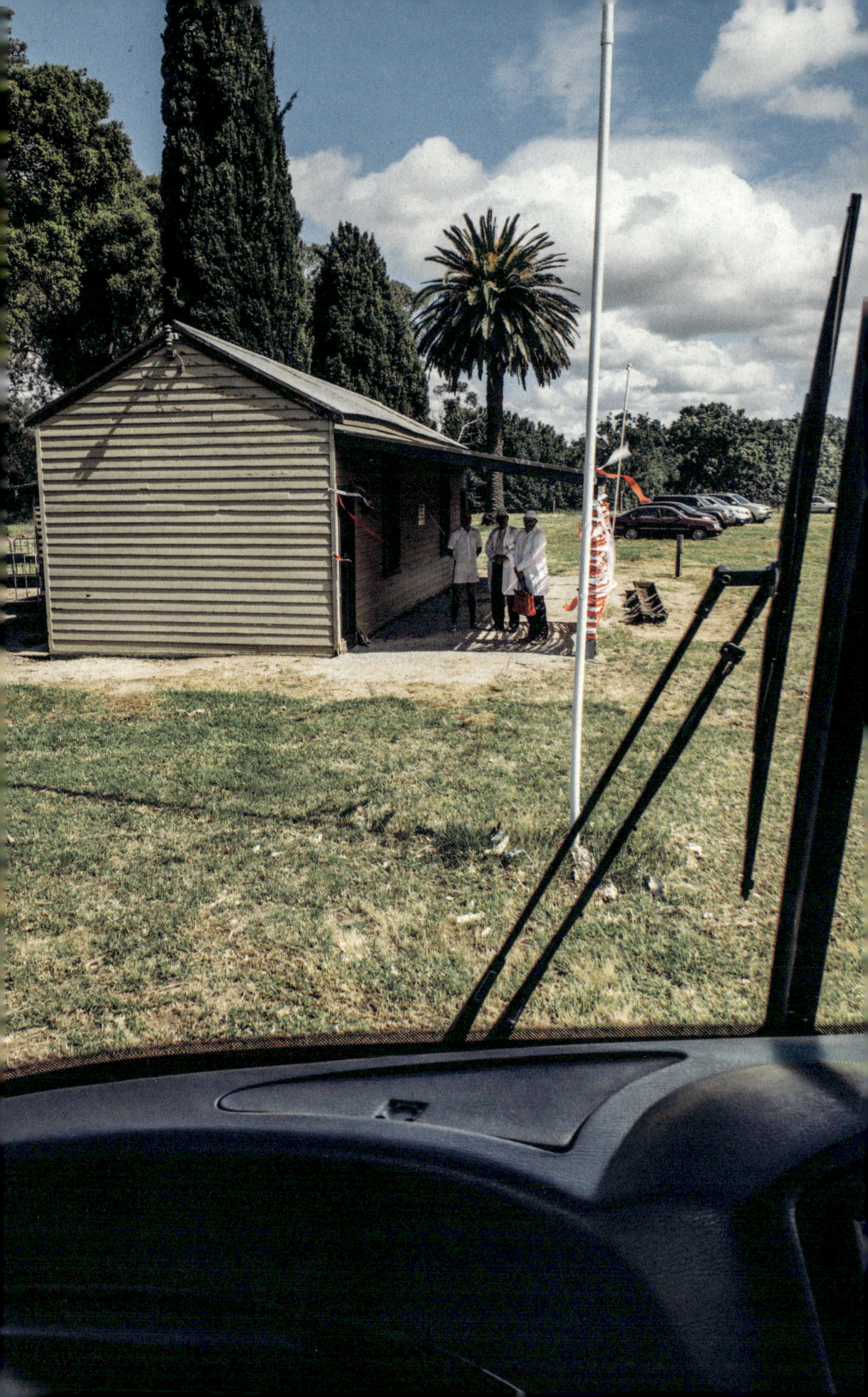

Treatment

COLOPHON

Treatment: Six Public Artworks at the Western Treatment Plant

Full details of the Cataloguing-in-Publication entry are available from the National Library of Australia. A record of this publication is held in the National Library of Australia and the State Library of Victoria.

Surpllus acknowledges the Wurundjeri people of the Kulin Nation as the traditional owners of the land upon which this book is published.

Editor: David Cross
Designer: Stuart Geddes

First edition 2017
ISBN 978-1-922099-21-1
Printed and bound in China,
by 1010 Printing
Edition of 600

Treatment:

Six Public Artworks at the Western Treatment Plant

Edited by
David Cross

Table of Contents

PREFACE

Melbourne Water is grateful for the opportunity to partner with Deakin University on the *Treatment* project in 2015; a playful public art exhibition exploring and interpreting the history, people and colour behind the Western Treatment Plant.

The Western Treatment Plant has been a much maligned landscape for generations despite playing a key role in Melbourne's history and being crucial to Melbourne's ongoing liveability. However, *Treatment* has helped broaden community perceptions of the Plant and celebrate the wonder of the site through art.

Just as the artwork offered degrees of abstraction, so too the landscape at the Western Treatment Plant could be seen to embody an amazing variety of forms. Its sights, sounds, textures and even smells have inspired an unimaginable body of artwork that explores different elements, challenging people—including Melbourne Water staff—to develop a new perspective of the Plant.

Treatment provides an encounter with an industrial process that offers moments of contemplation with our own impact on the environment, and helps flush out a landscape that represents a cultural blind spot that we don't often acknowledge; what happens to our waste?

This public art project has helped galvanise locals from surrounding communities, many of whom share personal connections with the Plant, while some are totally oblivious of the richness of this landscape.

Treatment is a celebration of imagination, creativity and ingenuity. Showcasing a unique landscape, the artworks outlined in this publication have rekindled a strong sense of history and indeed pride within Melbourne Water. Beyond its functionality, *Treatment* has brought about a realisation that the Western Treatment Plant is a unique landscape rich in both natural and cultural values, and a unique community resource to be managed and indeed celebrated for generations to come.

—Paul Balassone

INTRODUCTION

Treatment was a public art project that brought together six Australian artists who each developed temporary commissions in response to the extraordinary Melbourne Water Treatment Facility in Werribee, west of Melbourne. Invited by curator David Cross and associate curator Cameron Bishop to research the site across its many contexts, Catherine Bell, Bindi Cole Chocka, Megan Evans, Shane McGrath, Técha Noble and Spiros Panigirakis each created a place-responsive artwork that was experienced sequentially via a coach tour over two Saturdays in November 2015. The projects took place across an assortment of locations at the 10,000-hectare facility drawing on the rich diversity of geographical, technological and cultural histories of the former Metro Sewage Farm. As part of an ongoing research project at Deakin University, examining the formation of temporary communities via the commissioning of temporary public artworks, *Treatment* sought to identify and delineate a series of resonant contexts that were particular to the site and its extraordinary history.

The current treatment complex combines cutting-edge environmental engineering and energy capture with its key role as one of the world's leading bird sanctuaries. For some, the treatment facility is little more than the source of a ripe aroma that, in the past, depending on the wind direction, wafted across the outer west of the city and as far south as the Bellarine Peninsula. The pejorative associations of the 'poo plant' have served to mask a remarkable ecology and history, which serve as important reminders in the development of Melbourne.

This book captures many—but not all—of the resonances of the temporary traces activated by the six artists. Conceived by Melbourne designer Stuart Geddes, *Treatment* the book interrogates how an ephemeral public art project can best be located after the event through a series of still images and texts. In eschewing (or at least tempering) the iconic photograph in favour of a range of images of assorted qualities, foci and resonances, the book attempts to position the project as a complex series of moments, some stark and others decidedly murky. It seeks to animate for those who were not there the unique quality of the plant as a place where senses are continually working overtime. In addition to essays by the curators and noted public art thinker Rebecca Coates, the book also features texts by each of the artists who outline how the works emanated from new and existing research interests.

By inviting artists to work *in situ* and providing them with the resources to follow their interests and instincts, Melbourne Water have demonstrated a belief in the value of public art to instigate new encounters with place. They have set in train a complex and multifarious re-staging of the treatment plant, inviting us

to consider what we know about the outer west of Melbourne and how we might come to experience it anew.
—David Cross

ACKNOWLEDGEMENTS

The curators would like to thank and acknowledge the following people.

At Melbourne Water: Peter Kissonergis, Martin Bowles, Aaron Zanatta and Paul Balassone, Kim O'Hoy, Linton Marchant, Scott Crowhurst, Drew Ryan and the rest of the Woods crew for their assistance, Oliva Vincent, Anushia Sivanesan and Sheena Campbell, Liz Phillips, Robyn Brown, Dee Orgill, Dan Mooney, Daryl Zimmer, David Ezard, Jerome Peacock, Gerard Thurbon, Antonella D'Andrea-Tragas, Rachel Smith and Will Steele, Mim Holmes, Mary Catus-Wood, Heidi Ryan and Kim Carland.

At City of Wyndham: David Fitzsimmons, Bec Cole, Maree Clark, Dr Megan Evans, then Councillor Bob Fairclough and the Wyndham City Council.

At Deakin University: Professor Matthew Allen, Professor Brenda Cheridnichenko, Professor Jane den Hollander, Professor Chris Hickey, Associate Professor Geoff Boucher, Scott Allen, Brad Axiak, Jess Imam, Stephanie Moore, Holly Toyne, Flows and Catchments Research Group, Melanie Randell, Sean Redmond and Deakin Motion Lab Centre For Creative Arts Research, Katie Thompson, generous and supportive colleagues in the School of Communication and Creative Arts.

At Wyndham Community Cultural Foundation: Jan Goates and all of the board members.

Thanks to *Treatment* heroes Dr Fiona Lee, Ellie Boekman, Dr Luci Pangrazio, Simon Reis, Liz Taylor, Ella Forbes, George the coach driver, former residents of Cocoroc and the Metro Farm estate, Stuart Geddes, the entire team at WTP, Monica Schott, and especially the artists (Catherine Bell, Bindi Cole Chocka, Megan Evans, Shane McGrath, Técha Noble and Spiros Panigirakis), Rebecca Coates, all the performers and volunteers and everyone who made the pilgrimage.

Spiros Panigirakis would like to acknowledge Justine Makdessi, Jimmy Nuttall and Aaron Warren.

Shane McGrath would like to acknowledge his supporters: John Woodman and all those that donated to the Pozible campaign, Melbourne Water, Deakin University, Werribee Historic Society, Wyndham Community Cultural Foundation, all the ex-residents and Herefords of Cocoroc that contributed to the project, especially Vernon, David and Elizabeth McKane, and Leo Cooney. Filmographer & photographer: Kieran Watson-Bonnice. Performers: Ryan James, Julian McGrath, Luke Walker, Michael Monagle, John McGrath, Tim Blennerhassett, Rory Gove, Anthony Hack, Zach Stumer, Daniel Lord, Sam Barwell, Asher Hunter, Aaron Bensimon, Nick Percy, Oliver Pelling, Phill Howell, Dez Hunt, Tim Jedwab, Gervaise Netherway, Ollie Pelling. Catering: Maureen McGrath & Mia Grant.

Técha Noble would like to thank performers Edie Cross, Beth Sometimes, Liz Dunn, Caroline Anderson and John Micaleff. In addition to the immense production assistance of Ellie Boekman, Sophie Roberts, David Cross and Dixie Cross.

Treatment has been supported by Deakin University, City of Wyndham, Wyndham Community Cultural Foundation and Melbourne Water, along with generous funding from Creative Victoria.

We would like to acknowledge and pay our respects to the traditional custodians of the land on which this art project has taken place, the Woi wurrung, Boon wurrung, and Wada wurrung peoples of the Kulin nation, and their ancestors past and present.

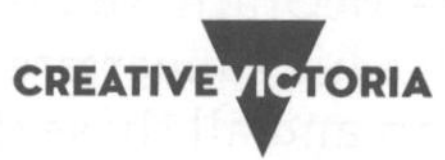

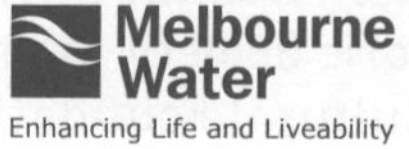

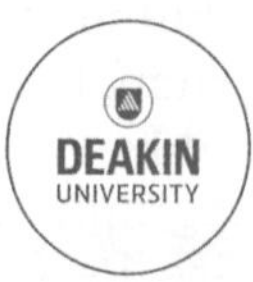

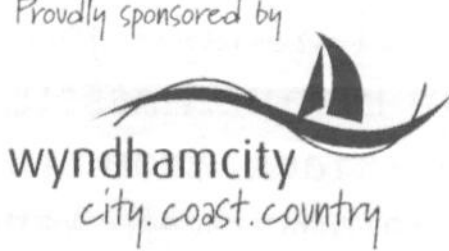

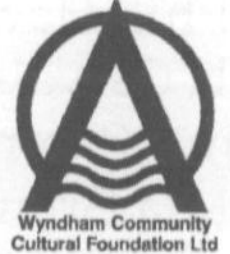

CONTRIBUTORS

Paul Balassone is Principal of Cultural Heritage in the Strategic and Water Asset Management, Service Delivery Group at Melbourne Water.

Catherine Bell is a Melbourne-based artist. She is an Associate Professor in the Bachelor of Visual Arts & Design degree, School of Arts, at Australian Catholic University. She is represented by Sutton Gallery, Melbourne.
suttongallery.com.au

Cameron Bishop is a Melbourne-based artist, writer and curator. He is Programme Director of Visual Arts at Deakin University.
cameronjbishop.com

Rebecca Coates is a curator, writer, Director of Shepparton Art Museum, and an Honorary Fellow at the University of Melbourne.

Bindi Cole Chocka is a Melbourne-based artist, curator, writer and PhD candidate at Deakin University.
bindicolechocka.com

David Cross is a Melbourne-based artist, writer, curator and Professor of Art and Performance at Deakin University.
davidcrossartist.com

Megan Evans is a Melbourne-based artist, writer and curator at Wyndham Arts Centre.
meganevansartist.com

Stuart Geddes is a Melbourne-based designer and Industry Fellow at RMIT University.
stuart.geddes.work

Shane McGrath is a Melbourne-based artist and PhD candidate at Deakin University.
shanemichaelmcgrath.com

Técha Noble is an artist based between Sydney and Berlin.

Spiros Panigirakis is a Melbourne-based artist. He is a Senior Lecturer in the Visual Arts program at Monash University and is represented by Sarah Scout Presents, Melbourne.
spirospanigirakis.com

On The Outer

Shane McGrath

When I would tell people about *On The Outer*, taking place out at the Western Treatment Plant in Werribee, the most common reply was 'where?'

'The poo-farm', I would reluctantly add, at which point they would understand. This casual ignorance became a thread that ran throughout this project—ignorance of the plant and its long history, as well as the people that helped create it. Personally, I had no idea about the existence of the now abandoned, small town of Cocoroc, located in the centre of the expansive landscape. Little remains but, surprisingly, the surviving feature that still dominates the site is the football oval—with its goal posts and changerooms both intact.

On first visiting the site my imagination conjured up players bursting from the rooms and taking to the field to restage an historic game. But, who used to play here? What was the history and significance of the team that called this once stinky oval home until 1964? What colours were they playing under and what did their team song speak of? All of these are questions that, I quickly found out, had very few answers. But I was confident a bit of detective work and digging around would uncover treasure.

I began my search by trying to track down anyone who once lived at Cocoroc, had relatives that played, or knew anything about the team. An elderly ex-player and local named A. J. 'Okie' McDermott came to my rescue with hints of information about some of the players, their country of origin (many European refugees and immigrants worked at the 'Farm', as it was and still is known), the scores of brothers and cousins that played together, as well as the generations that passed through the Club. All the players worked on the Farm in one way or another. Once the word got out that some artist was asking about the football team, I began to receive calls out of the blue with snippets of information, recollections and anecdotes about life at the club.

I learnt that they were called the *Metropolitan Farm Herefords*, named for the famous bovine that were raised on the Farm and, just like the cattle, the Herefords were Red and White. I learnt that at away games the women of Lara used their umbrellas to hit the *Herefords* as they ran onto and from the field, and that the opposition would refer to them as the '*sewer rats*' or '*shit-stirrers*'. While I was piecing together this history, I became acutely aware of the stigma that existed when discussing Werribee, and I uncovered examples of social and economical disadvantages linked to the postcode. There were even historical accounts of Cocoroc Hereford cattle being banned from competing at the Royal Melbourne Show due to the belief that the rich, fertilized grass gave the Cocoroc cattle an unfair advantage. Still today, you mention Werribee and most Melburnians dismiss it as the 'stink-town'. I'd bet most of those people are unaware that until the creation of the Werribee Sewage Treatment Plant, Melbourne was widely referred to as *Smellbourne*, due to our streets being awash in filth and excrement.

The stigma and subsequent isolation of all things Werribee became my point of focus when refining my project's conceptual framework. *On the Outer* became an exercise in exclusion and role reversal, where the audience is cast as the visiting team and outsiders. I went to great lengths to recreate the scene of a period football team with replica woollen jumpers, as well as field and goal umpires from the 1960s. As each busload of audience members arrived at the oval, the Herefords would leave the field, entering their rooms and shutting the audience out. The coach would give his address, which was informed by the collected anecdotes and personal accounts given by those who had occupied those rooms in the past. The audience had no choice but to listen in from the visitors' rooms and outside the pavillion. With the aroma of Dencorub in their nostrils and shouting ringing in their ears, the audience was back onto the bus before they knew it, clutching a stubby holder with the Hereford team song bursting forth from the speakers as the bus pulled away.

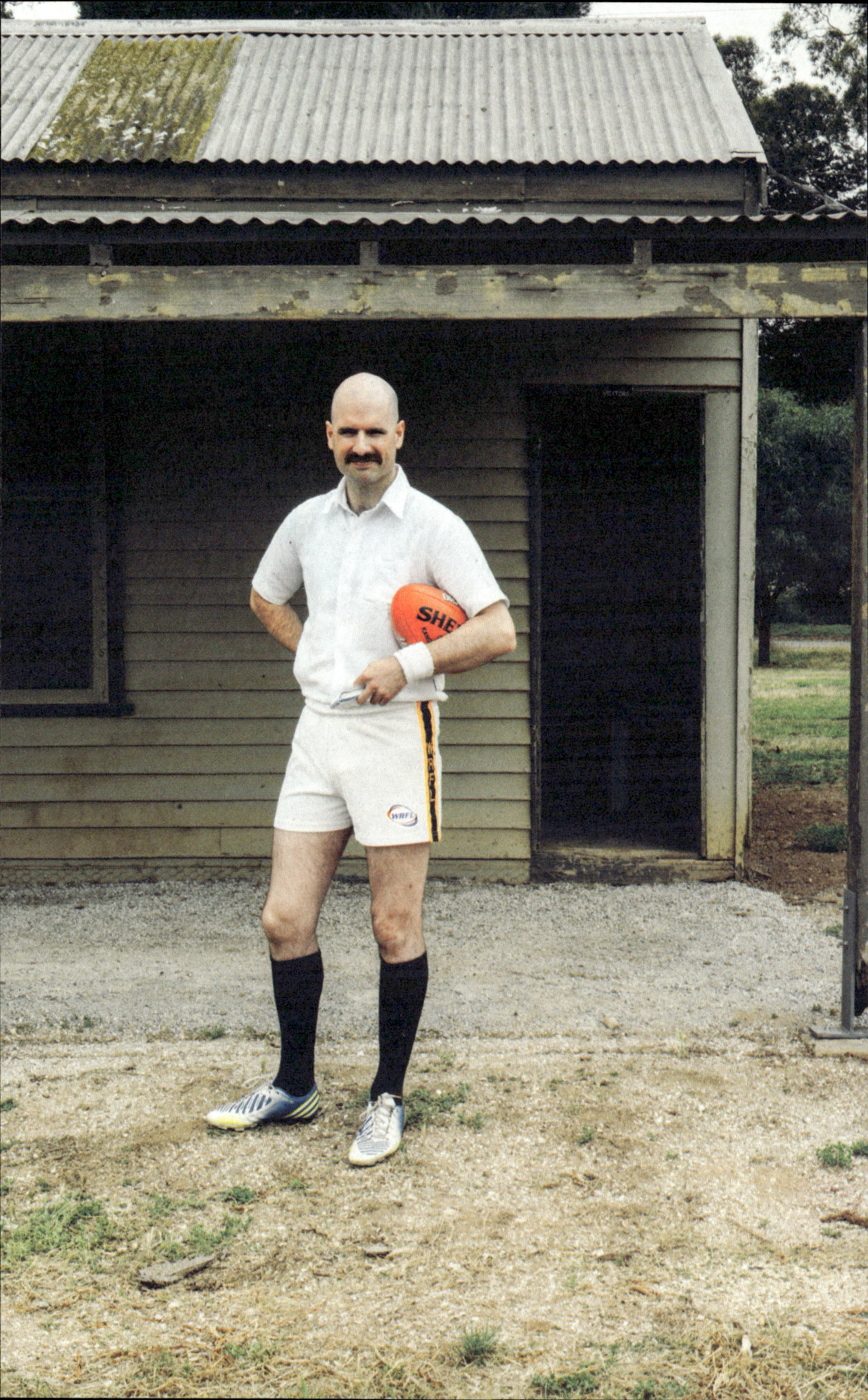
SHE
WRFL

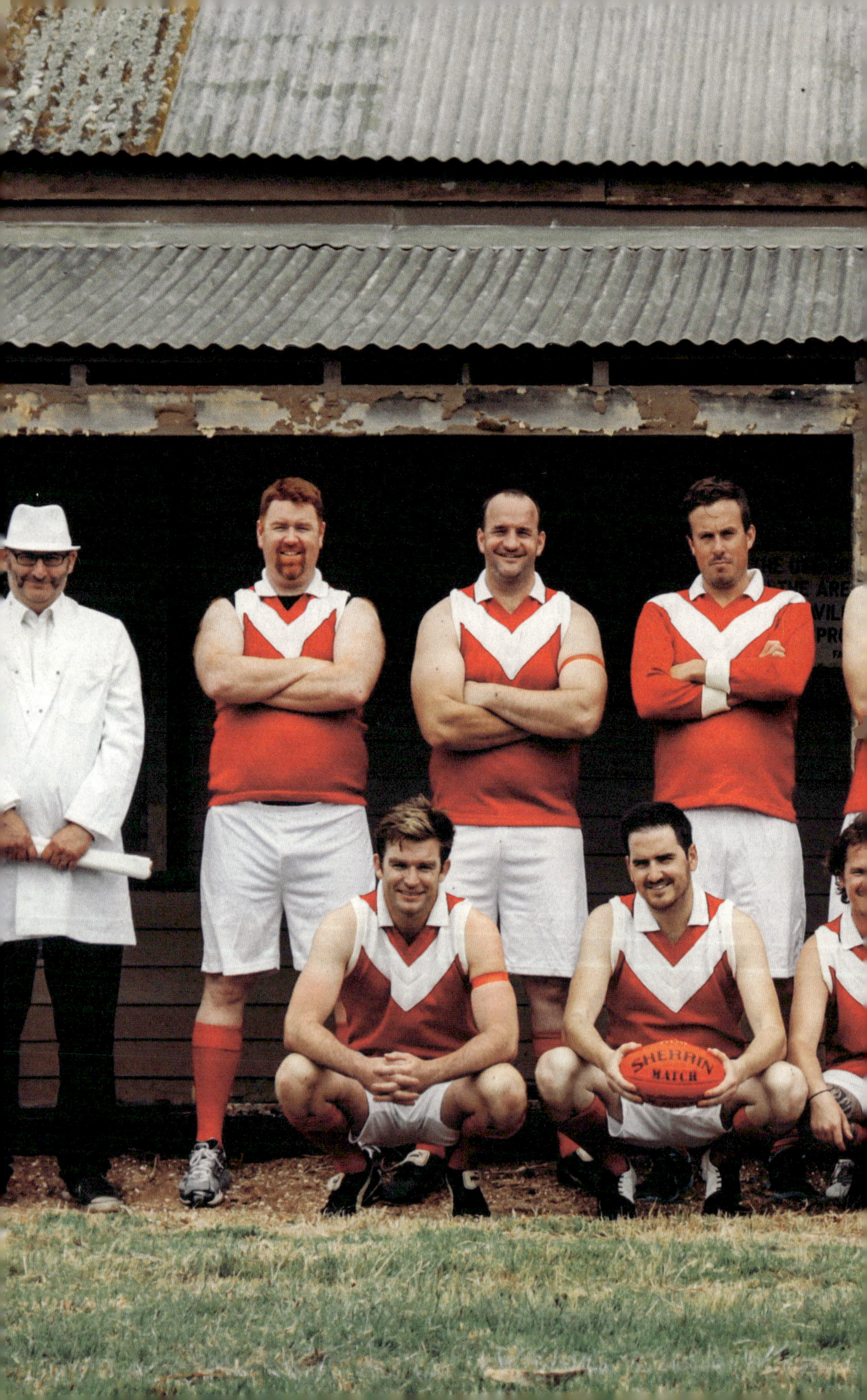
SHERRIN
MATCH

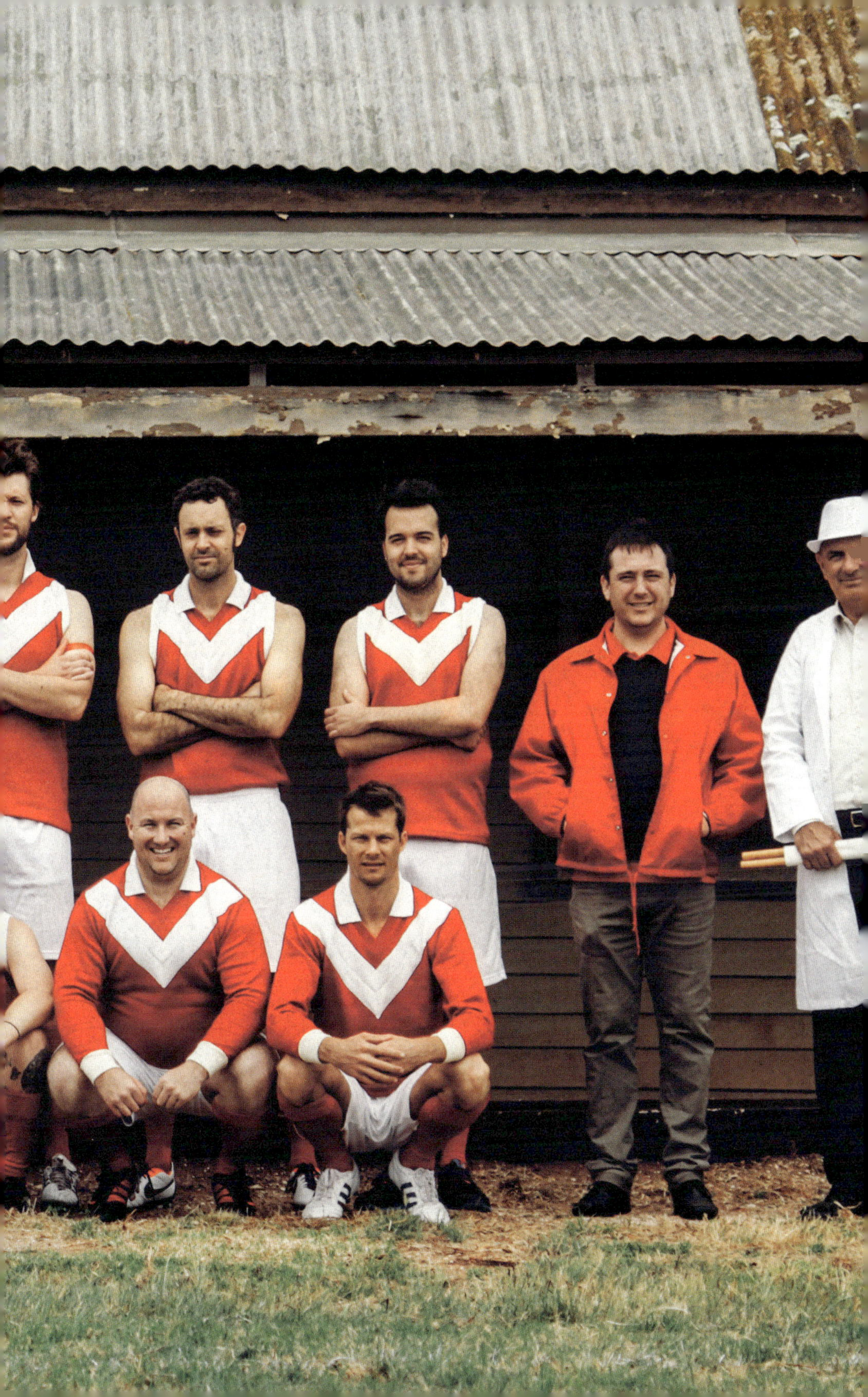

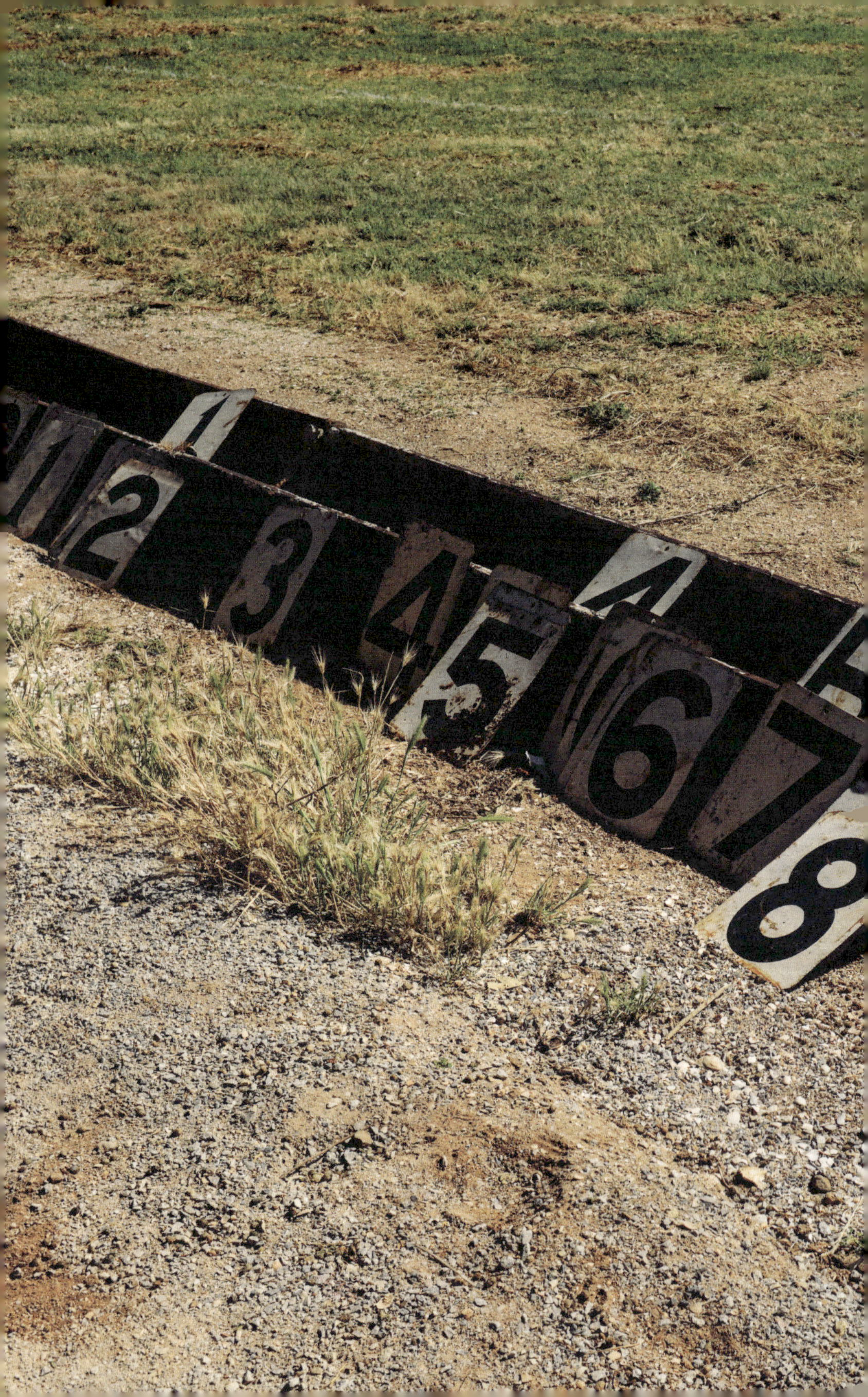
1
1
2
3
4
5
4
6
7
8

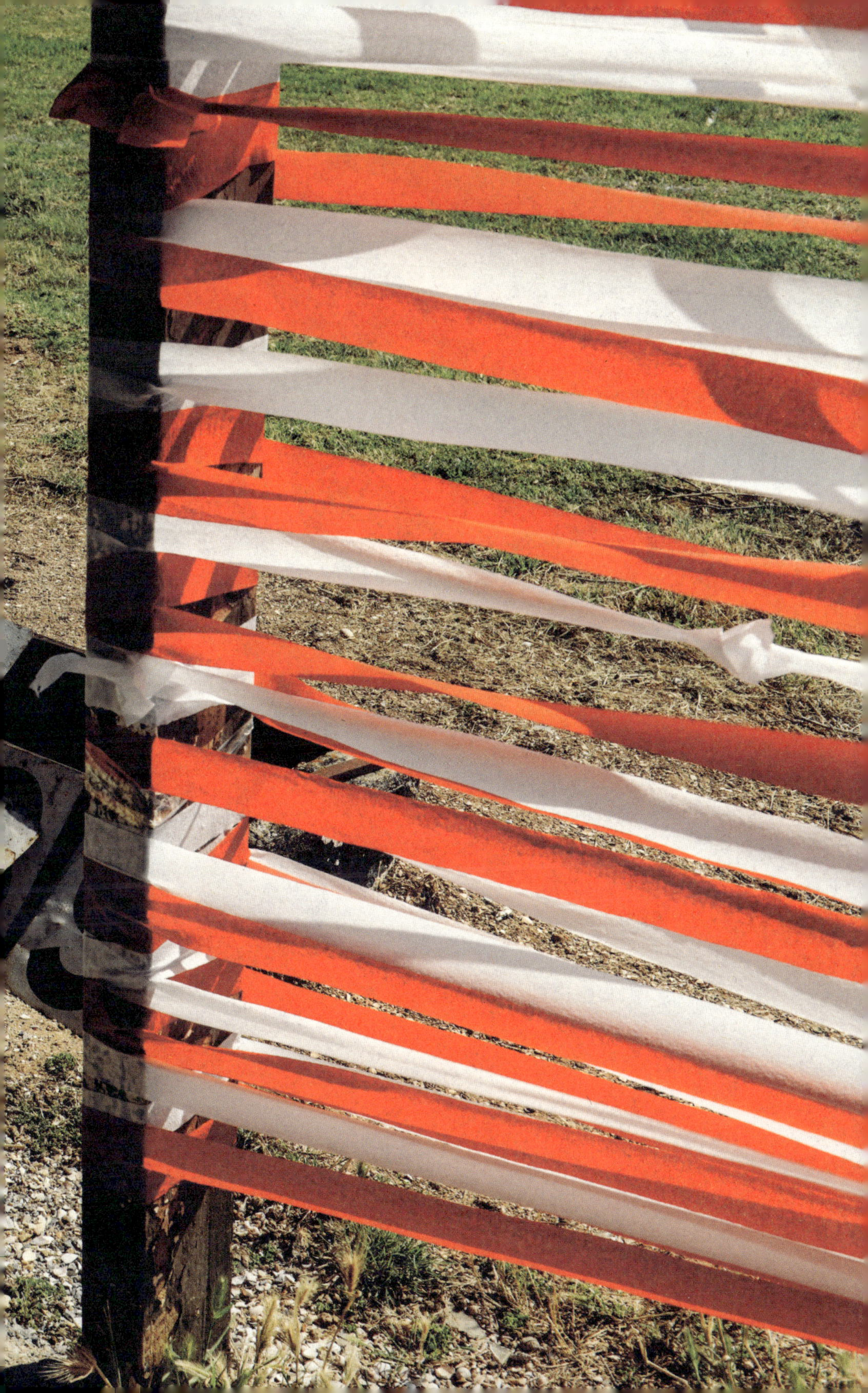

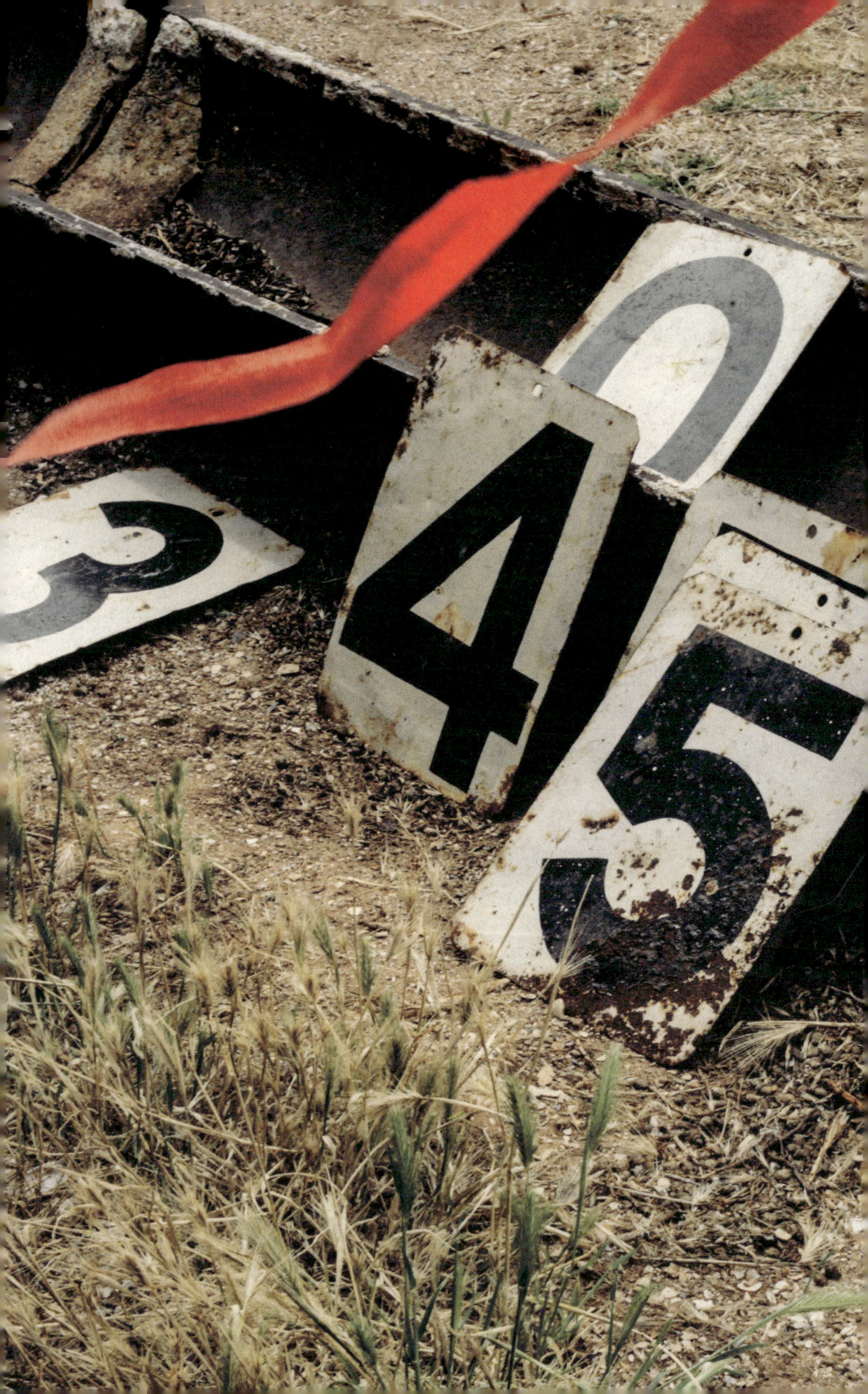
3
4
5

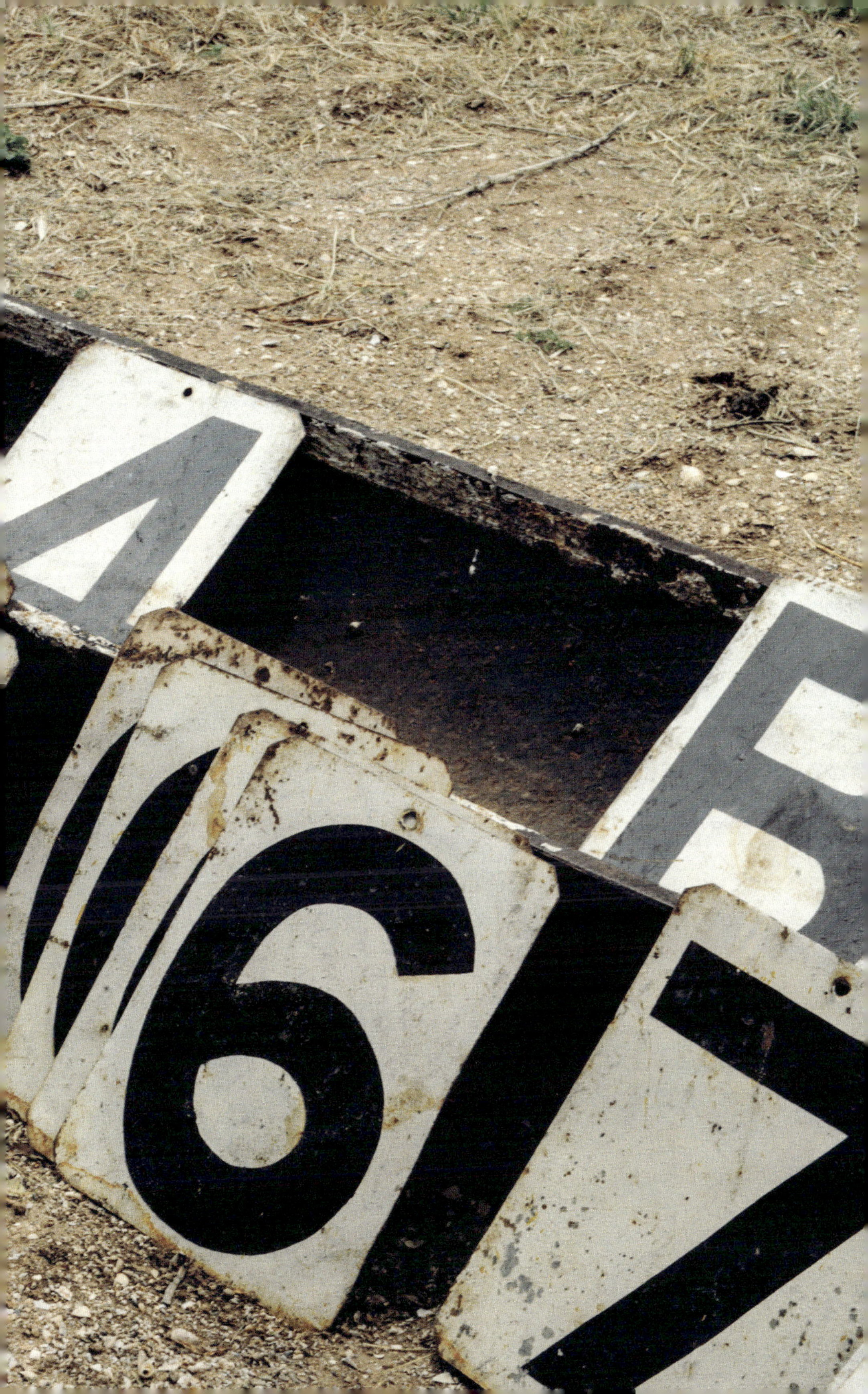
4
6
7

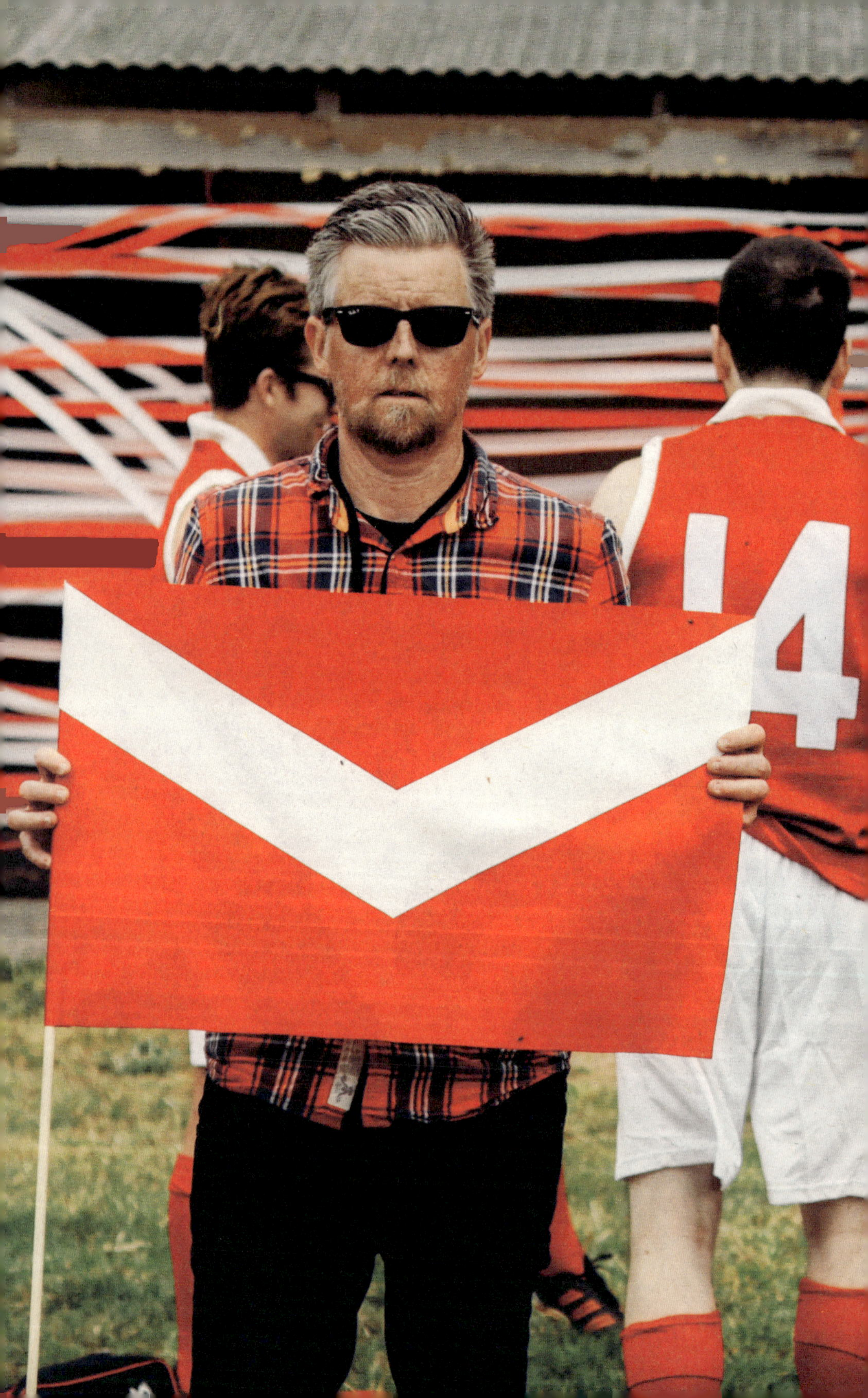
14

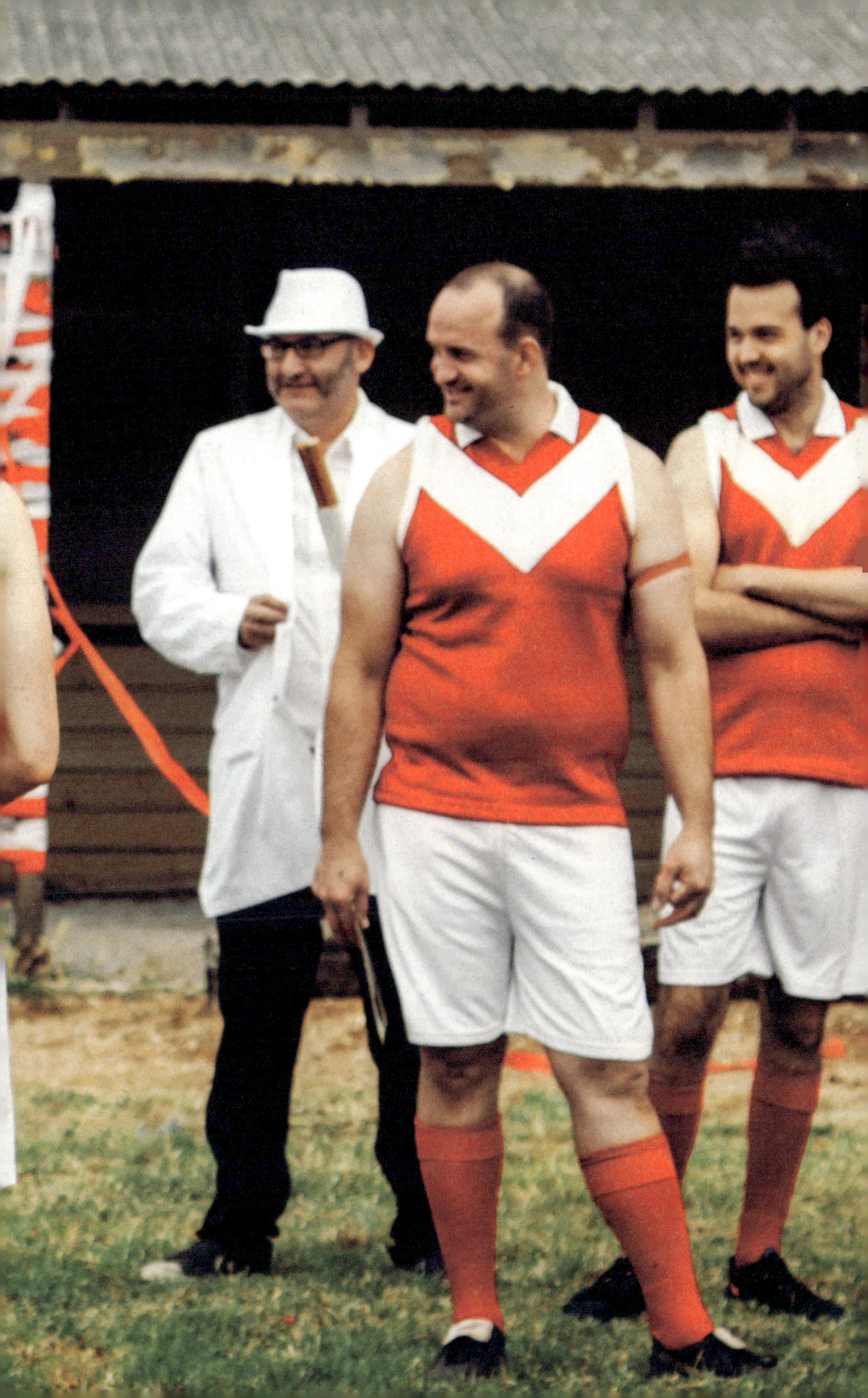

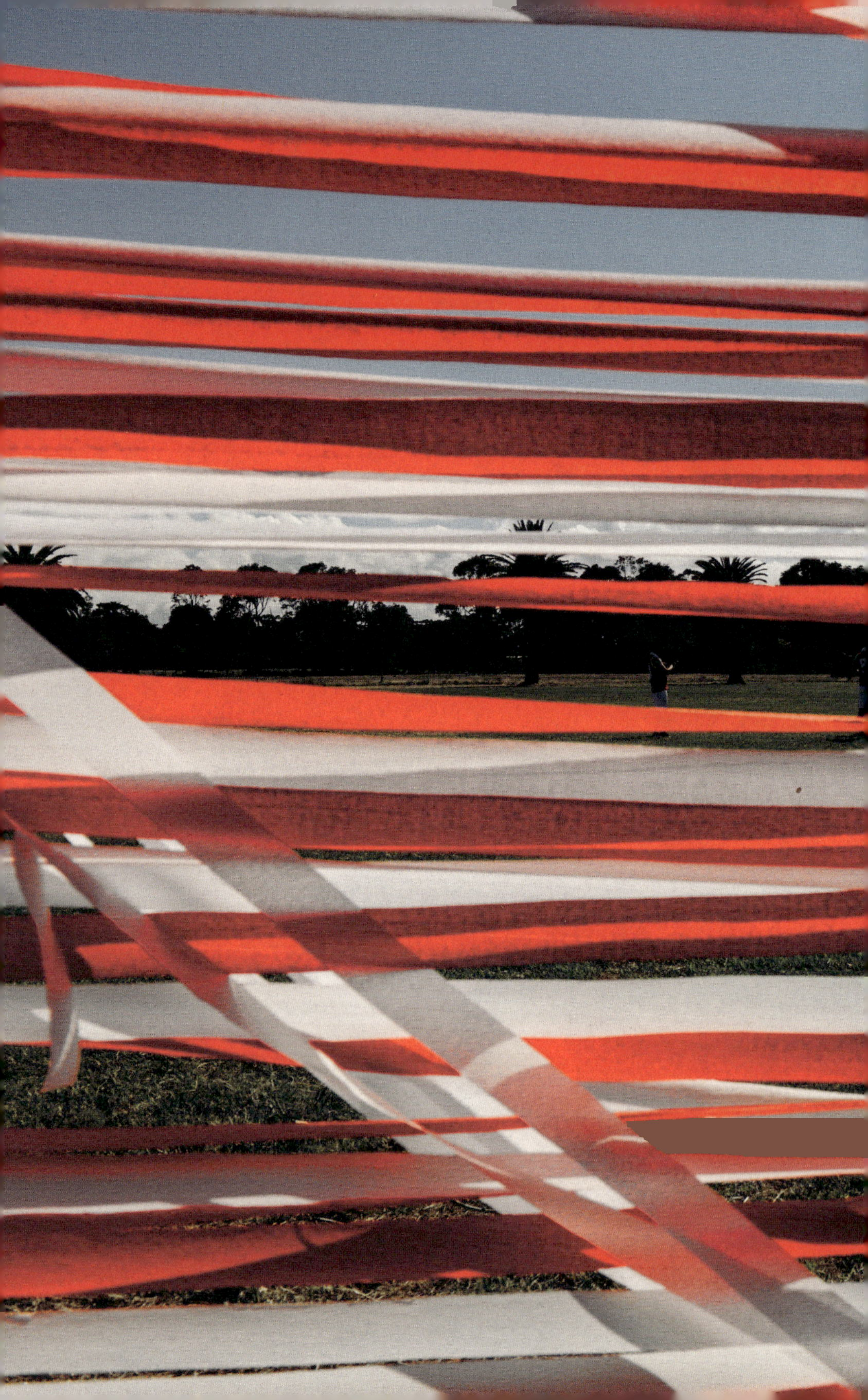

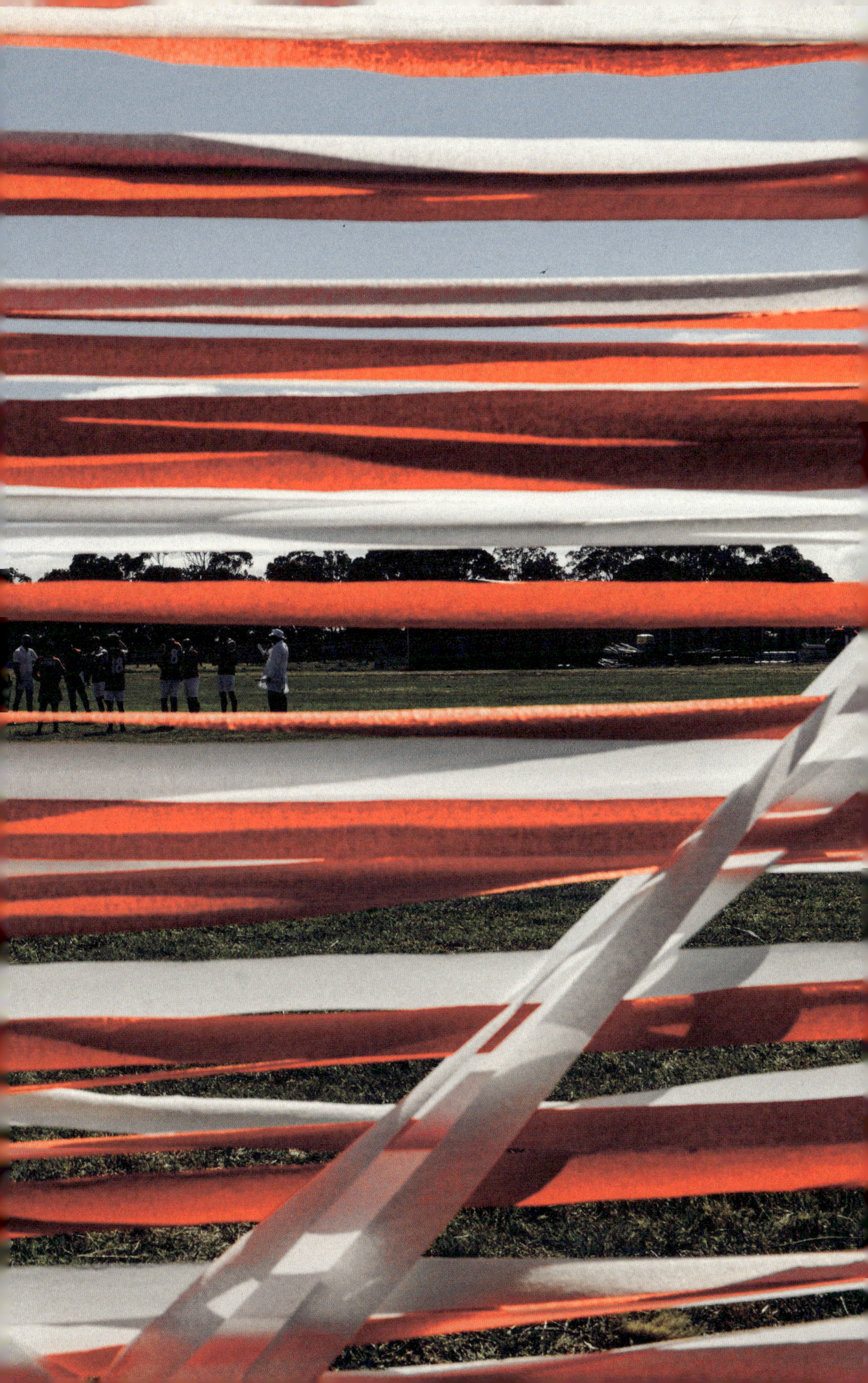

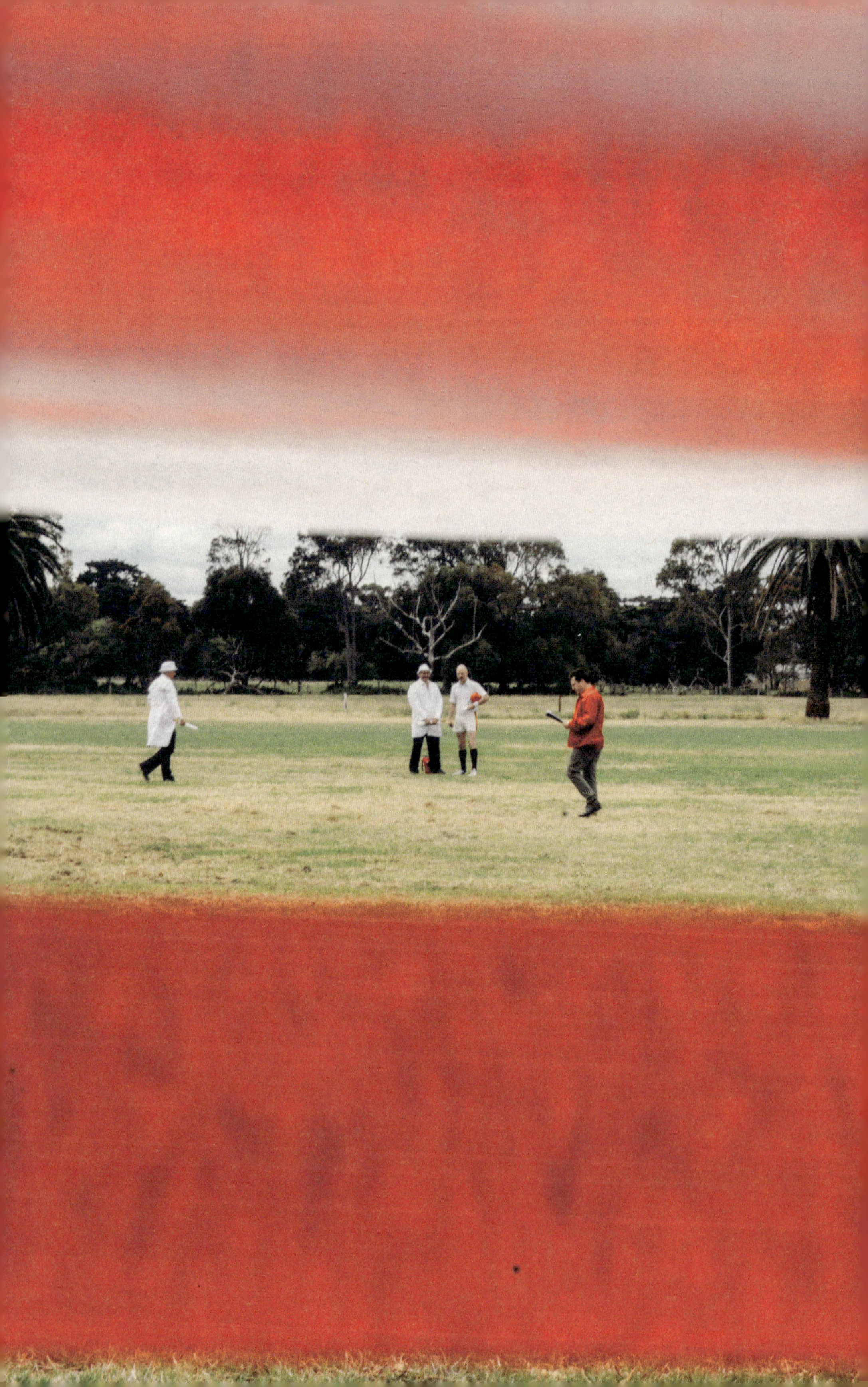

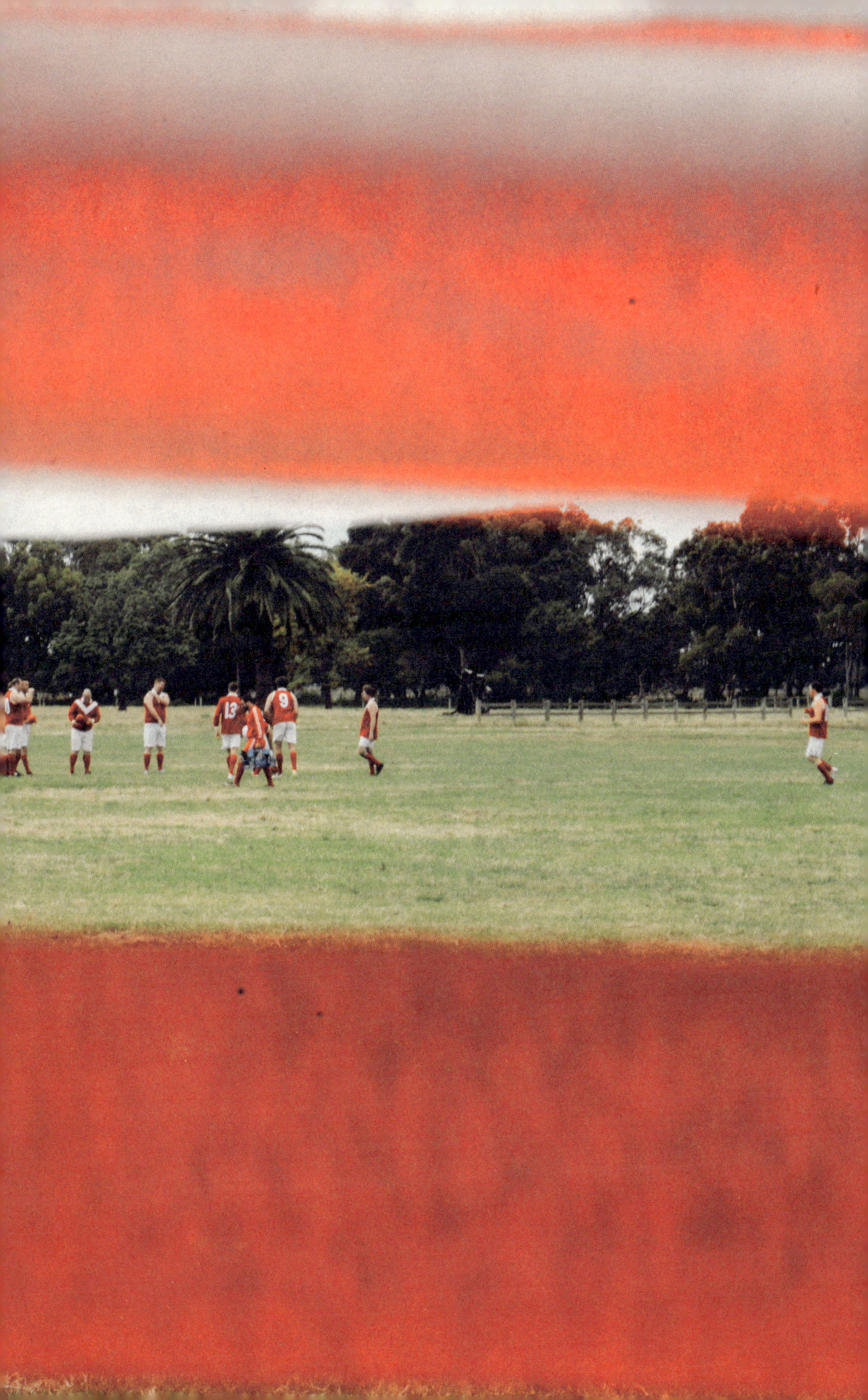

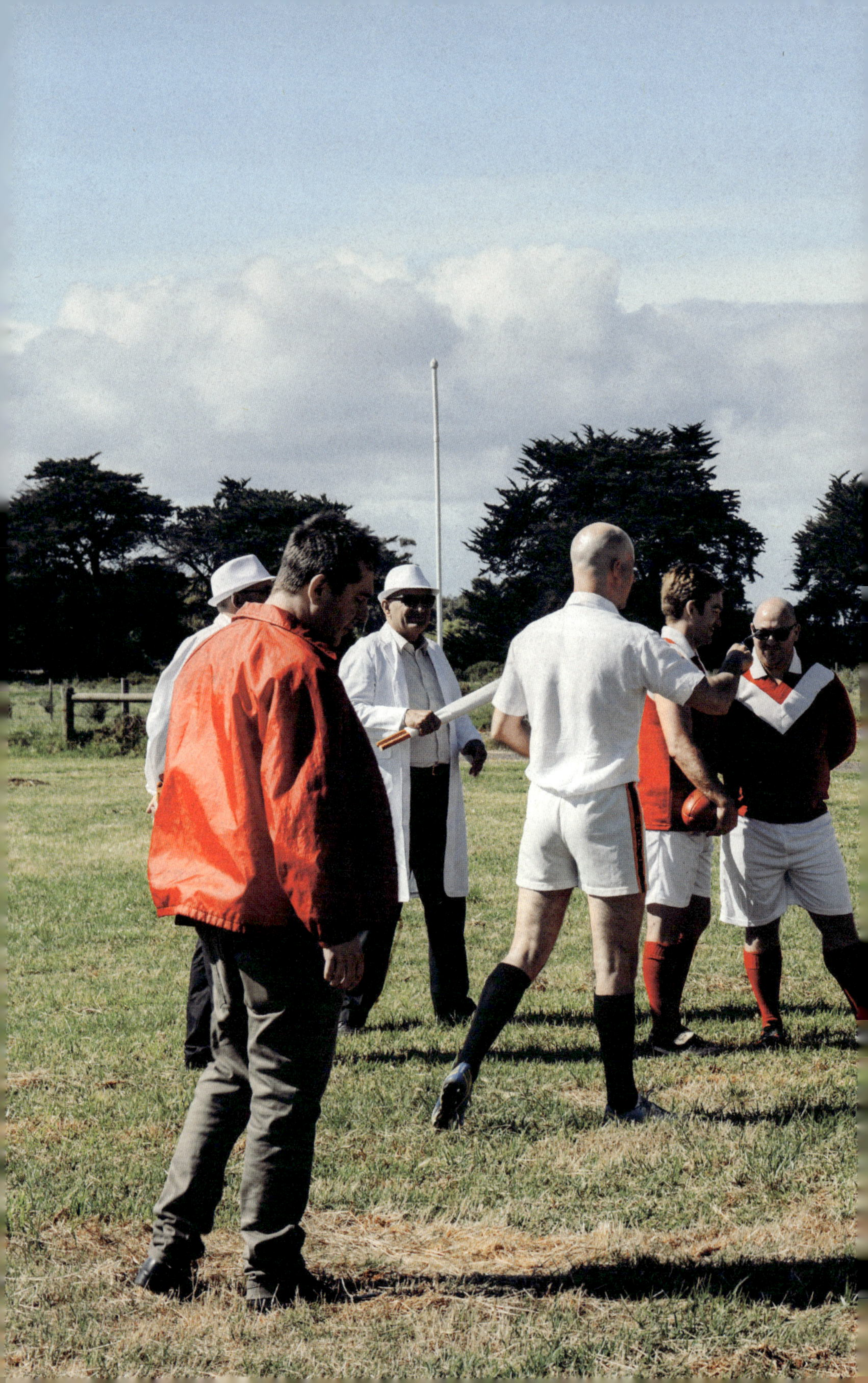

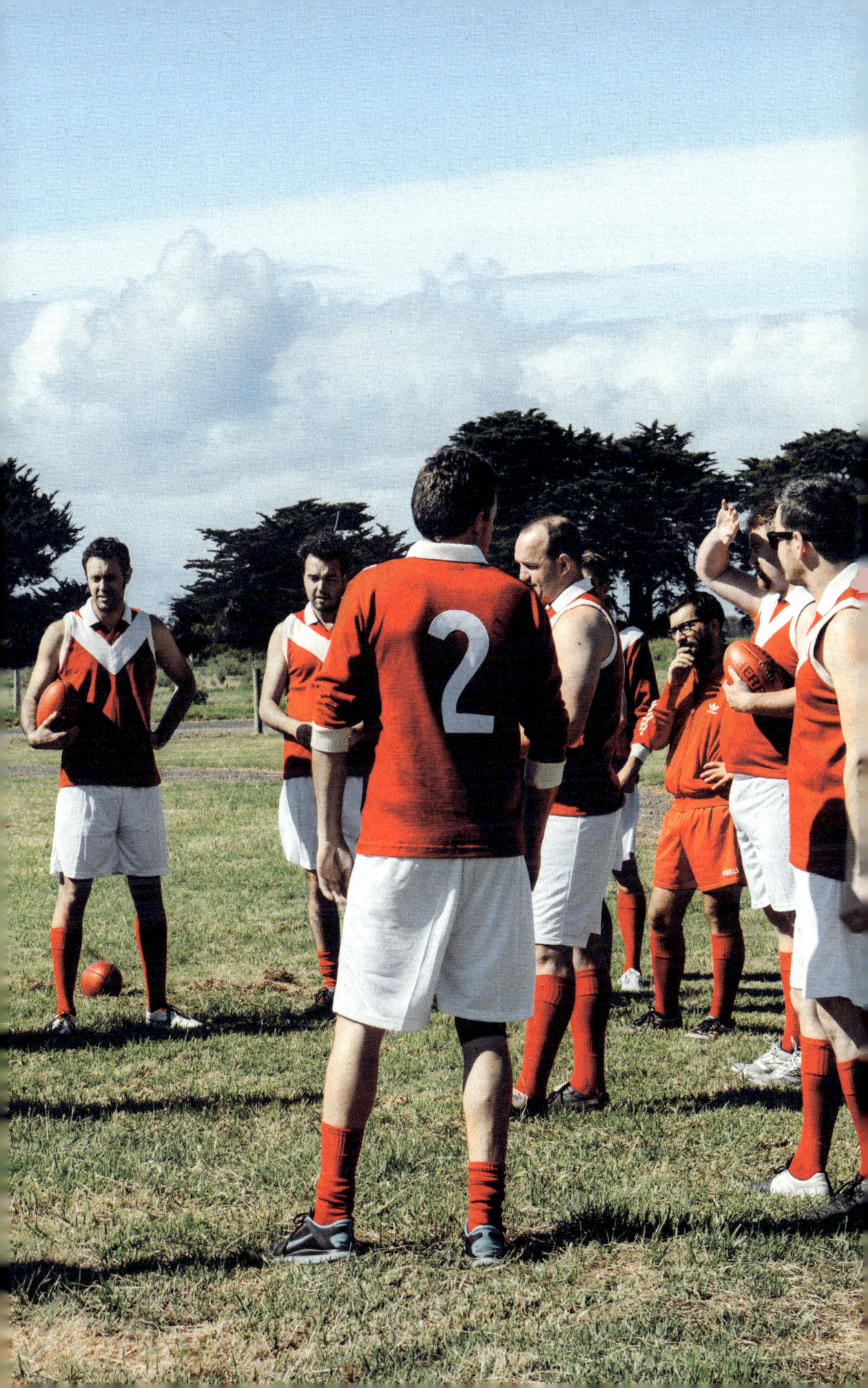
2

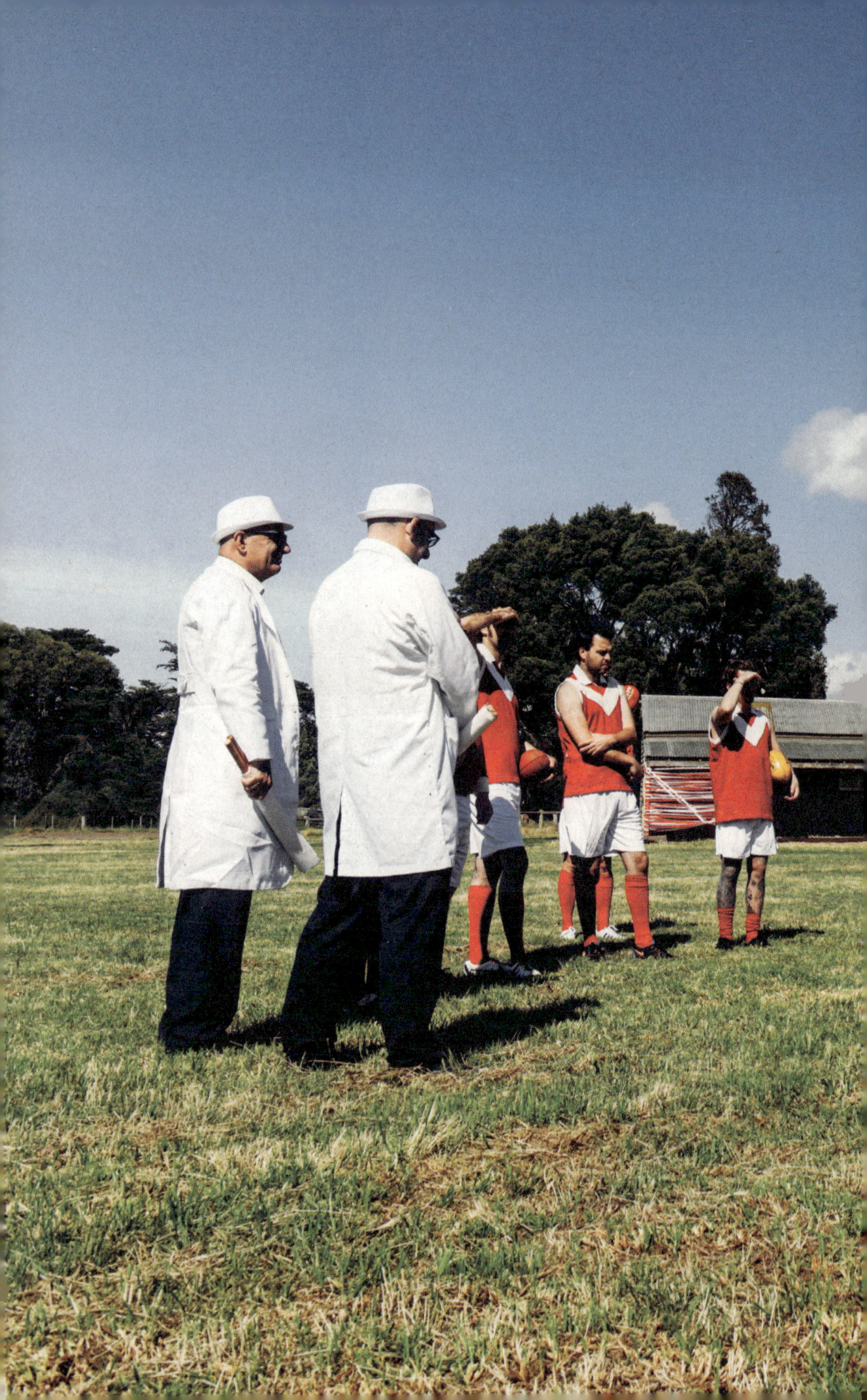

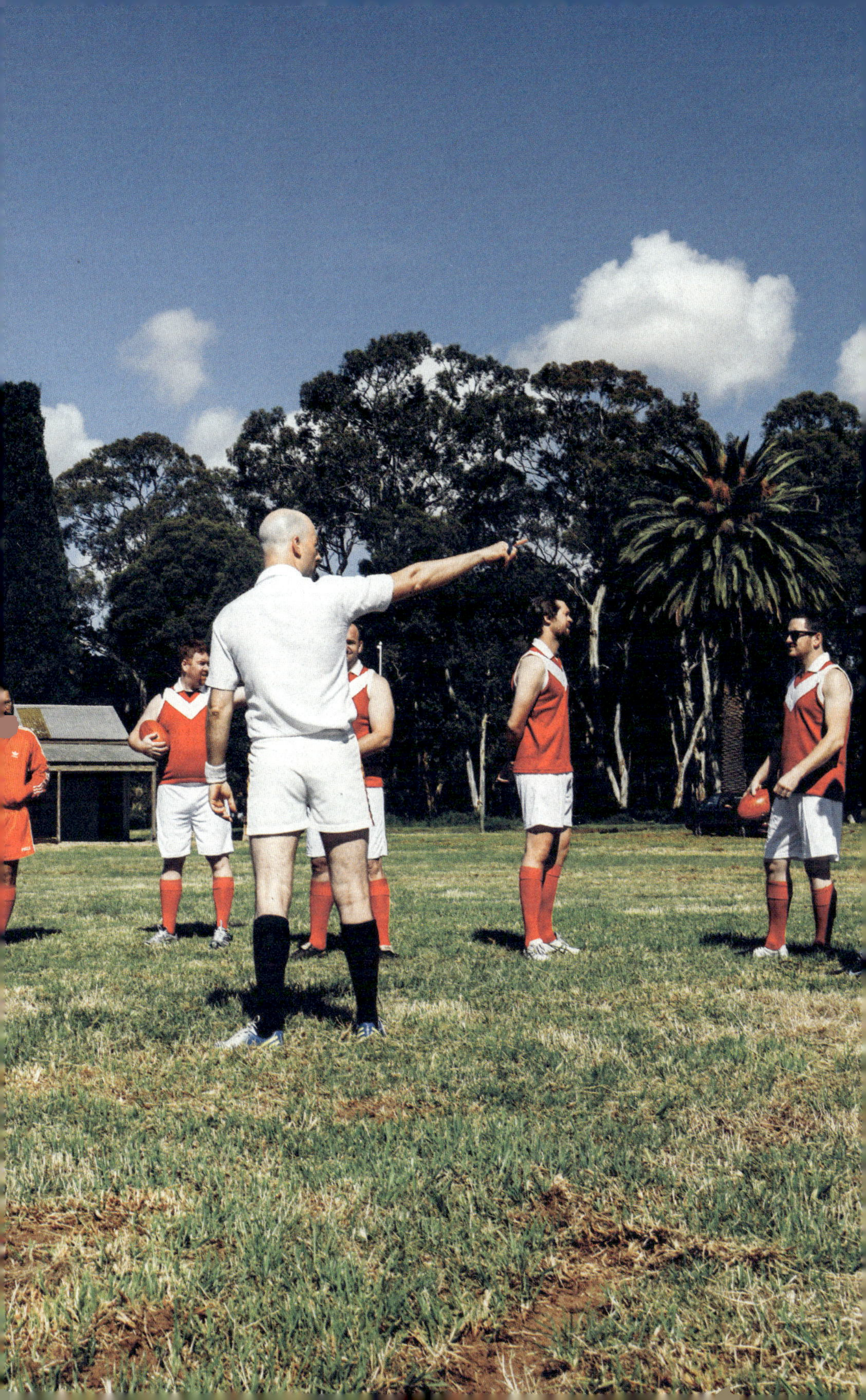

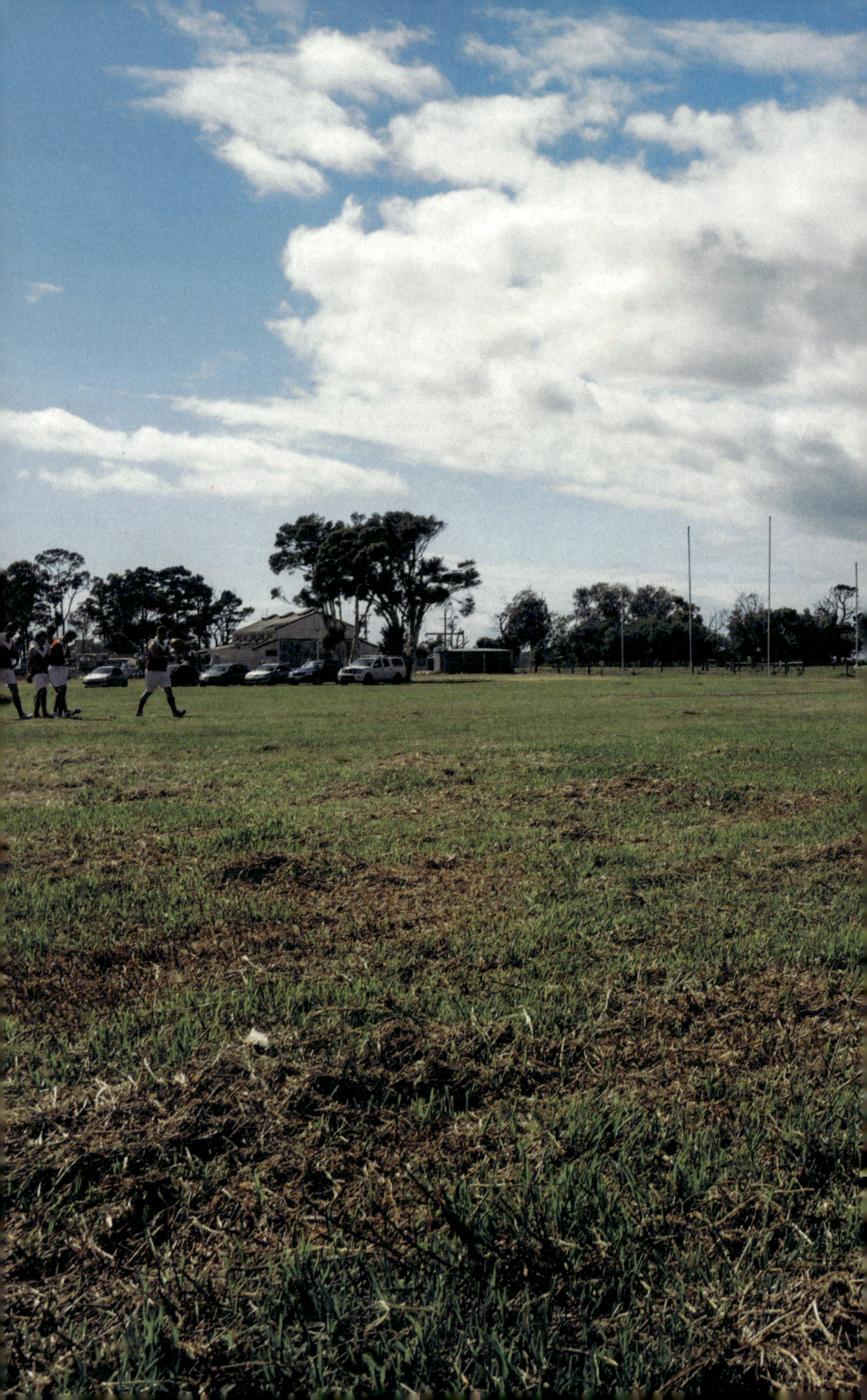

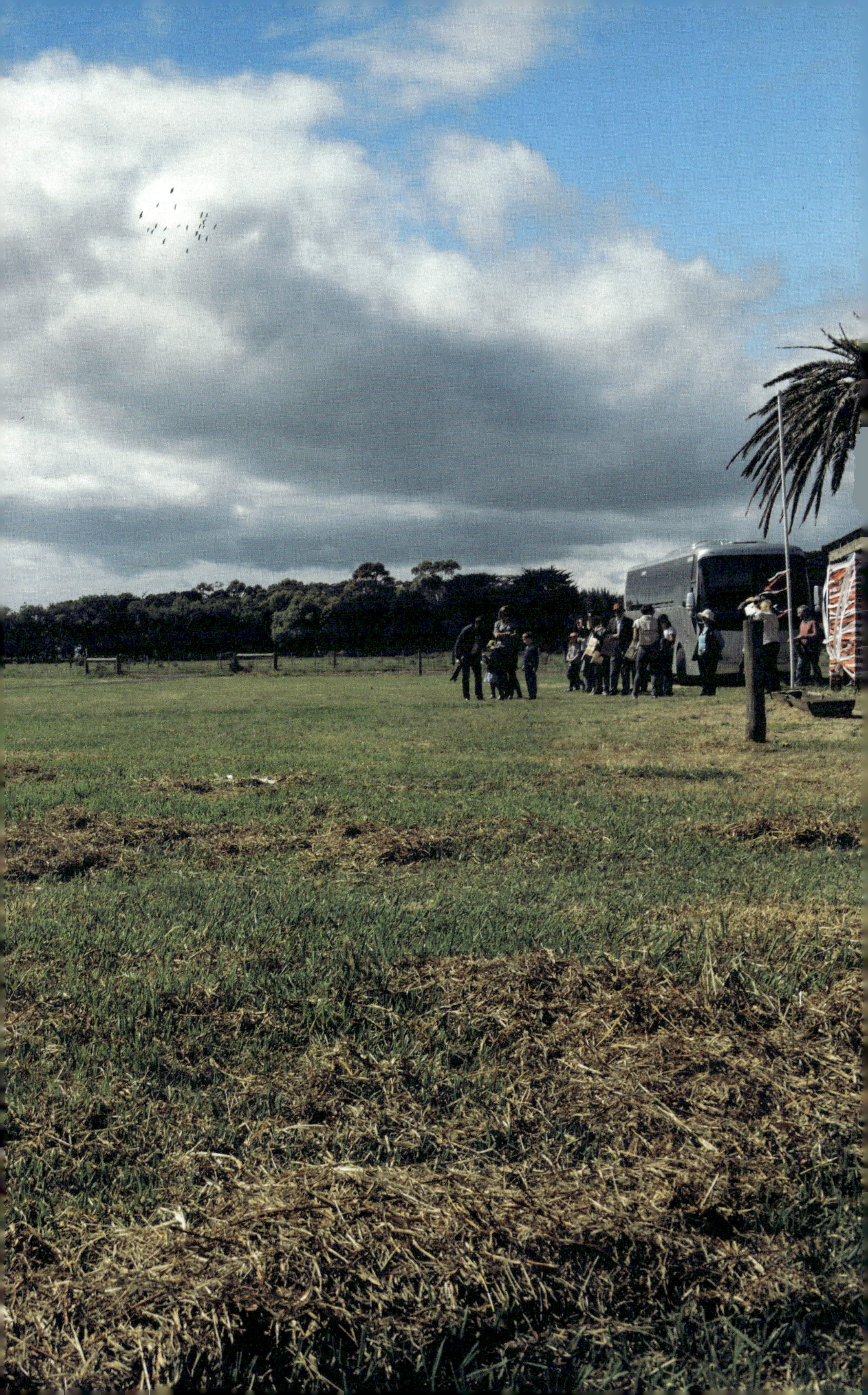

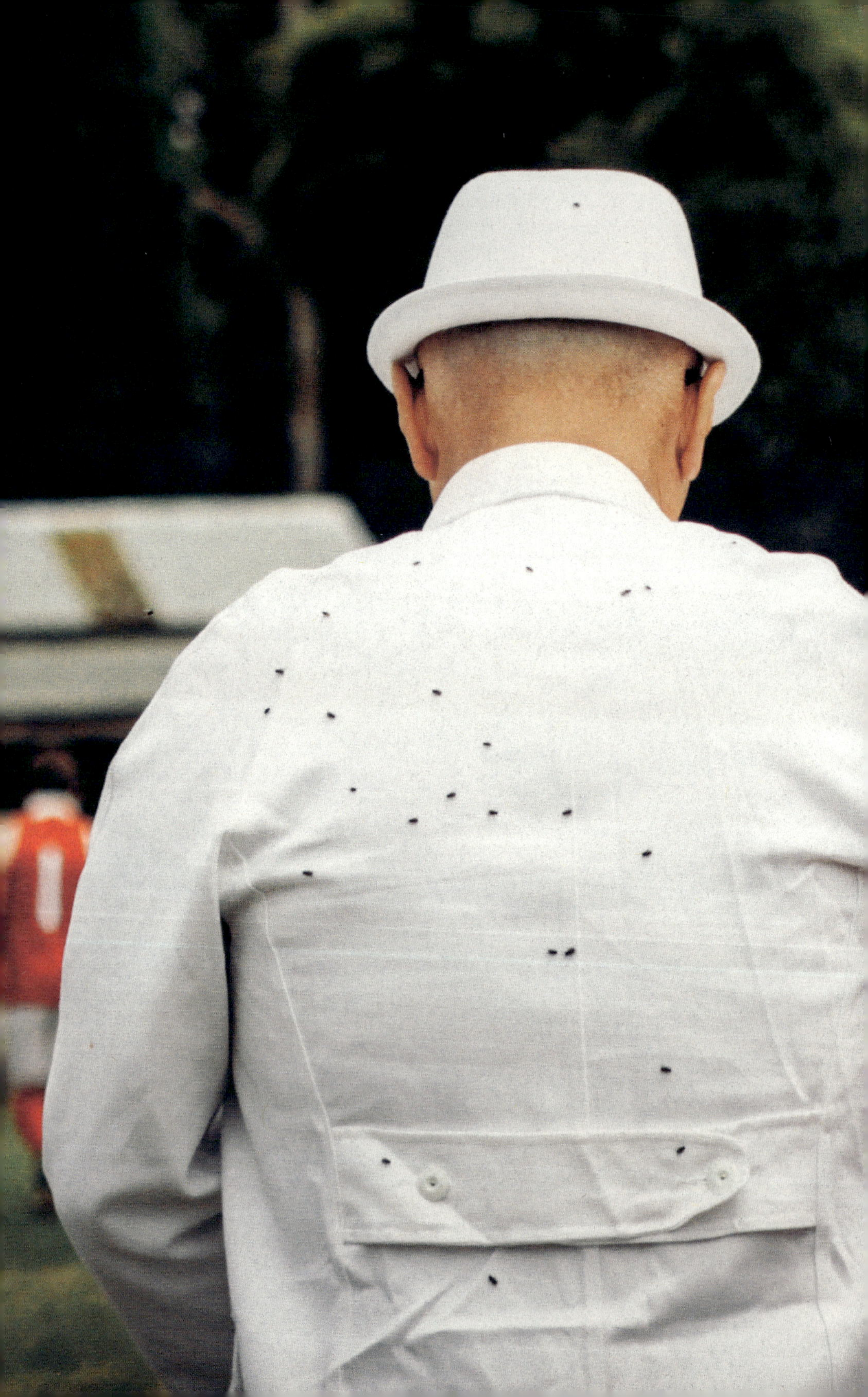

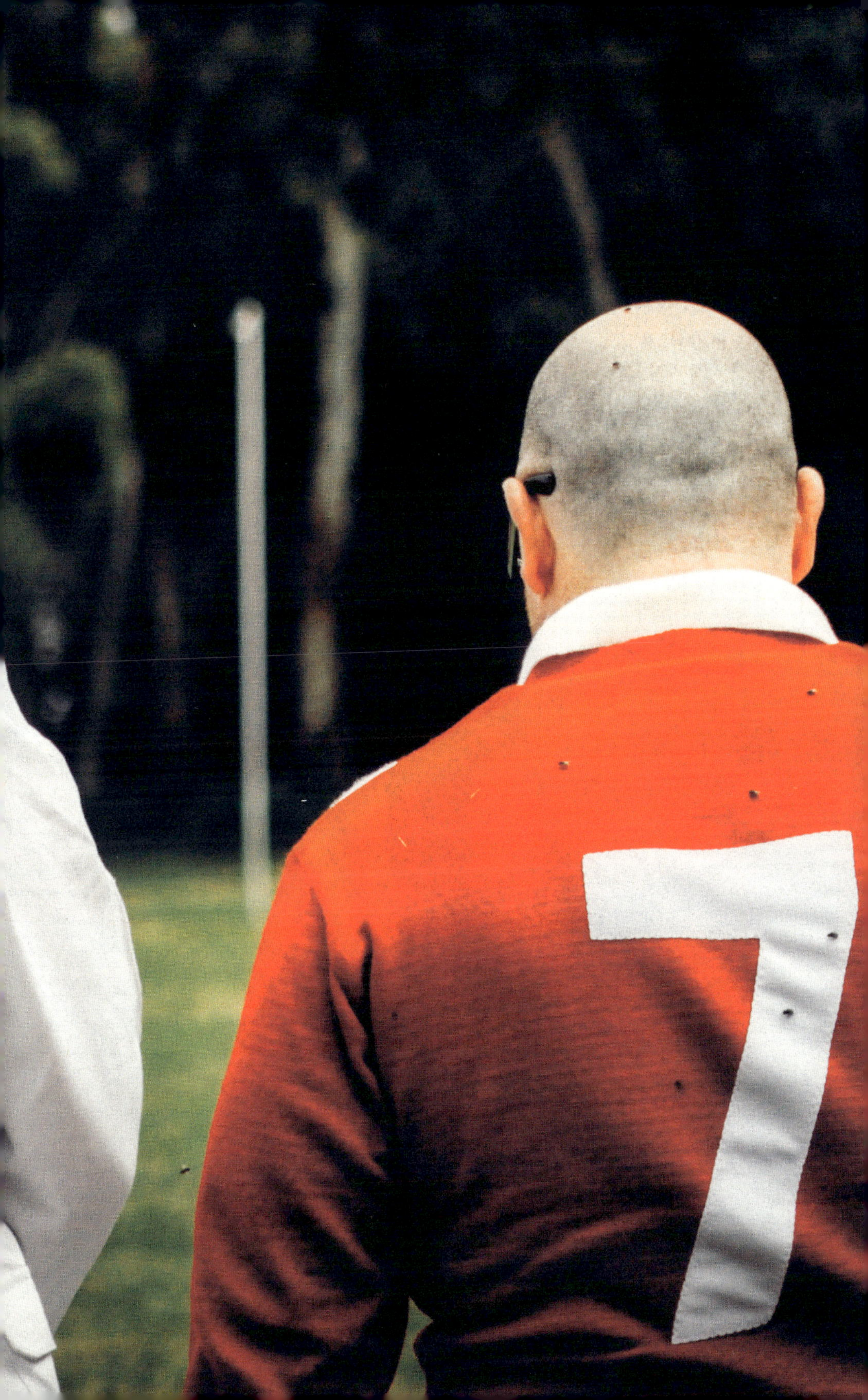

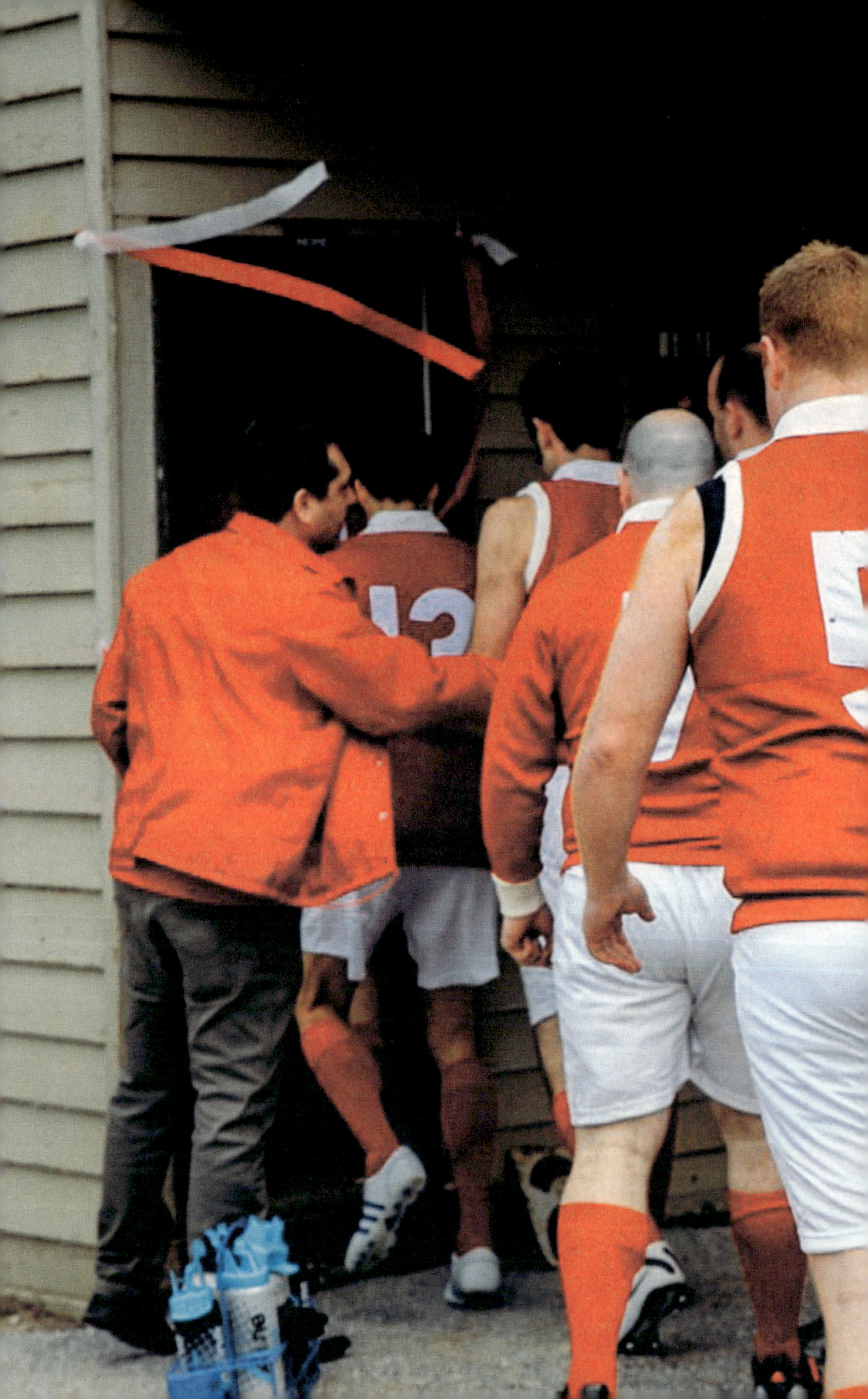

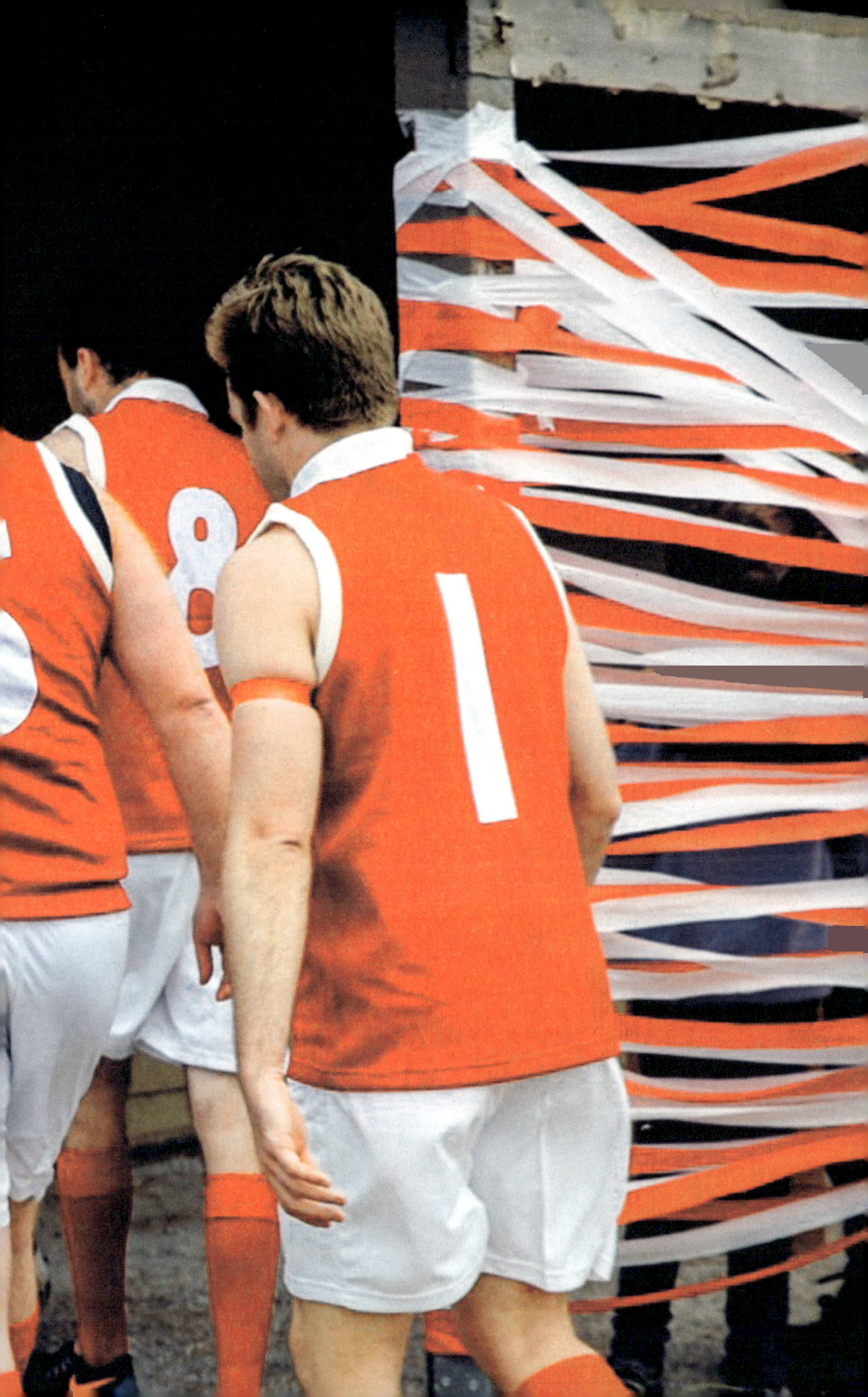
8
1

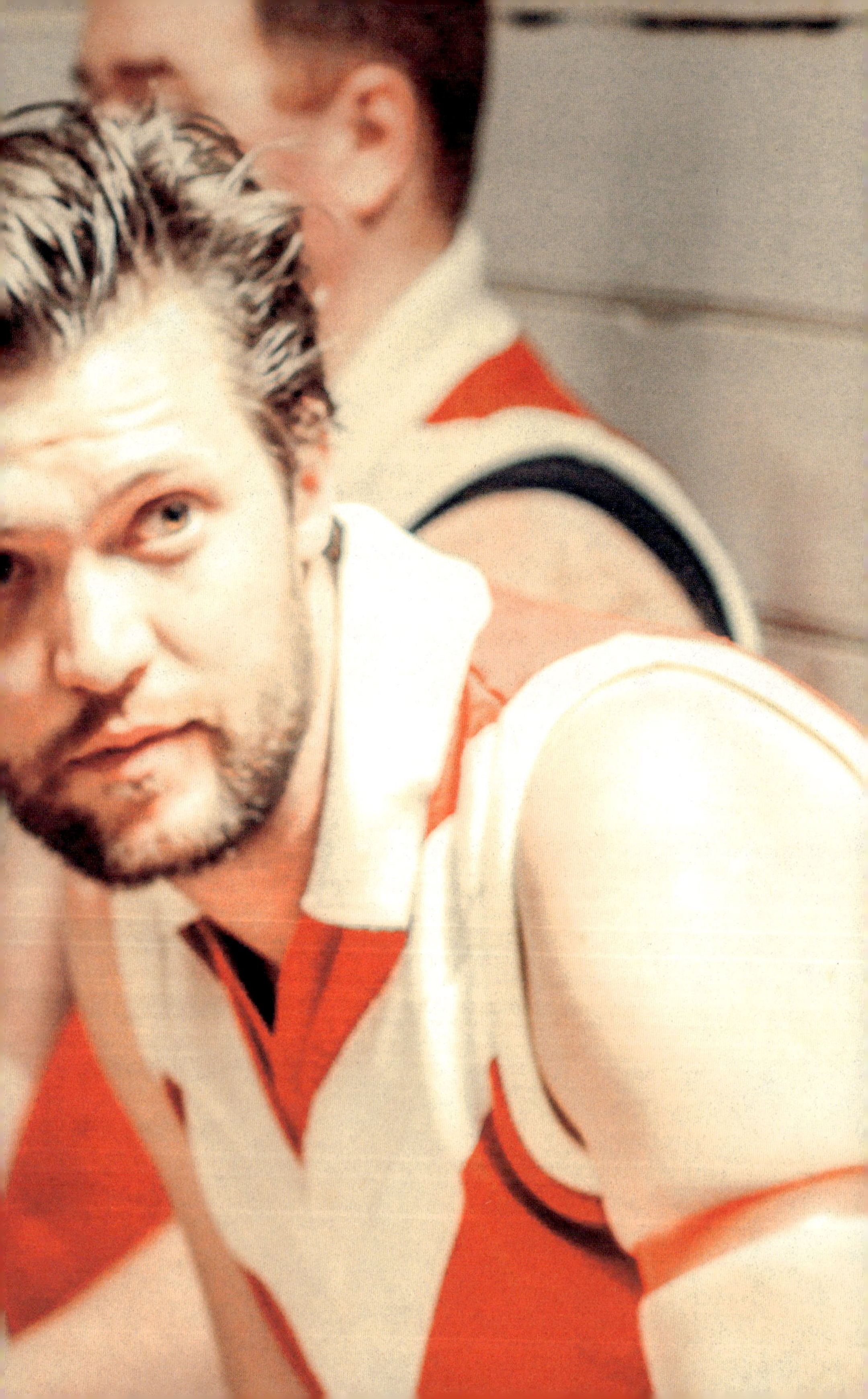

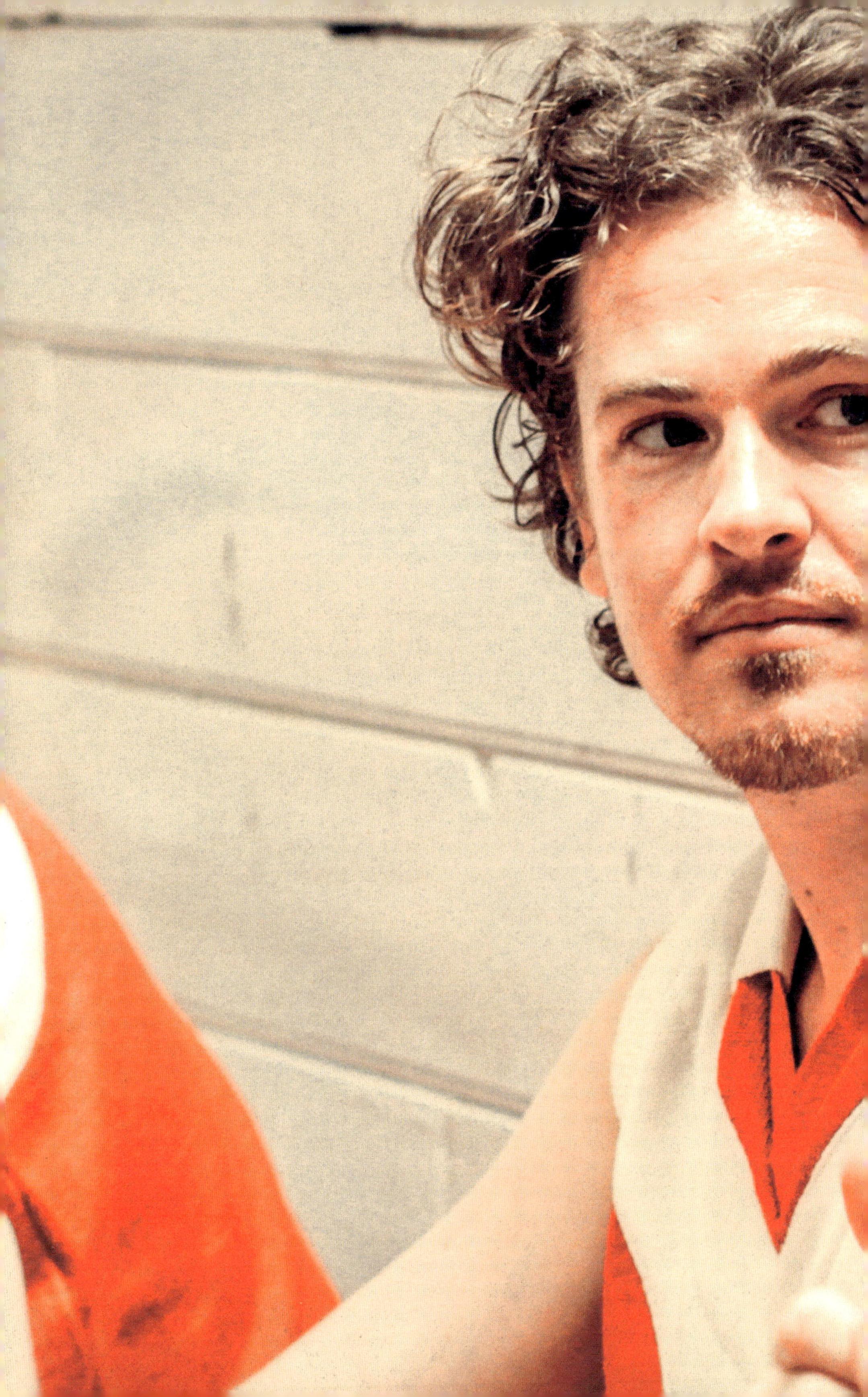

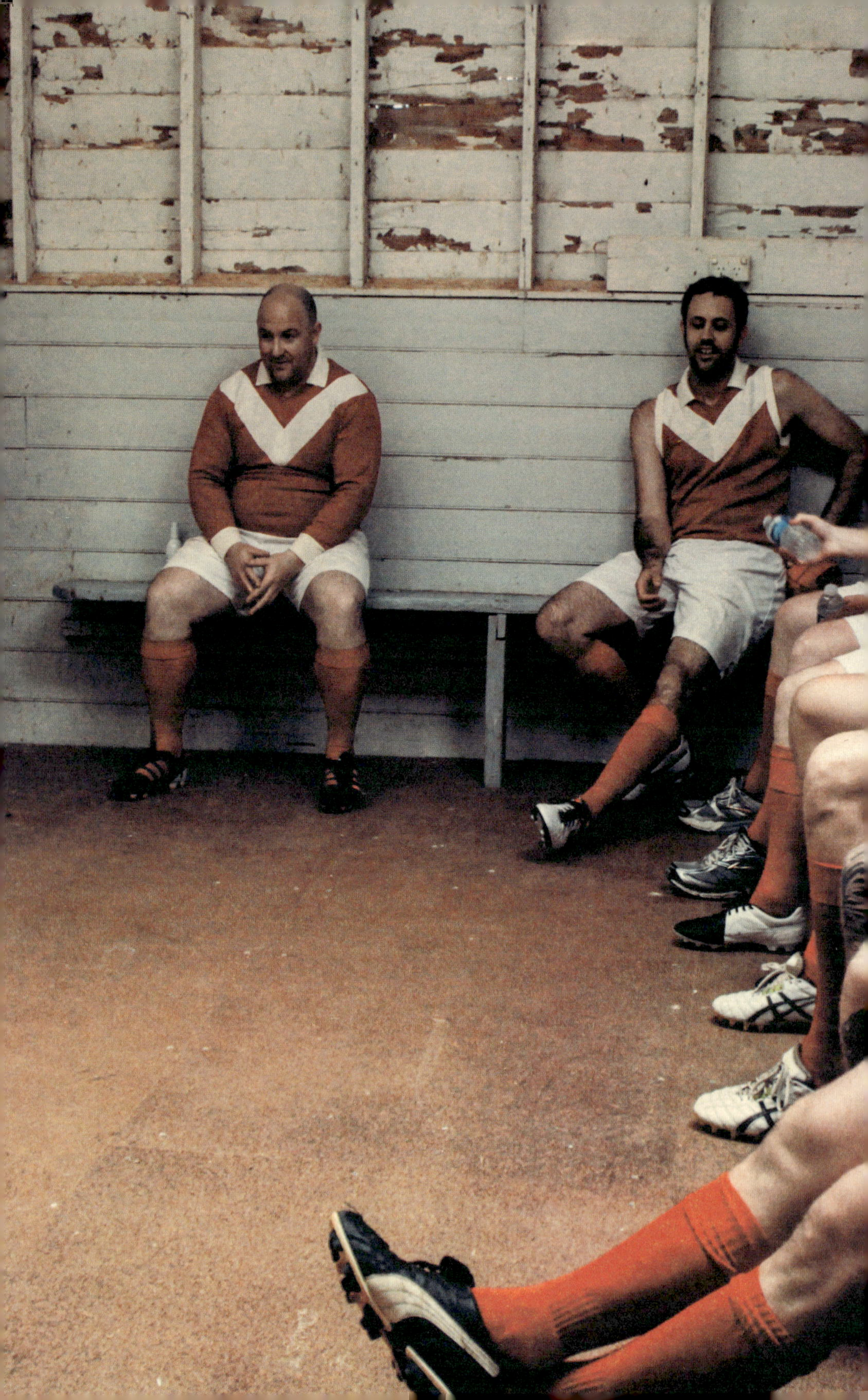

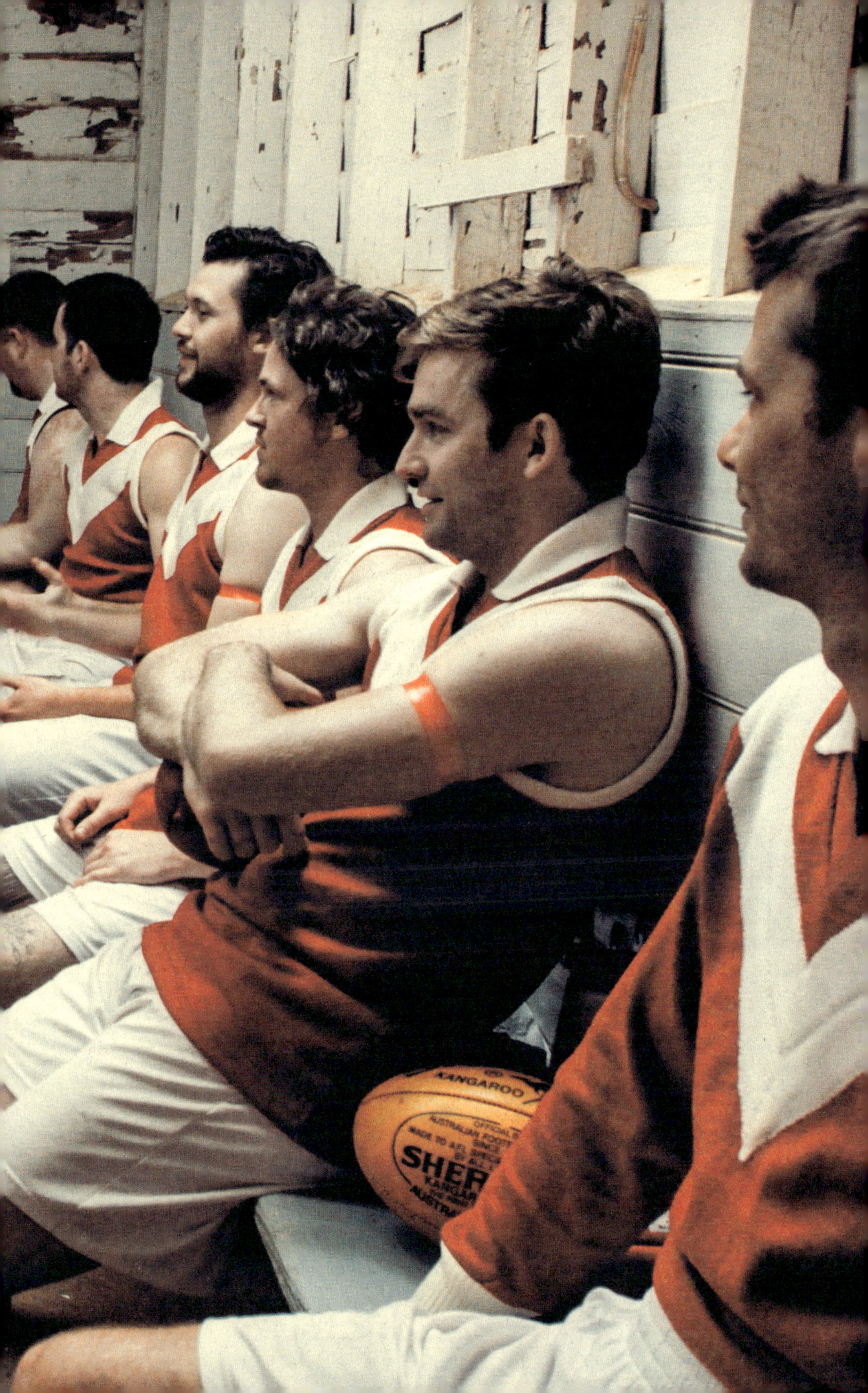
KANGAROO

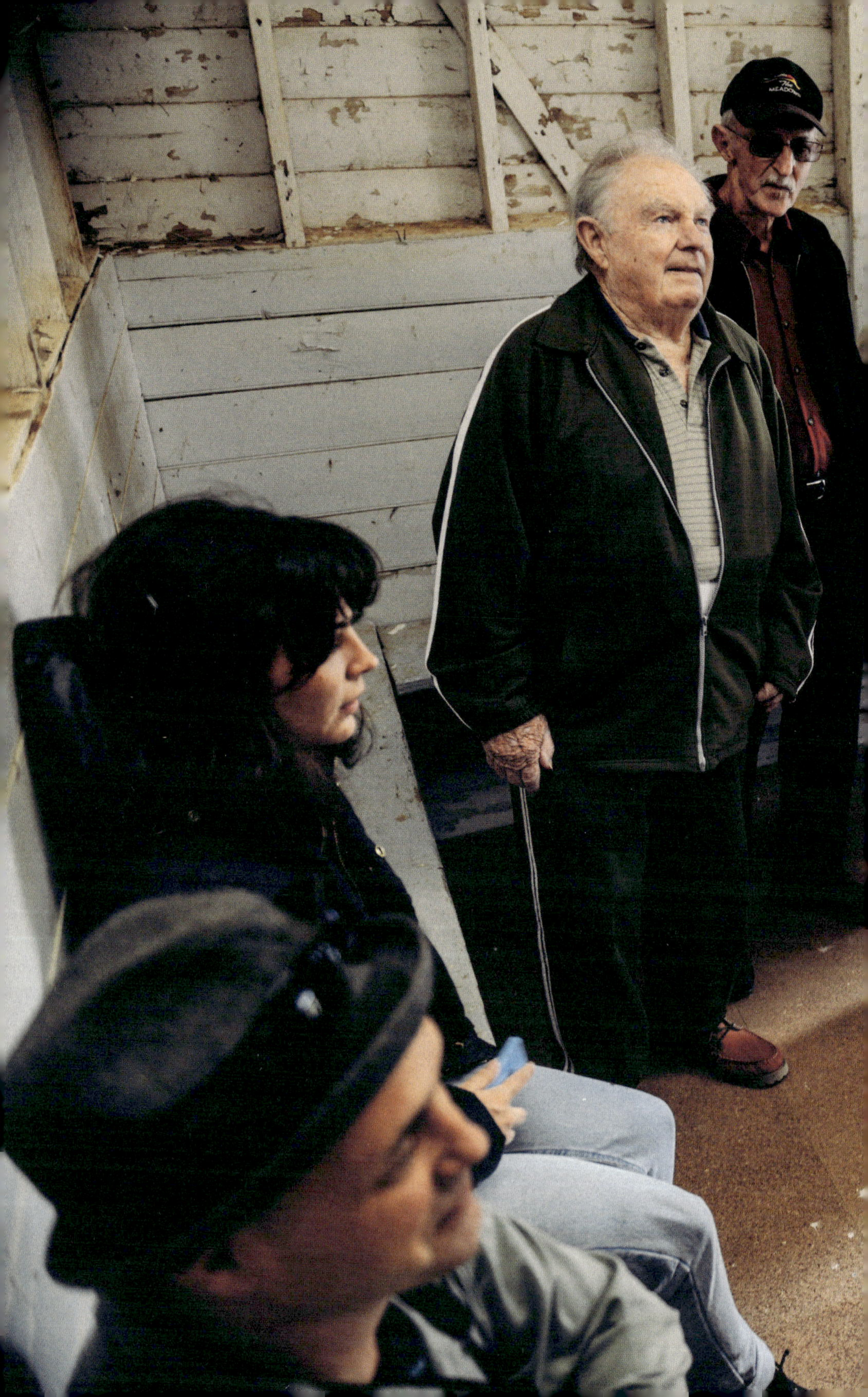

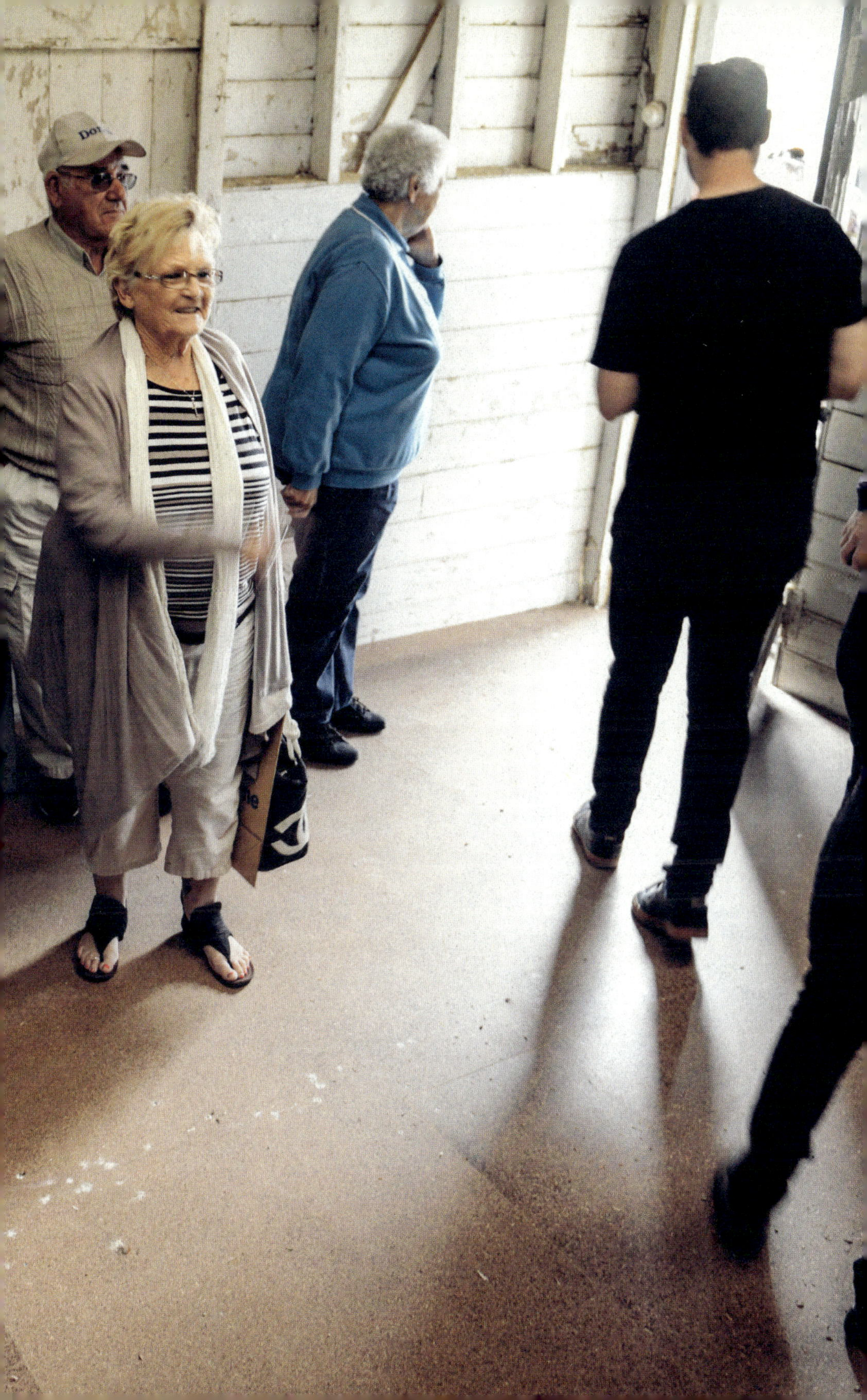

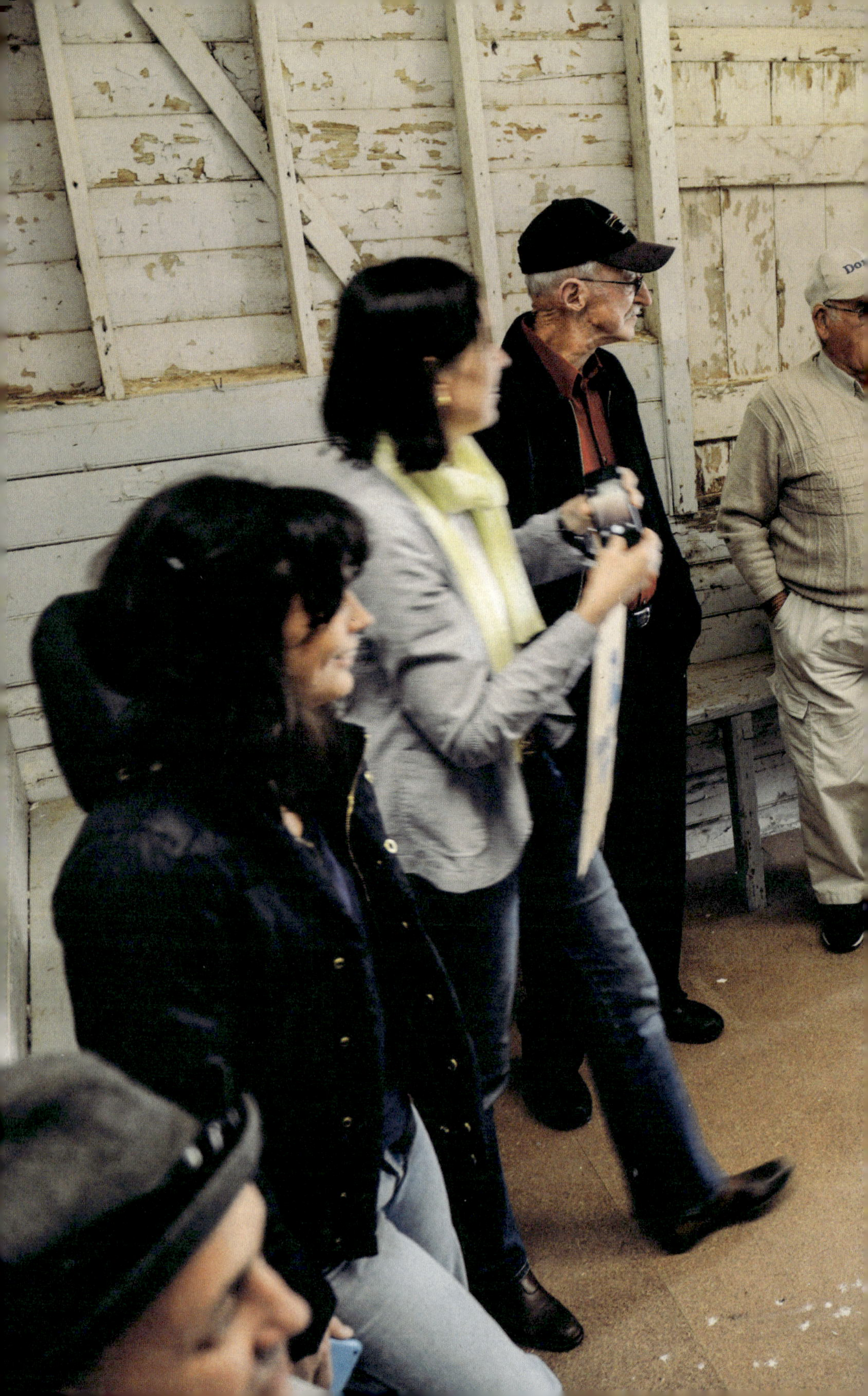

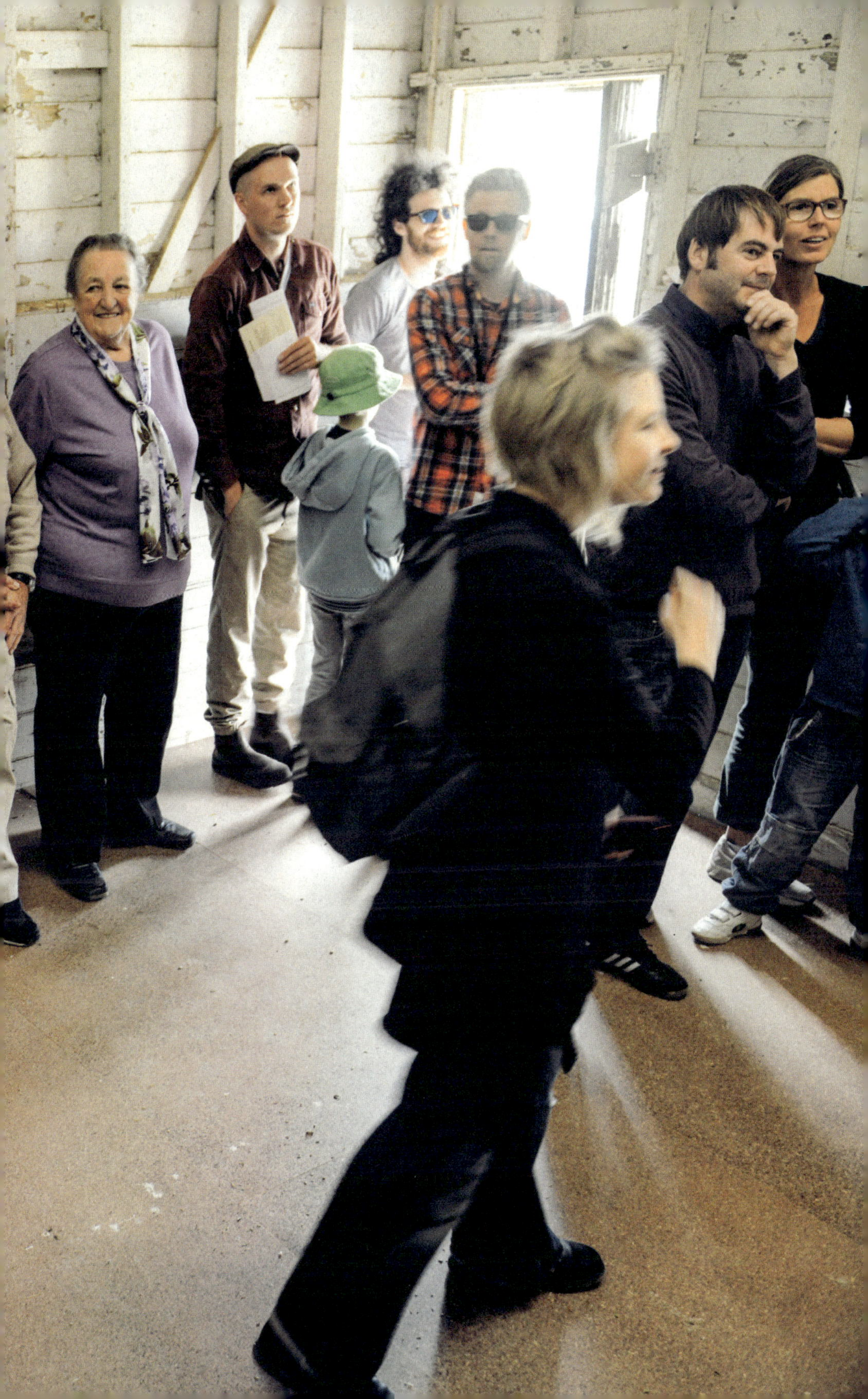

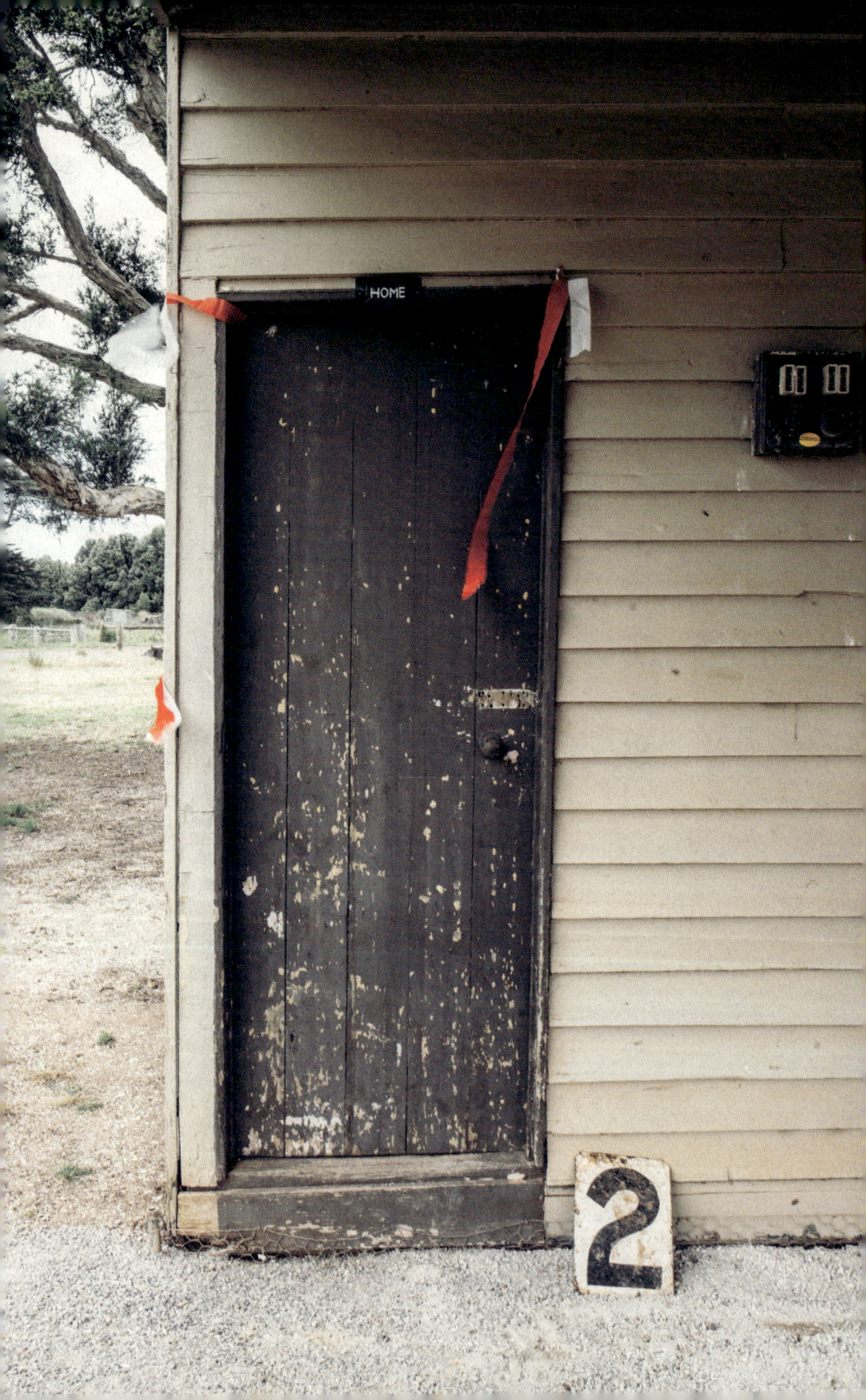
HOME
2

Treatment: Six Public Artworks at Melbourne Water

—David Cross

No doubt there are people who have pondered on the mysterious process of human waste removal set in train by the pressing of the toilet button. Yet, up until recently, I was not one of them. Sewage flowed somewhere, it was stored out of sight, the smell was likely to be off the radar, but beyond that I had no cogent understanding of public sanitation processes.

Driving through the gate at the Western Treatment Plant in Werribee, just outside of Melbourne, for the first time in late 2014, I was filled with juvenile prejudices but also a curiosity as to what lay inside the military-style security fences. In being invited to develop a public art project at one of the largest facilities of its kind in the southern hemisphere, I would at the very least learn about how civic authorities deal with the daily gift of literally millions of organic deposits: each one winding its way along the subterranean river network to Werribee.

At the time of writing this overview (almost a year after the project), I can potentially claim the status of a sewerage expert. At parties, I have reeled off details about the odour control facility ('OCF' in the trade) and how organisms are used to break down the smell of the raw sewage as it enters the plant. I have regaled bemused colleagues with stories of the fabulous mechanical aerators that churn (oxygenate) millions of litres of treated 'product' in a holding pond that is larger than the Melbourne Cricket Ground. And I have most likely appalled acquaintances with stories of the divers dressed like 19th-century underwater explorers, who disappear into the pitch brown pond to maintain the equipment. 'Visibility is zero', I add, for maximum impact.

In different company, I love to wax lyrical about the orange-bellied parrot, one of the world's most endangered birds, which breeds in Tasmania and flies north to Werribee for the winter. There are estimated to be no more than sixty birds in total left, and bird watchers the world over are desperate to see one. I have had to confess to mildly deflated looks that, in my year-long traversing of the site, I was not fortunate enough to encounter one, but they are out there, camouflaged by the millions of other birds that are blissfully indifferent to the variable water quality.

For these kernels of knowledge and a great deal more, I can thank the good people of Melbourne Water and the foresight of the City of Wyndham for the chance to make *Treatment: Six Public Artworks at Western Treatment Plant* in November 2015. The project brought together six Australian artists who each developed temporary commissions in response to specific aspects of the site. Catherine Bell, Bindi Cole Chocka, Megan Evans, Shane McGrath, Técha Noble and Spiros Panigirakis all developed a place-responsive artwork that was experienced sequentially via a coach tour across two Saturdays in November 2015.

The specs of the site are impressive and daunting: 11,000 hectares (almost the size of Malta); one of the largest bird sanctuaries/nesting sites in the world; a methane capture facility that powers the entire plant and an engineering process that manages to produce agricultural standard water without damaging the delicate ecosystem of Port Phillip Bay. As wonderful and spectacular as these things are, making artworks that speak to the site while holding their own ground was (and is) no small feat. This tension was, from the outset, a formative creative dilemma for the artists to negotiate, allayed only slightly by a significant six-month research period on site and by the extraordinary support and resources of Melbourne Water. Given unprecedented access to archives and to the site's many features and locations, the artists were able to benefit from the rich local knowledge of key personnel on the site, many of whom have worked at the plant since it was an authority of the Metropolitan Board of Works in the 1980s.

The wealth of anecdotal narratives and urban myths recounted by key Melbourne Water staff formed a crucial body of knowledge, from which the artists have responded to the site and its varied contexts. Of the many nuggets recounted by the plant's historian Paul Balassone, one in particular stood out. He outlined how, up until industrial-scale mechanisation replaced physical toil, many of the women whose husbands and partners worked on site were the beneficiaries of impressive jewellery collections. A small but potentially lucrative benefit of standing ankle-deep in 'bio-solids' all day was the possibility of finding something valuable. For the men who worked the fields, visual acuity was a hugely important attribute, enabling one to spot a gleaming valuable in a veritable sea of base material. Diamond rings, gold bracelets and other precious keepsakes that had been inadvertently sacrificed in a momentary act of clumsiness near the toilet bowl ended up in forensically-scrubbed private collections thirty-five kilometres west of Melbourne. Perhaps it was a measure of the narrative power of this anecdote that none of the artists chose to respond directly to it, preferring to let its mythical resonances float in the imaginary realm somewhere between truth and tall tale.

Most of the women with impressively well-stocked jewellery boxes lived in the township of Cocoroc in the northern part of the farm. Once a thriving community with schools, shops and recreational facilities serving over 600 hundred residents, the settlement closed down in the early 1970s. With advanced technological innovation on-site and improved transport enabling workers to commute from Werribee and surrounding areas, Cocoroc was no longer viable and many of its assorted buildings were transplanted to other areas in the district. Only a small proportion of the township remains, including the old swimming pools, the town hall, the football ground and, most impressively, a striking bluestone water tower. These features stand as evocative reminders of what was a burgeoning township and they became the focus of three of the projects.

It was not surprising that the artists were captivated by Cocoroc and wanted to make work that spoke to both the architecture and the history of this curious ghost town. Megan Evans, Catherine Bell and Shane McGrath chose to focus on the water tower, the swimming pool/changerooms and the football ground respectively. Each artist sought to reveal distinctly different aspects of the former township, some of which are visible or latent, but most of which are long gone. The spooky charisma of the ghost town in the middle of hectares of parched pasture compelled the artists to use the few architectural ciphers that remain to re-form, restage, or speculate on specific aspects of the township's life.

Evans was immediately drawn to the water tower, partly for its extraordinary form and beautiful interior acoustics, but also because of its status as a fundamental piece of Victorian infrastructure. The tower speaks to the 'civilising' effects of Western industrial engineering (proper sanitation) but also to the sense of authority and presence such a British structure is designed to evoke. Her interest in the tower was both for this signification of colonial civic status but also as a symbol of the dislocation of Indigenous people whose incremental ejection from Melbourne was due entirely to the concentric growth of the modern metropolis.

Working across sculpture and sound, Evans offered an installation of layered textures: acoustic resonances and beautifully formed materialities, all of which coaxed the audience to align finely wrought aesthetics with the brutal history of Aboriginal displacement. Configured inside the water tower as a series of dramatically lit theatrical stages or vignettes, each component deftly yet precisely imbricated the imported decorative crafts of colonialism with a concurrent narrative of exclusion. The reverberating pre-recorded sound of dripping water enhanced the dank interior, pressing home the critical purpose of the water tower as Melbourne's first source of safe drinking water. The artist makes the key point that, without this tower, Melbourne would have remained a small and fragile settlement. Evans's use of exquisite colonial craft and refinement, elided with the brutality of colonial expansion, established a beautifully painful counter-history to the bracing narrative of industrial development.

At the southern end of the old township, the Cocoroc oval exists in a state of elegant disrepair. When Shane McGrath first encountered the former home ground of the Metro Farm Herefords, the goal posts were crooked and almost entirely devoid of white paint, the grass was waist-high and yellow, and the old players' pavilion was collapsing with rabbit holes in the floor. It looked like a competitive game had not been played here since the advent of colour television. With some cursory research, McGrath pinpointed that 1964 was the last season in which the Herefords competed in the Werribee District Football league. It had been fifty-one years since the distinctive maroon and cream V guernsey had lit up Cocoroc oval.

McGrath's interest in vernacular culture is extensive, but sport, especially non-professional sport with its arcane codes, aesthetics and close community ties, is a staple of his sculptural and performative practice. The few lingering artefacts gathering layers of dust in the players' pavilion—such as rusting metal numbers from a long-gone scoreboard and an antique stretcher to carry injured players off the ground—piqued his interest in finding out more about the Cocoroc football team: their name; reputation, and hopefully what made them distinct from other clubs in the district. Uncovering through archival and oral history research a veritable treasure trove of information about the Herefords, from the jumper design to the club song to their nickname 'the sewer rats', McGrath decided that he wanted to bring the Herefords back to Cocoroc Oval.

In seeking to restage a game of football as his *Treatment* project, the artist had to regenerate every aspect of the site and produce a replica set of playing uniforms including, copies of the team's 1960s woollen jumpers. He also needed to find a team of players who approximated the diversity of body shape and facial hair of a 'typical' local football team. With enormous attention to detail and hugely complex staging, the audience disembarked from the bus in time to encounter a seven-minute interlude in the game when the players trudge off the field to be given a 'gee-up' by the coach in the changerooms. The audience, not sure what was transpiring or what to do as they disembarked from the bus, unwittingly took on the role of the football crowd, gathering outside the change room or wandering into the vacant visitors' room to hear the coach whip his players into a lather of competitive desperation. As the coach's rhetoric (built on stinging his players with opposition-inspired stereotypes of 'shit workers') rose to a crescendo, the room fell silent and the audience were ushered back onto the bus with a souvenir commemorative Herefords stubby holder and the sound of the club theme song ringing in their ears.

Adjacent to the oval, another Cocoroc recreation facility was also corroding and in a state of abject disrepair. The local outdoor swimming pools, one for adults, one for kids, had been a key gathering point in the township over many summers until left to gather mould, weeds and the requisite puddle of muddy water. Catherine Bell was compelled less by their dishevelled state than by the faint veneer of post-war civic optimism that the design of the pools retained. Like McGrath, Bell was intrigued by the lost charisma of the town's recreational amenities and wanted to imbue the swimming pools and the similarly putrid, wildlife-infested change rooms with a sense of their former spark and social pageantry.

In choosing to painstakingly restore the children's swimming pool back to a functional state, Bell sought to establish a marked contrast with the fetid adult pool parallel to it. With a glistening coat of 1950s-era blue paint, meticulously buffed tiles and the requisite sparkling water, the pool appeared delightfully incongruous in the landscape. This architectural gesture activated the experience of a bygone era, deftly shifting temporal registers of past and present.

While almost surreal in atmosphere, the work was further extended by a second component in the changerooms. In the Melbourne Water archives, Bell had discovered 8mm footage of children raucously playing in the pool in the late 1940s. The artist projected an edited sequence of this material directly onto the wall of the darkened changeroom with a soundtrack of jovial jazz from a similar era. The juxtaposition of joyful faces dive-bombing their friends, beamed on to a rotting wall in a ruined space that stank of rat droppings, was profound. Bell's alignment of two different kinds of assisted readymade, the modified pool and the film footage, offered a highly nuanced and generously open space for the audience to consider an almost lost history and to reflect on its previously dynamic and vital sense of lived experience.

The *Treatment* experience began and concluded at the Melbourne Water discovery centre, a 1970s modernist wonderland filled with interactive exhibits that outline the history of the site and the assorted processes by which sewage arrives and is treated. Spiros Panigirakis has more than a soft spot for high modernist art and design and was completely captivated by both the architecture and the slightly retro feel of the models and signage. Picking up on the decidedly optimistic flavour of this museum of sewerage, Panigirakis, via a performative installation in the foyer, sought to draw our attention to key aspects of the site and in particular to the curious yet complex languages of information display.

Throughout the course of both days, the artist and a small team of workers set about performing various acts of manual labour, each of which directed our attention to signage or architectural features that navigated the elusive boundary between modernist abstraction and Australian design vernacular. From vacuuming the Mies van der Rohe-style geometric foyer carpet, to assembling sculptural replicas of the enormous artificial bird perches that feature in the southern section of the plant, Panigirakis sought to draw our attention to the distinct imbrication of high and low art (international style confidence with a multi-modal learning centre on human waste) while speaking at the same time to the site's history of repetitive labour.

The casual, almost deadpan, tone of the performance meant that, for some of the audience, the activity appeared to register as building renovation rather than art. Part of the beauty of this especially subtle work was that the audience got to have a second experience of the work at the conclusion of the bus journey, arriving back to see the space slightly but significantly transformed. For some, this second bite was the point at which the work first registered as art: a denouement made manifest by having ninety minutes meandering in the landscape to contemplate what these actions could be. For others, the work provoked perplexed reflections on why building maintenance would be scheduled on the same day as the art exhibition.

In seeking to build an experience whereby a small number of artworks could resonate in and through an 11,000-hectare site without feeling slight and provisional, a number of key decisions were made about building an armature for the project as a whole. The device of the bus journey was one key mechanism through which we identified the possibility of shaping an art experience. By constructing the event as a schedule of ninety-minute bus tours, we had a mechanism that functioned to suture each of the commissions together around a carefully constructed journey. Beginning at the Melbourne Water Discovery Centre and then moving across the site via the township of Cocoroc, the bus tour was a frame, a curatorial conceit and a practical solution to the complexities of the site all in one. It also functioned as an air-conditioned viewing station, a mobile gallery, and a temporary community around which the experience of *Treatment* was collectively formed through shared conversation.

Both Técha Noble and Bindi Cole Chocka utilised the bus as a key feature of their respective works, accentuating its tourist-orientated role as a sightseeing vehicle. Cole Chocka had spent a significant amount of time on site courtesy of her role as the inaugural Wyndham/Melbourne Water artist-in-residence and this depth of knowledge resulted in two distinct works, a video projection that captured the sublime features of the landscape and a decidedly irreverent and playful work that addressed the sensory experience of smell. The video work *West of Wonka* in the discovery centre's large meeting room utilised footage taken on site that was then manipulated in post-production to render the landscape psychedelic, capturing the site as a continuous sequence of almost abstract hallucinations. The accompanying ambient soundtrack of music and birdsong accentuated the stark qualities of the landscape, pushing its repetitive features towards a mirage of sensory overload.

In contra-distinction to the video installation, Cole Chocka offered a second project that, while markedly different in tone, shared a sense of the strangeness of the landscape. Employing the 1970s birthday card staple of scratch and sniff, Cole Chocka used this retro sensory device to playfully reconfigure the firm association of Werribee with the smell of sewage.

Her two custom designed cards, each with an image of one of the plant's architectural features (the extraordinary odour control facility and the sewage pond aerators), offered a surprising and whimsical response to the aroma of human waste. As the bus passed both sites on the tour, the driver slowed the bus down and the audience was instructed to scratch the relevant card. In place of sewage, the audience was delighted to smell either cinnamon or chocolate in the air-conditioned and sanitised confines of the bus.

Noble's monumental and avowedly glam restaging of the life cycle of faeces took place in the vicinity of the sewage ponds. With the extraordinary aerators and engineering works as a backdrop, the artist choreographed the 'poo cycle' as a series of marvellous theatrical vignettes.

At each of the four 'stations', performers played out a component of the process garbed in outrageously elaborate costumes. Straddling the cosmic, the fantastical and the fetishistic, Noble offered a bespoke take on the specifics of this basic bodily process. The entire spectacle was played out in a cosmic time-space continuum as the bus, at a snail's pace, crawled its way around the performance site. The slowness of each performative action and the funereal pace of the bus added a layer of comic hilarity redolent of silent-era caper movies with a similar if languid, stylised and exaggerated performance of physical story telling.

Yet, in place of slapstick, Noble offered scenes that were certainly comic but also strangely foreign, perverse and marvellous in the surrealist sense of the word. The first tableau was a gigantic inflatable turd covered in a new-age astrology design of stars and cosmic patterns. Its softness and kinetic qualities enhanced by the wind, in tandem with its panel-van-art colour scheme, gave the form a striking, uncanny quality in the barren gravel landscape. This scene was closely followed by the extraordinary staging of two figures in protective gas suits performing an allegory of defecation, one figure extracting handfuls of gold dust from the other's posterior. Such a scatological performance, however, was tempered by the enhanced and highly stylised pimping of the suits. Noble's glam customisation of the suits with colour, mirrored reflection and a generous dose of science-fiction camp, gave the scene a striking, grandiloquent quality in contra-distinction to the subject matter. The work was completed when a young performer similarly resplendent of costume and with extended wings fluttering in the wind, guided the bus out of the sewage treatment area on its final journey back to the discovery centre.

Slavoj Žižek in his study of the event begins by describing it as an act of reframing. While going on to examine the event from a diversity of perspectives, including the idea that an event is an effect that exceeds its causes, this idea of reframing is a useful one in considering place-responsive temporary public art.[1] In creating an event whereby audience members are drawn to a specific place to consider it in dialogue with a series of artworks, a juxtaposition is established between the specificity of a place, its geographical features, use value, culture, etc, and the ways in which artists have chosen to re-frame these contexts.

For the artists in *Treatment*, Žižek's rhetorical question, *is an event a change in the way reality appears to us, or, is it a shattering transformation of reality itself?* could be seen as a useful provocation.[2] In seeking to respond to the Western Treatment Plant, while reframing its assorted contexts for an audience mostly unaware of any of the site's features, the artists sought to find an accord between reality and its appearance and their own distinct inflections. *Treatment* as an event sought to circumscribe the extraordinary features of both what is and what has been on this site, while at the same time transforming these contexts.

For the audience, there is a constantly shifting process between marvelling at the extraordinary scale of the plant, its harsh and denuded landscape interspersed with monumental industrial engineering, and the artists' assorted additions and subtractions. This process of drifting, between what is there and what has been inserted, is a fundamental condition of the experience.

While particular attention was paid to the artworks, the intervals between each individual work were crucial. These spaces—when we drove across kilometres of fields, past sewage ponds and odour control facilities—functioned as periods of liminality that enabled the audience to drift off into the passing landscape or to converse with fellow passengers. Former Cocoroc residents regaled strangers in these moments with personal anecdotes of growing up in the township, imparting first-hand experiences of swimming in the pool or watching the Herefords, thereby bringing the ghost town back into a lived community frame. The intervals also helped to build anticipation while allowing each work to be encountered discretely and distinctly on its own terms.

This strangely staccato journey across a unique landscape ensured the artworks and environment were in a constant process of push and pull, shifting in and out of alignment. That some of the works were experienced briefly on the bus and others over time in the township at the audience's leisure, meant that the tour was beautifully uneven. The audience was constantly seeking to identify the point at which each work began and when it had stopped evoking.

By inviting artists to work *in situ* and providing them with the resources to follow their interests and instincts, Melbourne Water and the City of Wyndham have demonstrated a belief in the value of public art to instigate new encounters with people and place. They have set in train a complex and multifarious staging of the treatment plant, inviting us to consider what we know about the outer west of Melbourne and how we might come to experience it anew.

As the Sunday painter equivalent of a sewerage expert, I, along with associate curator Cameron Bishop and the artists, have been consistently surprised and delighted by the curious and often profound goings-on behind that very expansive cyclone fence to Melbourne's west. *Treatment*, as a temporary public art project, offered a distinct set of pathways into the landscape, its people, history and the pleasures of experiencing art from a well-padded seat in air-conditioned comfort.

1 • • • • Žižek, Slavoj, *Event*, Penguin, London, 2014, p. 3.

2 • • • • ibid, p. 5.

UNreconciled

Stage three of *Keloid*
An intervention in history, as a part of *Treatment* at the Melbourne Water Western Treatment Plant 2016.

Megan Evans

When asked by David Cross to participate in *Treatment*, I knew straight away which site I would like to activate. Having been several times to Cocoroc, the Water Tower was not only a commanding presence in the landscape but it immediately resonated with my interest in Victorian history in Australia.

I had been working on *Keloid*, a long-term project which unfolds in stages, resulting from over 30 years of investigation into what displaces a sense of belonging in Australia.

Whilst my family history in this country can be traced back to the early 1800s, my late husband's Aboriginal culture is ancient. The establishment of my family in Australia took place at the expense of his.

UNreconciled is a response to the Water Tower as infrastructure of colonisation. 'The Tank', as it was called, was the first public water supply system reservoir in Victoria. It held reservoir water from 1857 to 1892 and sat on Eastern Hill near the corner of Albert and Gisborne St in East Melbourne. It was a prominent landmark in Melbourne until 1893 when it was relocated to Cocoroc at the Board of Works Farm in Werribee. My intervention in the space below the tank takes the point of view that water was vital in the growth and expansion of colonisation in Victoria.

I used sculpture, drawing, small object installations, photographs and sound to articulate the complexities associated with colonisation. These objects, symbolic of both personal and universal histories, are combined to unsettle traditional understandings of ownership, memory and identity.

The Victorian architecture that held up the tank is resonant of the bluestone structures across Victorian Melbourne, including Pentridge Prison. Underneath the tank, four cast iron water pipes had at one time brought water from the tank to outlets below. In the centre of these four pipes, I placed a work called *Stained*, a Victorian bedroom chair with legs extended using cut down steel pickets traditionally used for fencing. The original stains on the pale blue fabric of the chair have been exaggerated using embroidery and beading, with red beads spilling over the edge of the chair's seat, down to a pool on the ground.

Darkness created an immediate change of mood on entering the space. The twelve arches of the structure were illuminated by museum lights and the chair stood imposingly in the centre. The sound of rushing water pulsed from each corner of the space, with an occasional report from a gun shot in the distance. The installation emulated a museum, however the objects told another story. Jacinto Lageria, in an essay about Kader Attia, a French Algerian artist whose works looks at the concept of repair, says:

> The legal concept of 'civil reparations of History', which originated in the USA but is now internationally recognised and applicable, asserts that History can be held legally accountable and thus creates the possibility for victims to claim compensation—materially, politically and symbolically.[1]

UNreconciled asks the question: how do you take personal responsibility for actions taken in the past? In a sign that replicates the historical signage posted by Melbourne Water on the outside of the water tower, I have presented this as a dilemma yet to be solved. The mathematical equation states that the Water tower plus my ancestors' migration papers equals a map of massacres in Victoria. This is underlined graphically by a passage by Niel Black, written in 1839, two years after my ancestors landed in Australia, that reads,

> The best way [to procure a run] is to go outside and take up a new run, provided the conscience of the party is suffuiciently seared to enable him without remorse to slaughter natives right and left. It is universally and distinctly understood that the chances are very small indeed of a person taking up a new run being able to maintain possession of his place without having recourse to such means—sometimes by wholesale.[2]

The installation is made up of many small anti-monuments that present an alternative to the typical museum narrative, which is impersonal and holds history at a distance. I ask the viewer to consider their own personal story of occupation as I interrogate mine.

1 • • • • Lagiera, Jacinto, 'Repairing, Resisting', in Kader Attia, *The Repair from Occident to Extra-Occidental Cultures*, The Green Box, Berlin, 2014, p. 43.

2 • • • • Clarke, Ian, *Scars in the Landscape: A Register of Massacre Sites in Western Victoria, 1803–1859*, Australian Institute of Aboriginal and Torres Strait Islander Studies, Canberra, 1995, p. 1.

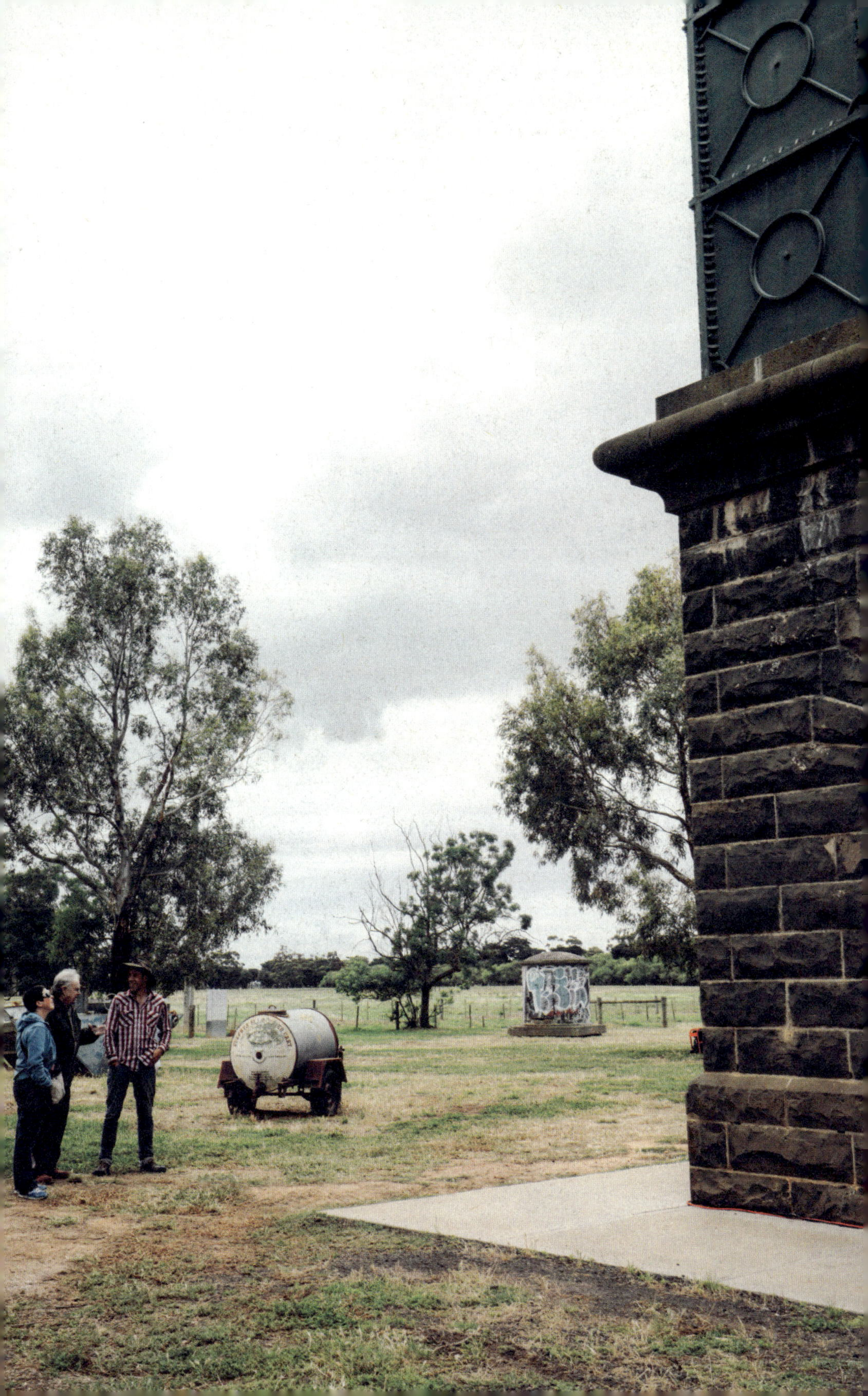

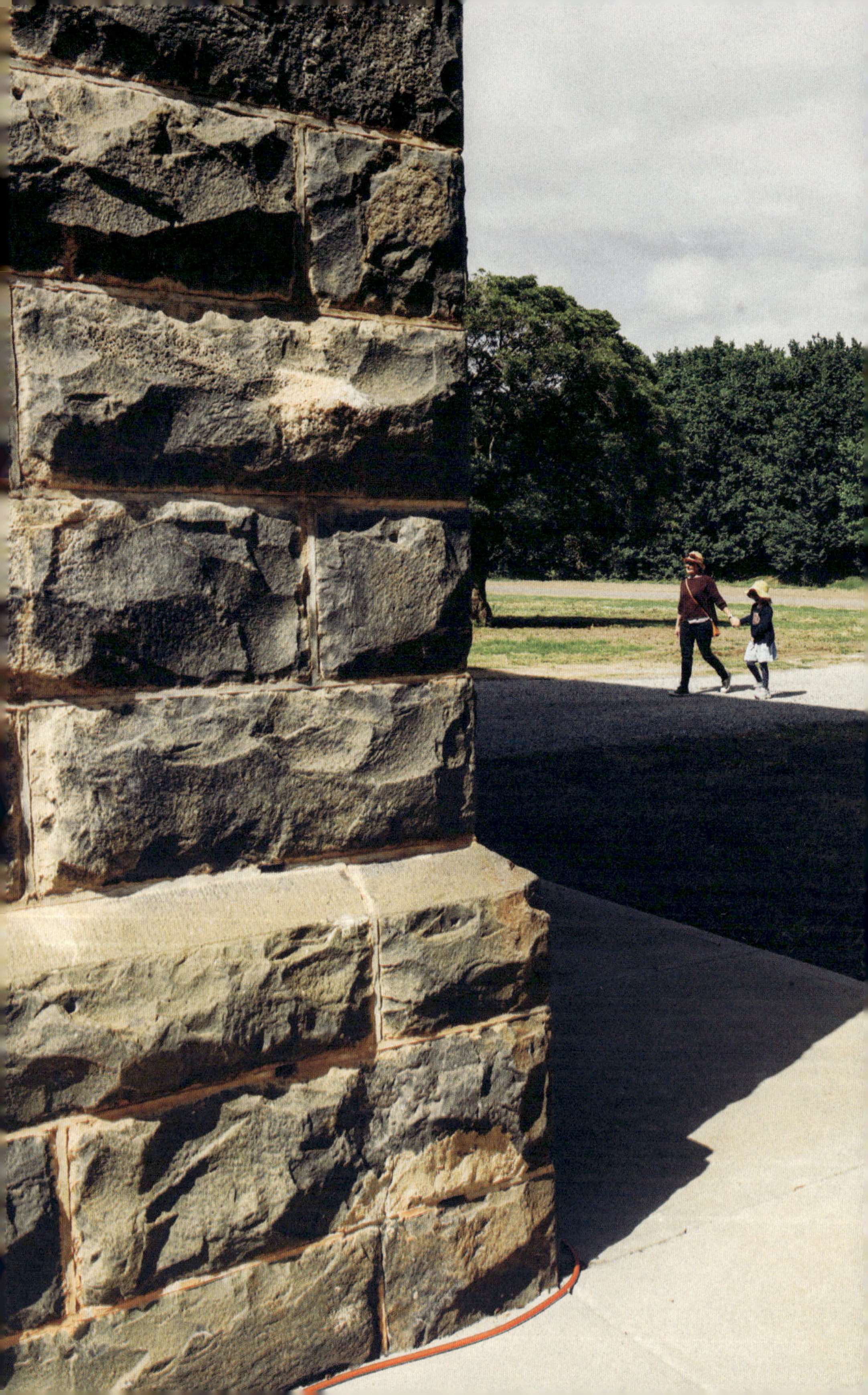

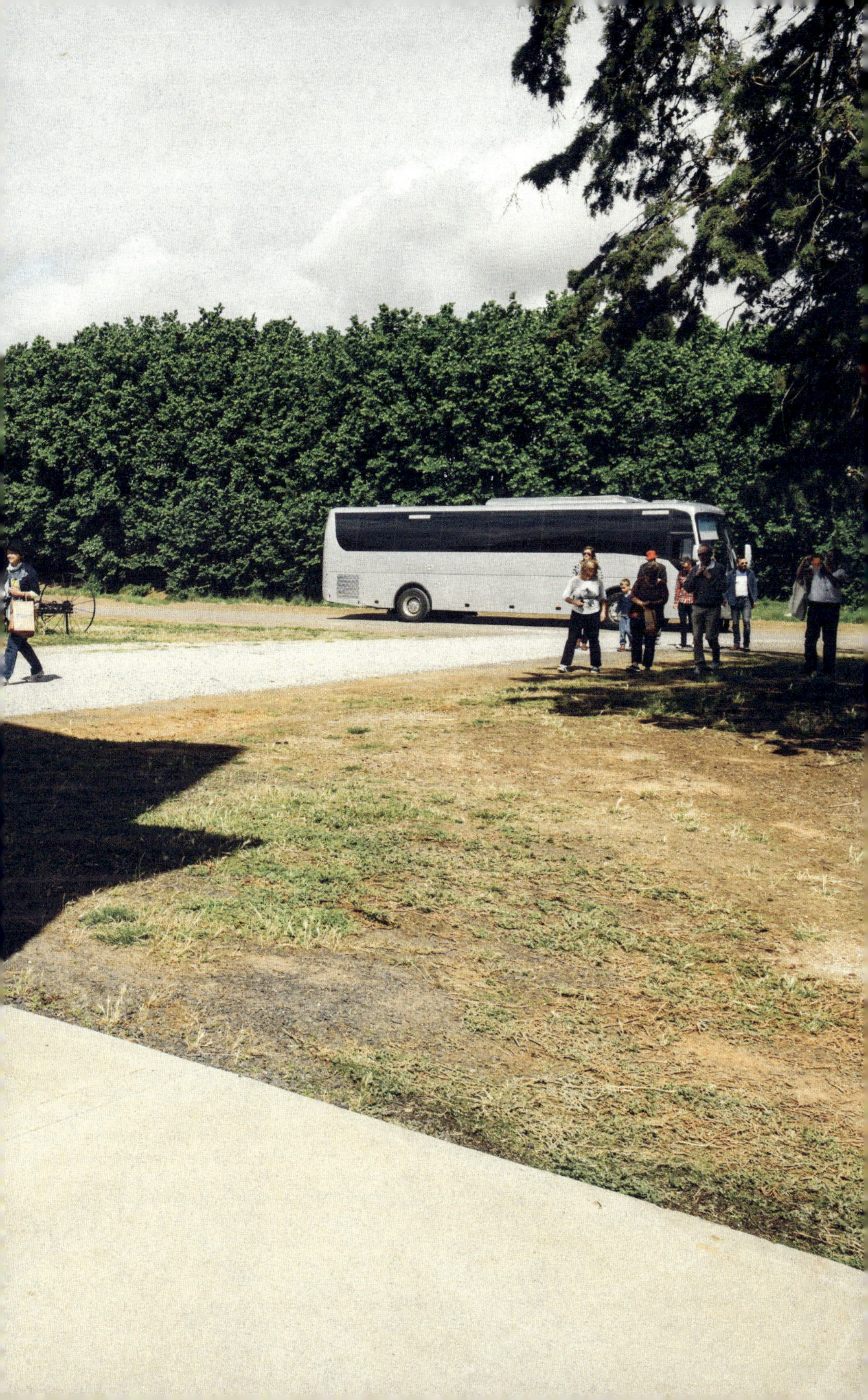

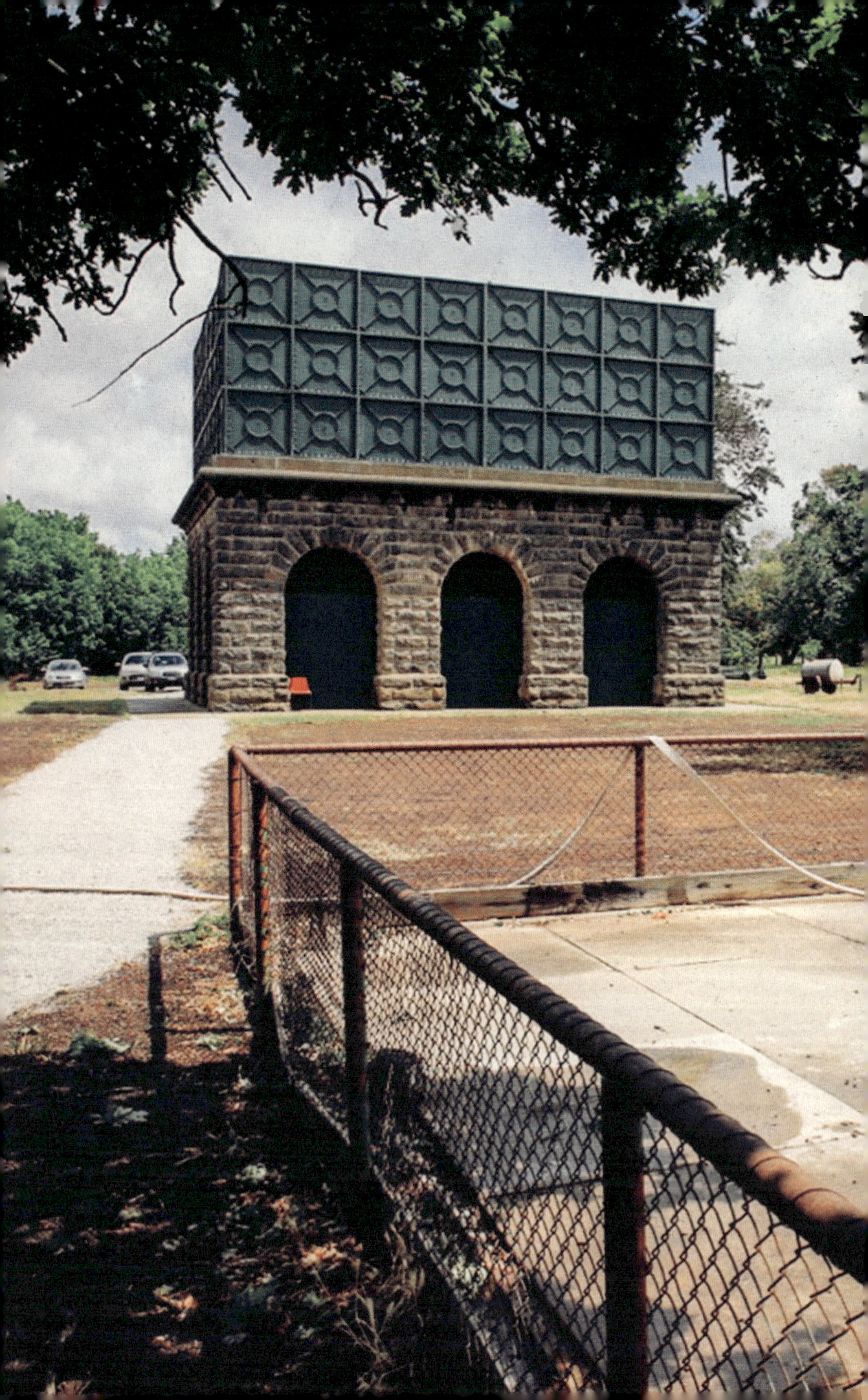

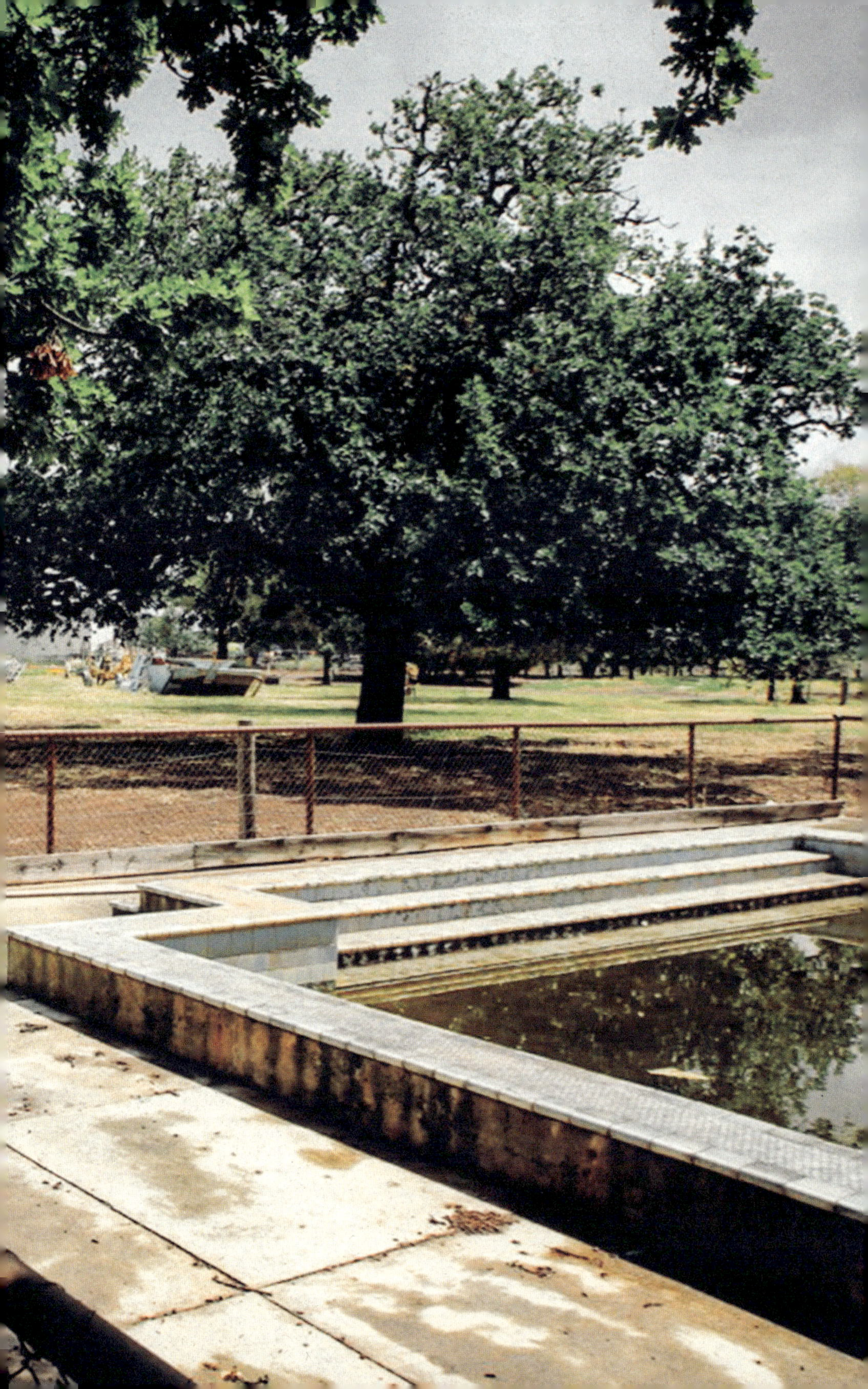

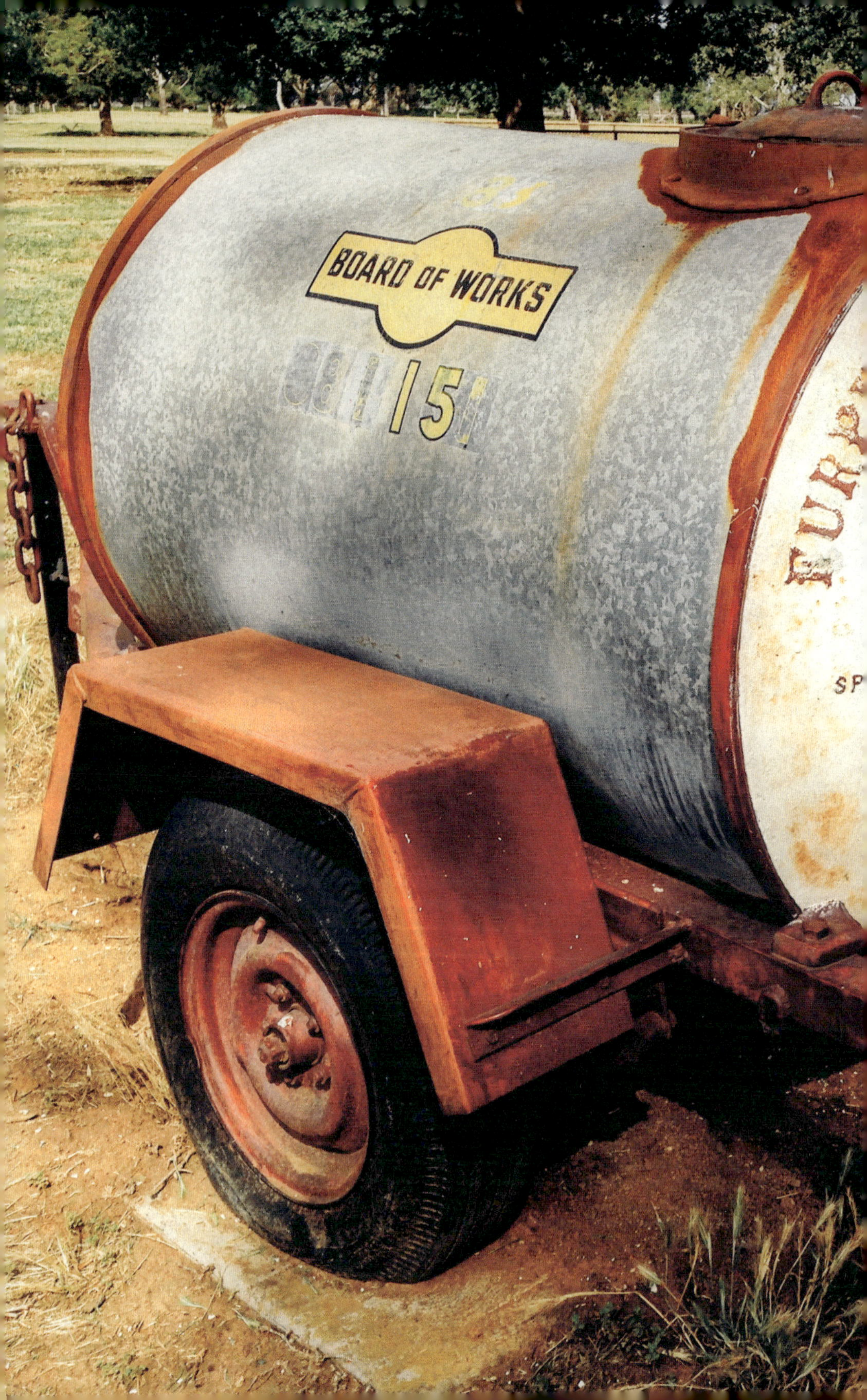
BOARD OF WORKS

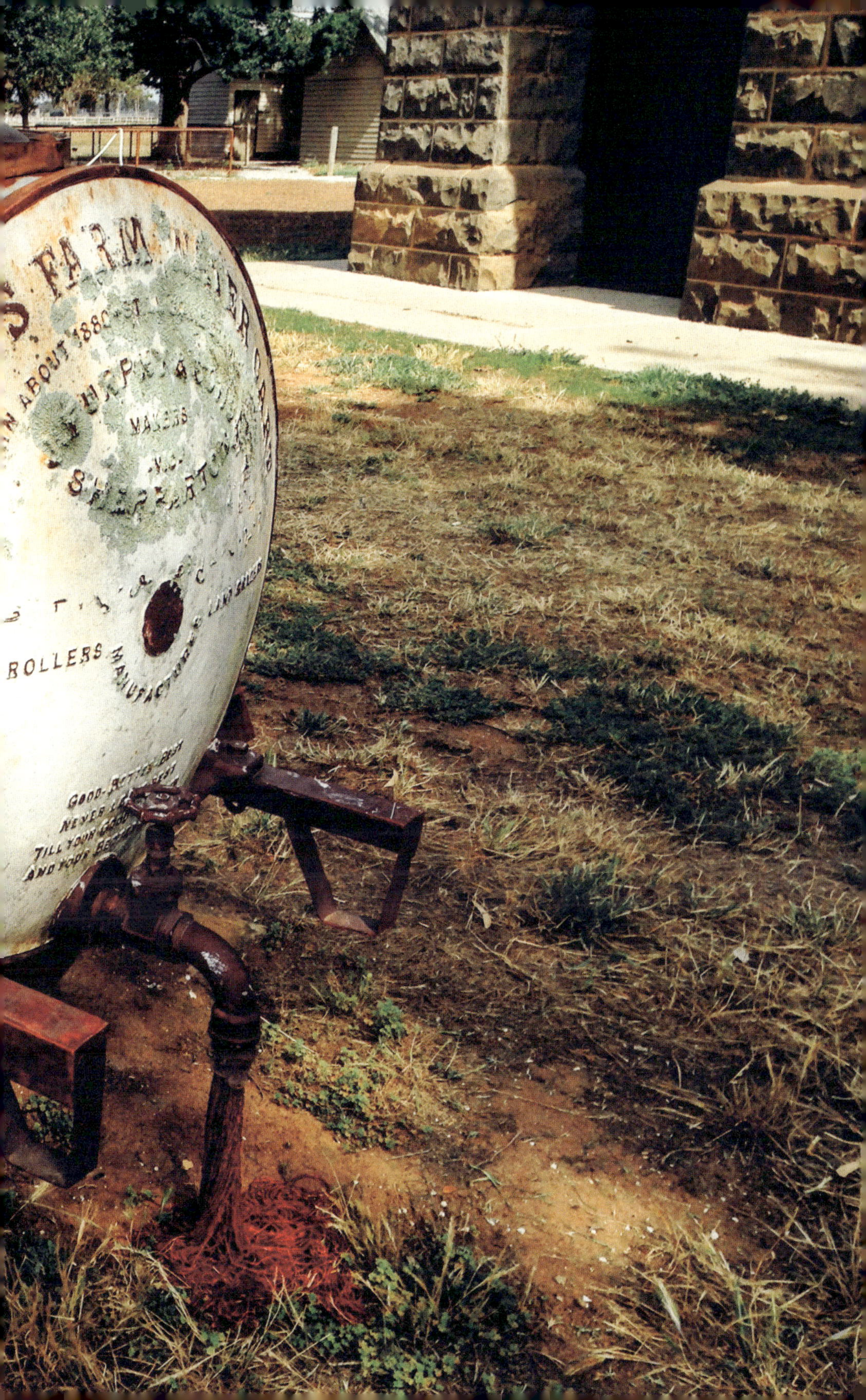
FARM
MAKERS
ROLLERS

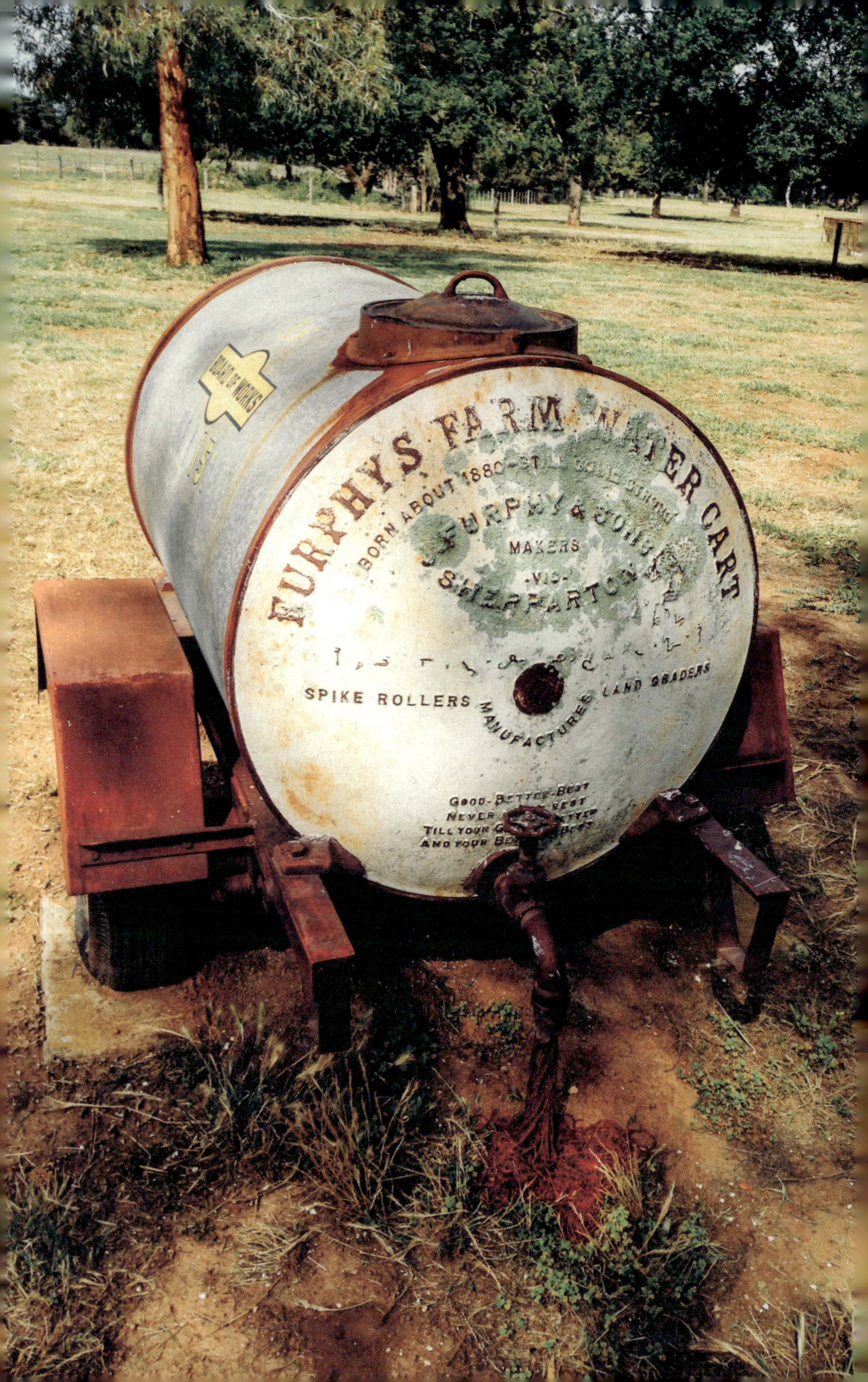
BOARD OF WORKS
FURPHYS FARM WATER CART
BORN ABOUT 1880
MAKERS
-VIC-
SPIKE ROLLERS
MANUFACTURES
LAND GRADERS
GOOD-BETTER-BEST

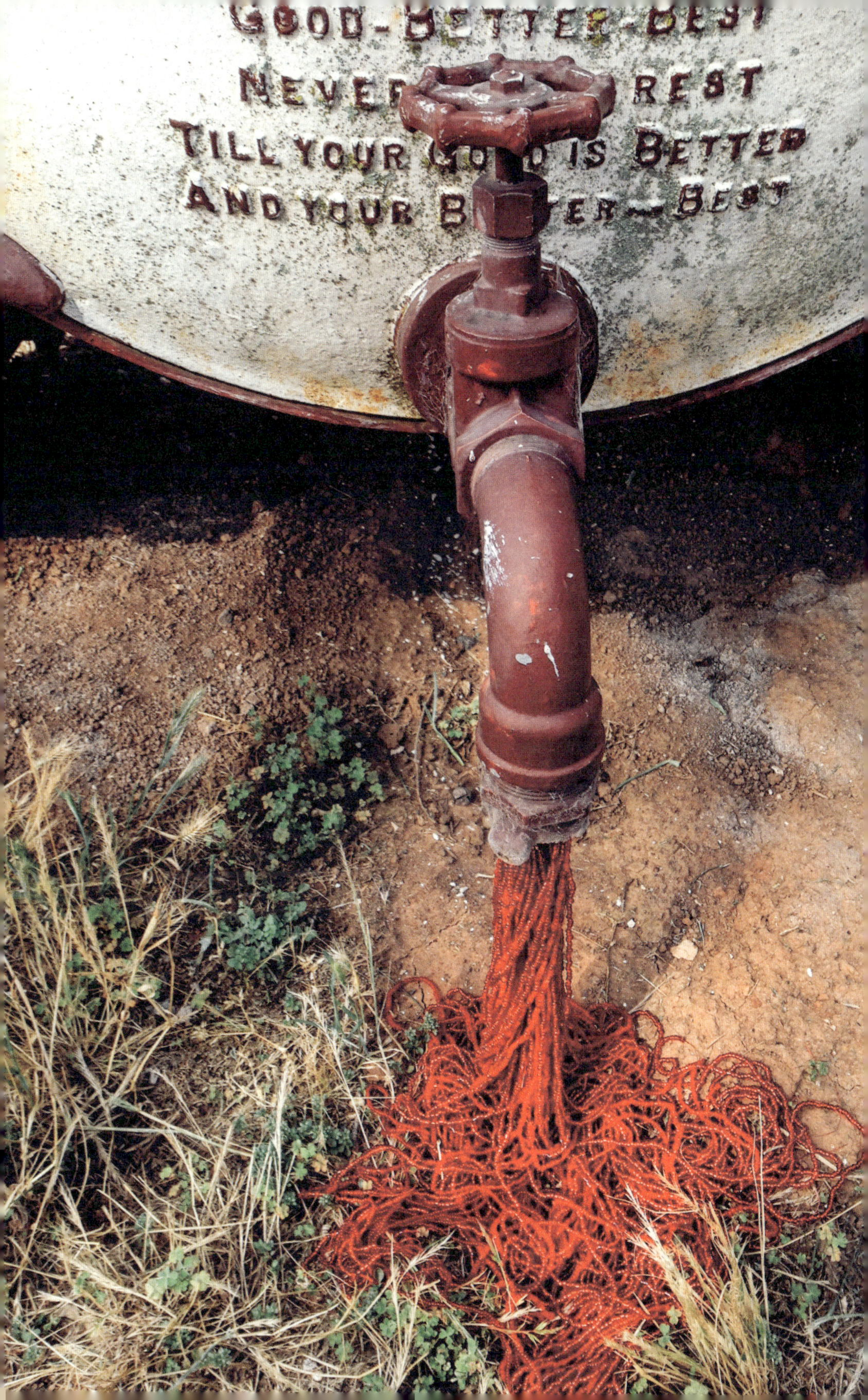
GOOD-BETTER-BEST
NEVE
REST
TILL YOUR
IS BETTER
AND YOUR B
ER—BEST

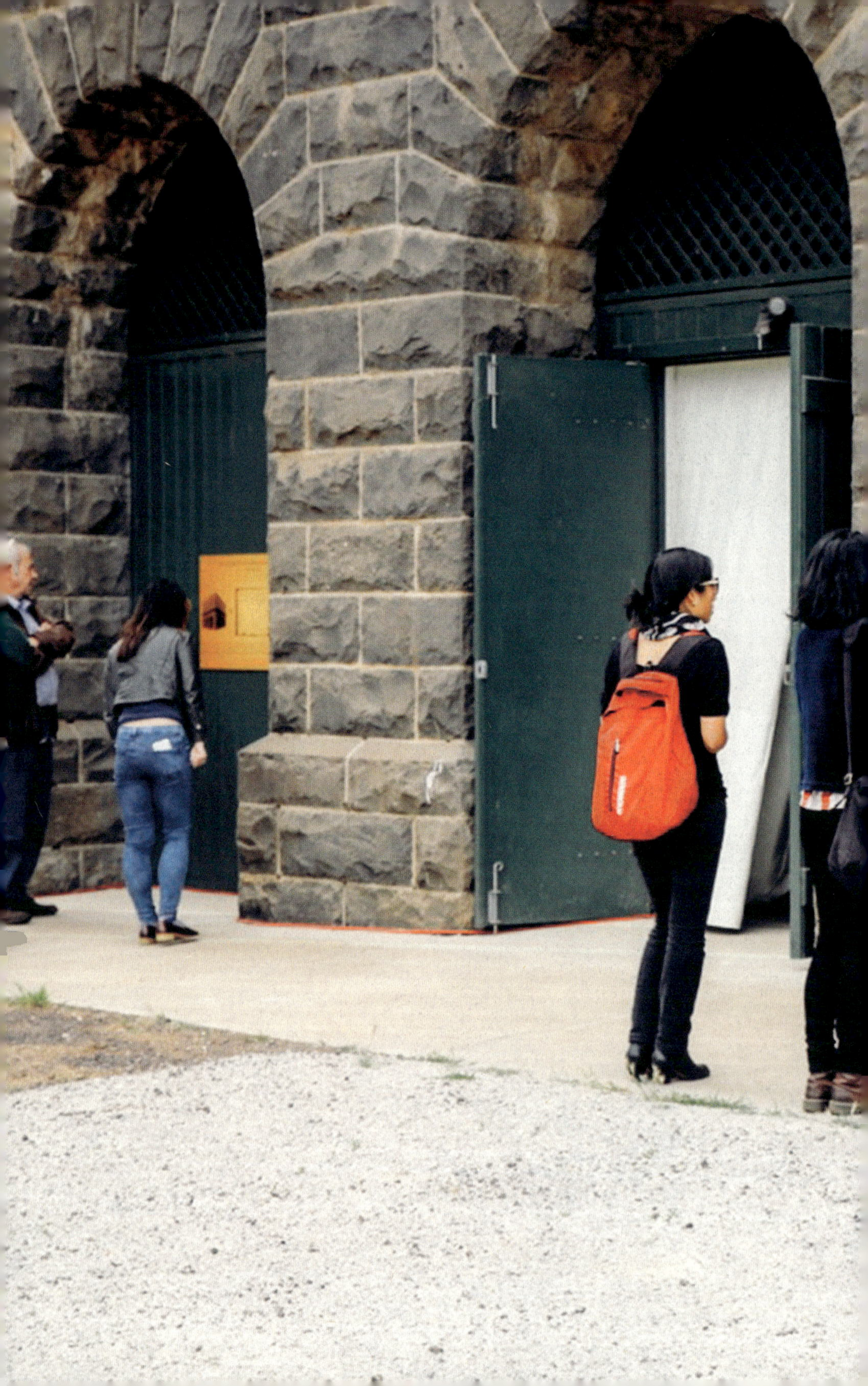

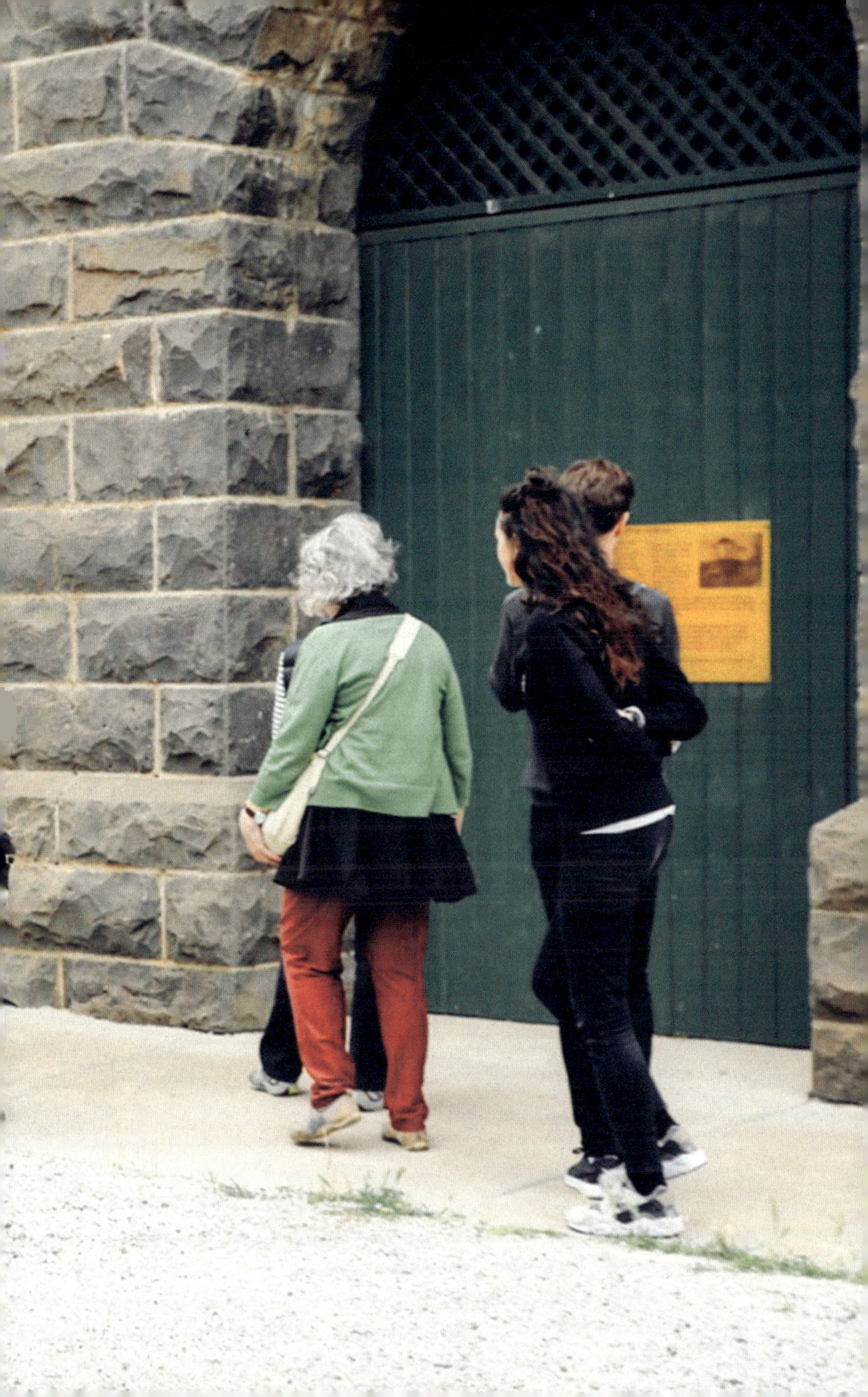

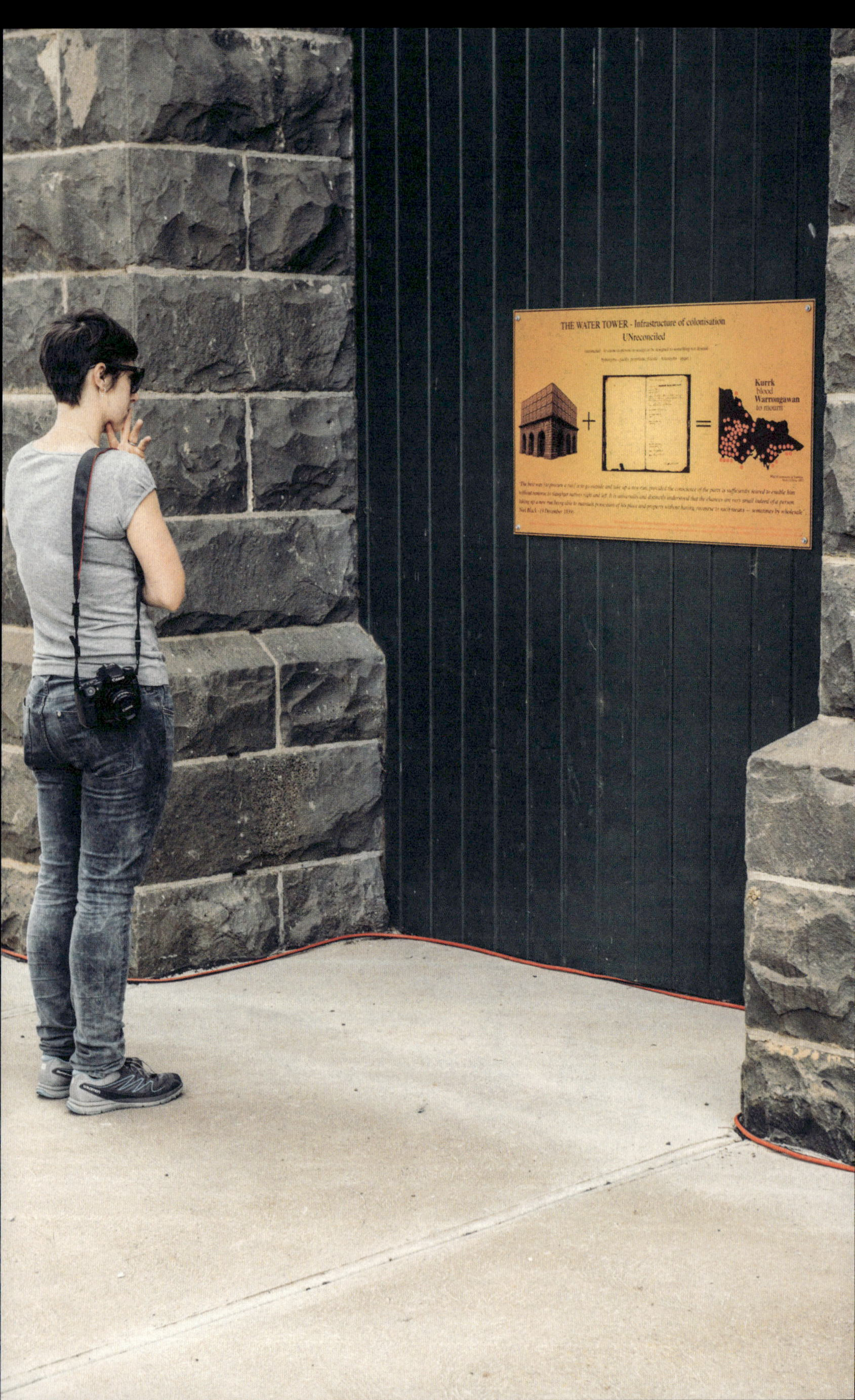
THE WATER TOWER - Infrastructure of colonisation
UNreconciled
Kurrk
blood
Warrongawan
to mourn

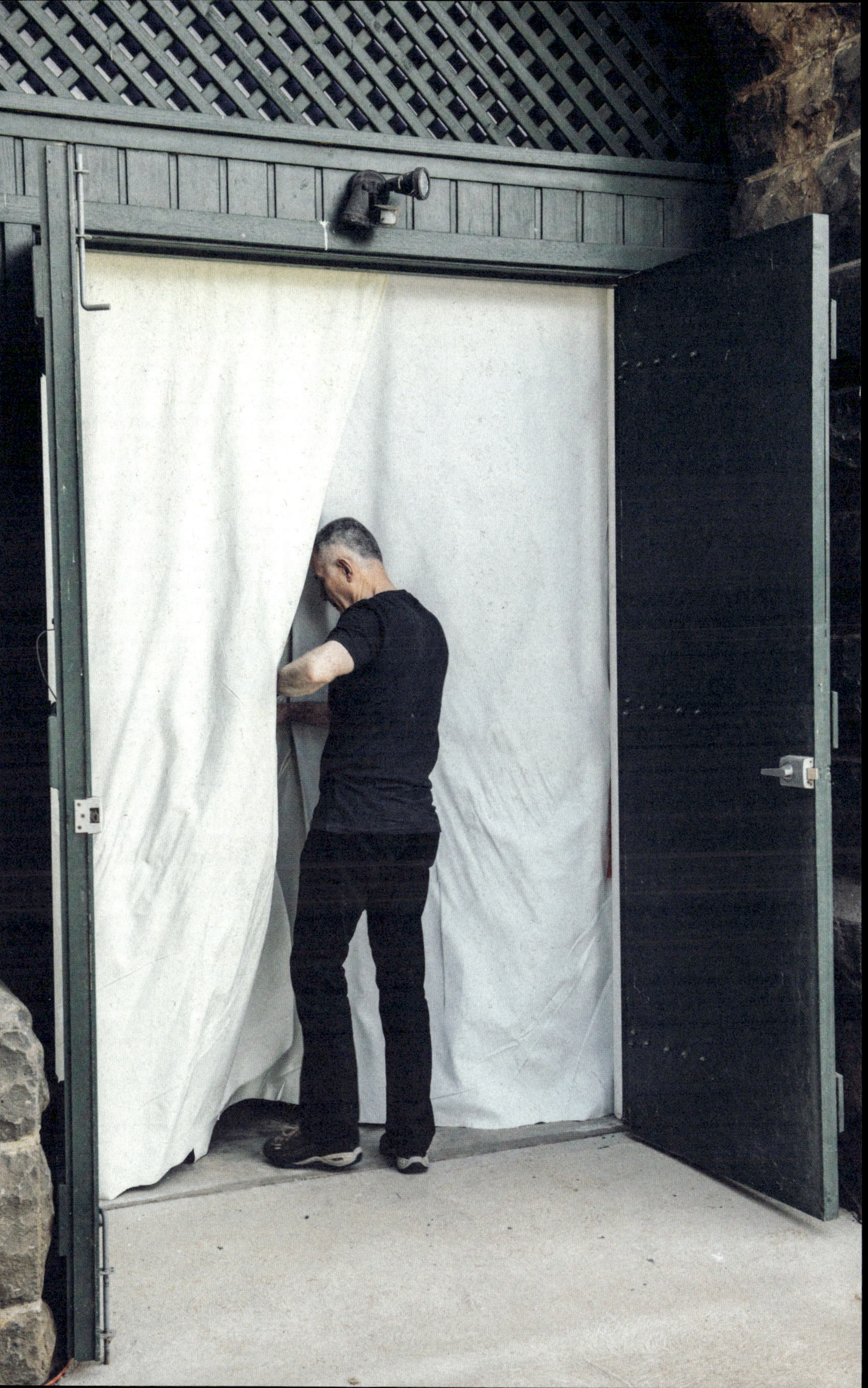

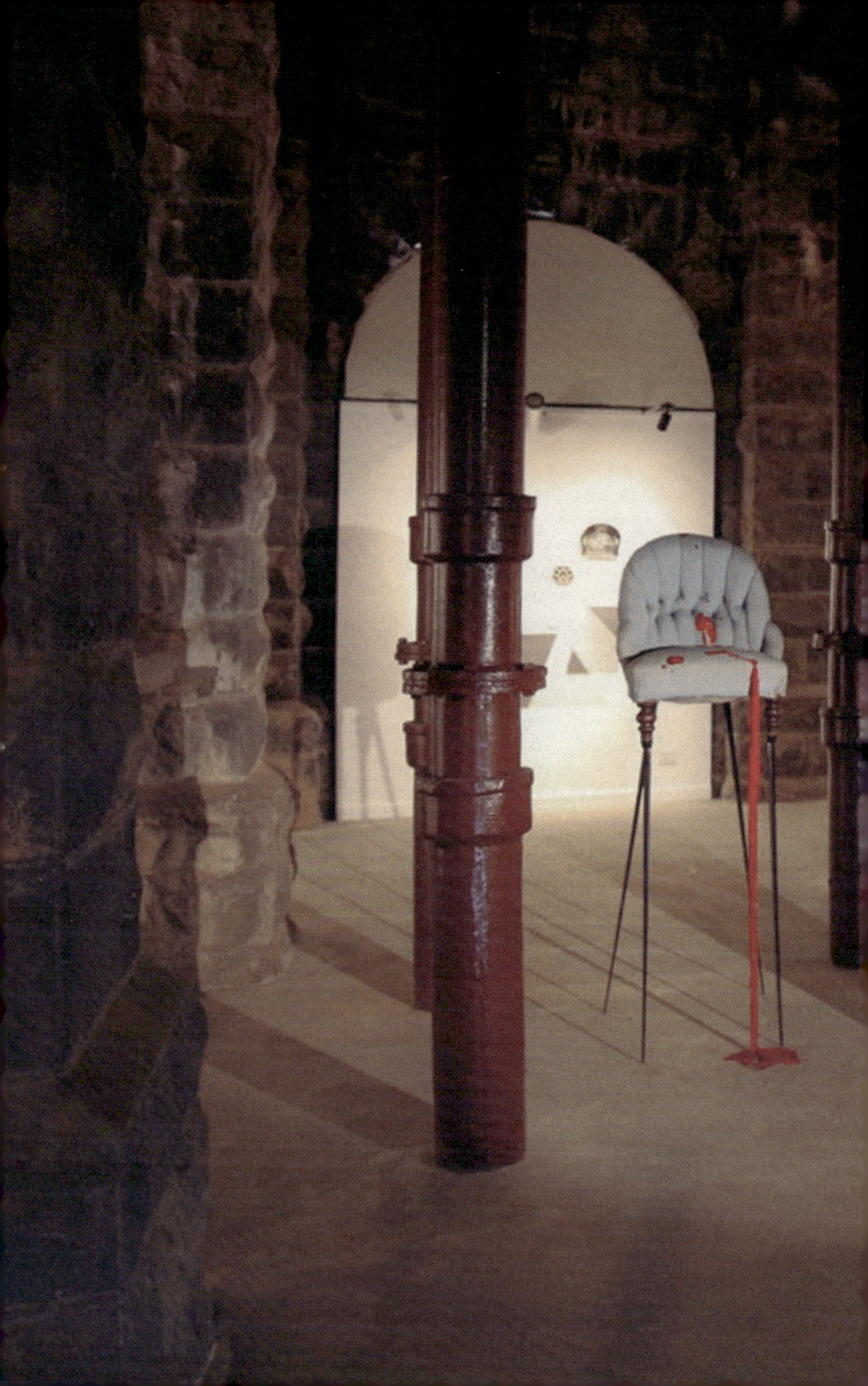

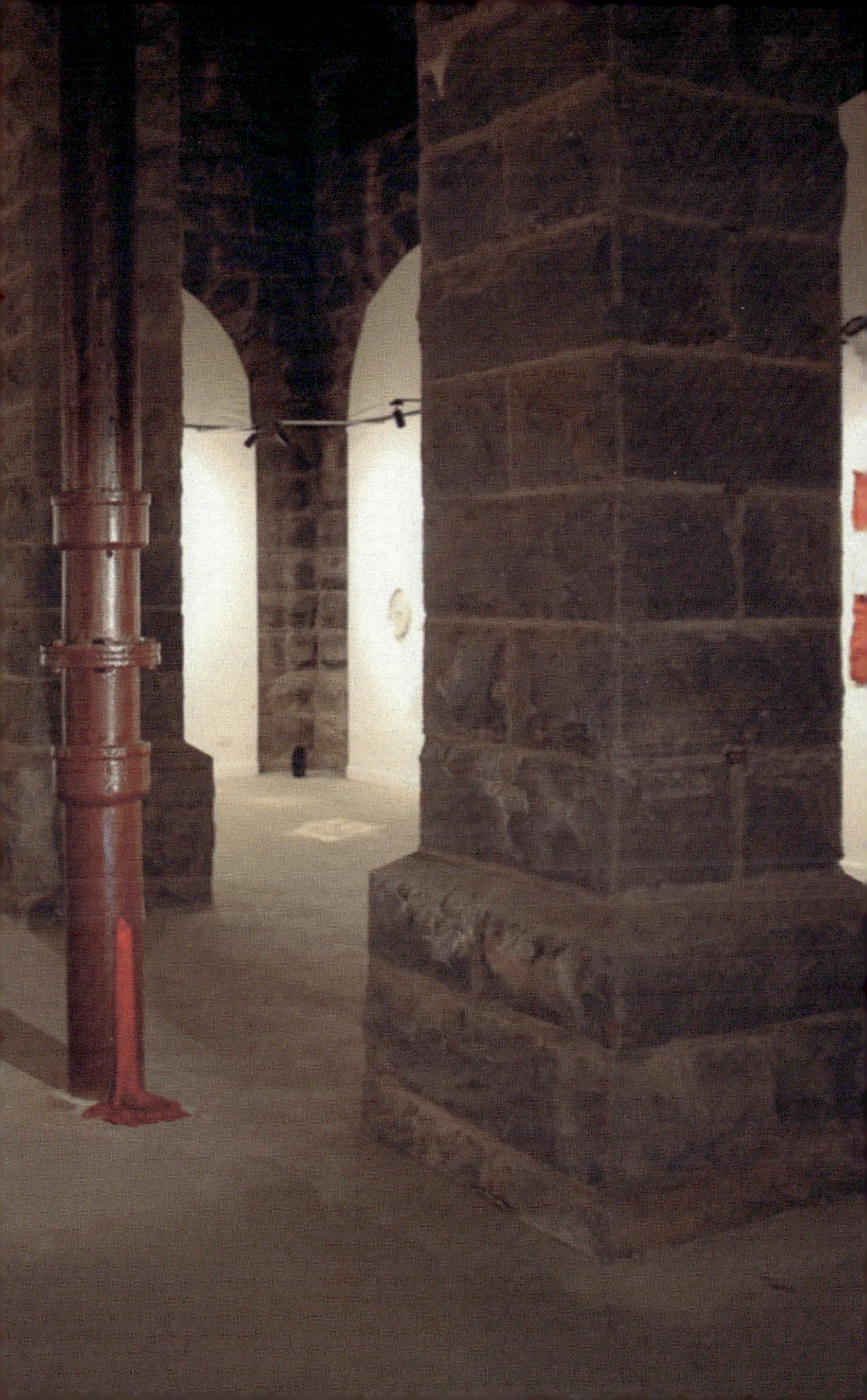

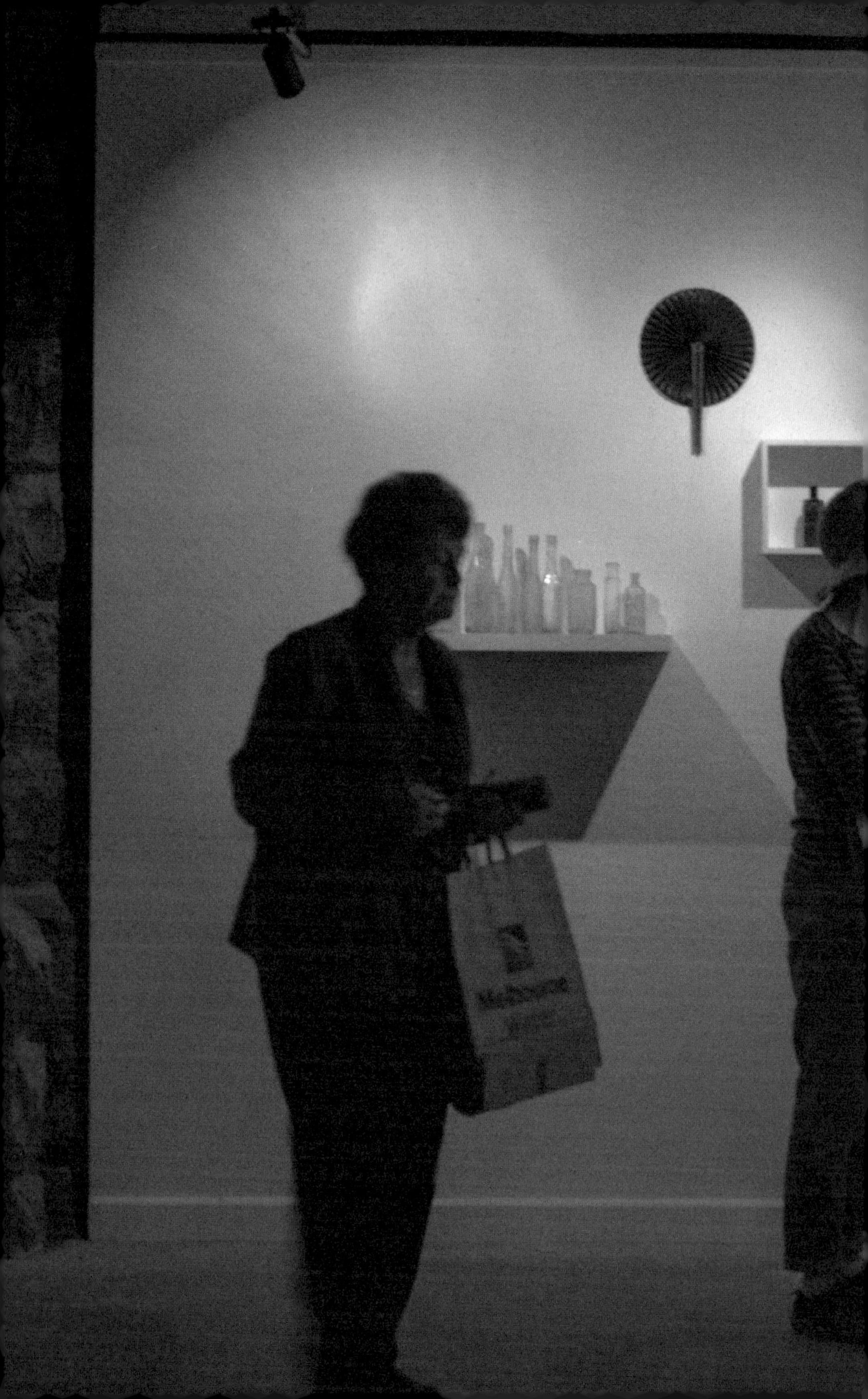

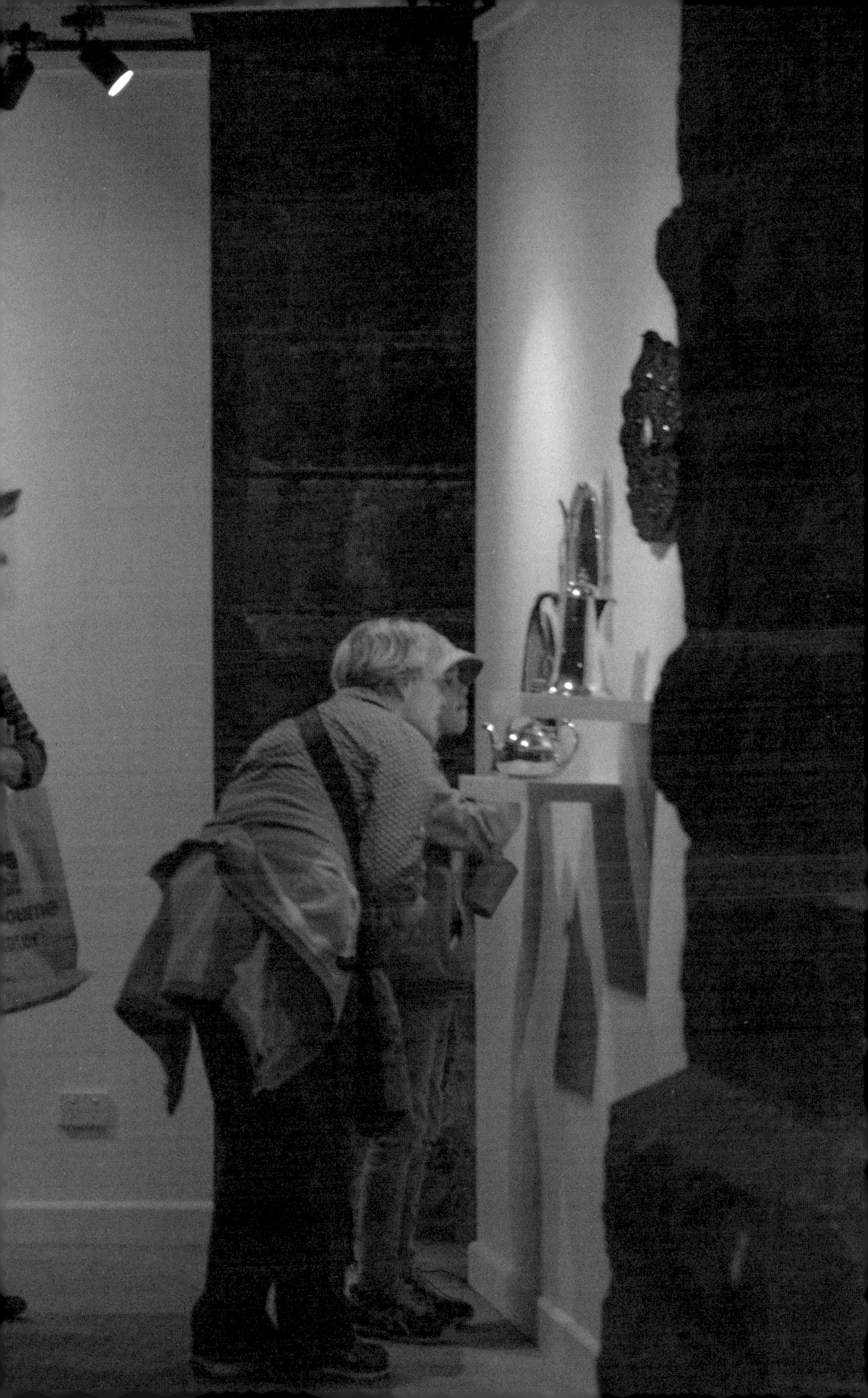

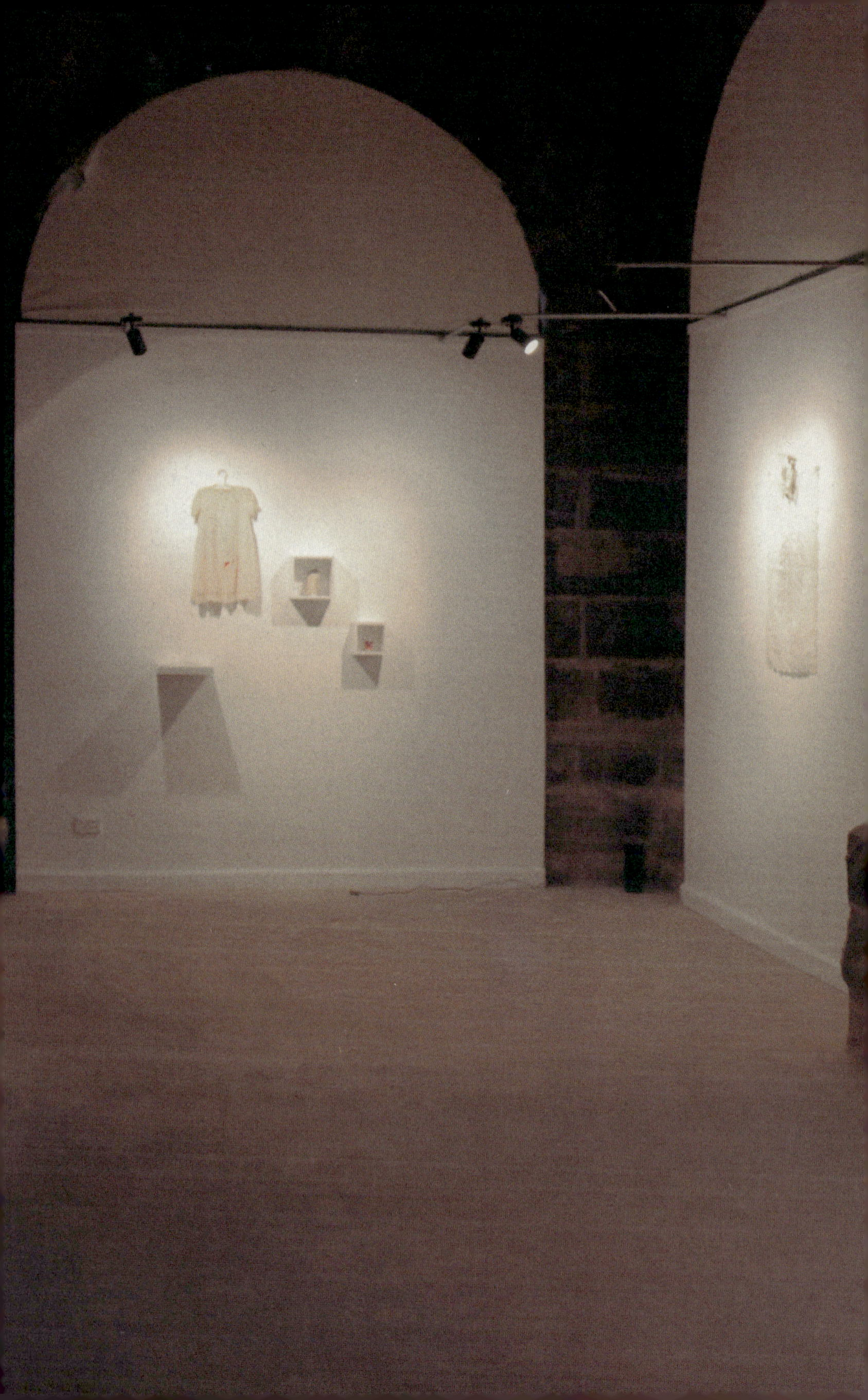

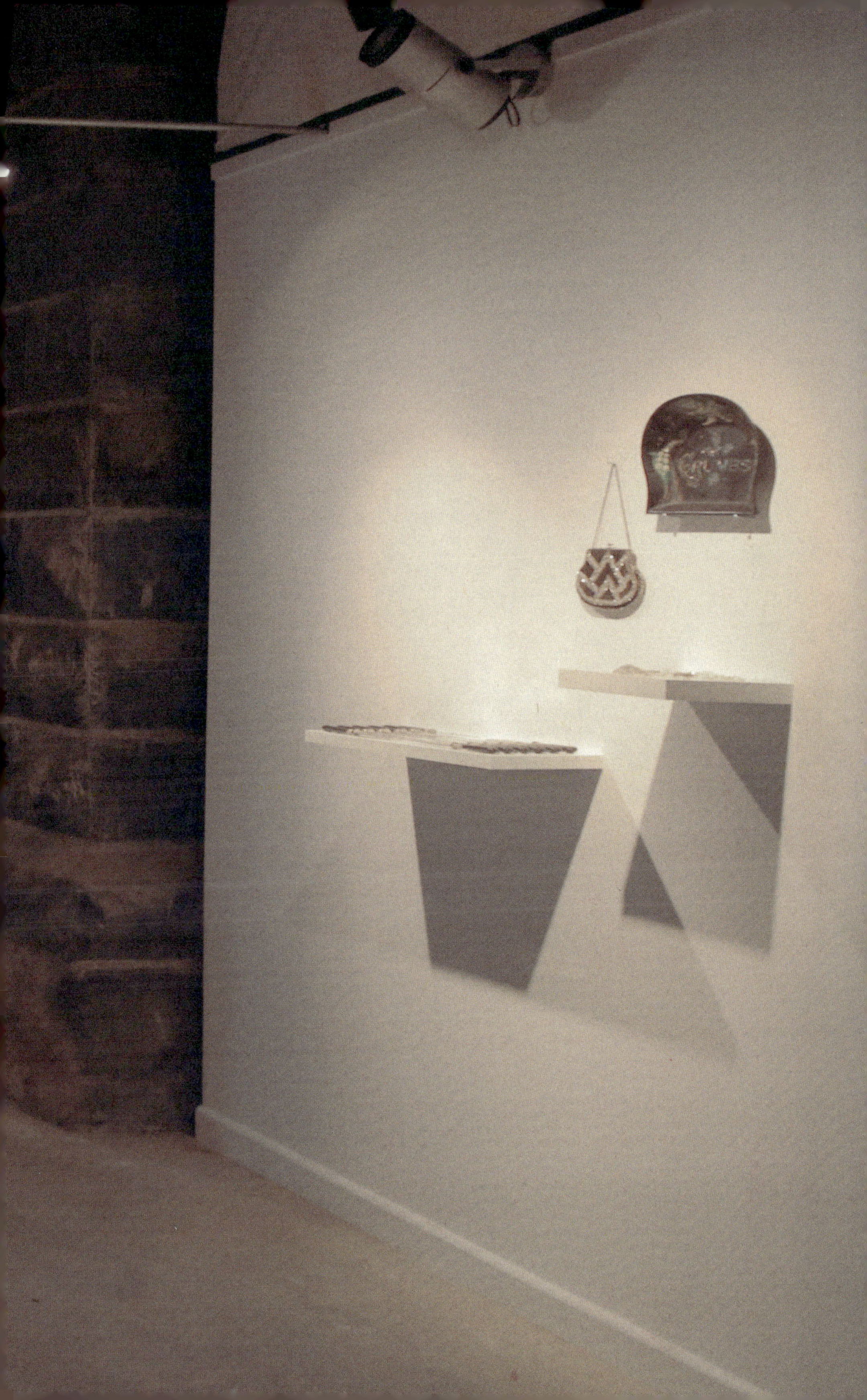

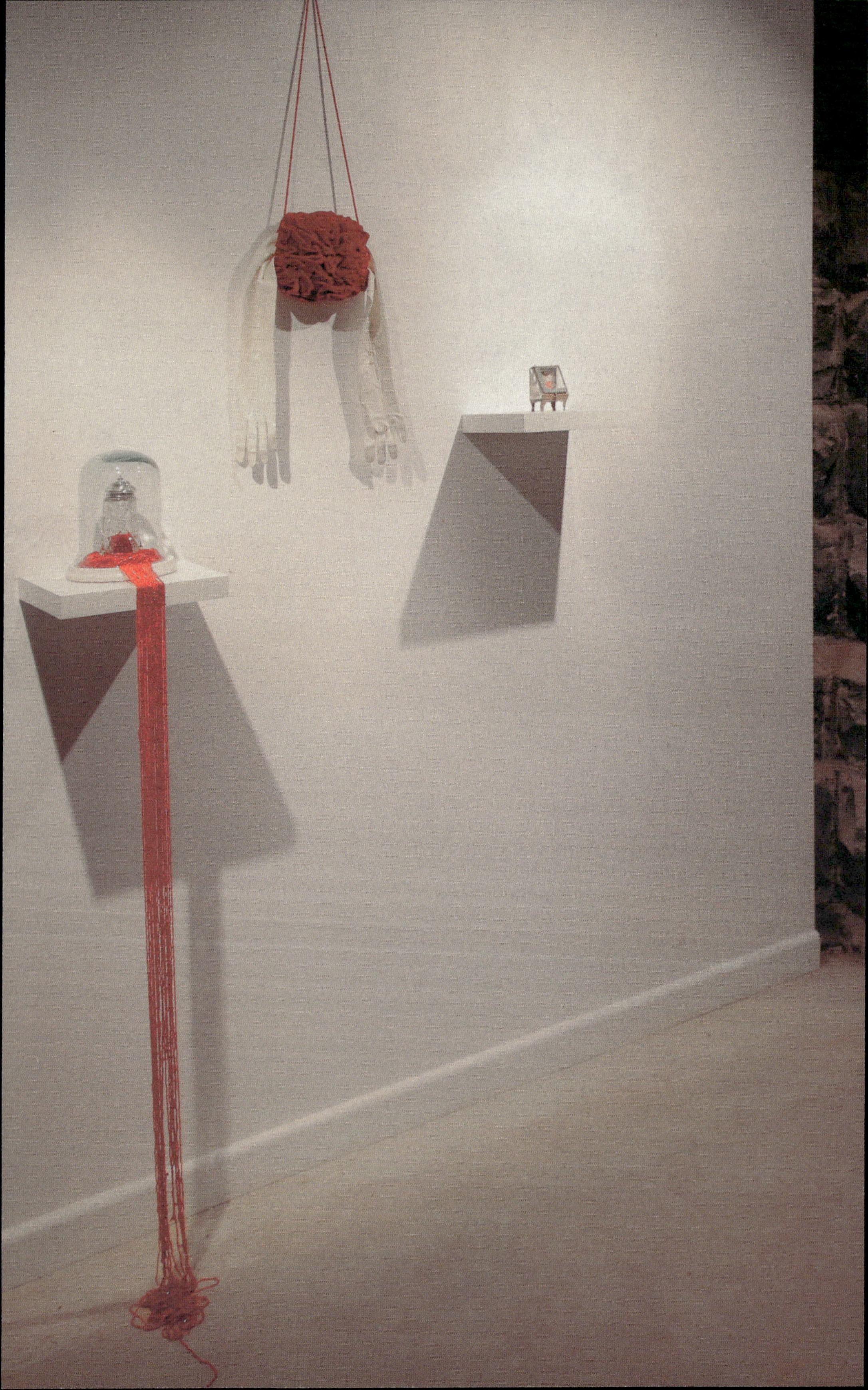

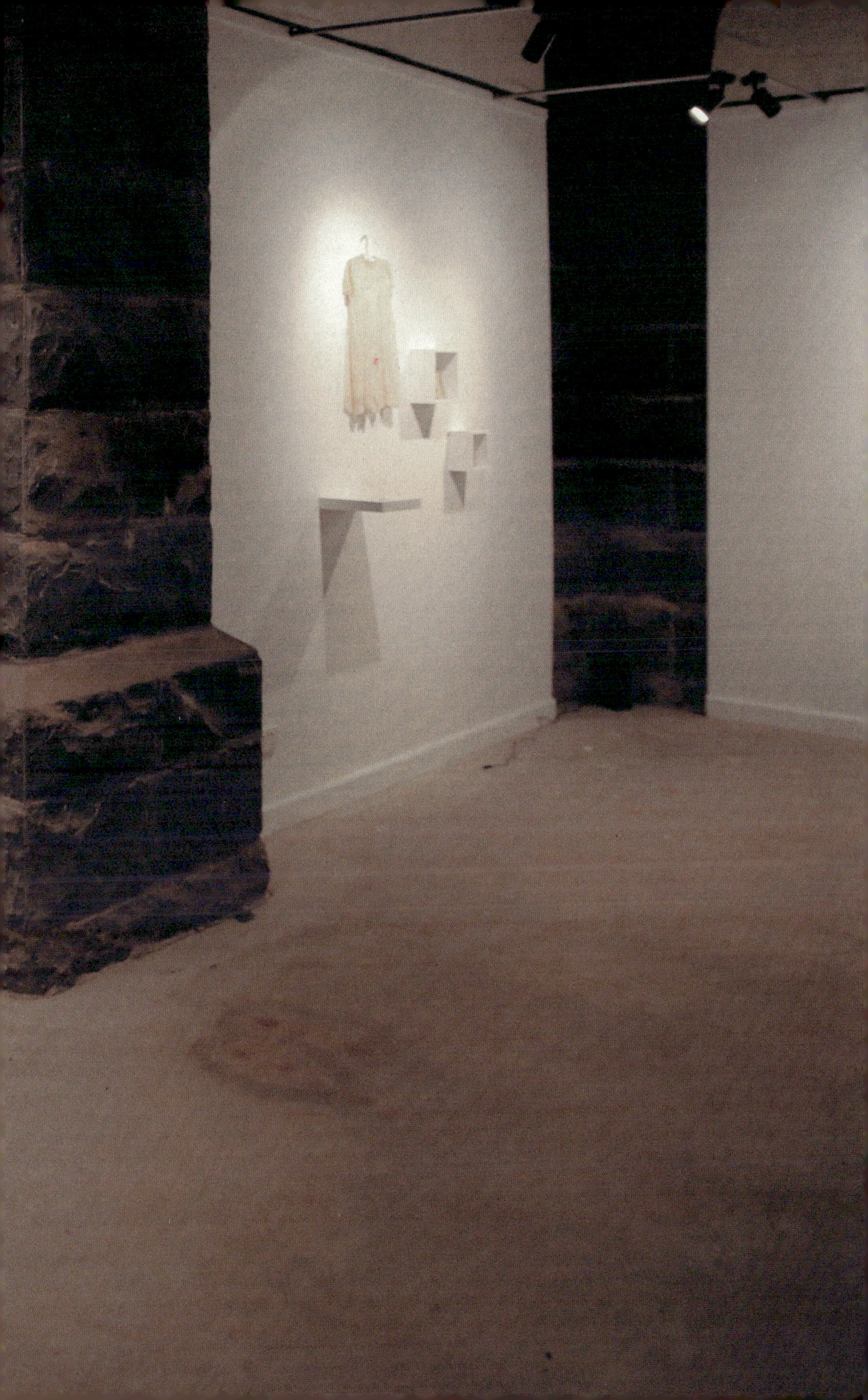

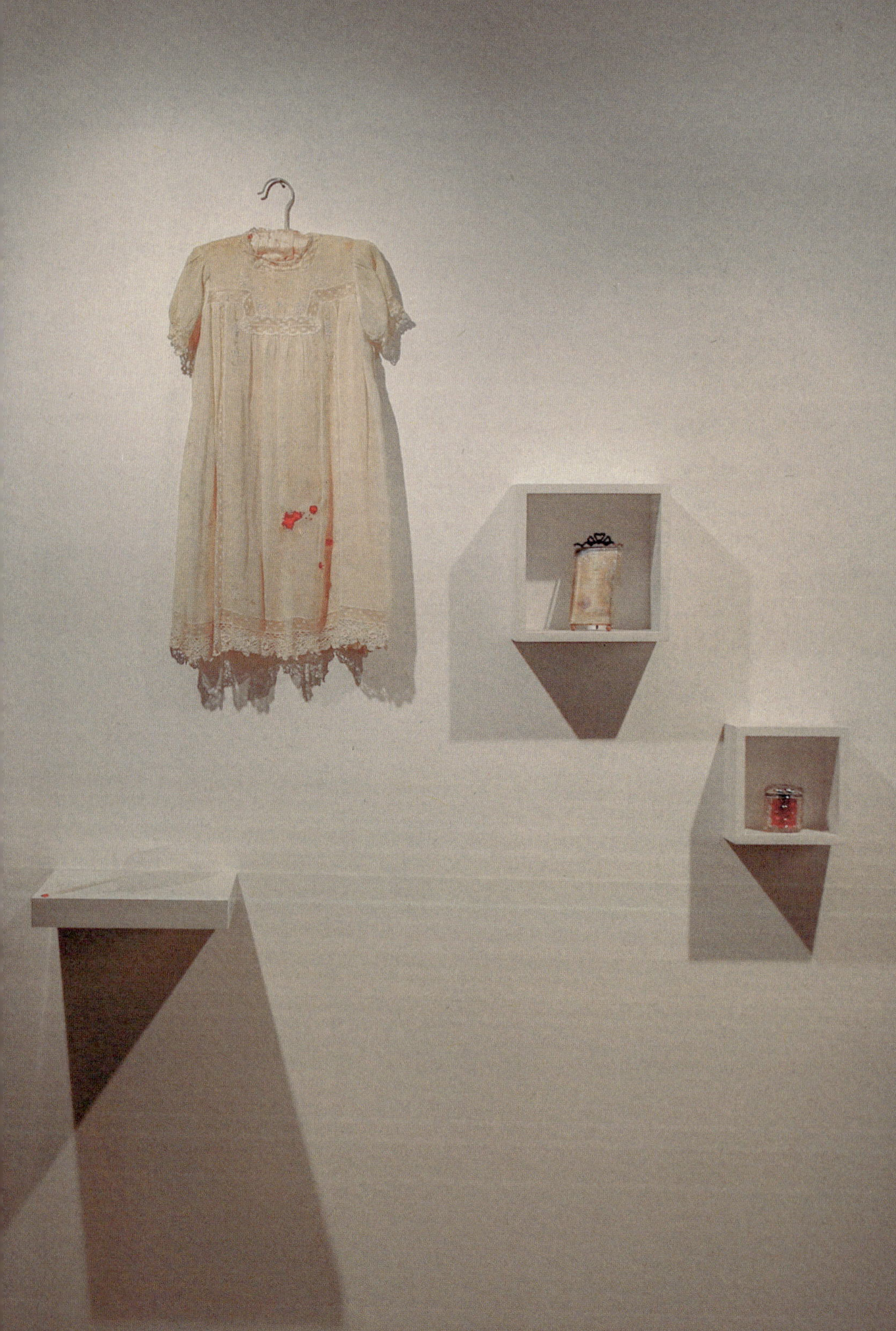

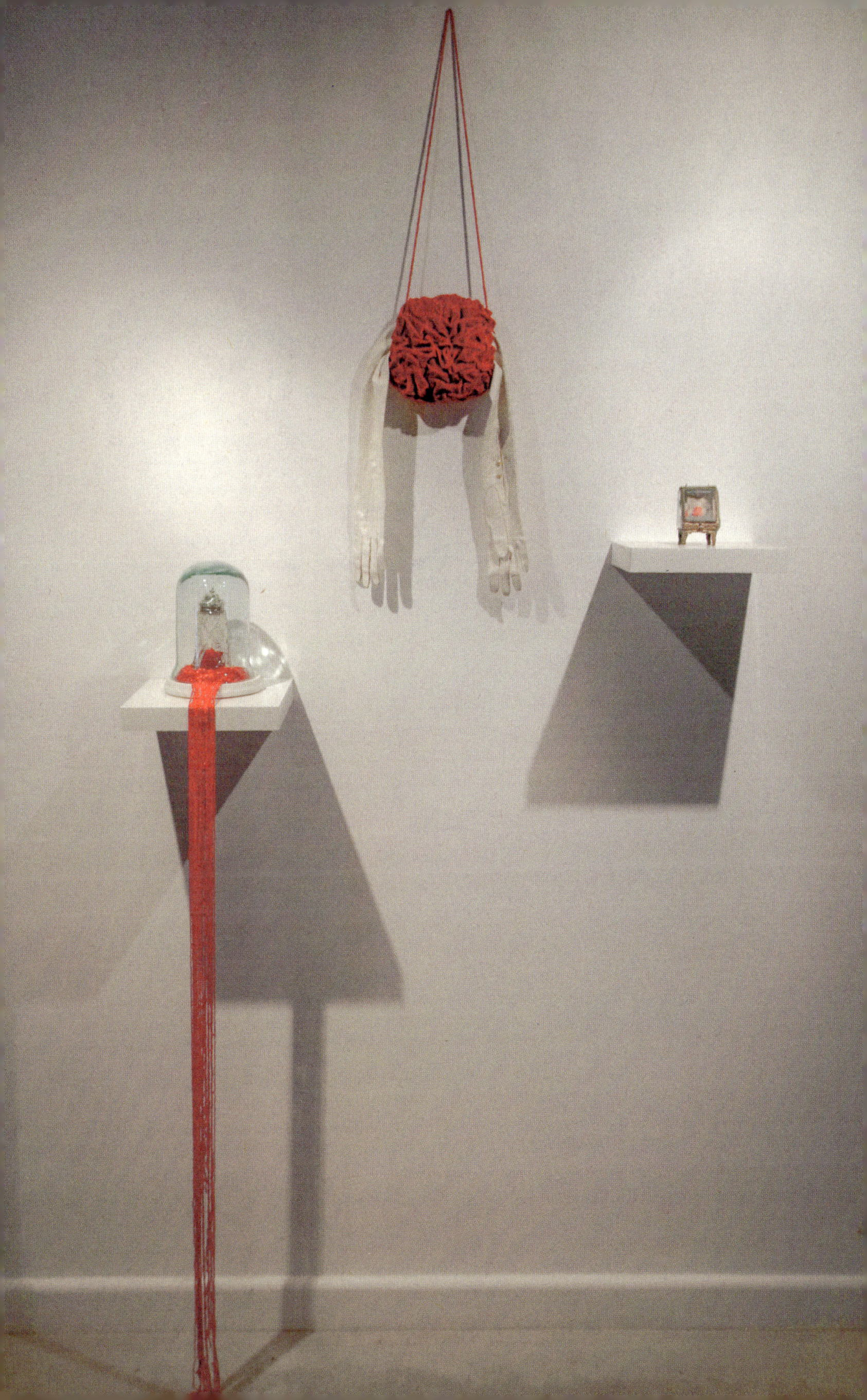

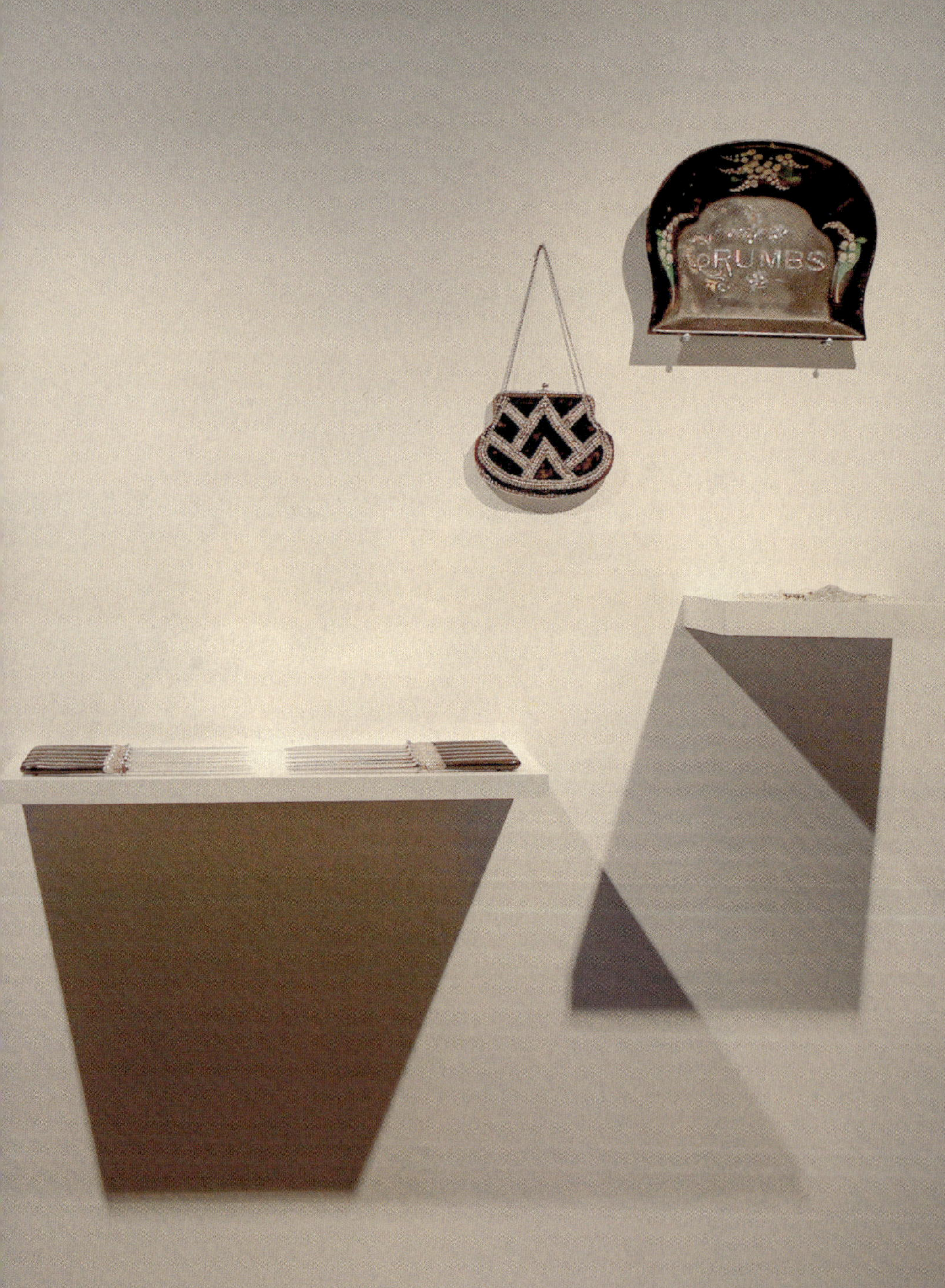
CRUMBS

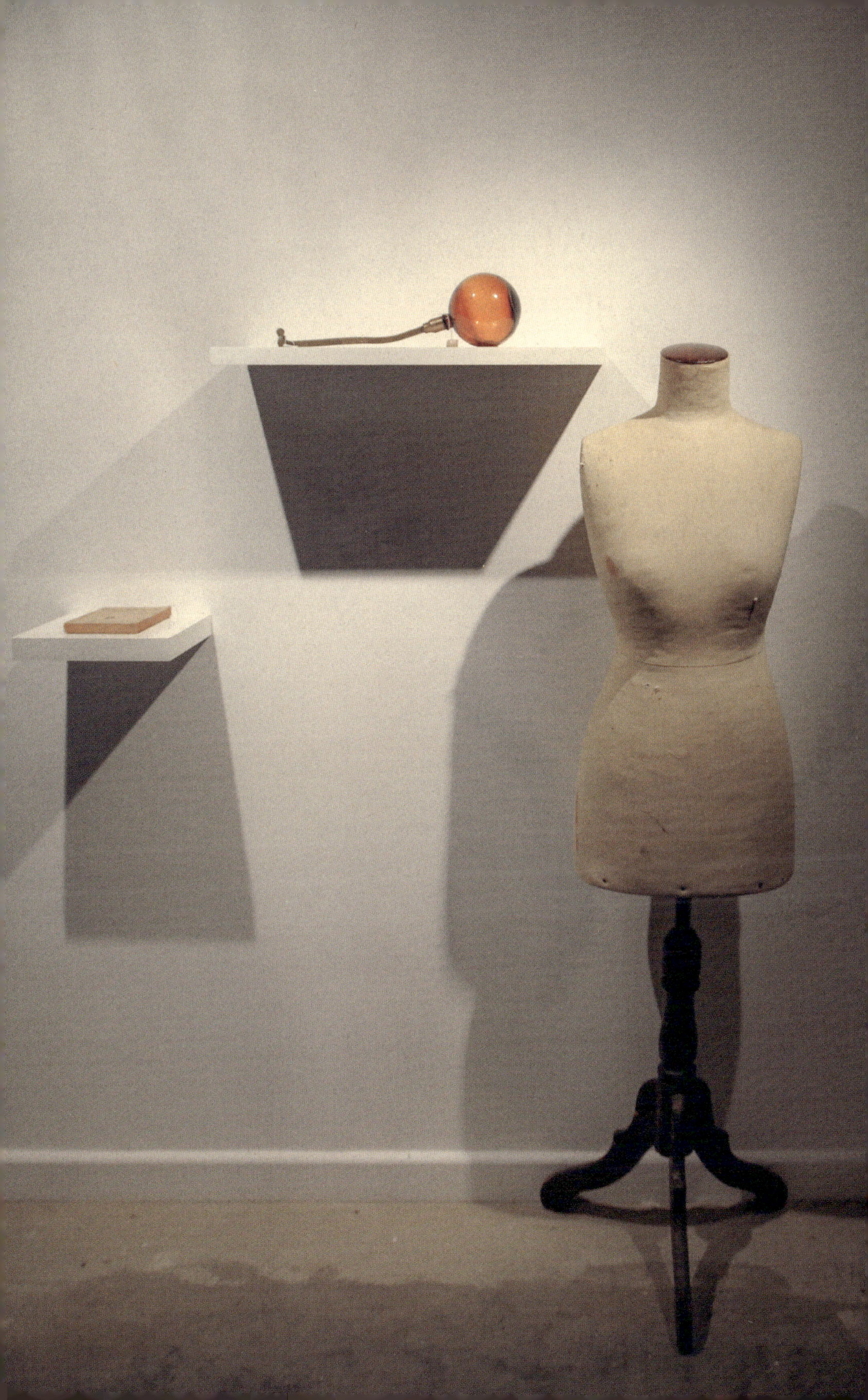

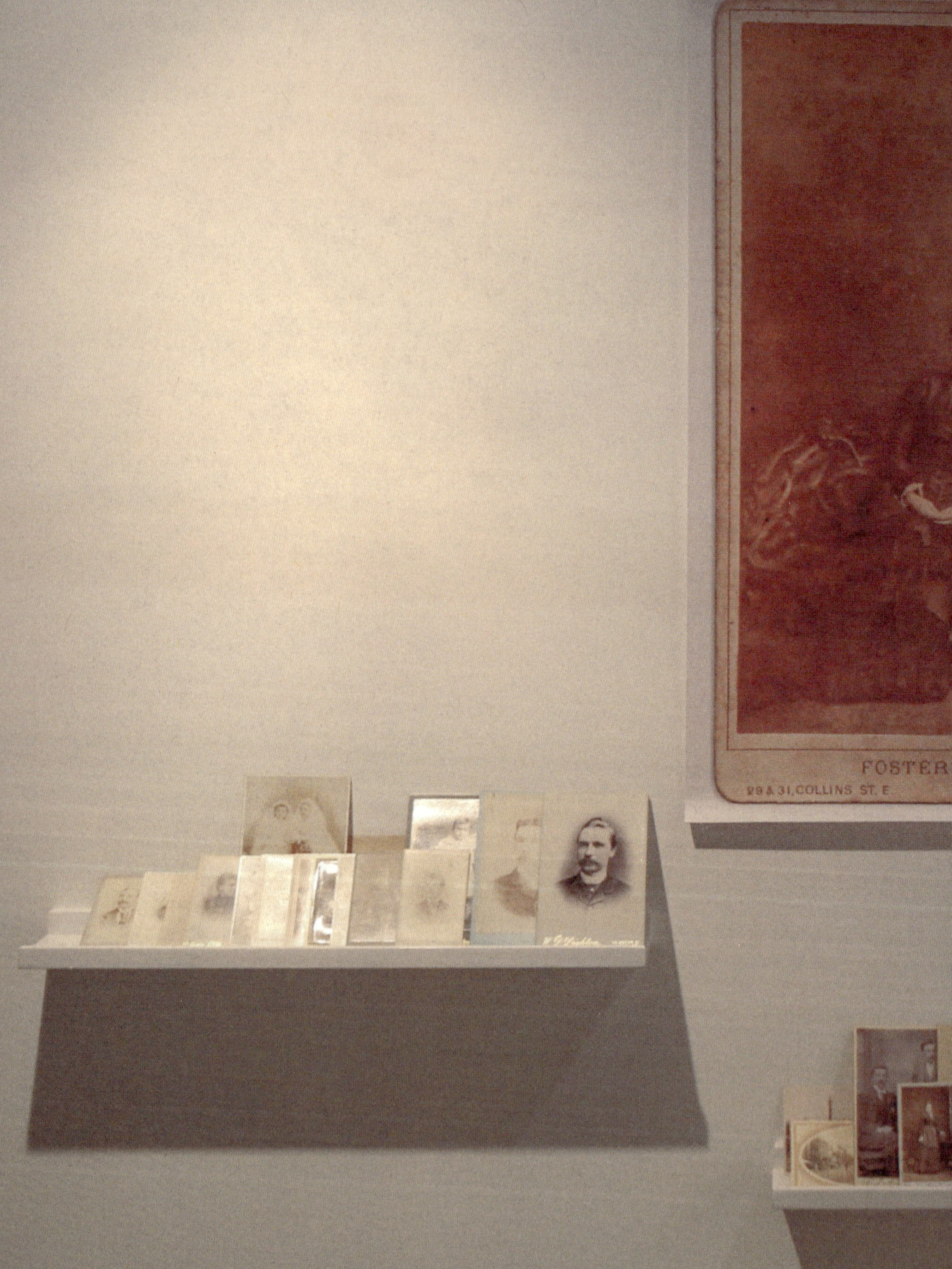
FOSTER
29 & 31, COLLINS ST. E.

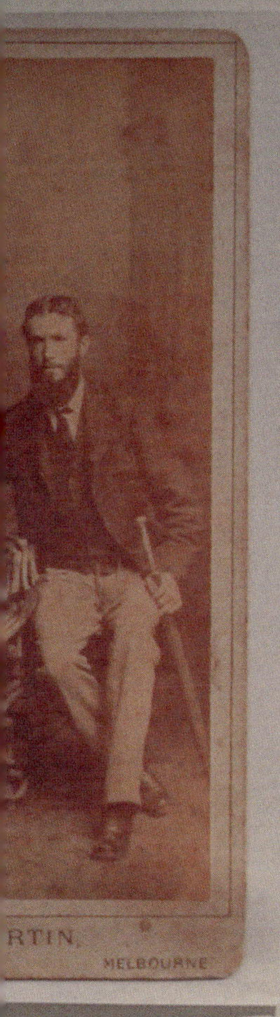
RTIN
MELBOURNE
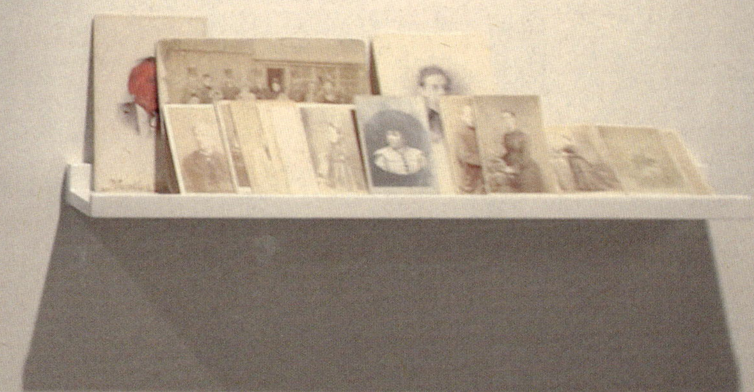

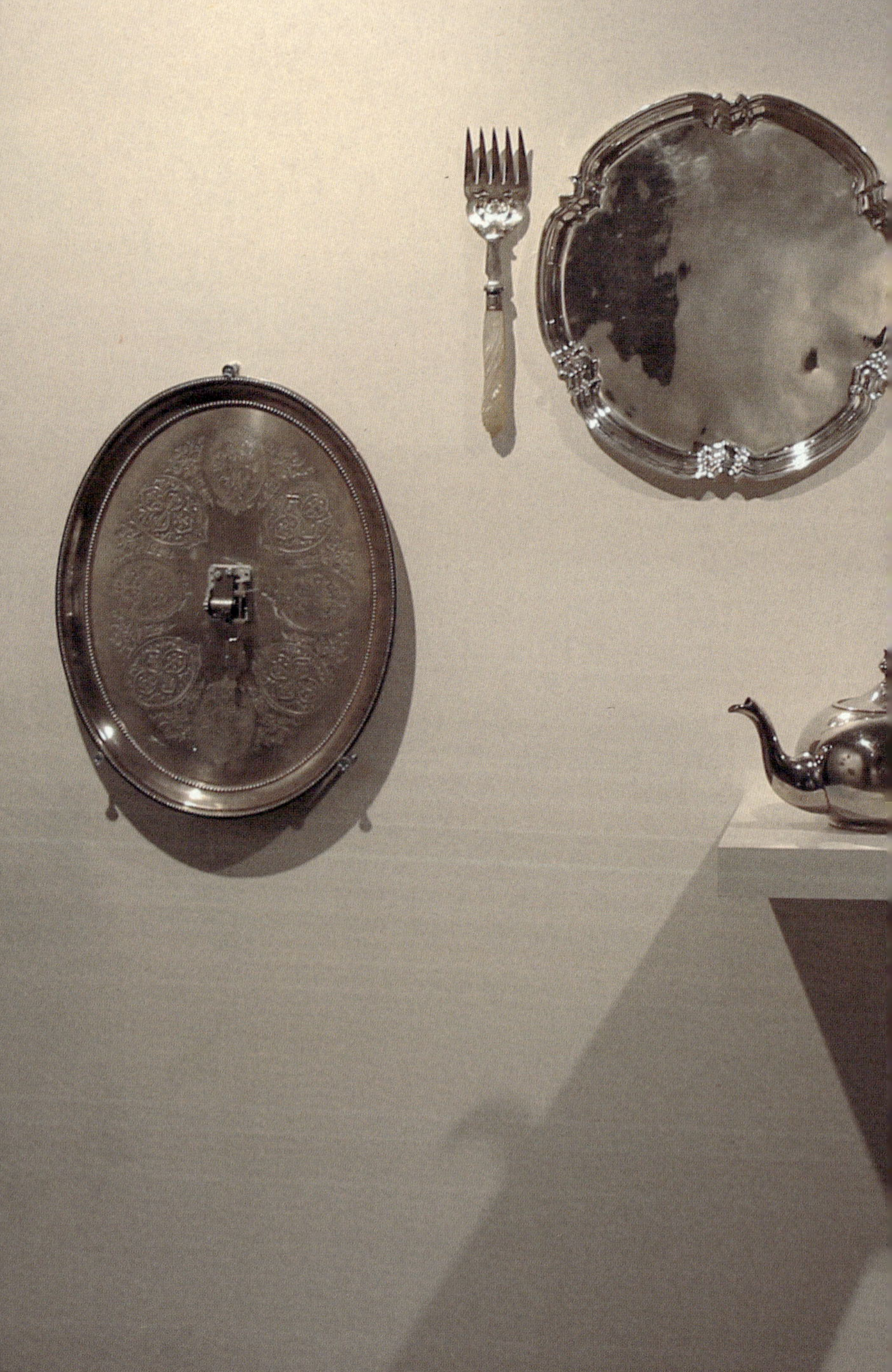

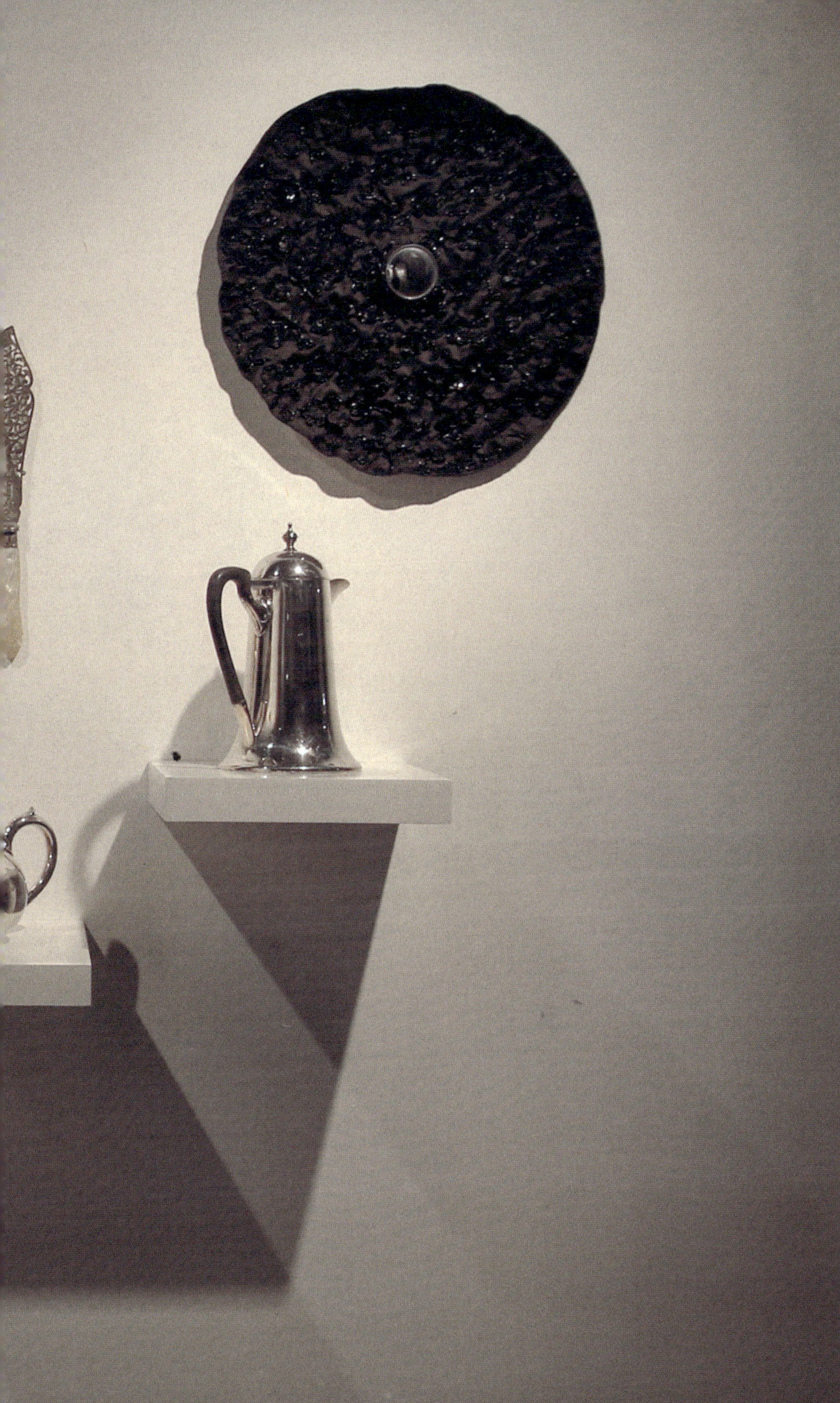

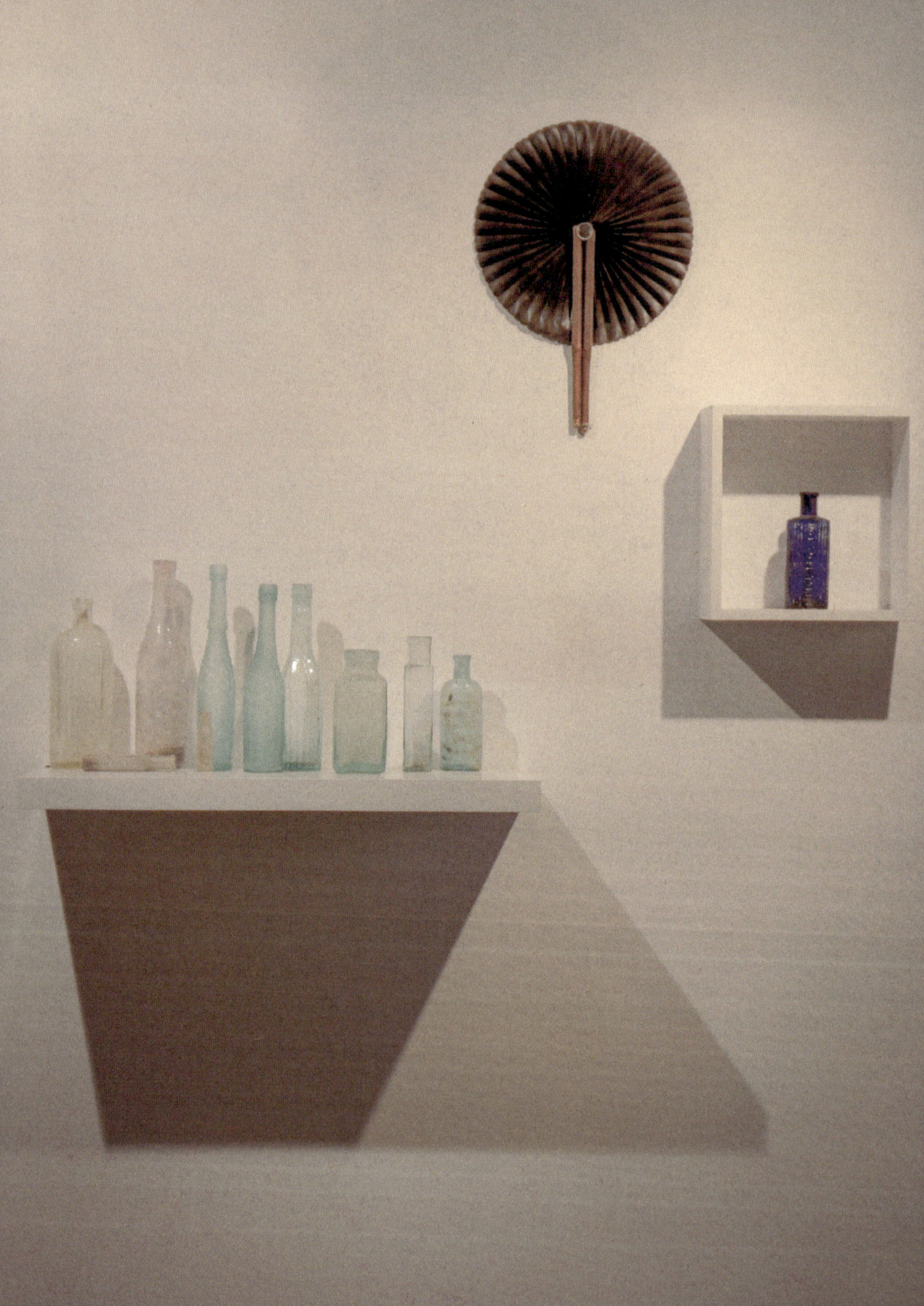

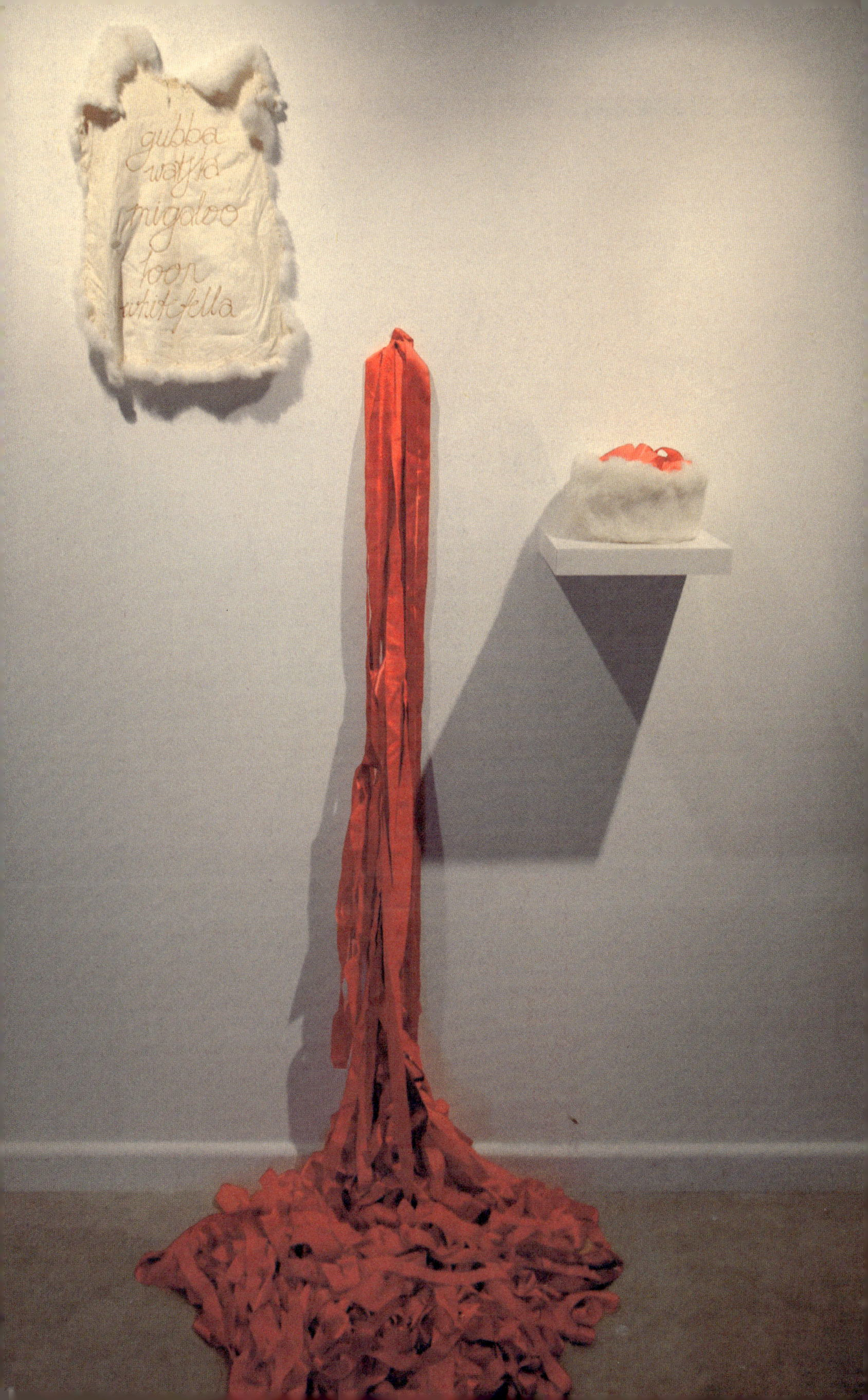
gubba
watjla
migaloo

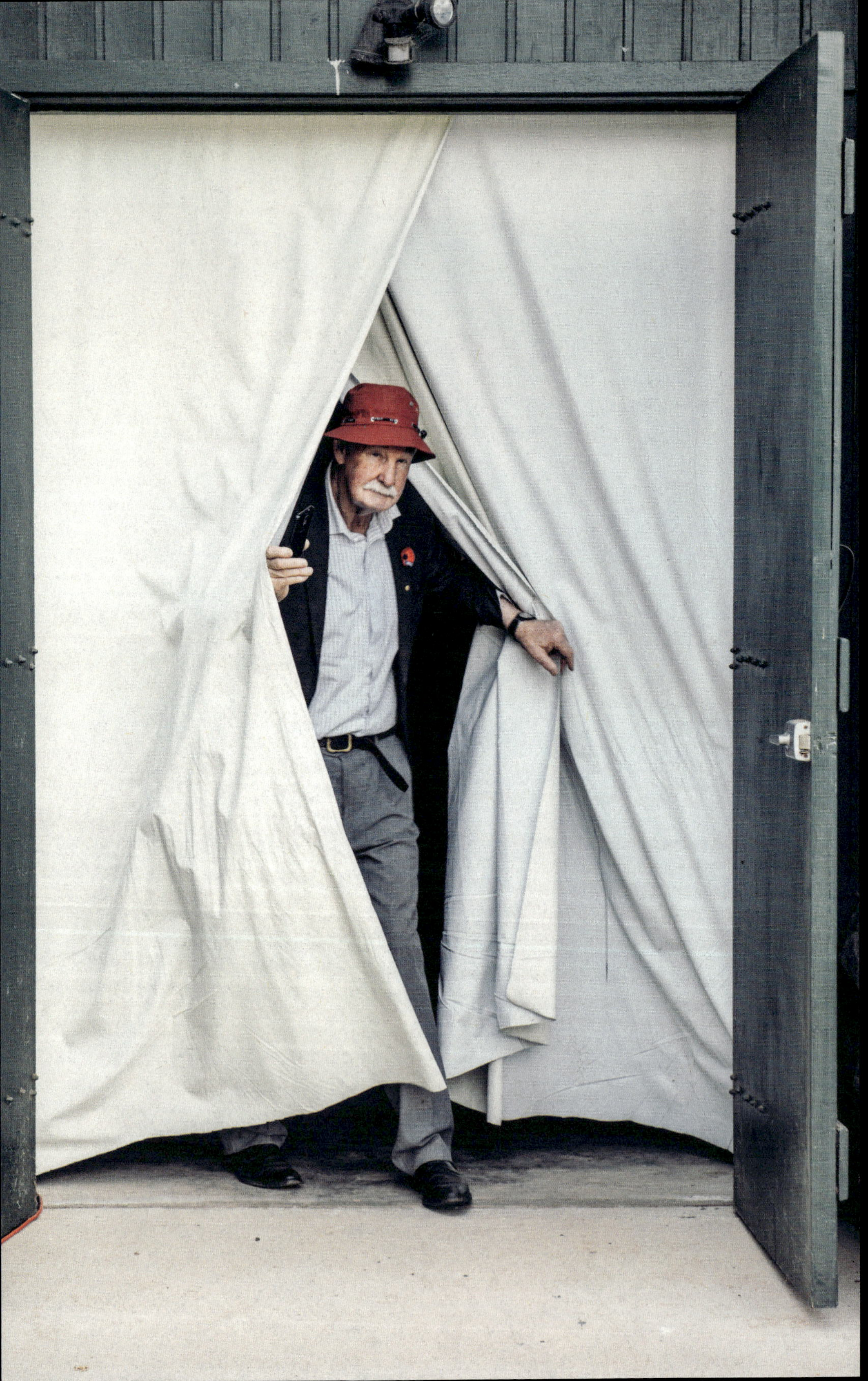

IMAGES FROM THE ARCHIVE

As an event, *Treatment* has moved from experience into archive. Documented in photographs, films, stories and books, it will join the rich collection of archival material Melbourne Water keeps. The archive here acts as a portal into other times, other narratives and other people's lives. In the images presented, we witness a community wedded to life's immediate productive forces. Through the film stills, taken from footage shot from the early 1900s to the 1950s, it becomes clear that the Western Treatment Plant (formerly The Metropolitan Farm) is a site undergoing a transformation—not only in the industrialisation of its technologies, but in its evolution as a community of workers, farmers, and families. What do we have left of them? Some of the ex-residents of Cocoroc visited the place for the first time in 50 years during the *Treatment* public art project in 2015. On viewing Catherine Bell's work, one woman, with tears in her eyes, was heard to say: 'I met my husband in that pool'. The site itself is multi-faceted in its technologies, a mix of old and new, ordinarily cut off from the metropolis it supports. In reactions like the one above, we might suggest that the site is more than an archive and not only a fertile ground for growing food and running cows. It operates at other deeply personal and collective registers for ex-residents, workers and indigenous people. Far from the project memorialising the site, the artists folded back its hidden layers to reveal a living culture, bound up in waste, stigma, pride, hard work, industry, community and diverse histories.

The Melbourne Water Heritage Team is responsible for the management of the collection of historic documents, photographs and ephemera related to the history of the business. The heritage collection is a source of knowledge, ideas, stories and memories. The collection is managed as a corporate and industry resource to educate and inform the business, the community and industry, and to contribute to the conservation of the history and heritage of the organisation and the wider water industry. The development, use and interpretation of the collection are the key means by which the mission is fulfilled.

—Cameron Bishop and Paul Balassone

Source for images:
Melbourne Water Archives

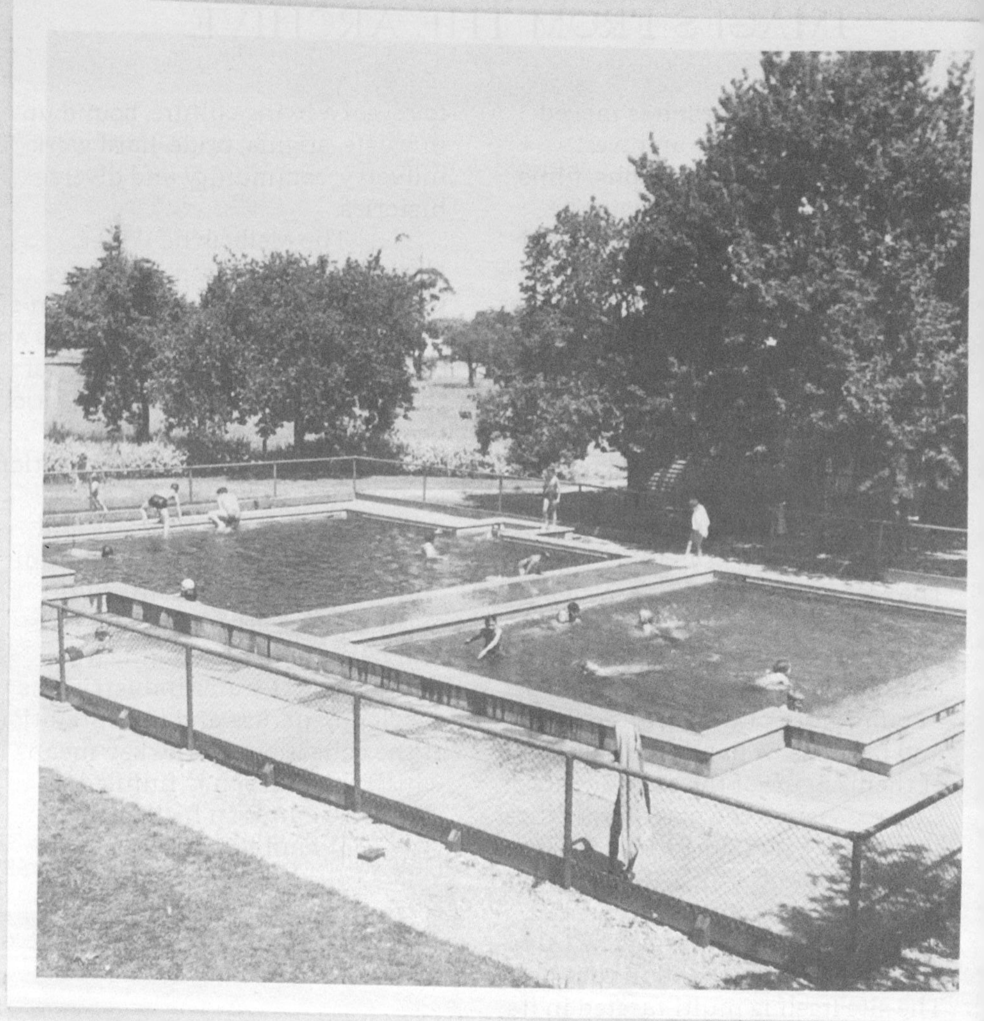

54-54

Swimming pool Metropolitan Farm.

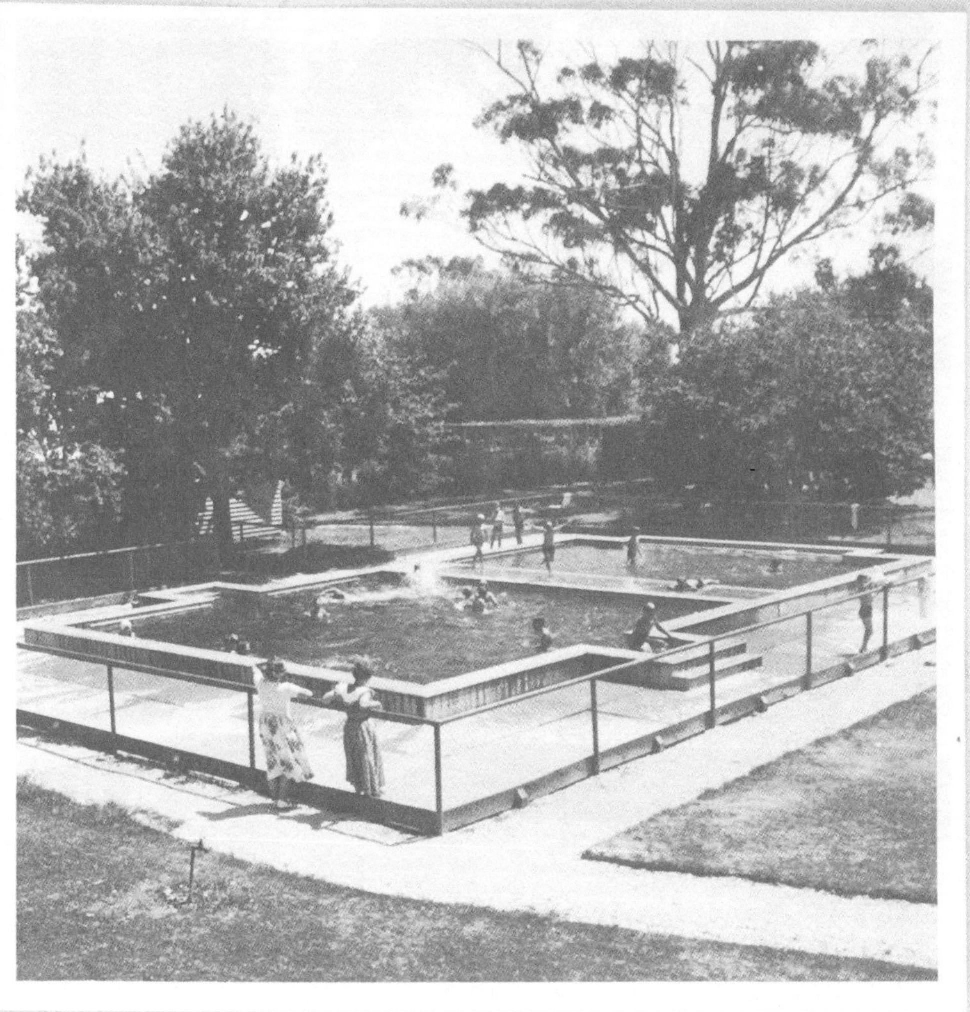

54-50

Swimming pool Metropolitan Farm.

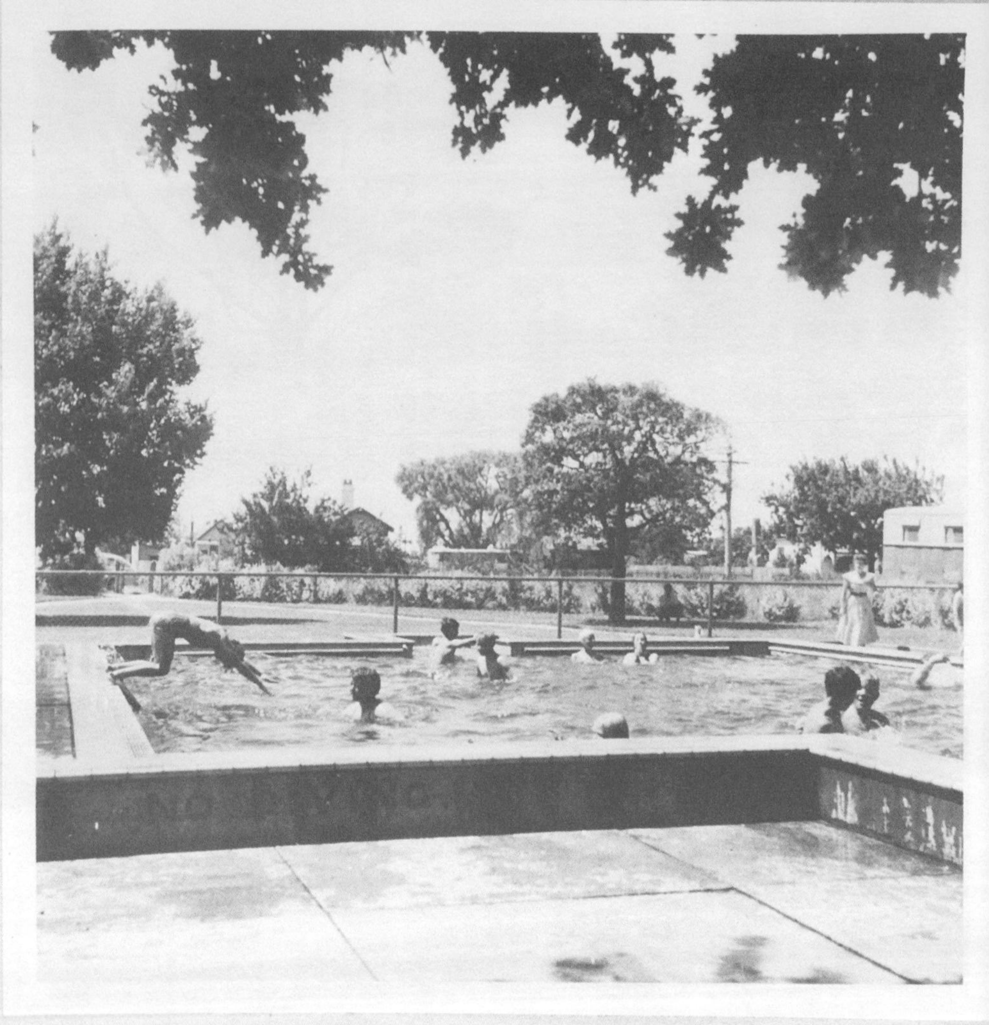

54-52

Swimming pool Metropolitan Farm.

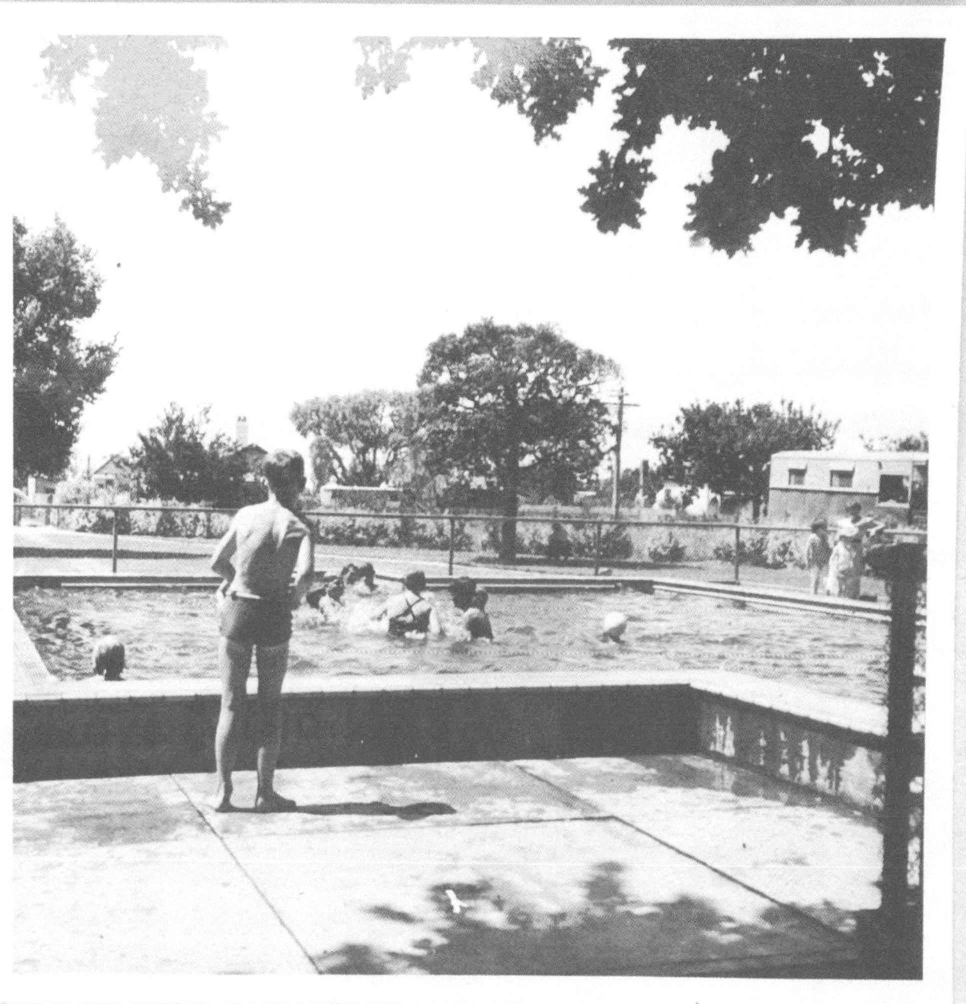

54-49

Swimming pool Metropolitan Farm.

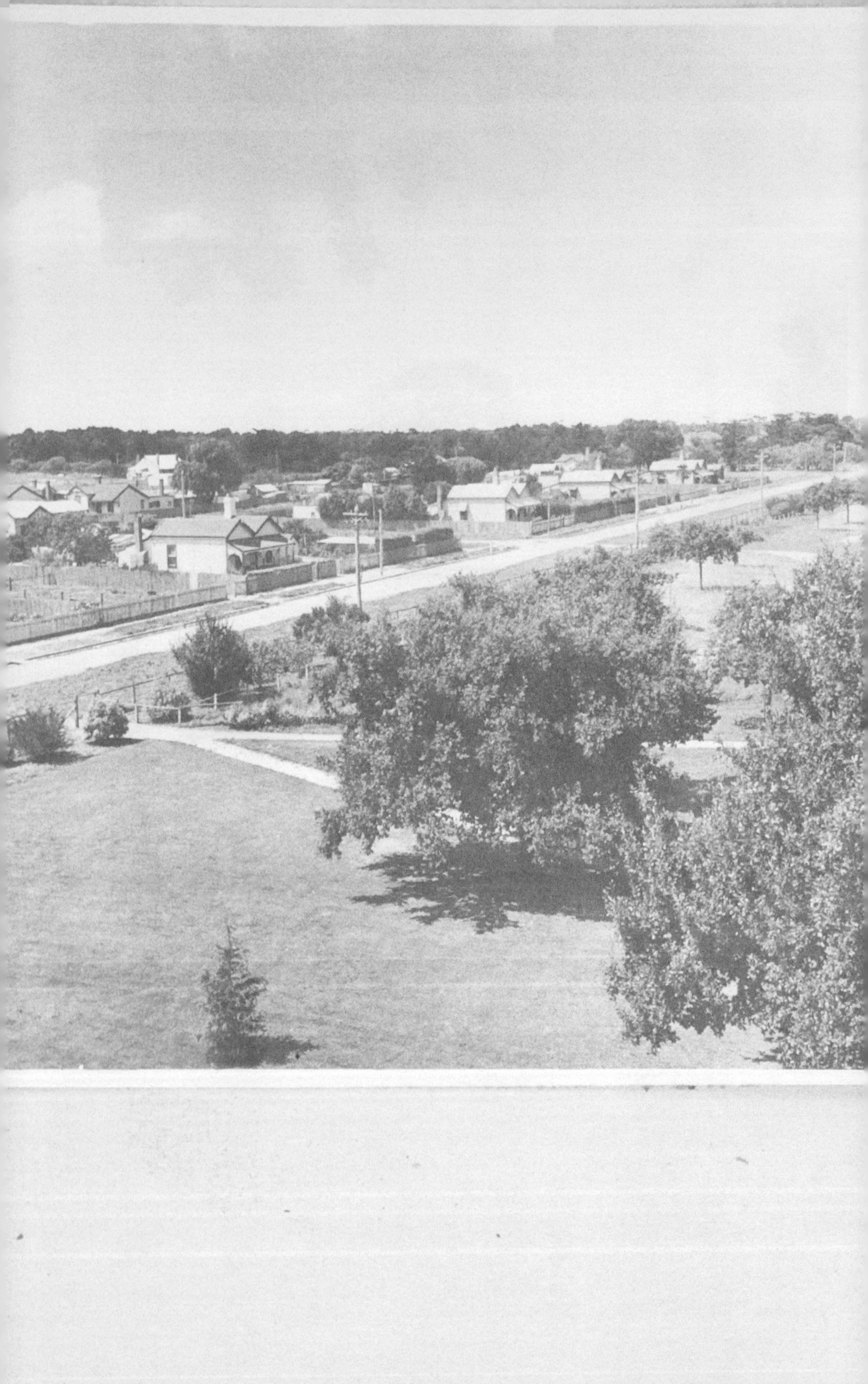

50-1R-8

Metropolitan Farm
township (from water
tower)

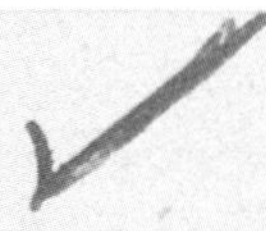

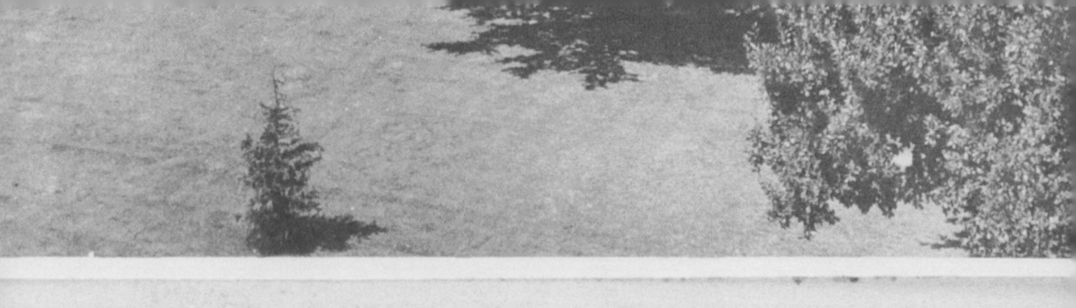

49-13R-7

Water tower
Metropolitan Farm

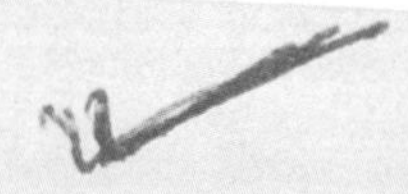

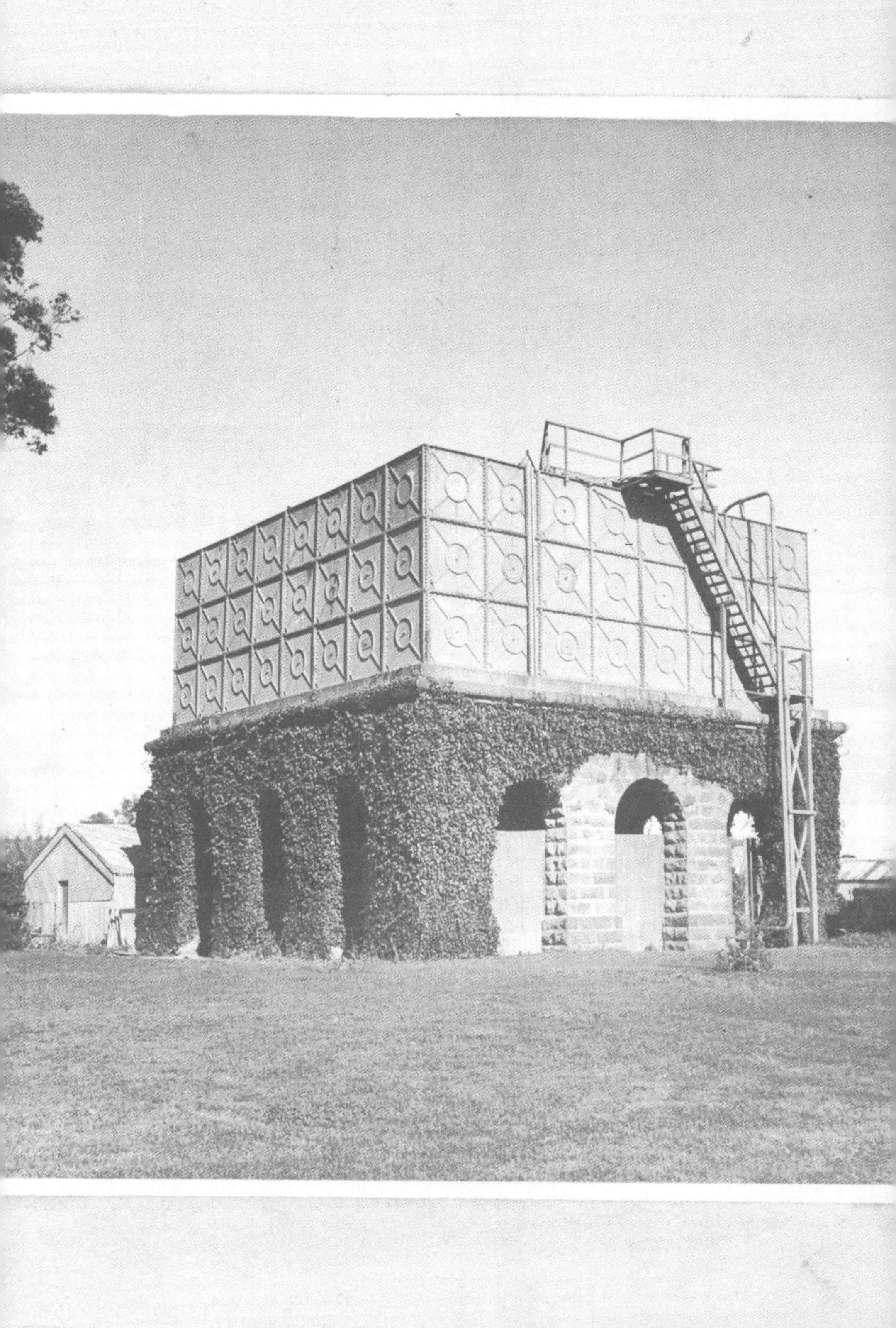

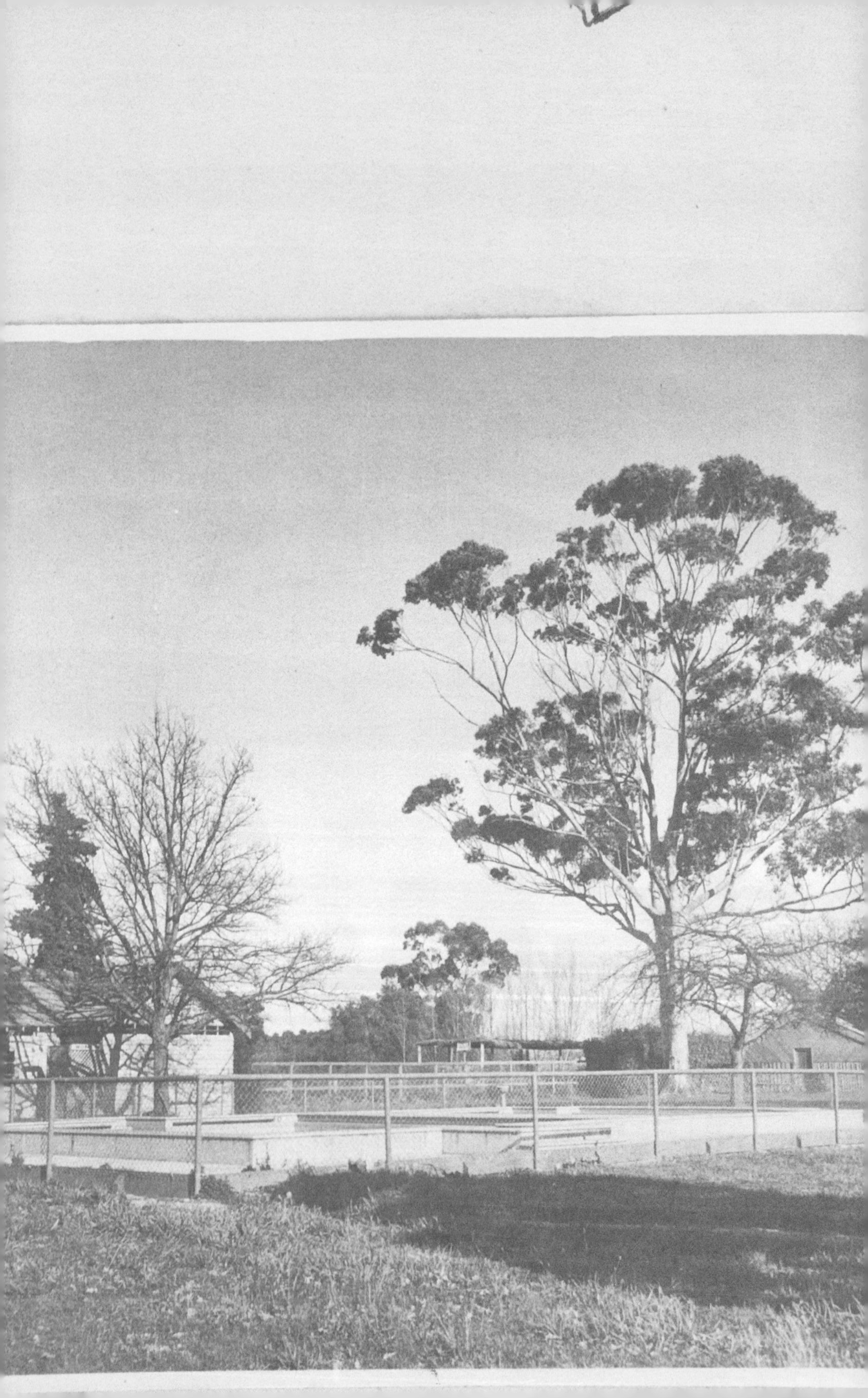

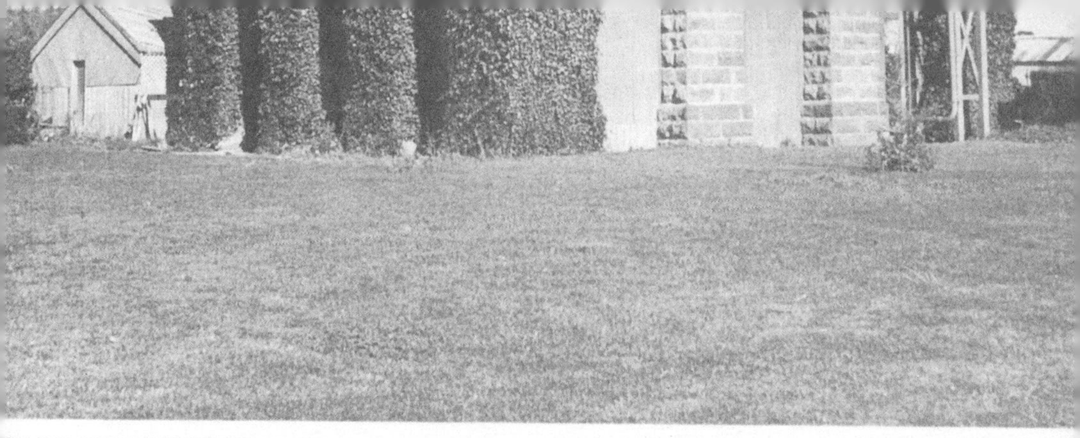

02 L
2363

49-13R-8

Swimming pool.
Metropolitan Farm

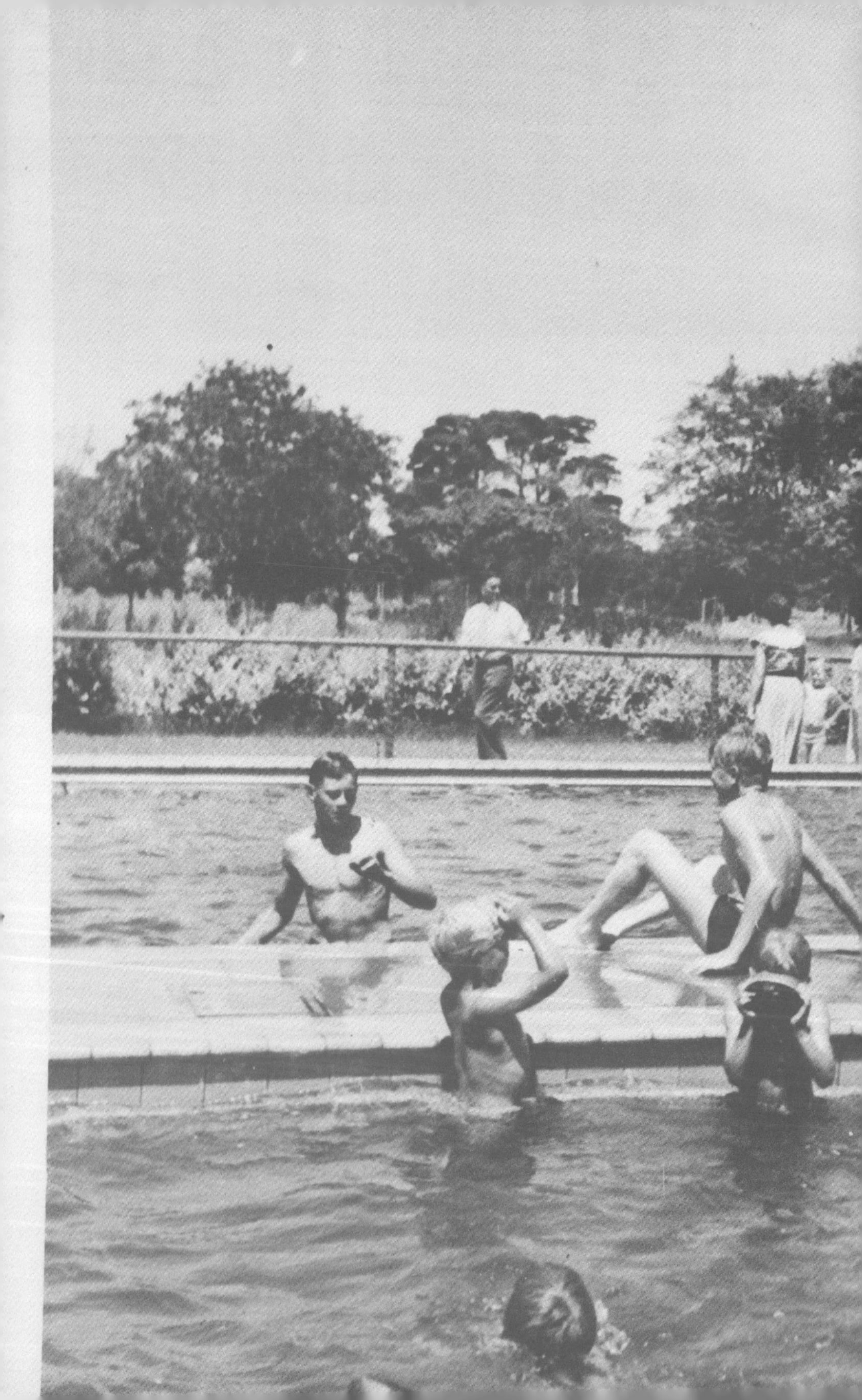

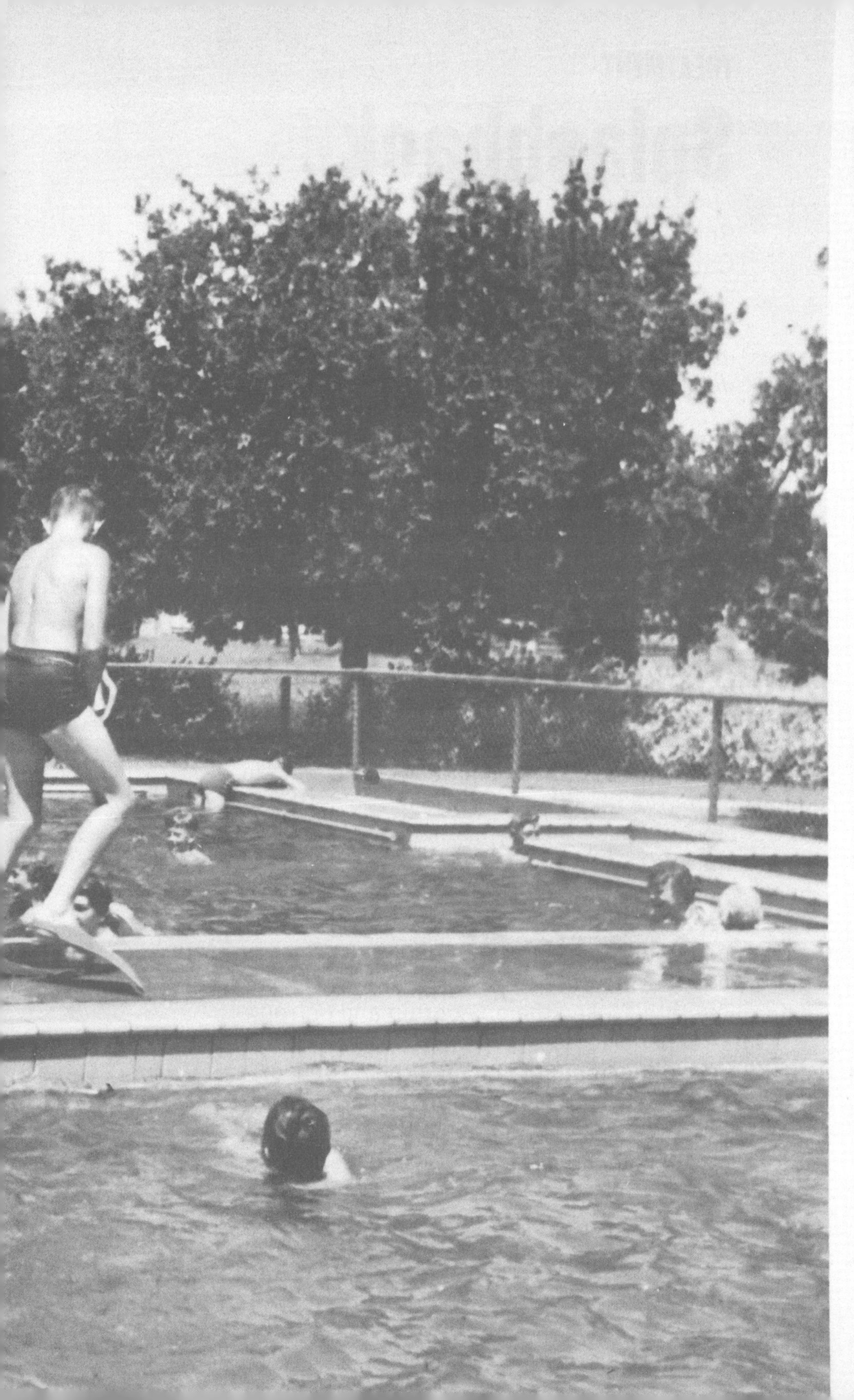

Splashback

Remembering Blue and Entropic Action

Catherine Bell

In the first instance archival artists seek to make historical information, often lost or displaced, physically present.[1]

Researching the archival footage at the Western Treatment Plant evokes the complexities and the pleasures of both looking and remembering, and highlights the artist's role and responsibility as both an interpreter and disseminator of cultural memory. I see the archive as the nexus between public and private space and I approached the documentary footage, filmed at the Western Treatment plant from the early 1900s, as a starting point to understanding how the archive acts as repository of history, memory, testimony and identity.[2]

I gravitated to the abandoned pools, built in the 1940s for the families that lived at the settlement of Cocoroc, because they symbolised a community lost, displaced and forgotten. The pools would have been an oasis for the families to escape the heat and sewage at the farm. The act of returning the abandoned children's swimming pool to its former glory while leaving the neighbouring adult pool in a derelict state evoked themes of ruin and entropy. The site-responsive intervention activated the location by juxtaposing the old and the new, past and present, functional and dysfunctional. Editing the sepia footage of children using the pools from the 1940s and colour 8mm film from the 1950s with a haunting 'Big-band' soundtrack created a portal into another time. Projected onto the back wall of the original changerooms located behind the pools, the footage generated an aura of timeless euphoria and community spirit.

There is an element of black humour embedded in the work because the pool's pristine appearance is an illusion; it is filled with effluent water. The crystal clear, blue water looked inviting but was toxic despite undergoing extensive 'treatment'. Ironically, public pools for children, although highly chlorinated, are a malodorous mix of bodily excretions, not so far removed from the 'treated' water used in the resurrected pool at Cocoroc. The archival footage emphasises the popularity of these pools and how communal bathing is an intimately visceral encounter. The pungent smell of animal droppings mixed with dank composted leaves in the changerooms delivered an abject viewing experience that tested the staying power of the audience. Sectioned off from the public, the pools were observed from a distance, and people intermingled at the congested observation points in earshot of the upbeat 'Swing' soundscape. The installation aimed to create a social space that united this temporary community in facing how future and past are compressed into the viewer's present.

The project was more than working with the physical site and researching the archives; I felt like I contributed to the lived experience of the place. Integral to the project was the self-reflexive approach to remembering, communicating and defining the colour blue. I was prompted by the curator to call the onsite contractor about the colour I wanted the pool to be painted. I left a detailed message that was like squirting every shade of blue pigment invented onto a palette and then meticulously describing how to mix the colours to achieve the vision of blue in my mind's eye. The poetic impulse of translating blue to a layperson suggested specific modes of reception that belong to the collective memory of public pools, thus engaging with the social temporalities of using these shared amenities.

The entropic action of the restored pool reverting to swamp at the conclusion of the project could be interpreted as melancholy, however ephemeral public art advocates that ruins are open to reinvention just as archives are open to summoning spectres.

1 • • • • Foster, Hal, 'An Archival Impulse', in *October*, no. 110, 2004, pp. 3–22.

2 • • • • See: Merewether, Charles (ed.), *The Archive*, Whitechapel Gallery and MIT Press, London and Cambridge, Mass., 2006; and Steedman, Carolyn, 'The space of memory: in an archive', *History of the Human Sciences*, vol. 11, no. 4, 1998, pp. 65–83.

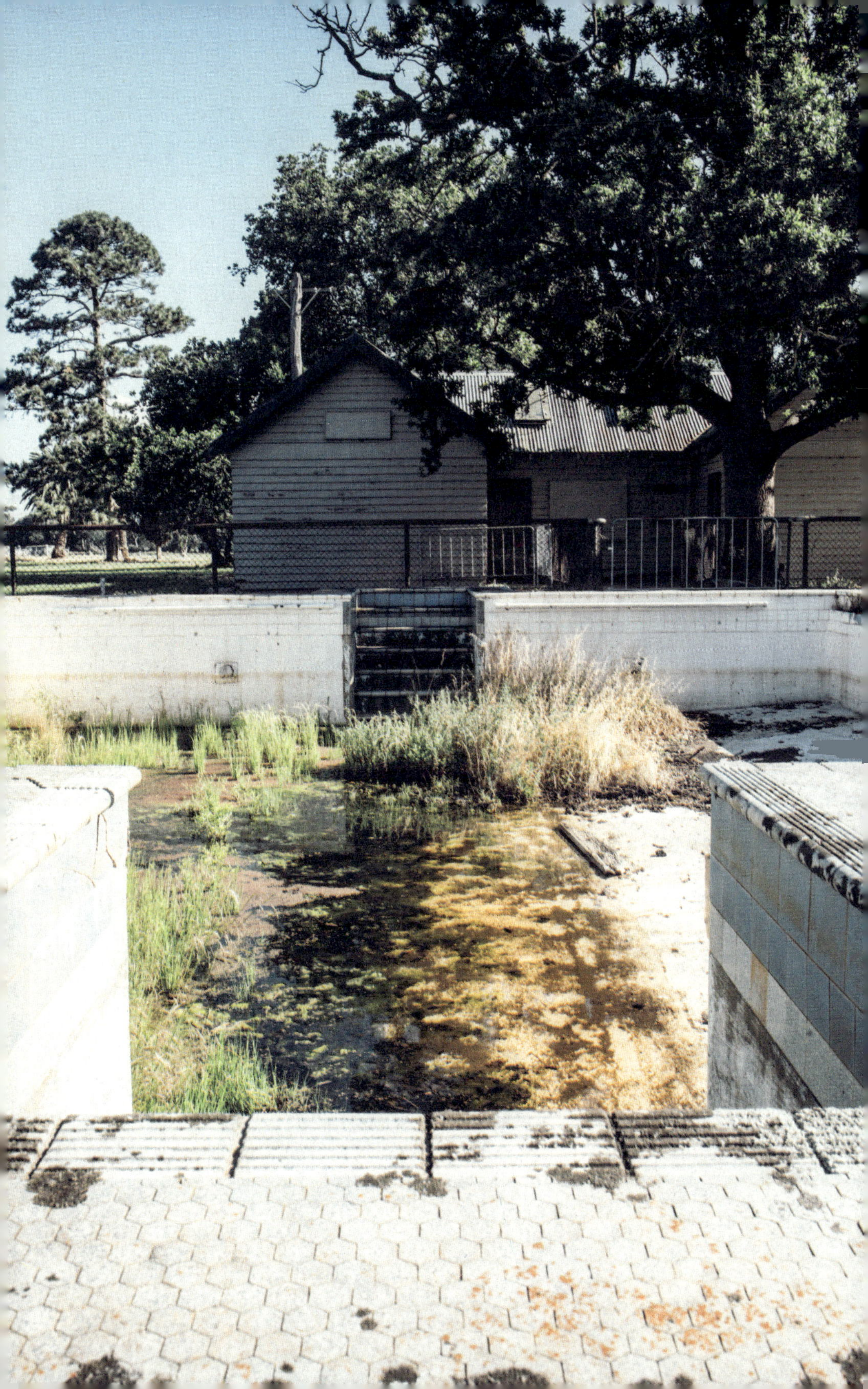

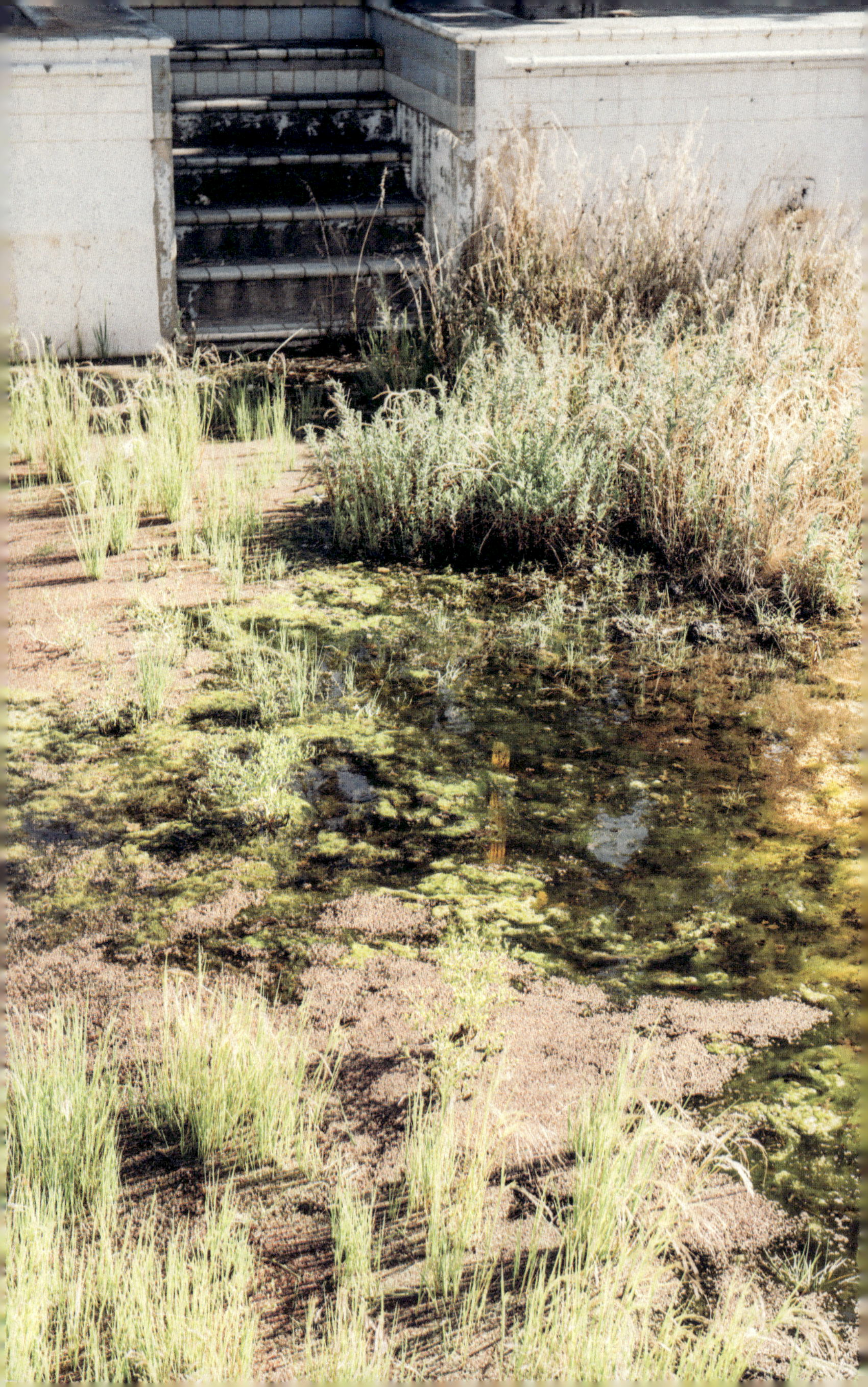

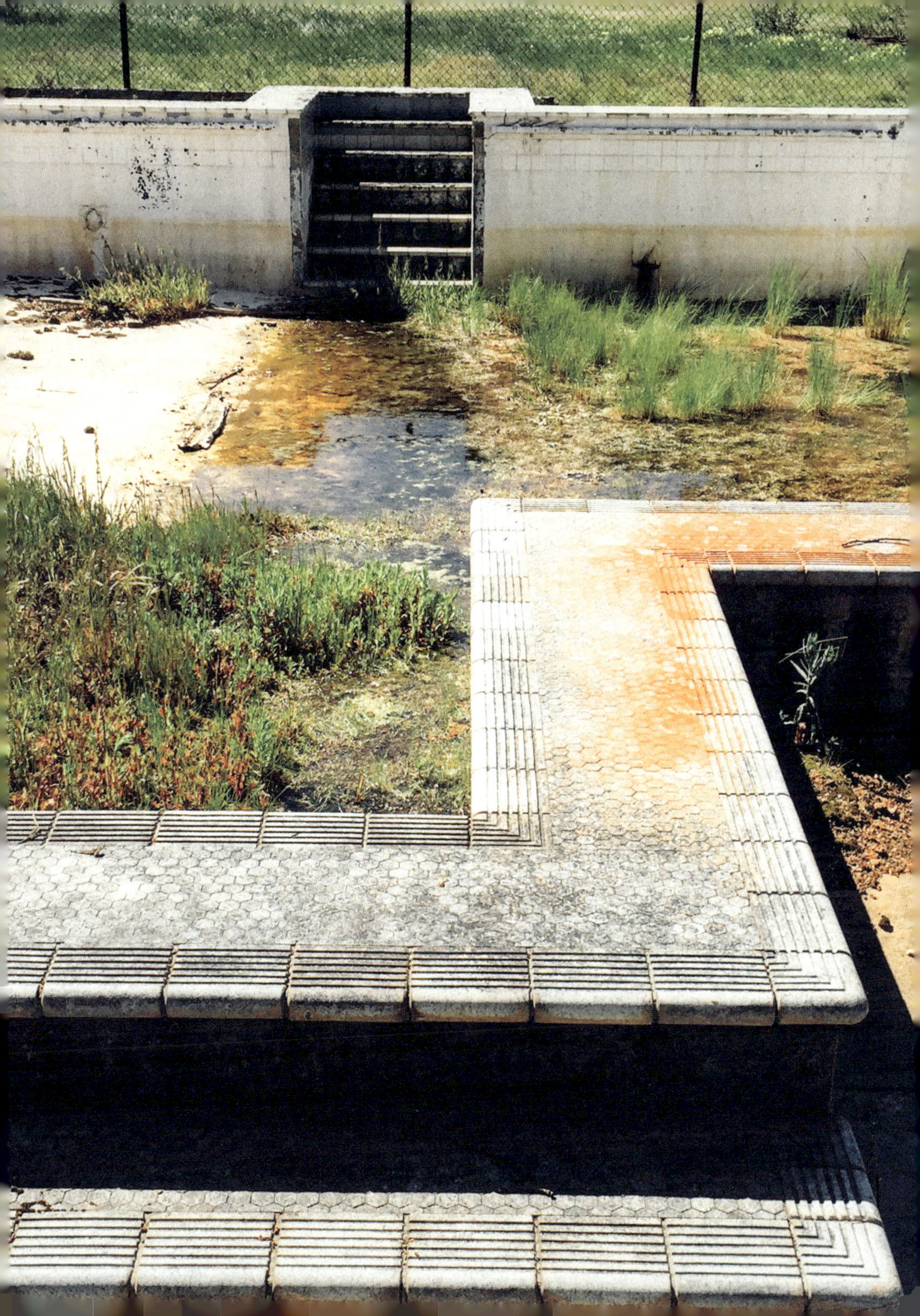

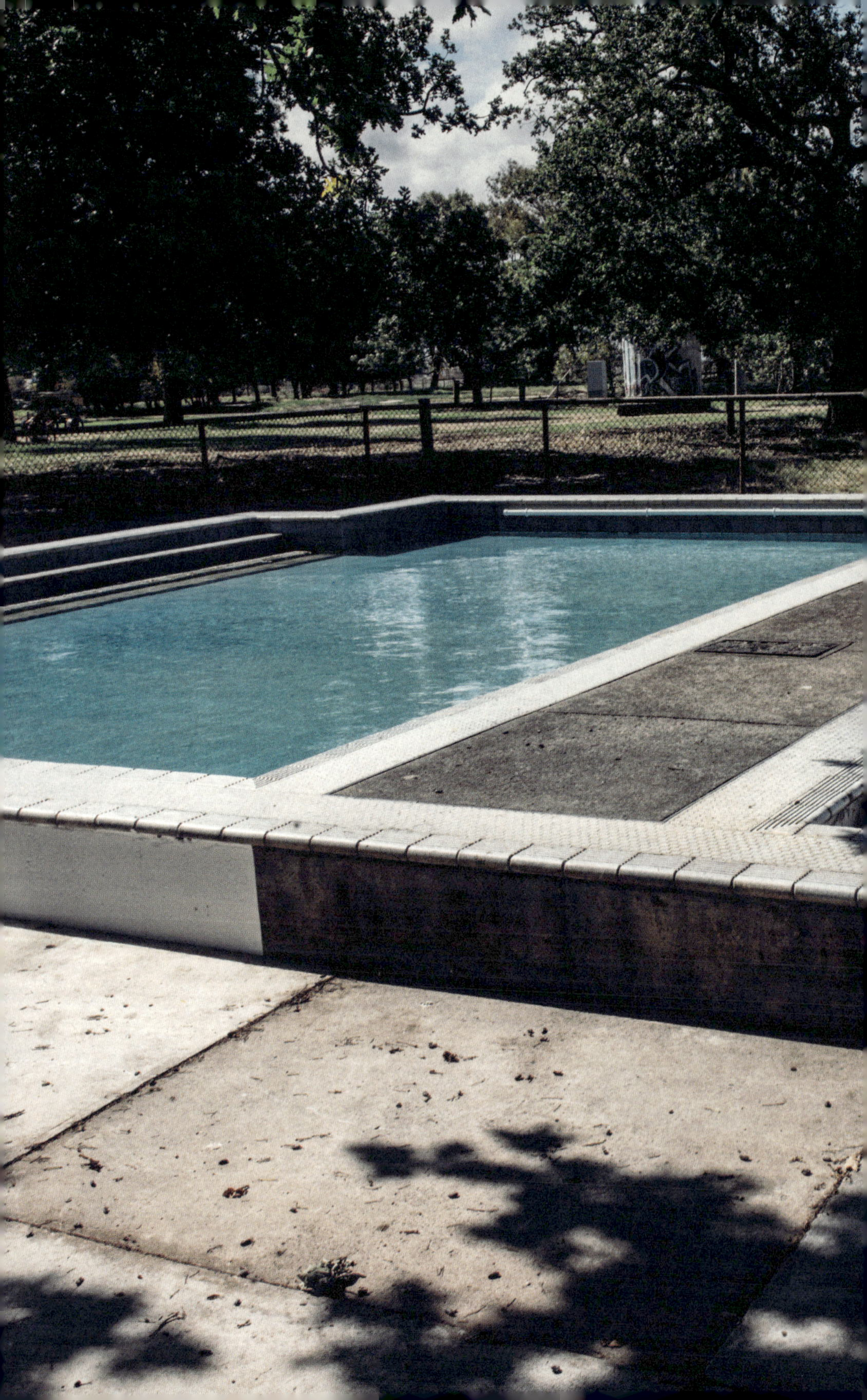

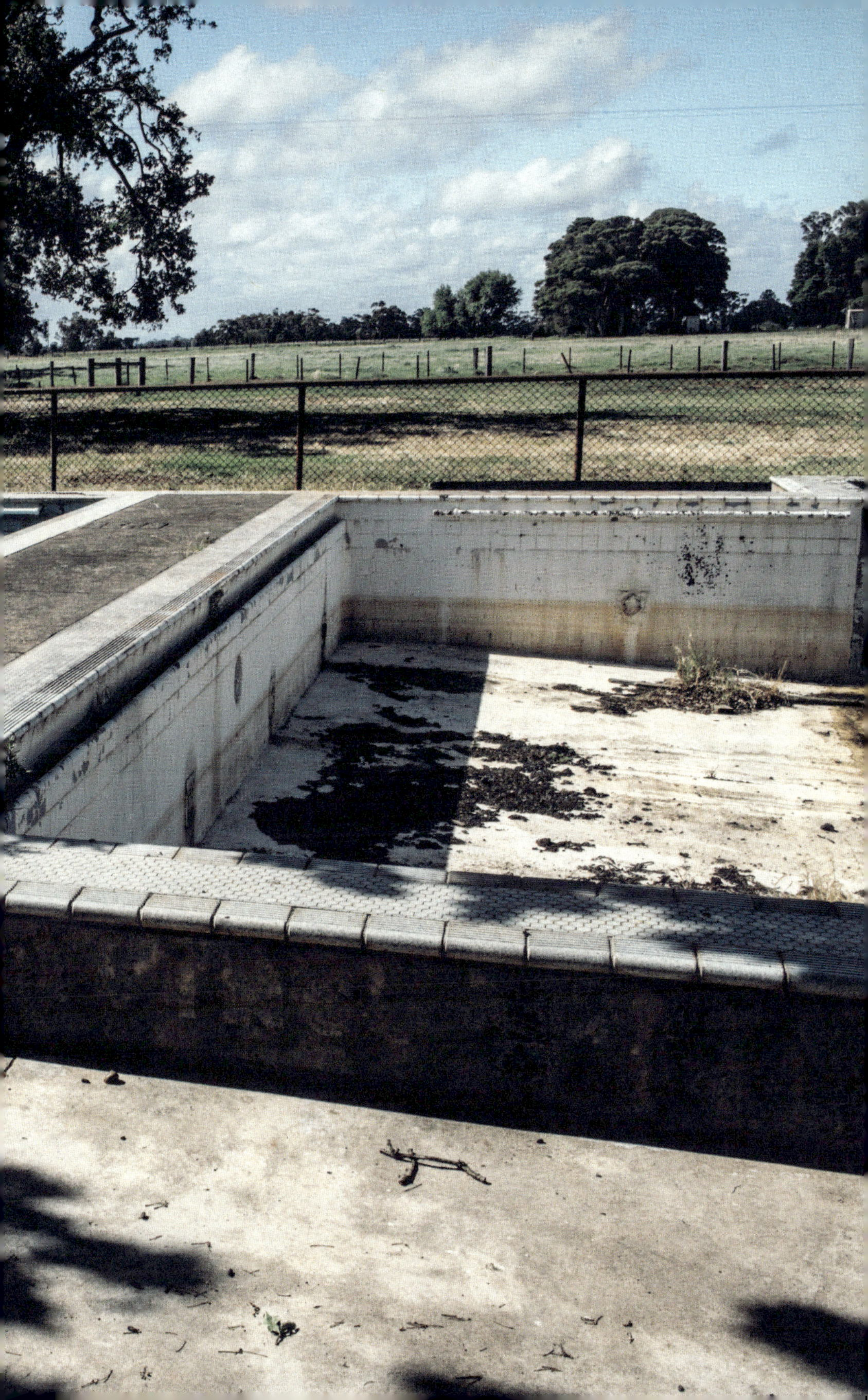

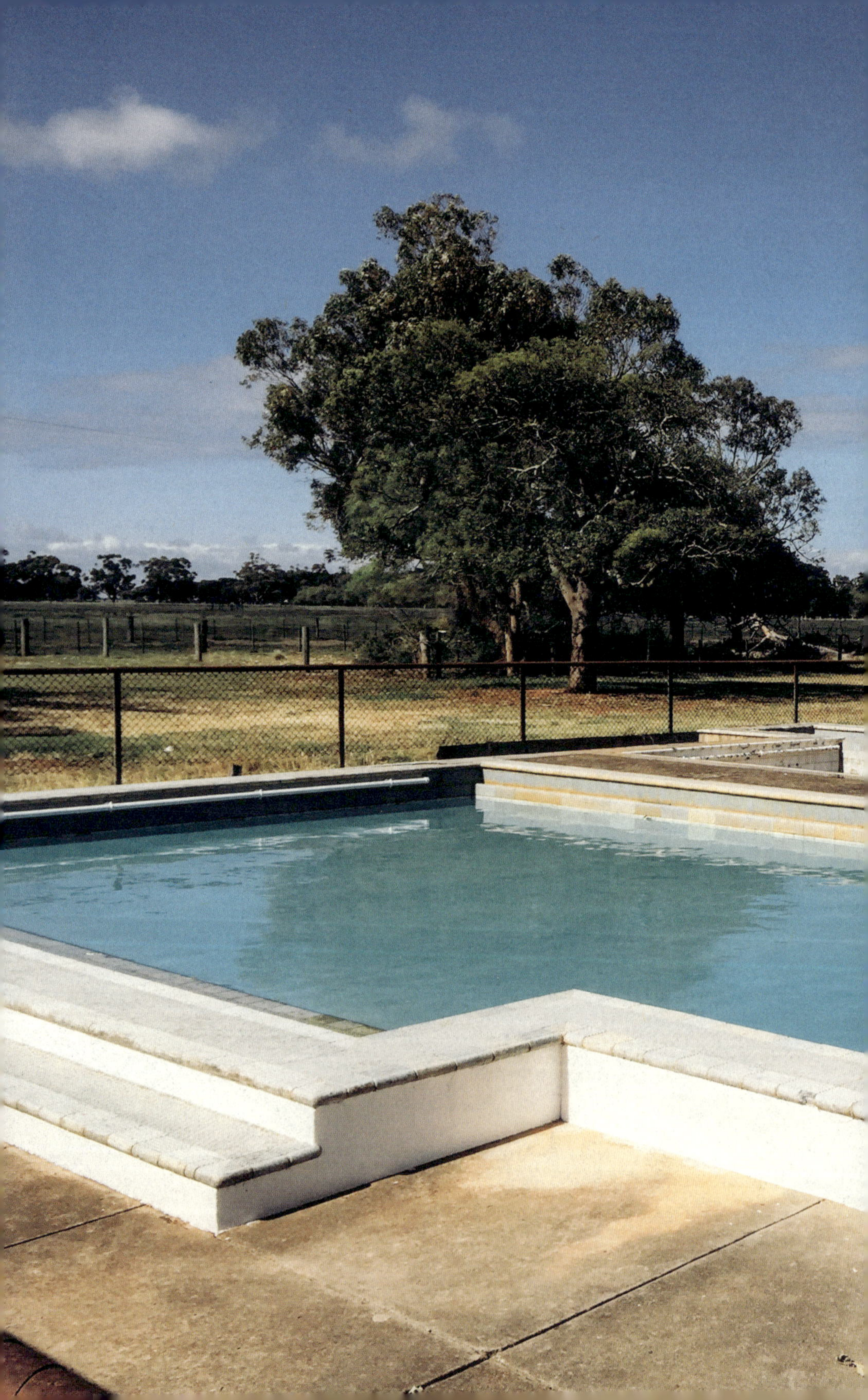

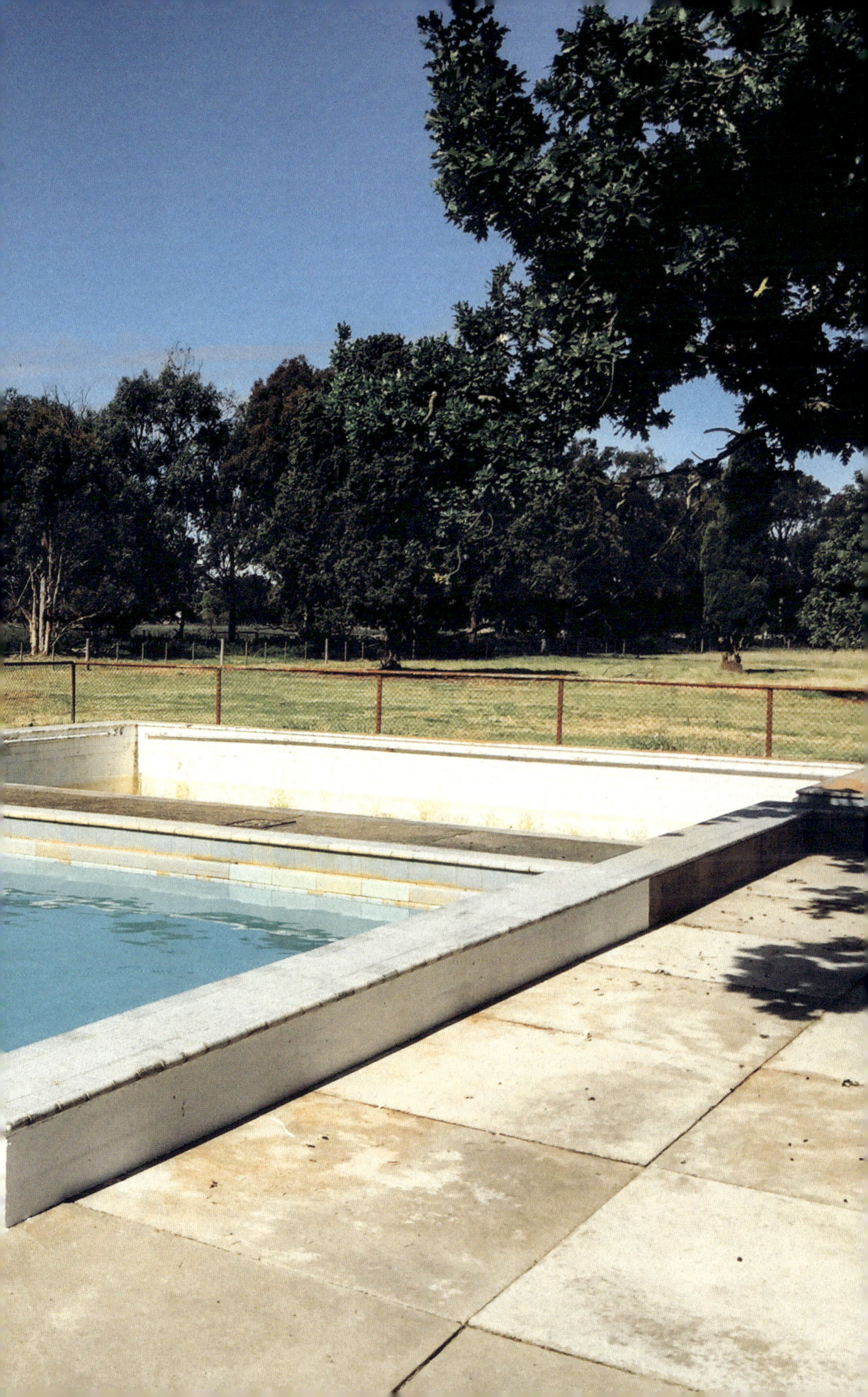

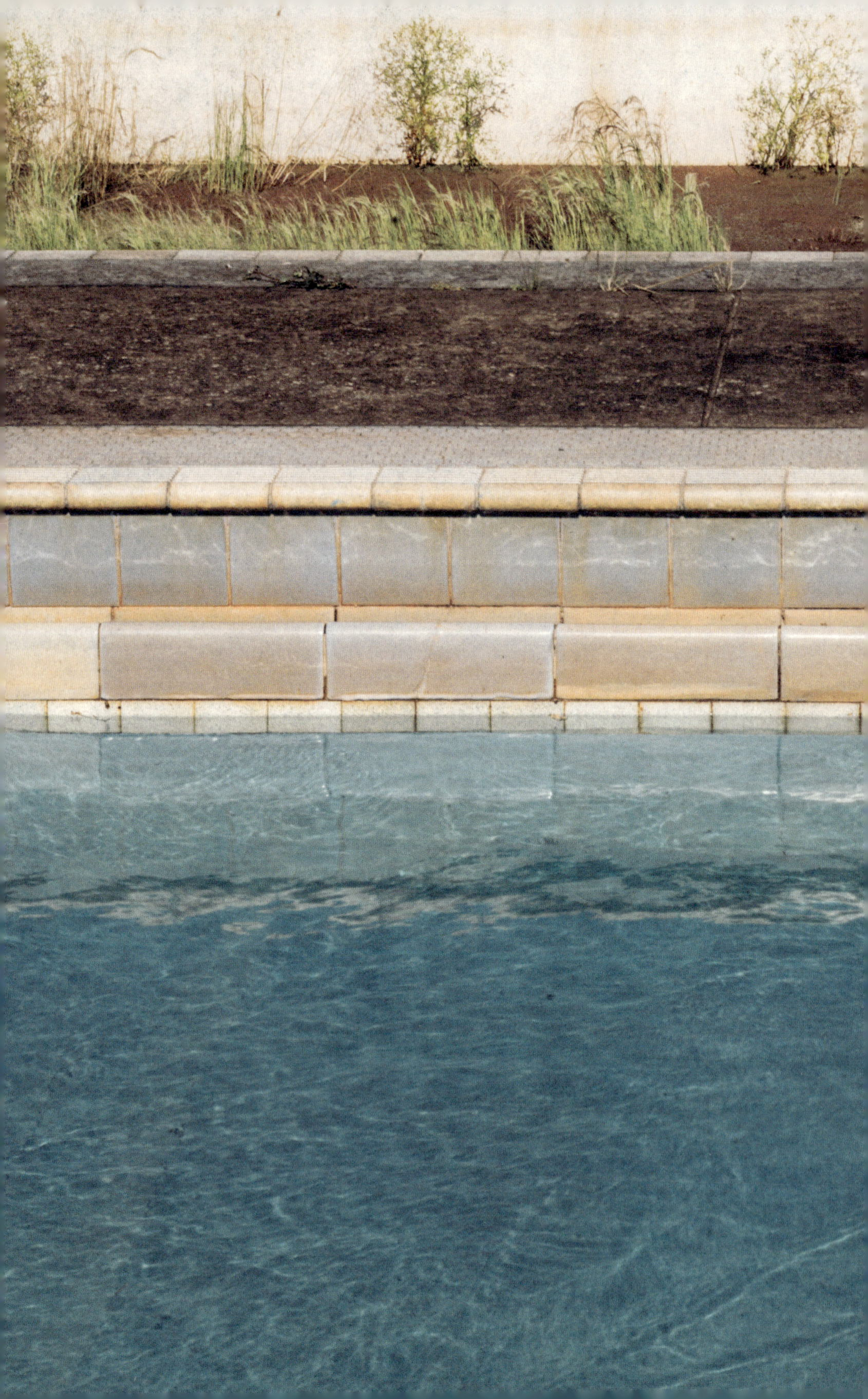

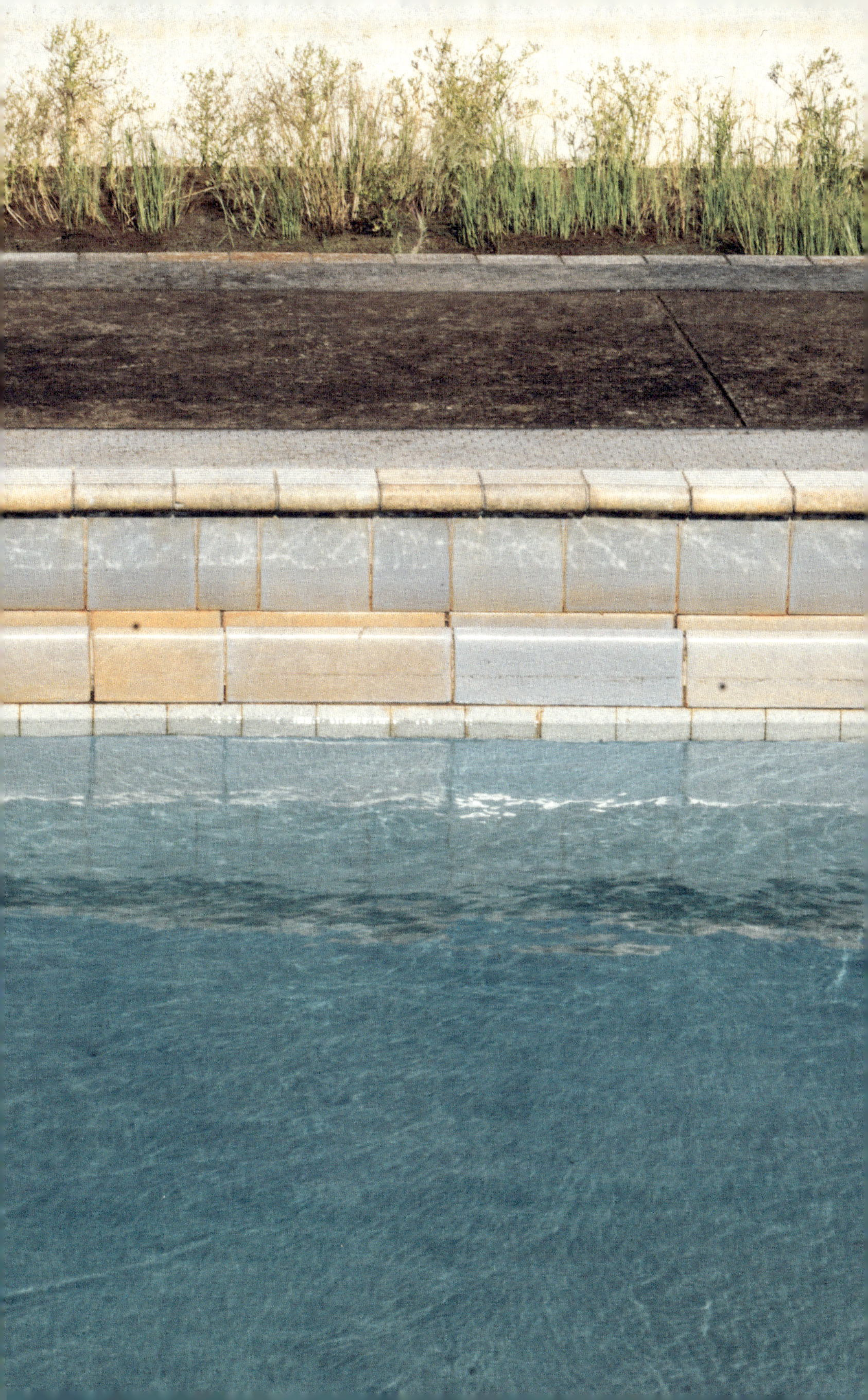

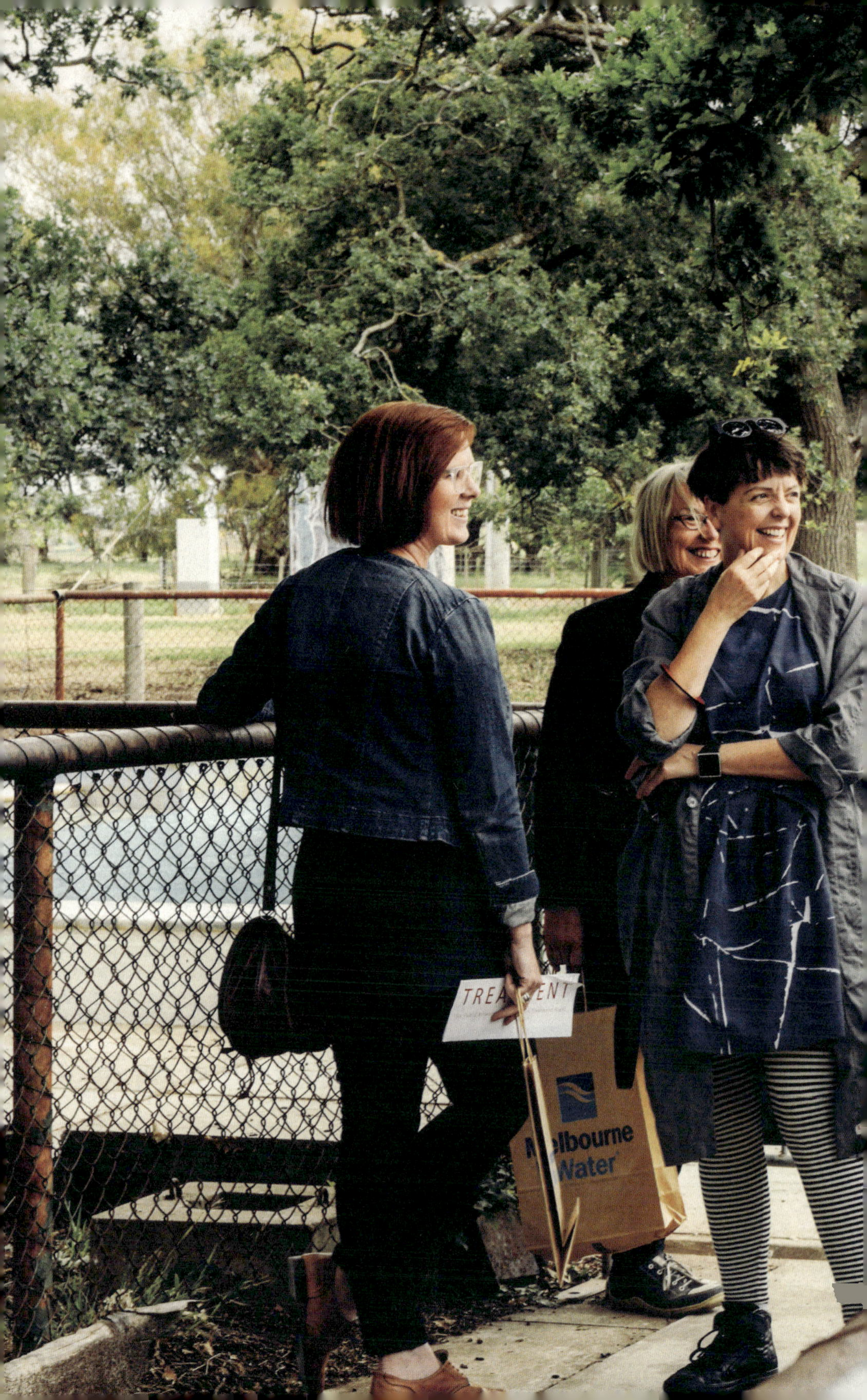

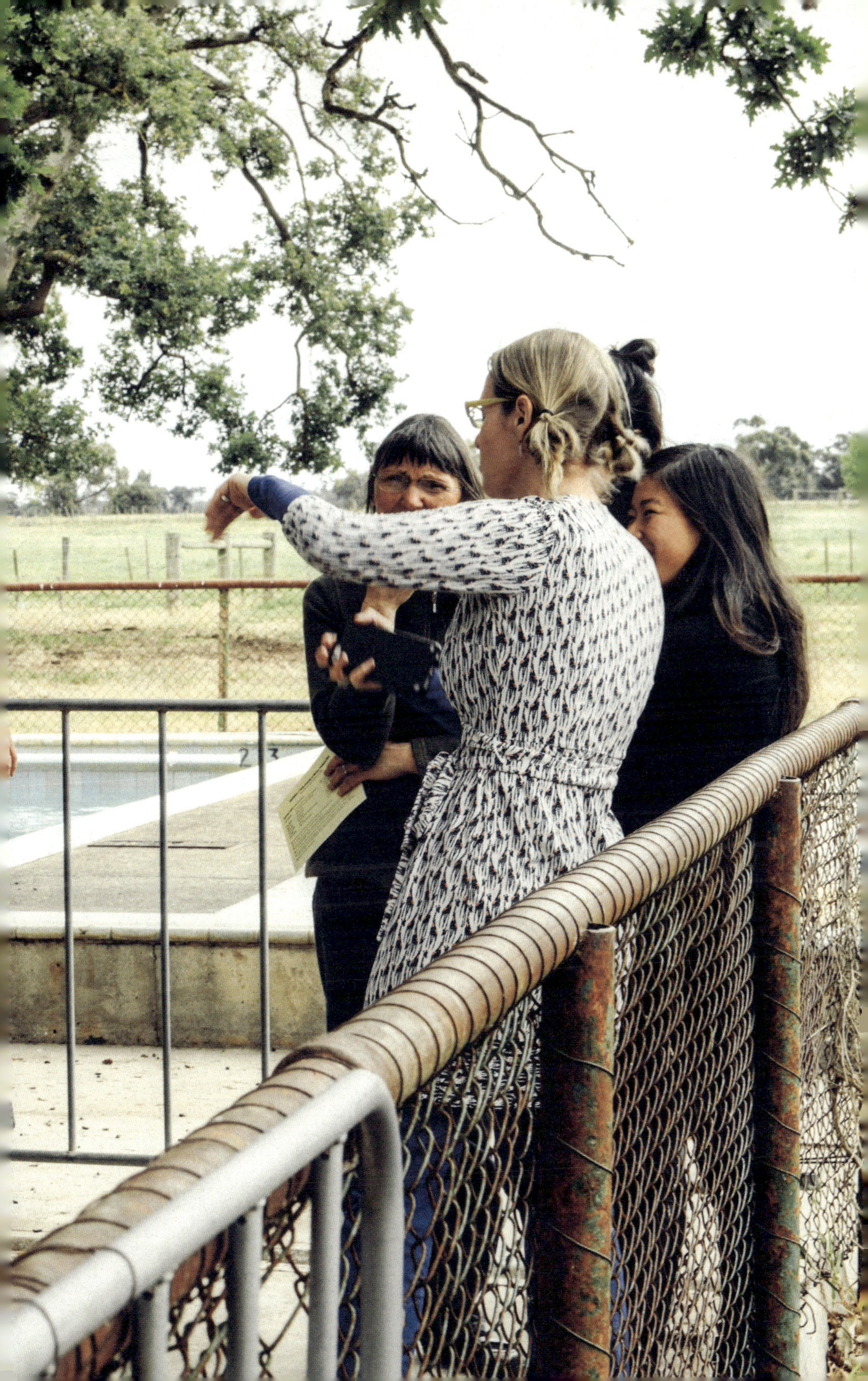

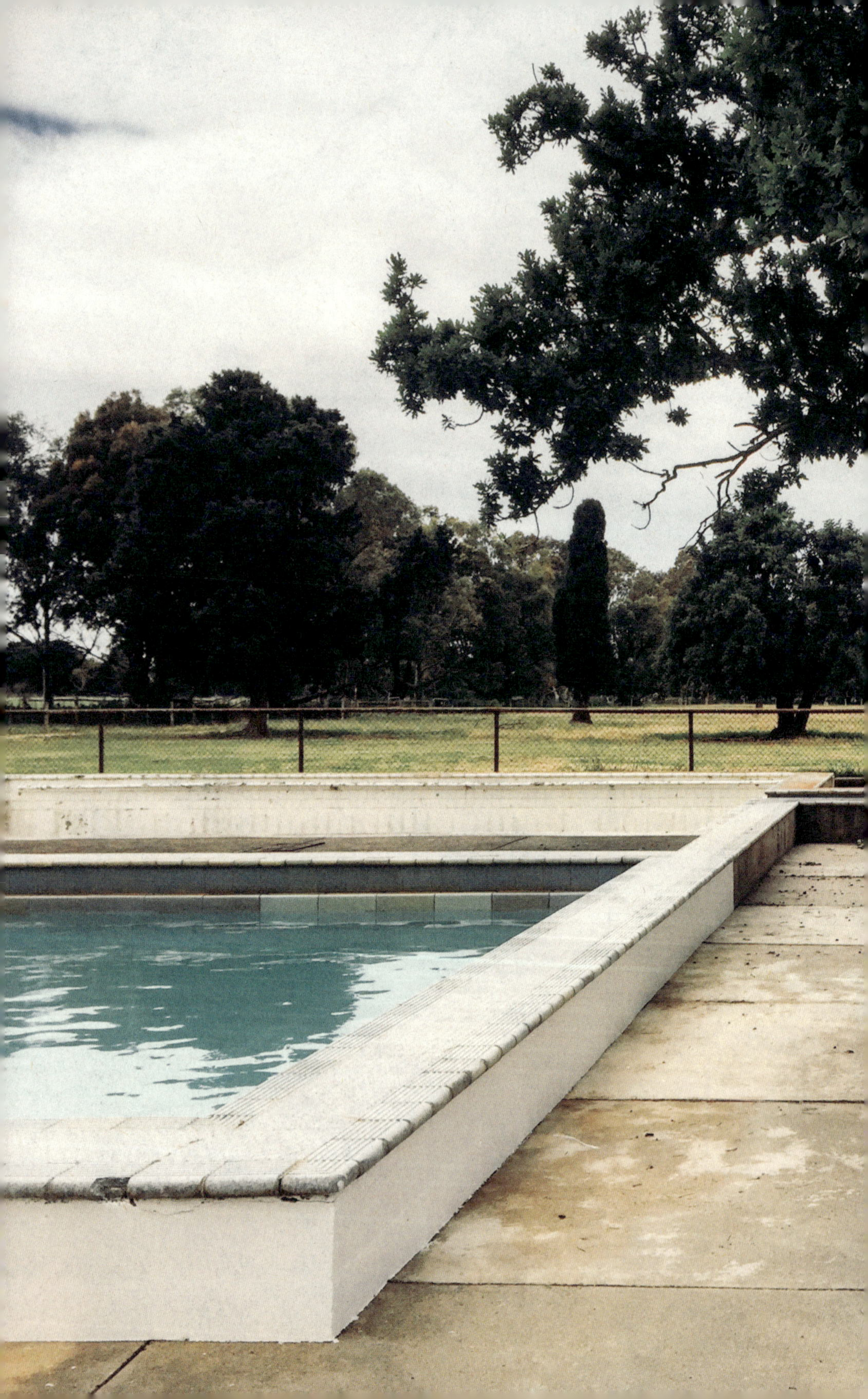

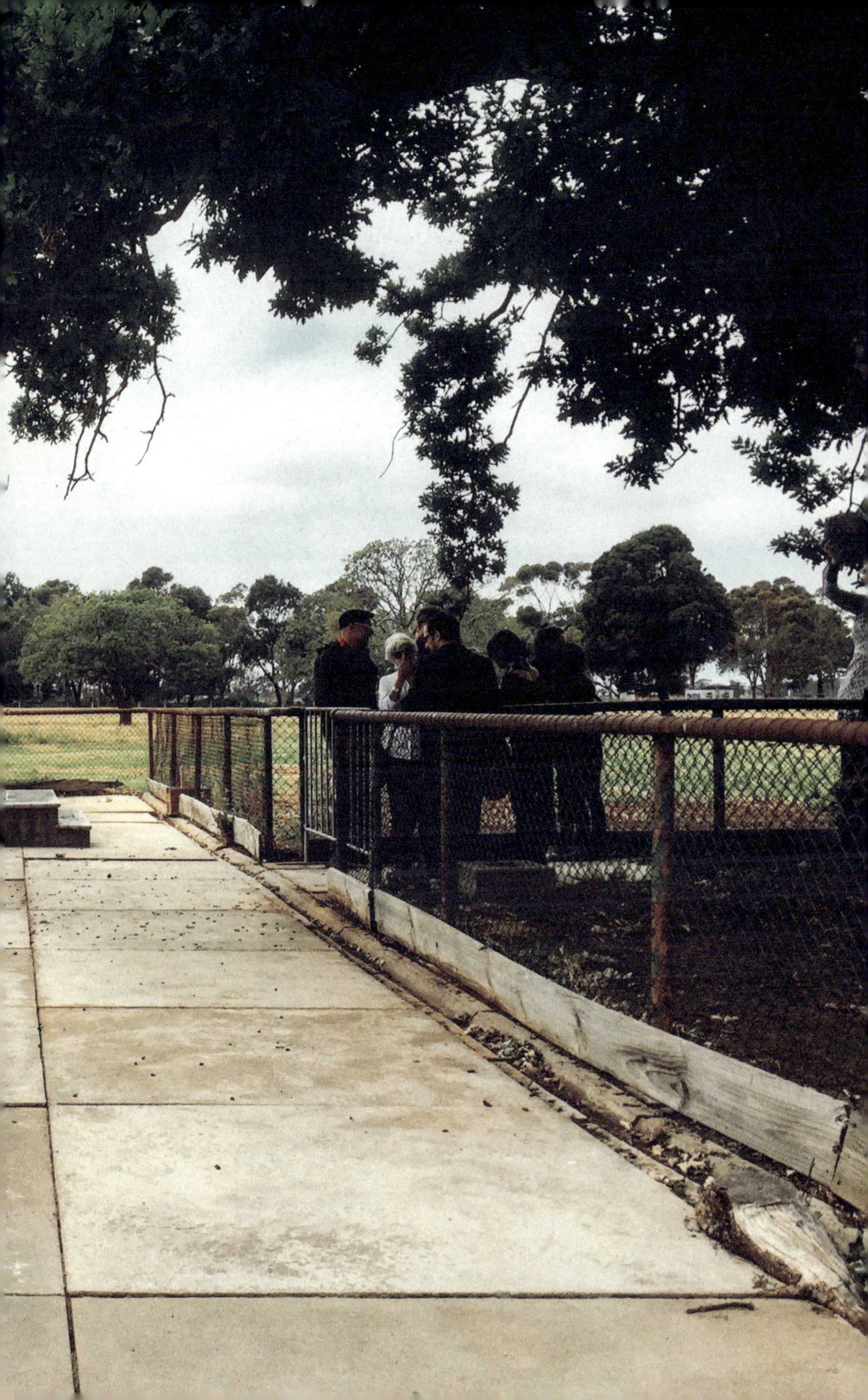

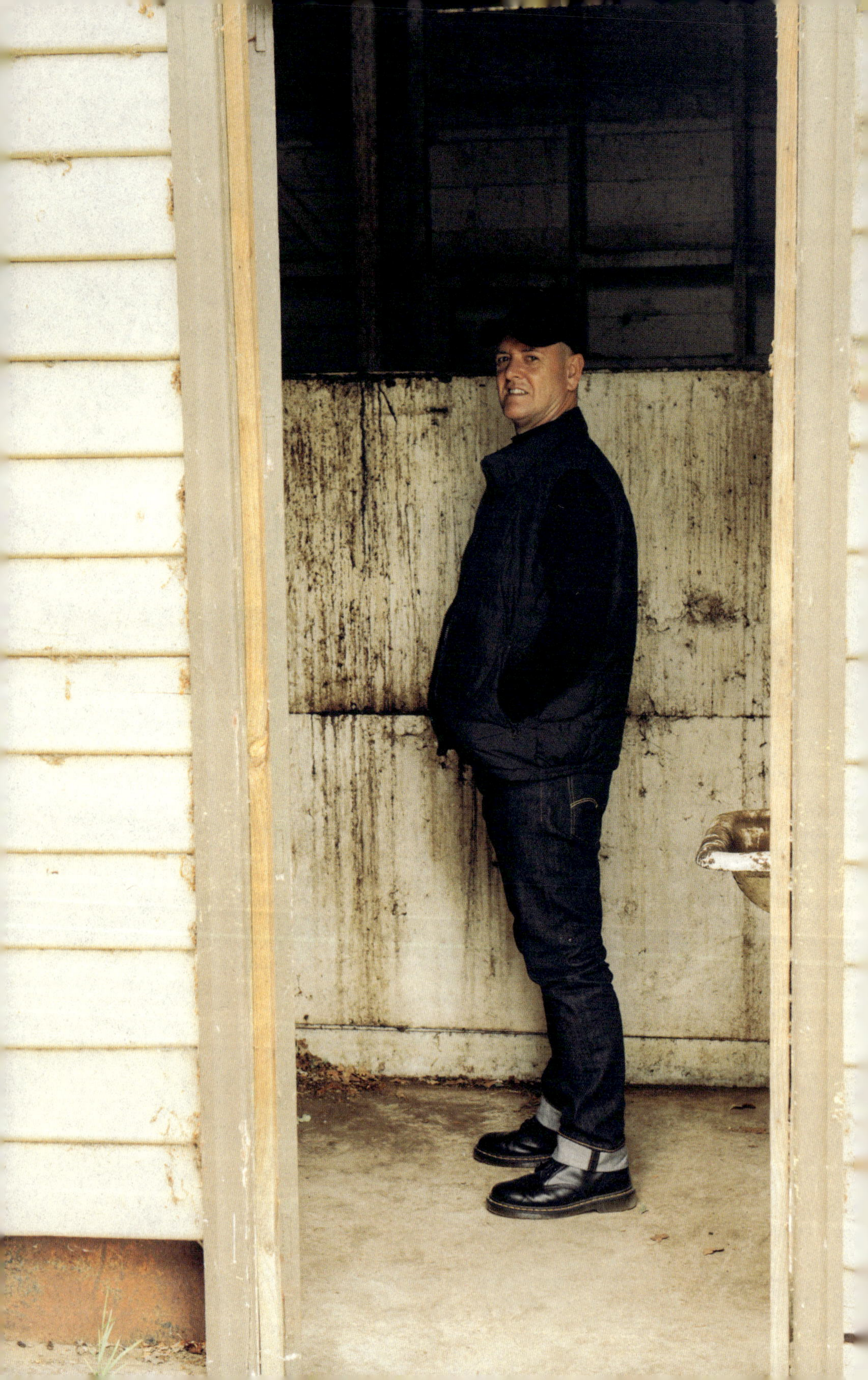

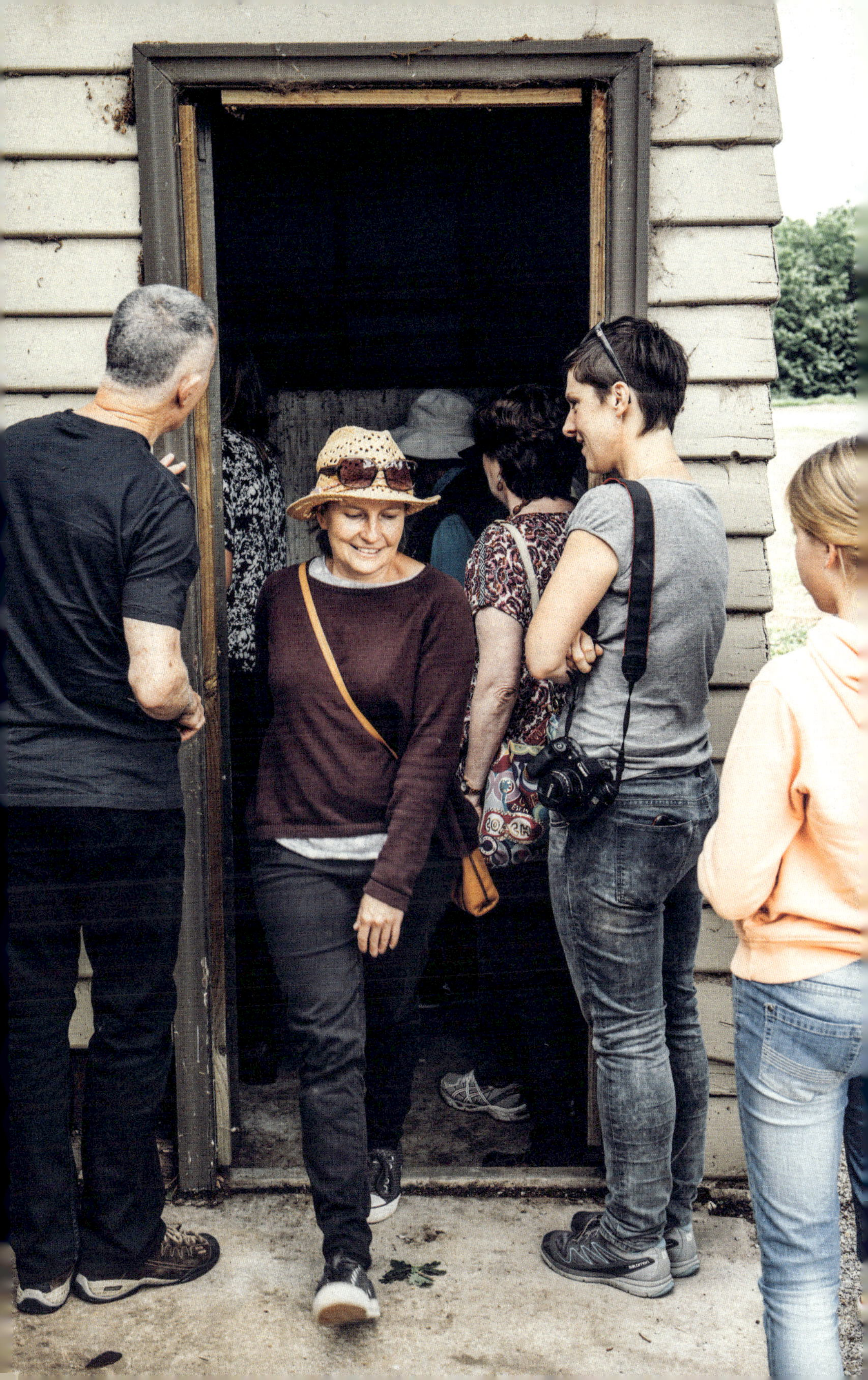

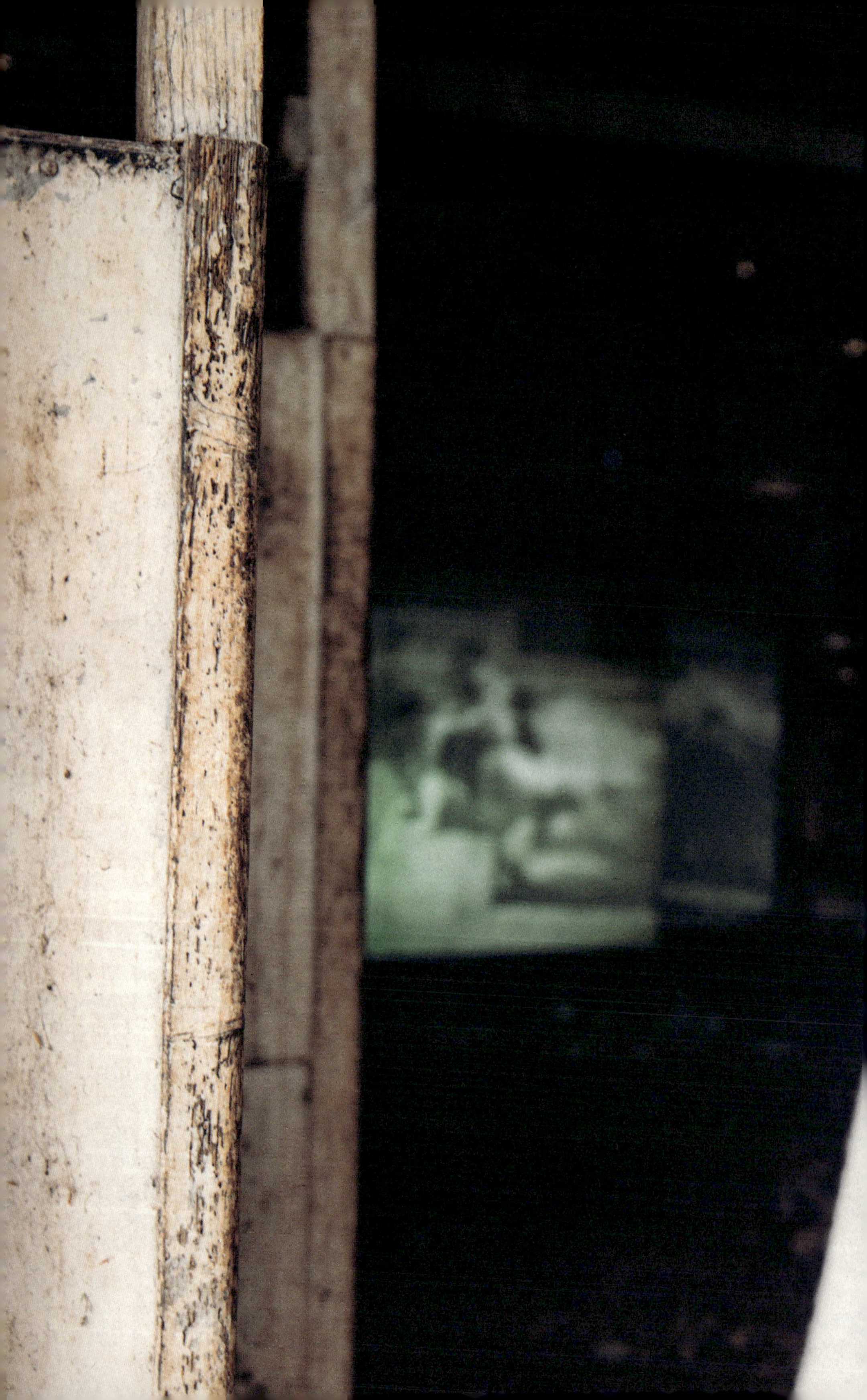

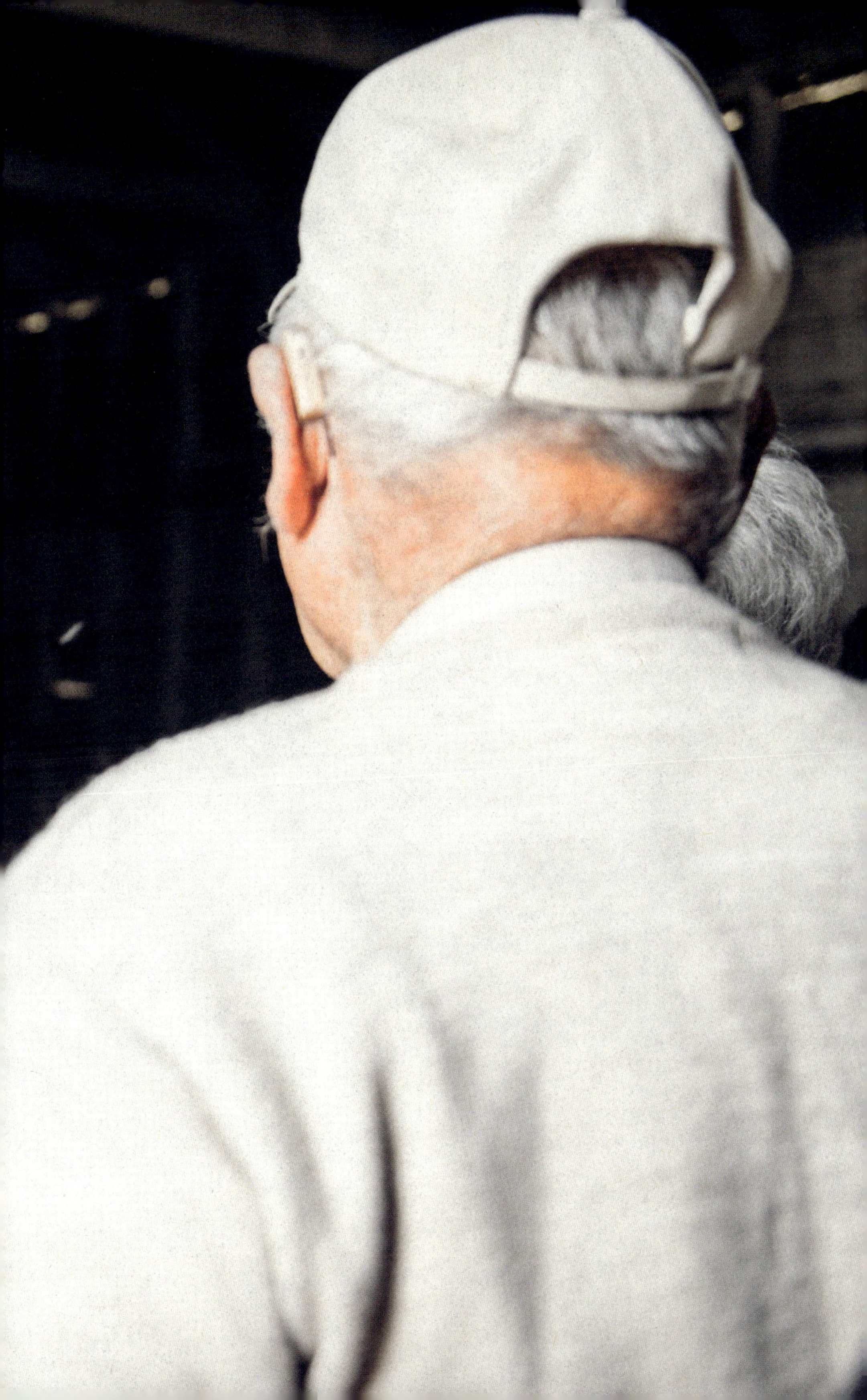

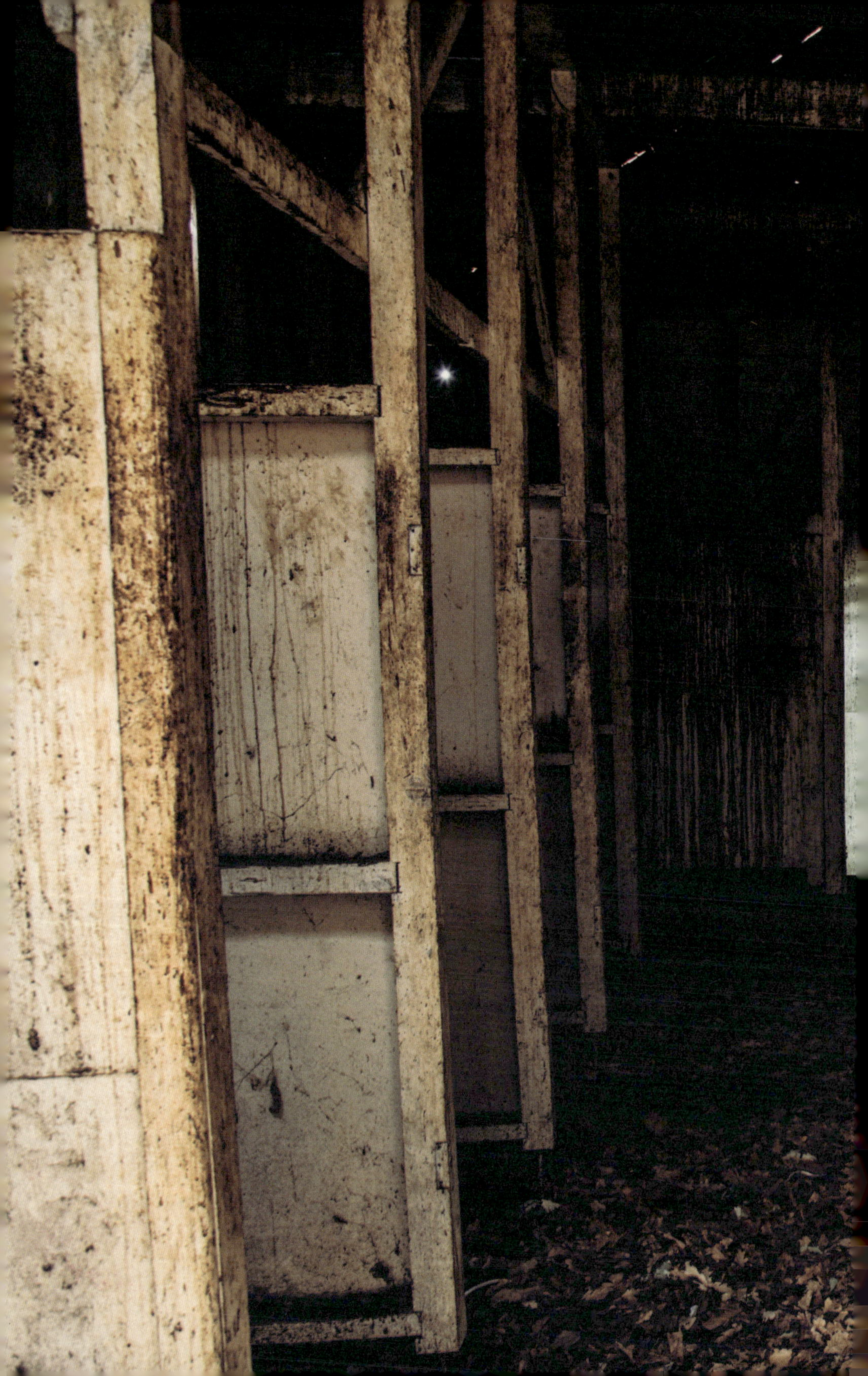

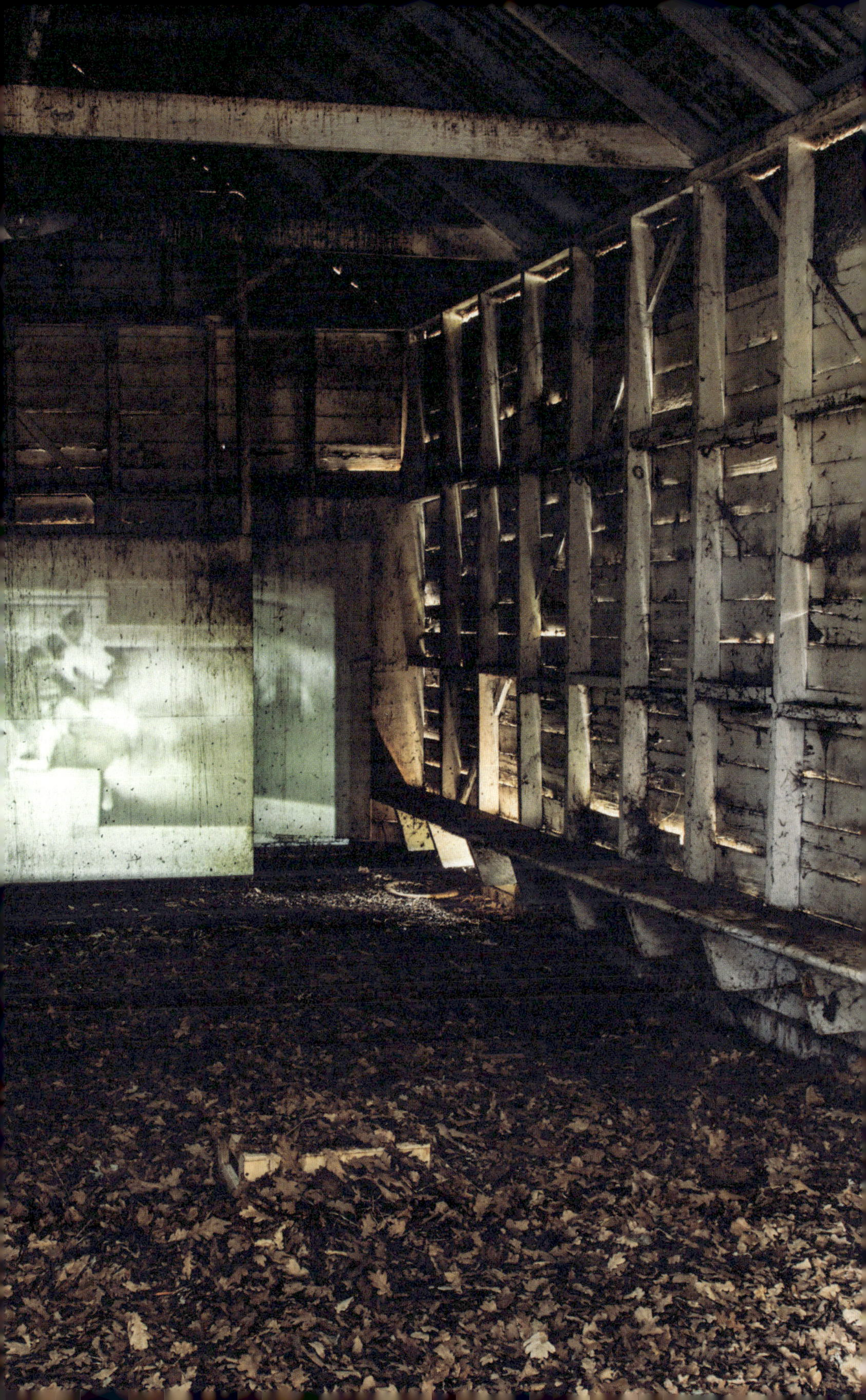

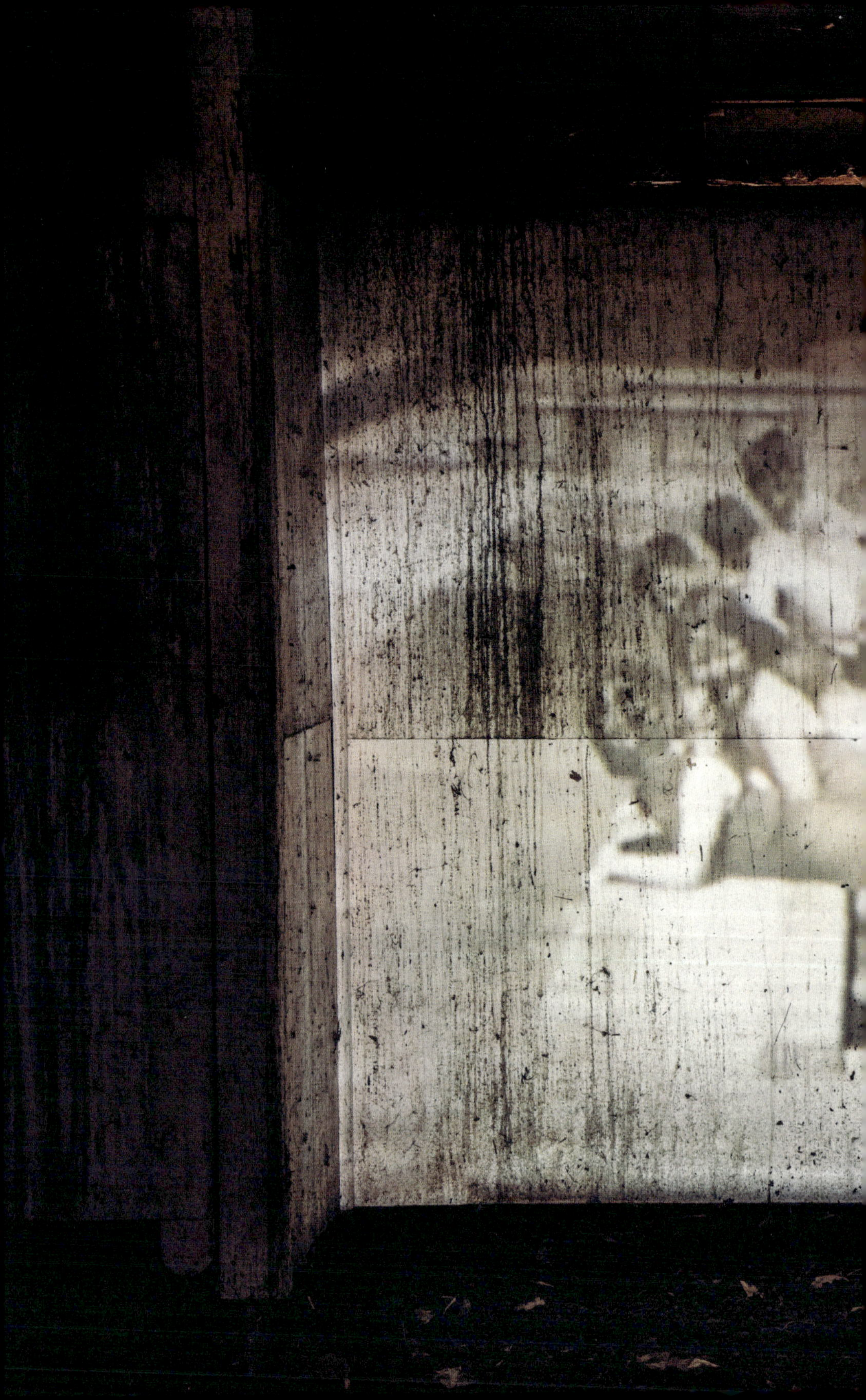

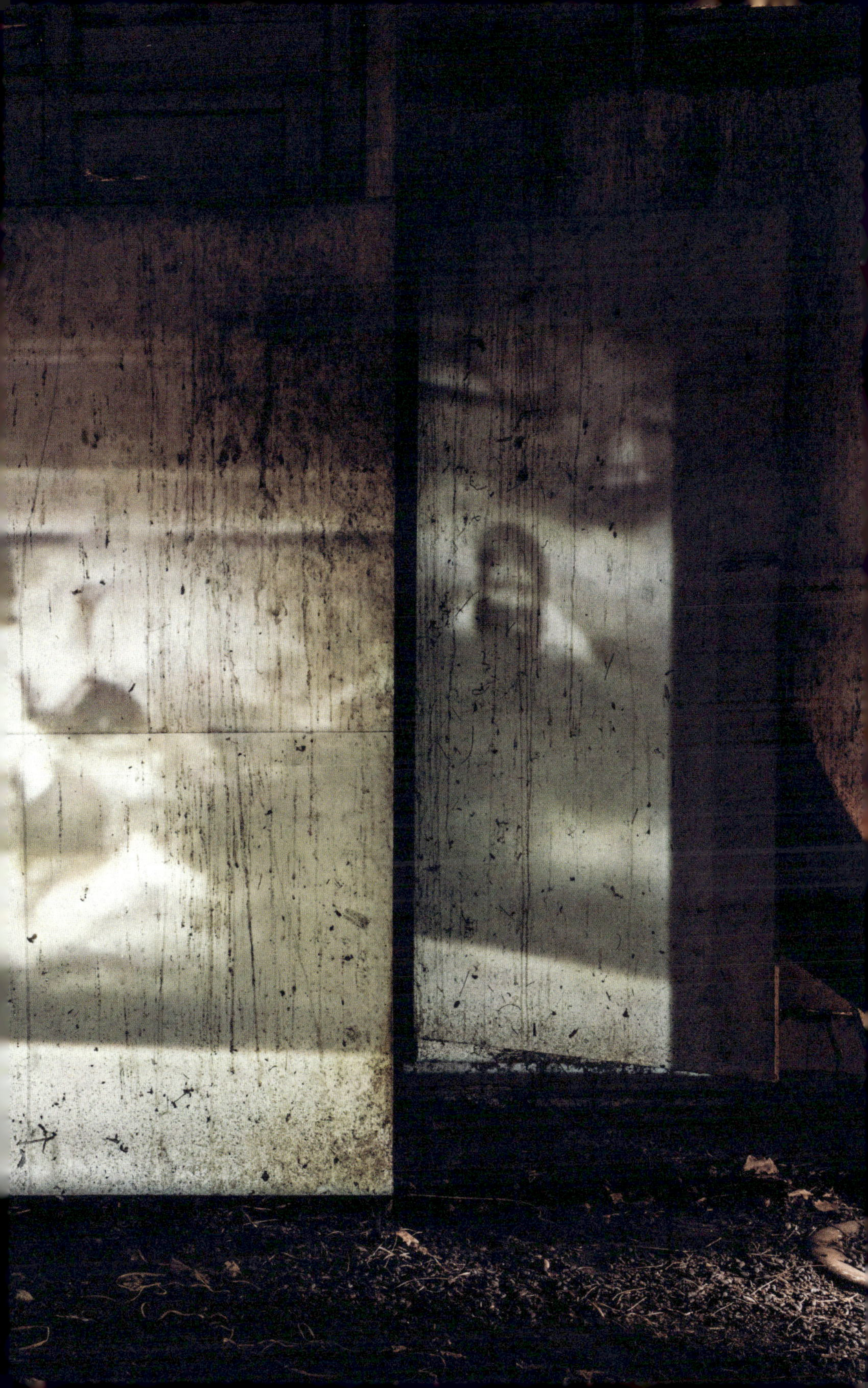

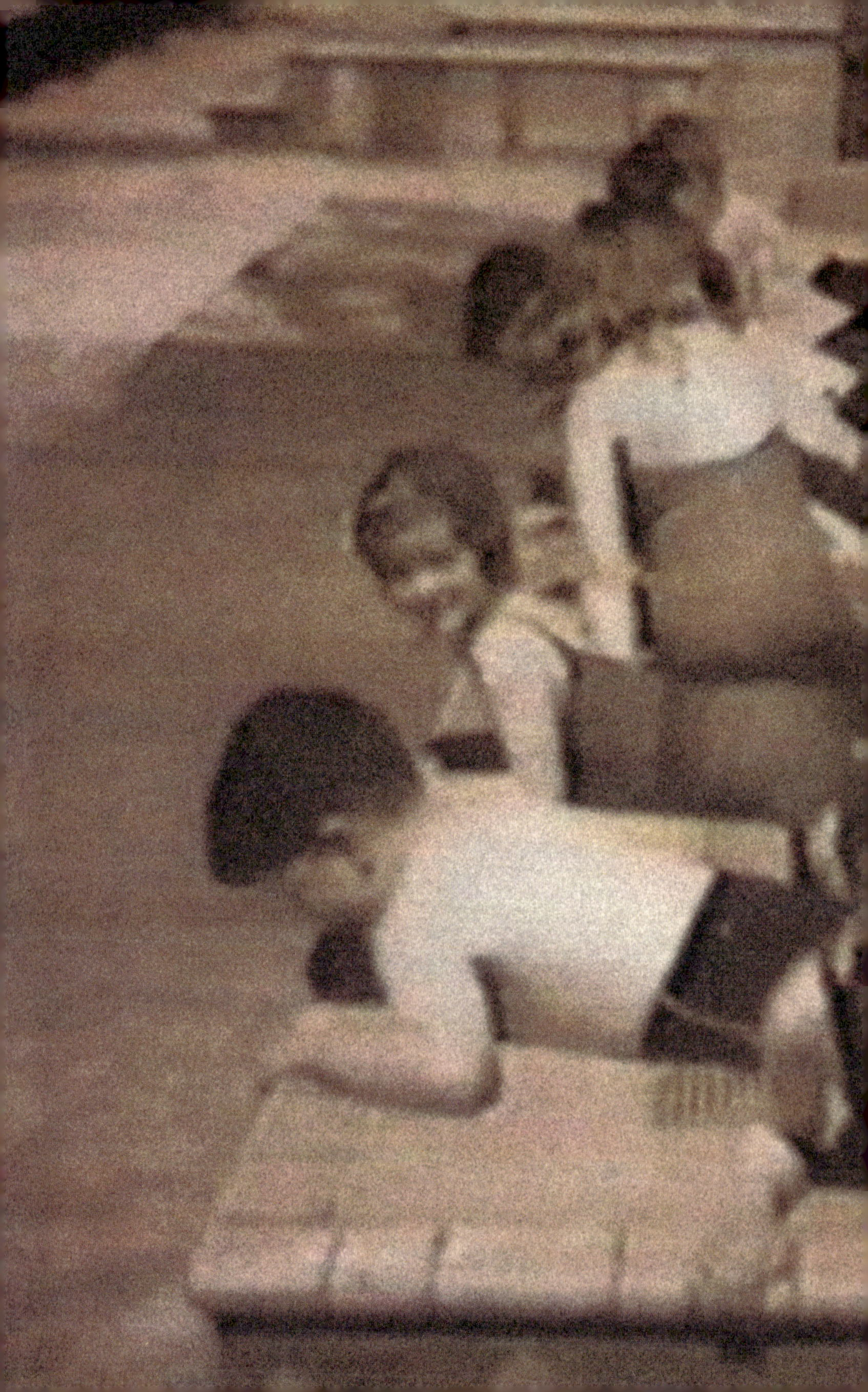

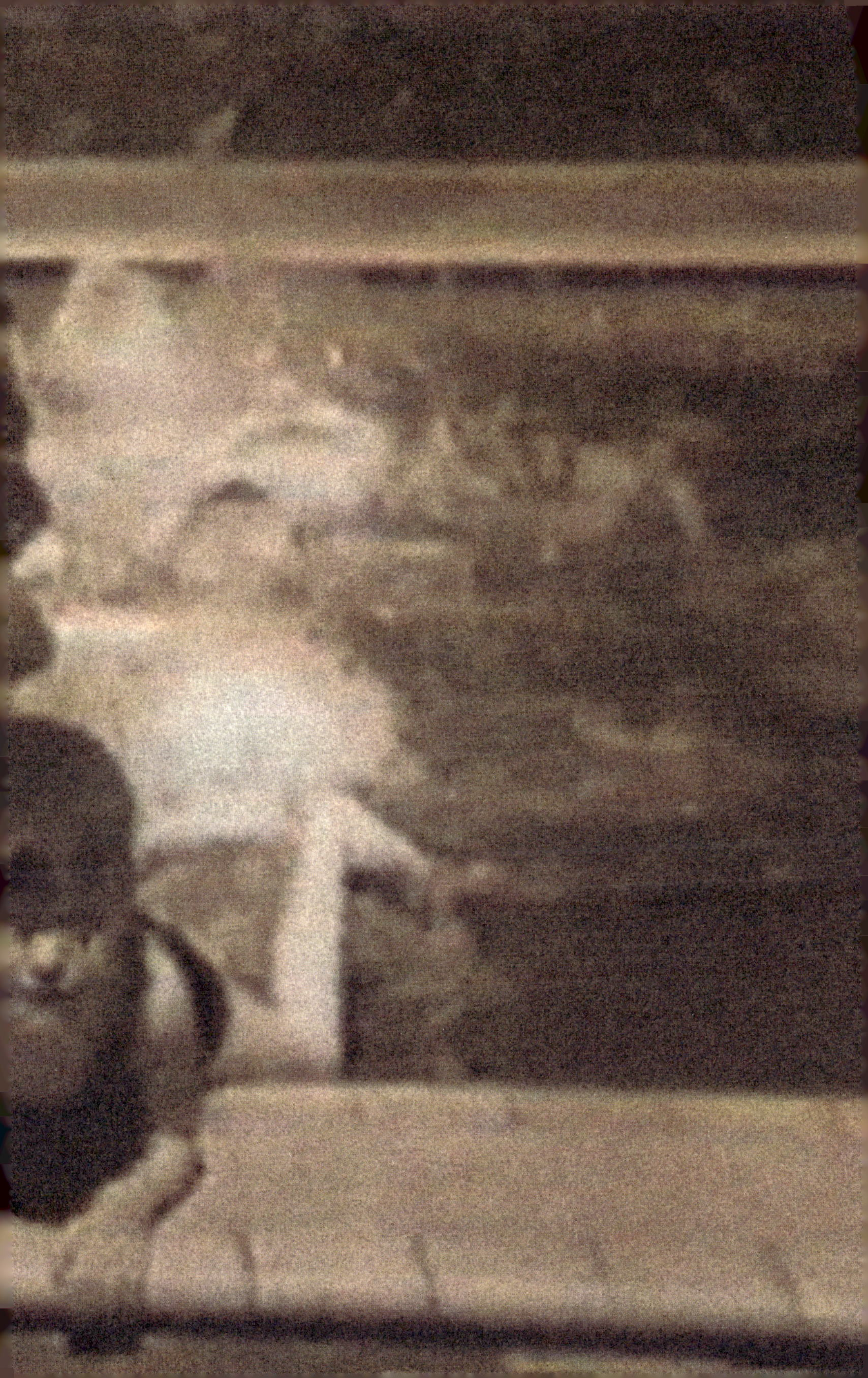

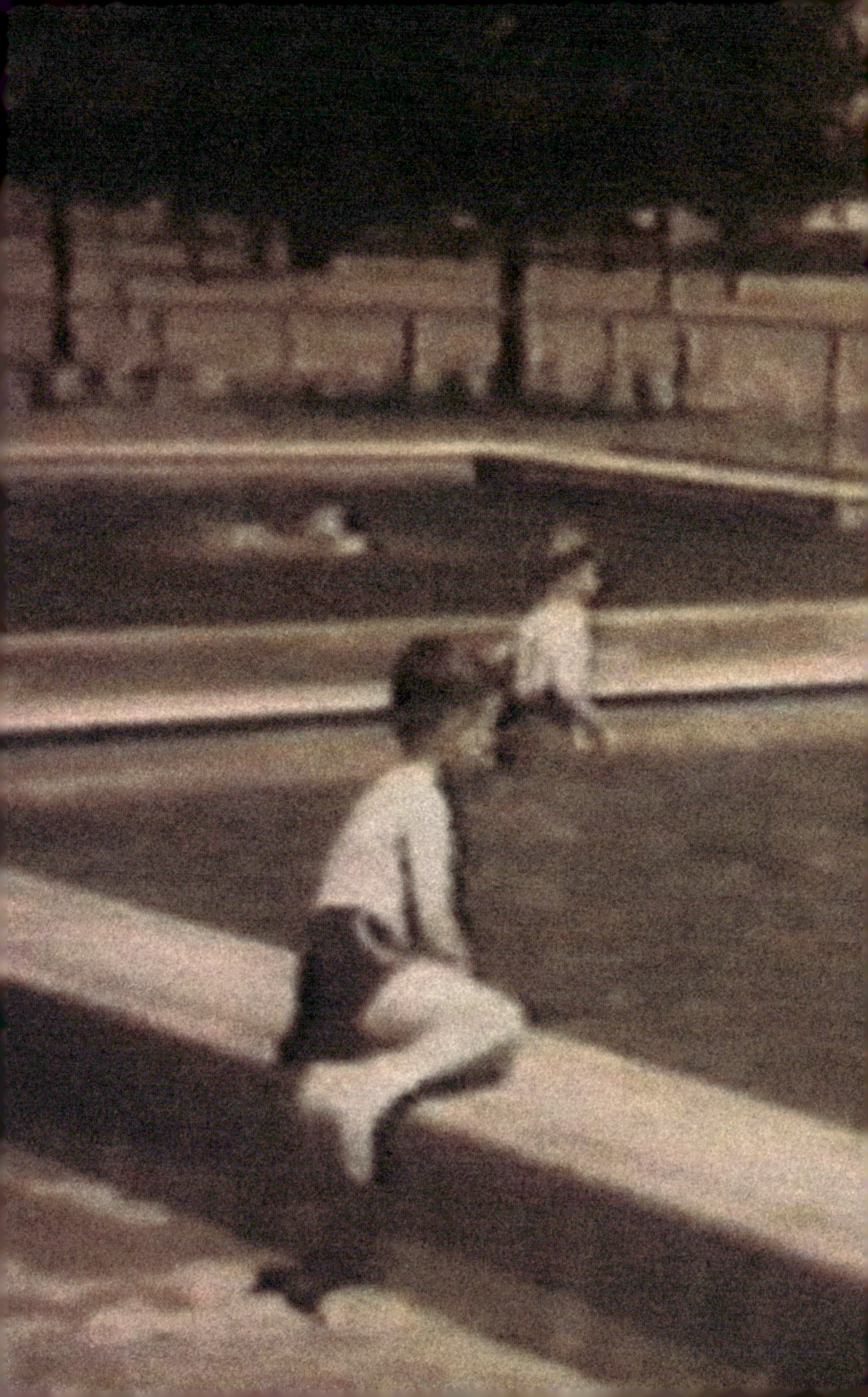

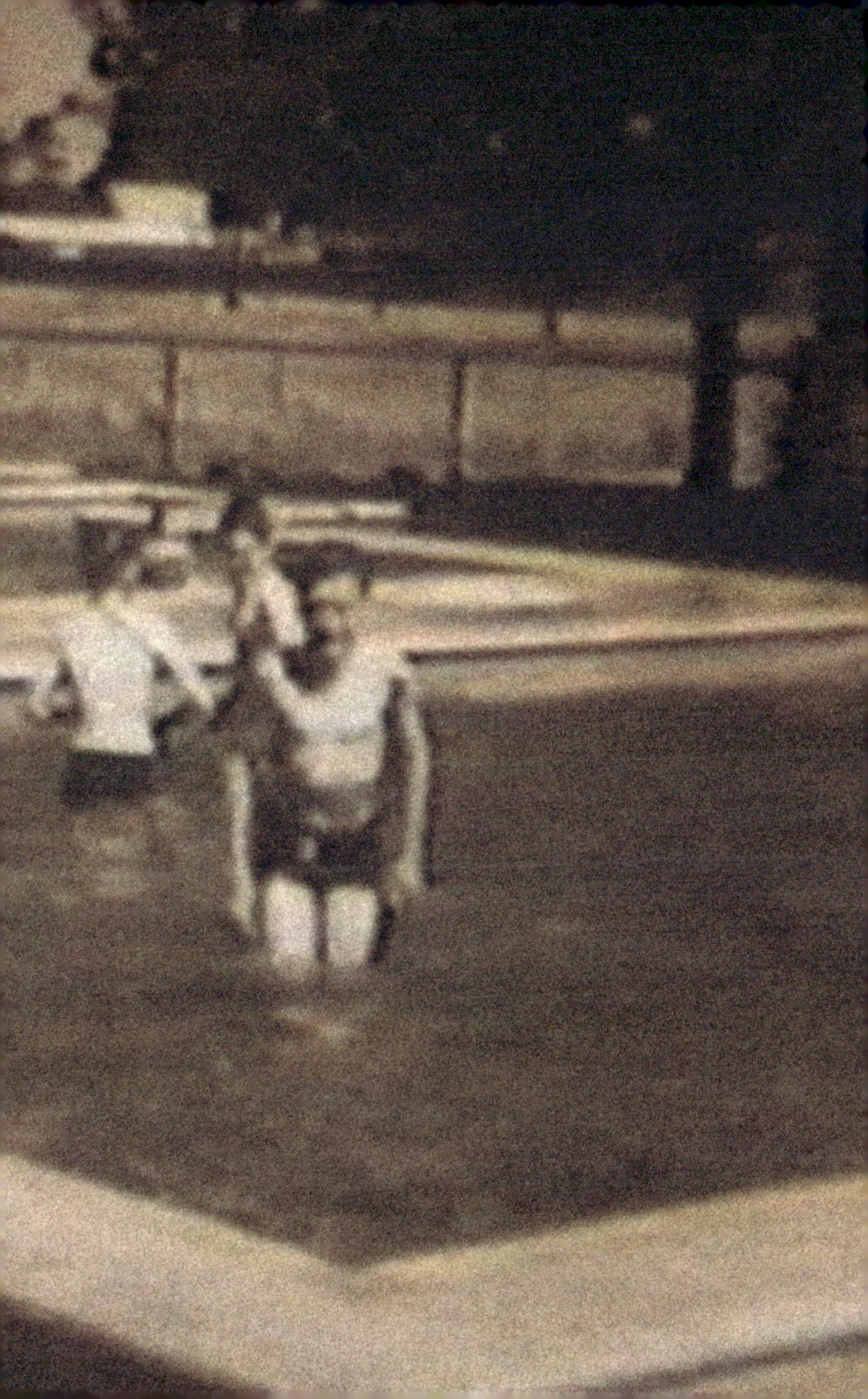

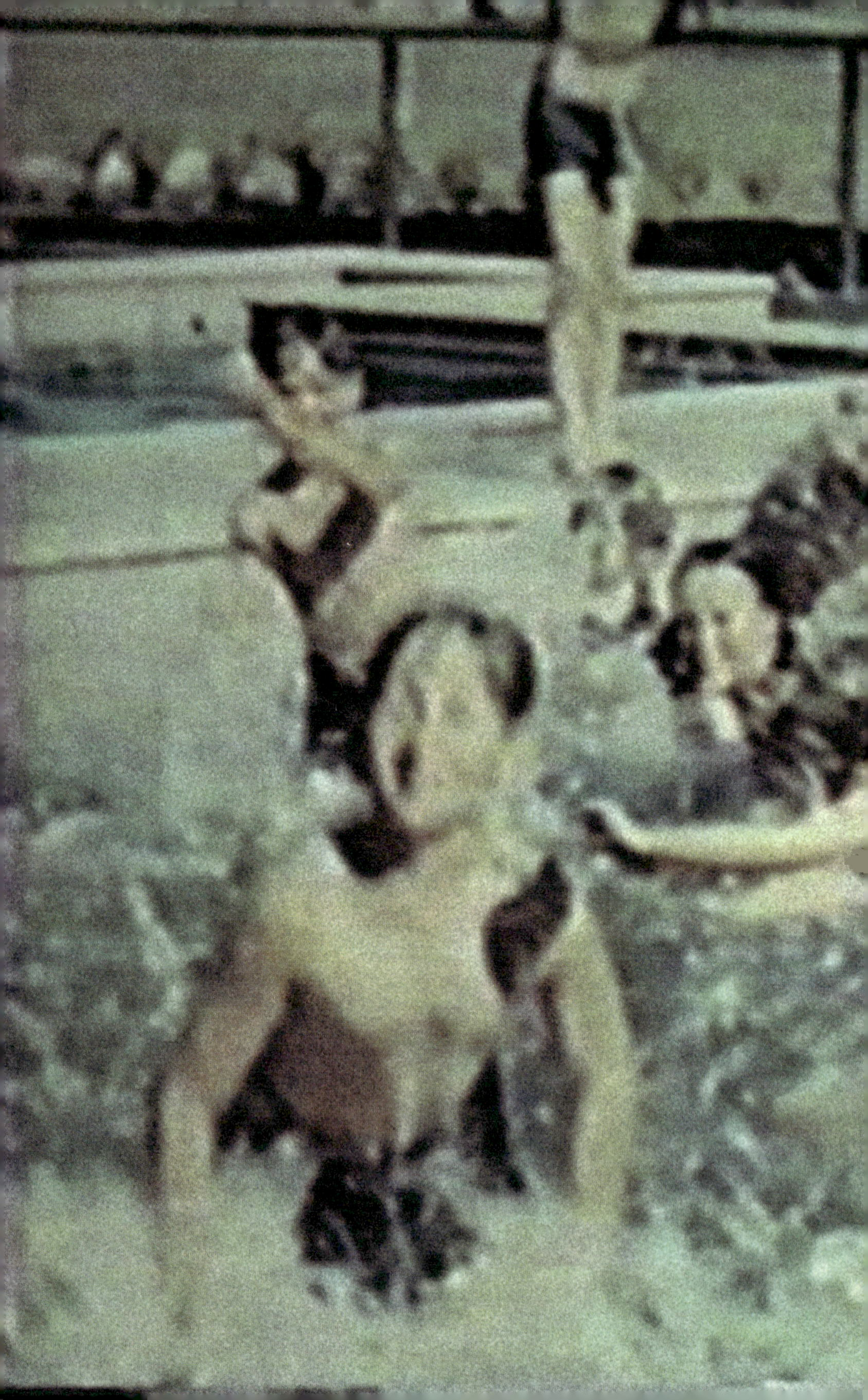

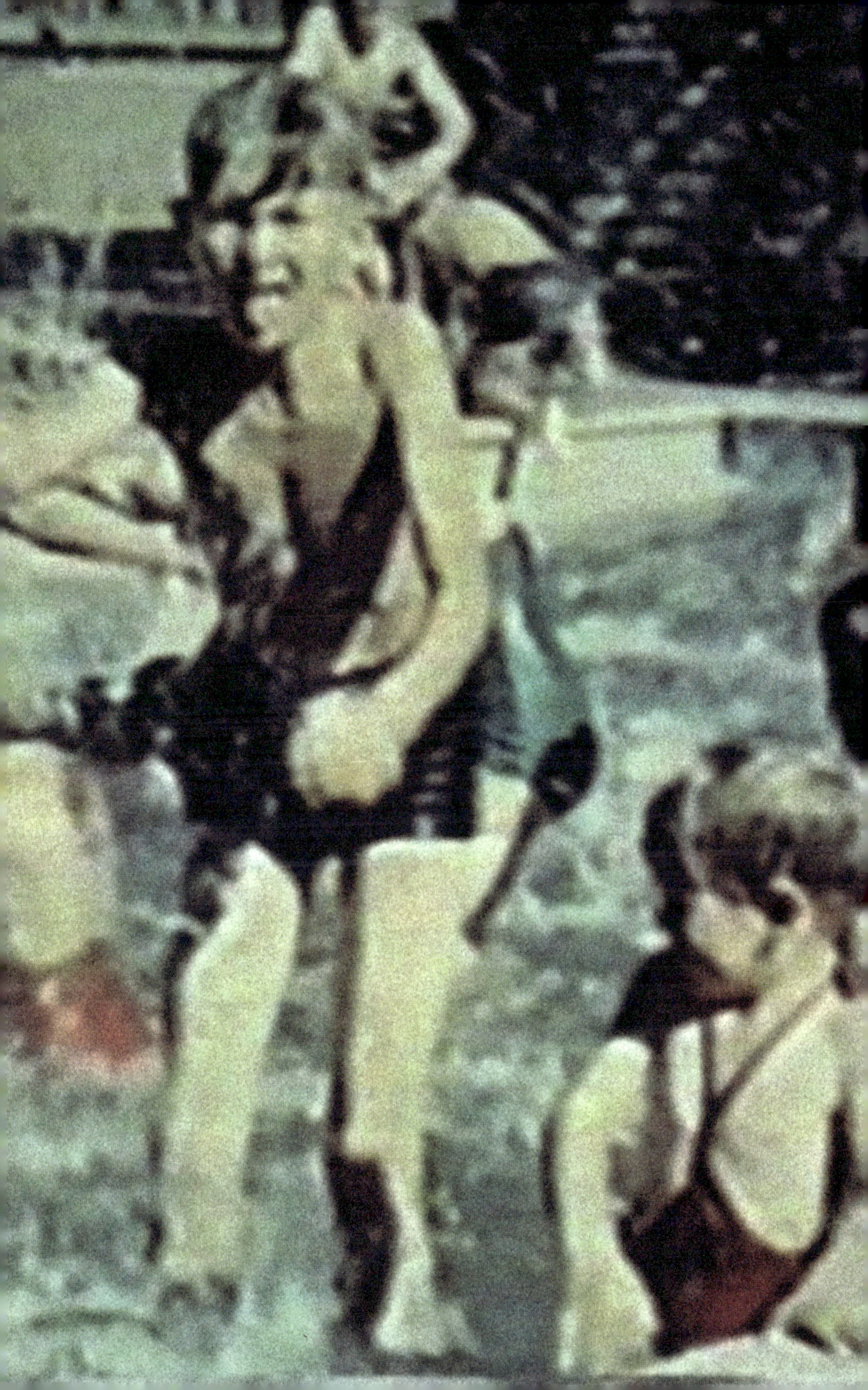

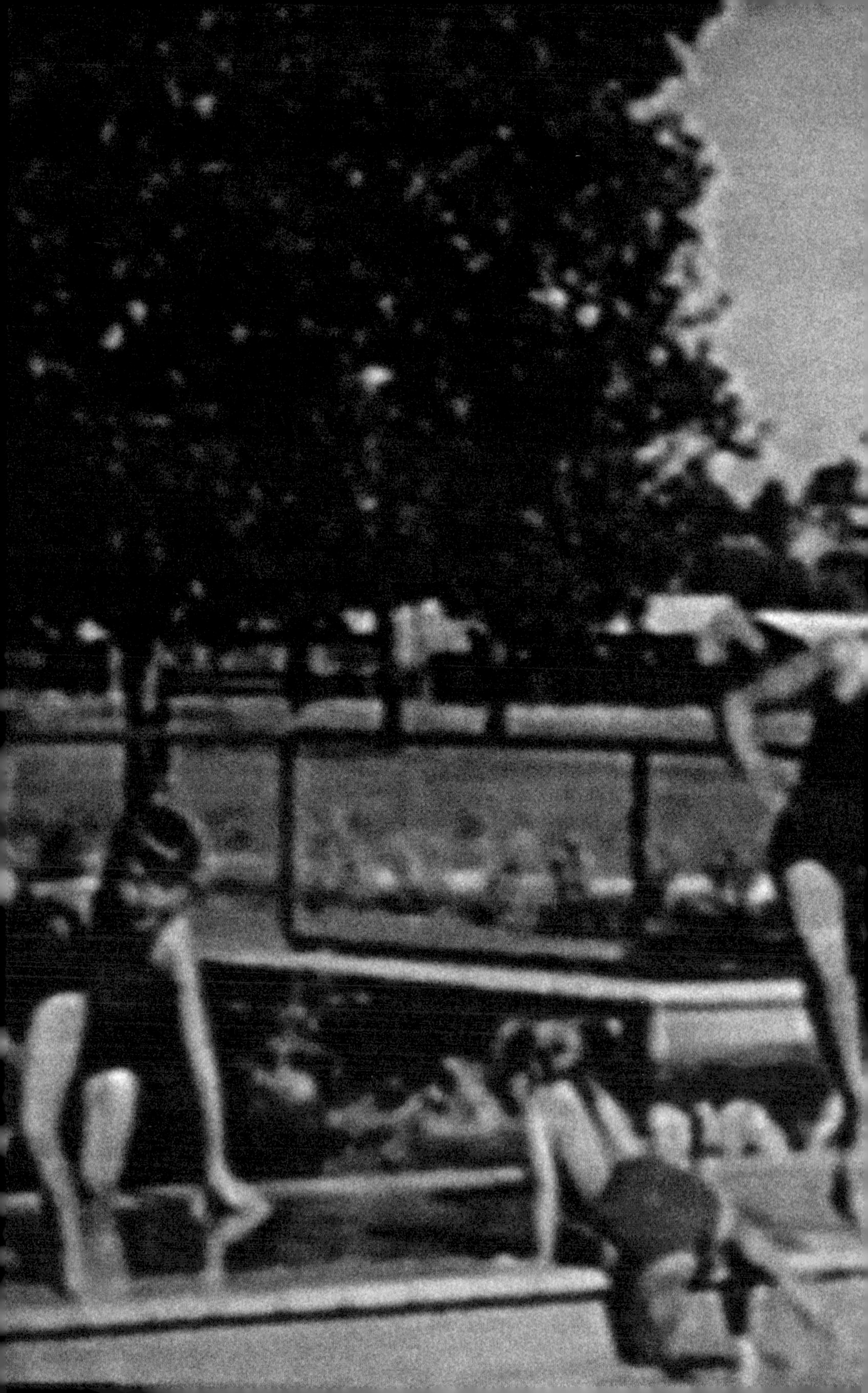

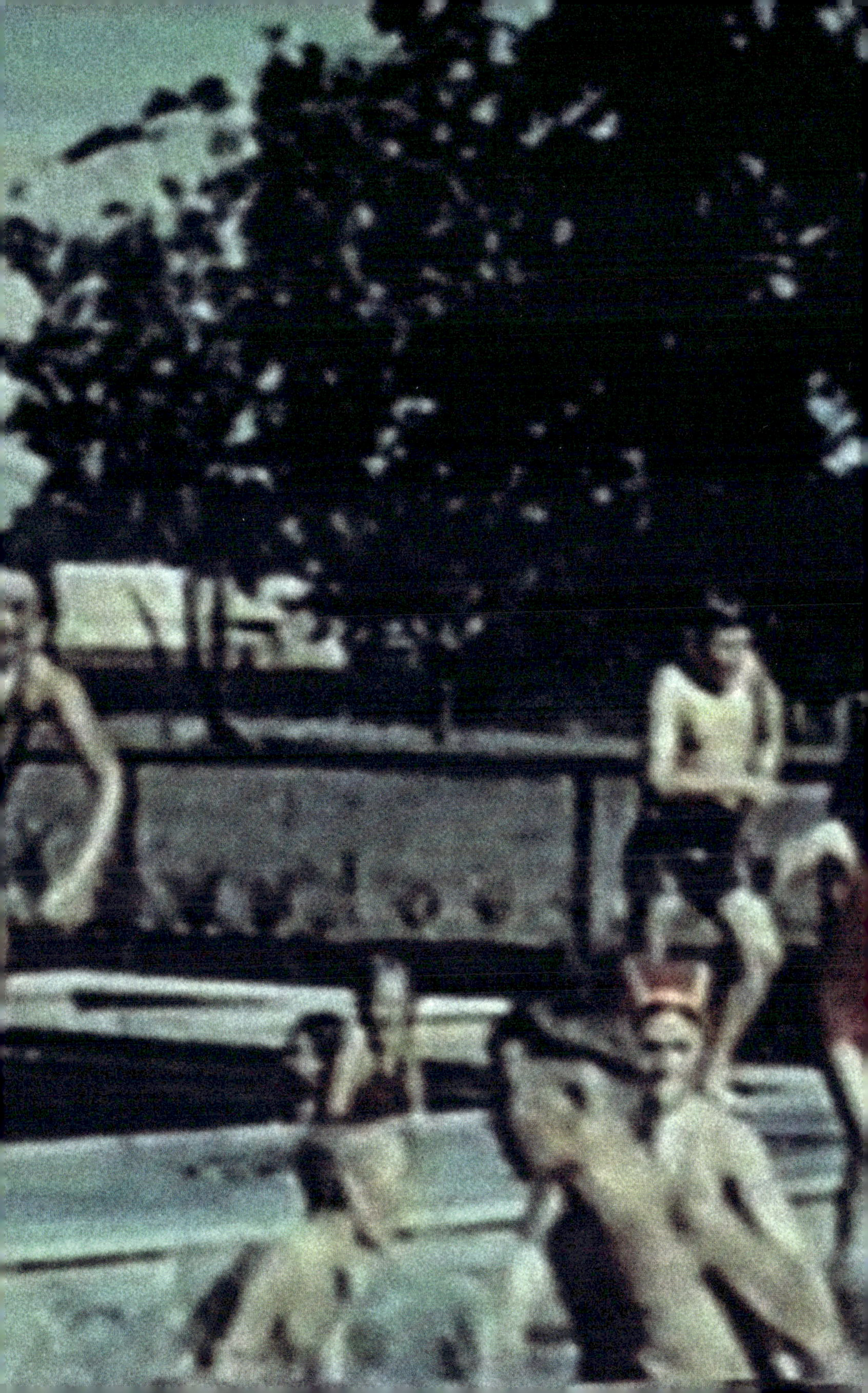

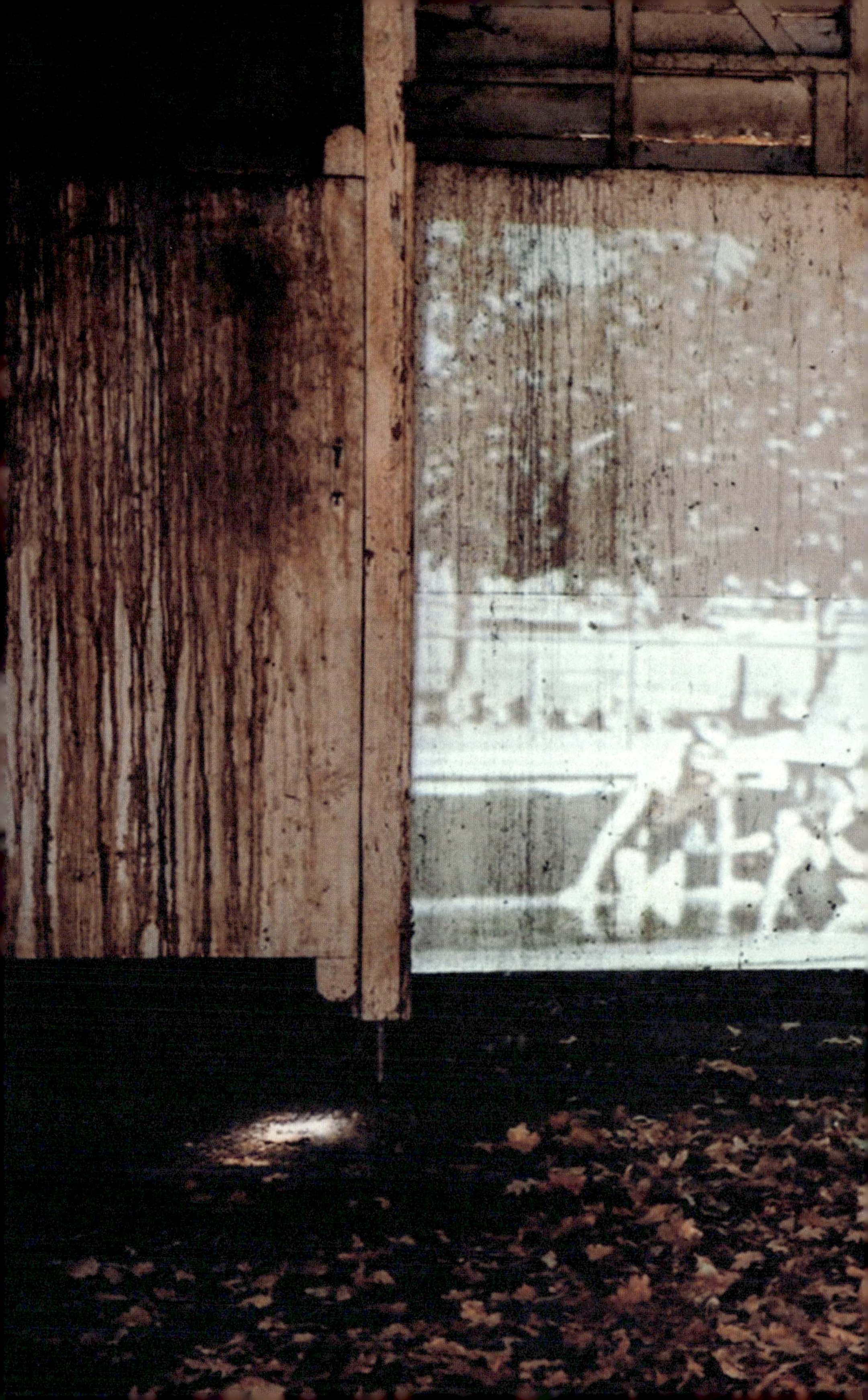

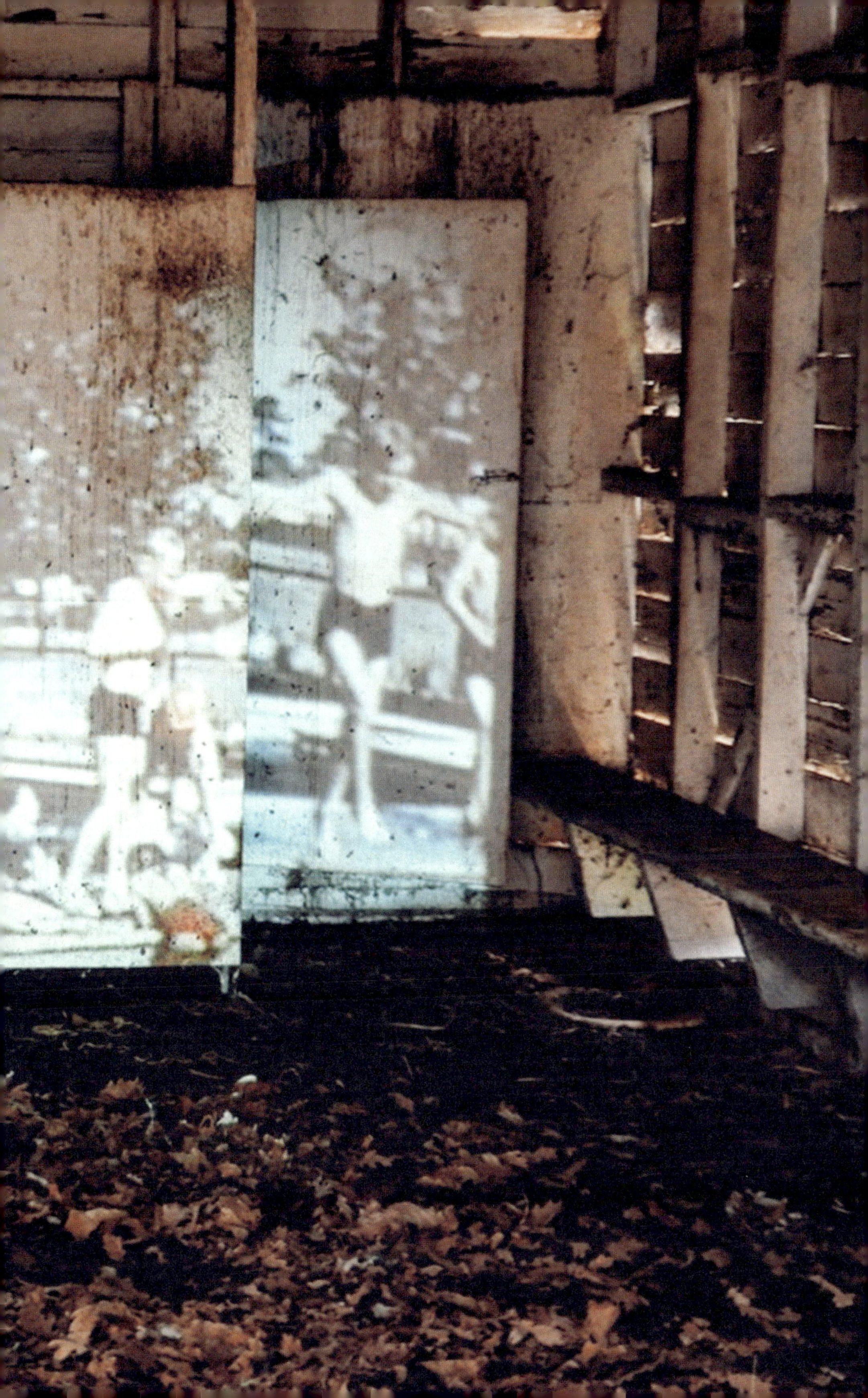

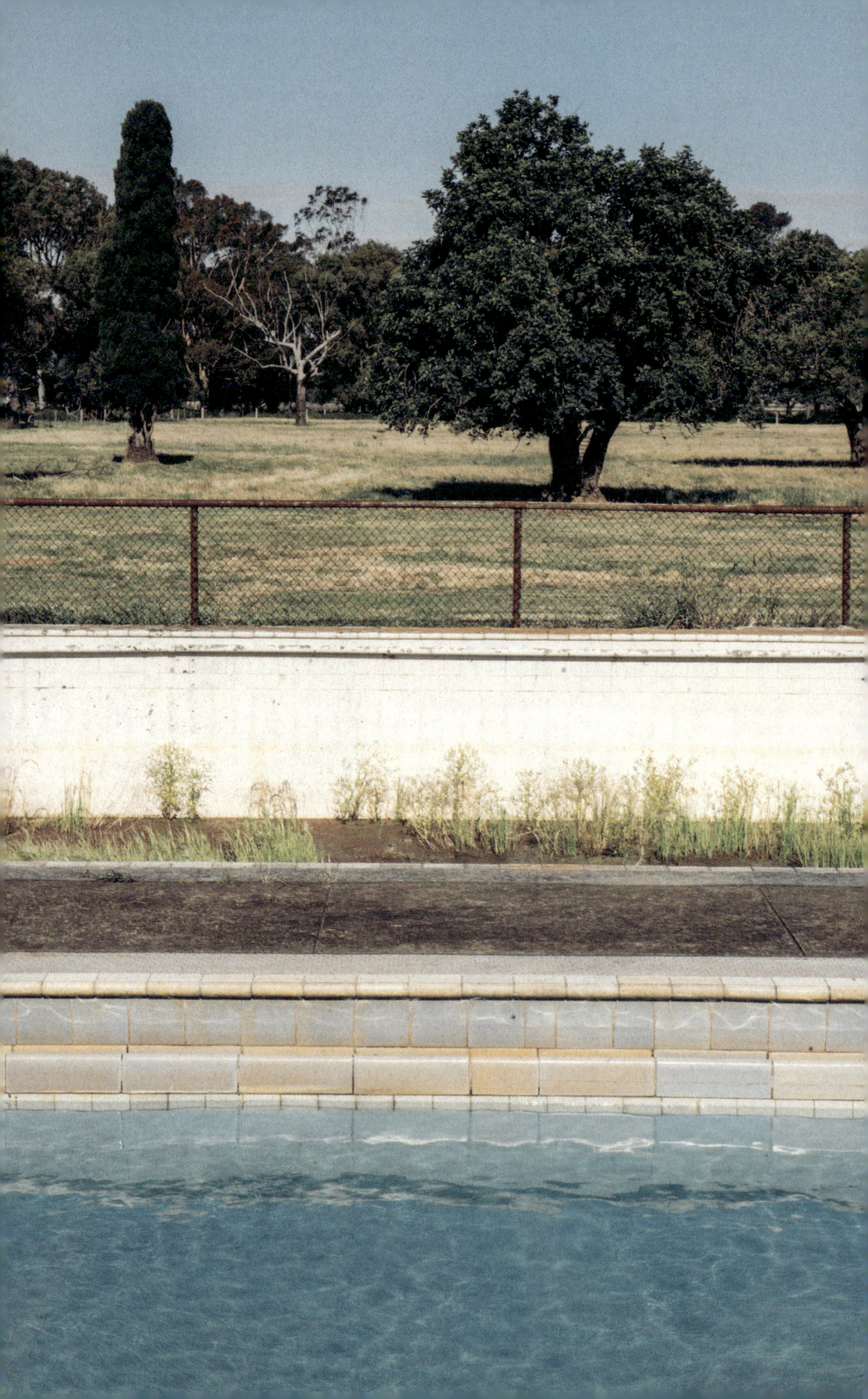

When the wind blows from the right direction...

—Rebecca Coates

Treatment starts with the weather, as do many good Australian and English conversations. I remember it as a blustery Melbourne day in late spring. All bright sunshine and high pollen count—when you wish you hadn't worn quite so many clothes, and it's still a little chilly out of the sun. For the first time ever, rather than sailing past Werribee Sewage Farm, I took a detour off the Geelong Road and found my way in. I've been driving, or have been driven, past this location all my life. As a child, in our early-model Holdens and Fords (some of which may well have been made in Geelong before the factory closed down), we would wind up the windows, melodramatically block noses, and claim that the smell of untreated sewage lingered for the rest of the journey. I'm not sure it did smell, but as a child with a vivid imagination, the glimpse of water ponds, and unidentified substances frothing on the surface (see, I am doing it again), evoked the smells associated with Melbourne's sewage treatment plant, whether they were really there or not.

Maps are not always my strong point, so on this more recent trip I managed to detour my way through Werribee town proper (the instructions given were excellent, the fault was mine, and VicRoads temporary detours helped). This small town echoed with another part of regional Victoria where I had recently started work: vernacular architecture (read: triple-fronted brick veneer); traces of industrial history; residues of modernisation; a high-street strip of sole operators (butcher, baker, newsagent); and the Golden Arches butted up against other 21st-century iconic takeaways.

Houses were single-storey, brick or weatherboard, and reminded me of the Australian dream of post-War quarter-acre blocks. If I said there were trimmed bushes, and buffalo grass nature strips and lawns, with the odd one unkempt and overgrown, that might be a bit of artistic licence. But the detour did provide a snapshot of the inhabitants and fabric of Werribee town, so important to the life and work of the Sewage Farm nearby.

Arriving at what was once the headquarters of the Board of Works, we alighted from cars and hopped on a bus. No self-guided tour this one: we had a self-appointed bus driving resident expat (also a certified bus driver), all part of a collective art experience. The curators aimed to locate a series of temporary art projects in a unique place, with a specific local history revealed through the language and ideas of a global contemporary art. Many of the works responded specifically to place, inviting visitors to rethink their understanding of the particular location, its history and inhabitants. Temporary artworks, performances and installations took place over the space of two weekends. The bus was full, although the occupants were mostly older, and not the customary art happening followers. Overhearing surrounding conversations, many were connected to the sewage farm and town, either growing up there themselves as children, or part of families who did so many years before.

I sat next to an older lady, who, despite initial suspicions, gradually got talking. She was with her sister, husband, and many of the nearby local community who had moved to Werribee, Geelong and further afield to find work, or when the town closed down. They had read about the event in the local newspaper, and hadn't been back to the scene of their early childhood years. The art experience was secondary to a trip down memory lane. As we drove into the farm proper, past paddocks and irrigation channels, with the plant structures visible across the flat paddocks ahead, my bus companion began to remember the people and places that had dispersed with the closure of the local Cocoroc town. From her rather capacious bag she shyly drew out an old picture featuring the old Cocoroc football club, which her father had played in and then coached to victory many years before. The local footy club was the glue that bound this small community—like so many other regional towns—together. But much of its history had been lost when the township closed down and the residents dispersed. It was a fitting overture to the first artwork.

We drew up at the old oval, with its small weatherboard club rooms. Disembarking from the bus, we saw a group of footballers in the middle of the oval playing Aussie Rules football, dressed in woollen jerseys, red with a white V around the neck. The Herefords, as the team were known, were finishing the quarter and leaving the field, jostling and shouting the usual things that men say when playing such games. They entered the clubhouse for the ubiquitous debrief, rub-down and men's business. We could hear them from the other half of the small weatherboard building. The smell of liniment was overwhelming, and when the sounds of fisticuffs broke out, we could only imagine the action on the other side of the partition.

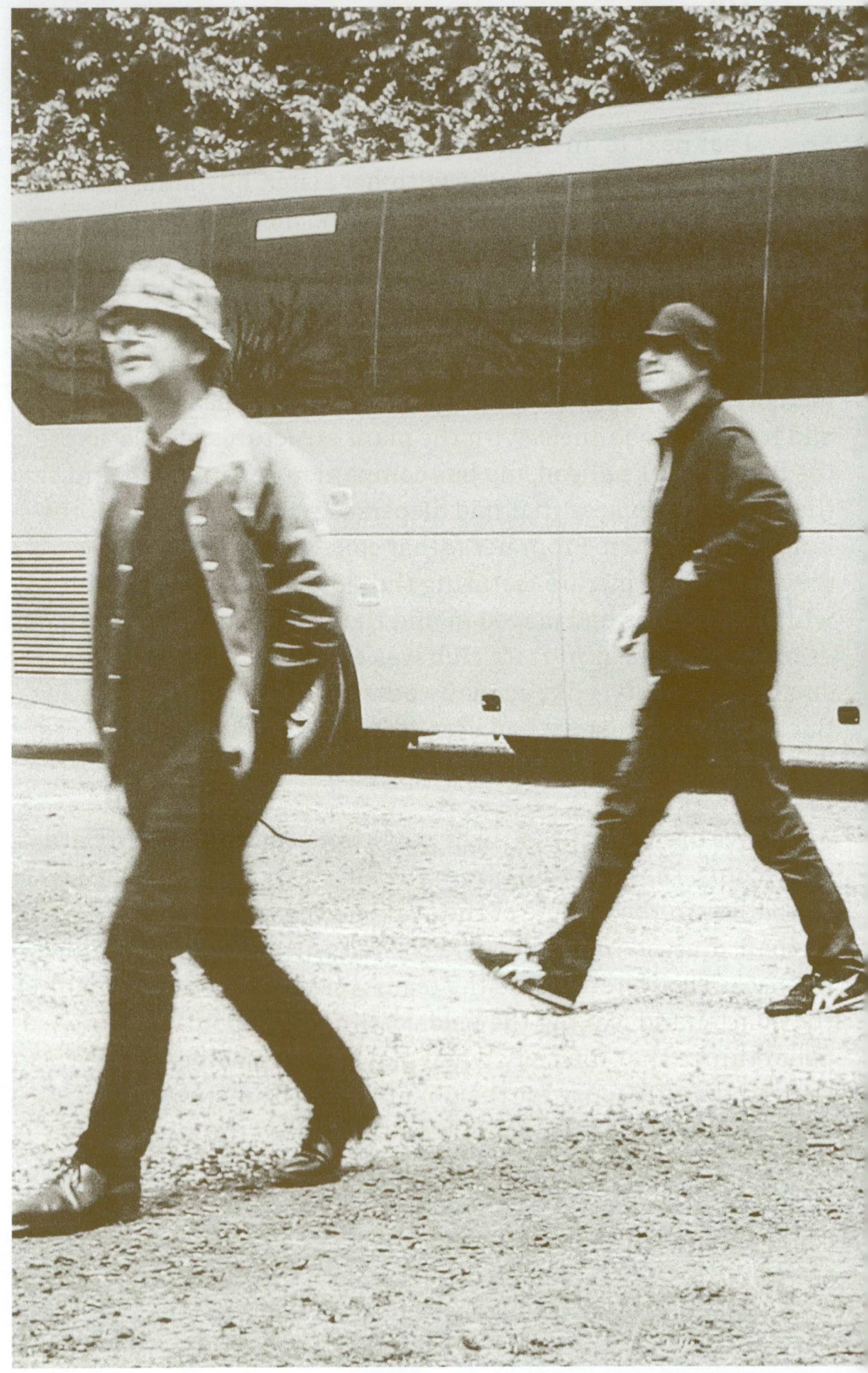

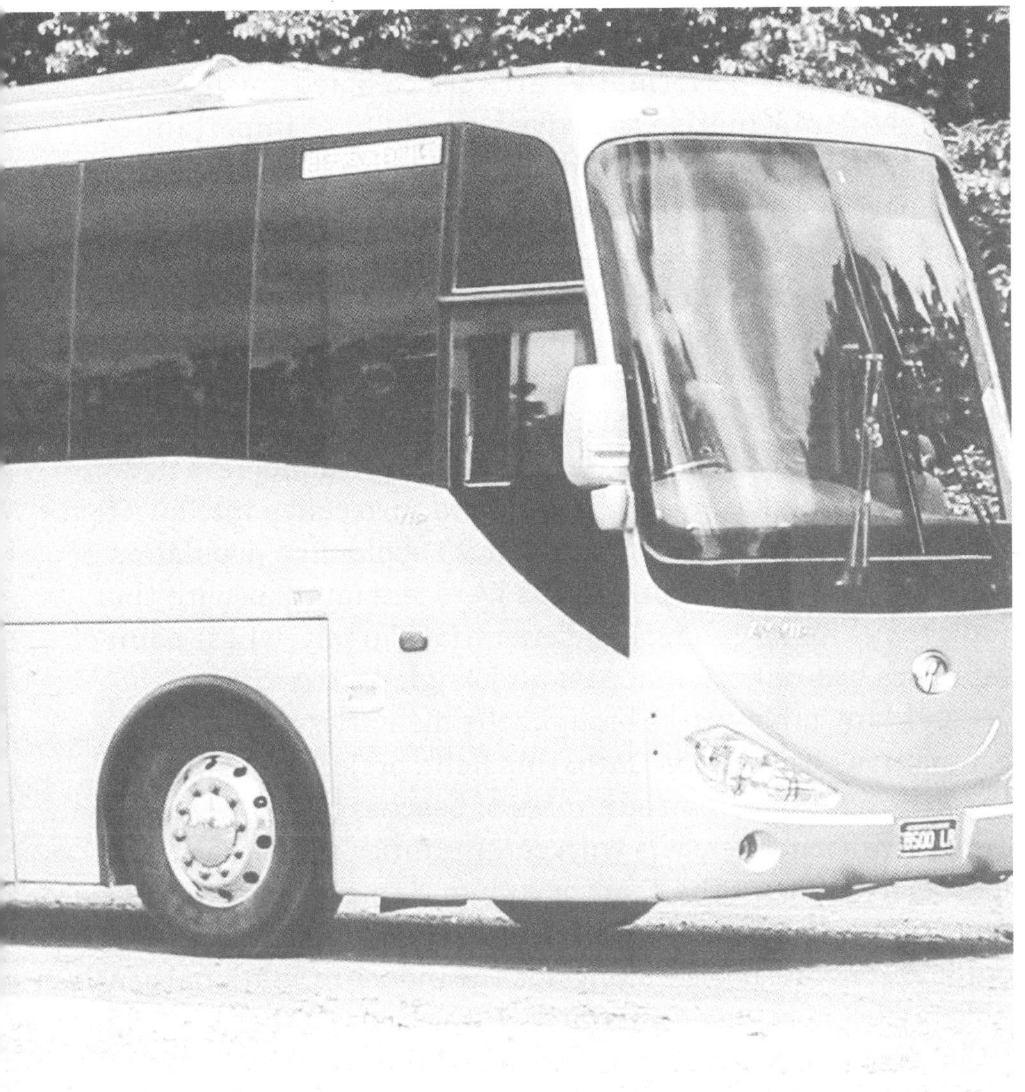

Shane McGrath's performative artwork co-opted smell, sound and a vivid imagination to revive an activity so important to bringing together a community, fostering pride and breaking down barriers. The performance reincarnated a past world of amateur footy and passed it on to a new generation.

The bus trip was a 90-minute orchestration of the past and present. We stopped at a monumental bluestone water tower, housing a work by Megan Evans. Originally built in the 1850s, the tower was moved to Cocoroc in the 1890s. Evans's installation, a multi-part narrative of text, sculpture and sound, revealed traces of colonial women's life which in turn called into question the impact of colonialism on the First Peoples, the population of the Kulin Nation. Most on the bus were less familiar with that Indigenous history—an older generation, largely, whose point of reference was our colonial past and Anglo-Saxon roots.

Many other works brought the memories of my bus companions back to life. Catherine Bell's project brought back the long, hot Australian summers of beaches (if you were lucky) or the local concrete pools with communities and rituals, like local footy clubs, at the heart of a town. Some local towns, like Shepparton, Chewton and Dalesford, have retained their old outdoor concrete pools—alongside the indoor recreational centres now preferred by older generations. As children, they stayed in the unheated waters until fingers wrinkled and skin puckered blue, and then warmed up 'star-fishing' on cooked concrete paths around the pool edge.

Bell's project reanimated the Cocoroc swimming pools which had become stagnant, green, and part-empty. She returned the wading pool to pristine blue and projected black and white films in the adjoining bathing pavilion. The nostalgia of families playing and splashing in the pools' halcyon days in the 1940s flickered in the darkened space. The rotted pavilion floor, though strewn with oak leaves, still reeked of the odour of possum and the other creatures now in residence. The restless passing of time and memories can be cruel.

My companion was tired. She and her friends had had a big day out. It had brought back long forgotten memories. The ABC radio journalist who had also been on the bus had loved her picture. He had recorded an interview in which she recalled how her dad coached the once-invincible footy team to use their home advantage when the wind blew from the right quarter. No doubt a nice cup of tea awaited her at home, and a further reminiscence with her neighbours. The fact that she had been viewing artworks all afternoon was unlikely to be a topic of conversation. Nonetheless, the day had been a resounding success.

WHO IS THE 'PUBLIC' OF PUBLIC ART?

Contemporary art projects such as *Treatment* rethink and redefine public art. They contrast with many permanent public artworks and they distinctively engage with 'publics' or audiences.

Curator David Cross has long been involved with curatorial initiatives that rethink publics, and art in the public realm. Cross and Claire Doherty (from Situations, UK) curated the critically acclaimed *One Day Sculpture* series, New Zealand (2008), developing a year-long progam of projects in a range of sites, each presented for just twenty-four hours. More recently, the City of Melbourne's inaugural Public Art Melbourne Biennial Lab (2016), curated by Natalie King, was presented at the Queen Victoria Market. Claire Doherty and David Cross led an intensive Lab model which developed eight temporary projects that were subsequently presented across various sites in the iconic market location. Each of these programs rethought public art, and its treatment of temporality, place, trace and, importantly, the public.

The question of who is the 'public' of 'public art' is a highly contested one. In art museums and galleries, they are the people

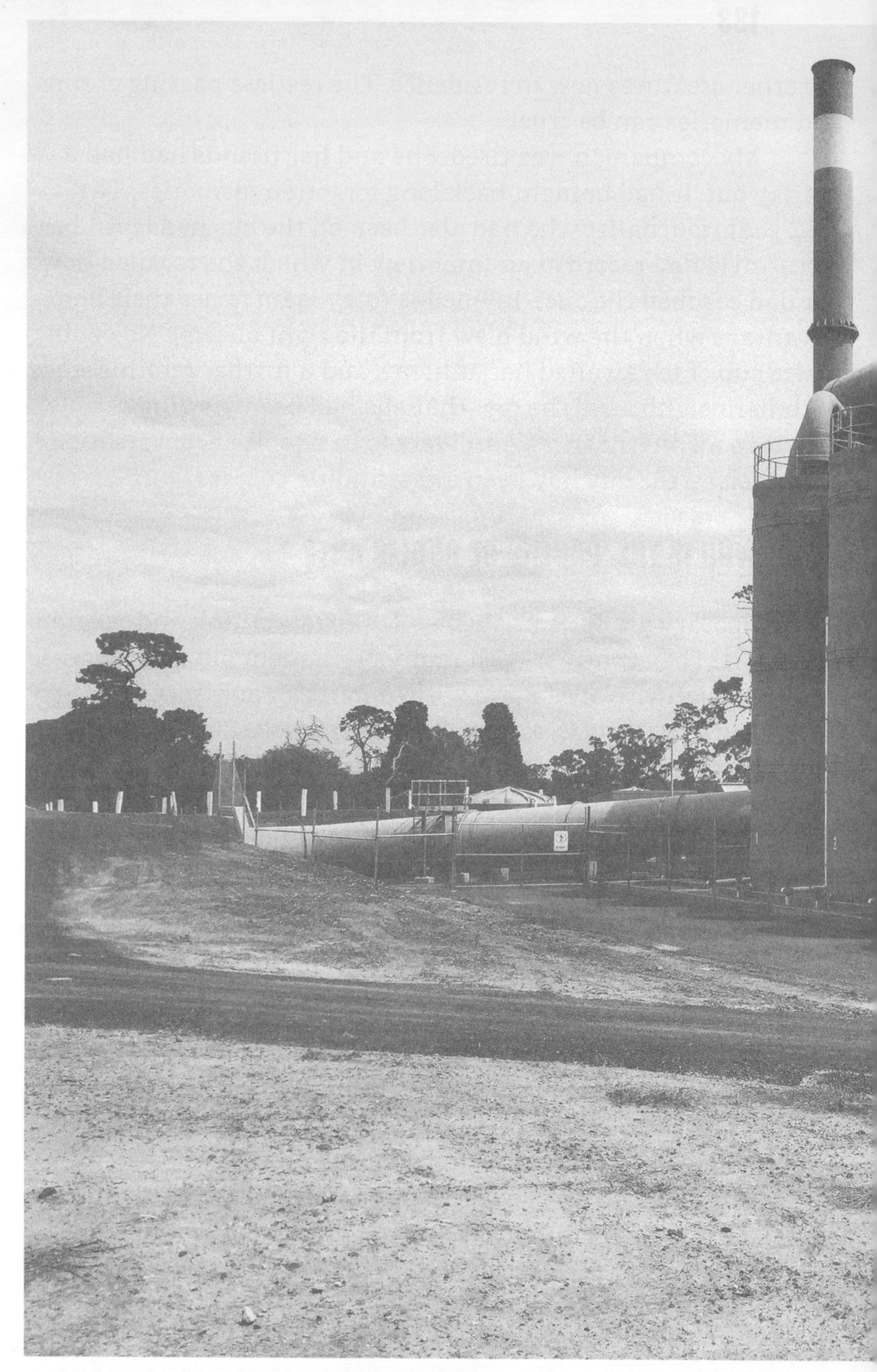

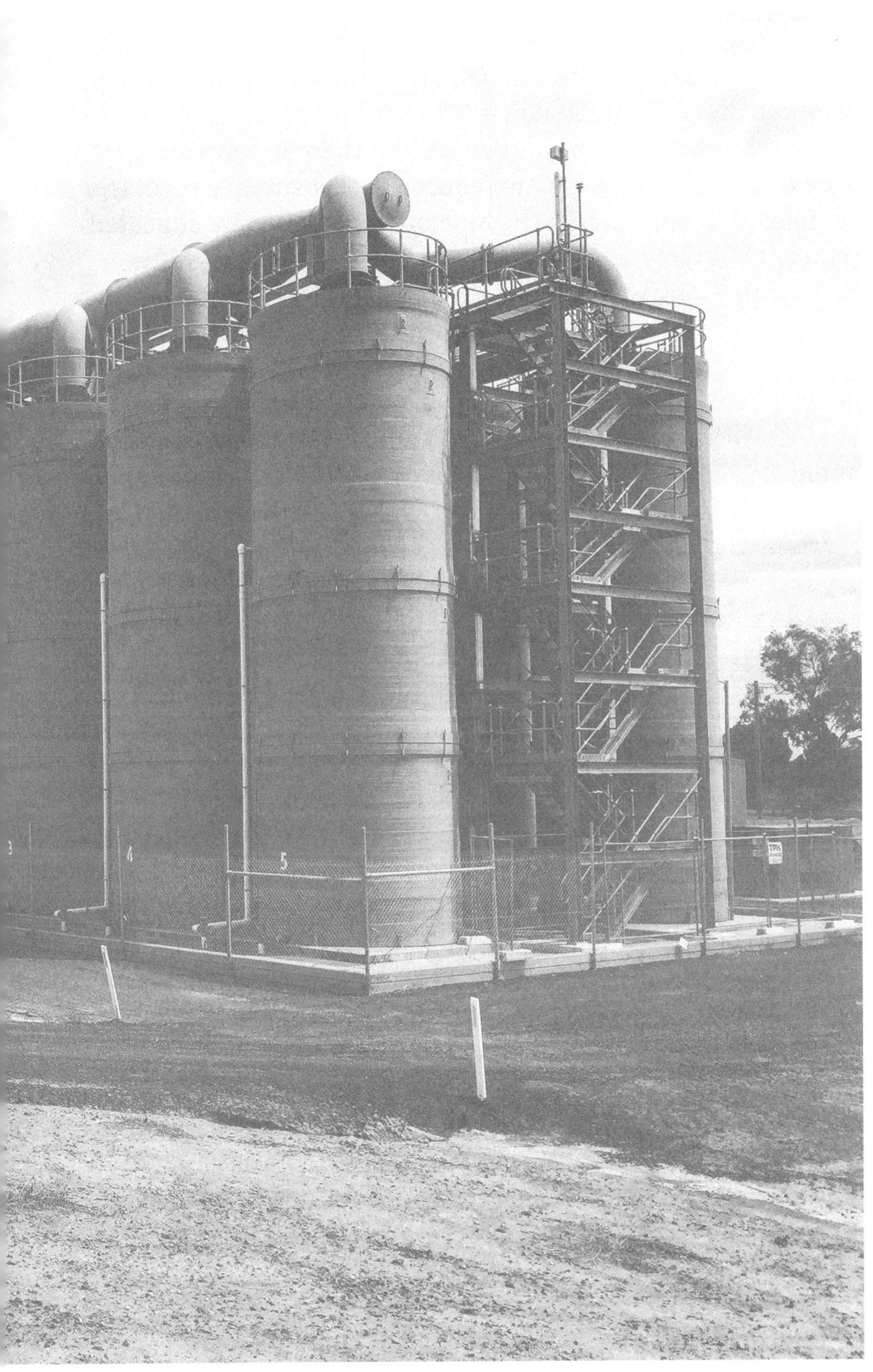

who come to exhibitions, participate in programs, and largely compose the viewing audience. The very act of visiting a gallery shapes the nature of the audiences and their commitment to the art experience. Postcodes are requested, and surveys regularly completed. Traditionally, the bulk of audiences were educated, white and largely female, but new thinking and programs have gone a long way in changing this tradition to attract more children, youth, and culturally diverse backgrounds.

Temporary artworks located in the public realm, however, are differently read. Art in freely accessible public urban or rural spaces will still attract an engaged and contemporary art-literate audience. But this art in the public domain also has other publics. Biennial Lab involved stallholders, market shoppers, and food tourists who have probably never attended a contemporary art opening. They may have stumbled across the artworks, experiencing them (if they noticed them) with no previous knowledge of the artist, artwork, context or event. *Treatment* was a destination experience, where all had to travel specifically to engage. But the curated program attracted various publics—from artworld-informed to general interest—to a water treatment station, not exactly a traditional artworld destination. The bus tour, with pre-determined itinerary, visited six temporary art projects, but it also explored unique local places and histories. The passengers included some who had come for the art, and others for the local content and history.

Artworks that directly engage audiences are often referred to as 'socially engaged' or 'community-based' art, though the latter term is not always positively meant. These largely refer to art projects that actively involve the audience or in which audience participation is central to realizing the work. Claire Bishop and Grant H. Kester's now-famous *Artforum* stoush of 2006 revealed the simmering tensions around participatory art, divided sharply along aesthetic and activist lines.[1] Both academics sought a standard for judging participatory works. Bishop took an historical approach to the subject, and argued that the essence of participatory art lies in its potential for social disruption, but maintained that an aesthetic criterion is essential. She argued that some socially engaged artists were more interested in using art as a means to alter the relations between people (activism) rather than as an end in itself. In contrast, Kester's approach to 'socially engaged art' was described by critic Eleanor Heartney as 'communitarian'—one in which he 'valorizes artworks that involve an immersion in local conditions, allowing artist to slowly develop solutions to very particularly sociopolitical problems through a sustained dialogue with specific communities'.[2] Both definitions, and positions, are useful in considering the temporary projects presented as *Treatment*.

Much has been written about the significance of place for site-specific temporary public art projects. The starting point is often Miwon Kwon's *One Place after Another: Site-Specific Art and Locational Identity* (2002).[3] It has generated numerous essays, articles and other publications by academics and artists that examine the curatorial imperative of 'place' for those involved in the many temporary exhibitions and biennials that have proliferated since the 1990s.

The desire to engage actively with a unique local context has been well documented. Context-specific curating became the touchstone for many organisations, curators and artists engaged in this sort of exhibition-making, where engagement, process and encounter often appear as key terms. Claire Doherty described it as a desire to shift away from a 'wide and shallow [engagement]' with place towards one with genuine engagement with the history and context of the place.[4] Using the 9th Istanbul Biennial (2005), curated by Charles Esche and Vasif Kortun, as her example, she described how the curators set out to commission artists to respond to the 'urban location and the imaginative charge that this city represents for the world'.[5] 'Glocal', as some described this shift, located local specificity within a global contemporary art world.

Cocoroc could never be accused of having either the history of context of the once capital of the Roman/Byzantine Empire, or the social and political complexity of contemporary Turkey, though Geelong is only a short way down the road. But both have unique local histories. That audiences respond to these specific histories and places is a testament to the strength of certain works to engage with this local context and place. The histories and experiences of people from a now-vanished small local town in regional Victoria were revealed through the six site-specific temporary public art projects that evoked memories shared by many other particular locales of regional and urban Australia. They in turn reveal the myriad of people and perspectives who make up the term 'public'.

1 • • • • The *Artforum* correspondence was generated by Claire Bishop's essay, 'The Social Turn: Collaboration and Its Discontents', *Artforum*, February 2006, pp. 179–185. Bishop, Claire, *Artificial Hells: Participatory Art and the Politics of Spectatorship*, Verso, New York, 2012; and Kester, Grant H., *The One and the many: Contemporary Collaborative Art in a Global Context*, Duke University Press, Durham, N.C., 2011.

2 • • • • Heartney, Eleanor, 'Can Art Change Lives?', *Art in America*, June/July, 2012, p. 68.

3 • • • • Kwon, Miwon, *One Place after Another: Site-Specific Art and Locational Identity*, MIT Press, Cambridge, Mass., 2002.

4 • • • • Istanbul Biennial Press Release, Curators: Charles Esche and Vasif Kortun, 9th Istanbul Biennial, 2005, cited in Doherty, Claire, 'Curating Wrong Places... Or Where Have All the Penguins Gone?', in O'Neill, Paul (ed.), *Curating Subjects*, Open Editions, London, 2007, p. 101.

5 • • • • ibid.

SIX PUBLIC ARTWORKS

Passage

Técha Noble

When I was presented with the opportunity to create a site-specific response to the Western Treatment Plant in Werribee, I thought it a ripe proposition. The project offered an opportunity to travel down the pipeline after you press flush, where an audience could contemplate our collective bodies in a soup of fundament—an offer impossible to refuse.

The site and the design of the event suggested the flow of energy and dynamic movement. This was in part achieved by the audience experiencing the site courtesy of a bus journey which wove through the landscape, echoing the constant flowing trajectory of effluent. The sense of flow through the mechanical system of the plant as it transitioned from pipeline to pond to tank to its final return to water system in a state of relative purity (shit to water) became the key route plan that informed my work.

The processing plant, on initial site visit, appeared like a giant digestive system unfolded across the Werribee landscape. The energetic journey of raw materials was, however, inverse to the human digestive path, as it began with the profane and ended in a state of clarity. I created my own map of entry to exits by colliding the bodily system with the Western Treatment Plant process.

solids in = mouth
grit removal, screening = liver
sedimentation = stomach
aeration = pancreas
clarification = small intestines

effluent holding basin = large intestine
water re-entry = anus

This parody of inverse paths and the collision of the sacred with the profane was the basis of the *Passage* piece. This inversion of movement in turn provoked an inverse use of materials to bring to the site. I decided to use 'mylar' glitter, traditionally used in burlesque contexts or celebratory glitter cannons, as a primary substance. I paired this with mirrored mosaic pieces, mirrorball adhesive and metallic gold and silver lamé as the basis of costume construction. This material was to sit in direct contrast to the site of the performance, the aerated sewage ponds. Affectionately called the 'shit milkshake', this pond is filled with giant mechanical aerators that turn the brown waste into a frothing filthy river of poo.

I created three costumed embodiments of the crucial stages of the water recycling process: Solids Entry; Clarification; Water Re-entry. All three costumes extended the body's natural boundaries or suggested alternative hierarchies for bodily functions. In keeping with the continual movement of audience and performers, the three performative moments connected to the buses' path around this section of the site with simple linking gestures that activated the costumes.

As part of my site-specific response process, I reworked disused gas suits from the Western Treatment Plant as a basis of the *Clarification* costume. In addition, I was lucky enough to have Edie Cross, the curator's 12-year-old daughter, embody the *Water Re-entry* costume, which brought a holistic completion to the *Passage* piece. As a result, the performance experimented with ways to give a sacred tonality to the raw effluent material, and made visible the alchemic potential of the plant's process.

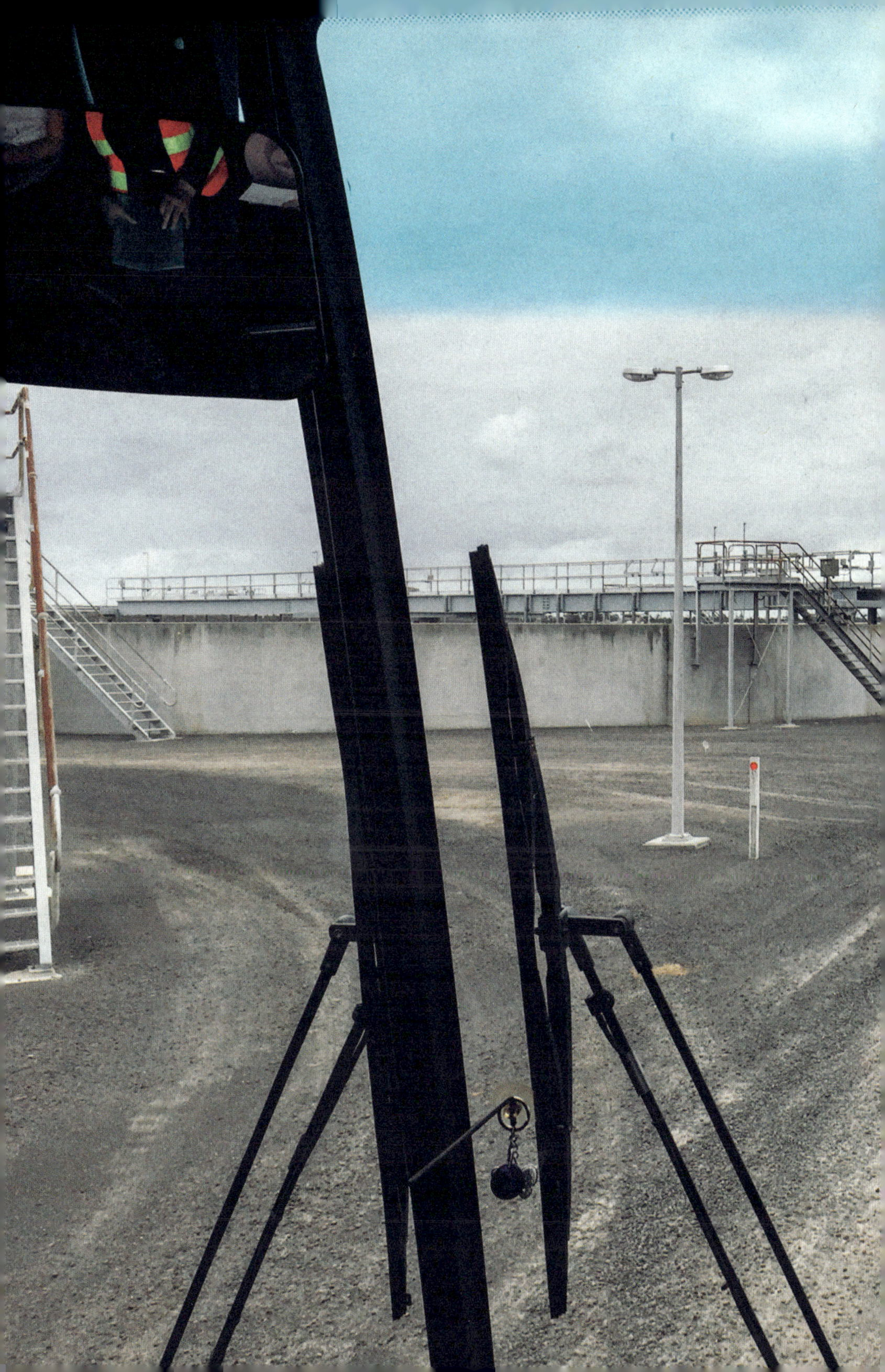

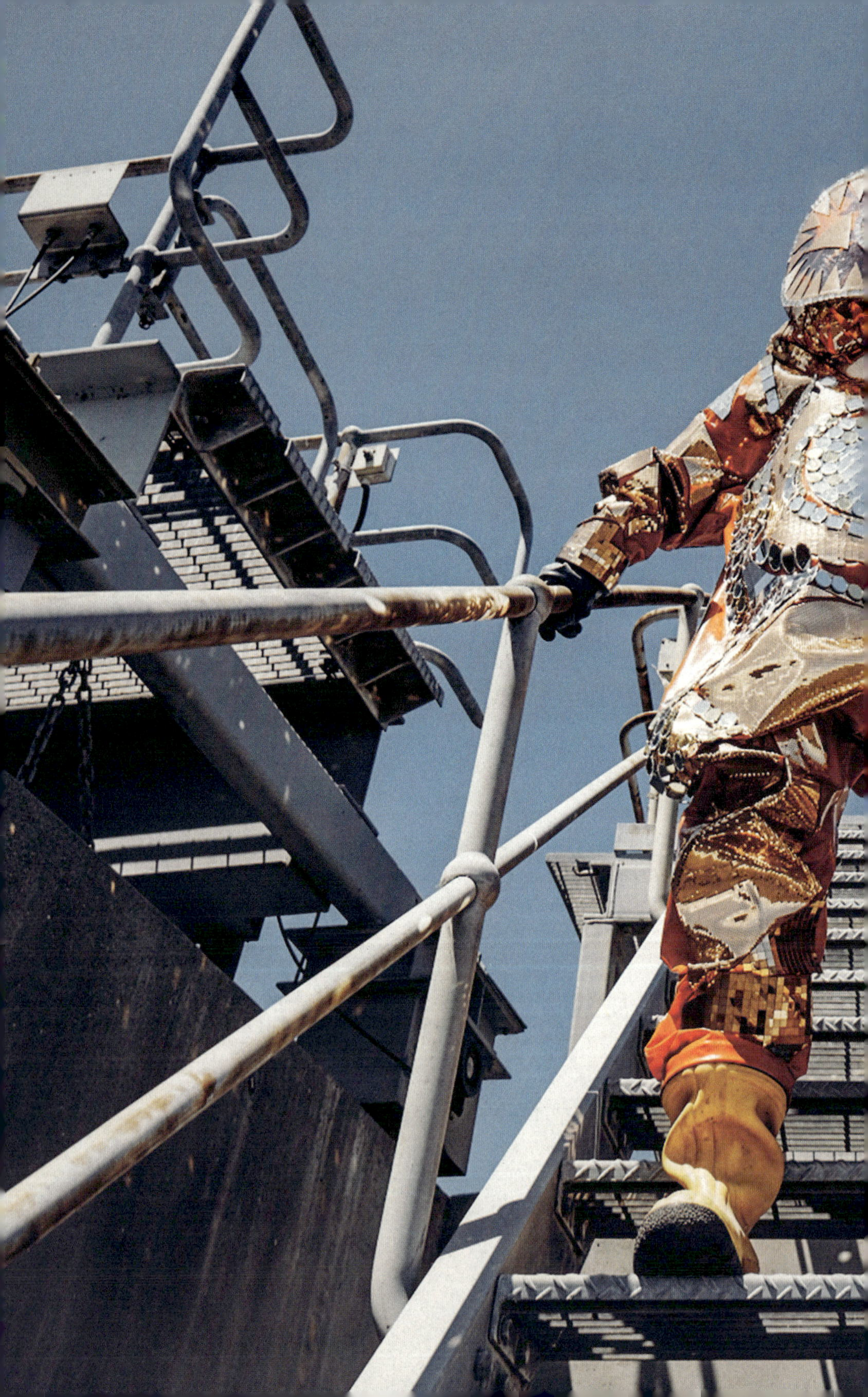

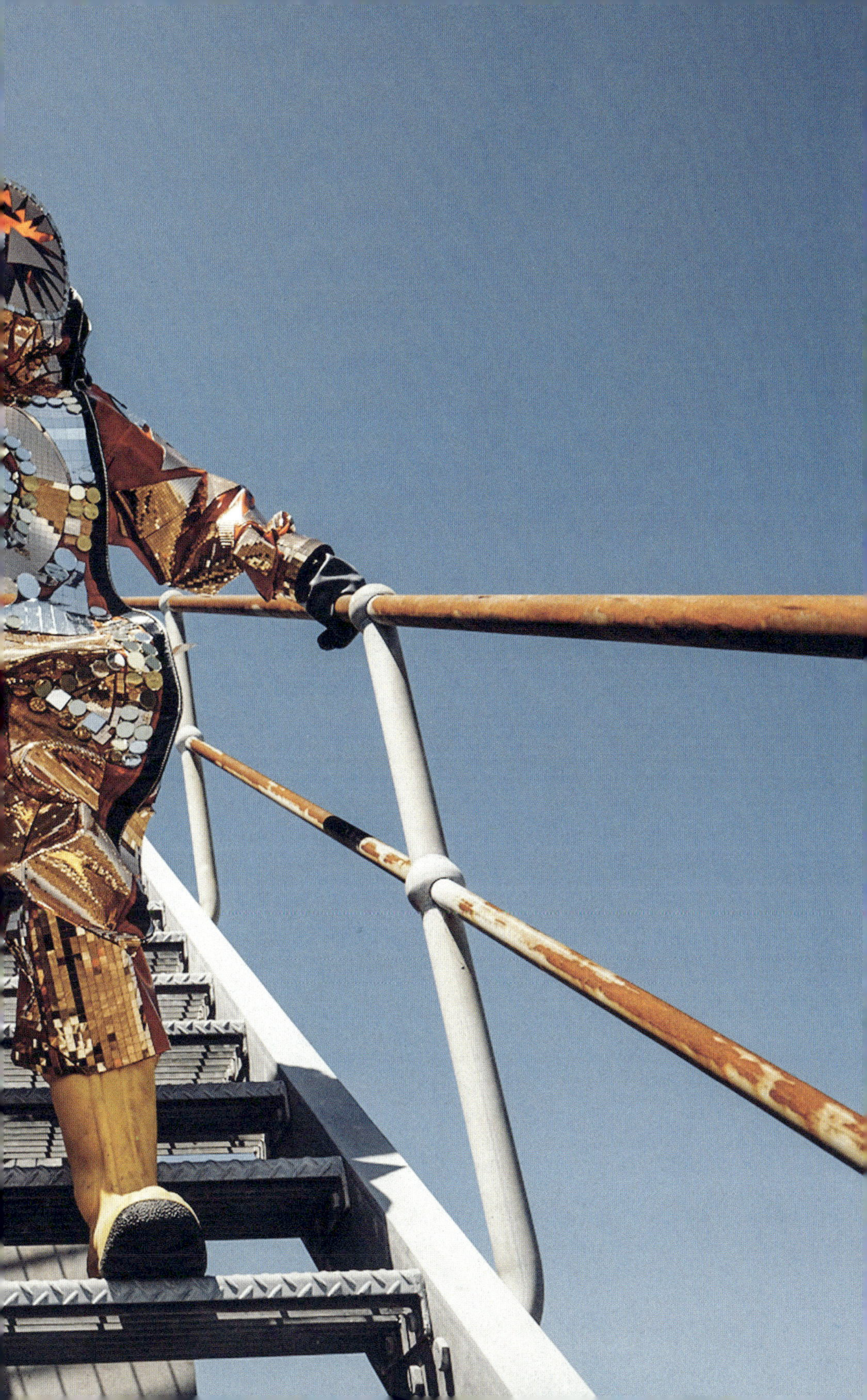

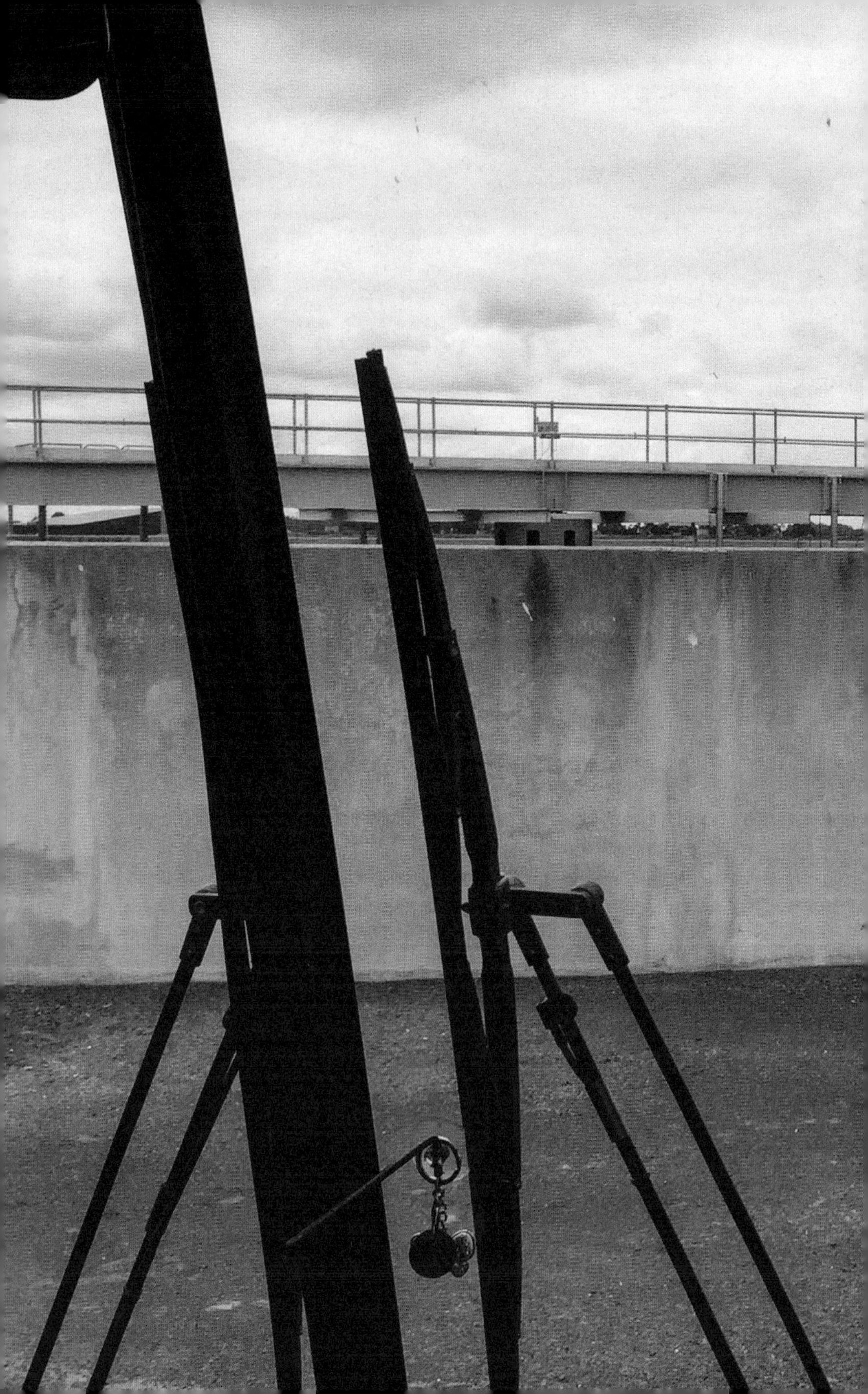

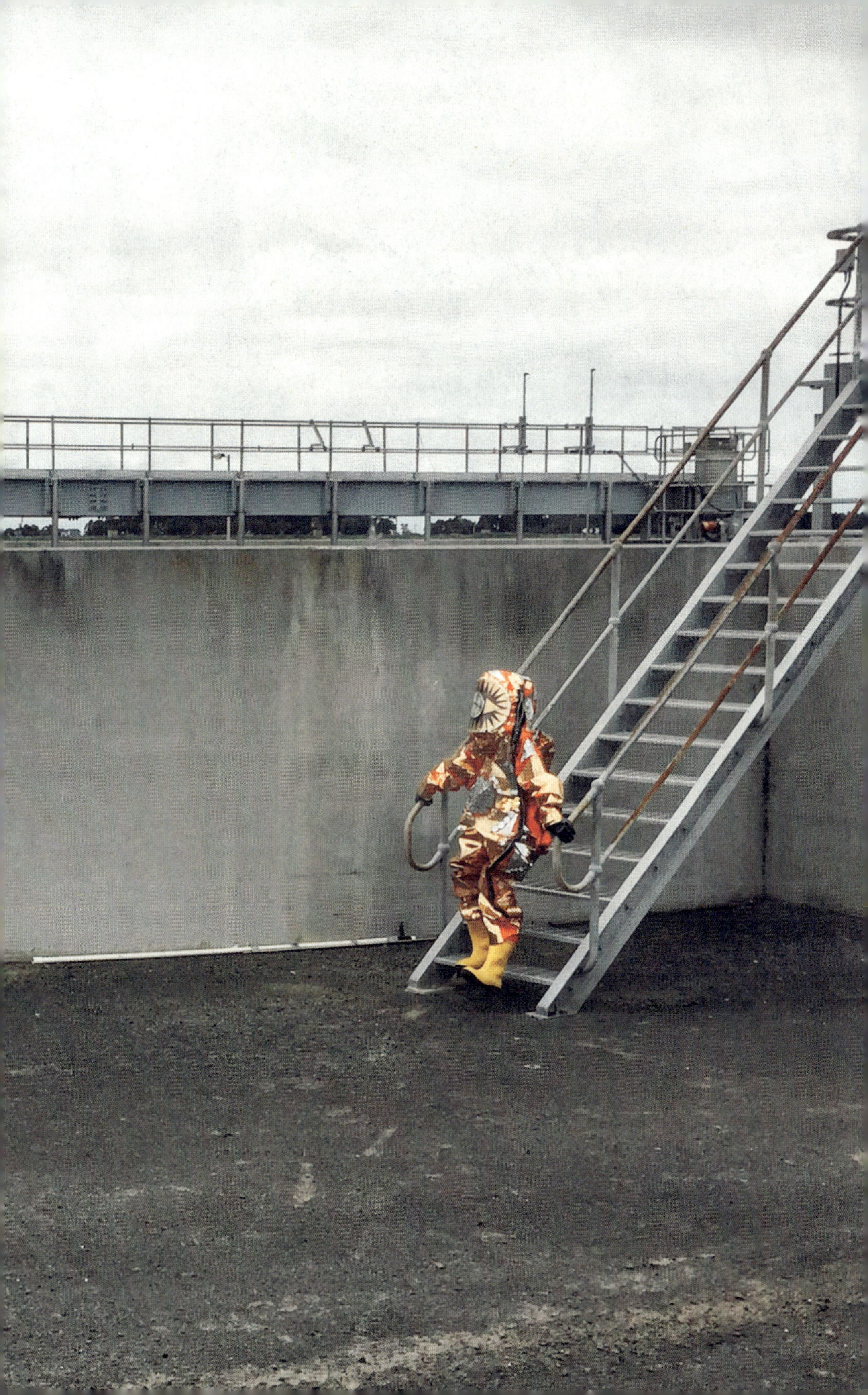

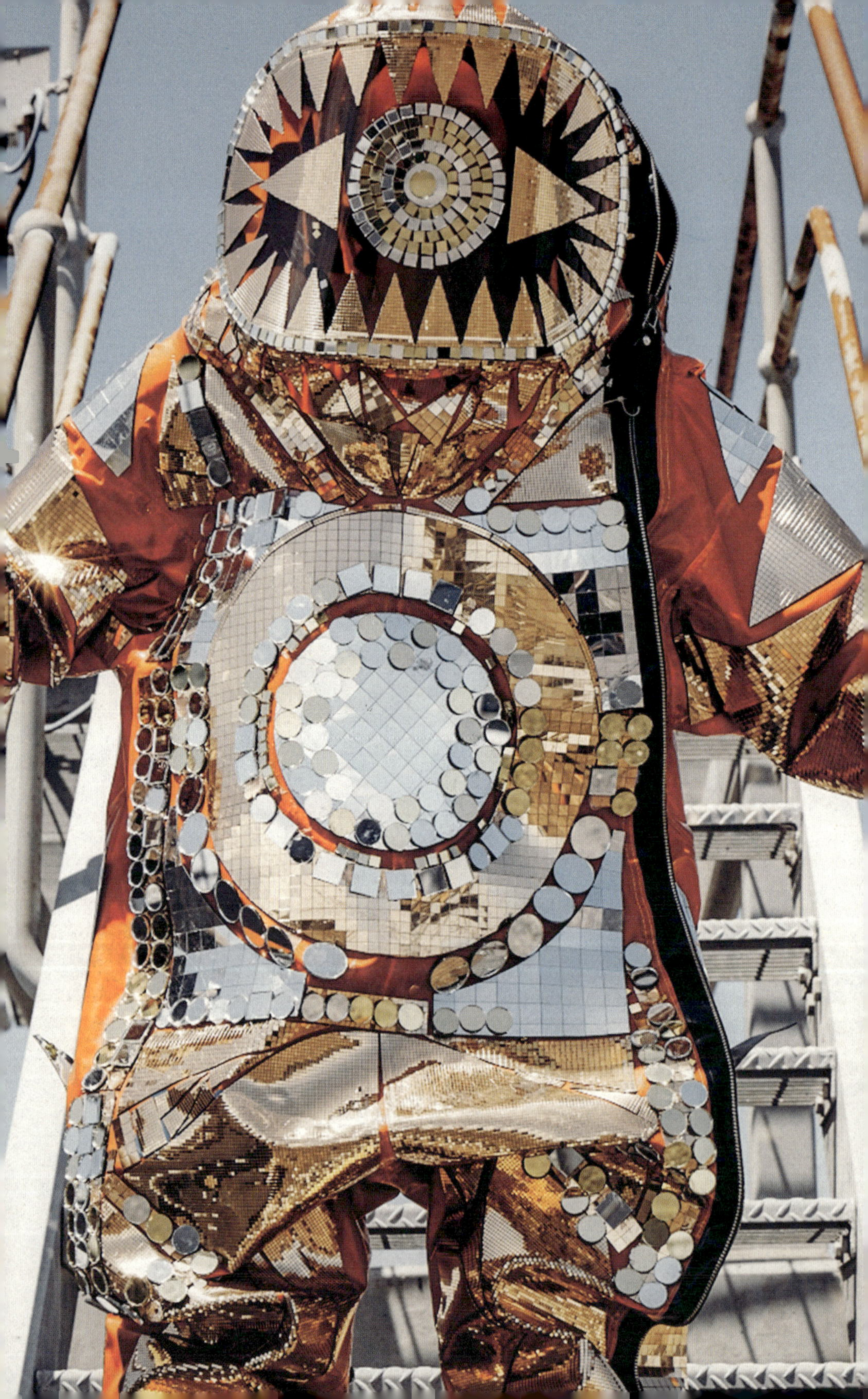

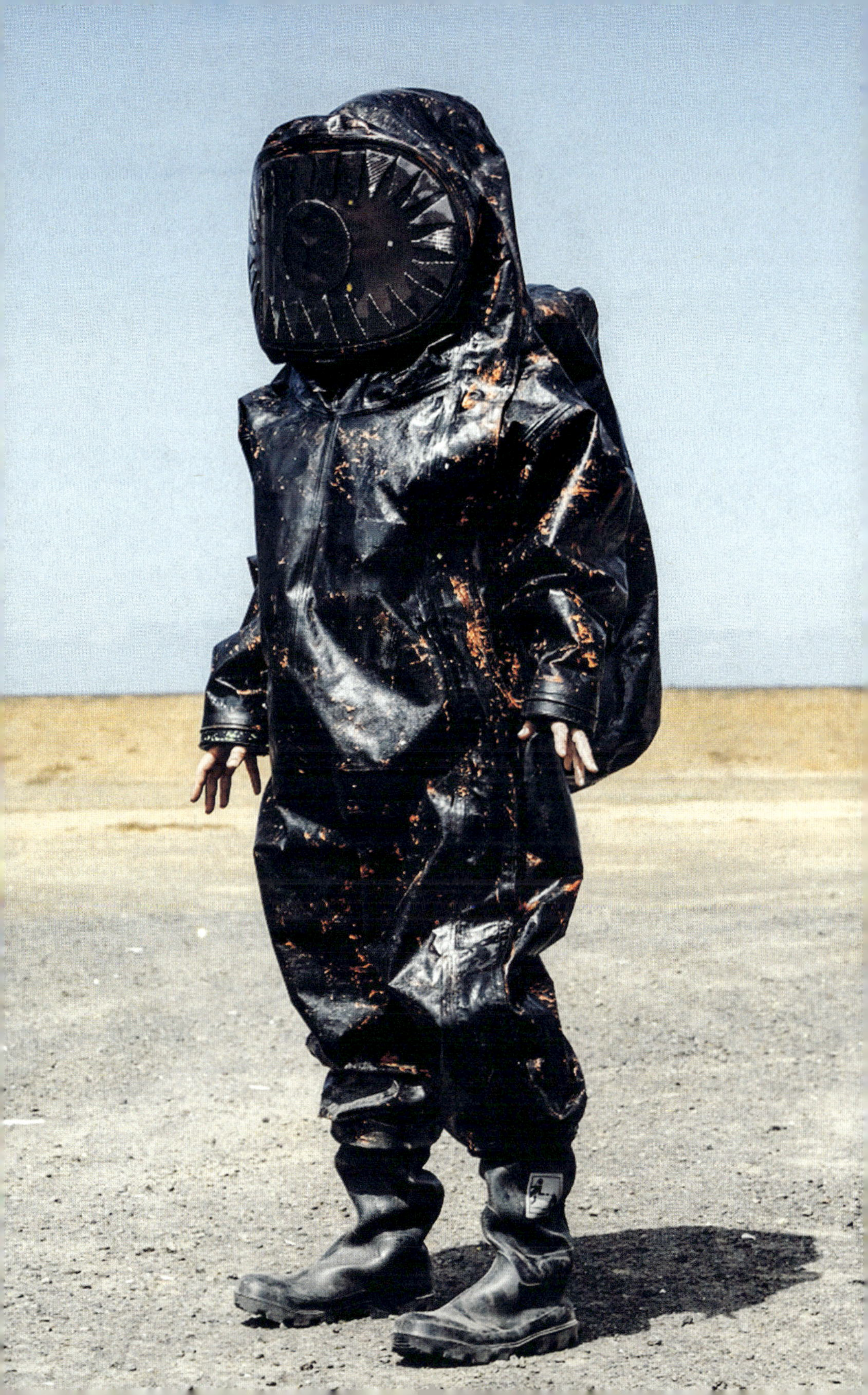

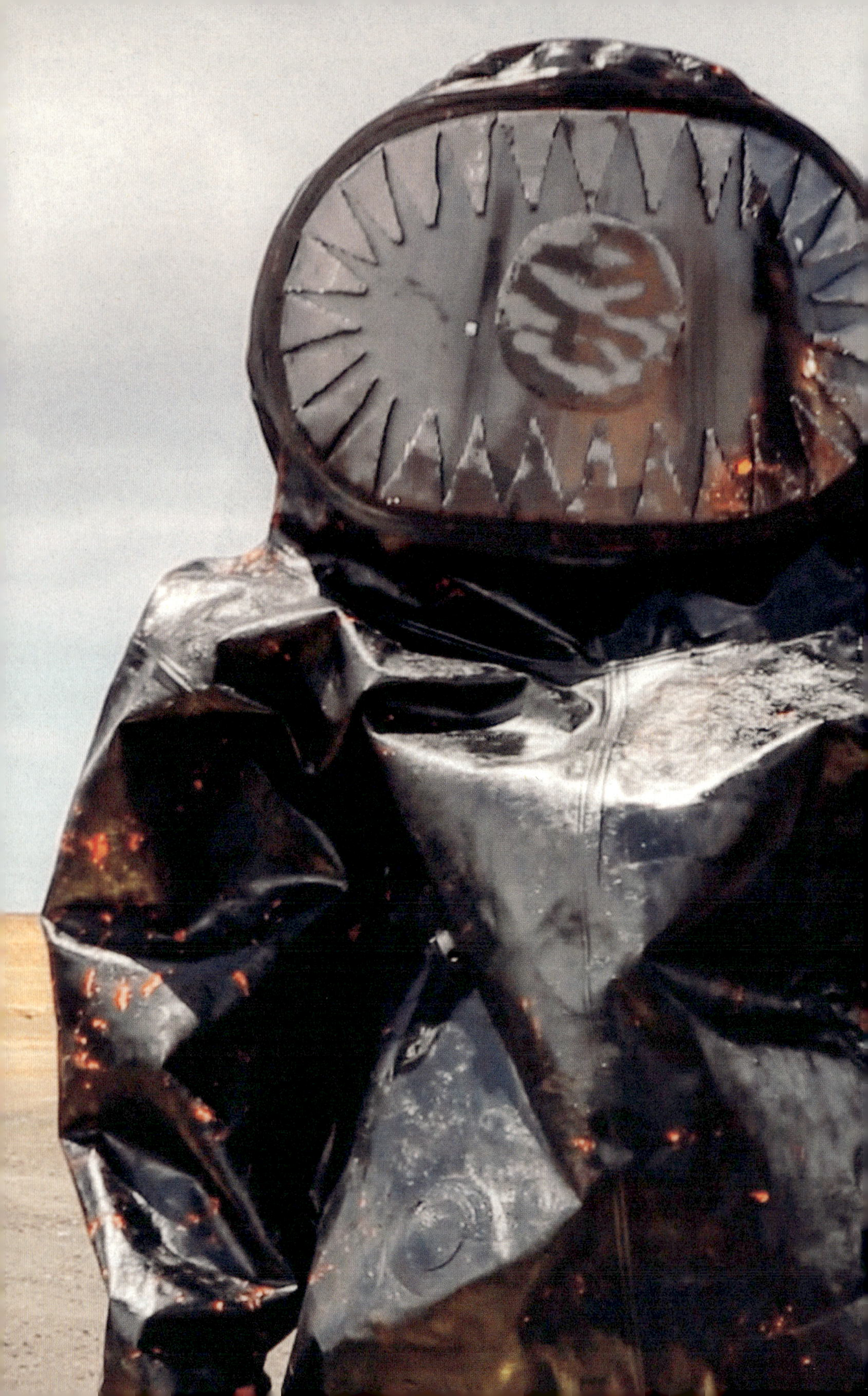

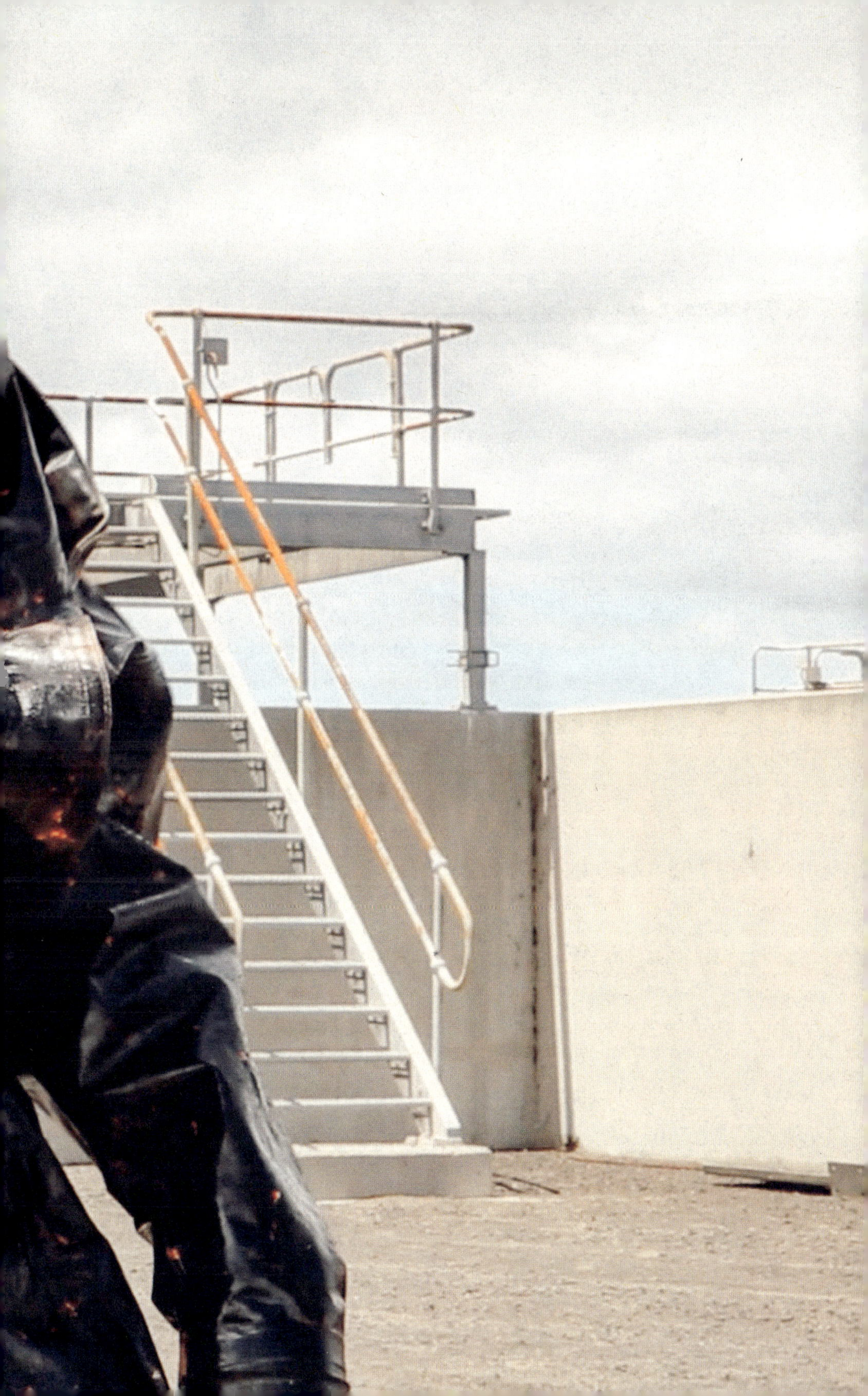

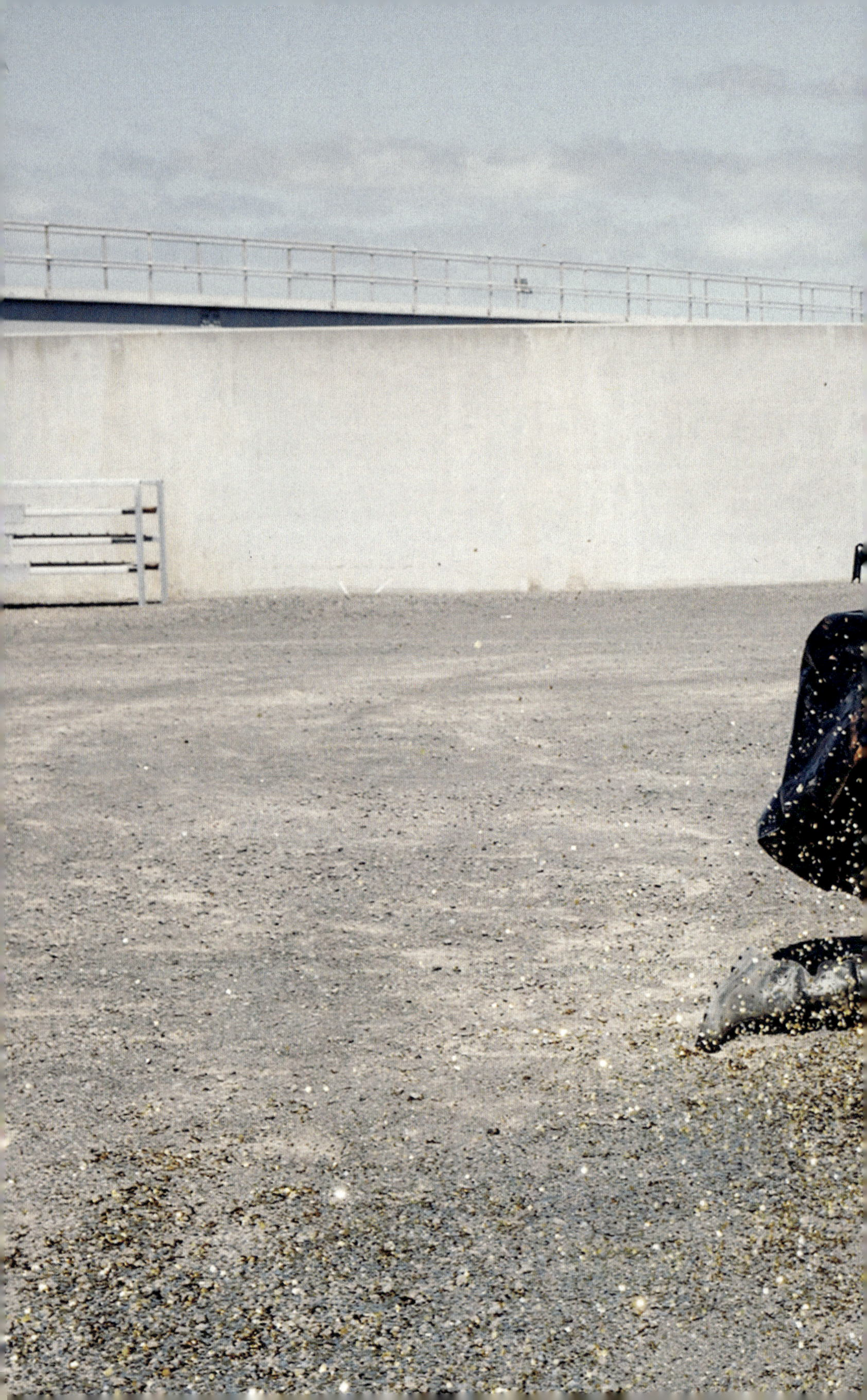

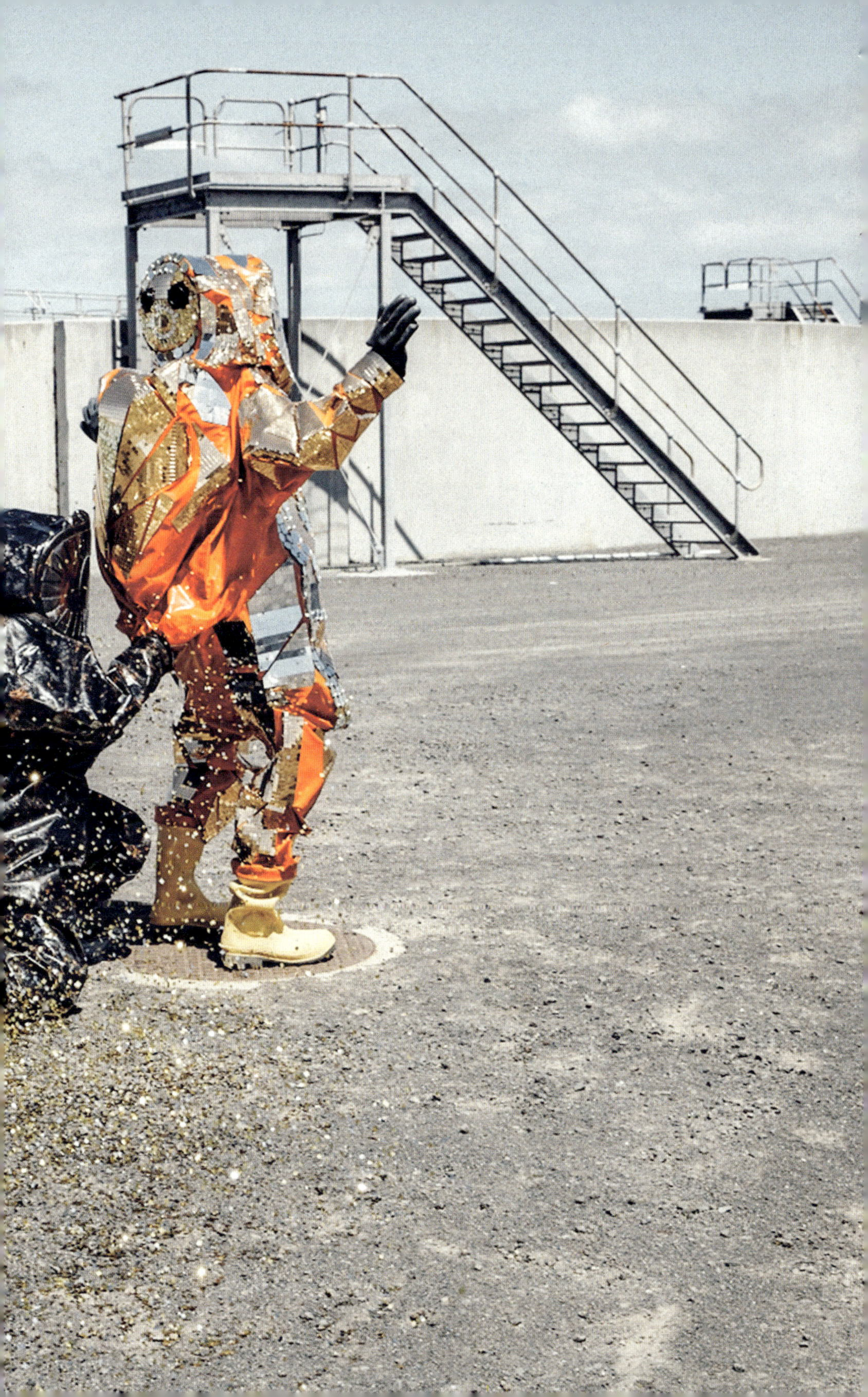

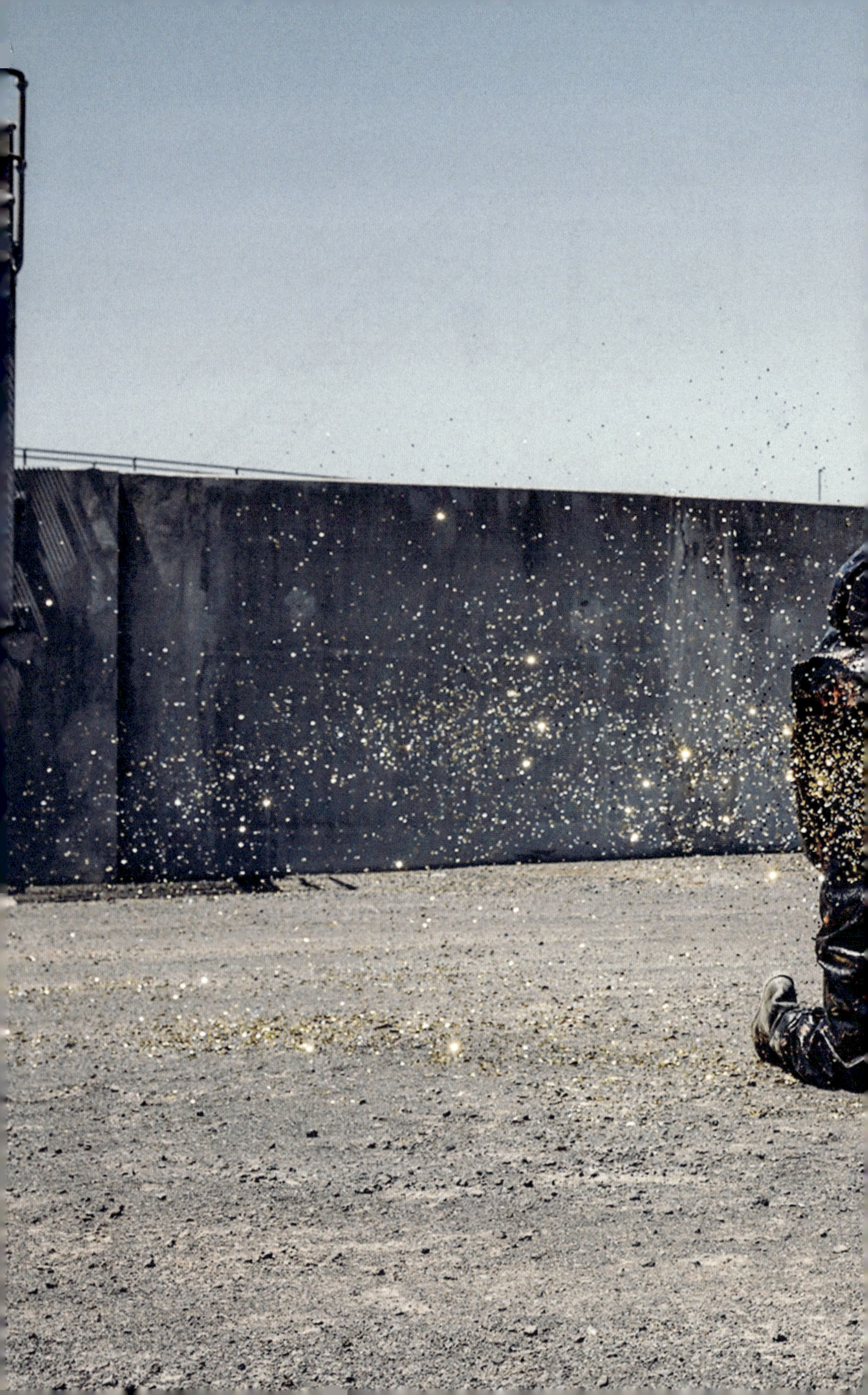

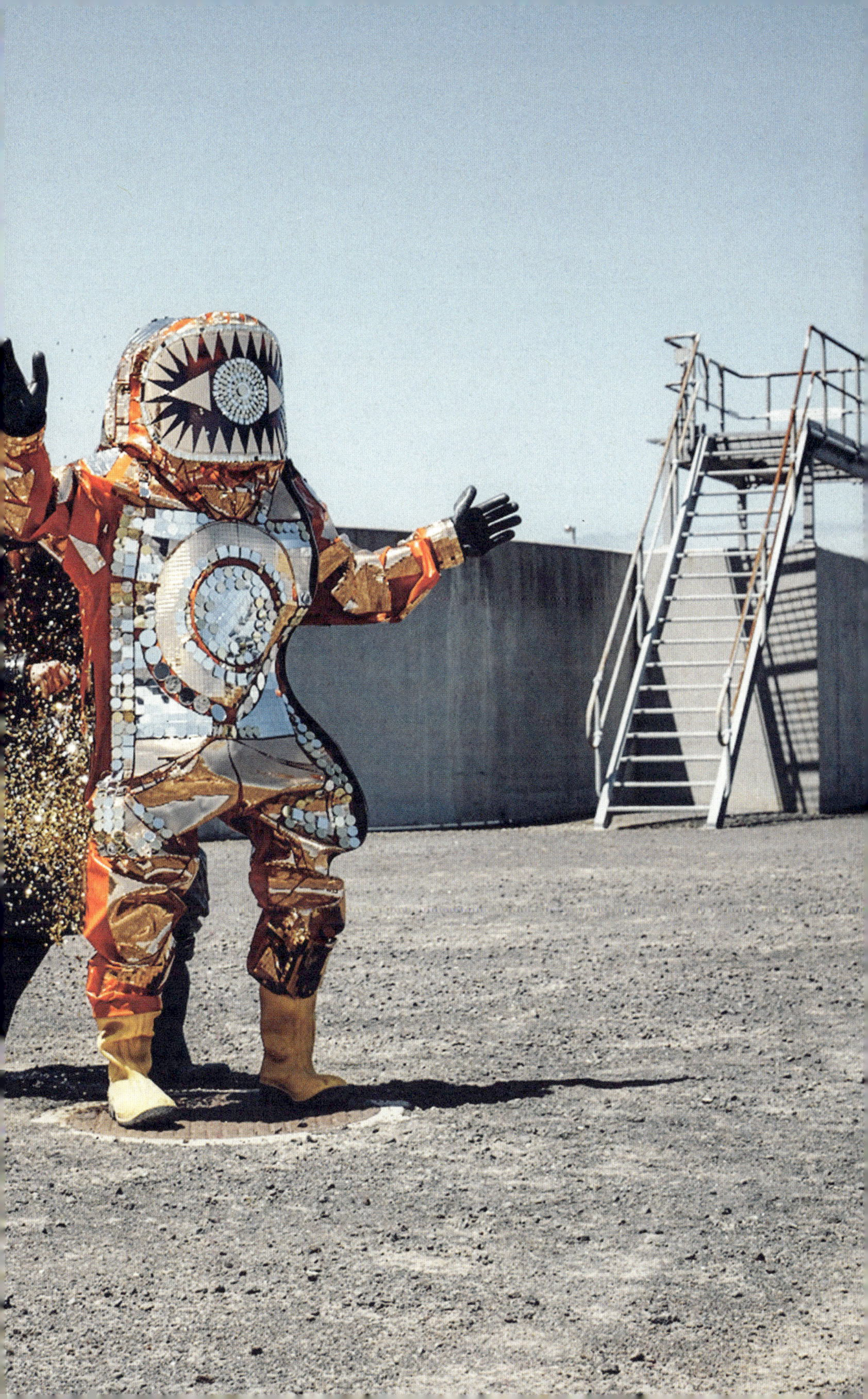

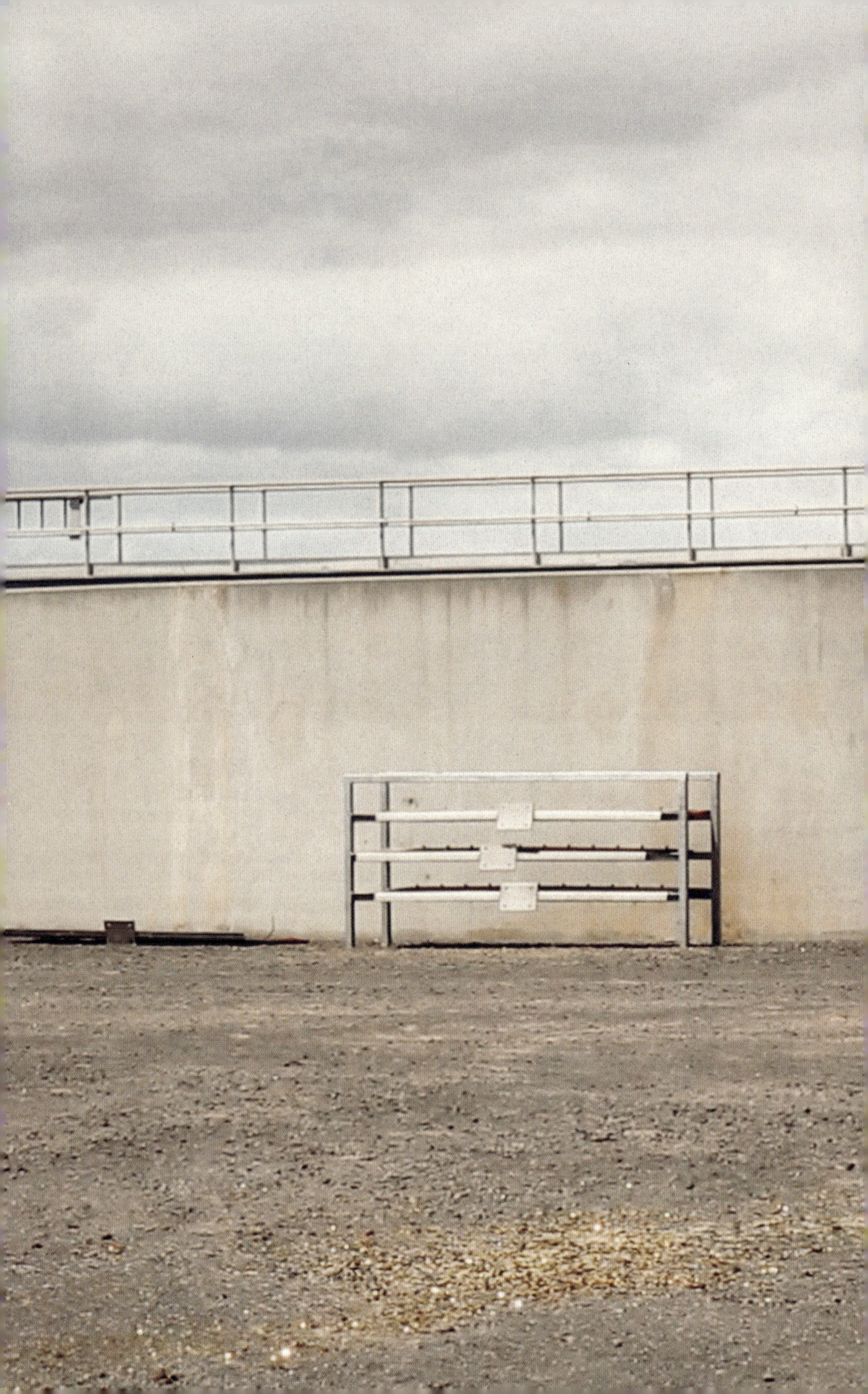

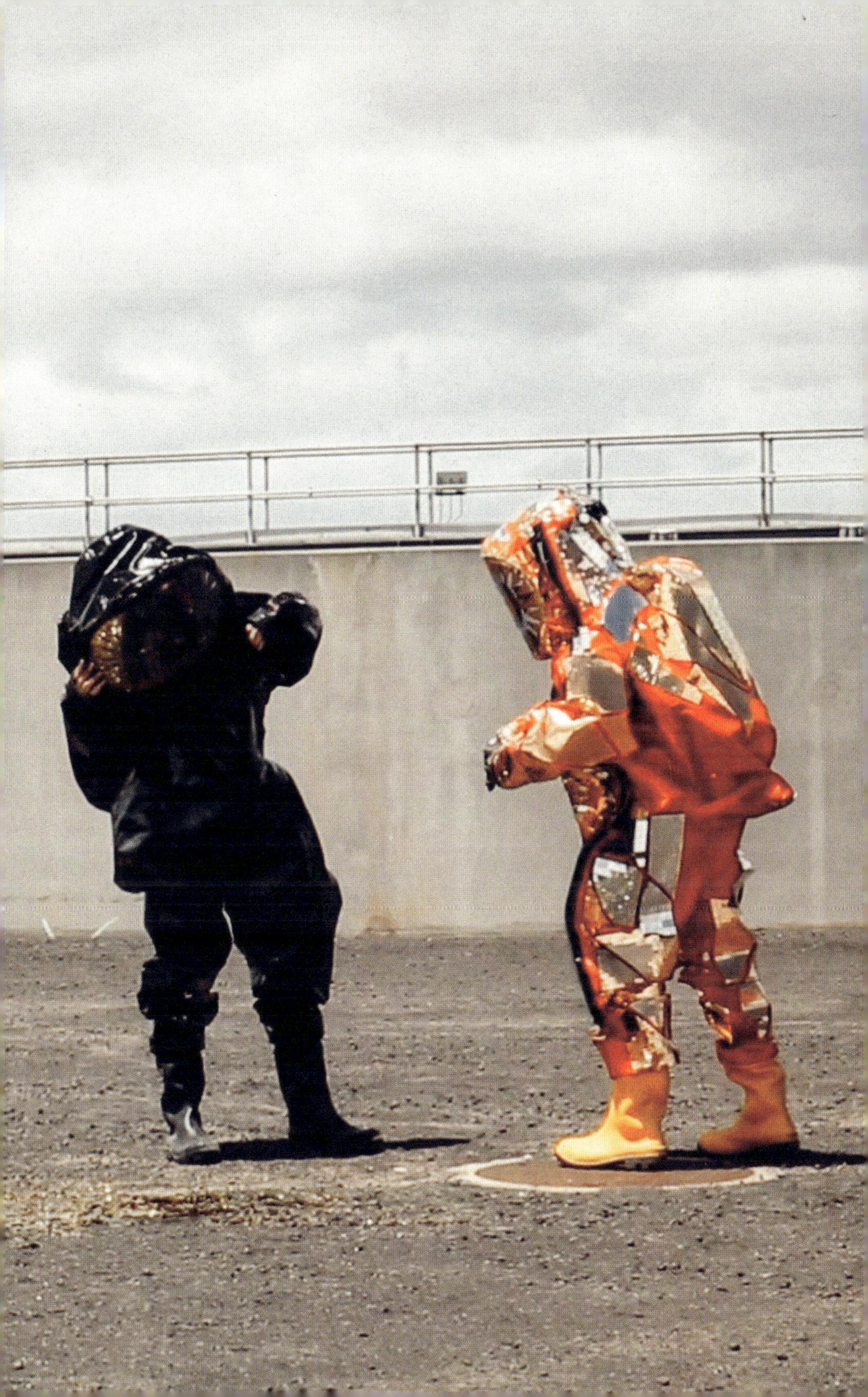

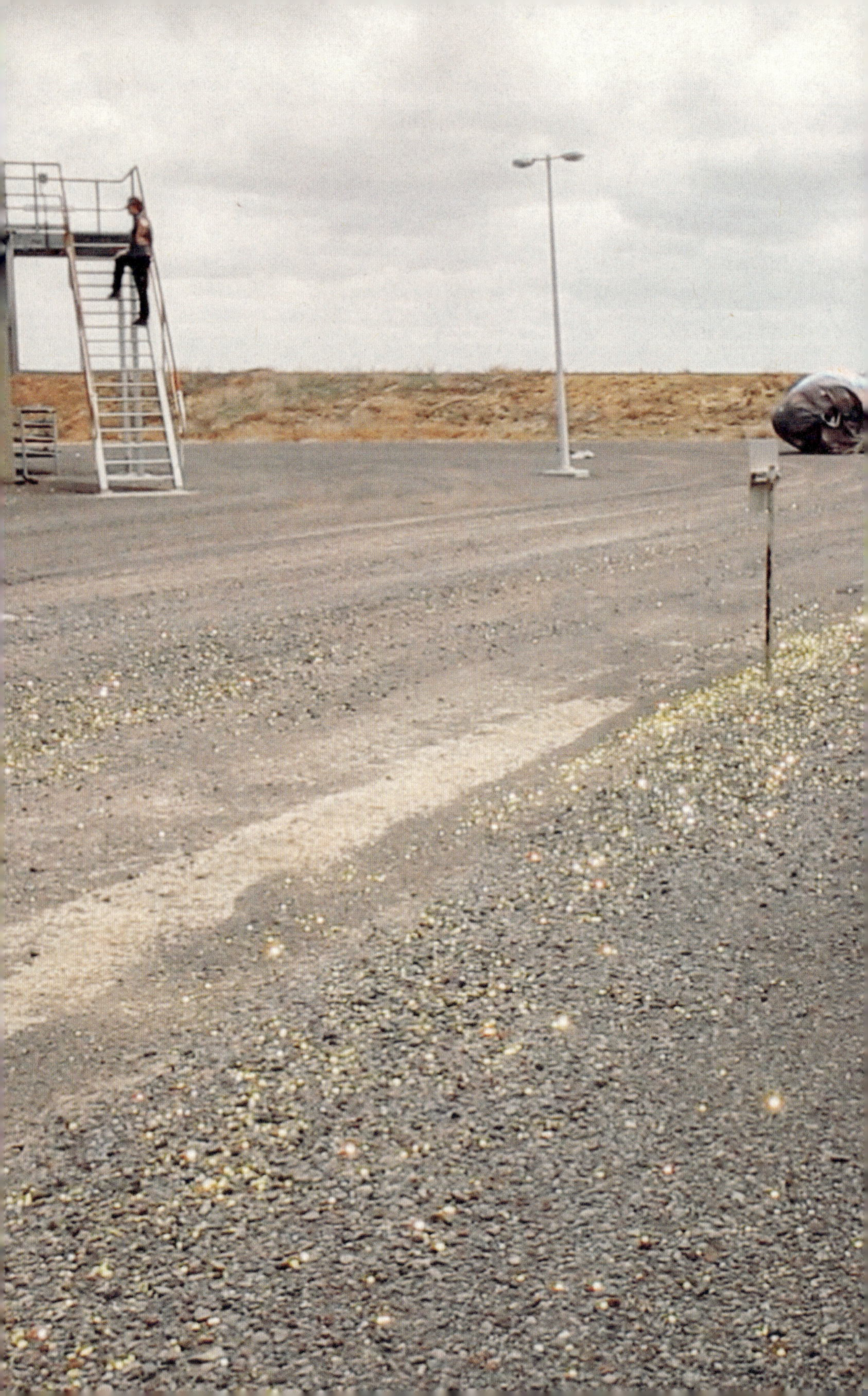

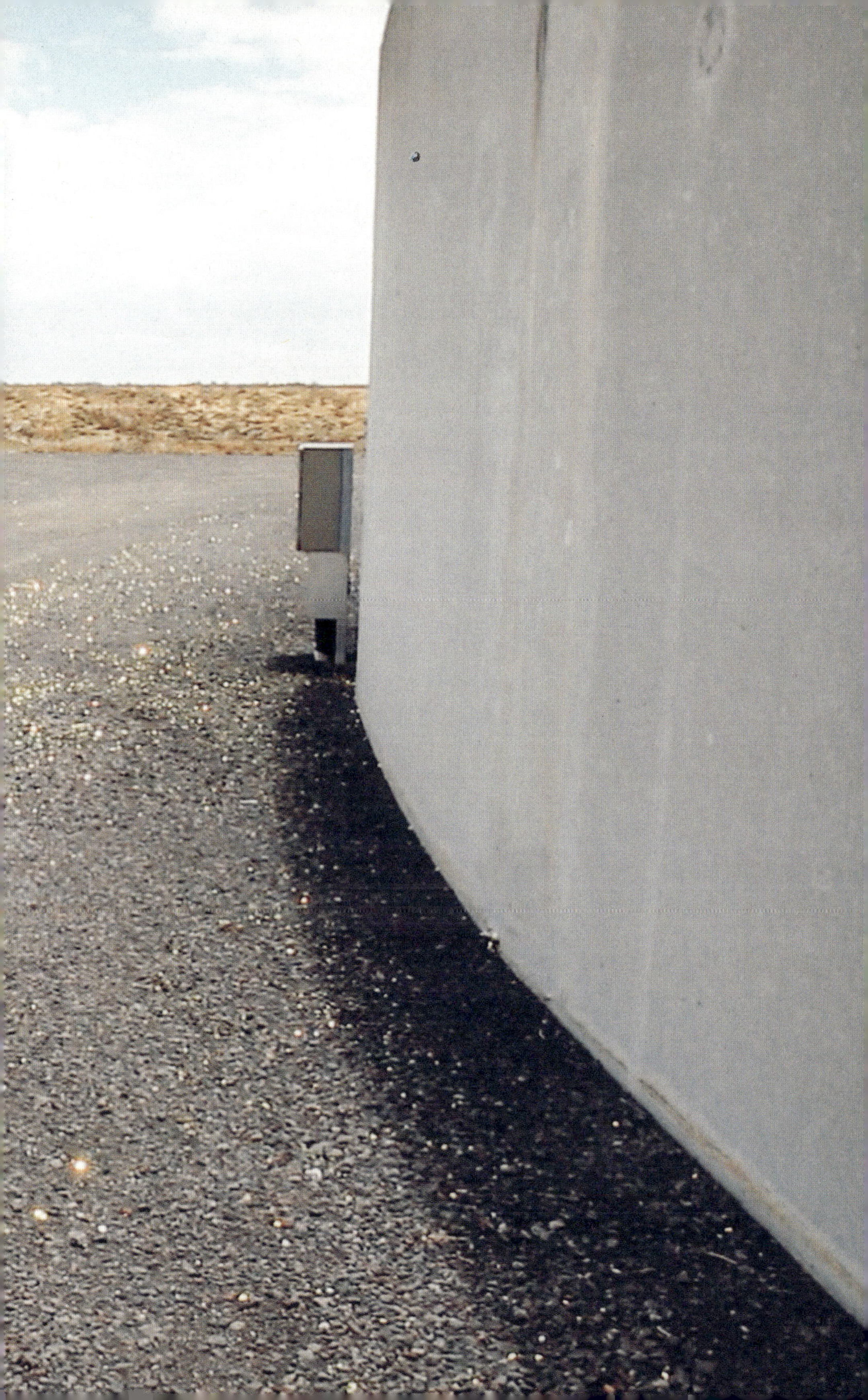

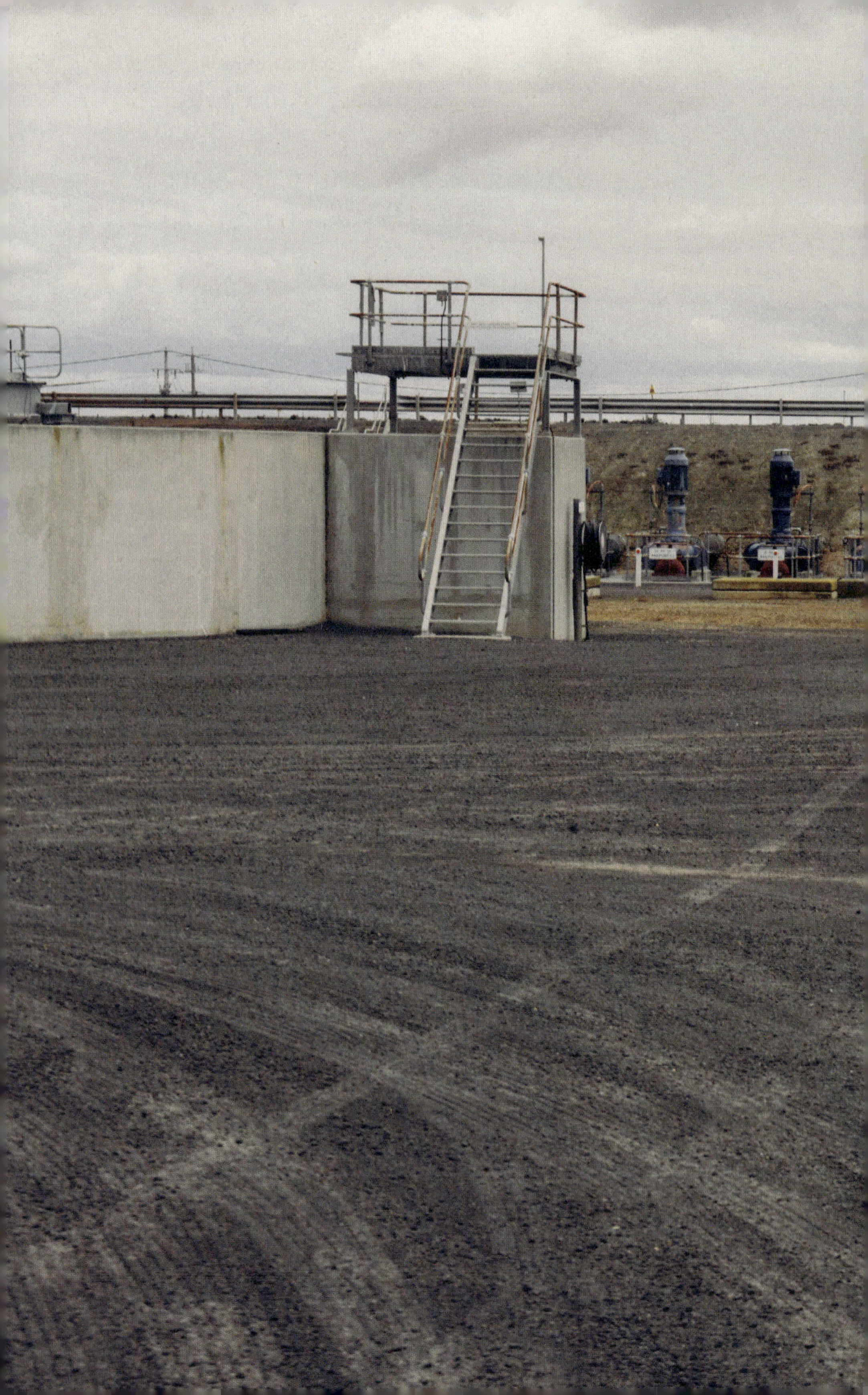

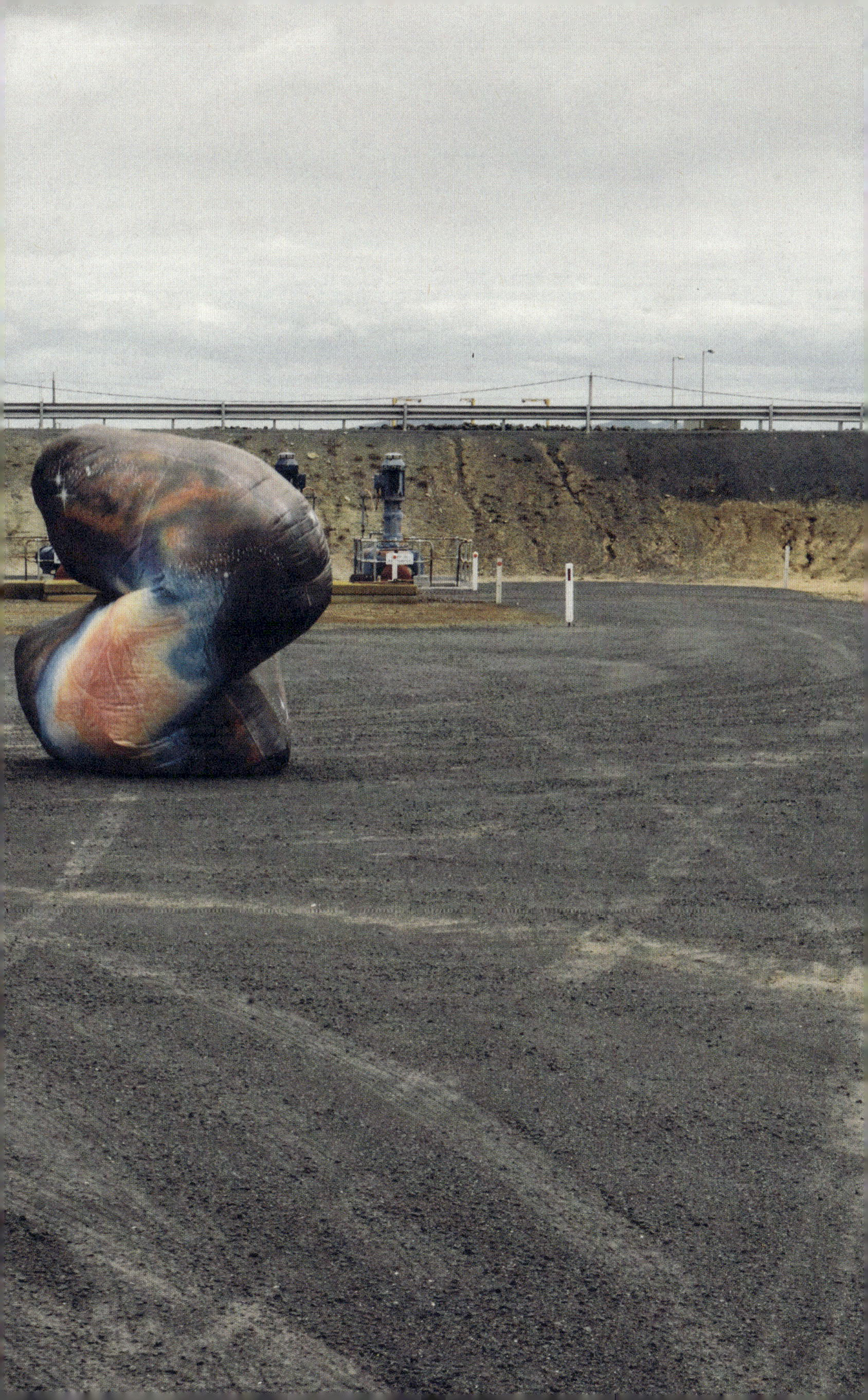

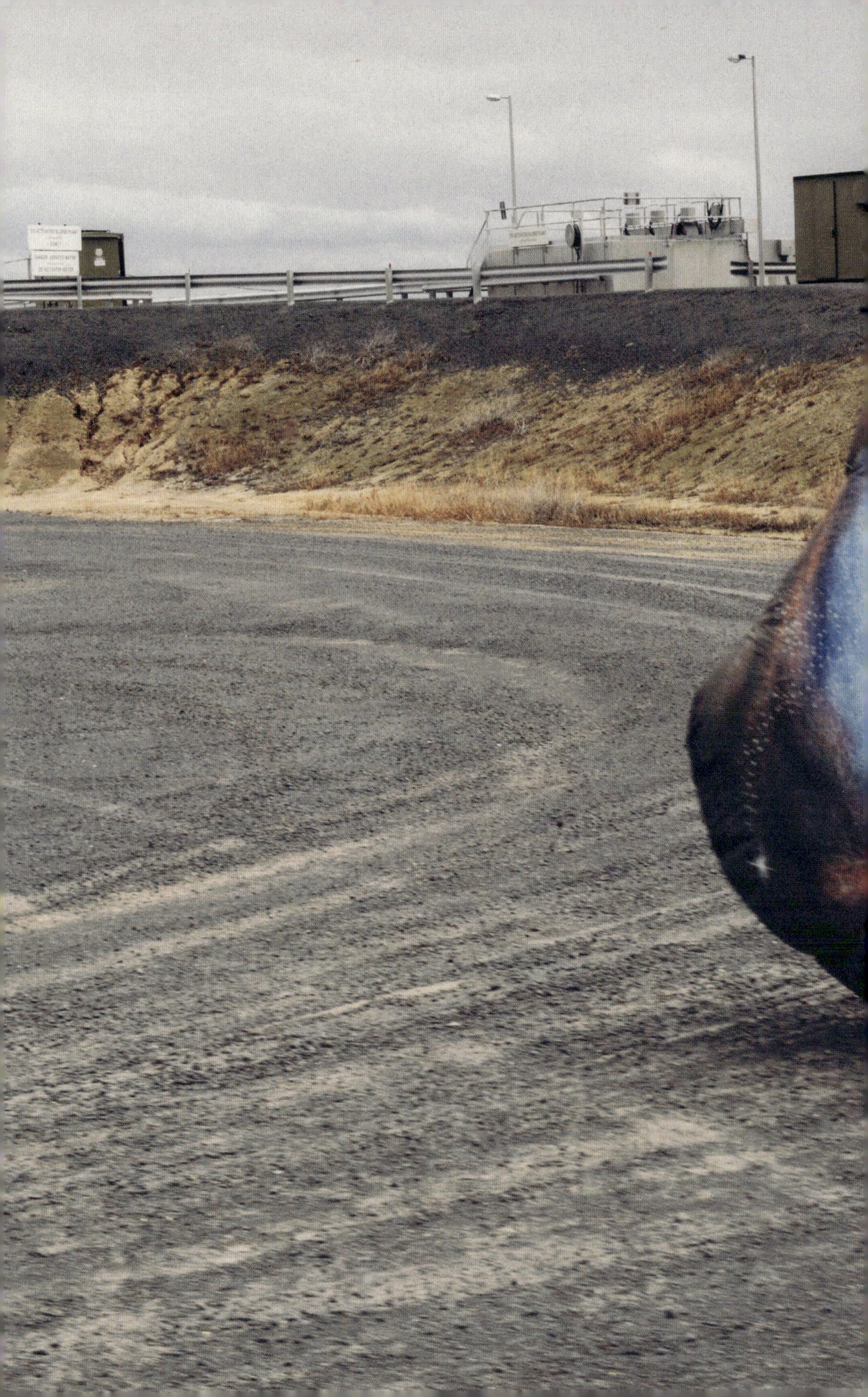

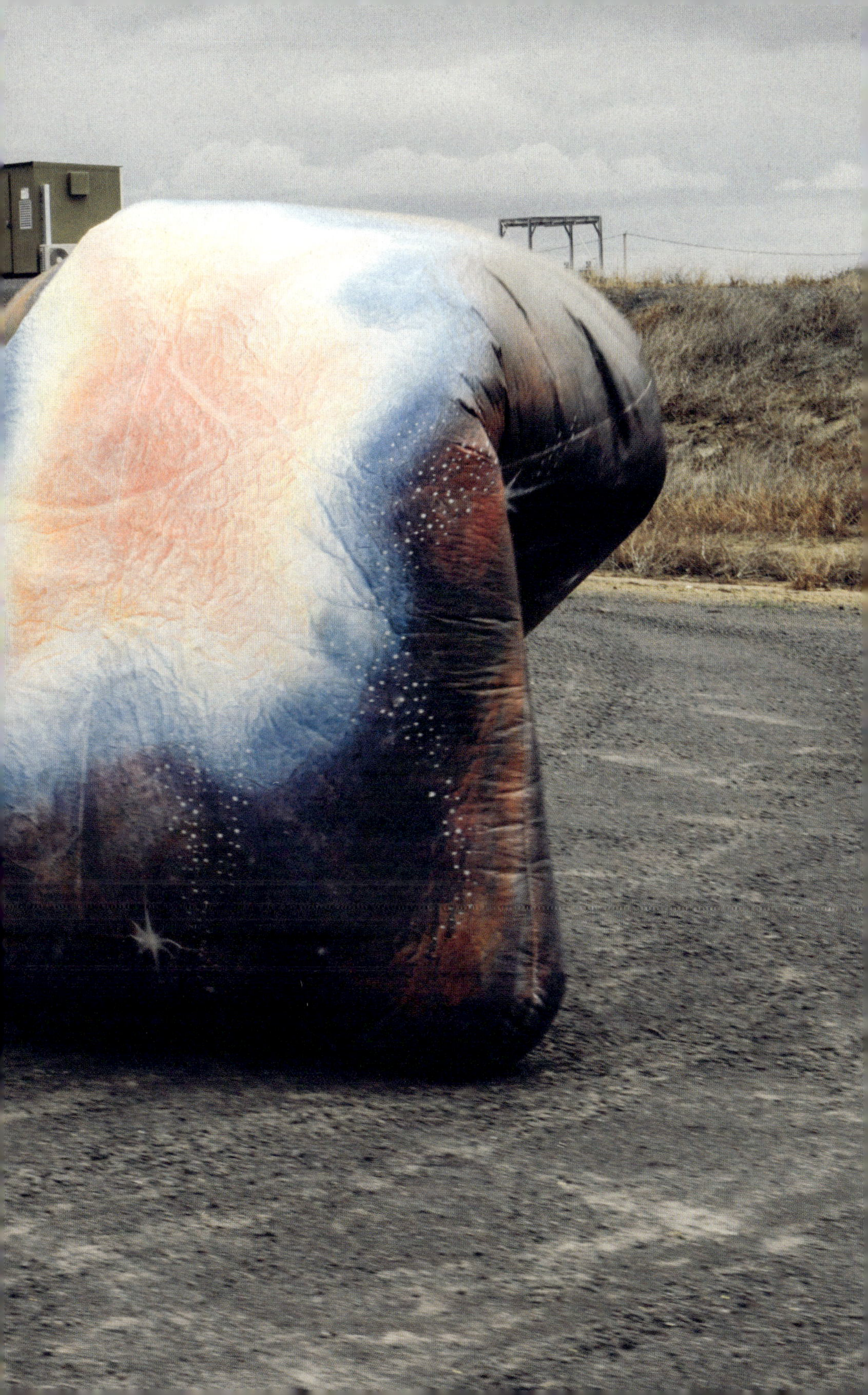

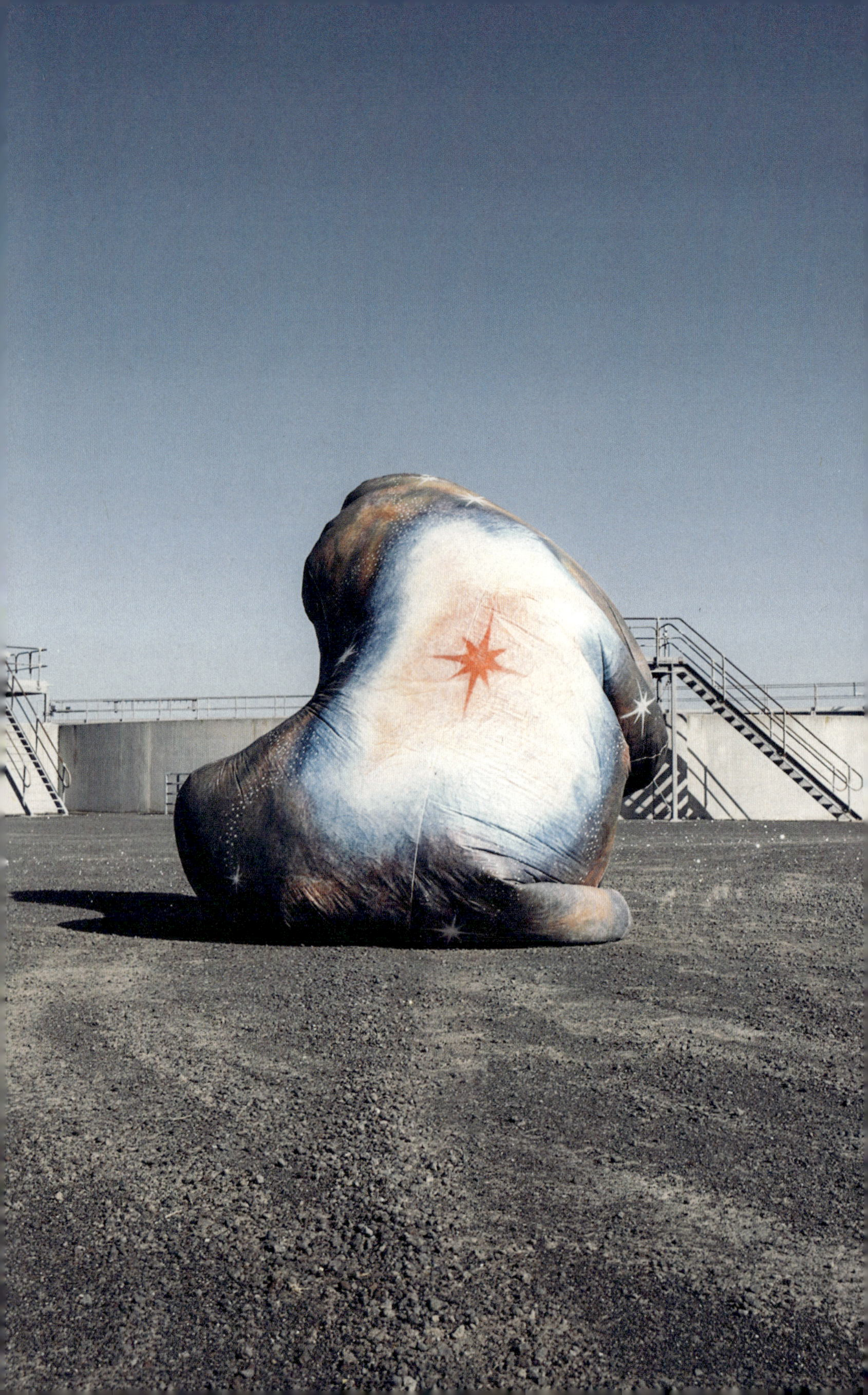

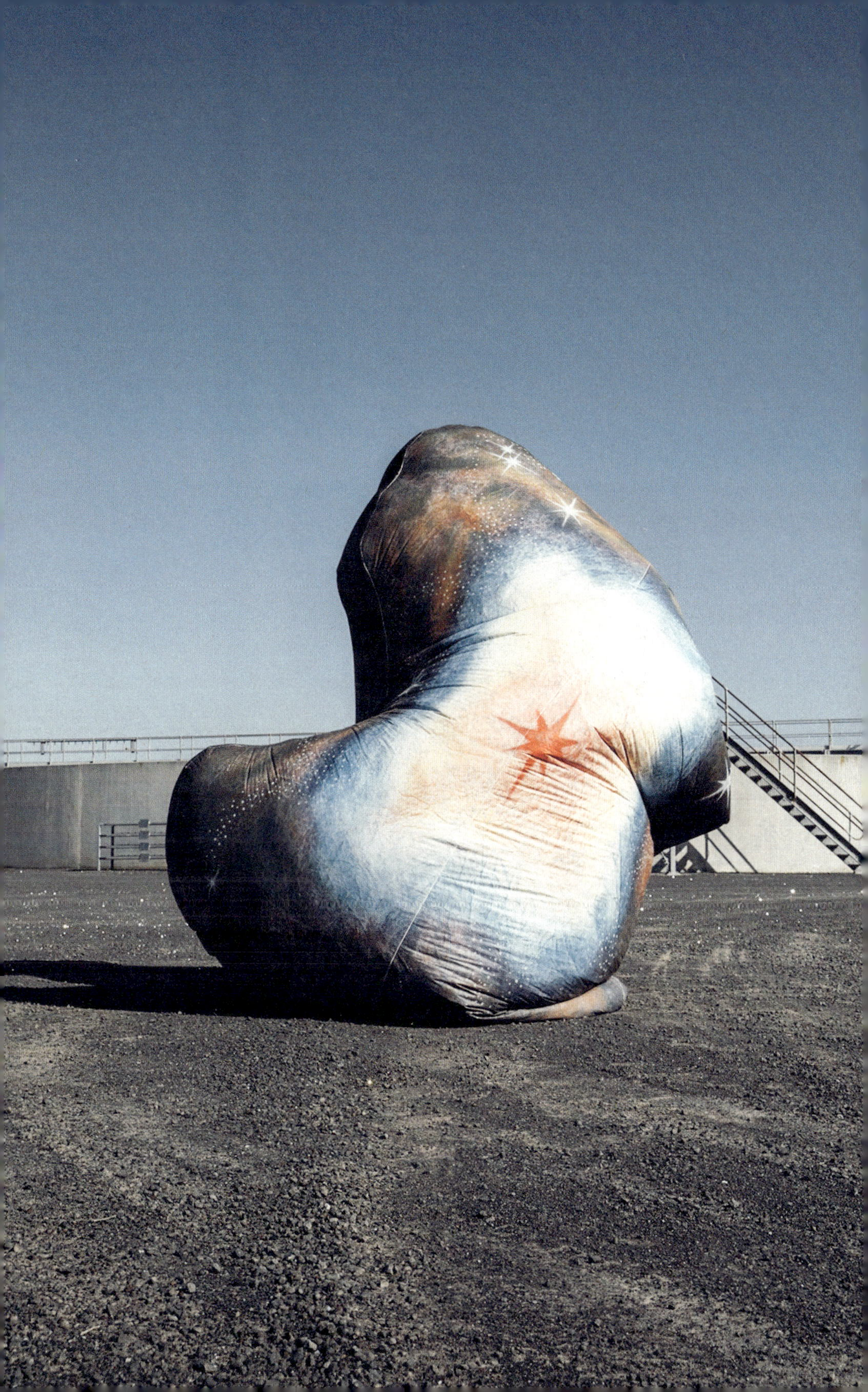

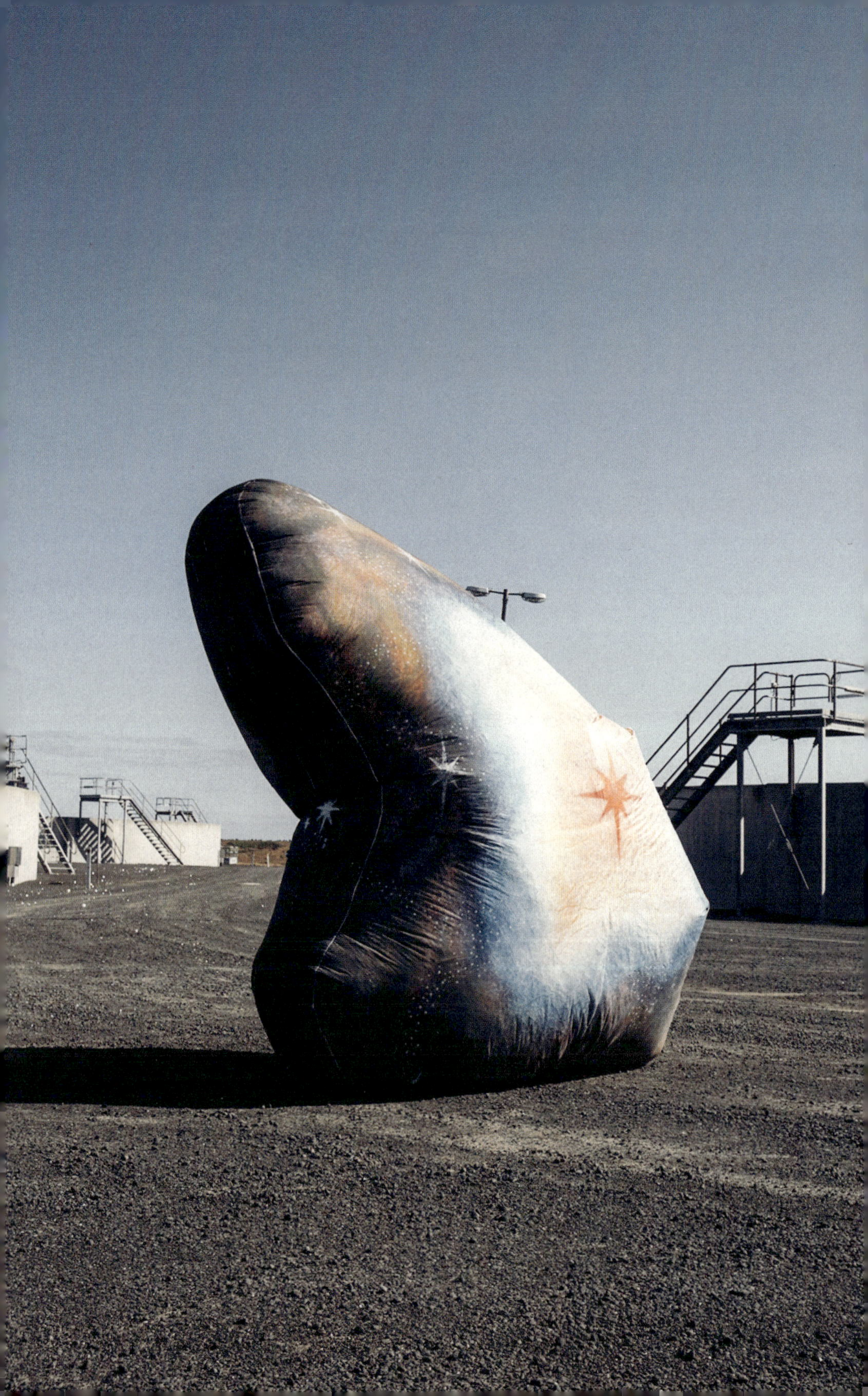

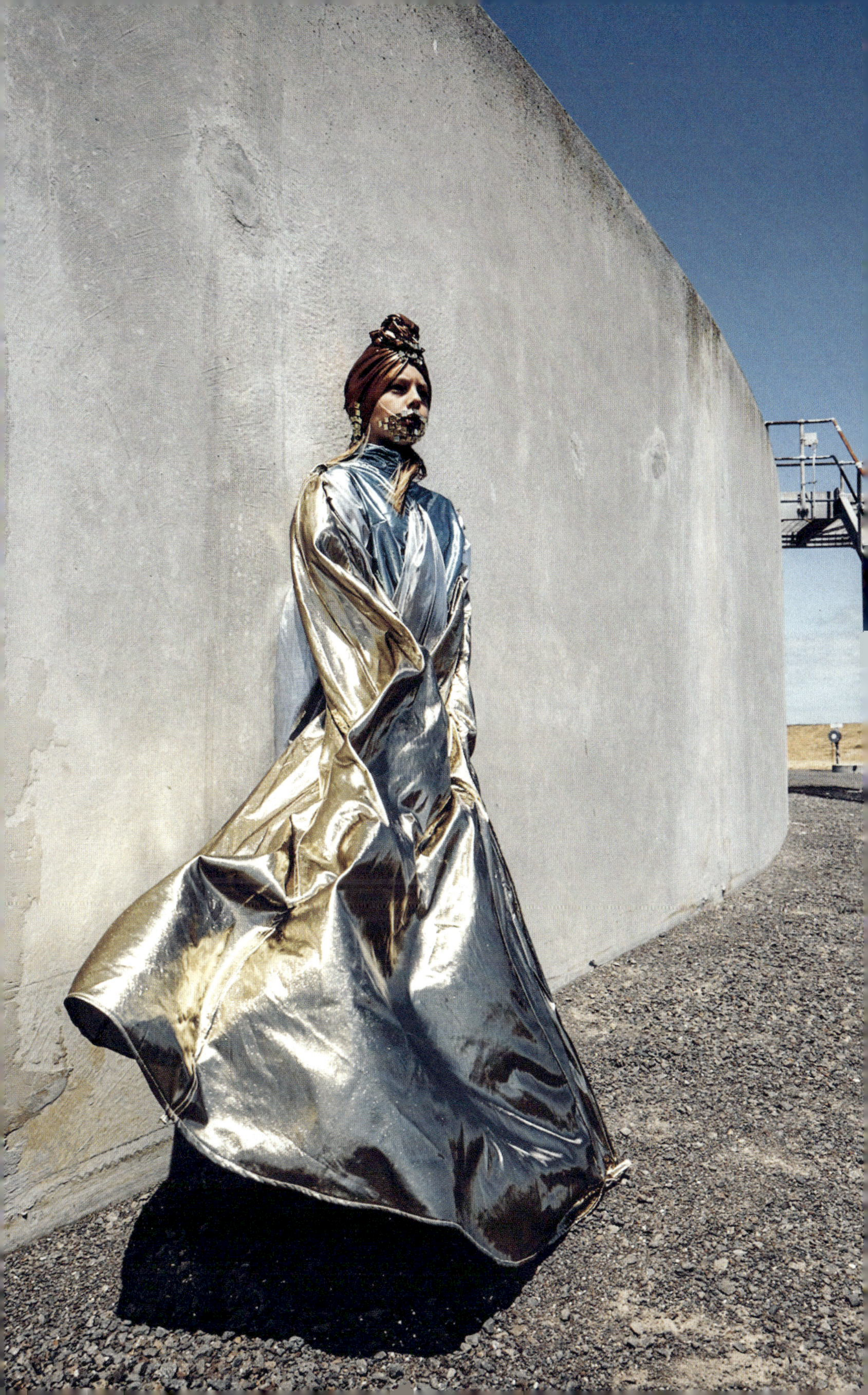

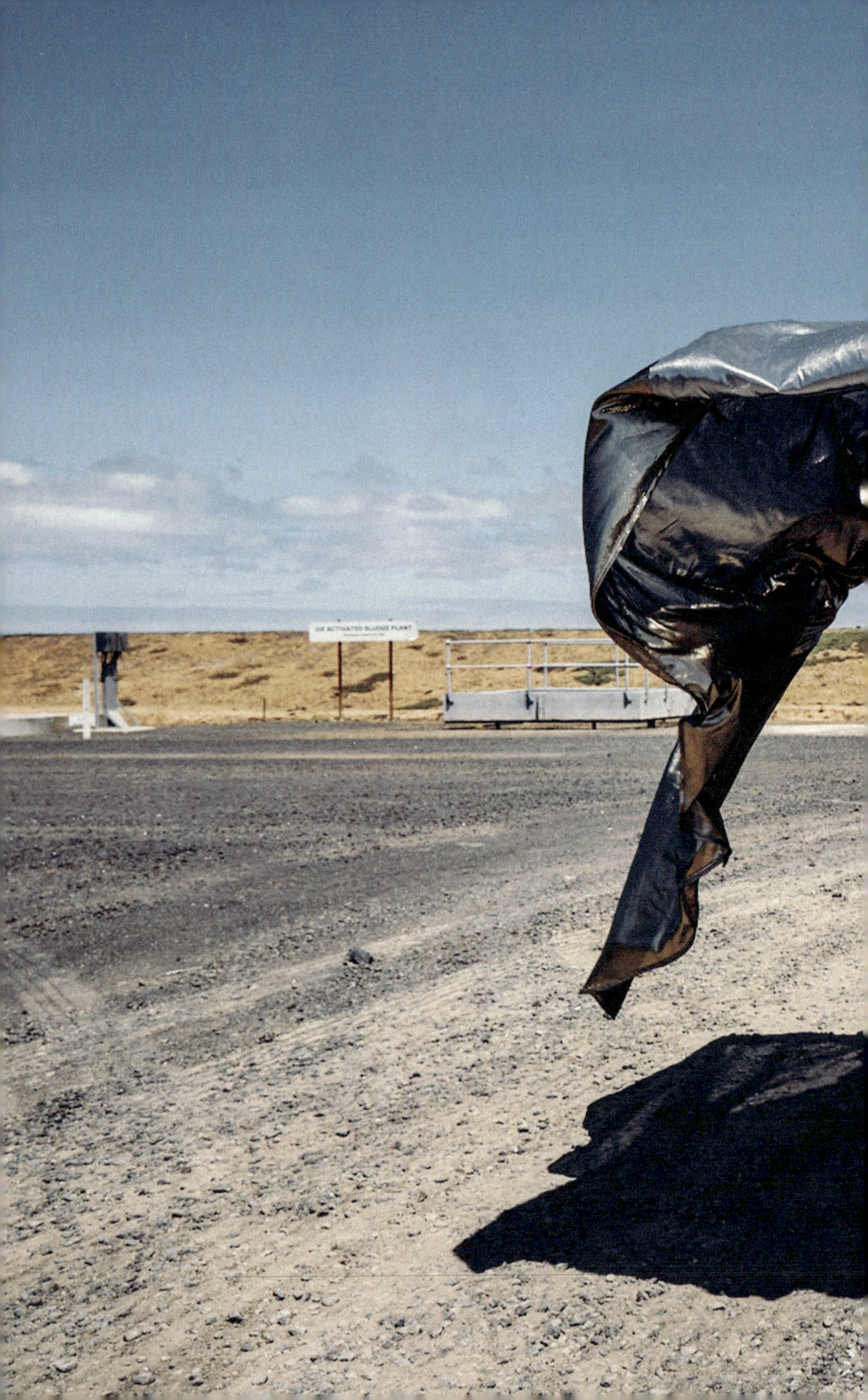
ACTIVATED SLUDGE PLANT

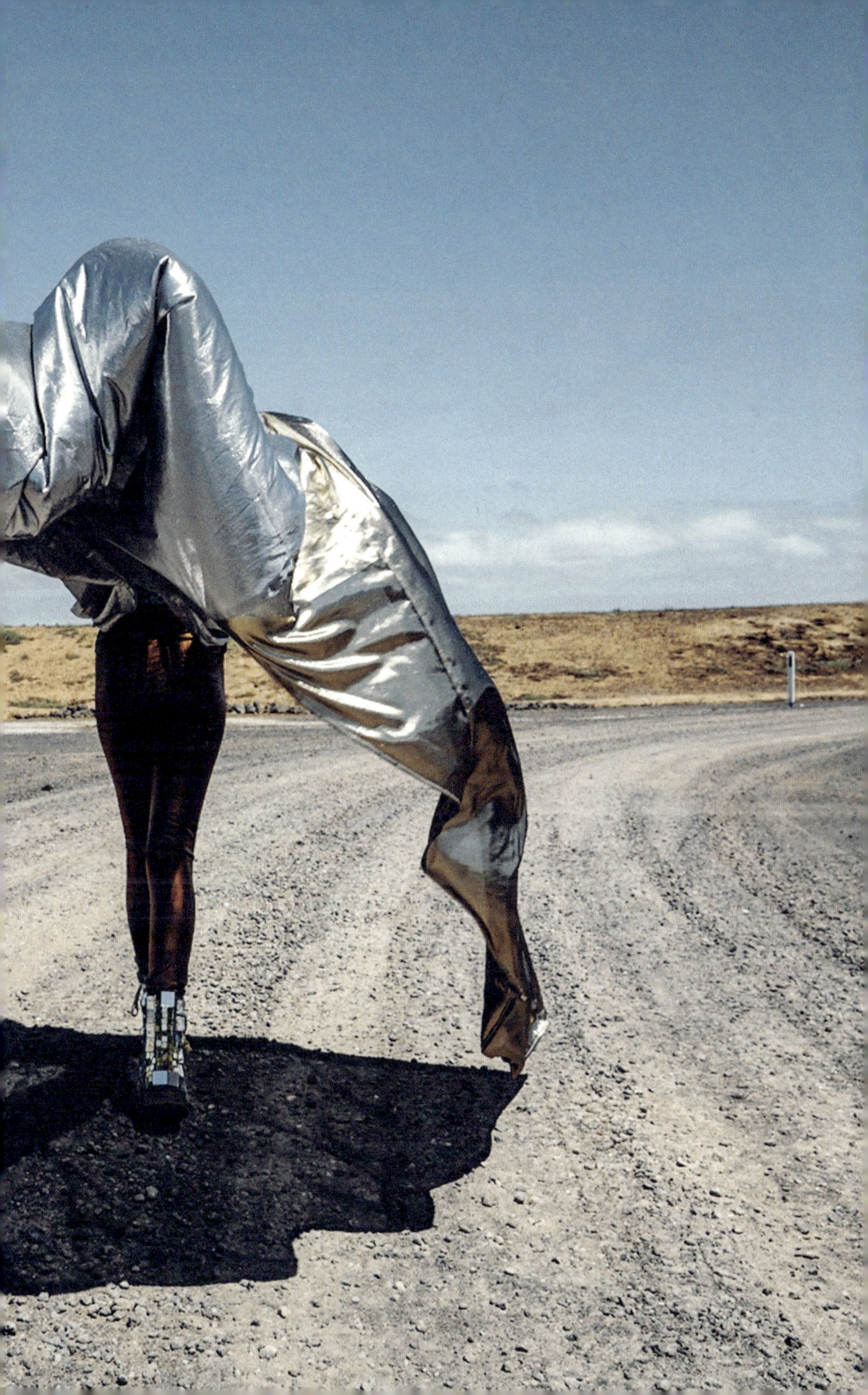

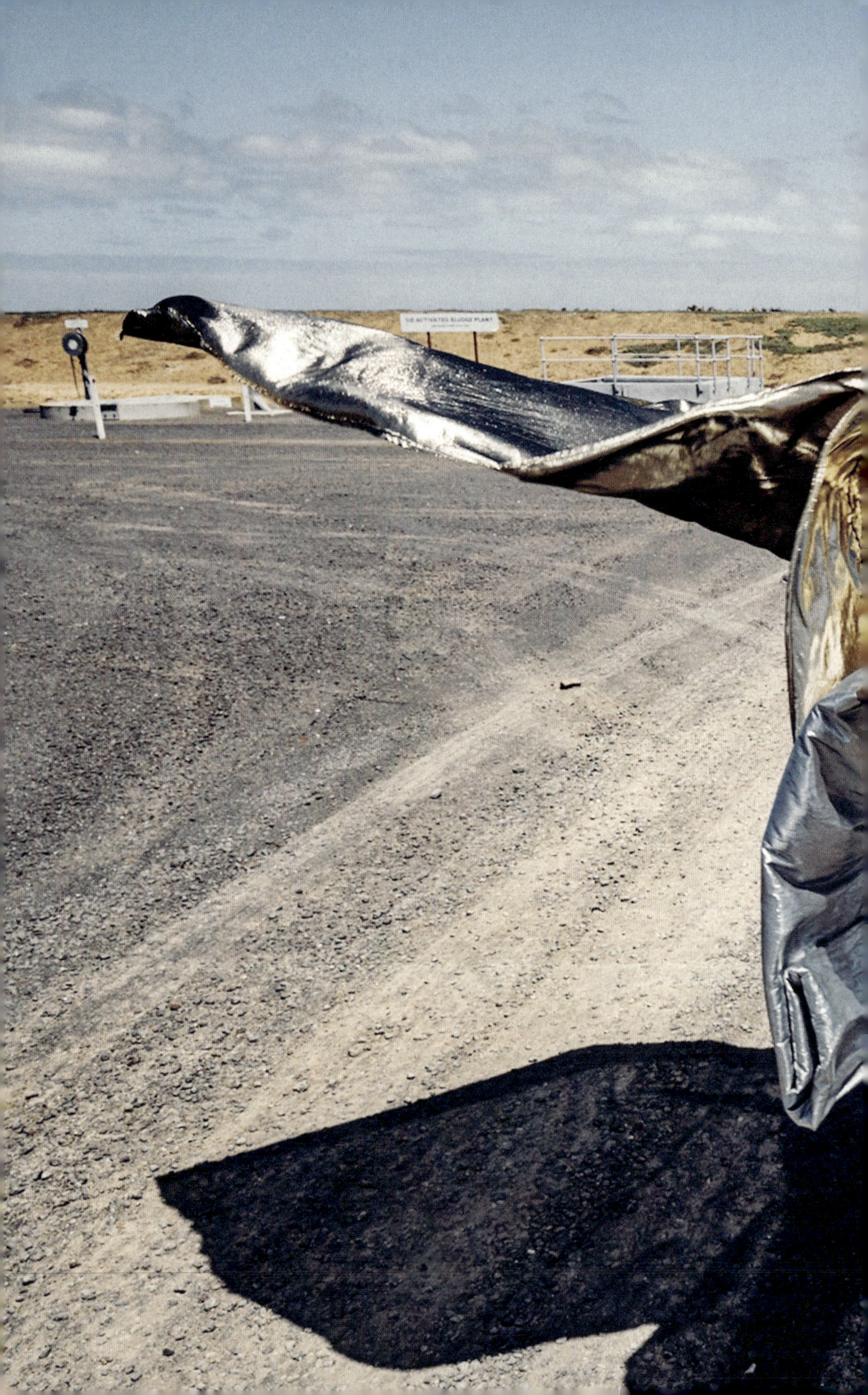
ACTIVATED SLUDGE PLANT

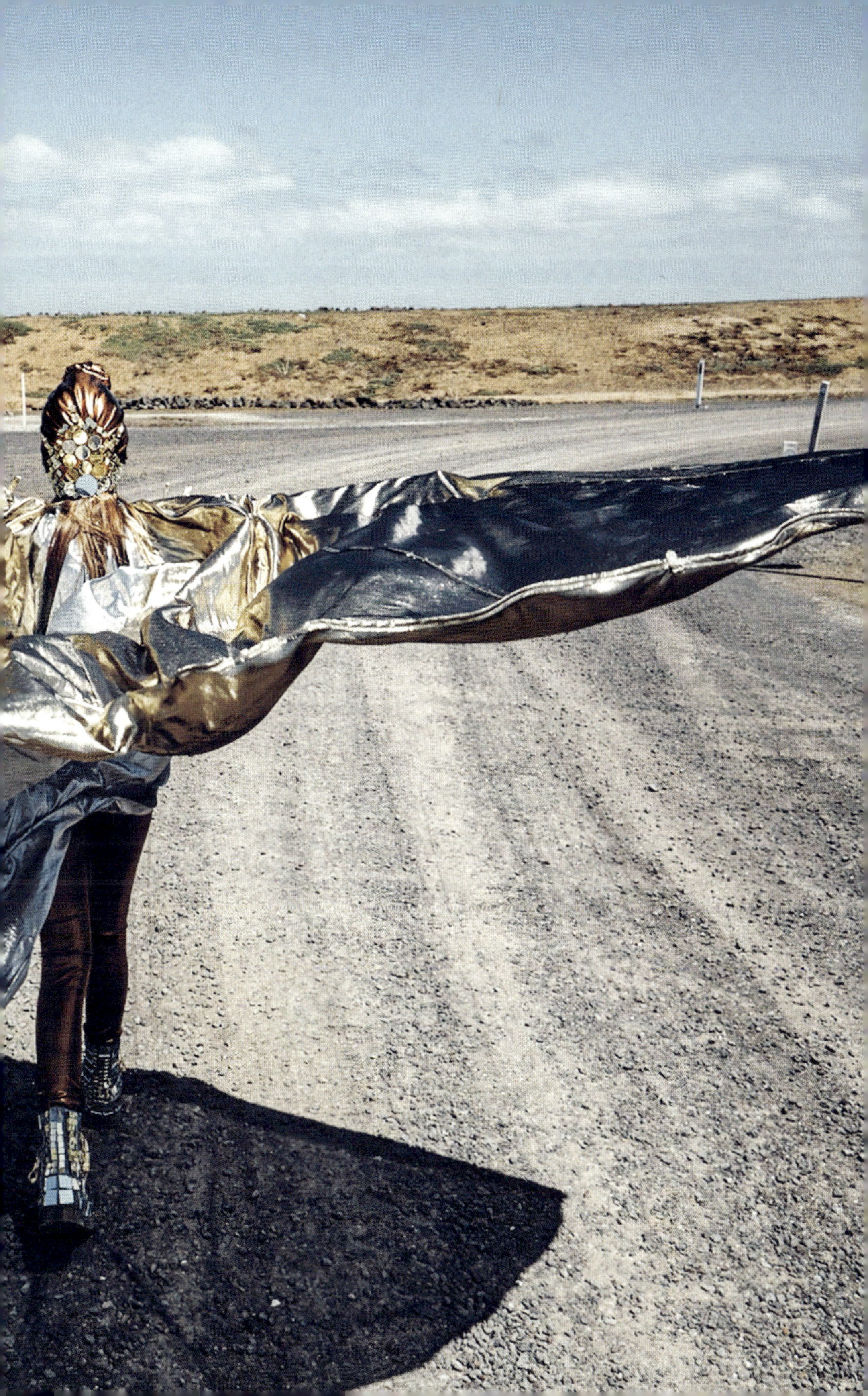

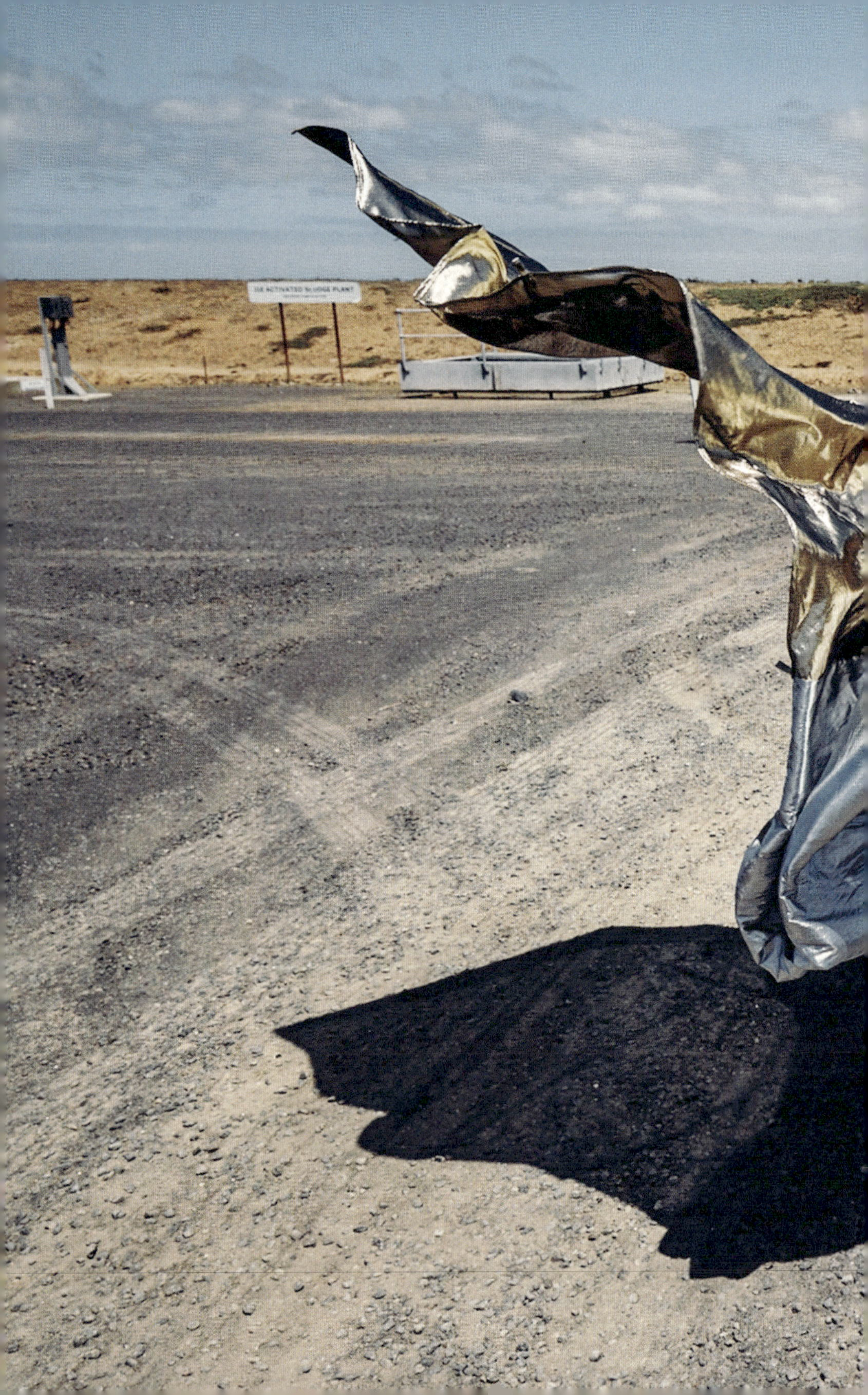
ACTIVATED SLUDGE PLANT

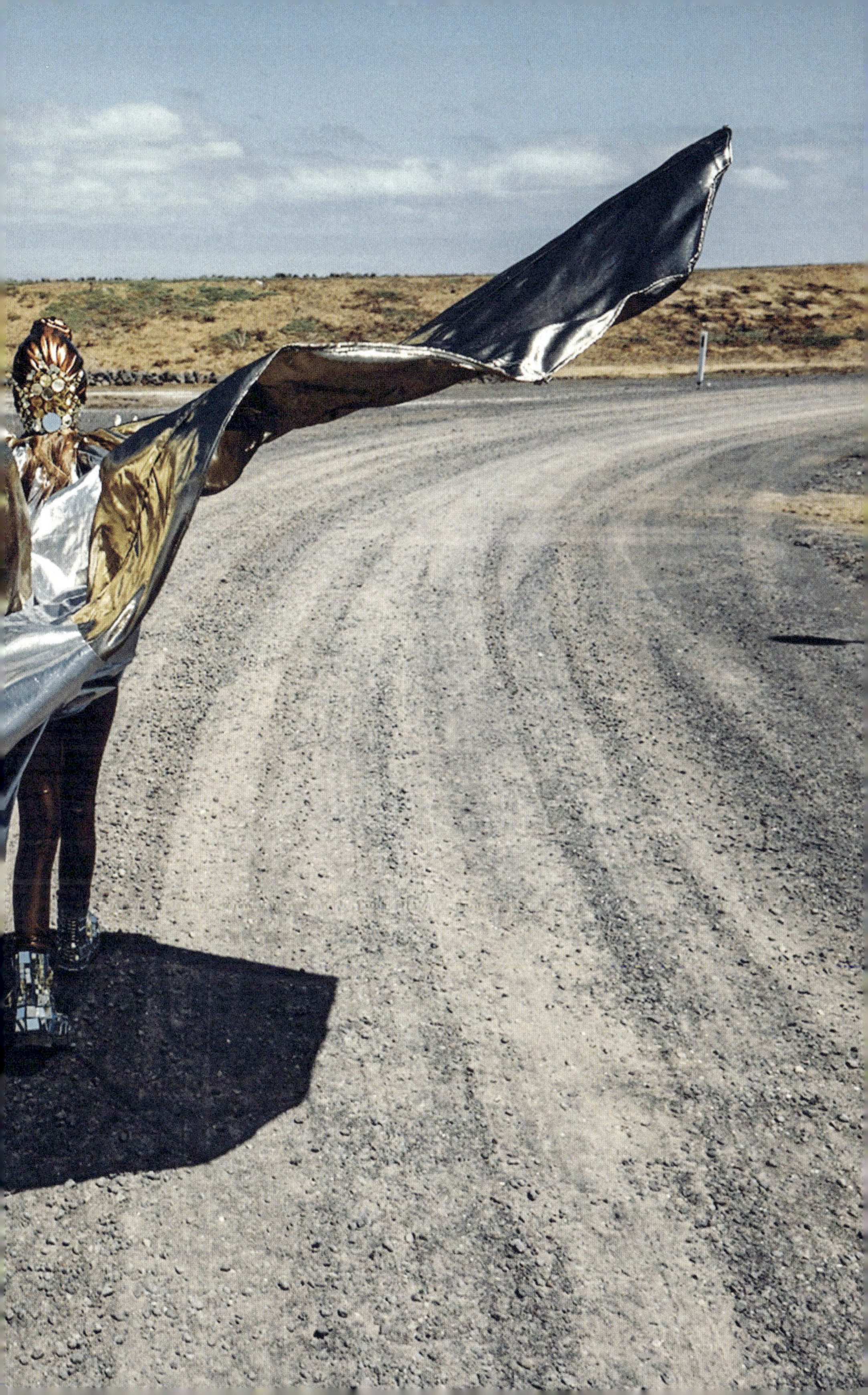

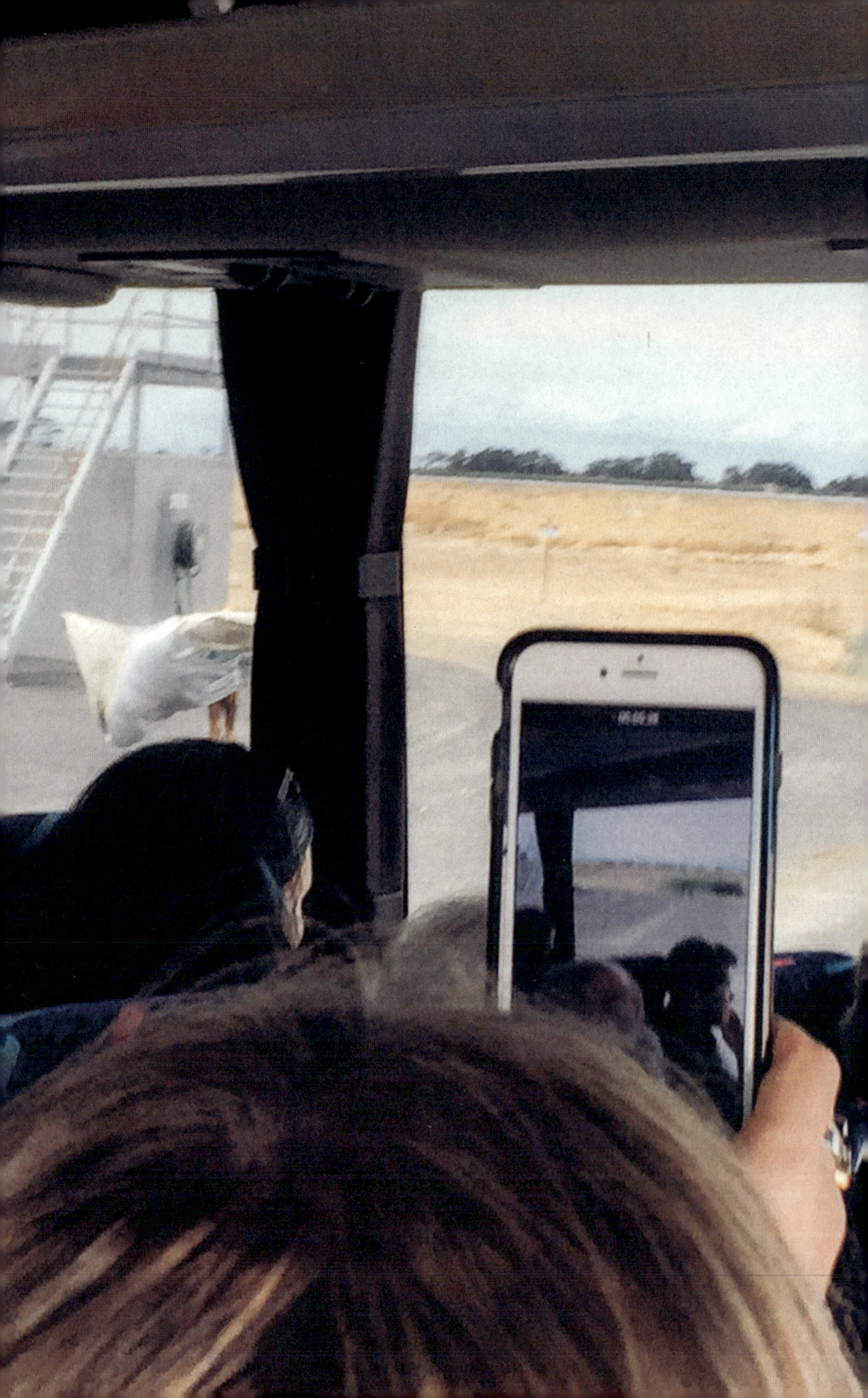

From Treatment to Treated: The Sacred Space becomes a Field of Play

—Cameron Bishop

The conflation of the artist's studio and the hidden network of pipes, tunnels and technologies that deal with our waste gives rise to jokes around the worth of much contemporary art, many of which would be spot on. To be sure, much contemporary art, as the artist and writer Hito Steyerl makes plain, is a 'hash for all that's opaque, unintelligible, and unfair, for top-down class war and all-out inequality'.[1] I argue, though, that curated projects like *Treatment* take contemporary art practice, in its many forms, into cultures and spaces to enrich them in spectacular, irreverent and sometimes undetectable ways. In *Treatment*, a public art project at the Western Treatment Plant (WTP), it was the space and the culture that surrounded it that mattered as much as the site-responsive works that triggered such strong audience reaction and repeated participation. It is with this in mind that, far from treating sewage as a joke in this essay, I make the suggestion that the Western Treatment Plant is a sacred space—for the simple fact that it is ordinarily invisible to us.

Alongside my role as associate curator on *Treatment*, I curated the follow-up exhibition, *Treated*, exhibited at Wyndham Art Gallery from late November 2015 to January 2016. The name suggested that we were at the back end of the process, one that picked up the artefacts (waste products) produced by the temporary art event, *Treatment*, and re-distributed them in the gallery. More than a legacy exhibition, though, it sought to re-present the artefacts from the works at the Western Treatment Plant to further explore them, as a massed collection, in the static space of the gallery. In this layering of object and space, I make the slightly controversial suggestion that art might be seen as a mechanism through which to recast our relationship with what we expel, and the sites we choose to do it in, from the toilet, to the treatment plant, to the gallery and the rubbish tip.

The philosopher Giorgio Agamben suggests that 'defecation ... in our society ... is isolated and hidden by means of a series of devices and prohibitions that concern both behaviour and language'.[2] Our waste is flushed, to be sure, but at the same time, it is separated out and forgotten as something that was once a part of us. When broaching the ordinarily taboo topic of human waste, we often guild our language with humour, which saves us from thinking about it—where it goes, its treatment, and its transformation. For seventy years from the 1890s, on the site of what was once the Metro Farm and subsequently the Weribee Sewage Plant, a community of people engineered, laboured, farmed and played on the land in an effort to treat Melbourne's effluent and to keep diseases, like cholera, in check. Until the 1970s, the public was free to enter, as they are any suburb, until the township at its centre, Cocoroc, was de-commissioned due to the combined attributes of technology and capital. Since the 1970s, the goings-on inside the WTP have been a mystery to those travelling along the road between Melbourne and Geelong. While it is indeed the case that the assorted technologies and engineering are a marvel of modern science, it is the perception we have of it as a closed or hidden space that helps to exacerbate the disconnect between what we consume and what we produce.

This separation also works to elaborate the relationship we have to the notion of the sacred in our society. The philosopher George Bataille took a controversial view of the sacred by suggesting that it designates a space beyond our everyday social- and capital-oriented practices. The sacred constitutes those things that cannot be assimilated or appropriated by conventional, capitalist society including 'the waste products of the human body and certain analogous matter (trash, vermin)...'[3] Sewage, as Agamben asserts, is a field of thought and practice that opens up a 'polar tension between nature and culture, private and public, singular and common.'[4] And it is in this common aspect of waste, realised in a singular, usually private act but re-materialised in shared industry, that we might recognise parallels between what is constituted in the artist's studio and what ends up in the common space of the gallery. For Bataille, our intimate bodily expulsions—from defecation to laughter—constitute a sacred realm disconnected from a 'homogeneous representation of the world'; a representation that emphasises a staid, unchanging value system.[5] Bataille advocates a radical difference that understands the sacred as inhabited by foreign bodies—a space for the rejected, abject other that cannot be appropriated by the conventional order. This goes for the biological body as much as for the social one, which can be imagined as a local community or a nation state. Following Bataille, I suggest that the Western Treatment Plant is perhaps a curious embodiment of a sacred space.

So it is for now, in these precarious times, that we might equate the art gallery with the sewage treatment plant, and, even in a leap of faith, with the detention centre. Each offers a site for the control of potentially disruptive forces, and in this project the Wyndham Art Gallery was conflated with the sacred space of the treatment plant. The two spaces, both public and private, in different ways intersected for a brief moment in time. Objects, performances and social entanglements that would usually only be activated by a space such as a gallery, or in a designated public space of 'allocated participation',[6] used the treatment plant as a site to channel issues related to our waste and our denial of it. The sacred space of the WTP became, if only for a short time, a field of play for the artists. From this came a series of works that spoke to our collective and silenced histories, to our communities, stories, technologies and, in many cases, directly to our emotions. In reaction to the works, people cheered and jeered, sang, laughed and cried—immediate and expulsive reactions to particular elements in the art, caught as they were in the sacred space of the WTP.

Expulsion and Re-presentation

The idea of expulsion can be invoked in many ways: by what we flush in the morning; the sites and practices left behind by new technologies; colonisation and elimination; and in the privileging of resolved object over the processes that brought it into being. *Treated* took from *Treatment* and traced some of the elements from the temporary public art project through the one space—Wyndham Art Gallery. The artworks, preserved and re-presented in various forms including film, photographs, archival collections, objects and seminars, found themselves in the static space of the gallery, but tricked up to mimic and play with certain features from the WTP—such as the beautiful wood panelling in the Melbourne Water Discovery Centre. The gallery exhibition sought to contrast and conflate the sacred glitter and alien figures from Técha Noble's *Passage* with Megan Evans's precious Victorian tear catchers and red beads, which, exhibited in the watertower at Cocoroc, showcased the technology and alien aesthetic that proved powerful in the attempted elimination of the original occupants of the land. Shane McGrath's project, *On the Outer*, in its exploration of stereotype and prejudice through re-animating lost local cultural, and essentially male, practices, finds its critical partner in Spiros Panigirakis's *Scarecrow*'s working party, frustratingly leisurely and without end, and seemingly without purpose. His performance/display abstracted and activated the visual cues of the WTP landscape, Melbourne Water's Discovery Centre and, ultimately, various parts of the Wyndham Cultural Centre, and picked up on the sometimes fine line between labour and leisure (signified in the worker's high-vis dressing gown).

The loss of leisurely practices and its association to site played out in a related but distinctly different form in Catherine Bell's work, *Splashback*. Like McGrath's work, it prevented the viewer from crossing the threshold into actually engaging with a key aspect of it, the renovated children's pool. The audience could only look at how it sparkled in contrast to the adult's empty, dilapidated vessel next to it. In *Treated*, it remained re-presented, but disengaged from site and, like the archival film of the children playing in the pool projected onto the old walls of the swimming shed, a memorial to a time past. The site's serious and newer technologies, activated as sites of play, as in Noble's and Bindi Cole Chocka's work, gave rise to notions of the sacred and the profane as they disconnected the technologies from their practical function, but re-connect the audience with their senses. In answer to both works, it might be said that, sometimes, a poo is just a poo, but in chocolate and glitter our associations to the sites are transformed, if only for a second to transform our perception of the utilitarian technologies of the WTP's Odour Control Facility and aerators. They might also be described as sacred technologies, which, in part, serve to keep ourselves from knowing ourselves. We humans are abject, and like all creatures we are smelly; we are, in our waste, equally expulsive.

Returning the Object to Common Use

The waste disposal centre, once known as the tip (another sacred space), is a site that, like our biological acts, reminds us that we are equal before what we expel—the discarded objects consumer capitalism rejects tells us so. In the early 1980s, one of the most curious and interesting things I did with my father was visit the local tip. On entering the facility, and rounding the dirt mounds, from afar, the discarded objects seemed as if they had been spewed into a singular mass. Initially it looked like hundreds and thousands clinging to a scoop of chocolate yoghurt, but the closer we got to the rubbish heap, the more it looked like what it was—a dirt mound about to trap the objects in stratum, landfill. Equal, in their valueless heap. The tip is gone, moved north to become a 'waste refuse centre'—in its place there are two BP petrol stations, great beacons for the car, and for the spectre of capitalism and progress. In the 1980s, though, figuratively speaking, I would forage for gold. For most people, the objects had moved past their use-by date; for some their obsolescence was their saving grace for they could be re-constituted, and put back into the field of play—spruced up and re-used as what they were (in the case of toys), but for everyday materials, broken up, recombined and given new life, if only for a short time.

To profane means to 'return things to the free use' of all people and, as in the case of children, perform a special kind of 'negligence' on the object, one that Agamben describes simply as 'play'.[7] At the suburban tip the object did not carry the cultural weight that it once had because it had been discarded—it was free to be played with. Taken out of the economic sphere the object at the tip—or any object in a child's hands before they are given over to the abstract concept of value—is profaned because it is no longer understood as property—which signifies status, something owned, or to be exchanged for something of an object of equal symbolic value. The art object in *Treatment*—that is, the thing looked at and participated in from the bus and on the sites around Cocoroc—entered into a new relationship with the space when activated by the audience. Like children, the artist finds new combinations for objects, sites and bodies in the studio. The artists in *Treated* and *Treatment* both celebrated and profaned the sites they worked with. The characters they imagined into being, the objects they constructed, the sites they cleaned and inhabited, are to be read outside of our usual experience of the world—in this case, our economies of consumer culture and waste management. It is in this spirit that, although compacted and re-presented in a gallery format for *Treated*, the artefacts were re-ordered, picking up on a number of the abstract and sometimes literal threads of the works. The objects were not for sale but they are precious for what they conjured, in remembering the project, the site, its inhabitation and the audience reaction.

The academic Gay Hawkins suggests that waste is the 'shit end of capitalism'.[8] We hide it so well now that our infrastructure allows us no view of what we expel, but sometimes it just bubbles up—like a blocked toilet. The Western Treatment Plant receives a good portion of Melbourne's ablutions; it is a technology spread out over ten-and-a-half thousand hectares and, at its scale, the city cannot afford for it to get blocked. It is a wonder for what it does and its technologies are key to our civilisation. As a total work, a sacred technology and a space removed from the people it serves, it is enigmatic, but it hums. From the methane gas extraction, to the on-site engineers and community of workers, and the filtration process of the anaerobic and aerobic ponds, the plant, for all its histories and mythologies, is an infrastructure we should get to know.

The events, *Treatment* and *Treated*, reacquainted many Werribee people with a place they were cut off from in the 1960s. For the audience and participants from elsewhere, the deep connections we have to this place are more abstract, but the artists brought us closer to it in acts of making and presenting a part of ourselves we usually keep hidden. More than cloaking our waste in cheap puns and jokes—however tempting that may be—the artists researched the site for its vexed histories, the various work and social practices it has hosted, its aesthetics and its close ties to the Werribee community. The project demonstrates that Melbourne Water's Western Treatment Plant resonates with us in more ways than one.

1 • • • • Steyerl, Hito, 'A Tank on a Pedestal, Museums in an Age of Planetary Civil War', in *e-flux Journal*, no. 70, 2016.

2 • • • • Agamben, Giorgio, *Profanations*, Zone Books, New York, 2007, p. 73.

3 • • • • Bataille, Georges, *Visions of Excess: Selected Writings, 1927–1939*, University of Minnesota Press, Minneapolis, 1985, p. 142.

4 • • • • Agamben, *Profanations*, p. 73.

5 • • • • Bataille, *Visions of Excess*, p. 97.

6 • • • • Bishop, Claire, *Artificial Hells: Participatory Art and the Politics of Spectatorship*, Verso, London, 2012, p. 283.

7 • • • • Agamben, *Profanations*, p. 73.

8 • • • • Hawkins, Gay, *The Ethics of Waste: How We Relate to Rubbish*, Roman and Littlefield, Oxford, 2006, p. vii.

SIX PUBLIC ARTWORKS

West of Wonka

Bindi Cole Chocka

Willy Wonka: [singing] If you want to view paradise, simply look around and view it. Anything you want to, do it; want to change the world... there's nothing to it.

In 2008, I invited my father (Uncle Bryon Powell) to sit for a portrait as part of a new photographic series I was creating titled 'Not Really Aboriginal'. I suggested that he might like to choose the location. He took me to the Werribee Treatment Plant (WTP) grounds and chose a picturesque spot overlooking the Werribee River, which is the border to our traditional Wadawurrung country. At the time I remember thinking how beautiful, lush and fertile this personally significant land was.

In 2015, I was invited to produce a work for *Treatment*. At the same time, I won the inaugural artist-in-residence position at WTP, working in conjunction with the Wyndham Art Centre. Consequently, I had the opportunity to spend months in wide-eyed exploration of the massive site, most often alone and for hours at a time.

Willy Wonka: Little surprises around every corner, but nothing dangerous. So don't be alarmed.

As I began to explore and learn, I became surprisingly passionate and started to feel like a little girl, an adventurer in a novel, regularly allowing myself to get lost while letting my imagination run wild.

Willy Wonka: [singing] There is no life I know to compare with pure imagination. Living there, you'll be free if you truly wish to be.

The thing I didn't realise about the plant is that most of the land (which is almost the size of Malta) is open, untouched, sublime beachside country. The plant's lagoons, grasslands and coastline provide an ideal habitat for birds with a constant water supply, abundance of food, and little intrusion from humans. In comparison, there's a small (but highly fascinating) presence of industry so it's easy to almost forget that you are on a poo farm. Yet, for all its beauty and charm, there's really no denying that fact and I couldn't shake the idea of the similarity between the WTP and *Charlie and the Chocolate Factory* by Roald Dahl. A magical place that only a few ever gain access to, of absolute intrigue and mystery but with a dark and dangerous (and occasionally smelly) undertone.

Mrs. Gloop: What a disgusting, dirty river!
Mr. Salt: Industrial waste, that. You've ruined your watershed Wonka: it's polluted.
Willy Wonka: It's chocolate.
Veruca Salt: That's chocolate?
Charlie Bucket: That's chocolate!

As an only child with a propensity for escapist novels, I read voraciously when I was young. I considered my books my friends and would reread the same book over and over. Children's literature has always been full of dangerous and subversive material. Writers such as Roald Dahl and the Brothers Grimm created worlds inhabited by evil villains, fairies, Oompa Loompas and talking animals, where innocents are tested and bravery and honesty rewarded. Danger lurks around every corner and nothing is quite as it seems. 'The danger doesn't have to be present explicitly but can be more ambiguous'.[1] This is done well by Roald Dahl, who also includes a healthy dose of humour. It was this idea that kept coming back to me as I ventured through the plant, a forbidden, dark and twisted place that looks seductively sweet with its beautiful and captivating landscapes.

Willy Wonka: No other factory in the world mixes its chocolate by waterfall.
[gently whispering in Mr. Salt's ear]
Willy Wonka: But it's the only way if you want it just right.

As a result, I created two distinct artworks. The first, a twin set of scratch'n'sniff cards, reminiscent of both my childhood and the scratch'n'sniff wallpaper in the 1971 American musical movie, *Willy Wonka and the Chocolate Factory*, directed by Mel Stuart and starring Gene Wilder. The audience was instructed to activate (scratch) the cards at certain intervals. I received feedback that participants were hesitant to scratch the cards as they believed they would release the smell of excrement. I loved this element of danger and messing with the audience's minds, just as Roald Dahl did with Willy Wonka. Of course, the smell was chocolate, another layer of the twist—looking at poop while inhaling a sweet-smelling cocoa scent. 'Employed correctly, danger is evocative and powerful, and oftentimes resides alongside magic'[2]

Willy Wonka: A little nonsense now and then is relished by the wisest men.

The second project was a video landscape inspired by the psychedelic and seemingly dangerous boat ride taken down the chocolate river in the same movie. Hours of footage of the WTP's landscapes were edited down, manipulated and overlaid with an evocative soundscape. This was situated as the final stop on the tour and seemed a fitting and mesmerizing end to the experience.

> *Willy Wonka: There's no earthly way of knowing | Which direction they are going... There's no knowing where they're rowing...*
> *Mr. Salt: [weakly echoing] Rowing...*
> *Willy Wonka: Or which way the river's flowing... Is it raining, is it snowing? | Is a hurricane a-blowing?*
> *[sharp gasp]*
> *Willy Wonka: Not a speck of light is showing | So the danger must be growing... Are the fires of Hell a-glowing? | Is the grisly Reaper mowing? | Yes! The danger must be growing | 'Cause the rowers keep on rowing |*
> *[practically screaming]*
> *Willy Wonka: And they're certainly not showing | Any sign that they are slowing!*
> *[lets out a high-pitched, almost unearthly scream]*

Dangerously dark imagery inspires the imagination, yet, for all of the danger awaiting any visitor to the Plant, it remains one of the most unspoiled and beautiful areas of land I've experienced in Victoria.

1 • • • • Richter, Barbara B., 'Roald Dahl and Danger in Children's Literature', *Sewanee Review*, vol. 123, no. 2, 2015, p. 325.

2 • • • • ibid.

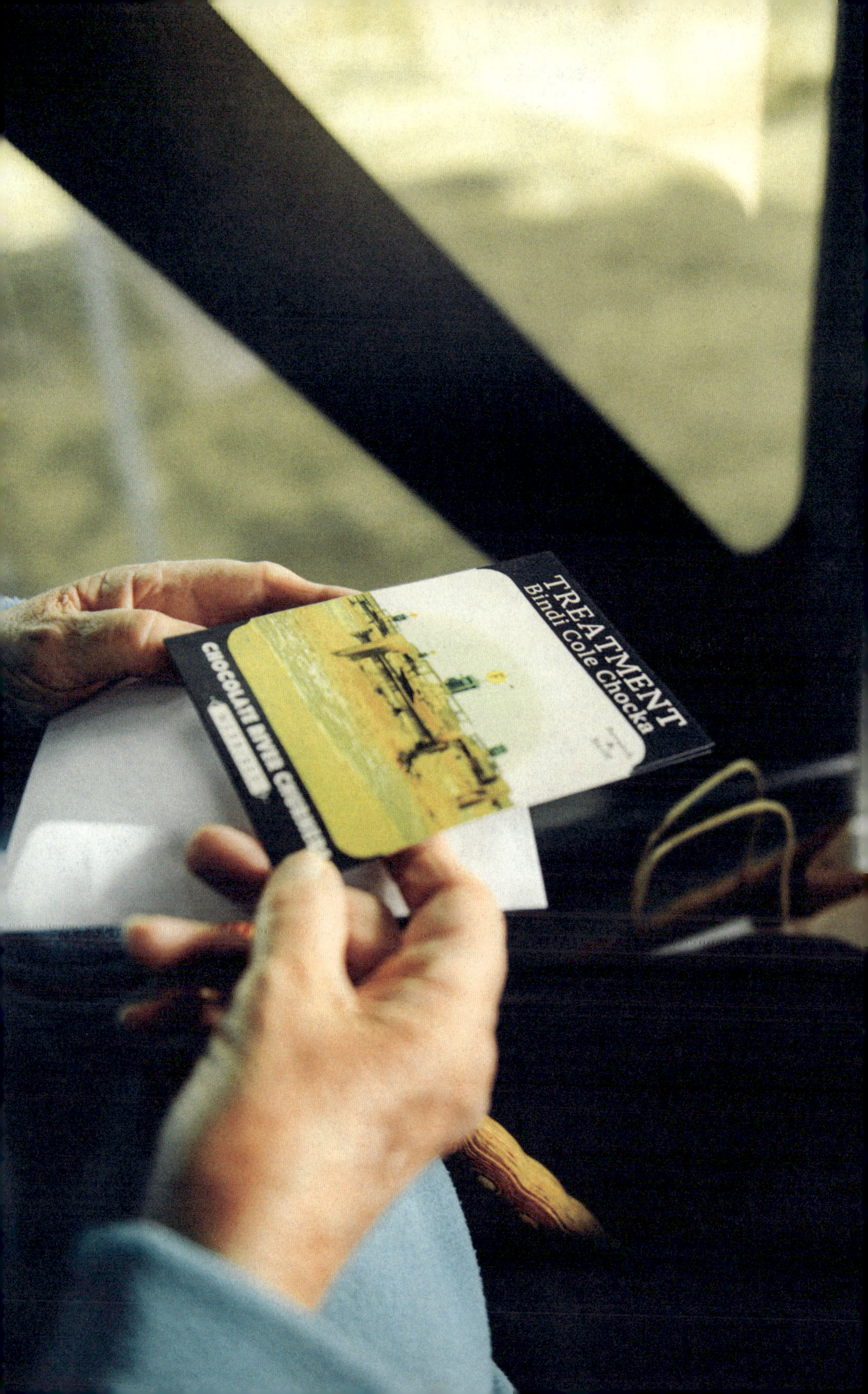
TREATMENT
Bindi Cole Chocka

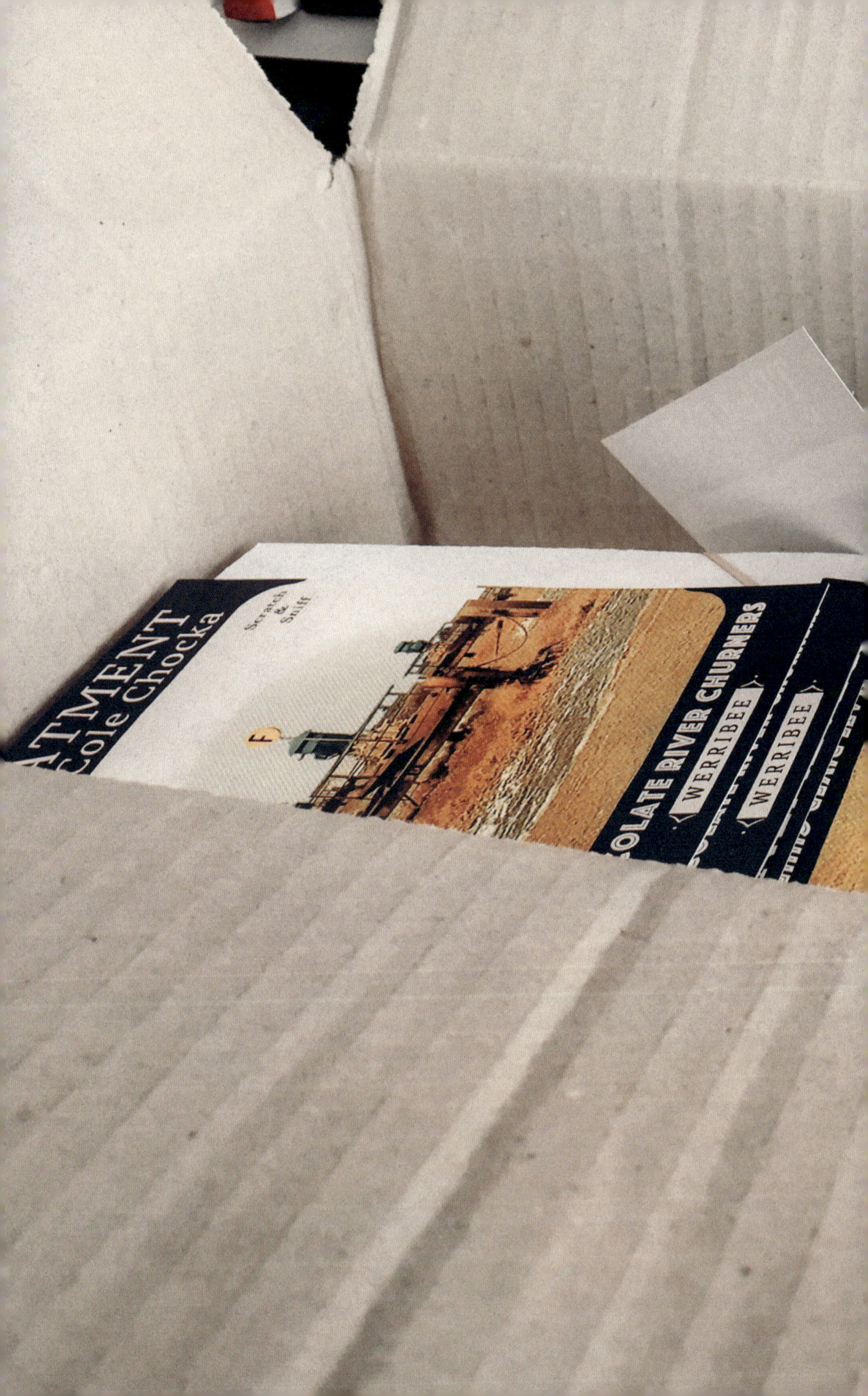
Scratch & Sniff
WERRIBEE
WERRIBEE

TREATMENT
Bindi Cole Chocka

Scratch
&
Sniff

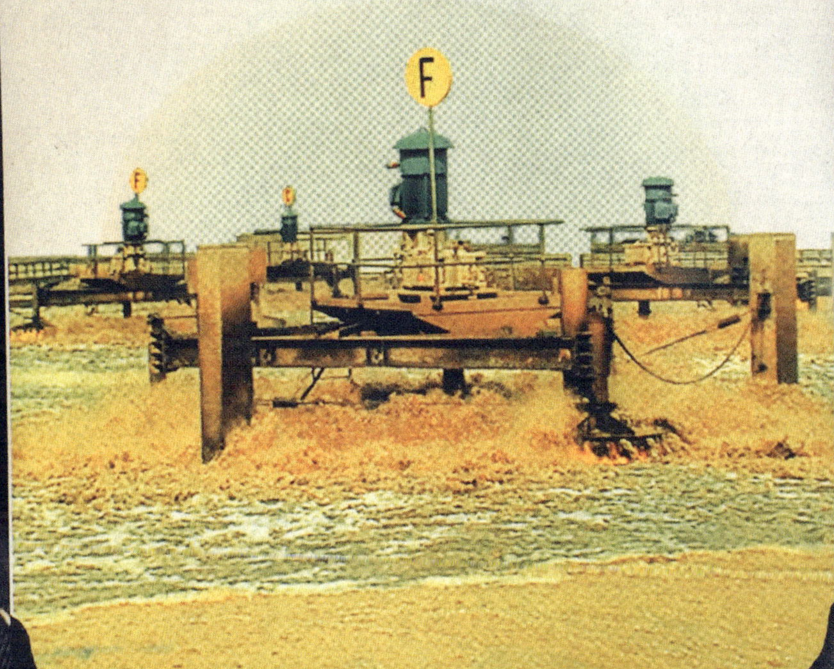

CHOCOLATE RIVER CHURNERS

WERRIBEE

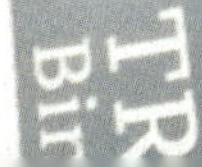

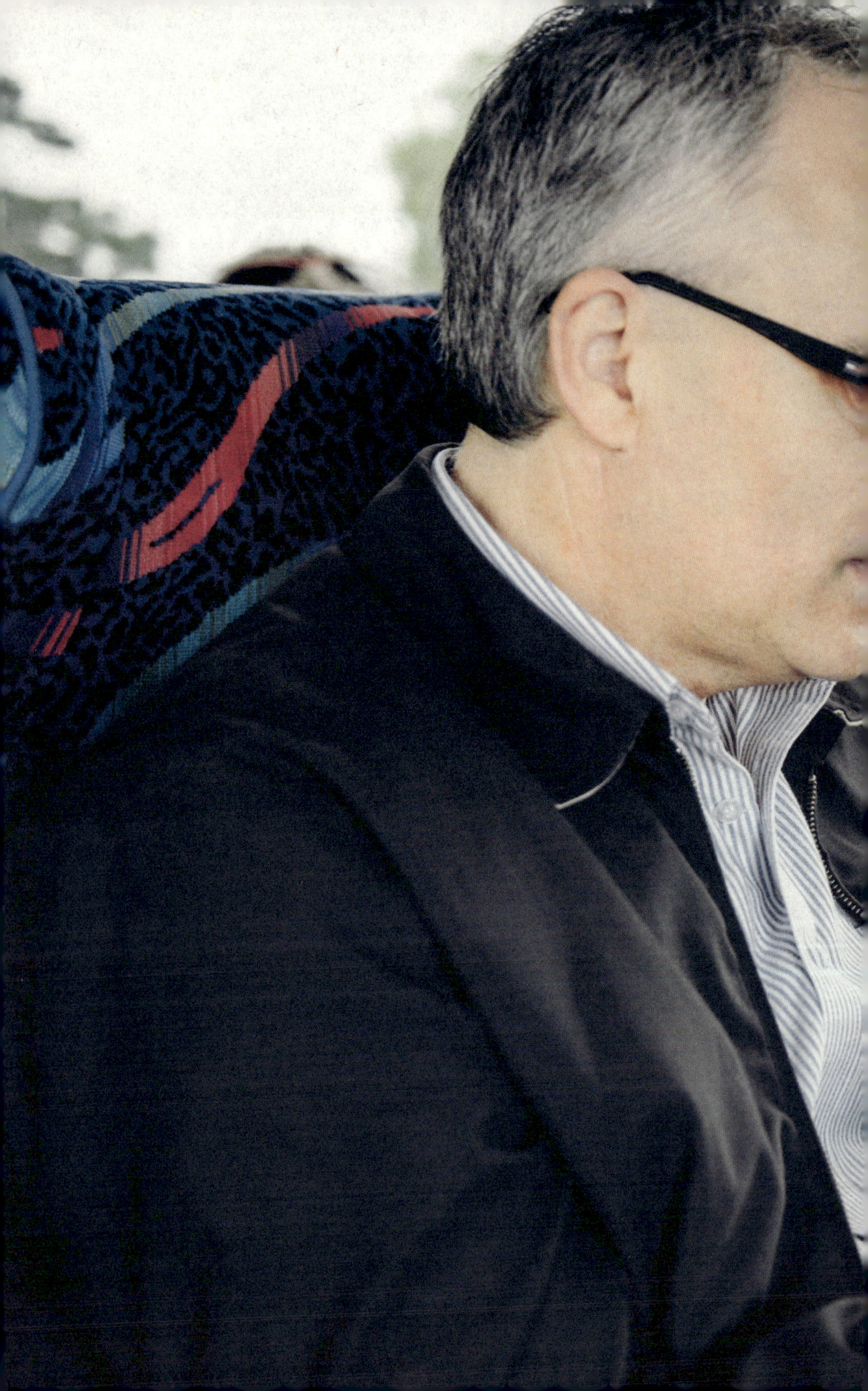

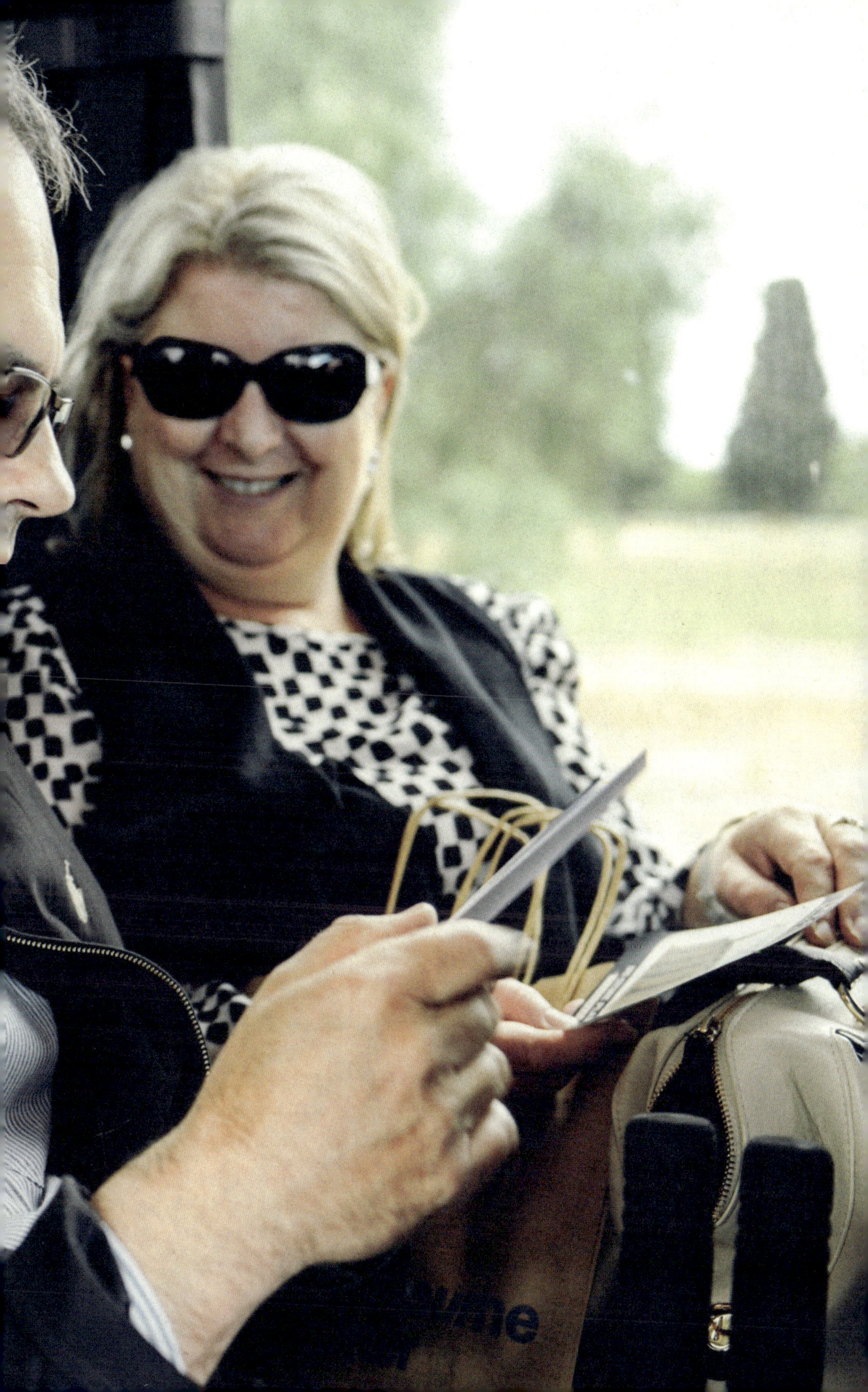

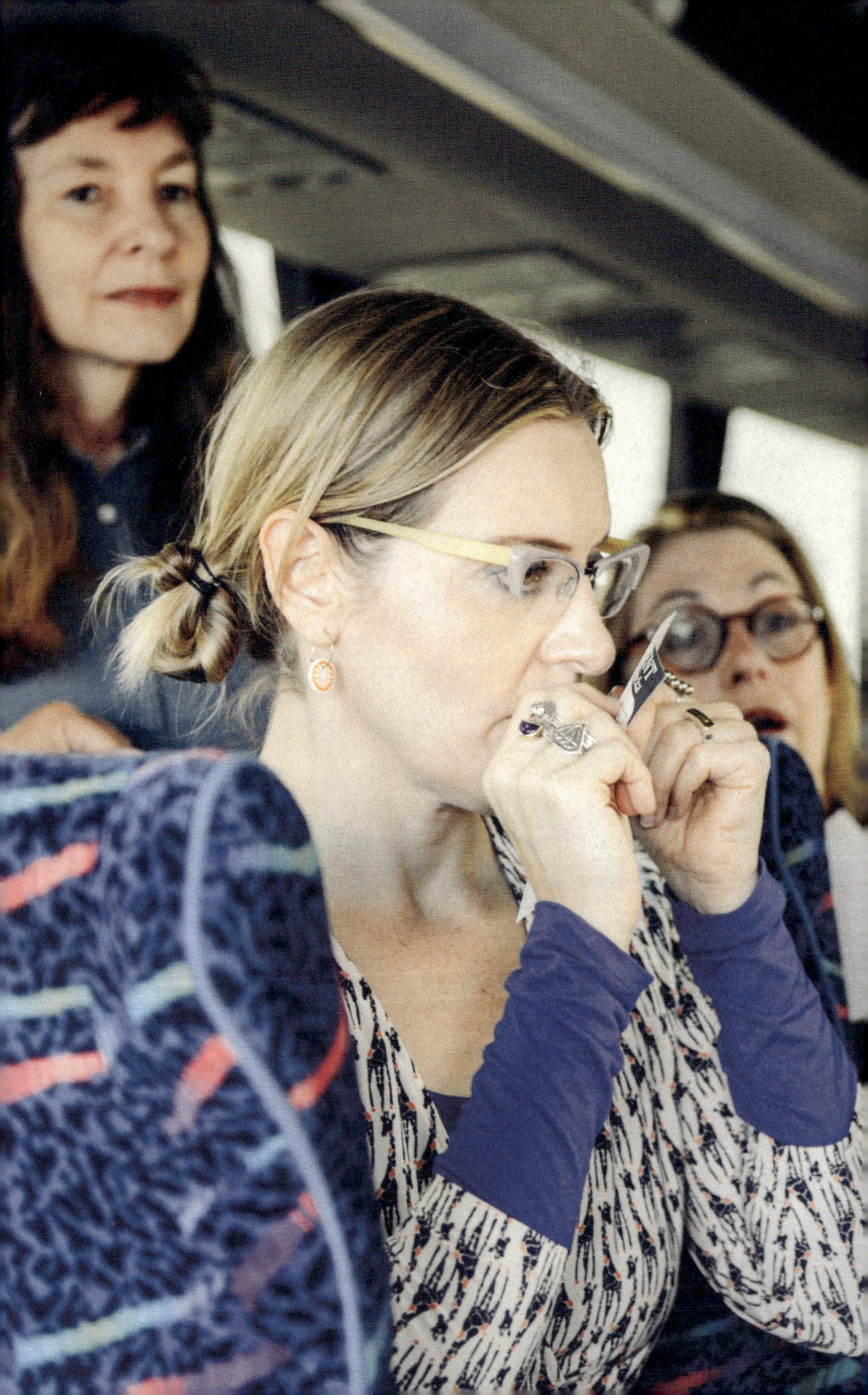

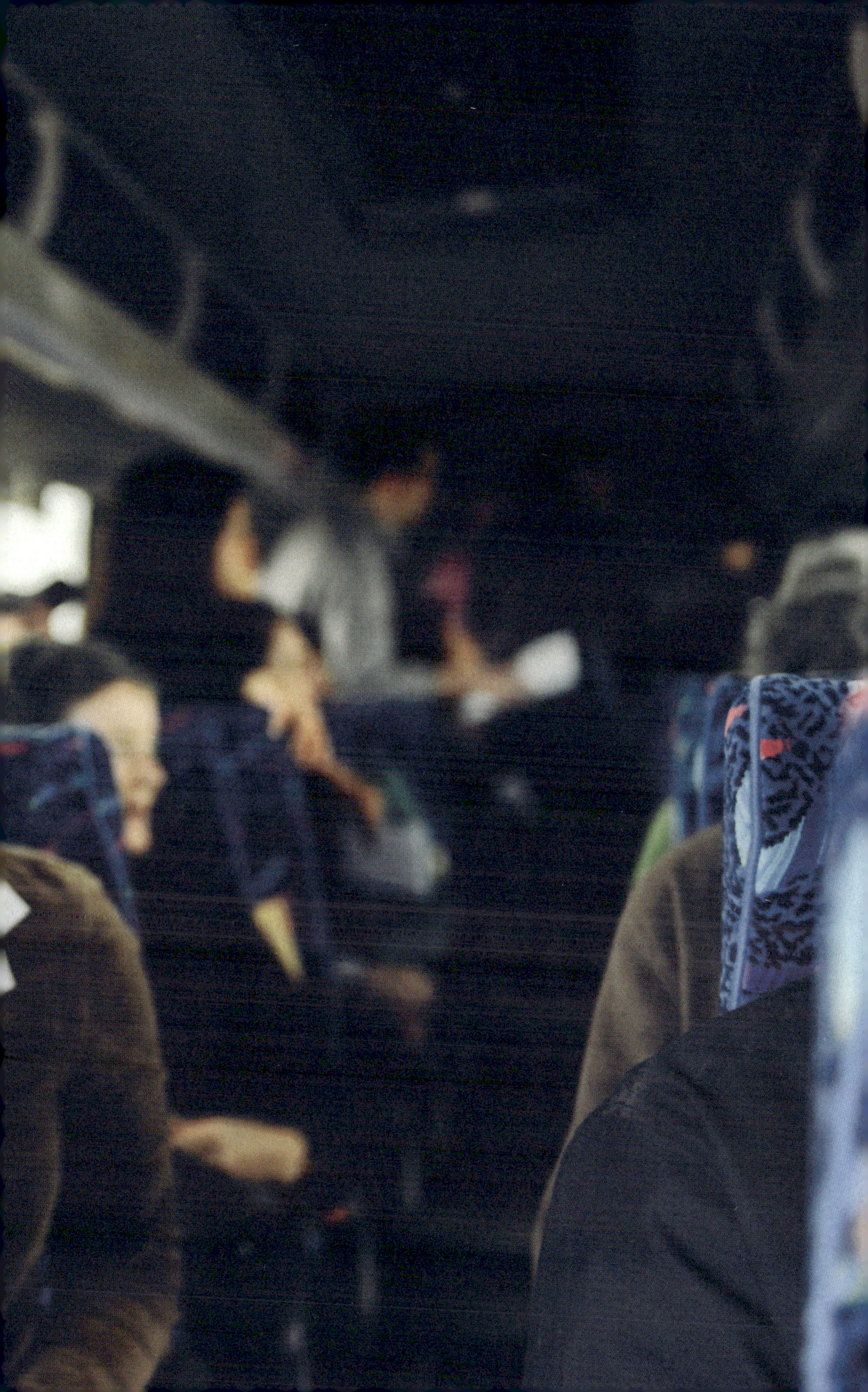

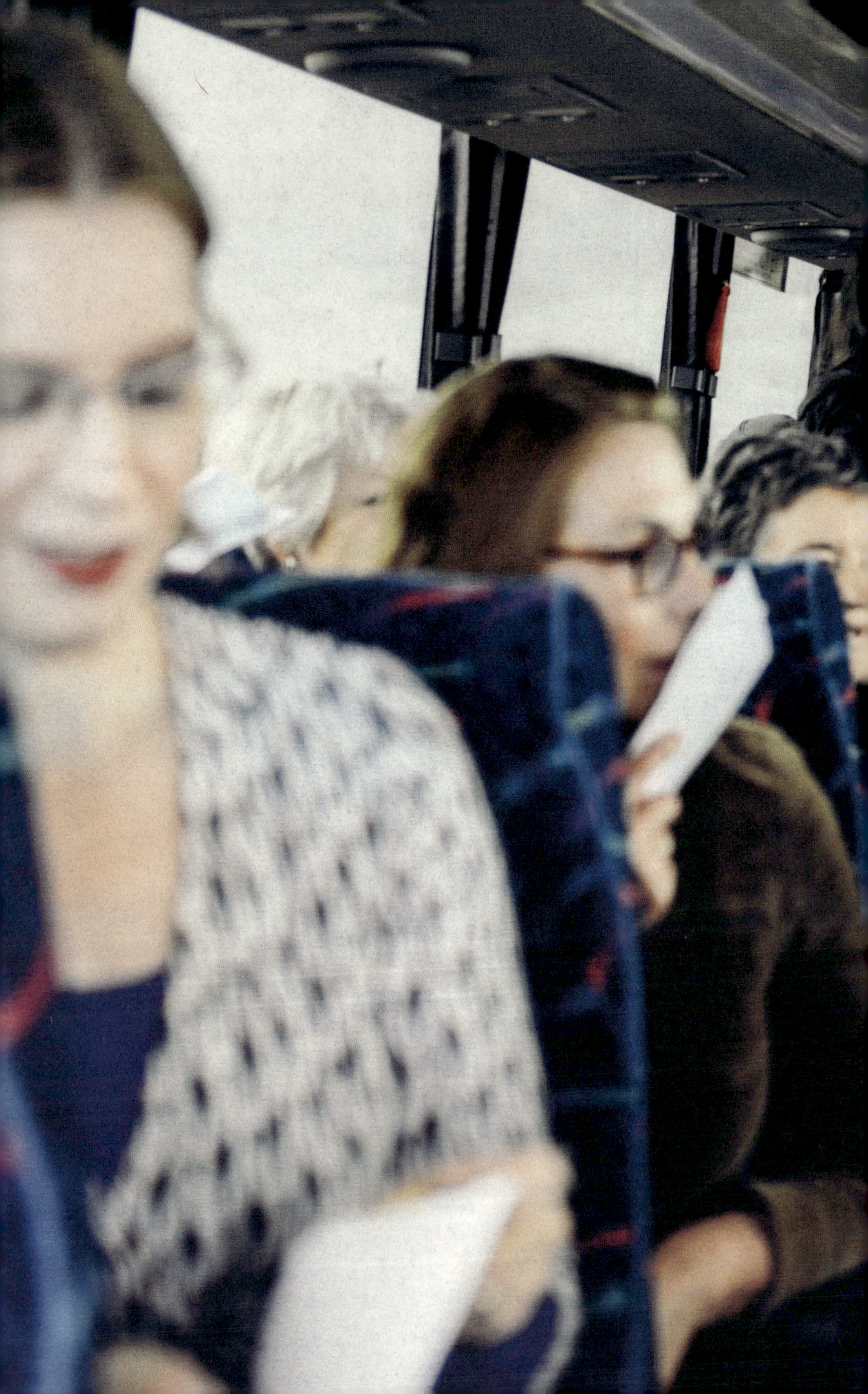

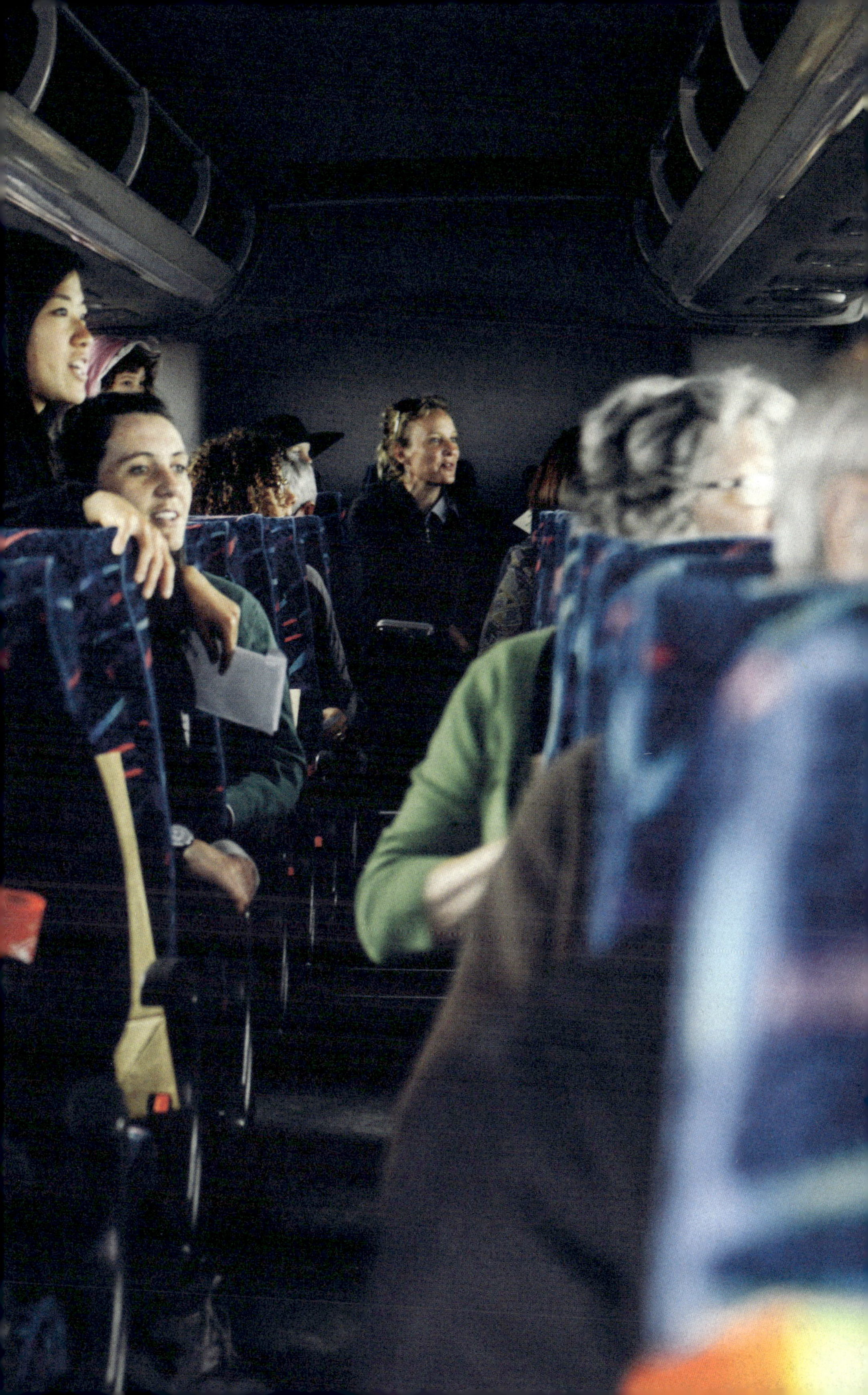

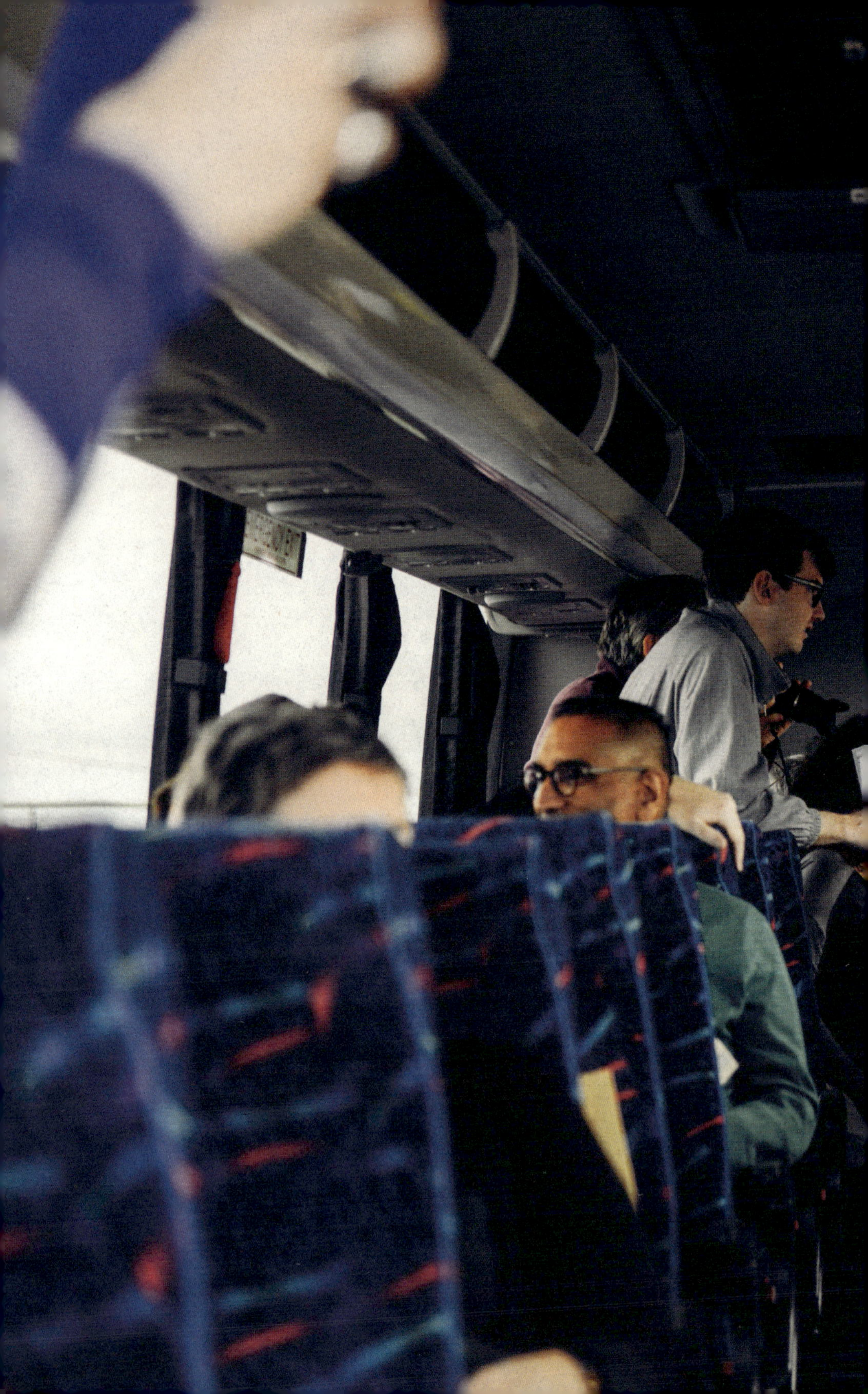

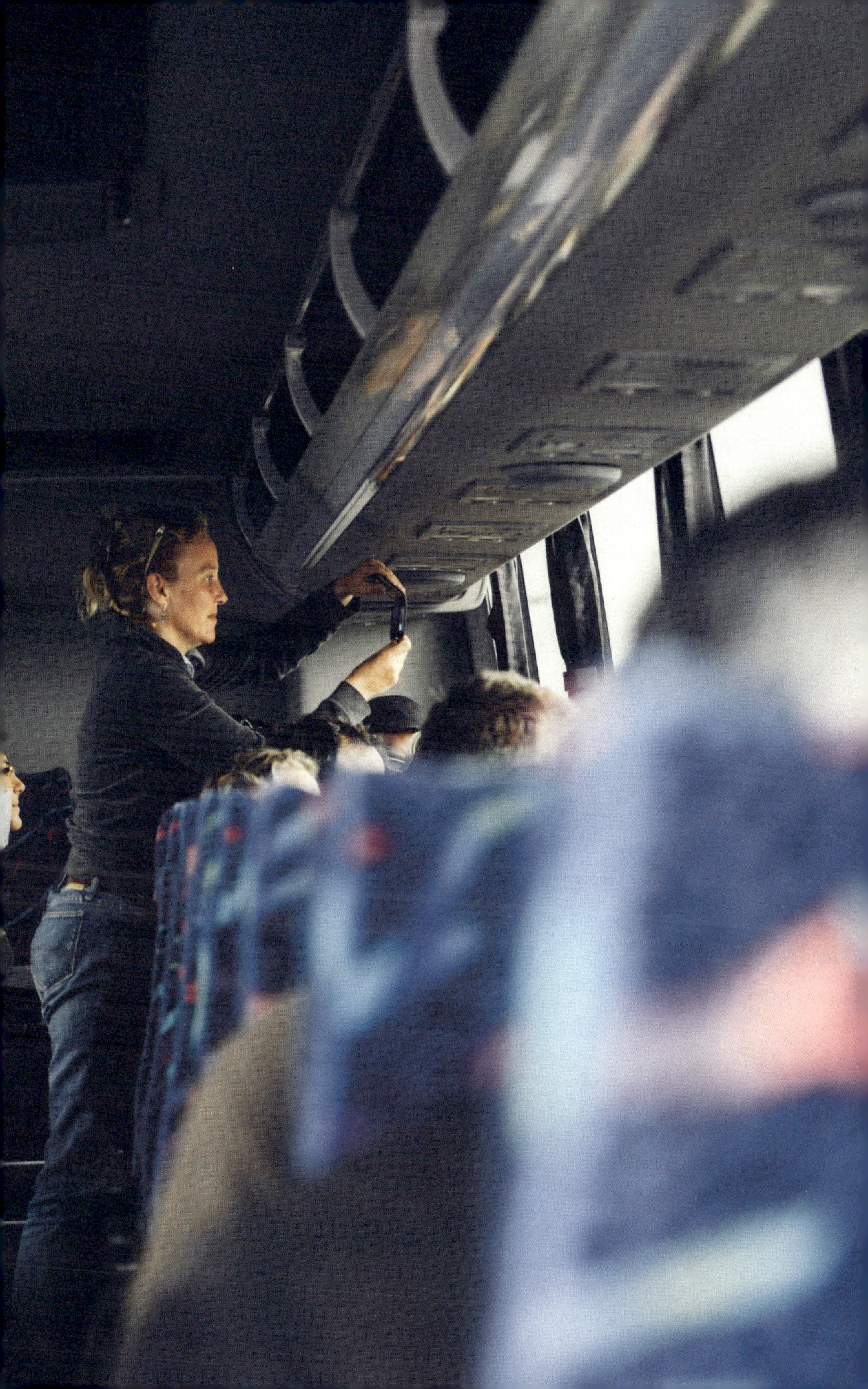

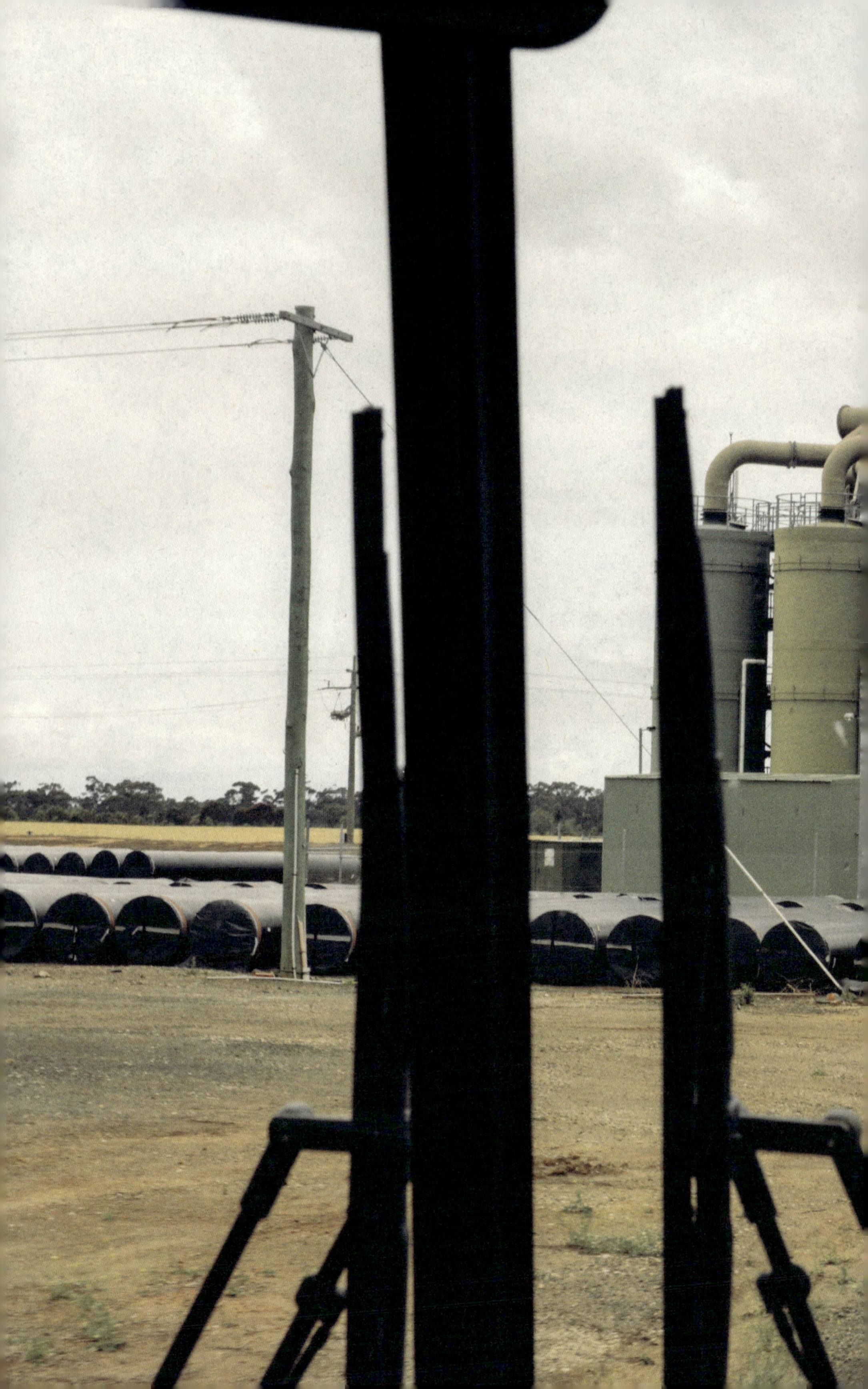

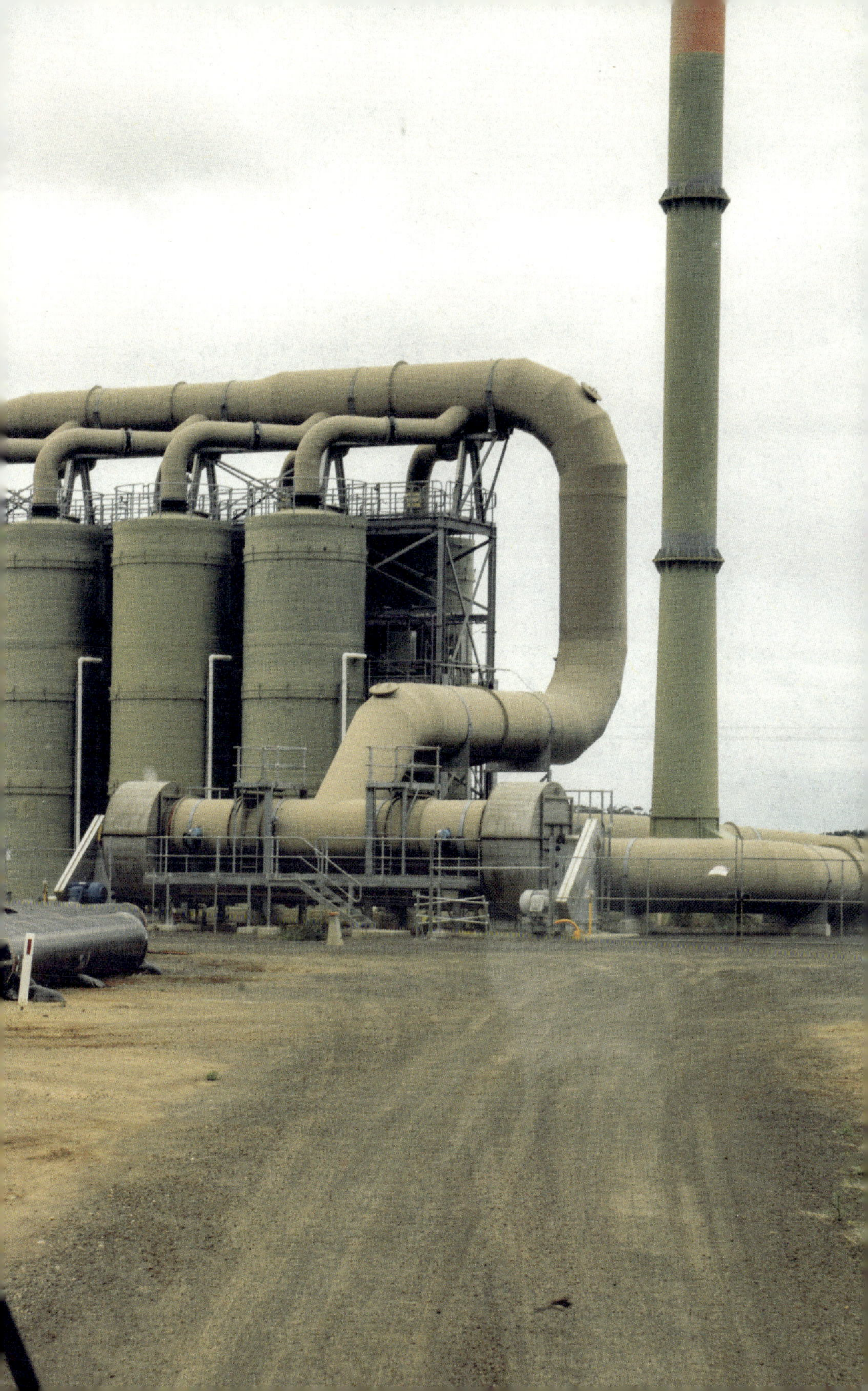

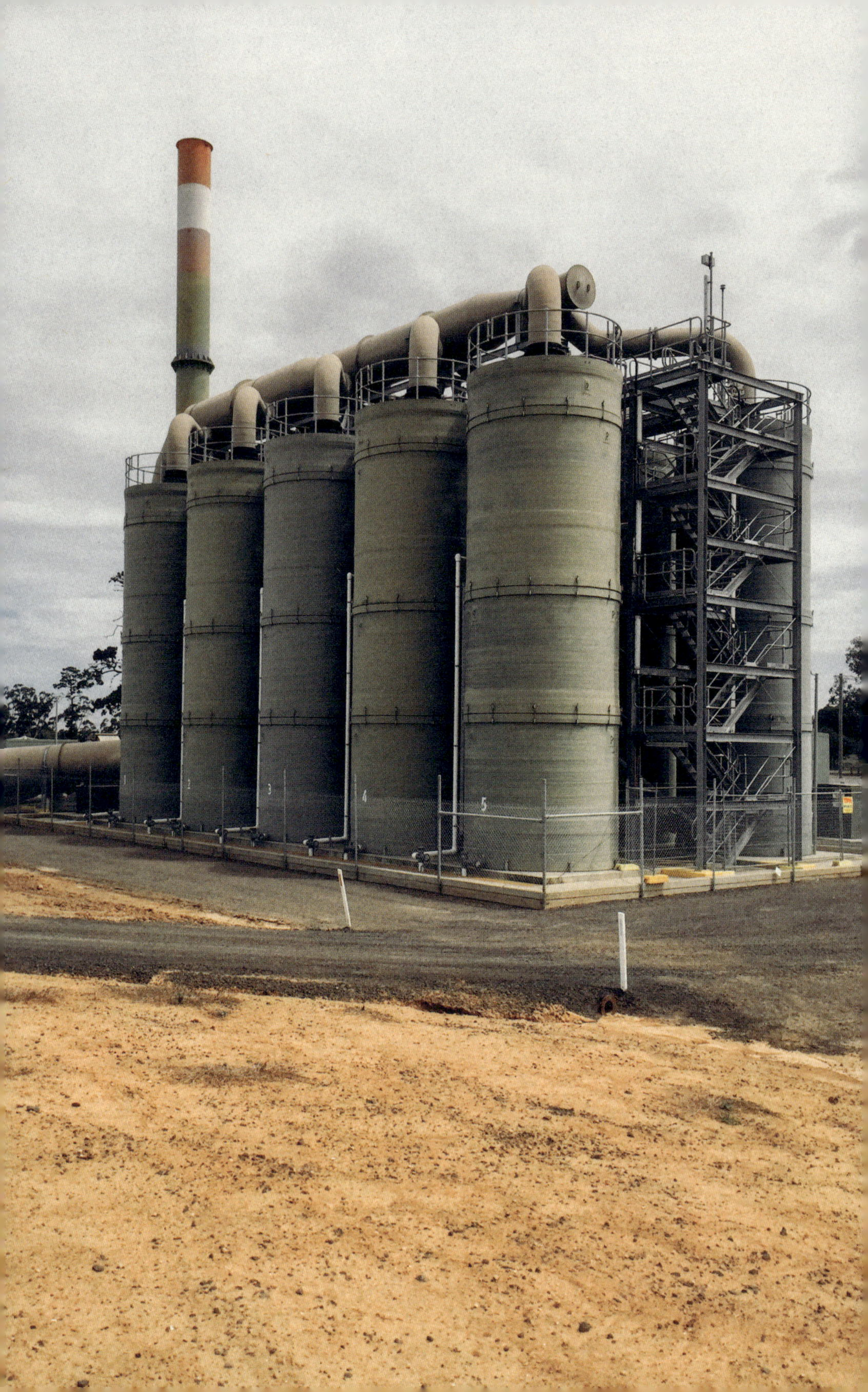

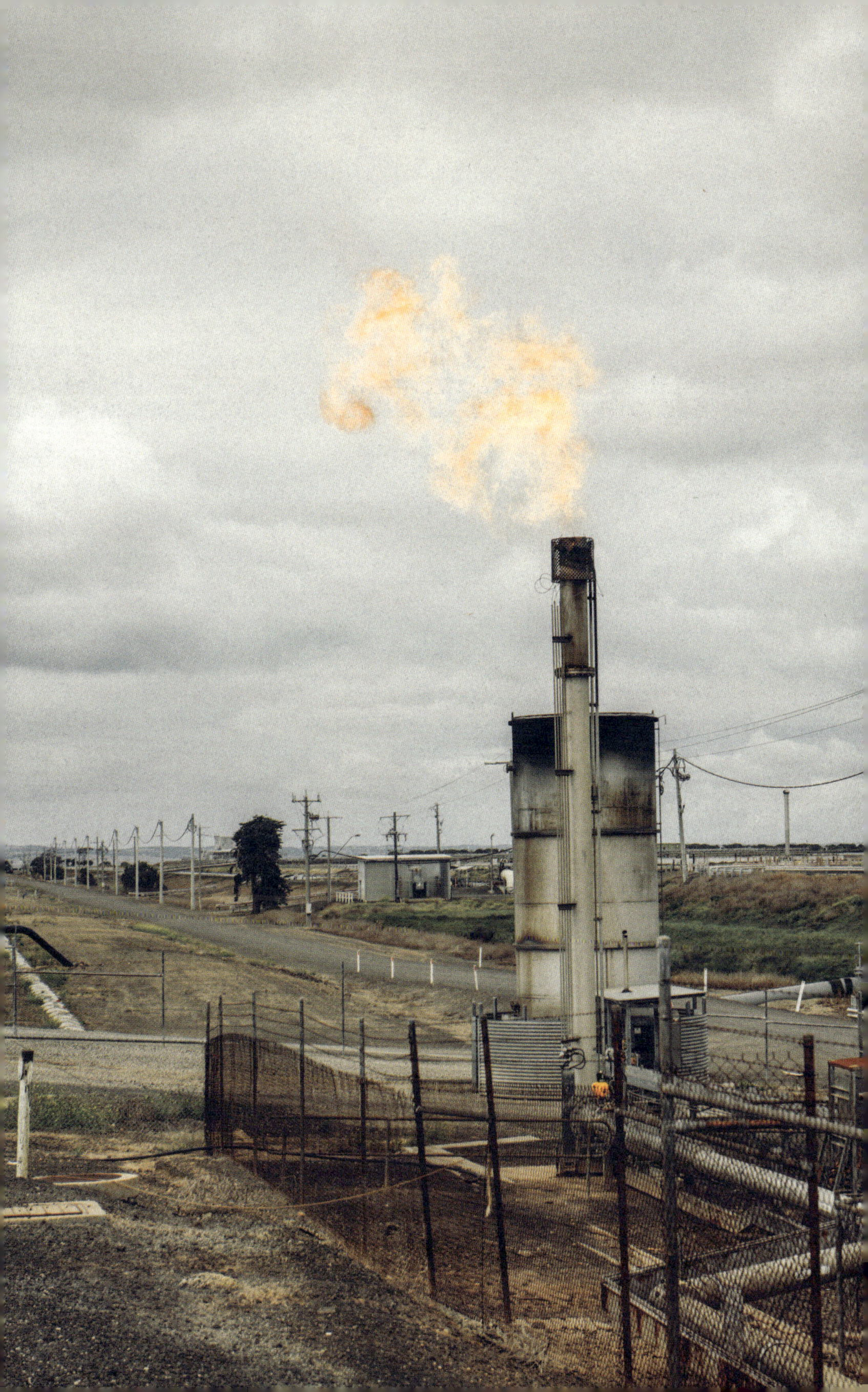

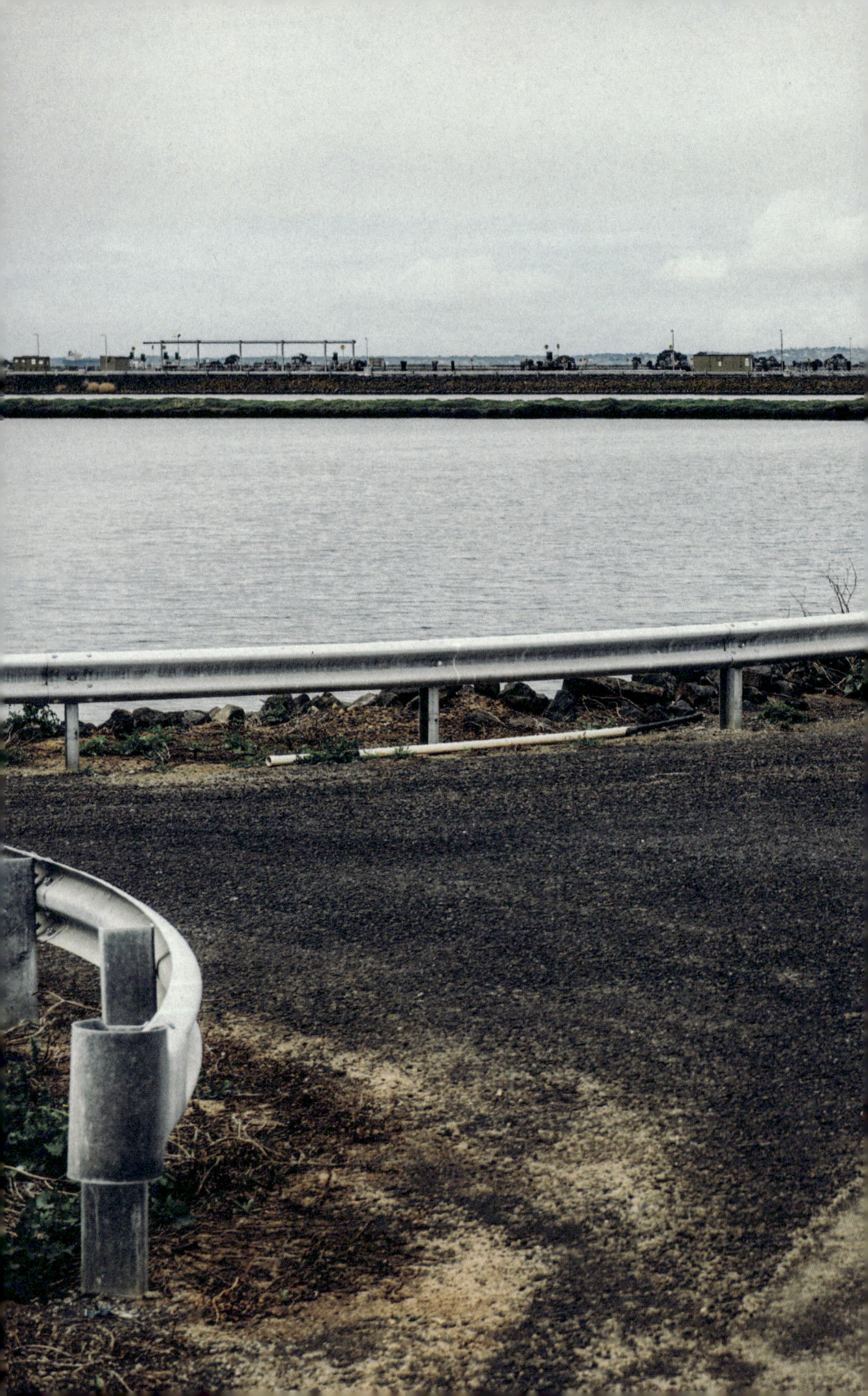

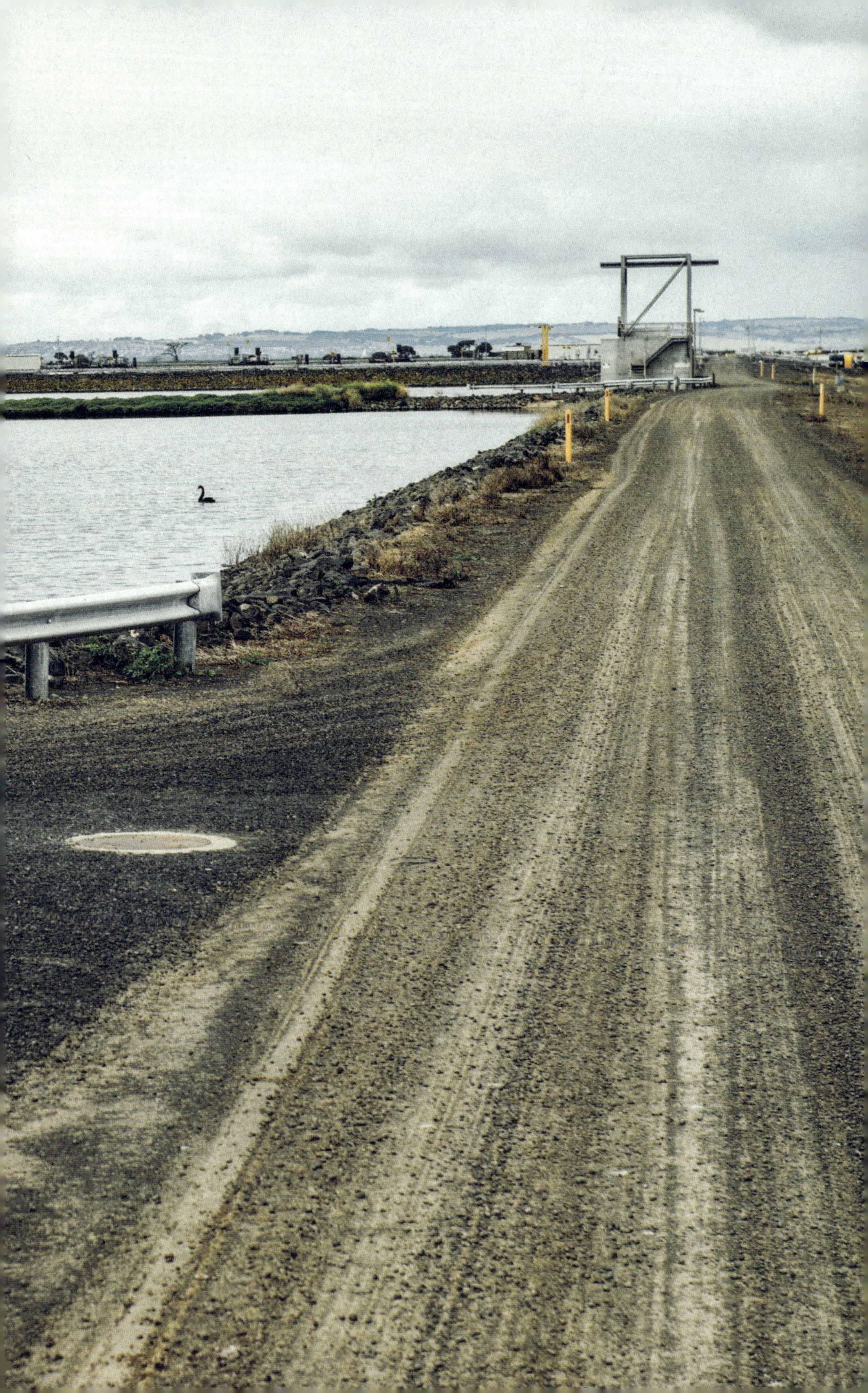

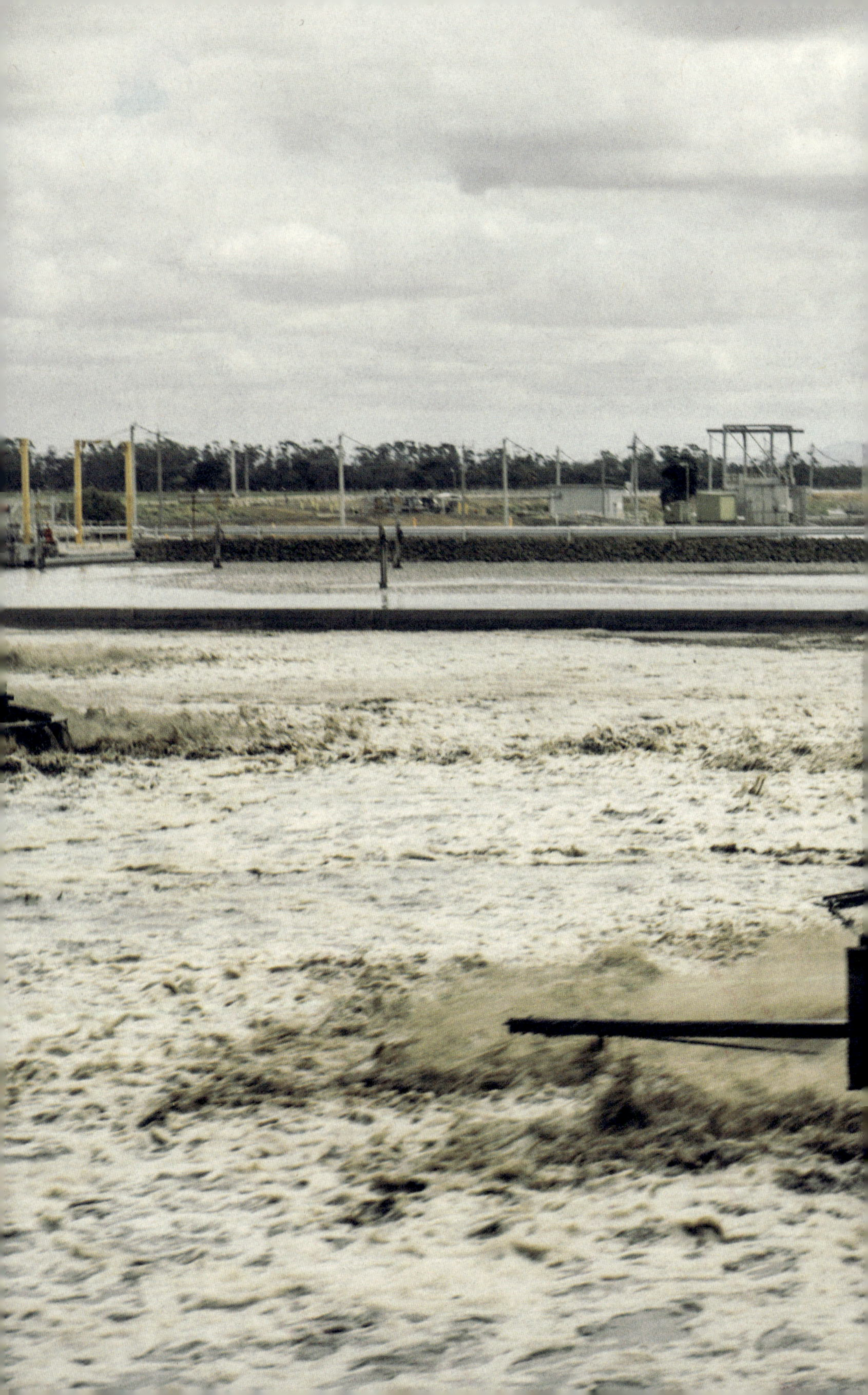

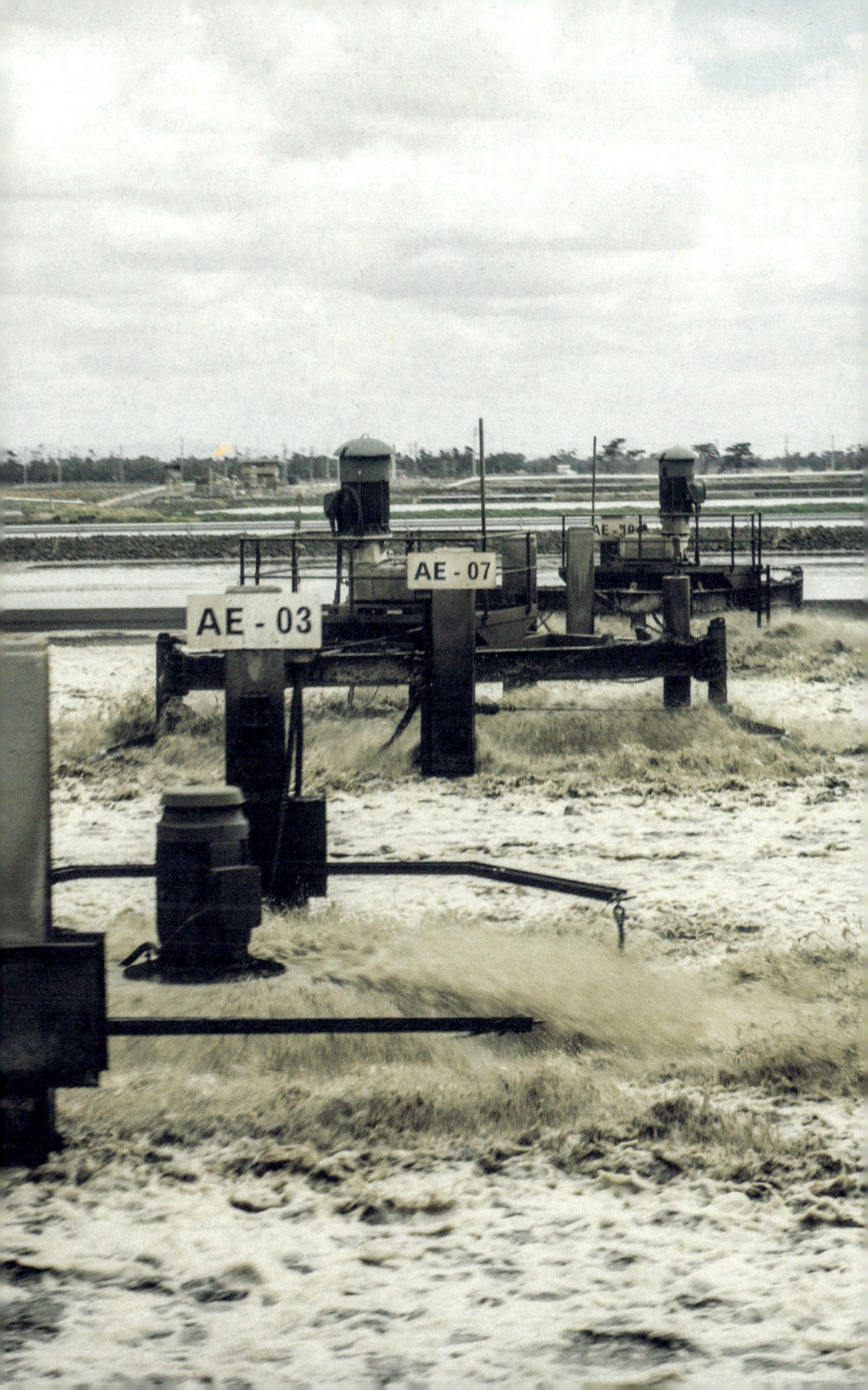
AE - 03
AE - 07

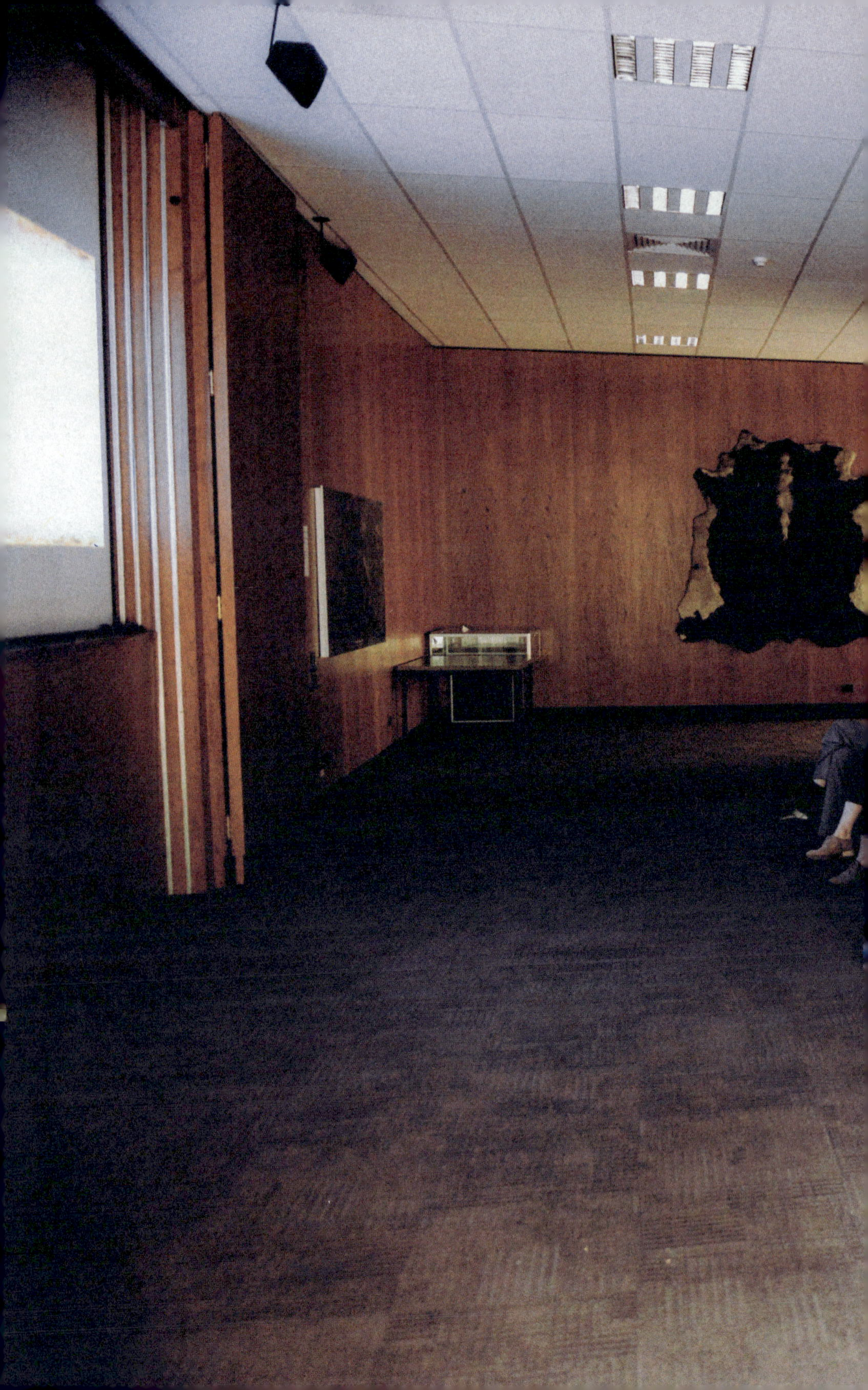

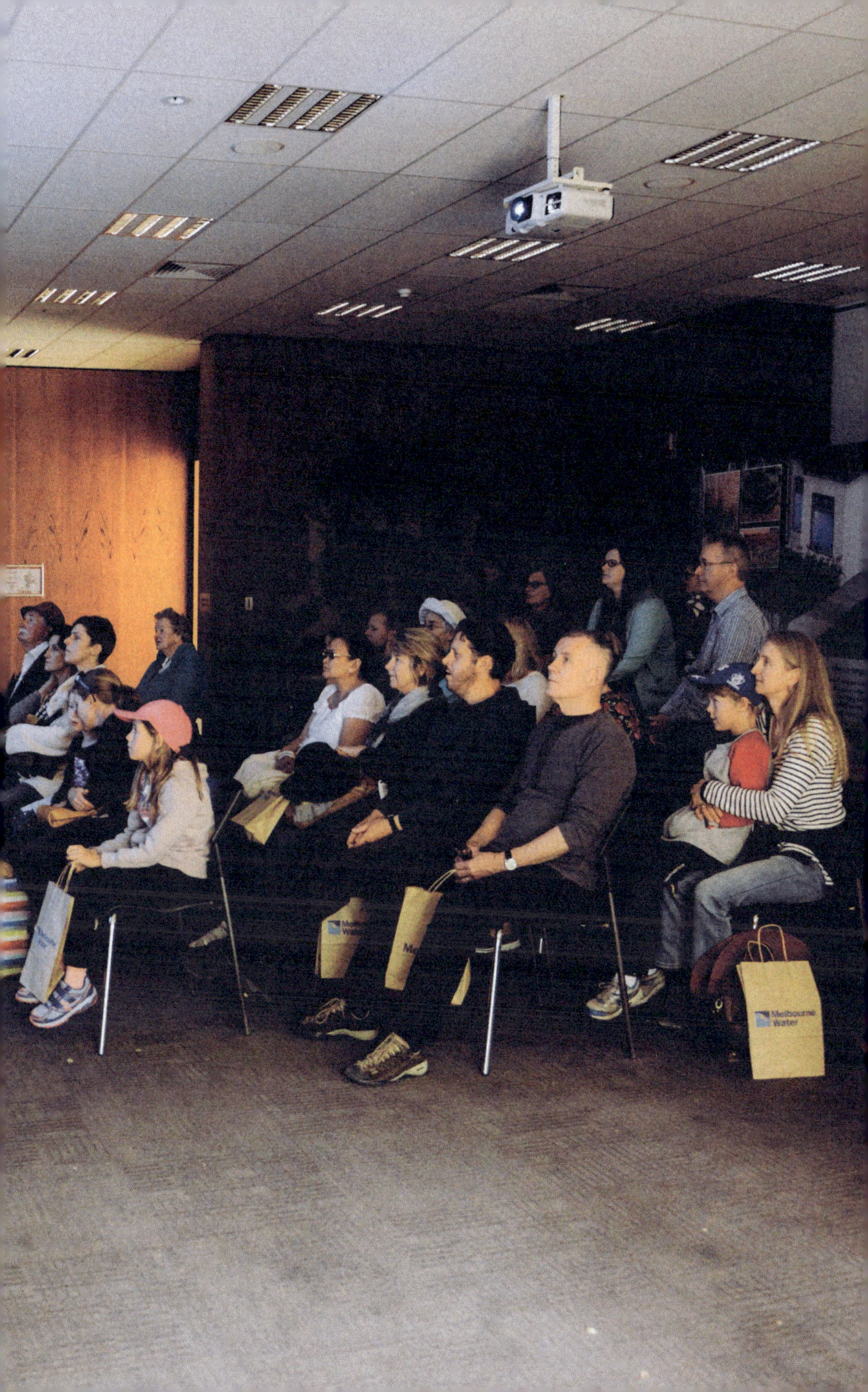
Melbourne Water

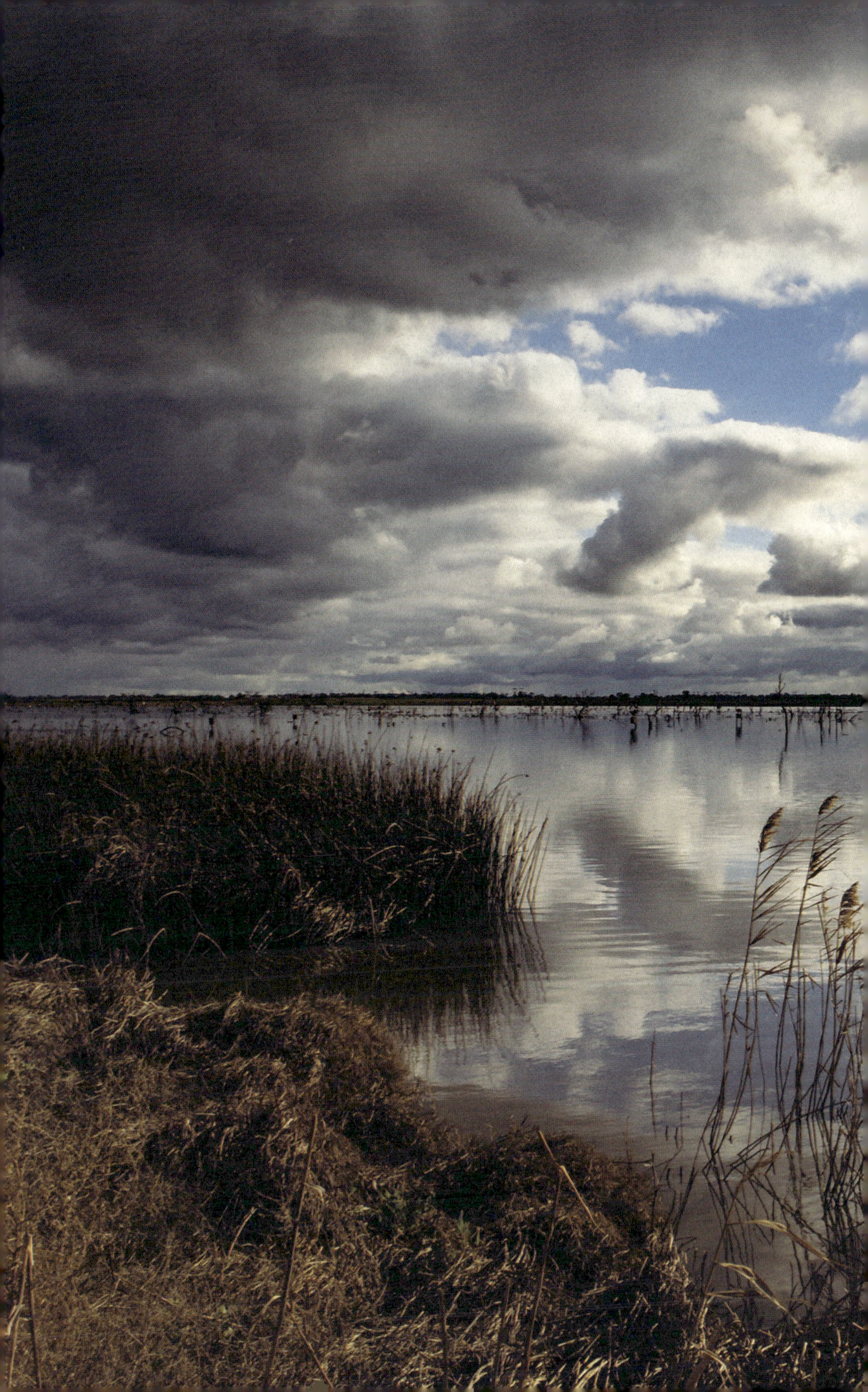

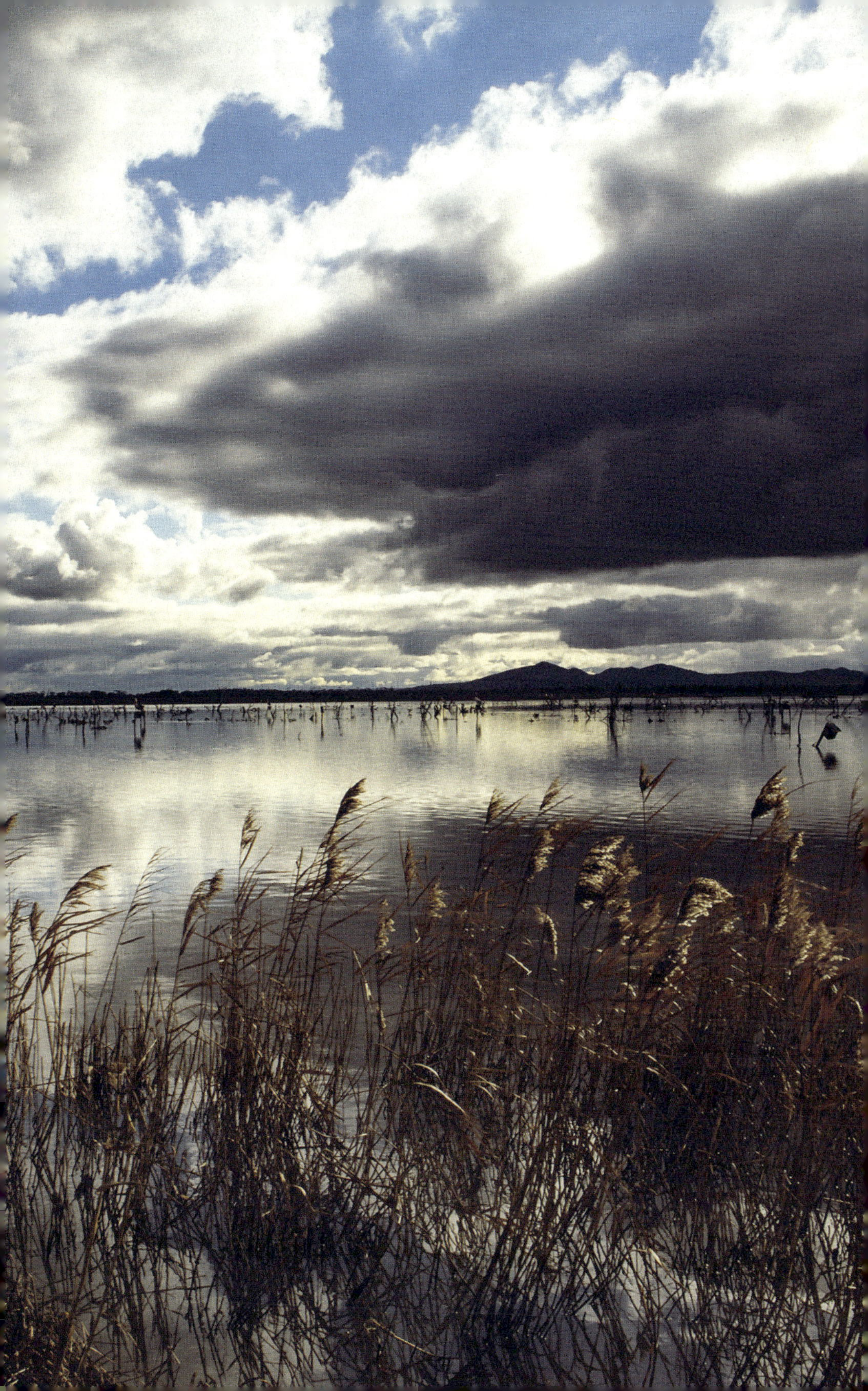

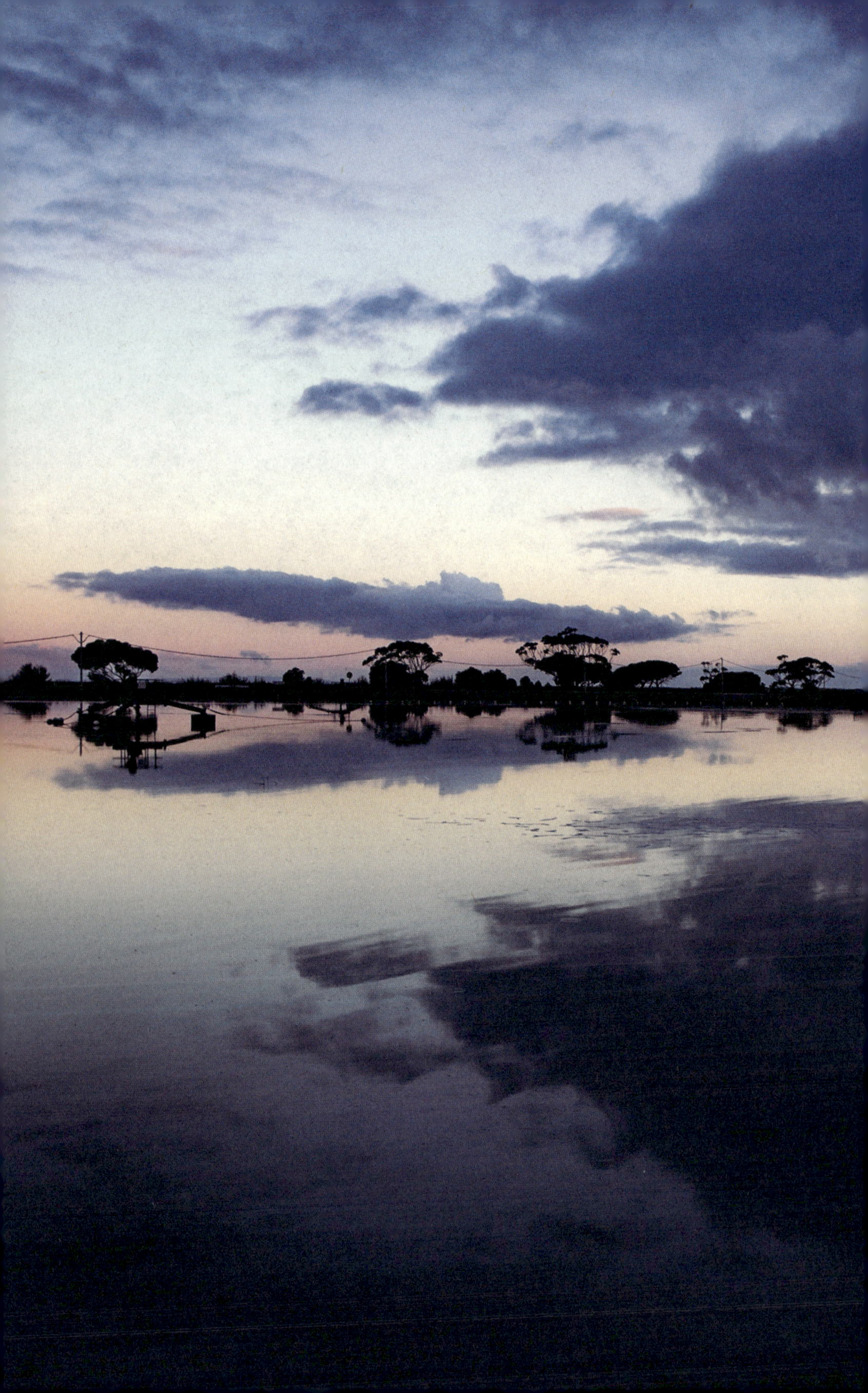

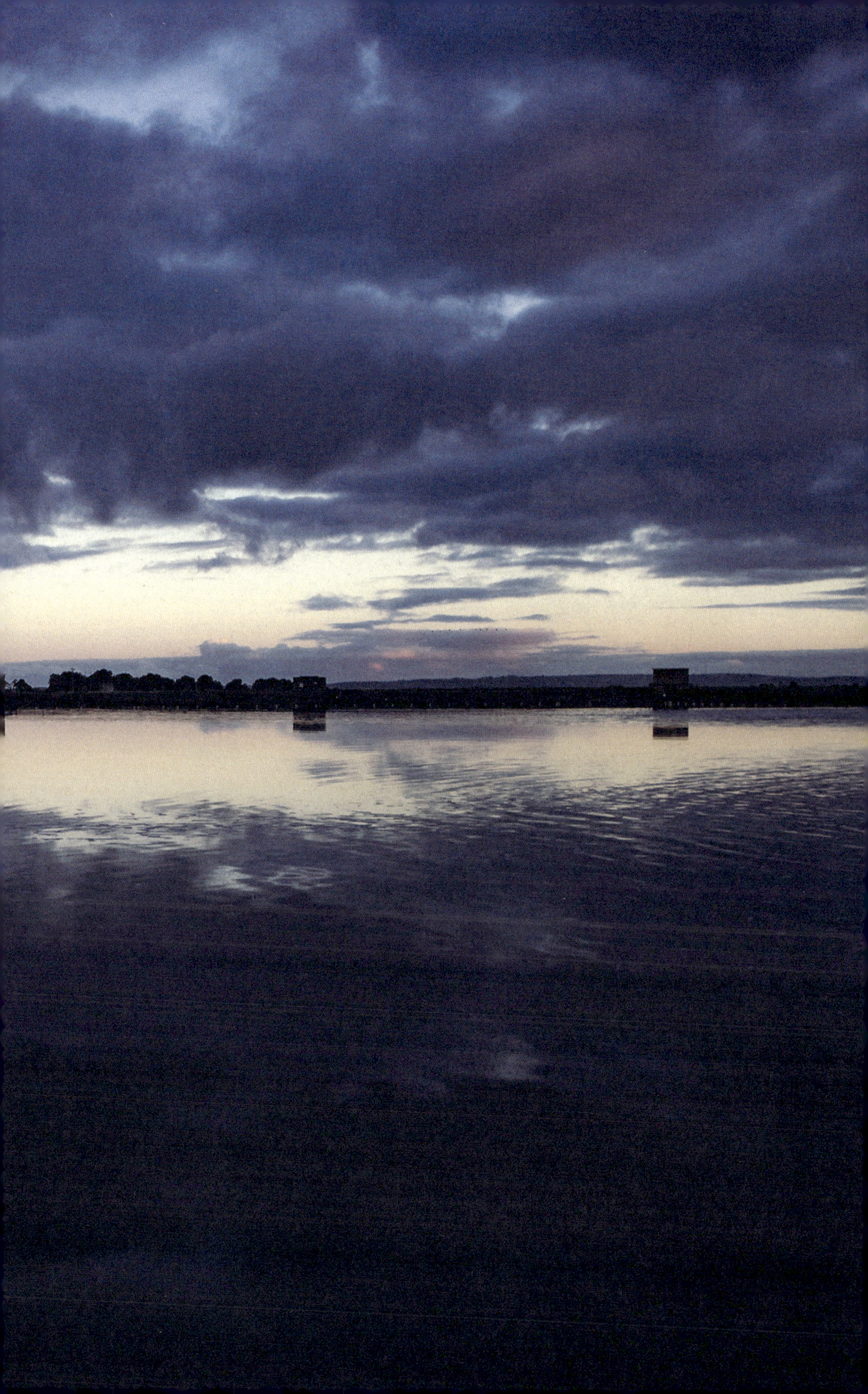

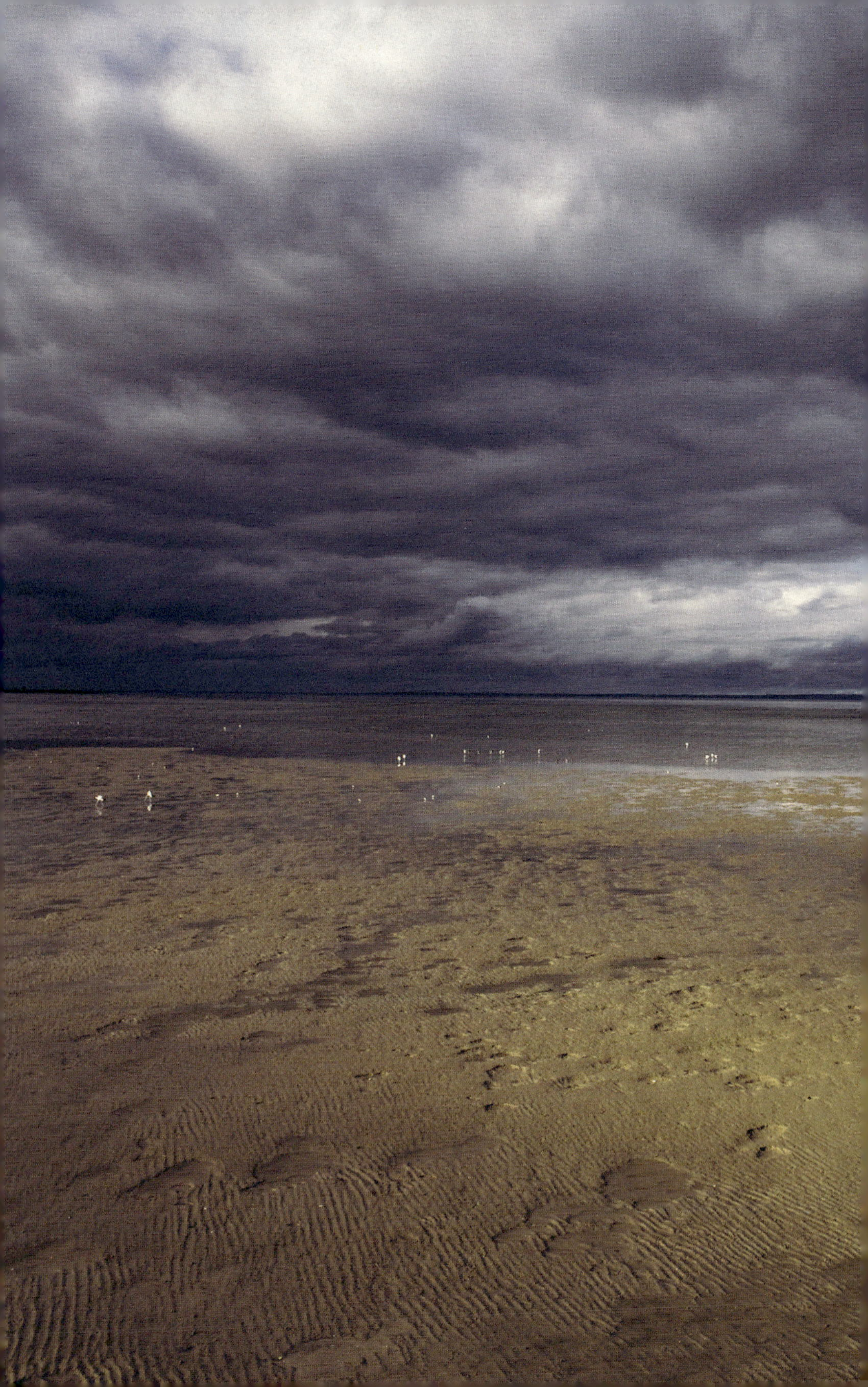

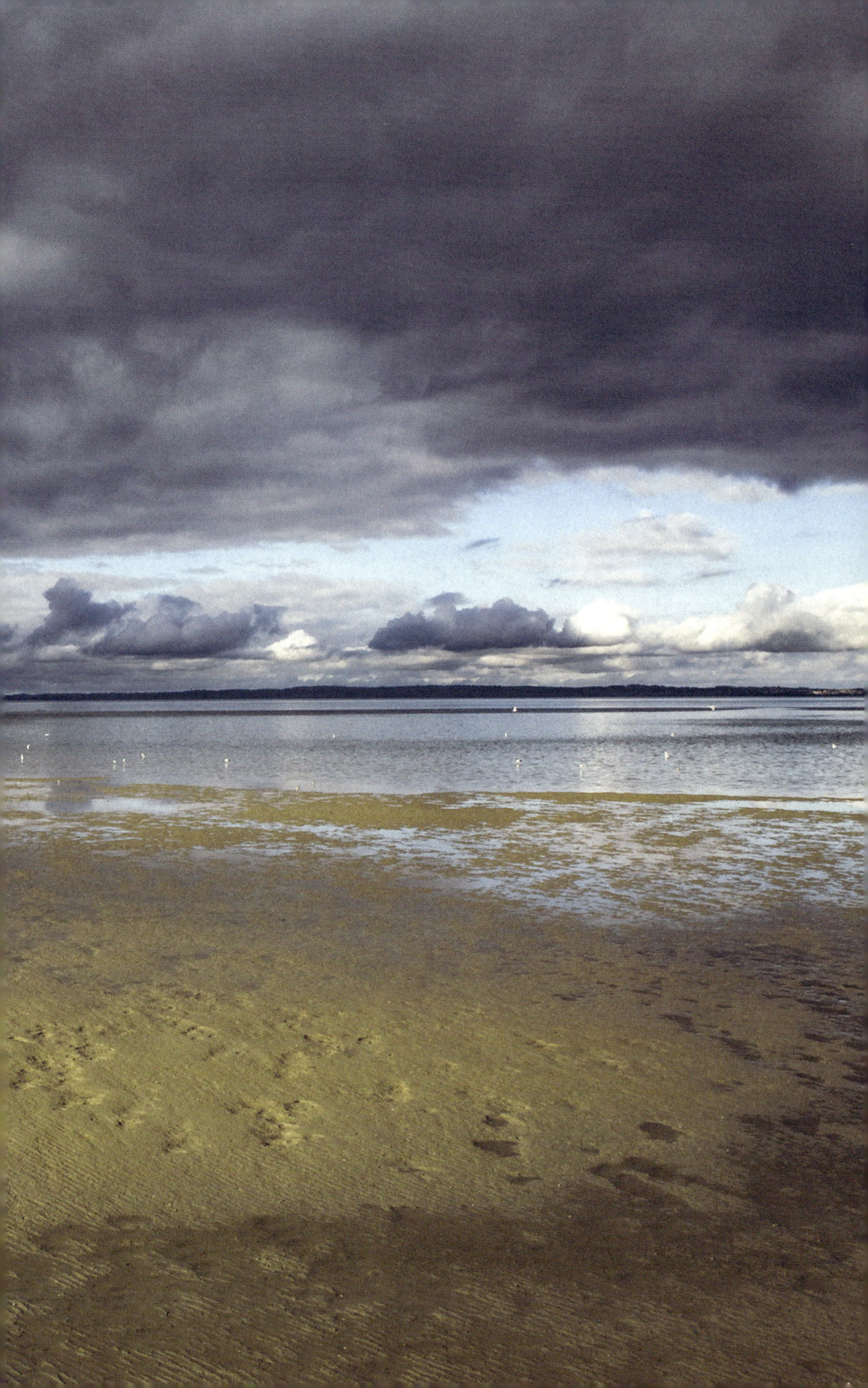

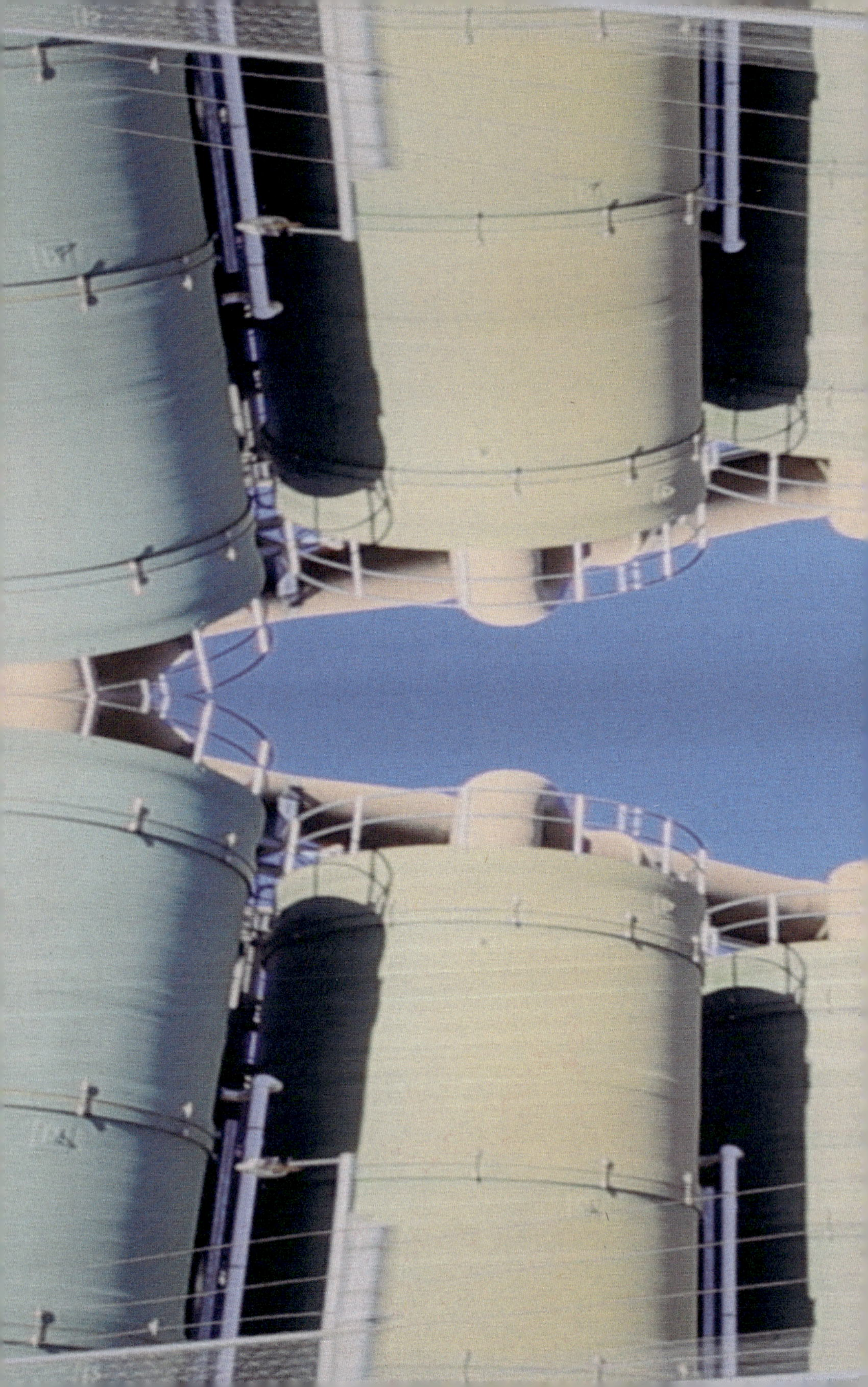

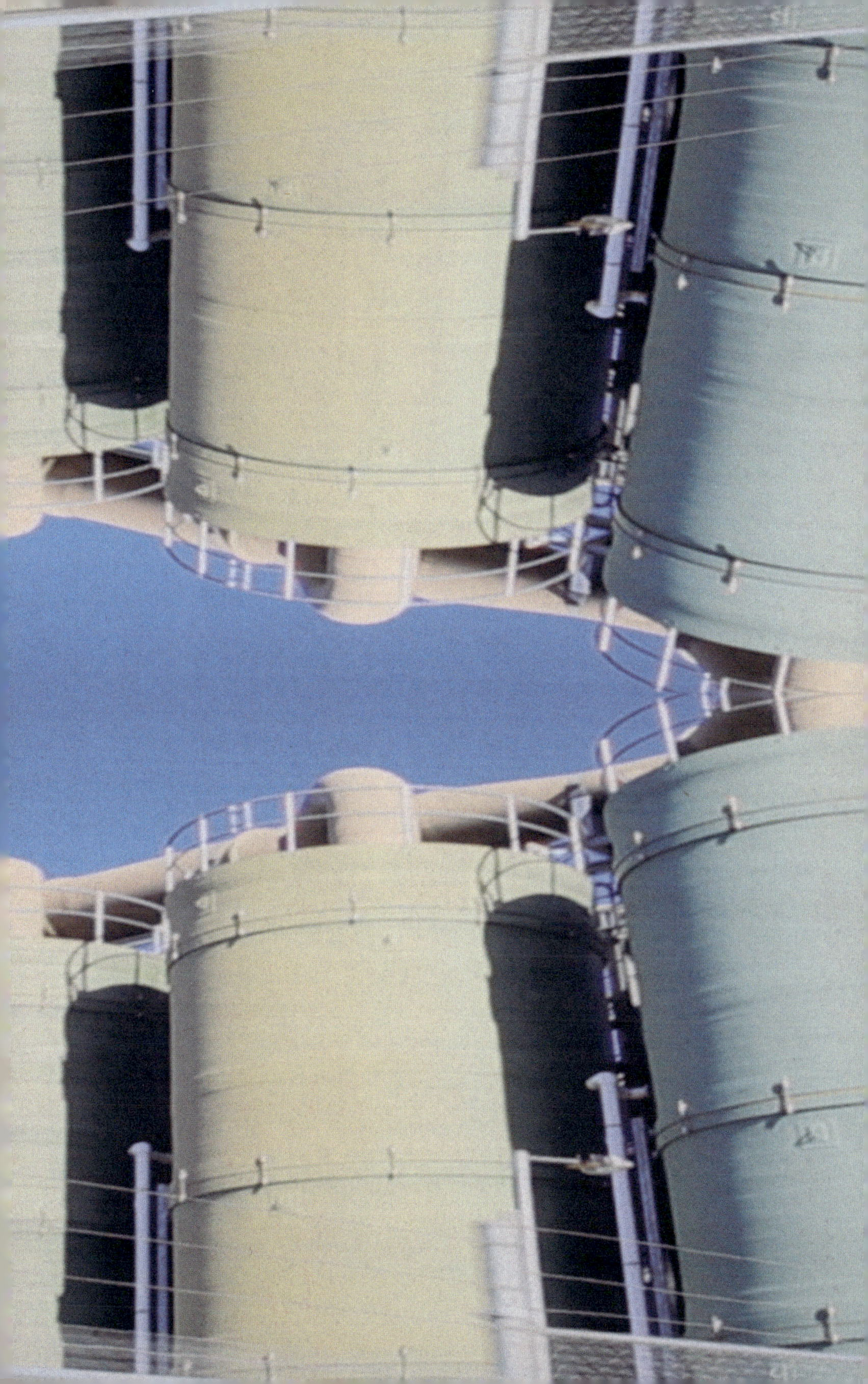

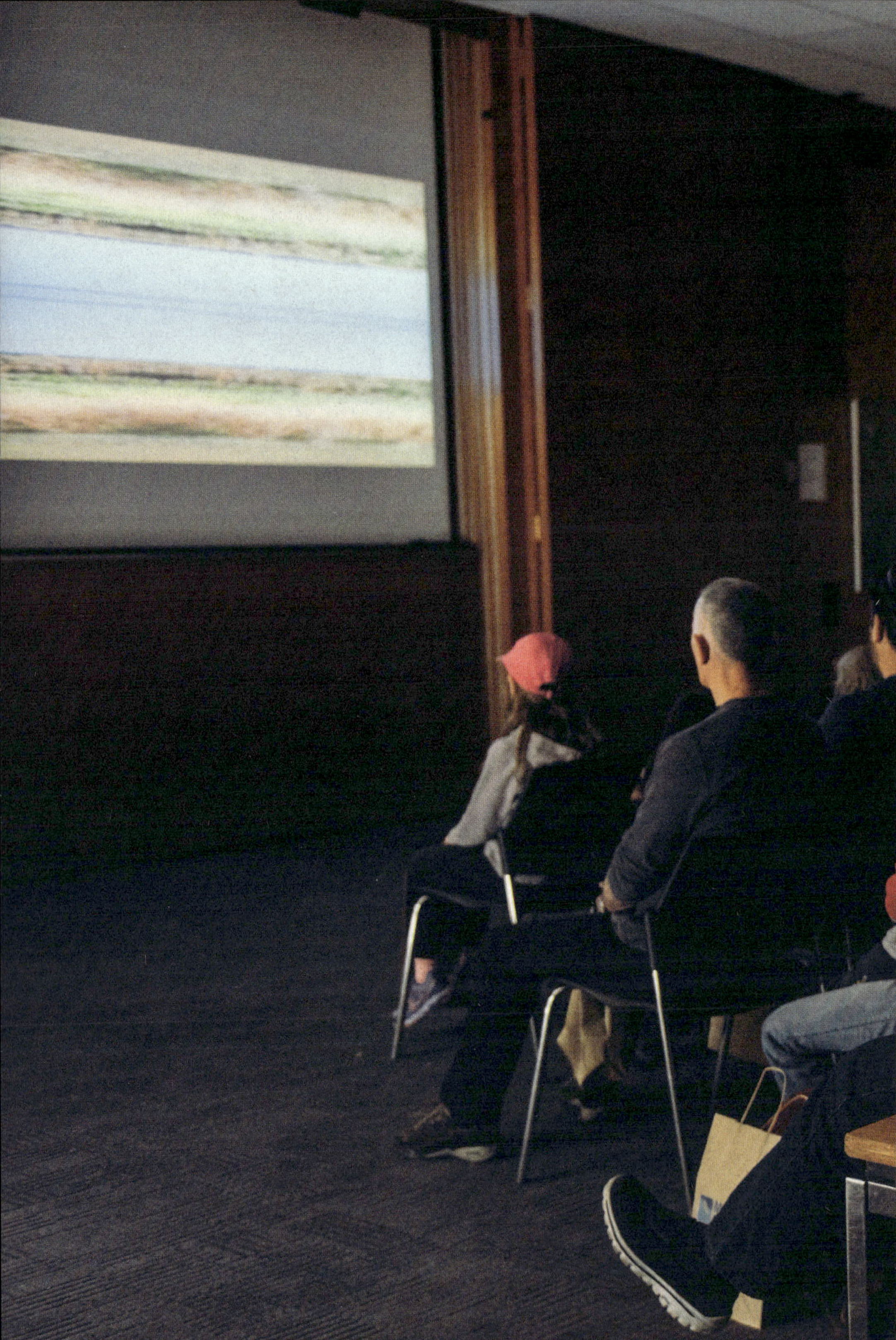

The Metropolitan Farm at Werribee

—A film by The Melbourne Metropolitan Board of Works

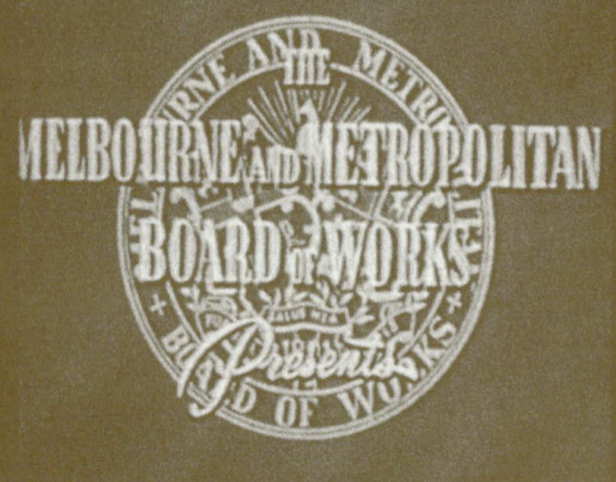
MELBOURNE AND METROPOLITAN
BOARD OF WORKS
Presents

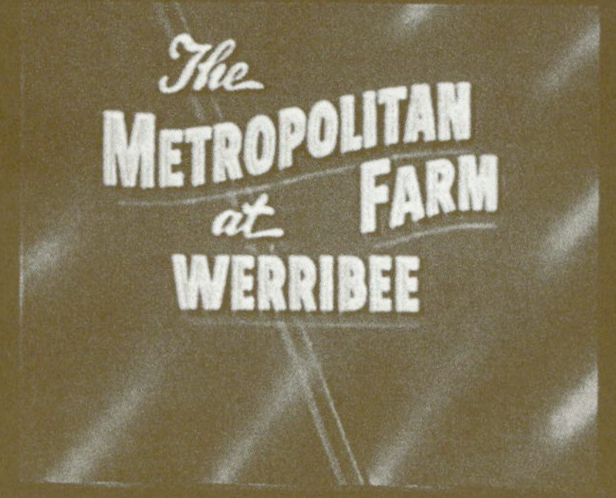
The
METROPOLITAN
FARM
at
WERRIBEE

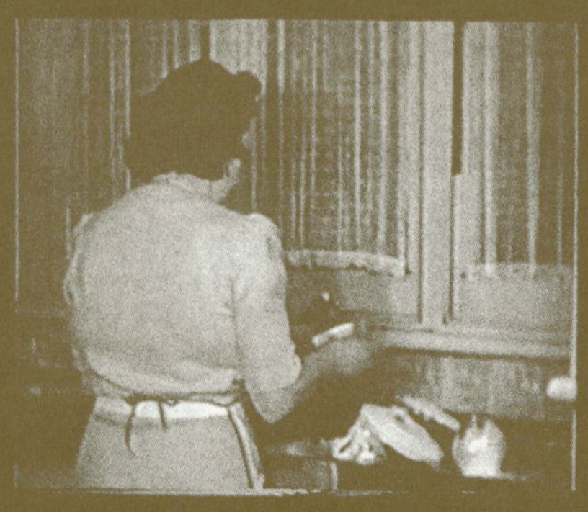

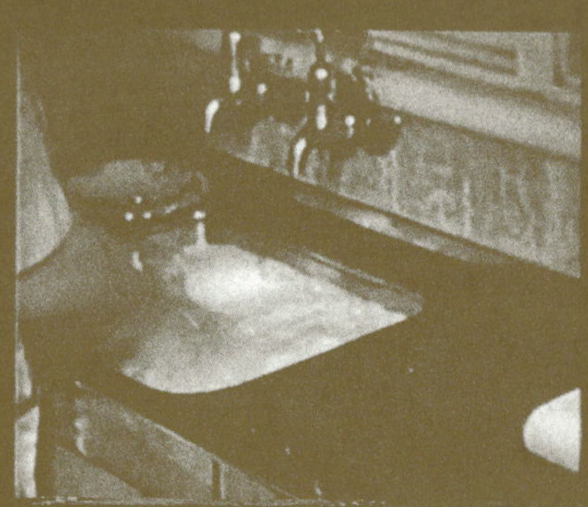

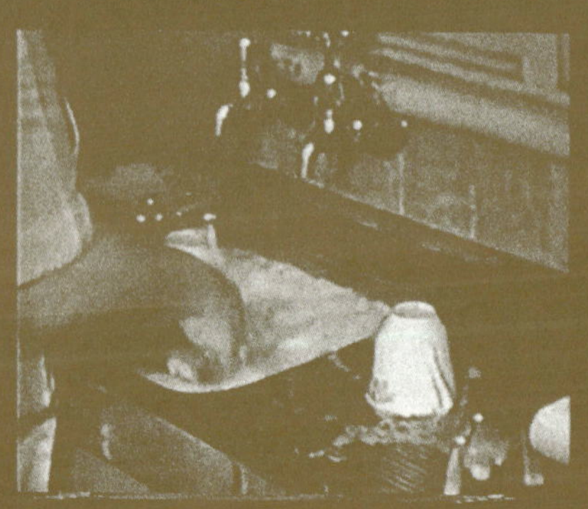

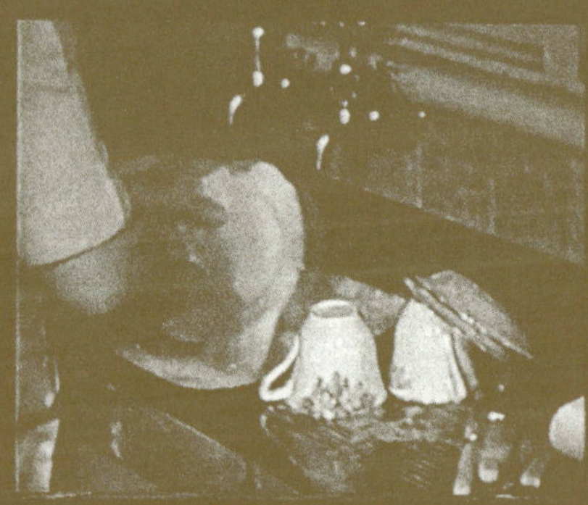

How many of us have considered the problem created by pollution of water by normal house-hold and industrial usage

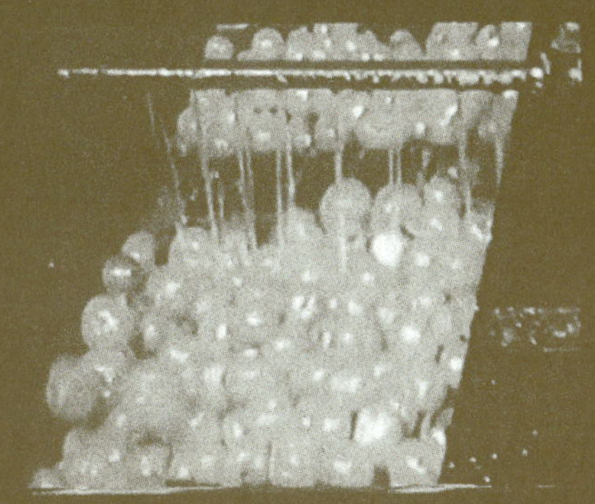

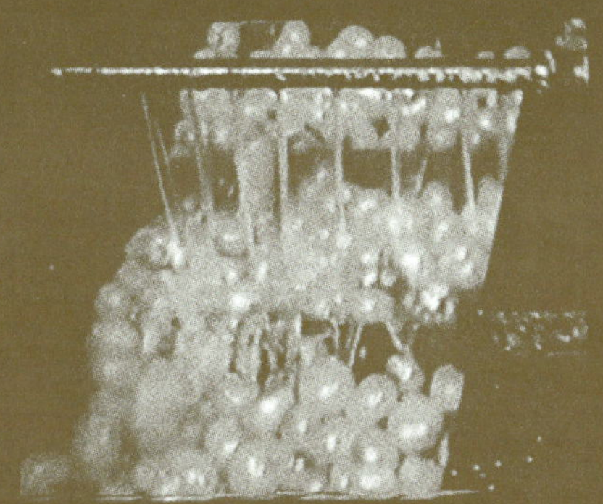

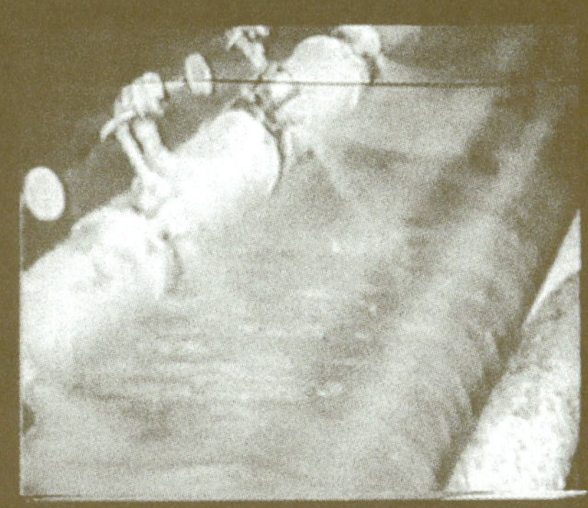

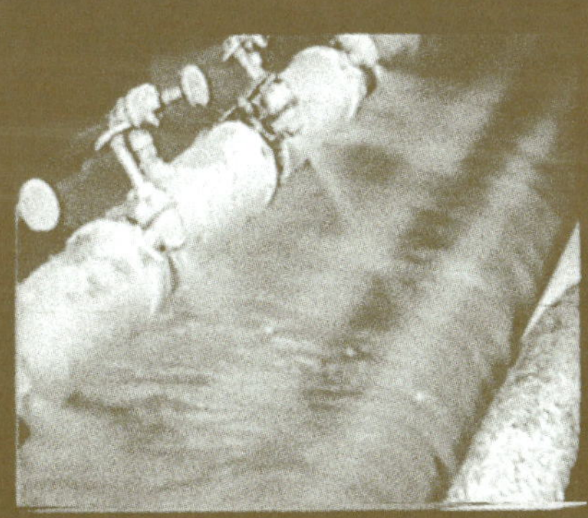

If the water so polluted were not re-moved from the vicinity of our homes and work places and disposed of in a proper manner,

of our homes and work places and disposed of in a proper manner, noxious and offensive conditions would be set up and epidemics would

up and epidemics would occur. This film depicts how these dangers to health are prevented in Melbourne.

2723 Miles of underground conduits collect the sanitary drainage and converge at the Spotswood Pumping Station

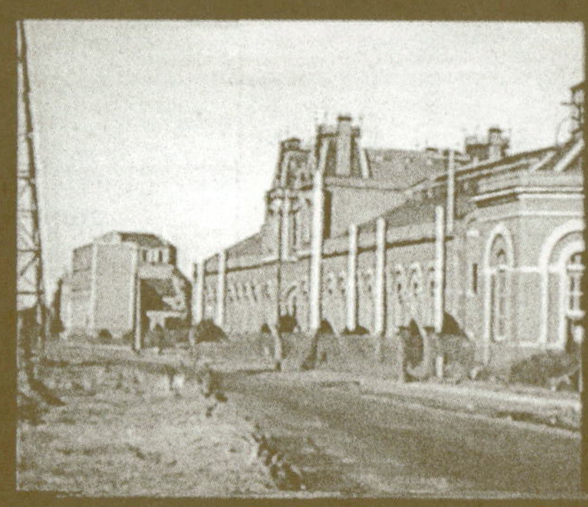

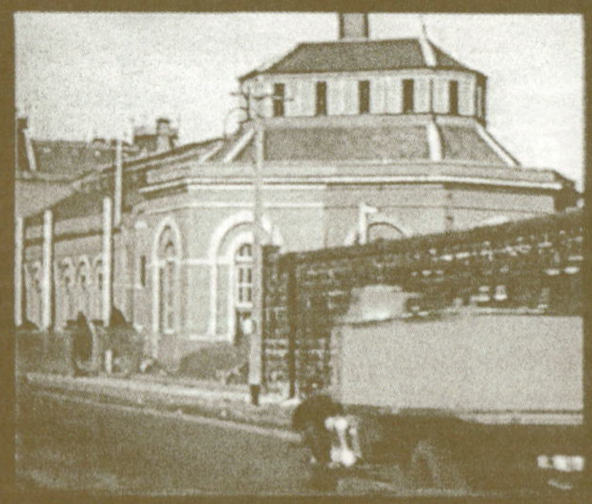

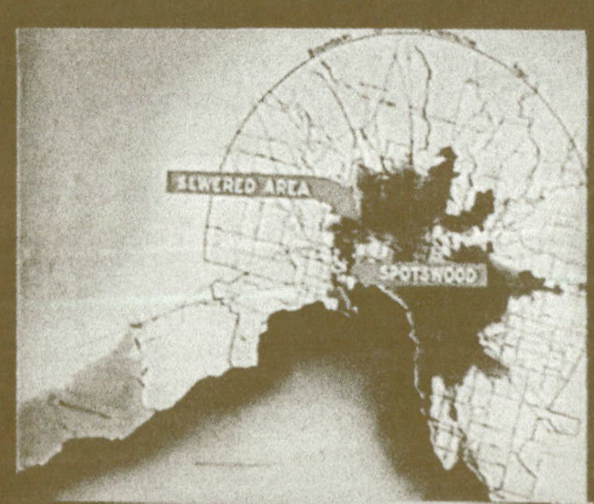

Sewage is lifted by pumps through a height of 108 feet to Brooklyn.

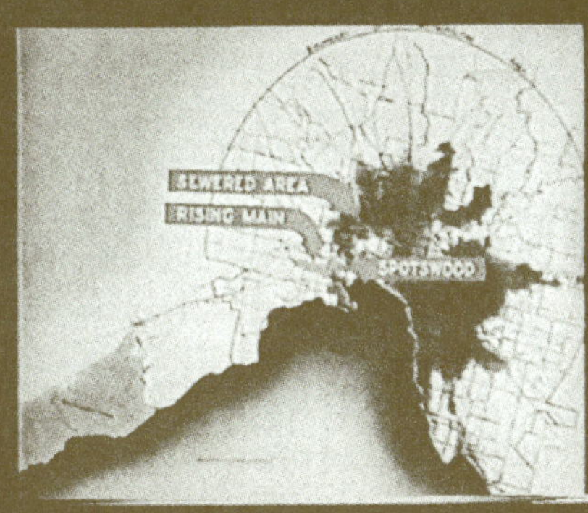

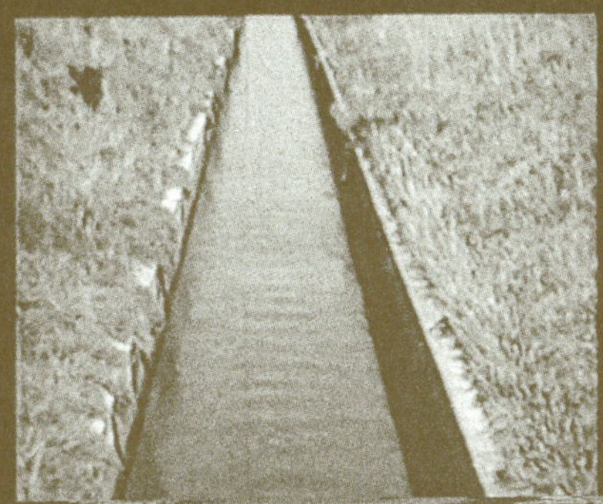

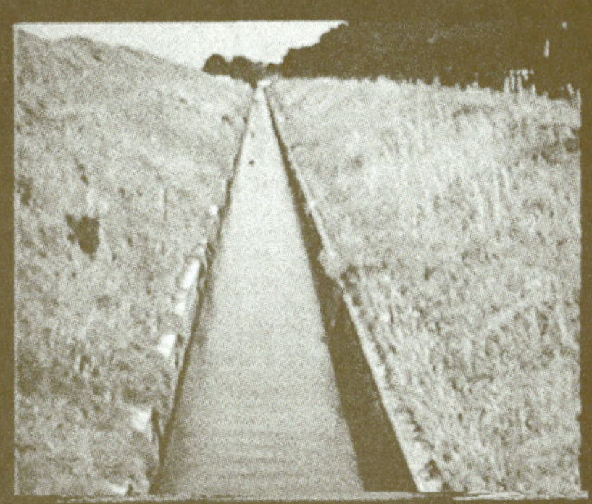

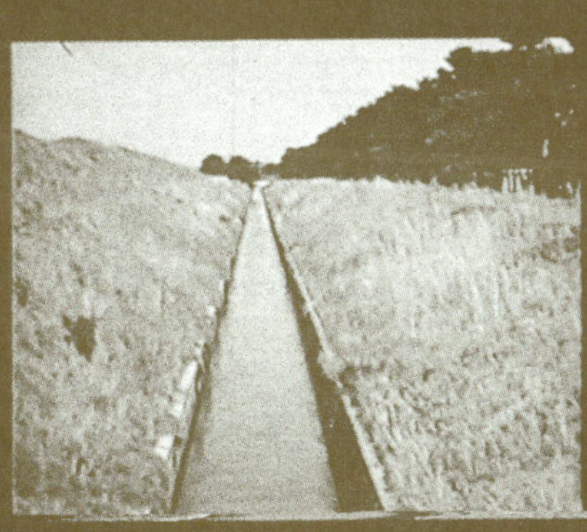

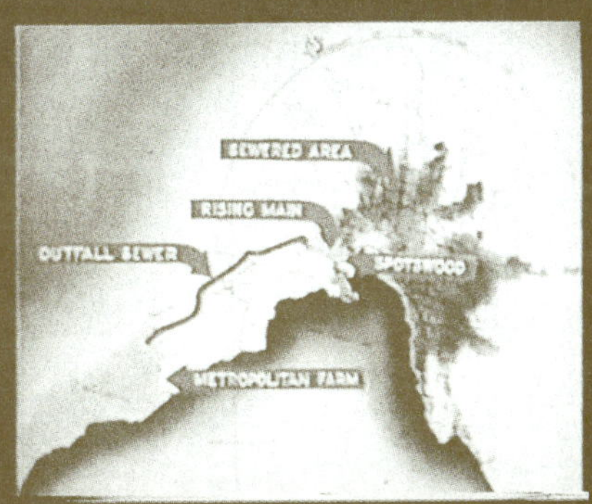

When in 1891 Parliament created the Melbourne and Metropolitan Board of Works and charged it with the duty of providing a sewerage system for the metropolis, land treatment was the most suitable method known for the purification of sewage

the purification of sewage of a large city. For this purpose an area at the mouth of the Werribee River was purchased and the Metropolitan Farm established. The Farm is controlled by the Board's Farm Committee consisting of . . . The Chairman of the Board . . .

Committee consisting of . . . The Chairman of the Board . . .
. . . . J.C.Jessop, Esq., J.P.
Cr. A.H.Woodfull, LL.M., Vice-Chairman . . . . . City of Prahran
Cr. G.A.Rogers, J.P. . . . . City of Port Melbourne
Cr. R.Nuzum, J.P. . . . . City of South Melbourne

. . . . . City of Port Melbourne
Cr. R.Nuzum, J.P. . . . . City of South Melbourne
Cr. J.B.Naughton, J.P. . . . . City of Melbourne
Cr. H.Moroney, J.P. . . . . City of St. Kilda
Cr. the Hon. W.Barry, M.L.A. . . . . City of Melbourne
Cr. A.J.G.Sinclair, J.P. . . . . .

Cr. the Hon. W.Barry, M.L.A. . . . . City of Melbourne
Cr. A.J.G.Sinclair, J.P. . . . . .
. . . . City of Caulfield
Cr. K.Parlon, J.P. . . . . City of Fitzroy
Cr. J.T.Ryan . . City of Fitzroy
The Committee's chief technical advisers are . . . .

Cr. K.Parlon, J.P. . . . . City of Fitzroy
Cr. J.T.Ryan . . City of Fitzroy
The Committee's chief technical advisers are . . . .
Mr. E.F.Borrie, M.C., M.C.E., M.I.E., Aust. . . . Chief Engineer of Sewerage
Mr. C.L.Lock . . . Farm Manager.

To reach the farm
we travel through
Werribee township.

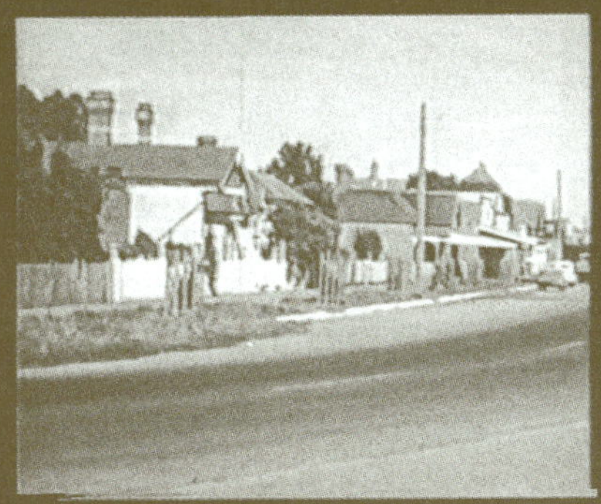

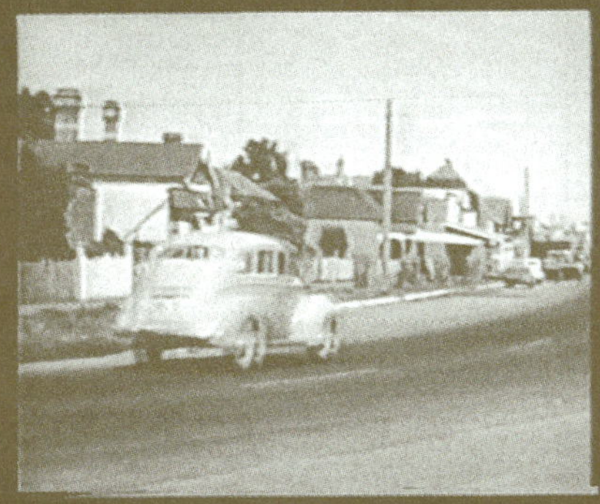

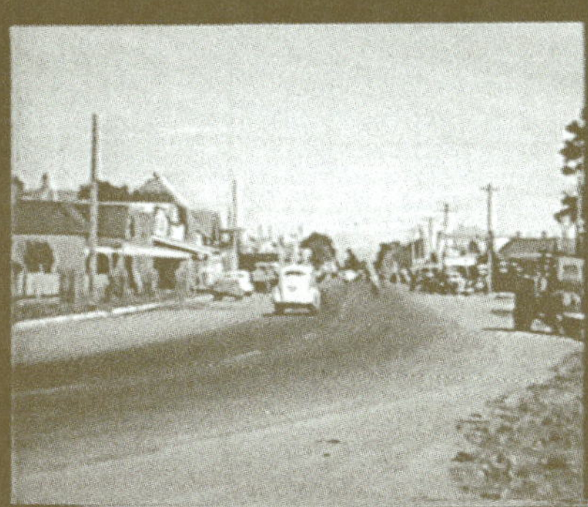

After crossing the
Werribee River,

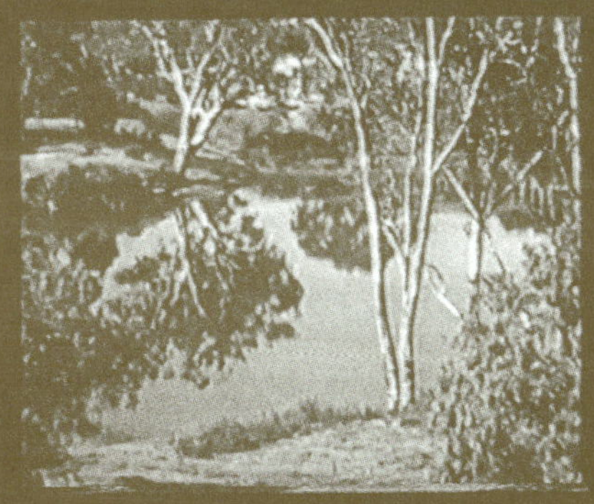

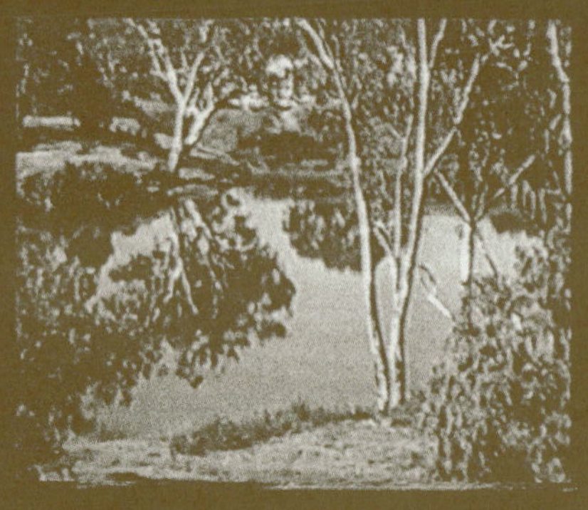

......we leave the main road and travel a further three miles before reaching the administrative buildings

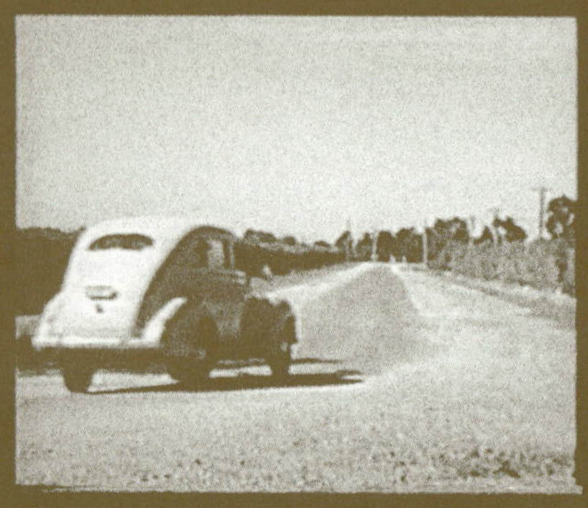

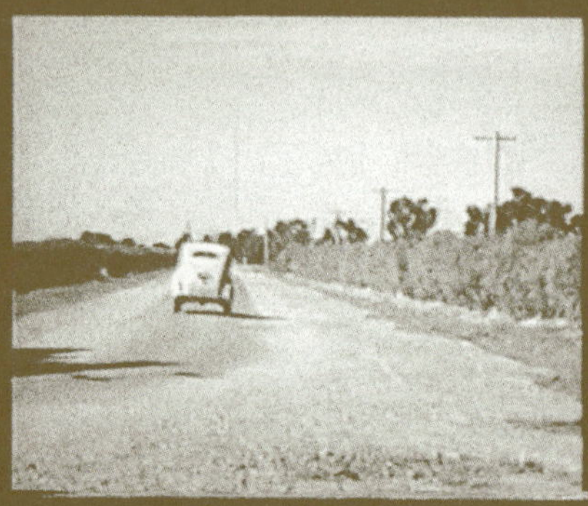

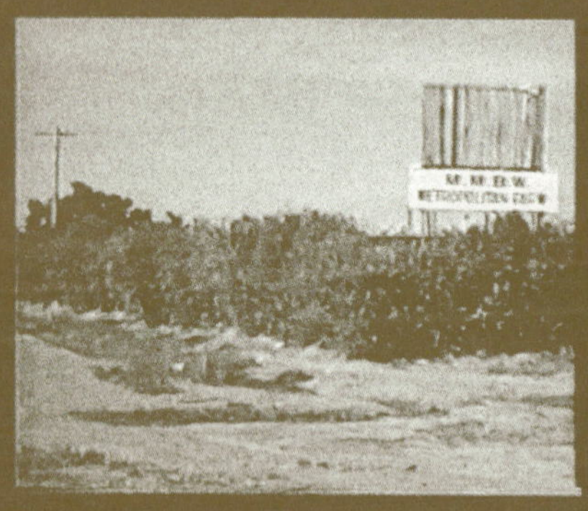

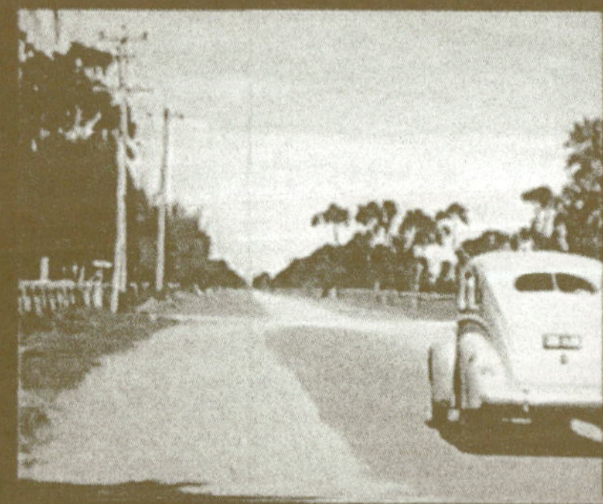

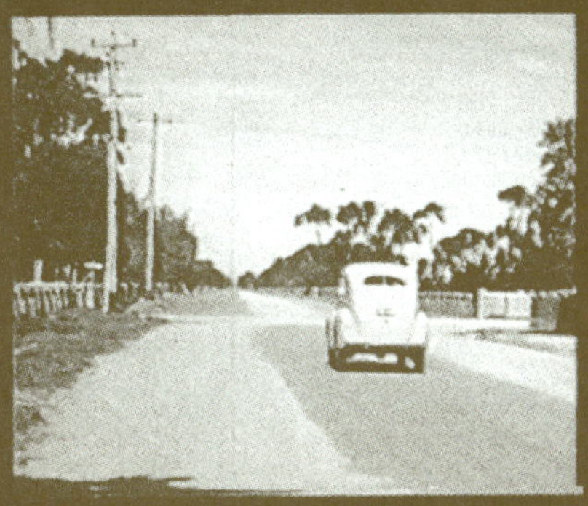
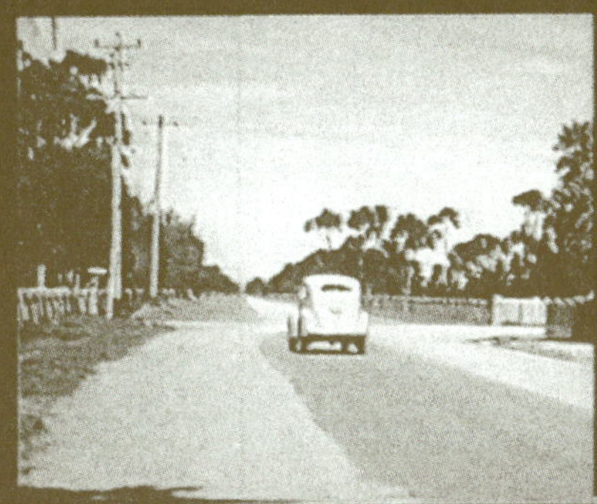
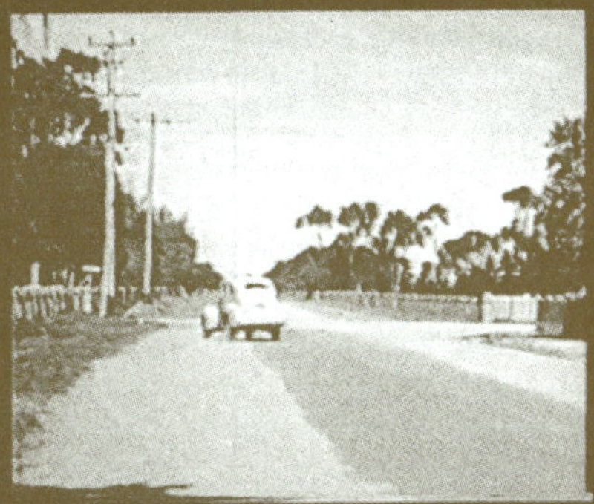
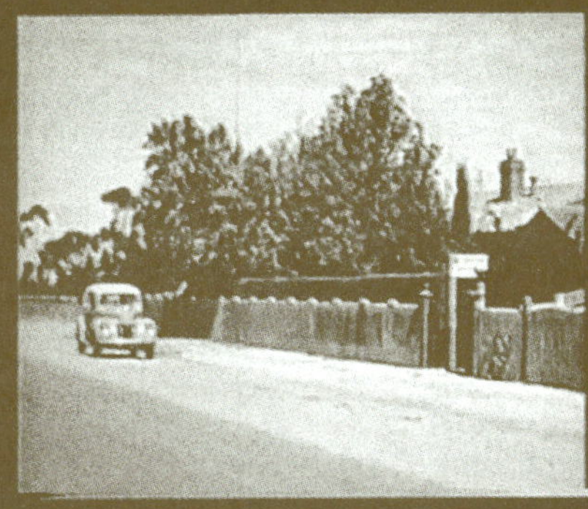
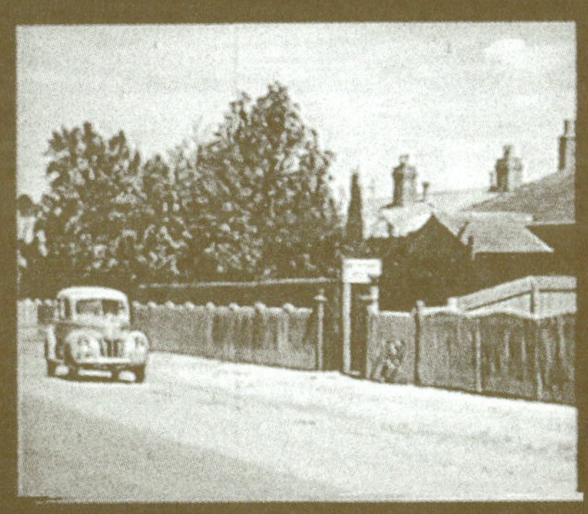
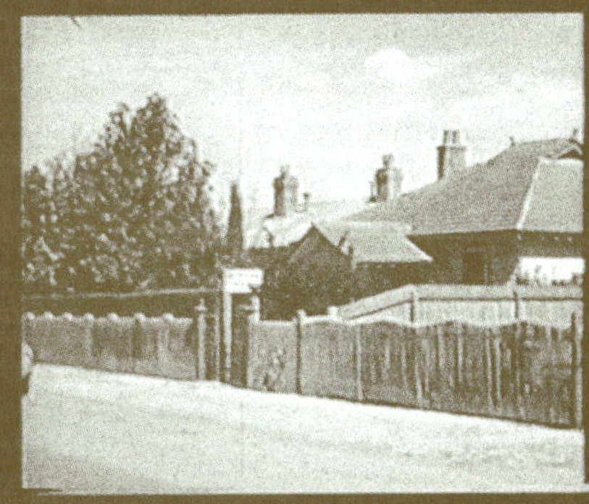

SIX PUBLIC ARTWORKS

Today, the Farm comprises an area of 24,579 acres. One can appreciate its extent when it is superimposed upon the sewered area.

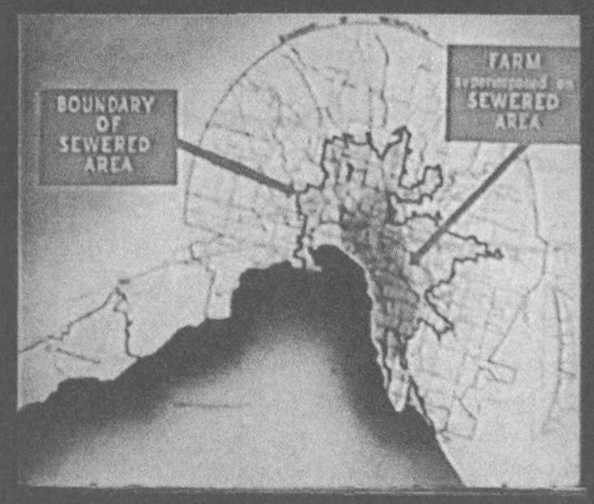

The primary function of the farm is the purification of Melbourne's sewage before it is discharged into Port Phillip Bay.

Thorough preparation of the land is essential. The first step is to break up the sub-soil to improve its permeability.

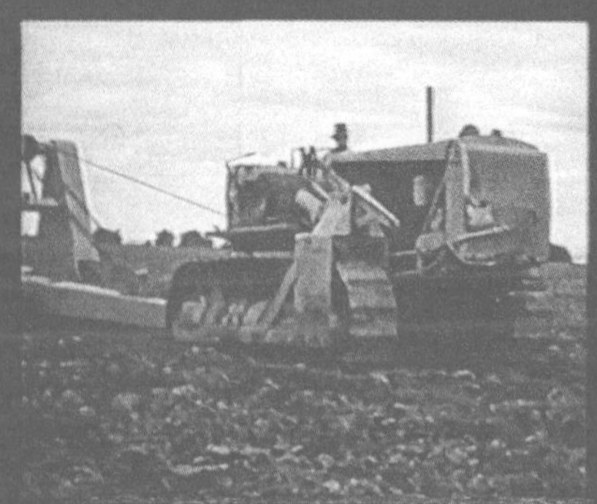

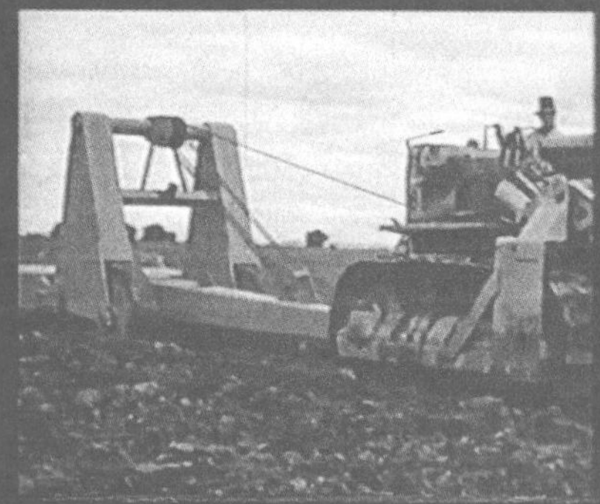

WERRIBEE
FARM
POST
WORLD WAR
TWO

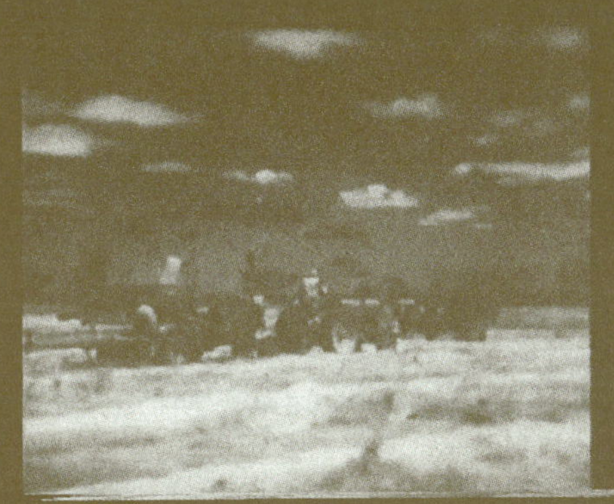

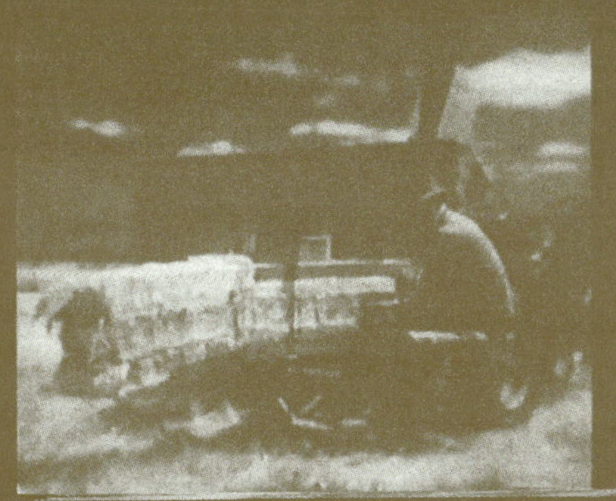

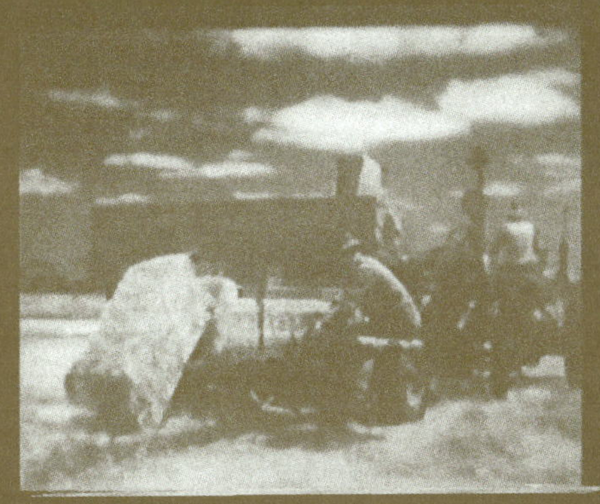

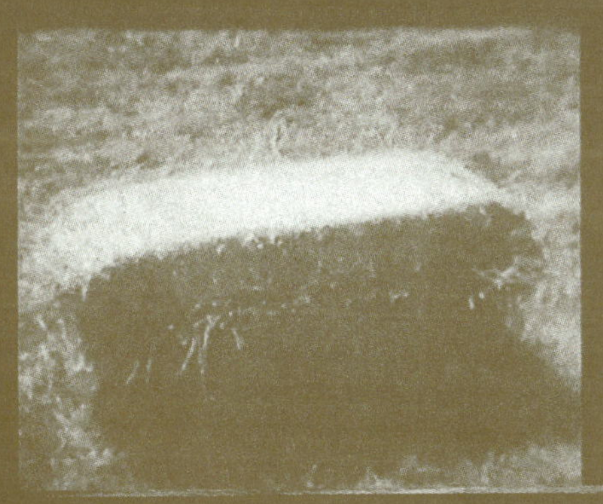

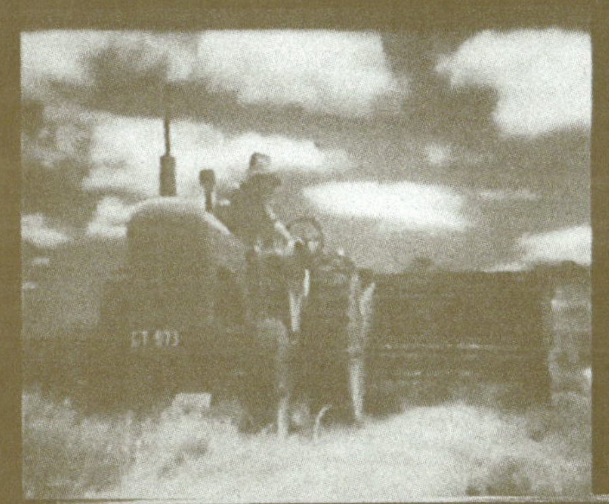

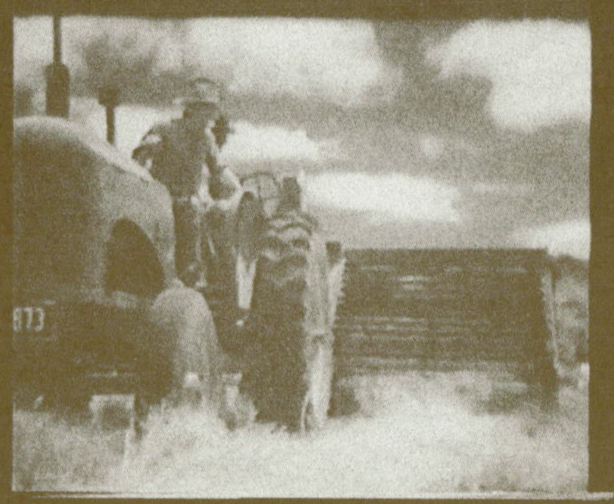
873

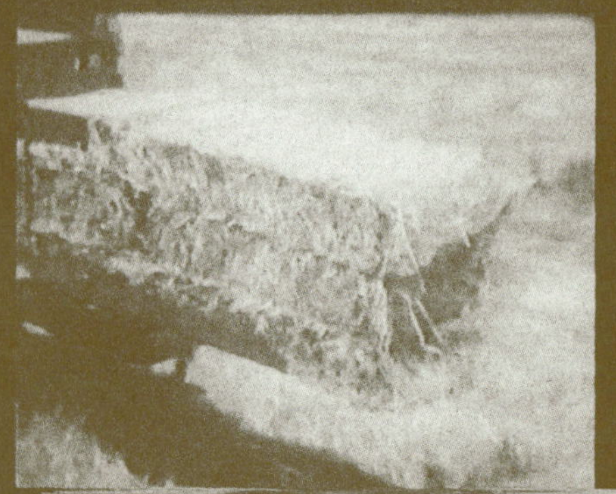

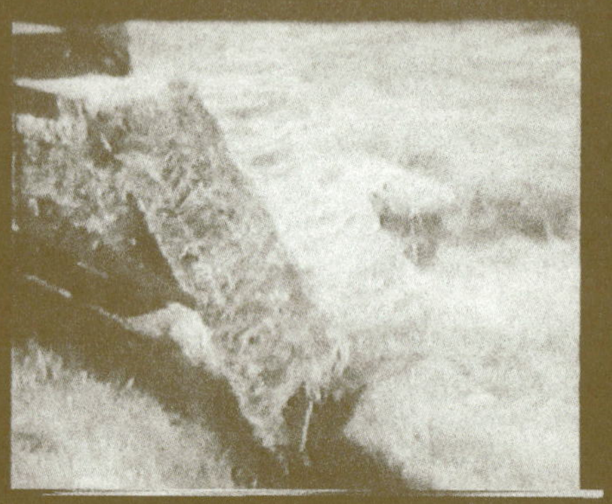

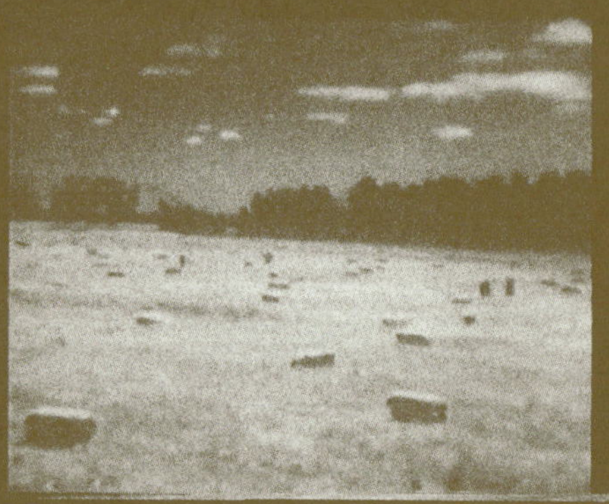

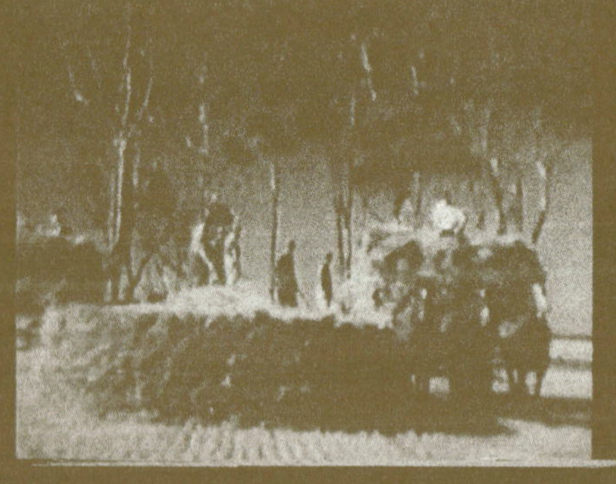

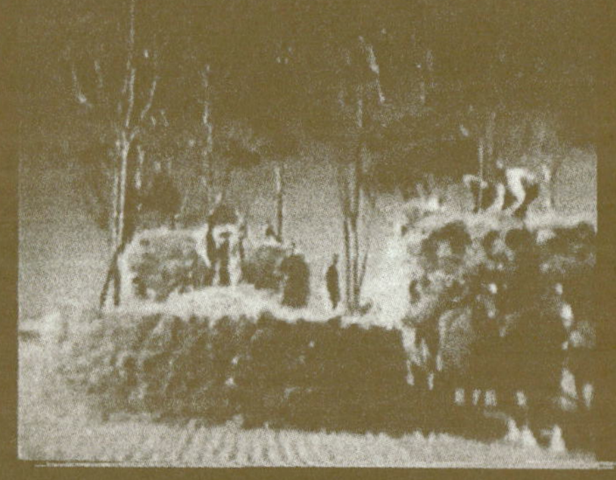

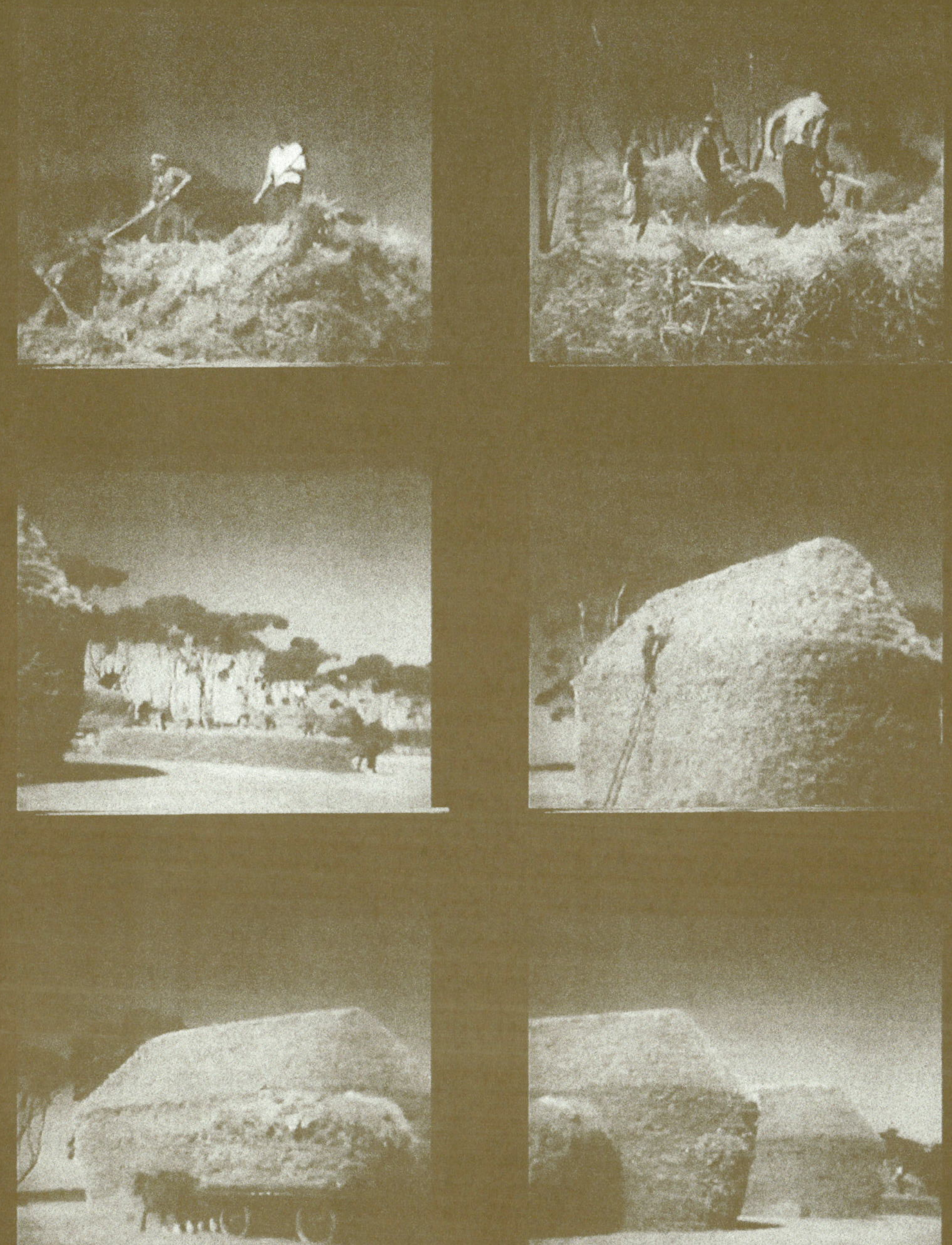

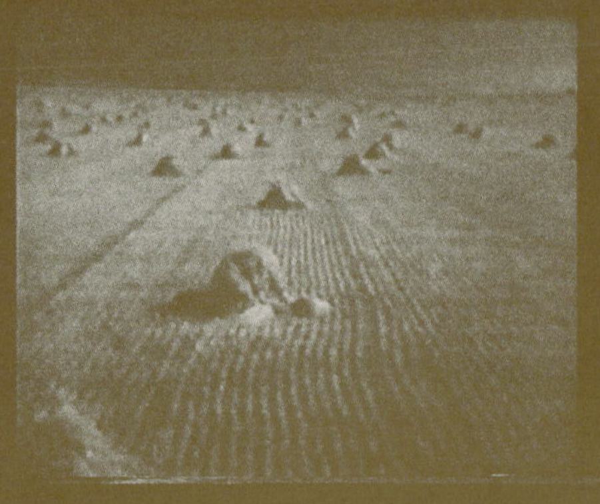

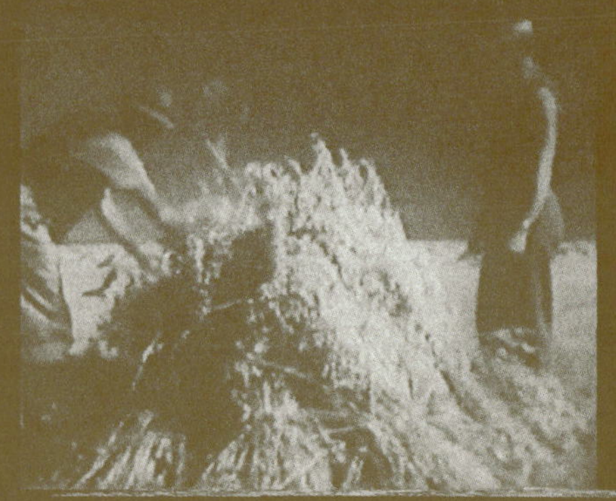

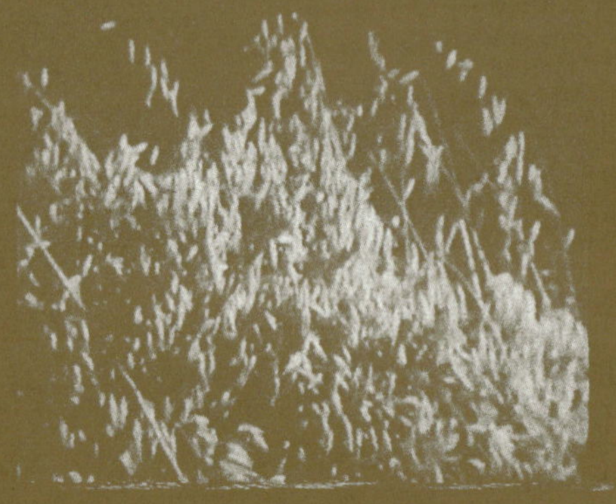

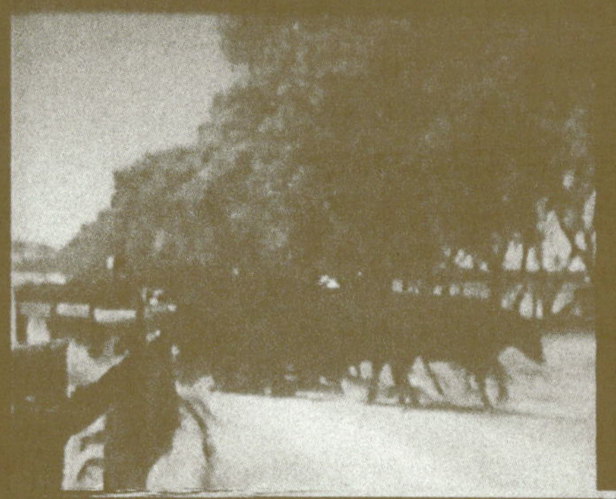

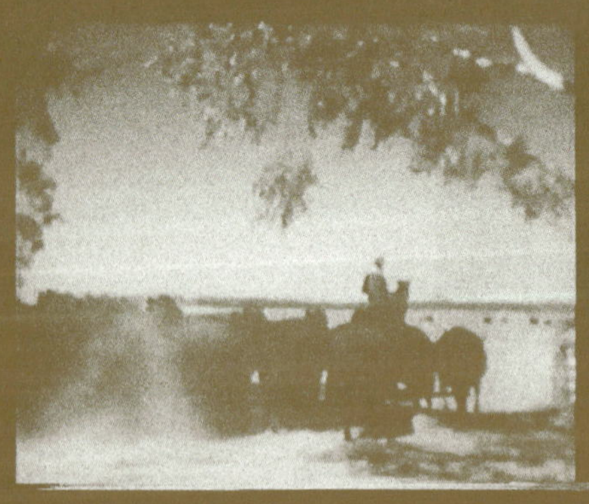

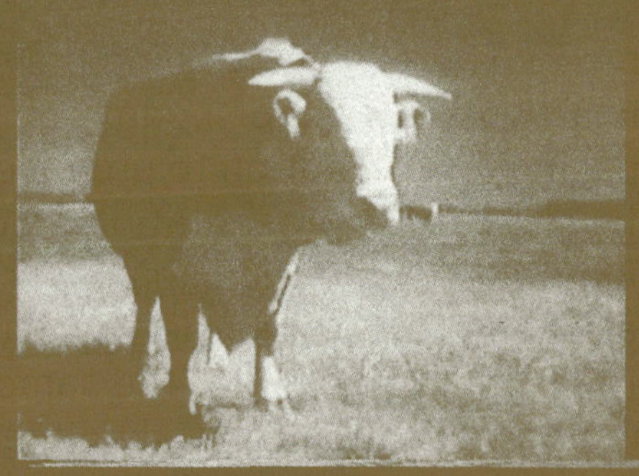

Notes for a scarecrow

Spiros Panigirakis

1. Welcome to Melbourne Water. The architectural program of the foyer generates this welcoming. But underpinning this congeniality is an efficient administration of activity. This is a space that determines access to labour, state infrastructure, education and leisure. The spatial dynamic of this foyer is dominated by the dissemination of information produced by a map and a model. The model, made up of geometric prisms of solid perspex, could be a polite abstract sculpture but instead its formal language is used to communicate how sewage is transformed across a geographic terrain. The giant floor-based map of Melbourne continues to somewhat perversely work against the late-modern architectural style to signpost a particular place—potentially your place.

2. There is no avoiding the sited conditions of an artwork. It is an orthodoxy of contemporary art making and reception to produce meaning through the site of art's presentation. Regardless of the potential dislocating capacity of the approach taken to site, the over-determination of the artistic framework via site is at the same time tired. This is arguably the case even when the artistic response to the site in question is disruptive. The public relations rhetoric for the site intervention is one of virtuousness—the artist is, after all, being thoughtful.

However, to counter this tendency is to be somewhat deluded. The geometric prism that is plonked into a foyer is no less problematic in the site-less conditions it asks the visitor to imagine.

3. The commercial imperative of the fashion industry embeds obsolescence within an understanding of style. This can be interpreted as a highly responsive relation to social, political and environmental shifts over time. The mass exploitation associated with certain sectors of production makes the investment of labour and material resources associated with the production of clothing questionable. There are, of course, some design exceptions and subcultural resistances to this fast fashion. But another way of framing this perpetual cycle is to understand the stylistic shift as something that always flips within a certain period of time—a response to a question that can never be resolved. Definitive it is not.

4. A rudimentary definition of role play within an artwork can be understood as the identification of the artist's process within a broader social framework. So this might mean the mode of production and how this labour is valued, named and understood by others. Role play's more dominant connotation relates to the performative construction of self through social acts. Whilst there is no authentic here, play is often used as a tool to understand and model social relations. With or without a script, we fumble through staged assertions of ourselves—lethargic, horny and/or hungry.

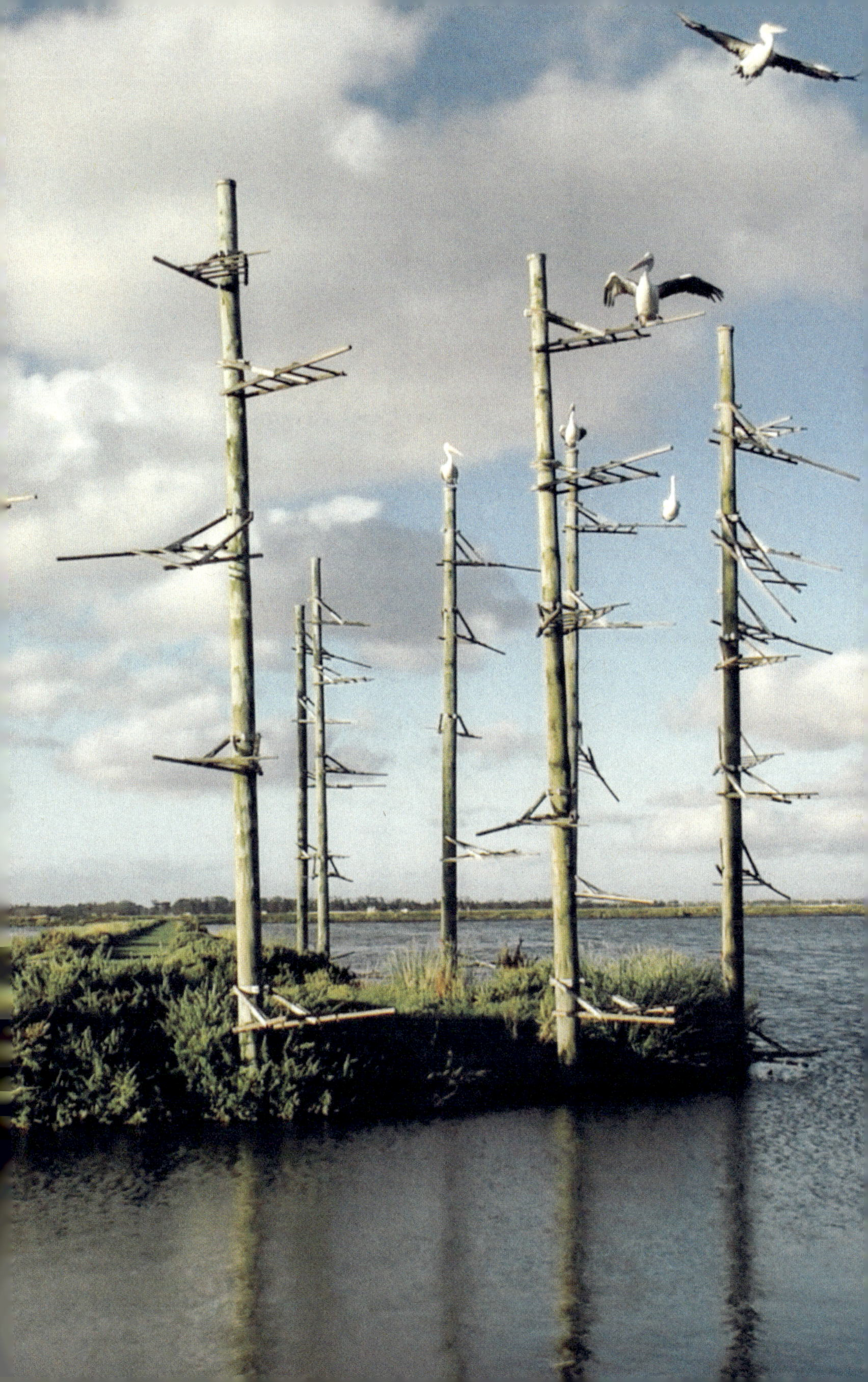

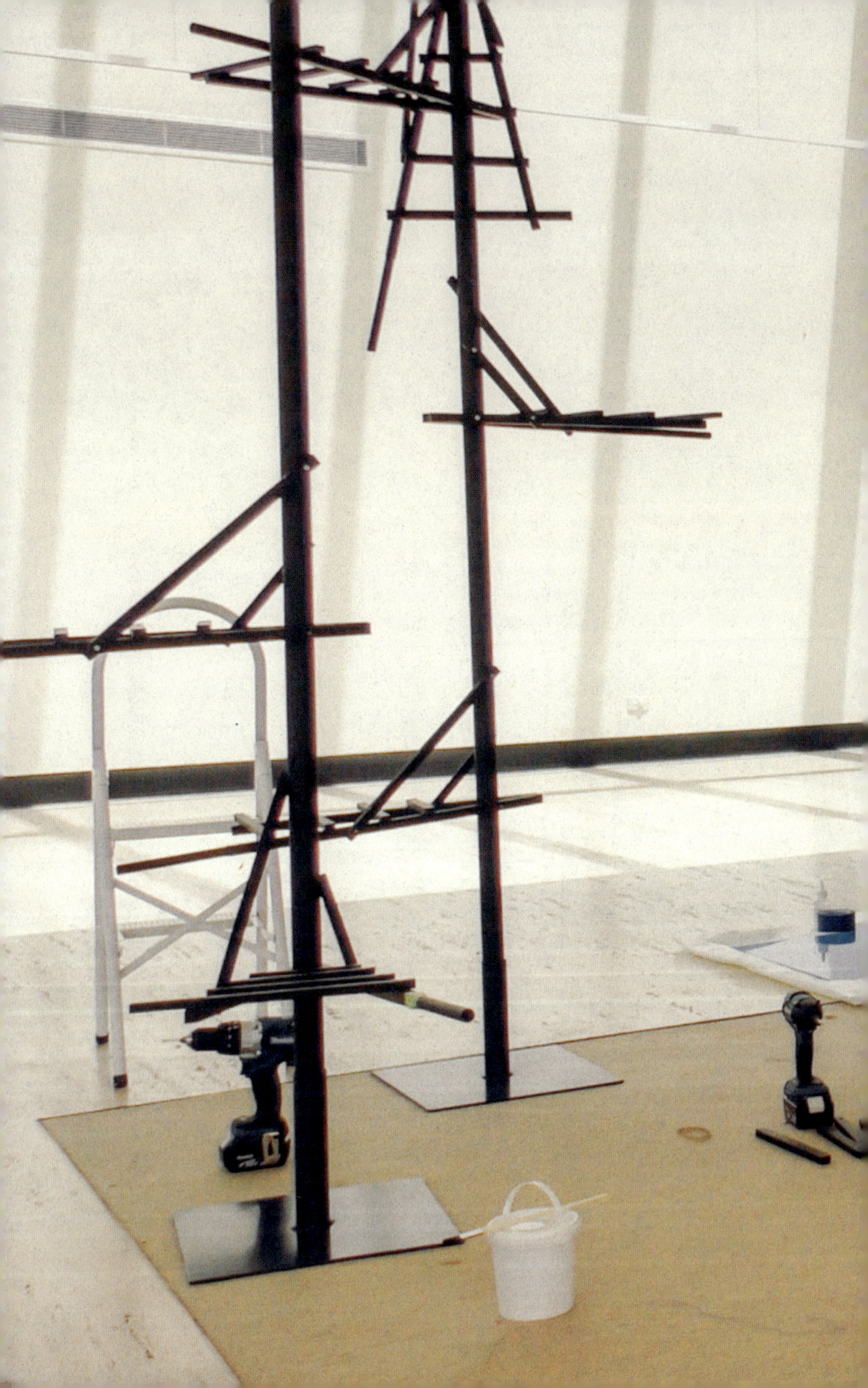

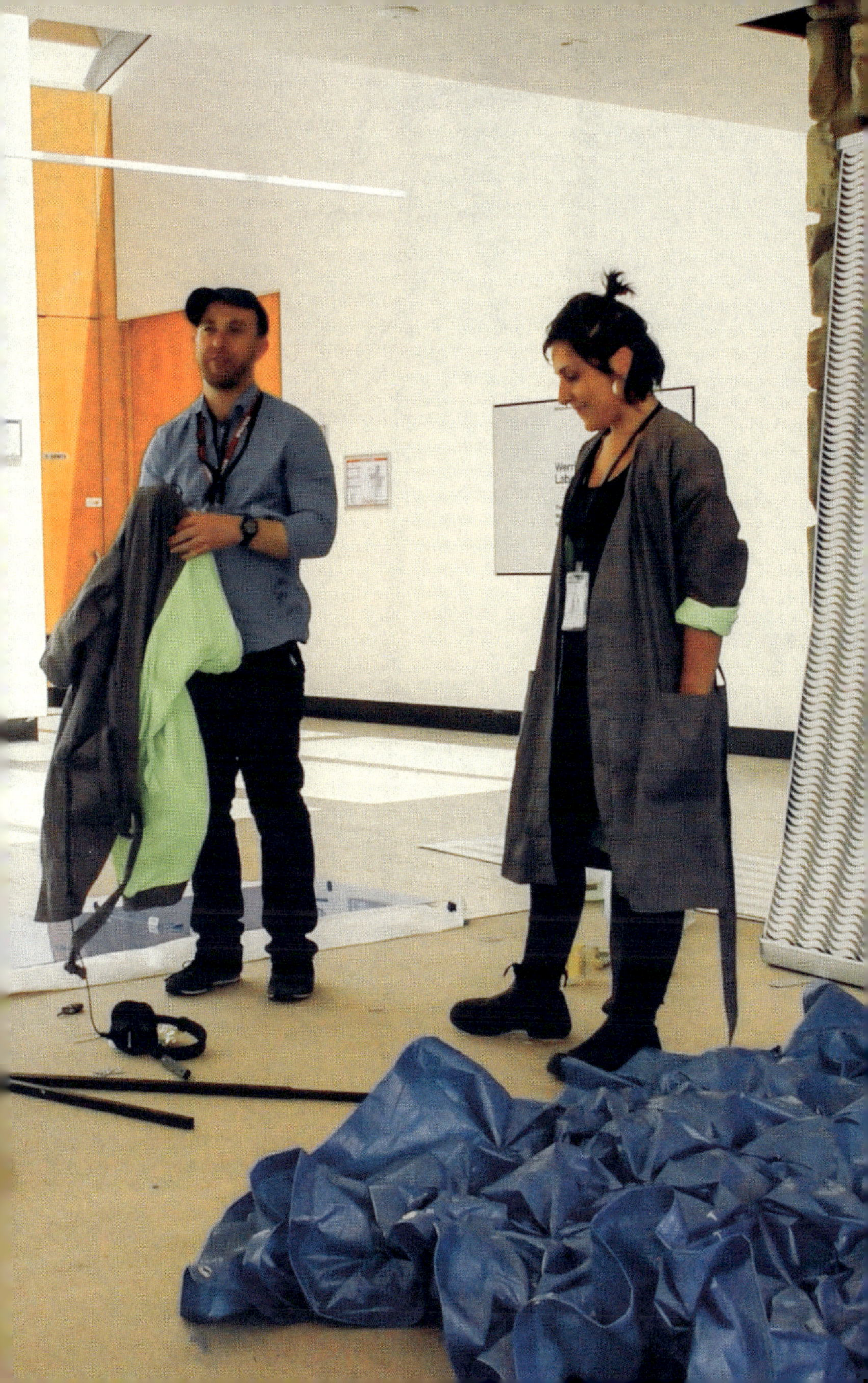

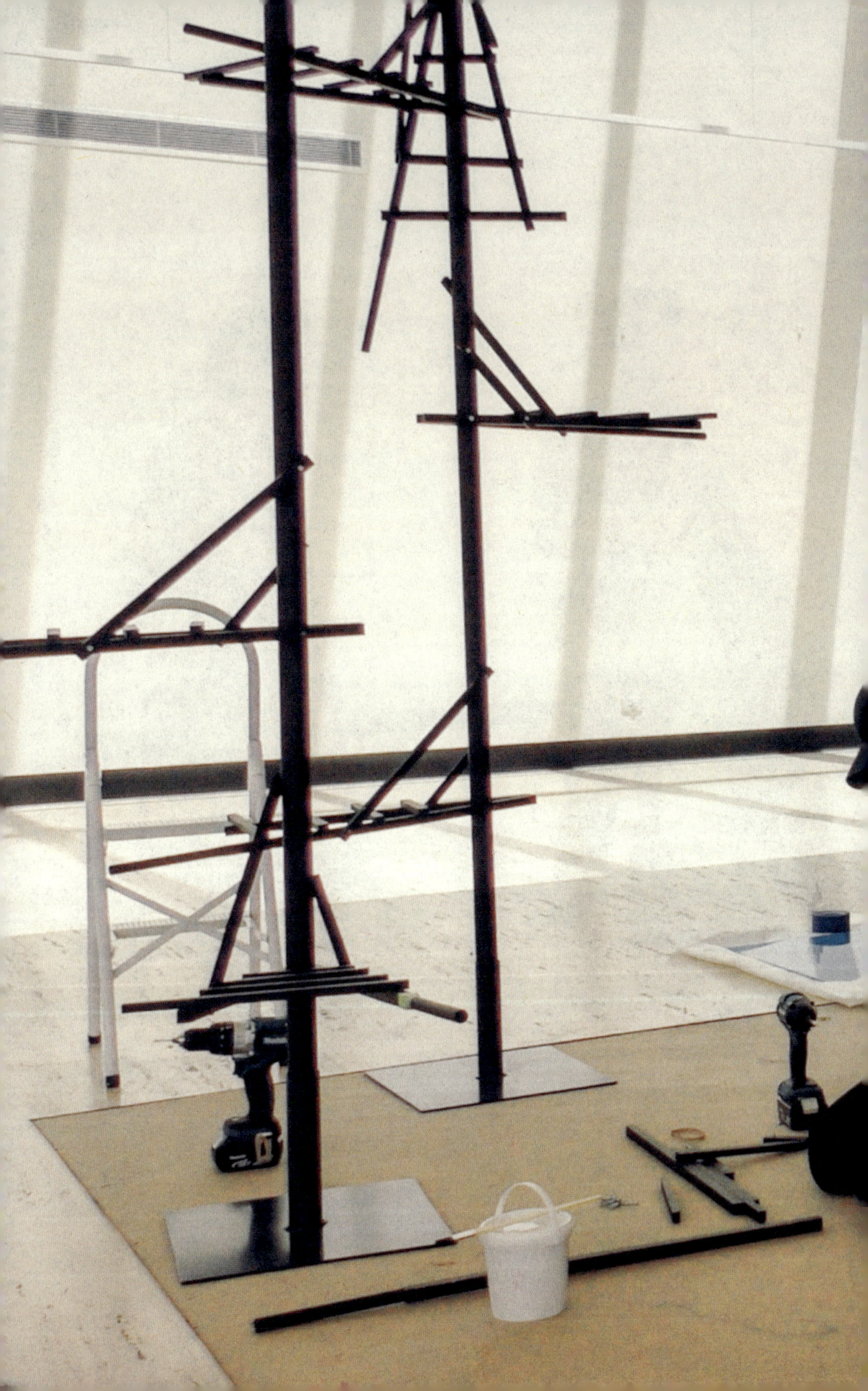

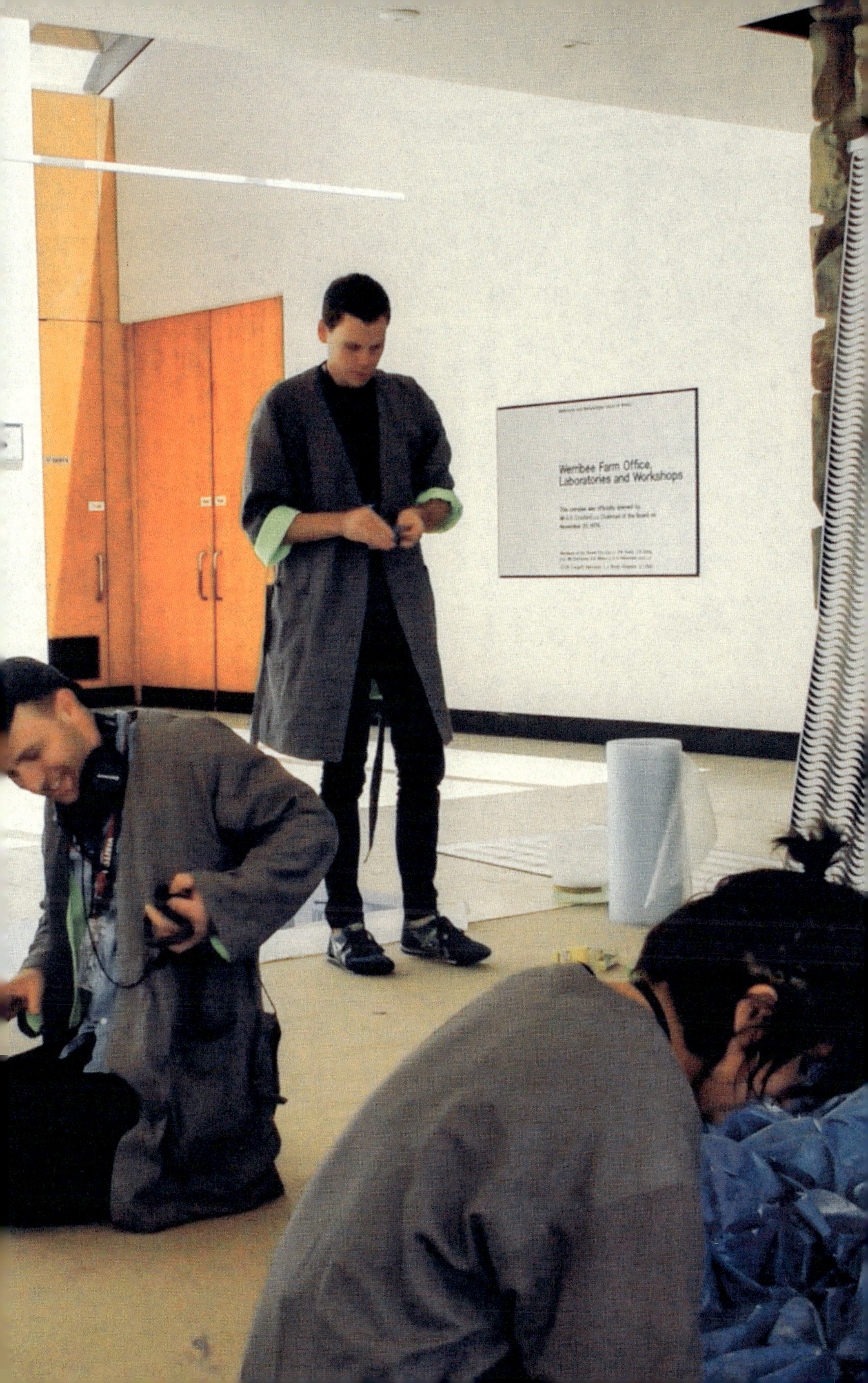
Werribee Farm Office,
Laboratories and Workshops

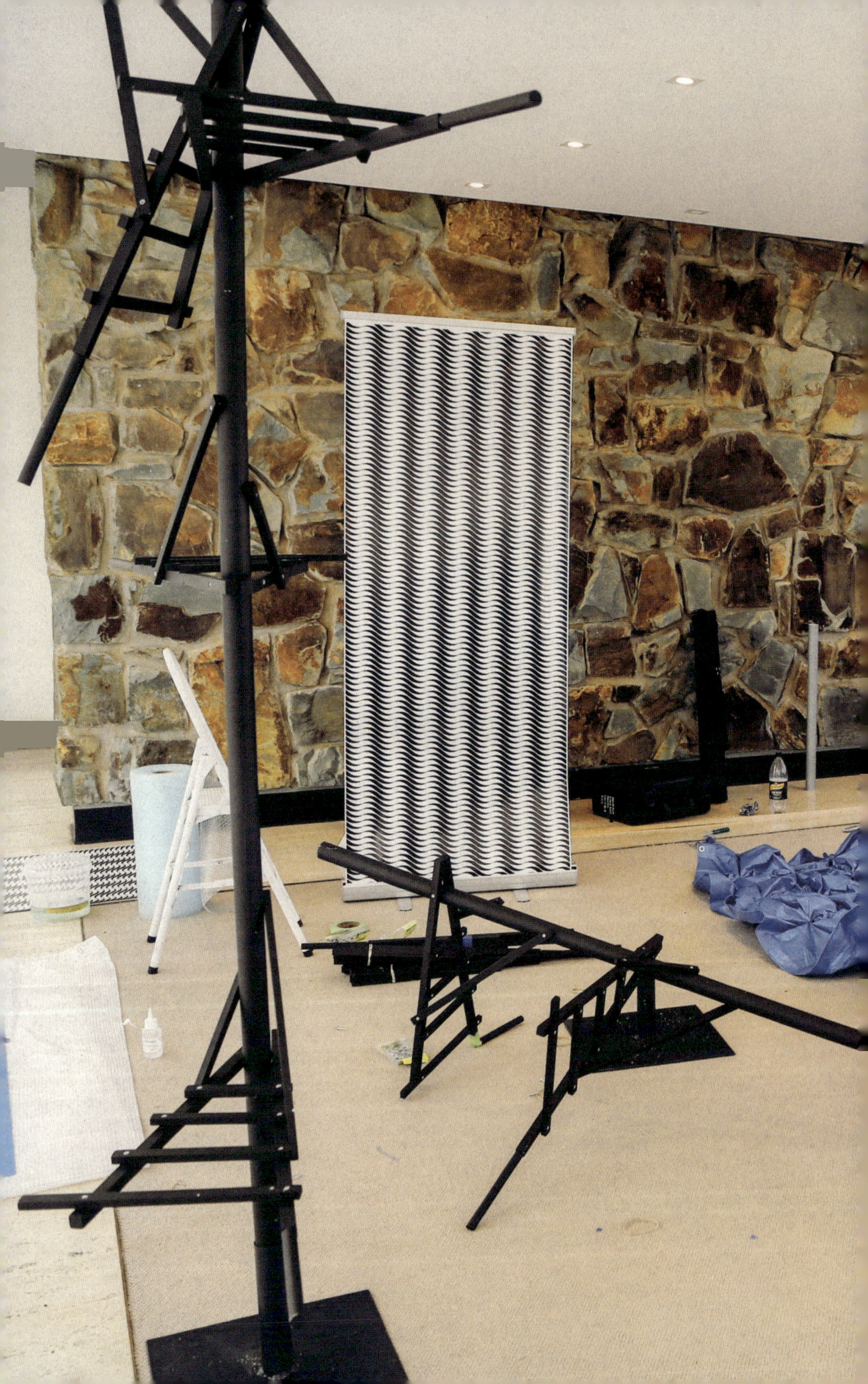

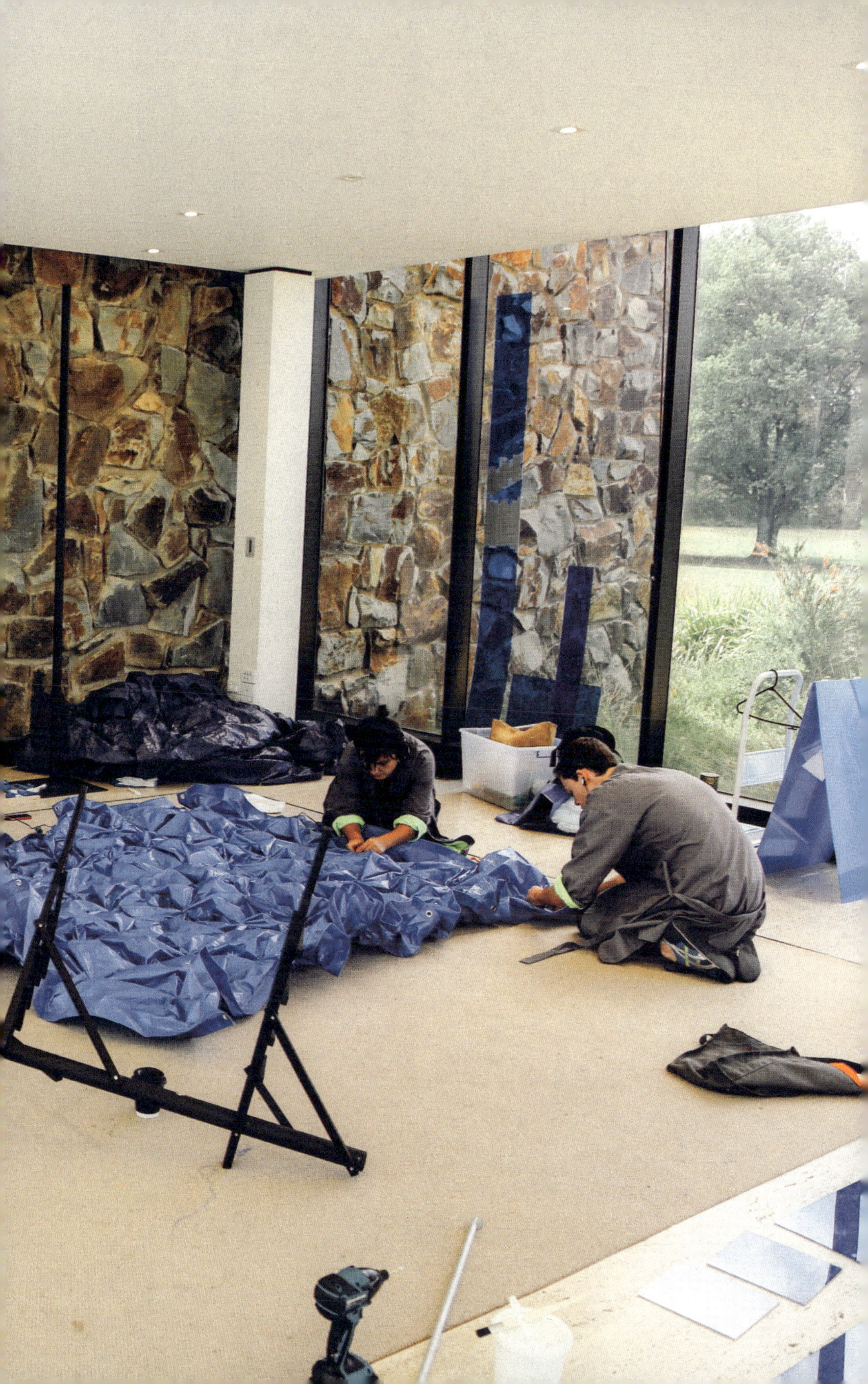

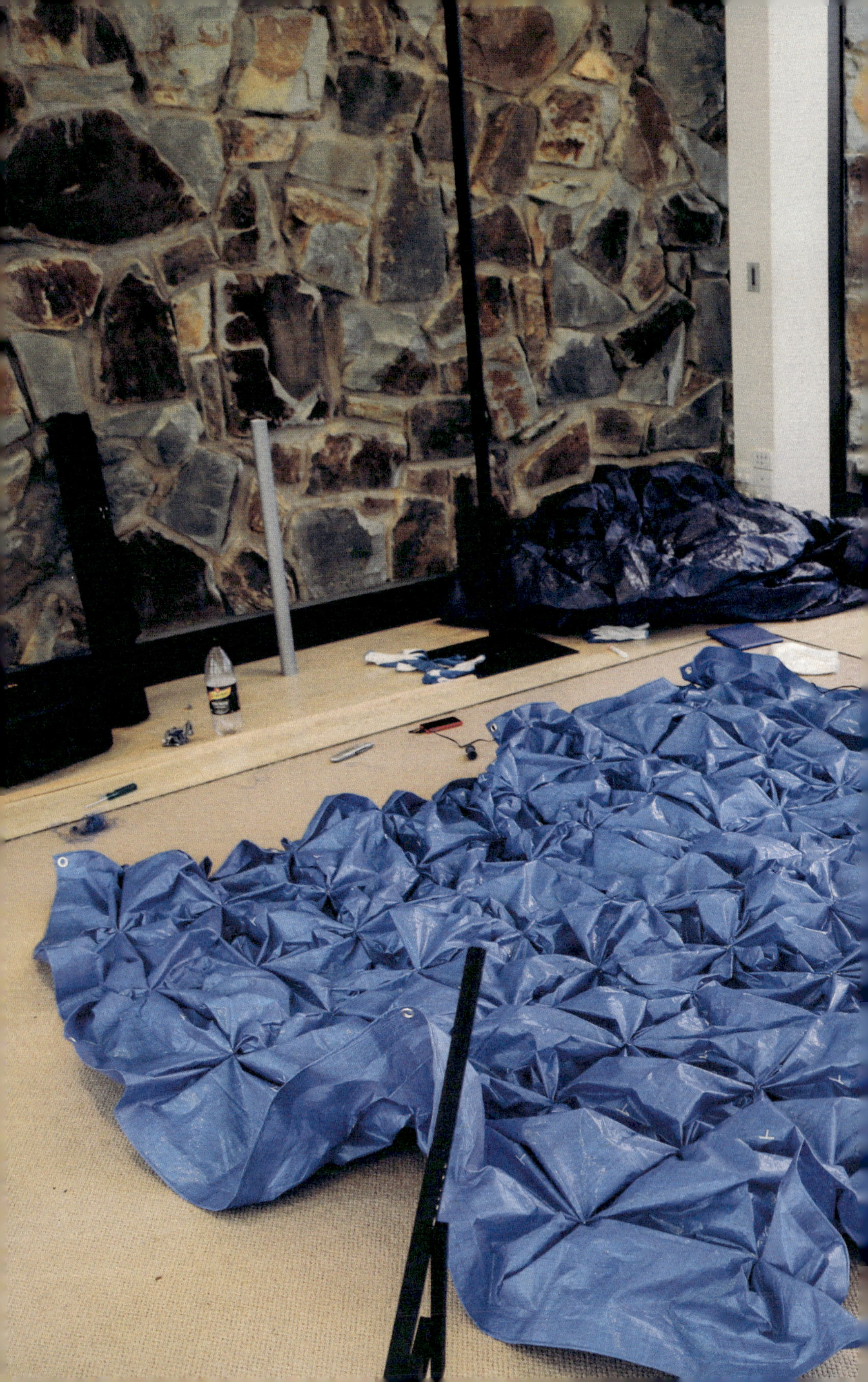

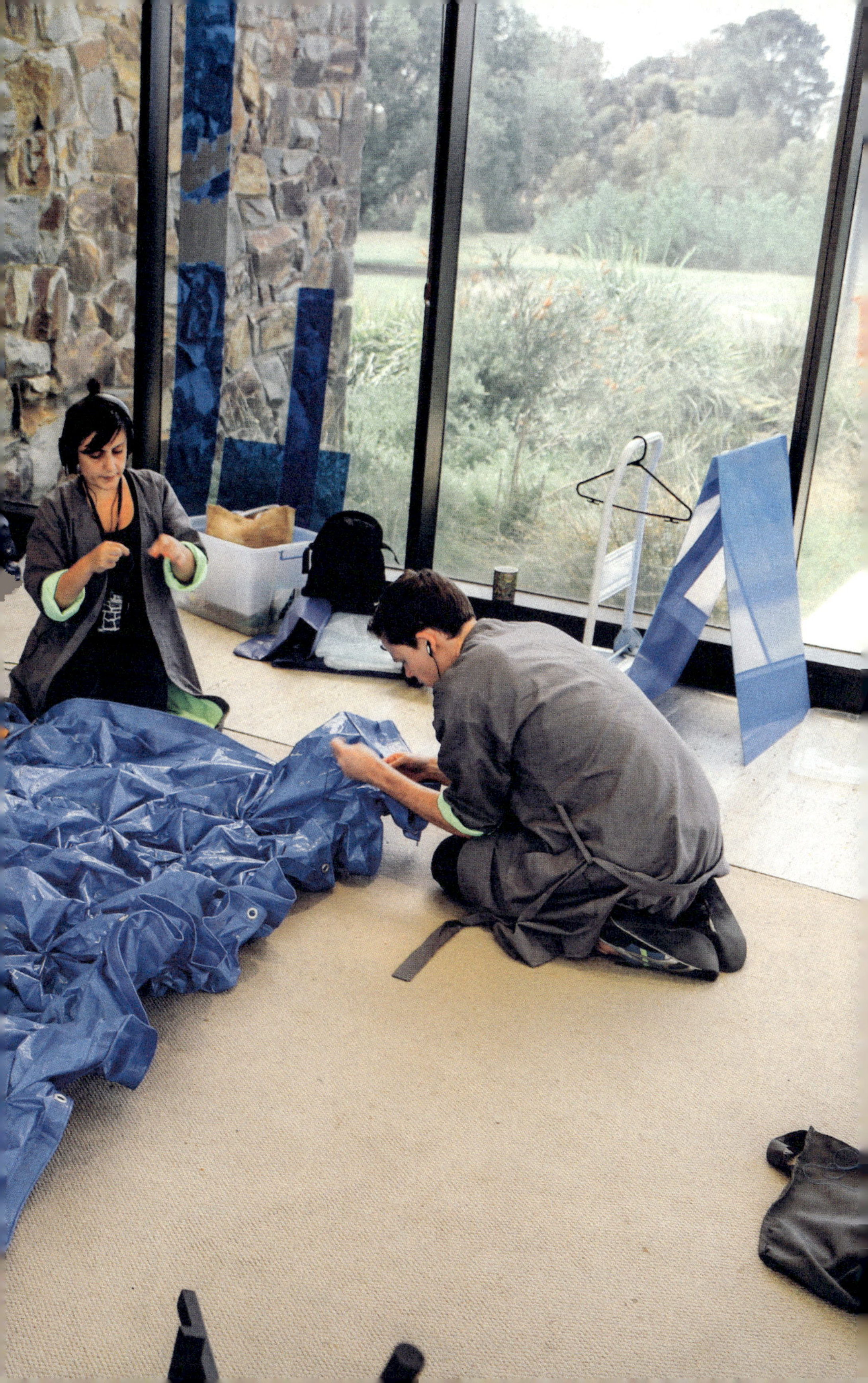

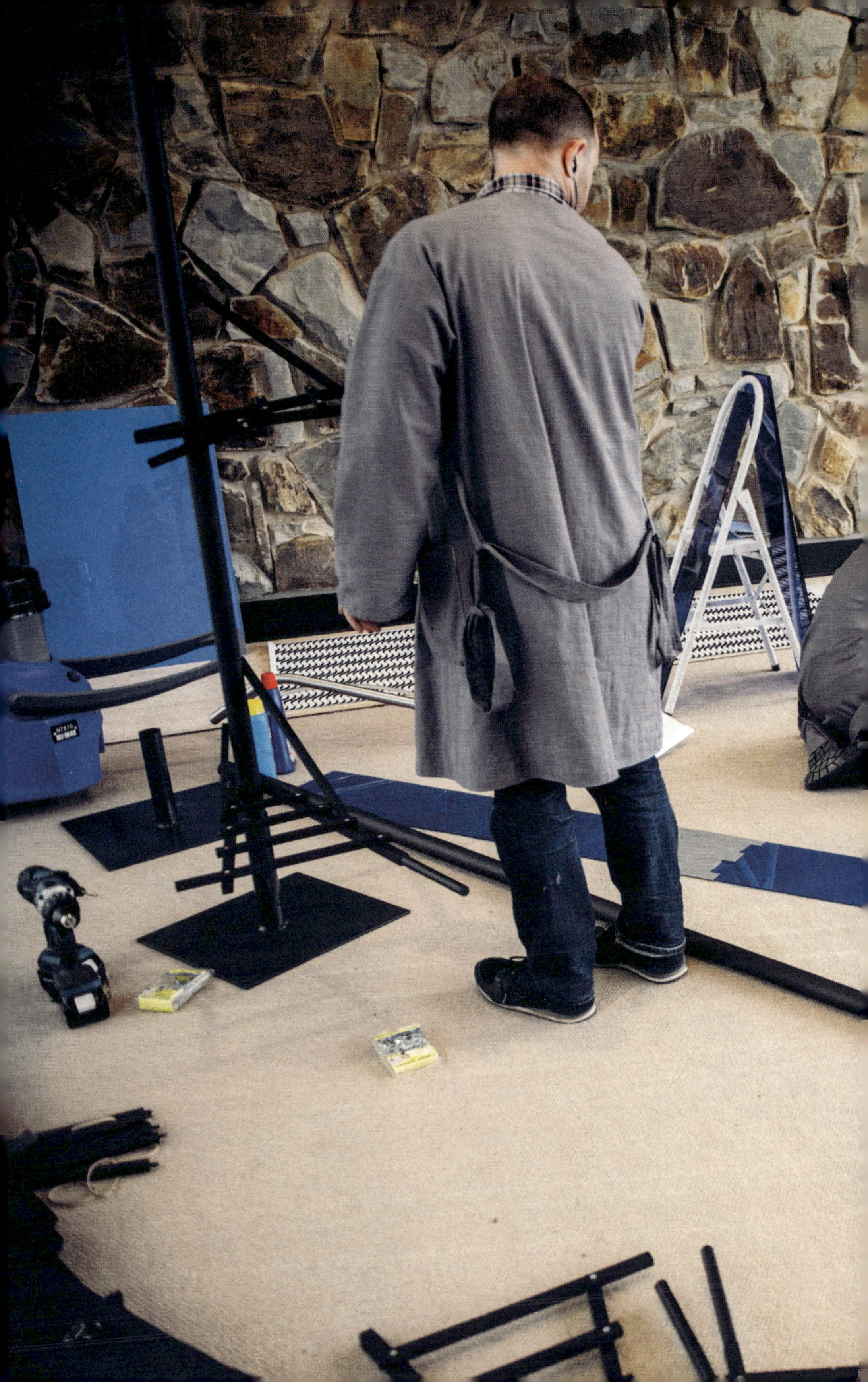

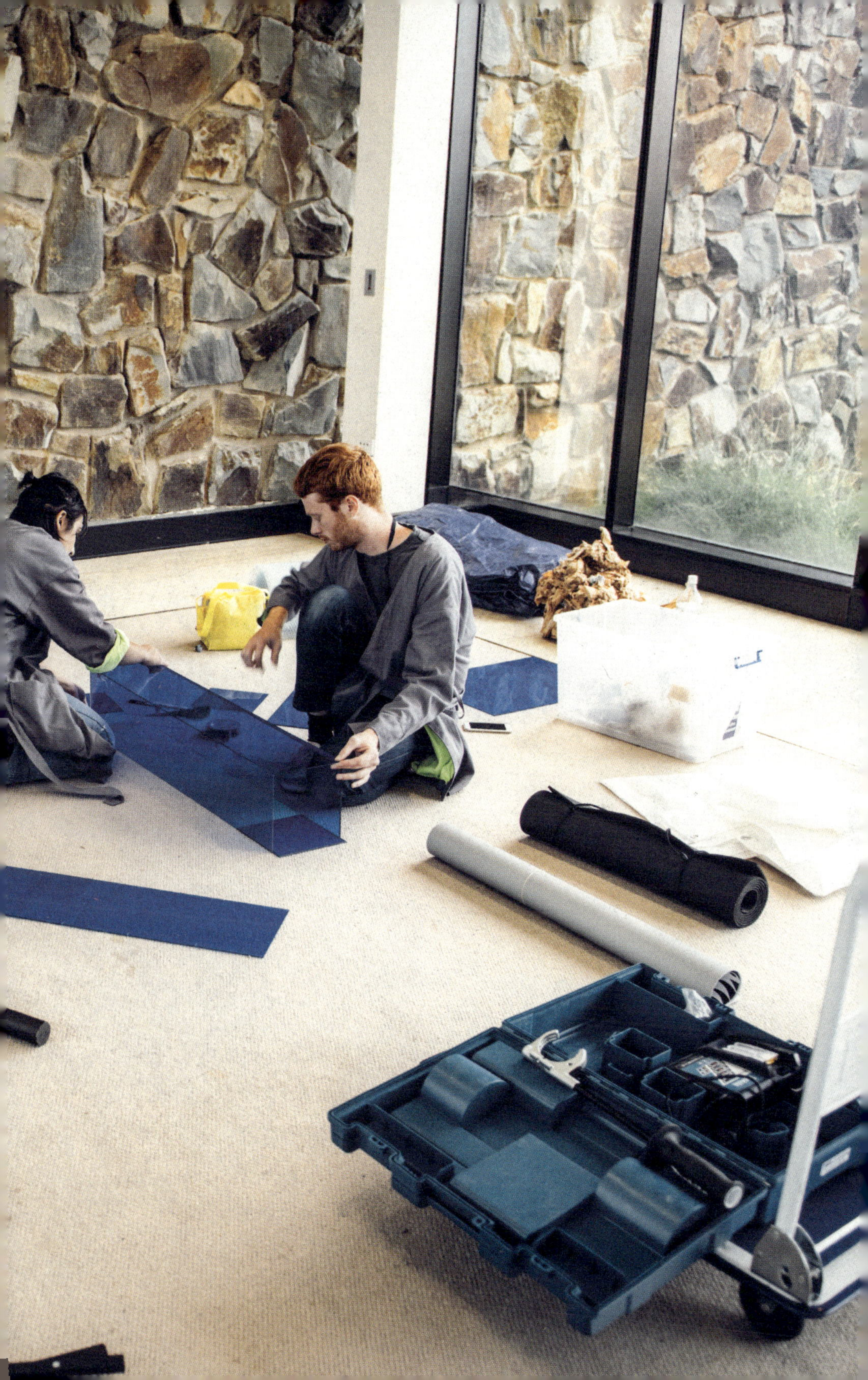

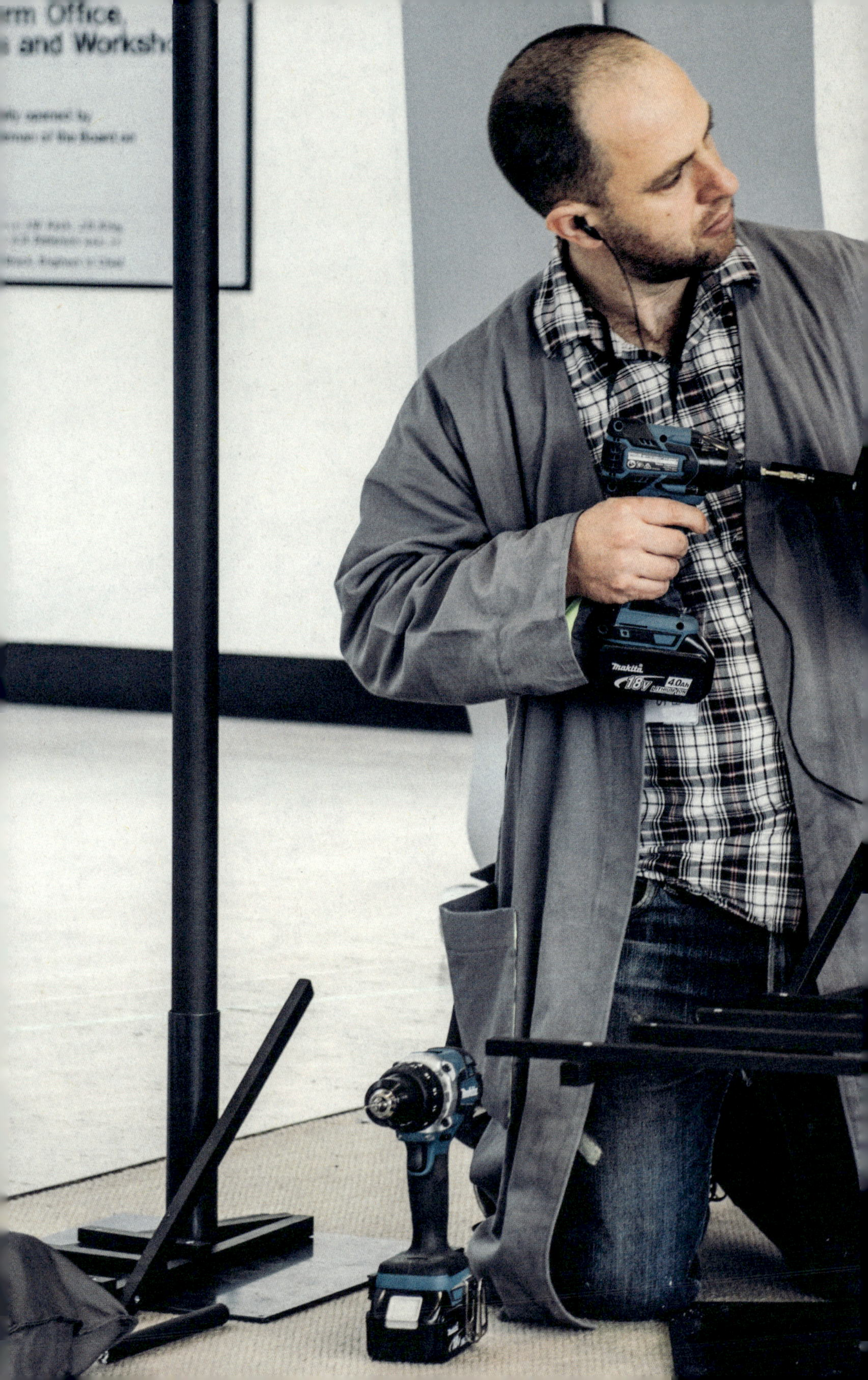
makita
18V 4.0Ah

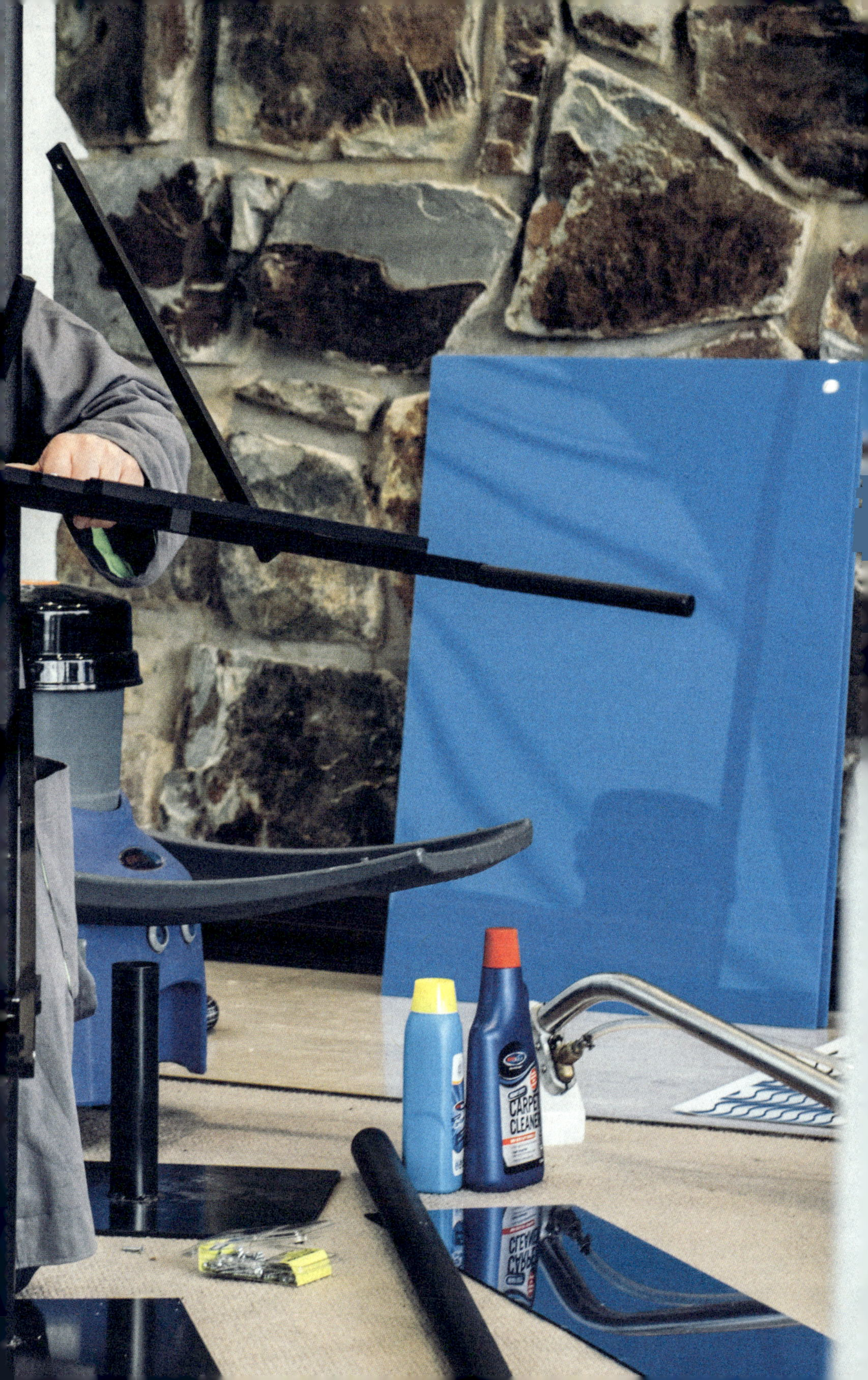
CARPE
CLEANE

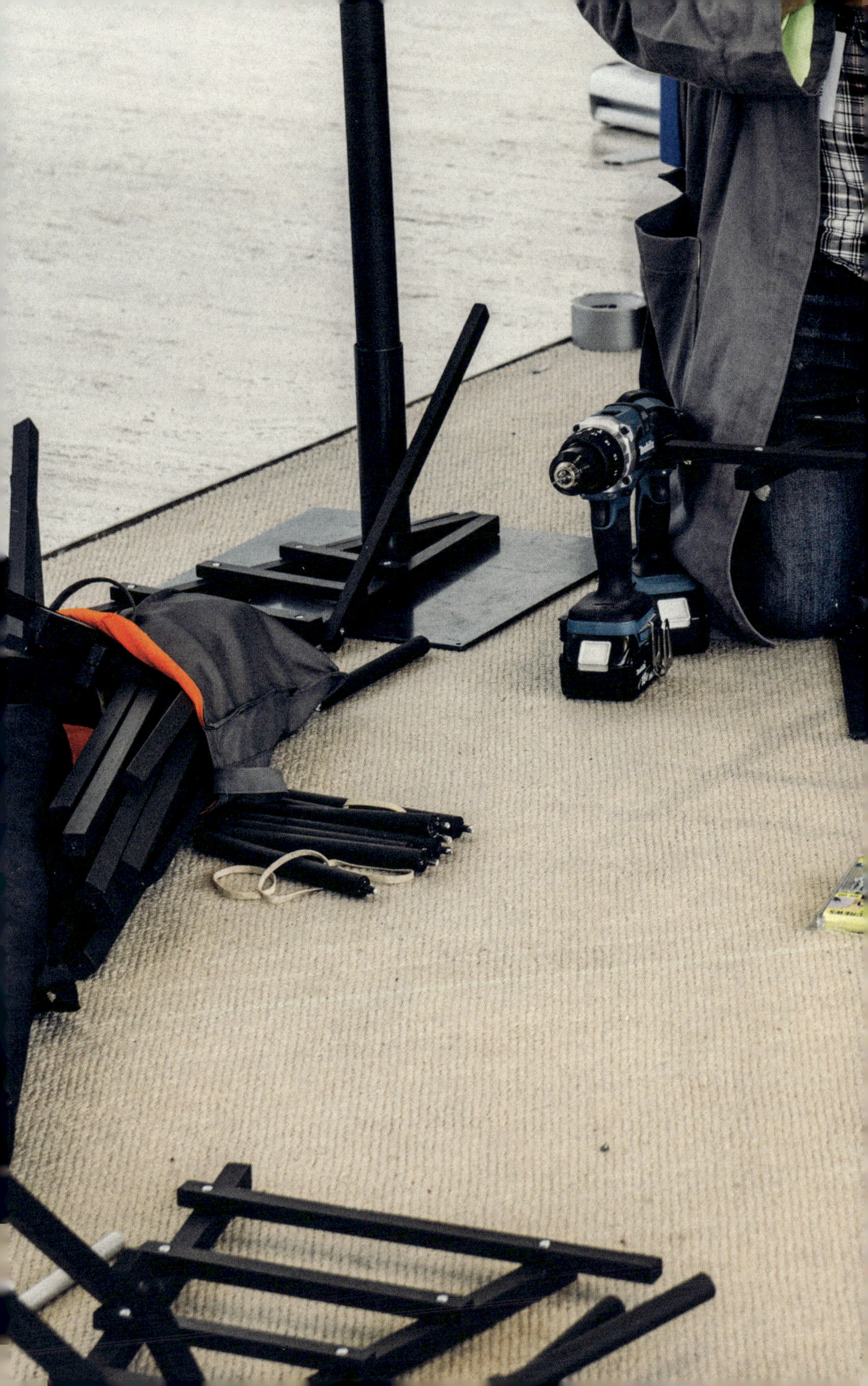

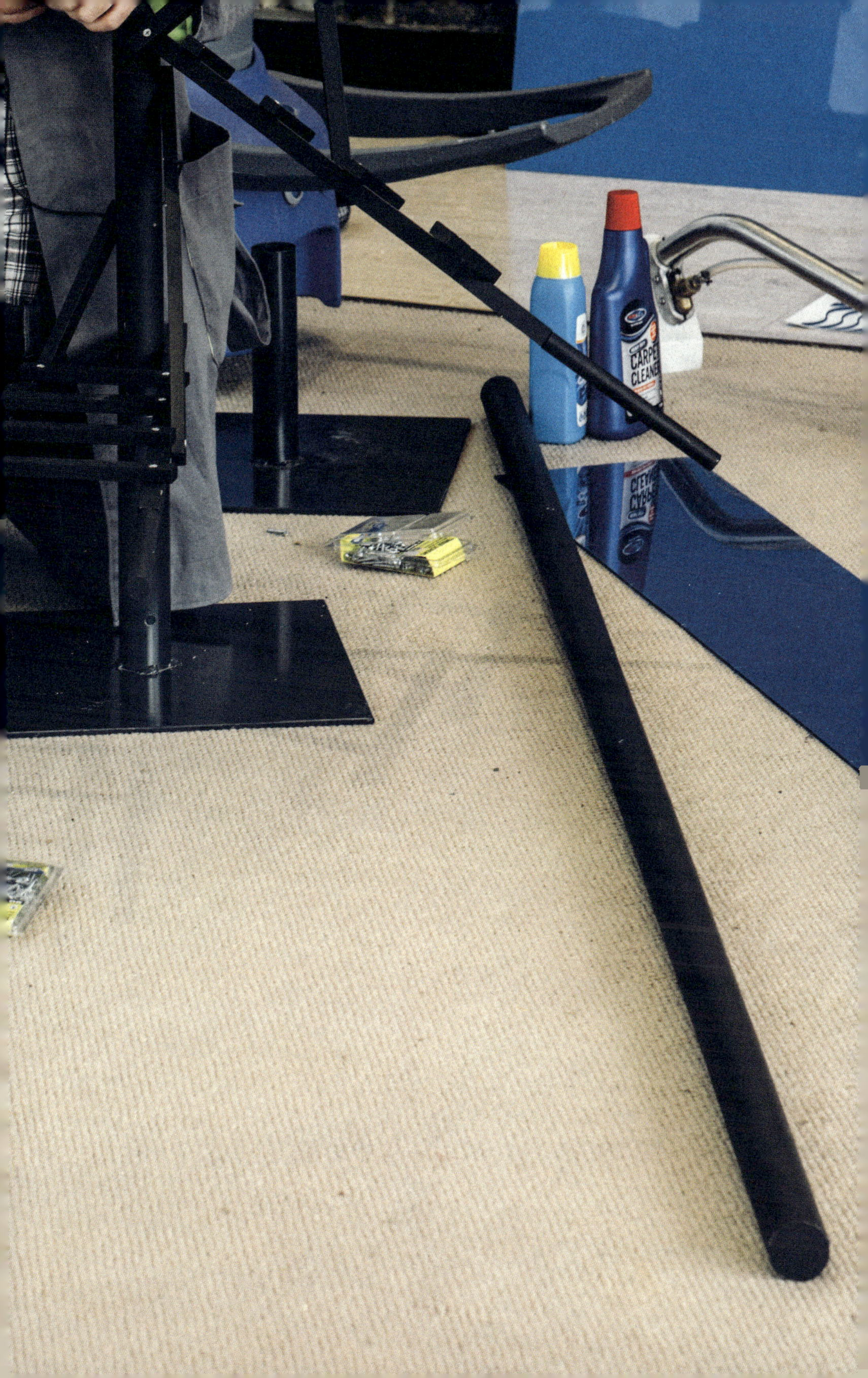

CARPE
CLEANE

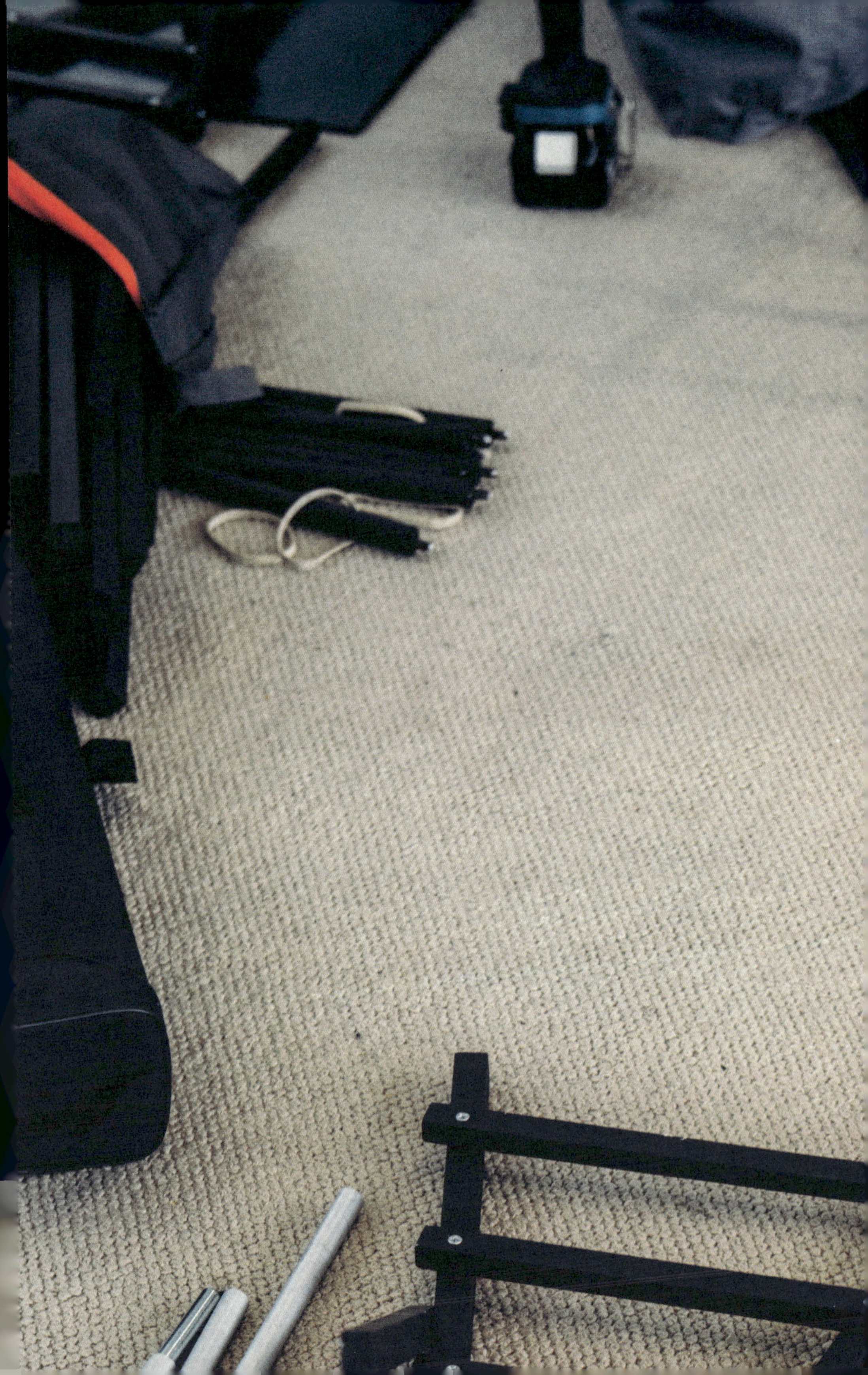

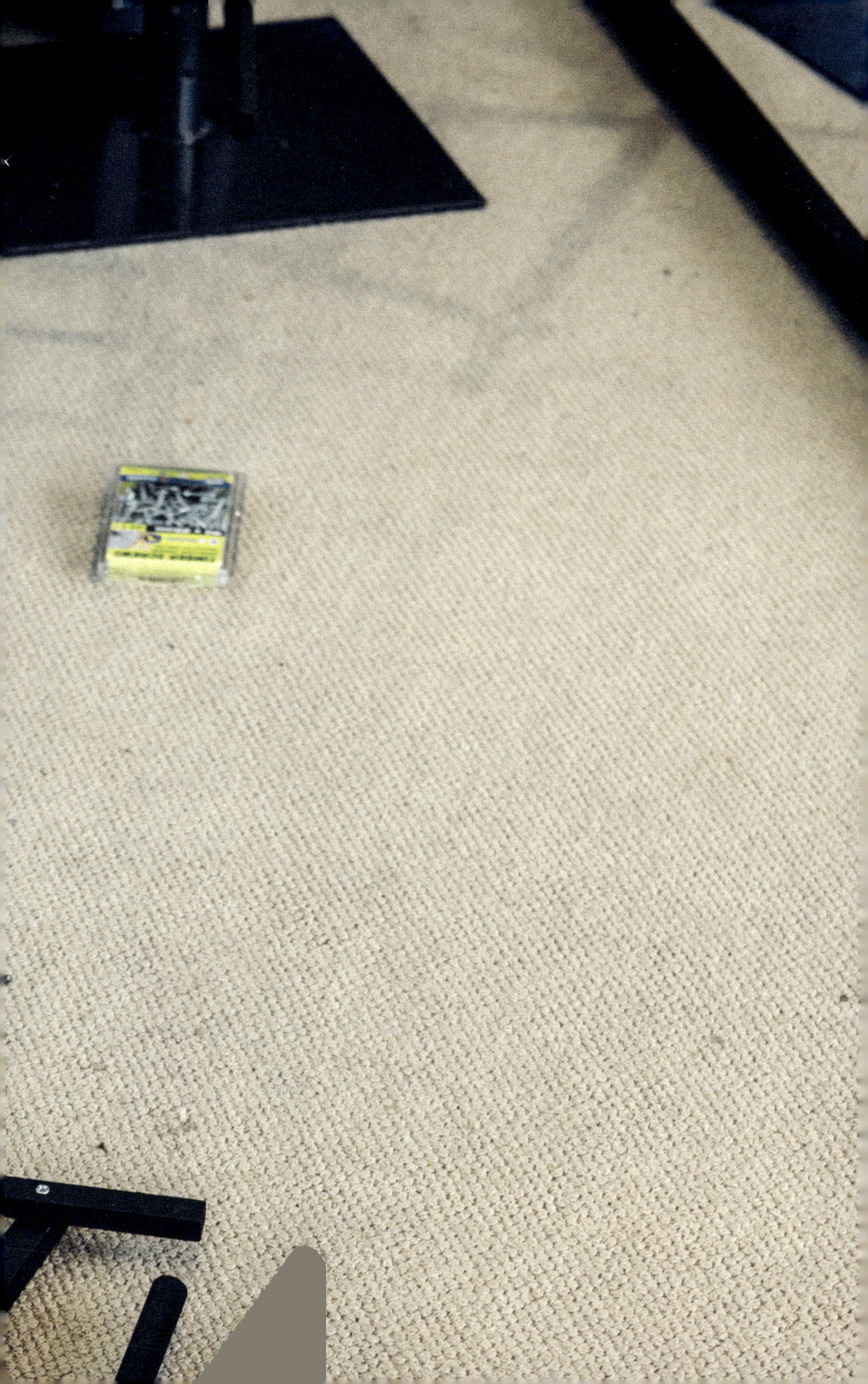

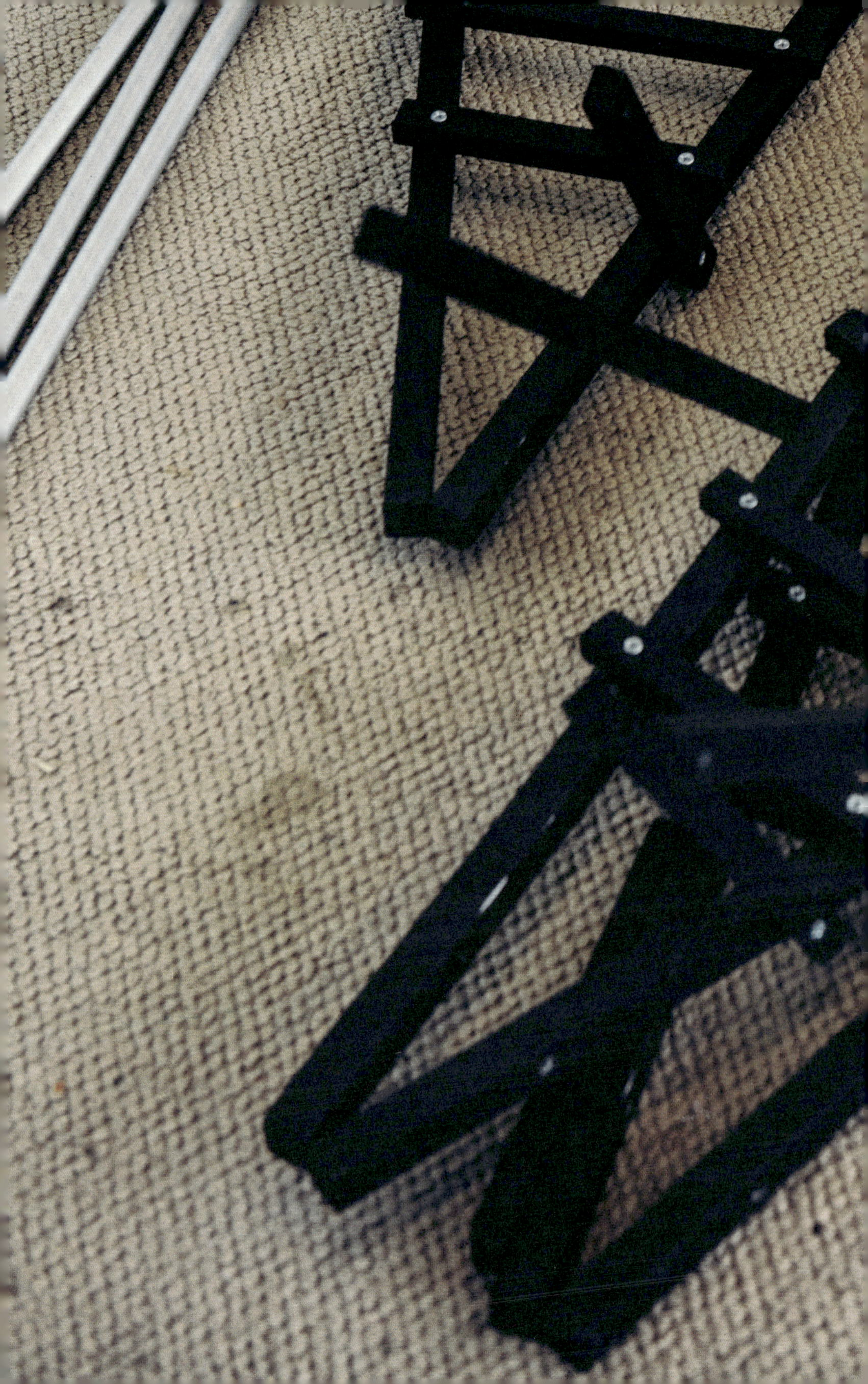

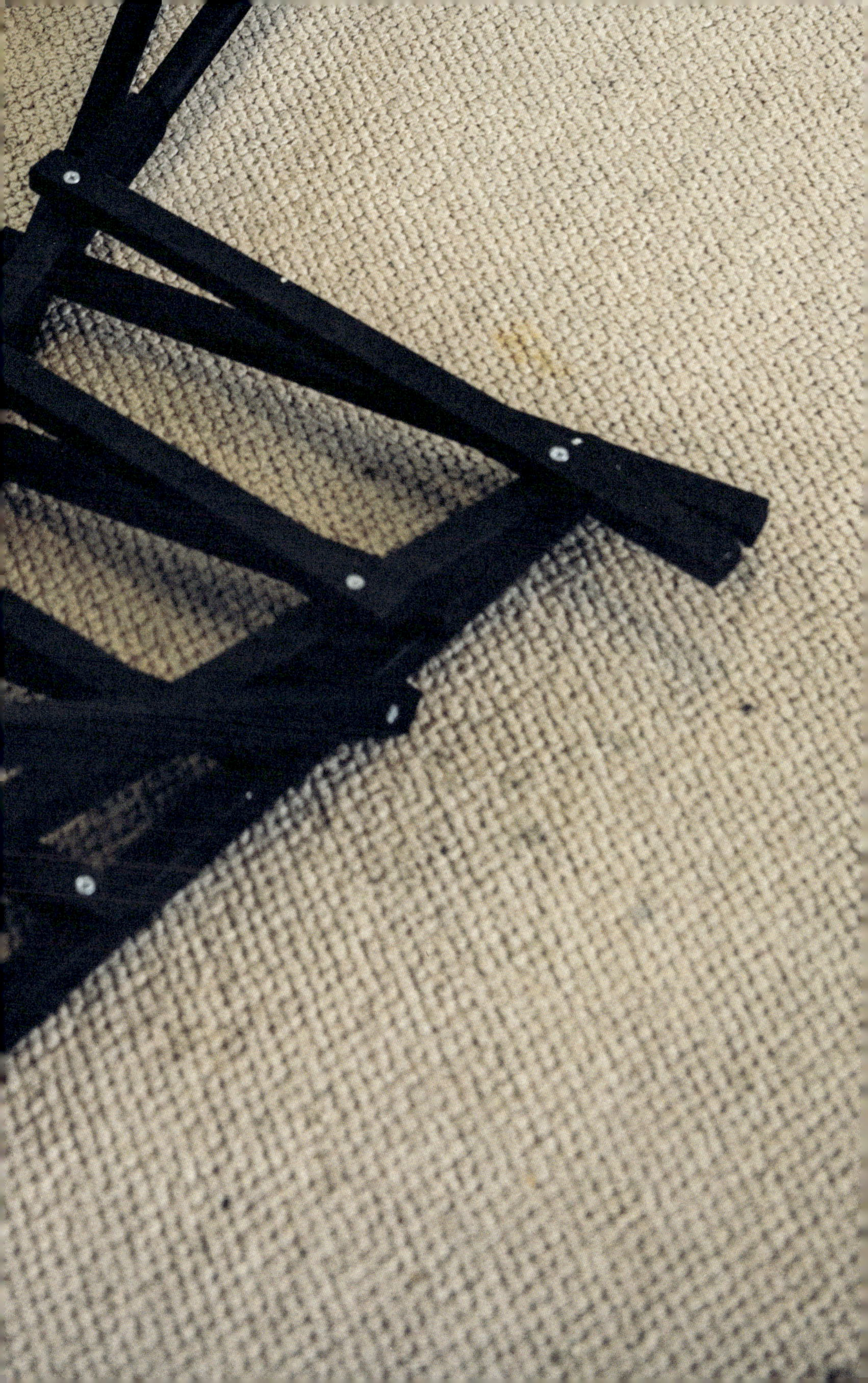

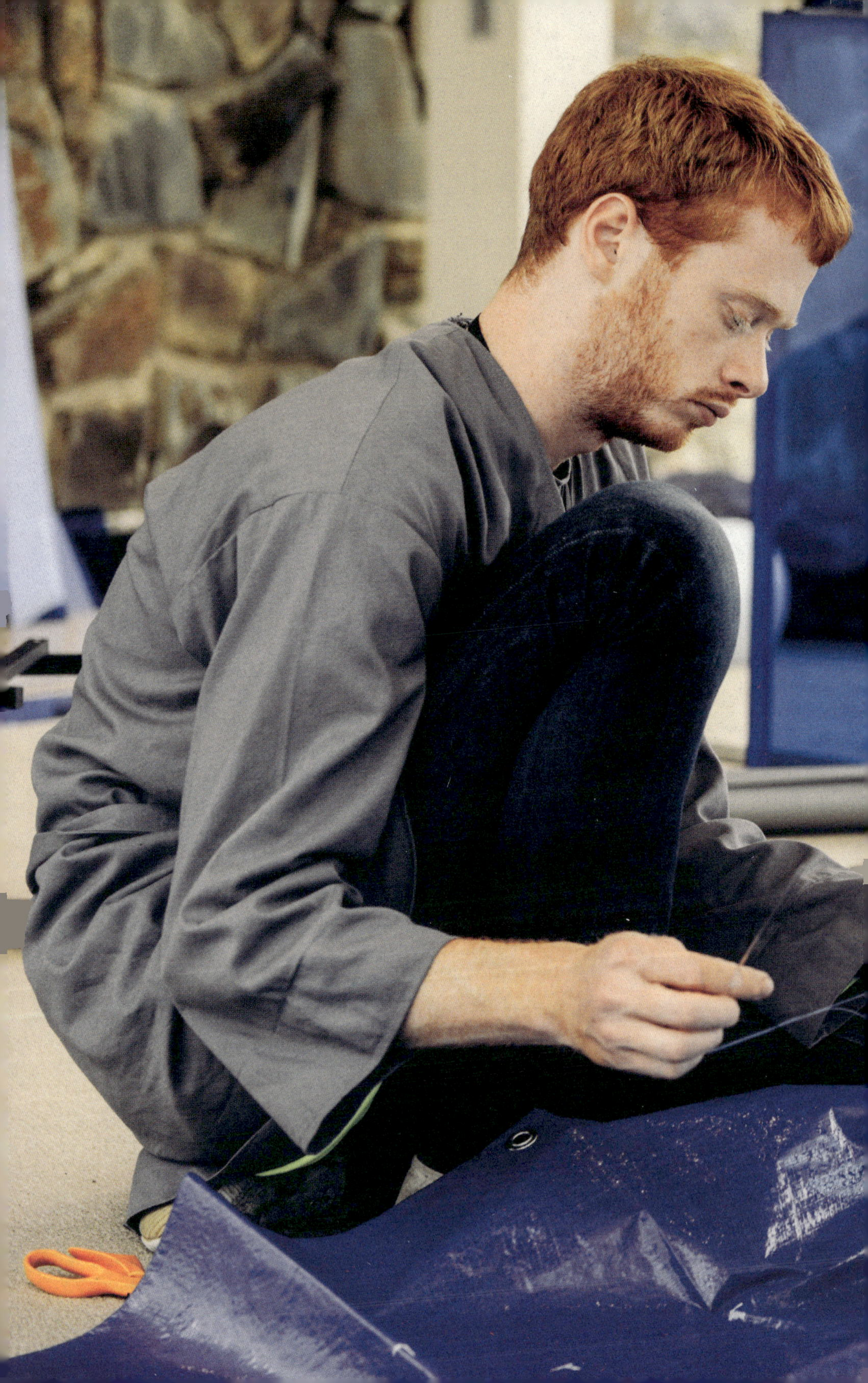

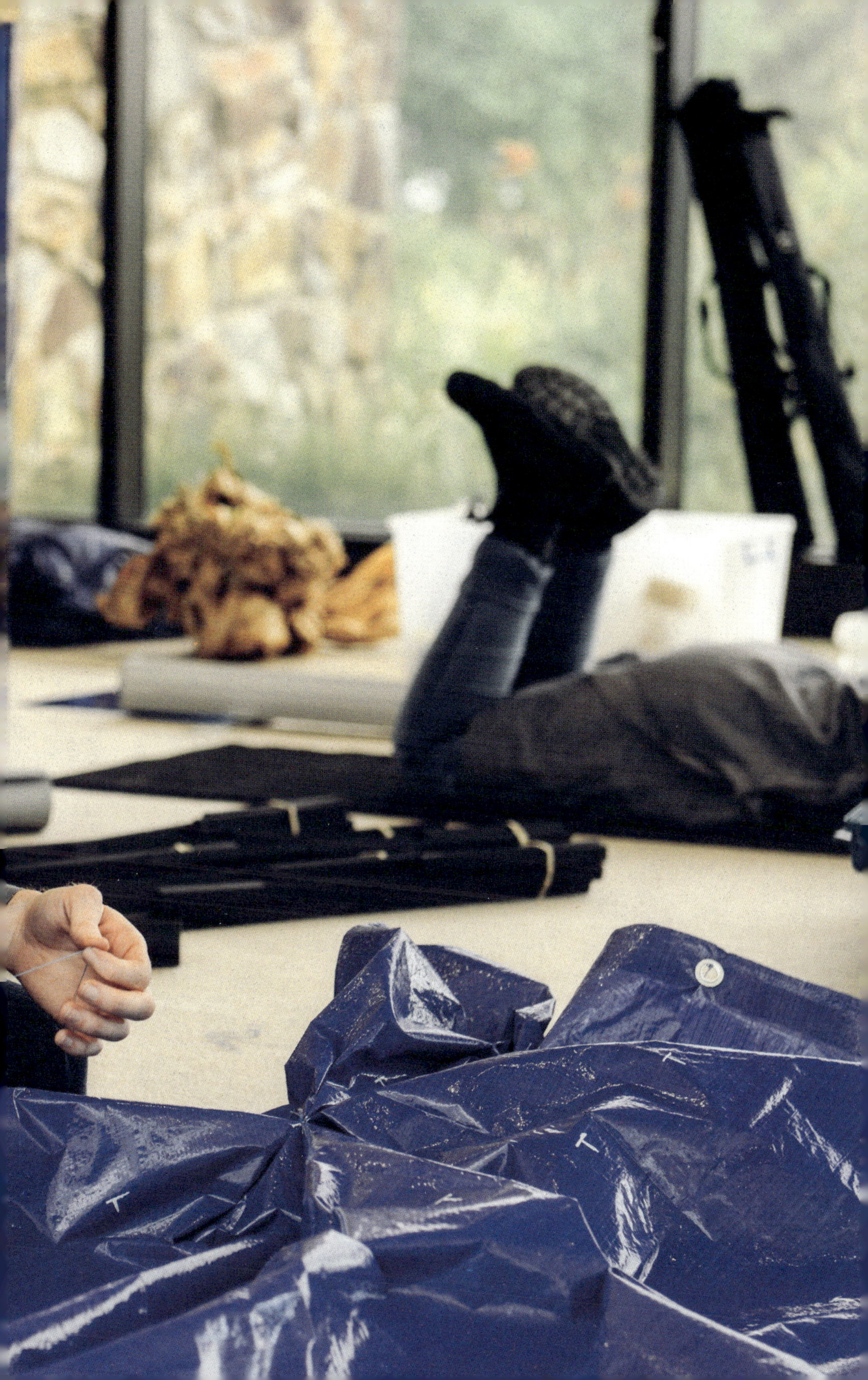

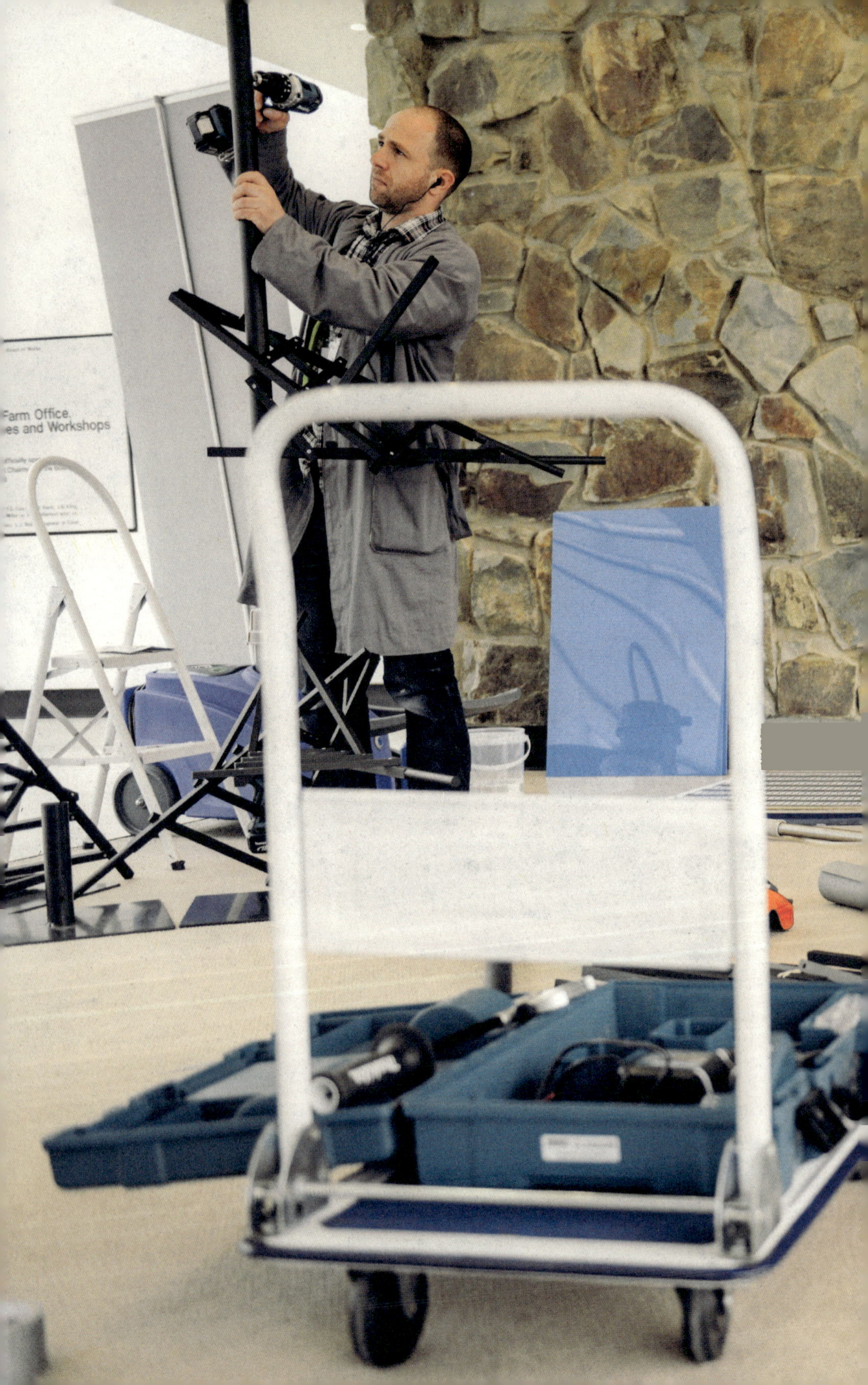
Farm Office,
es and Workshops

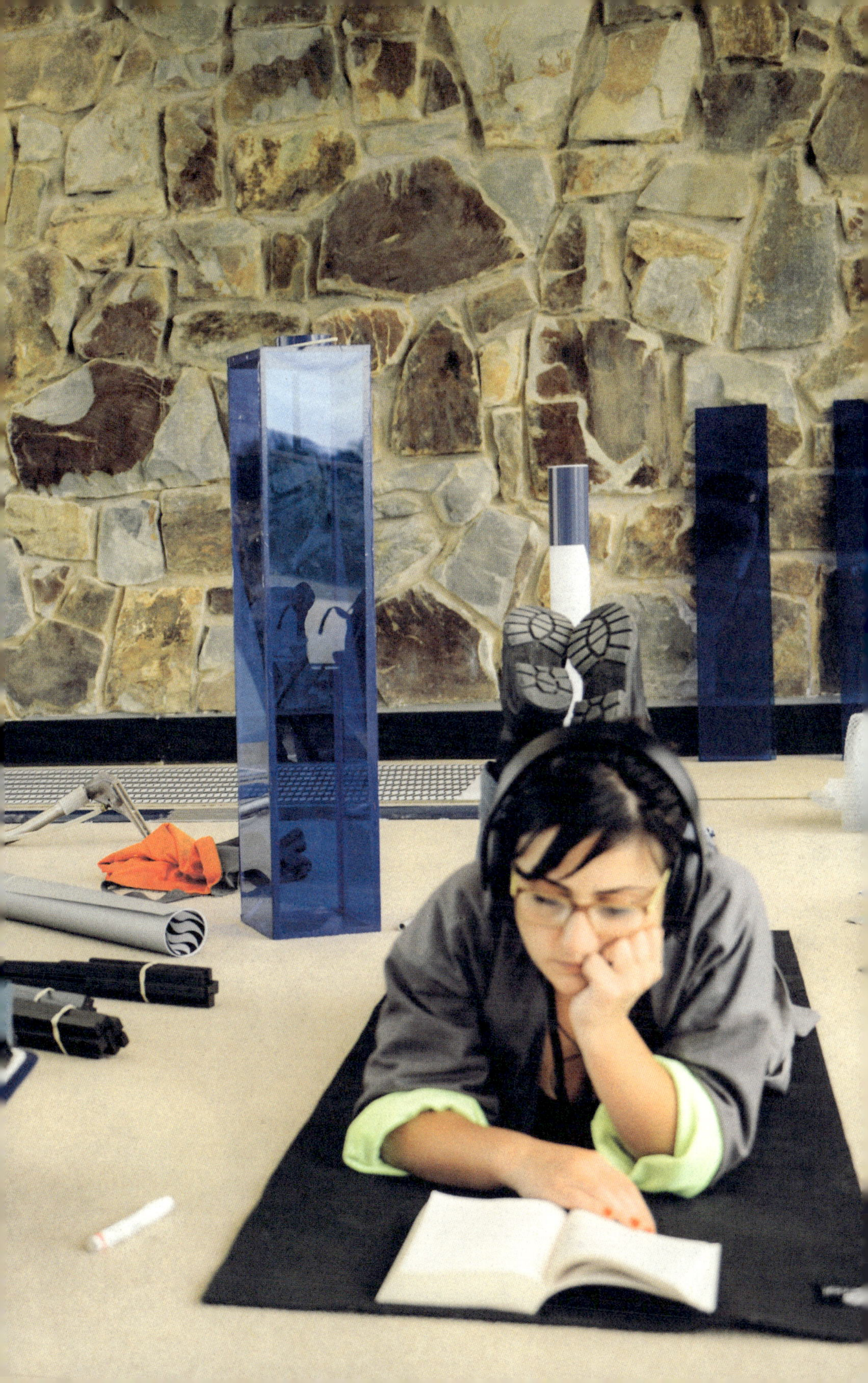

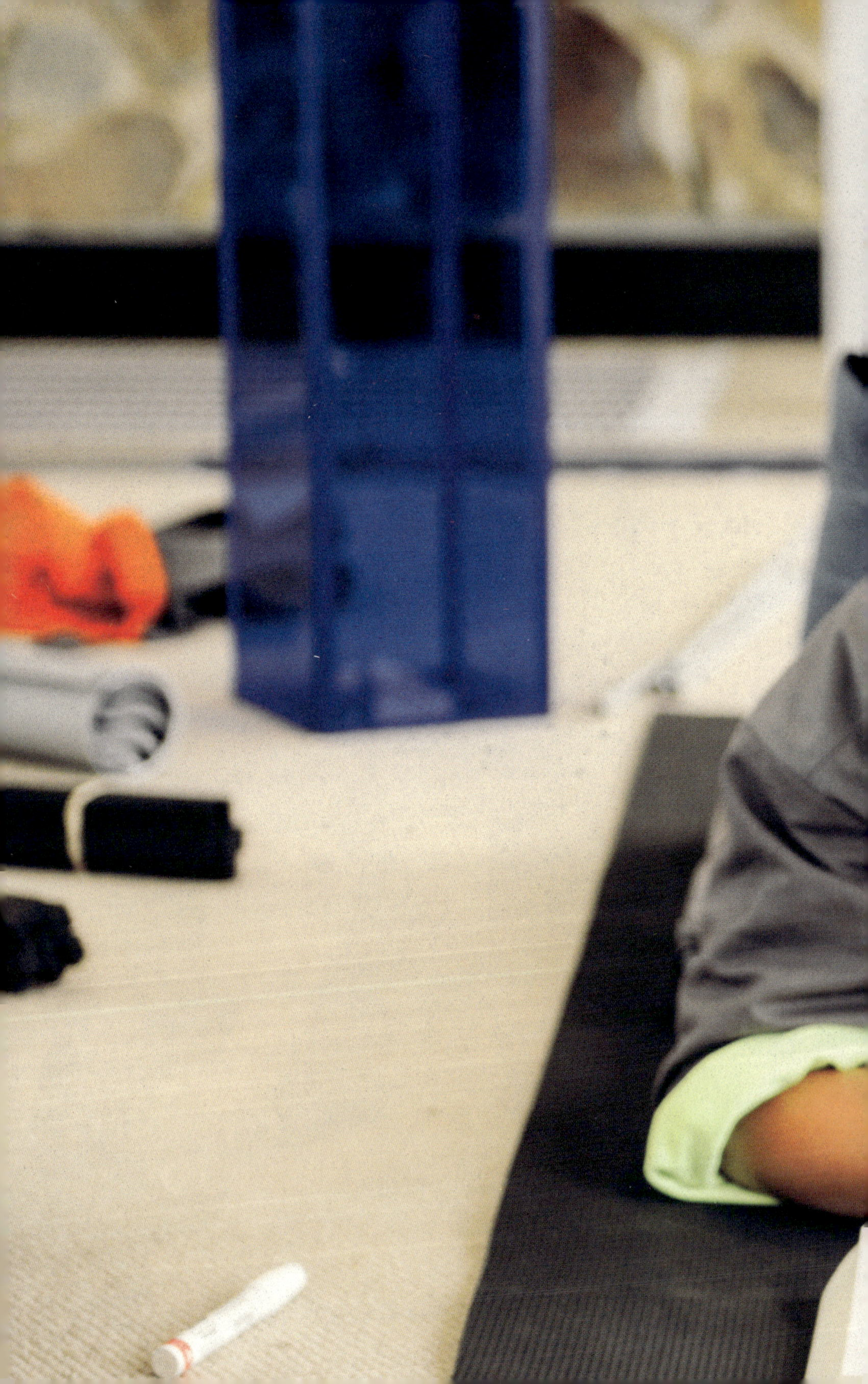

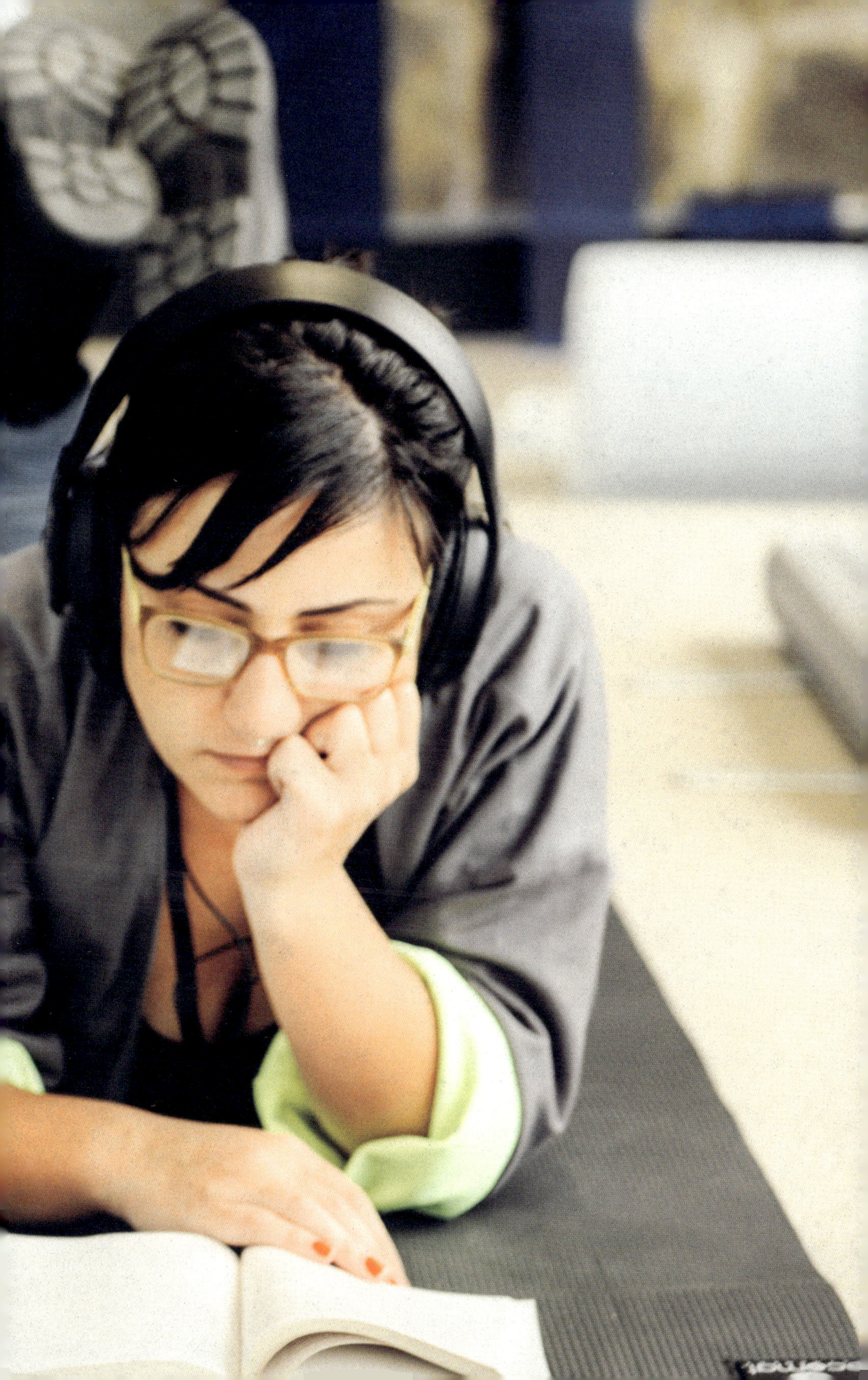

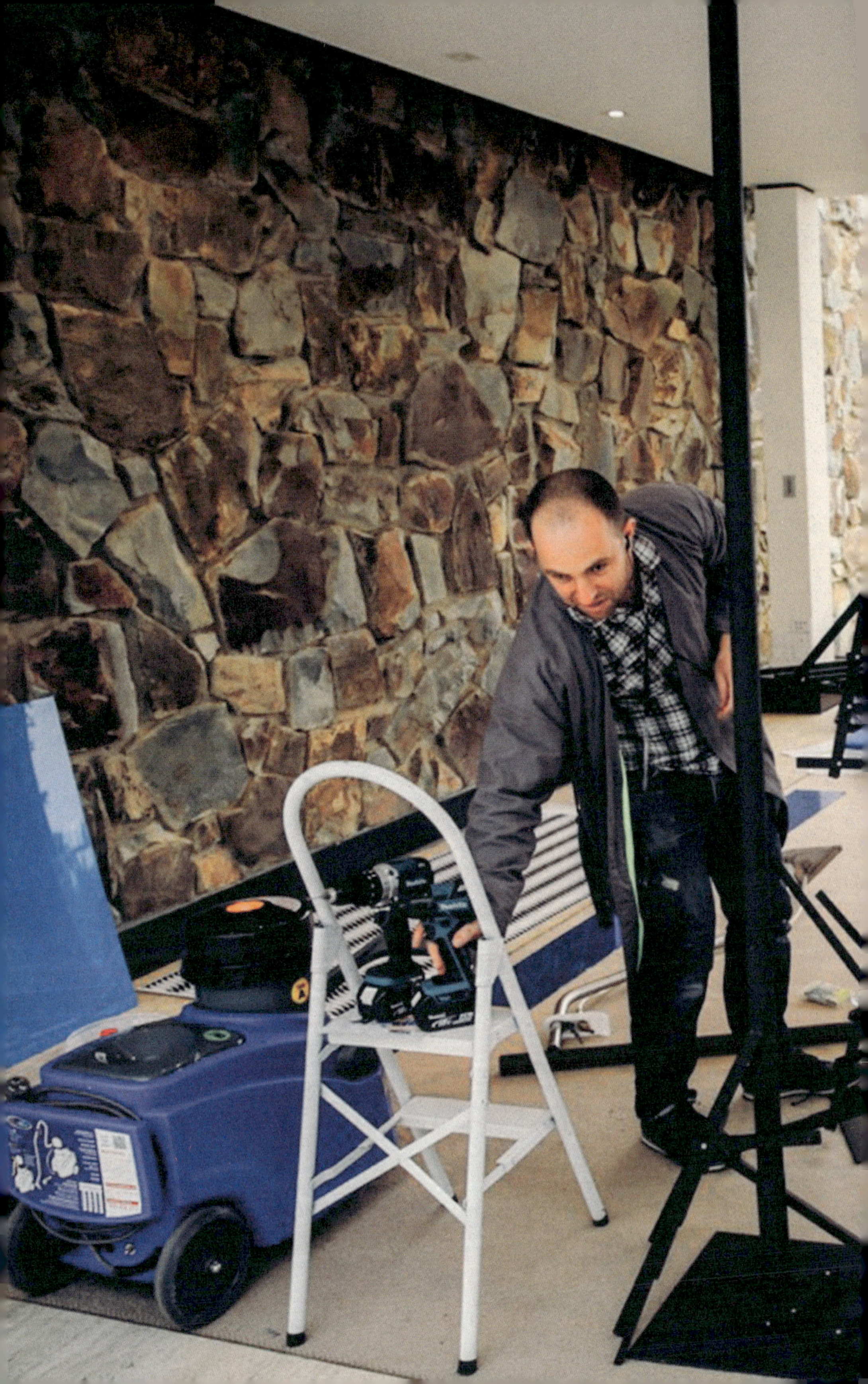

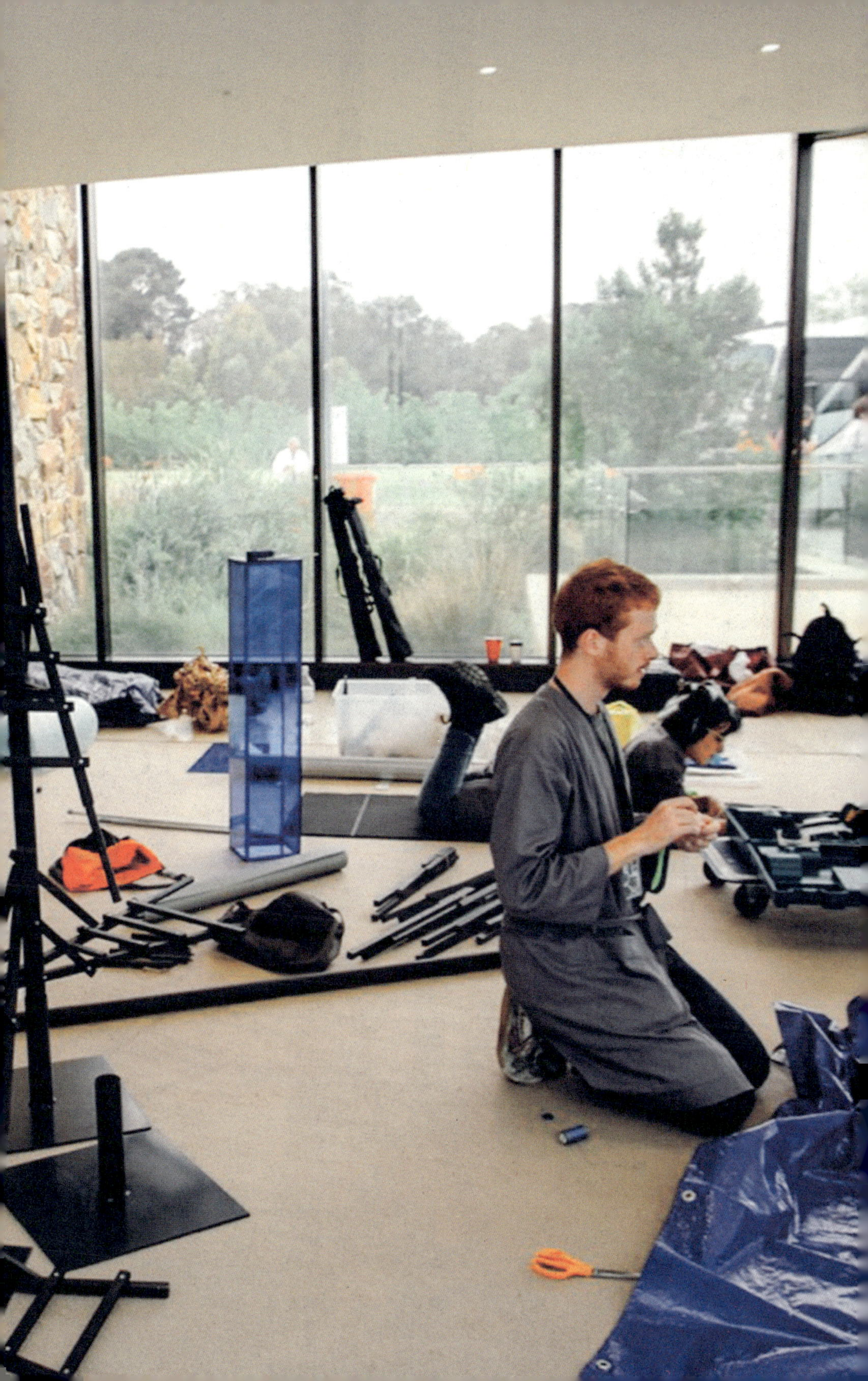

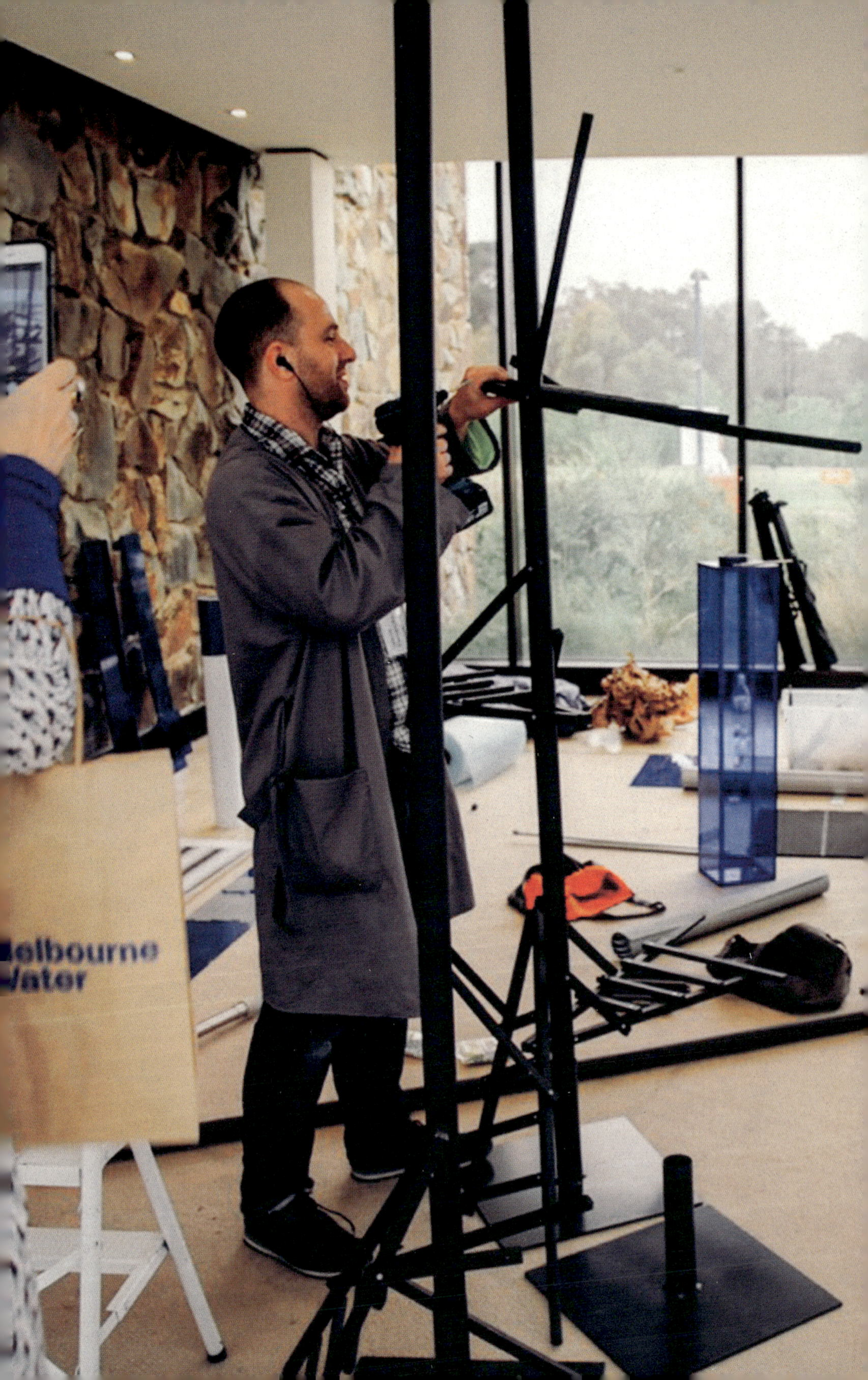
elbourne
Water

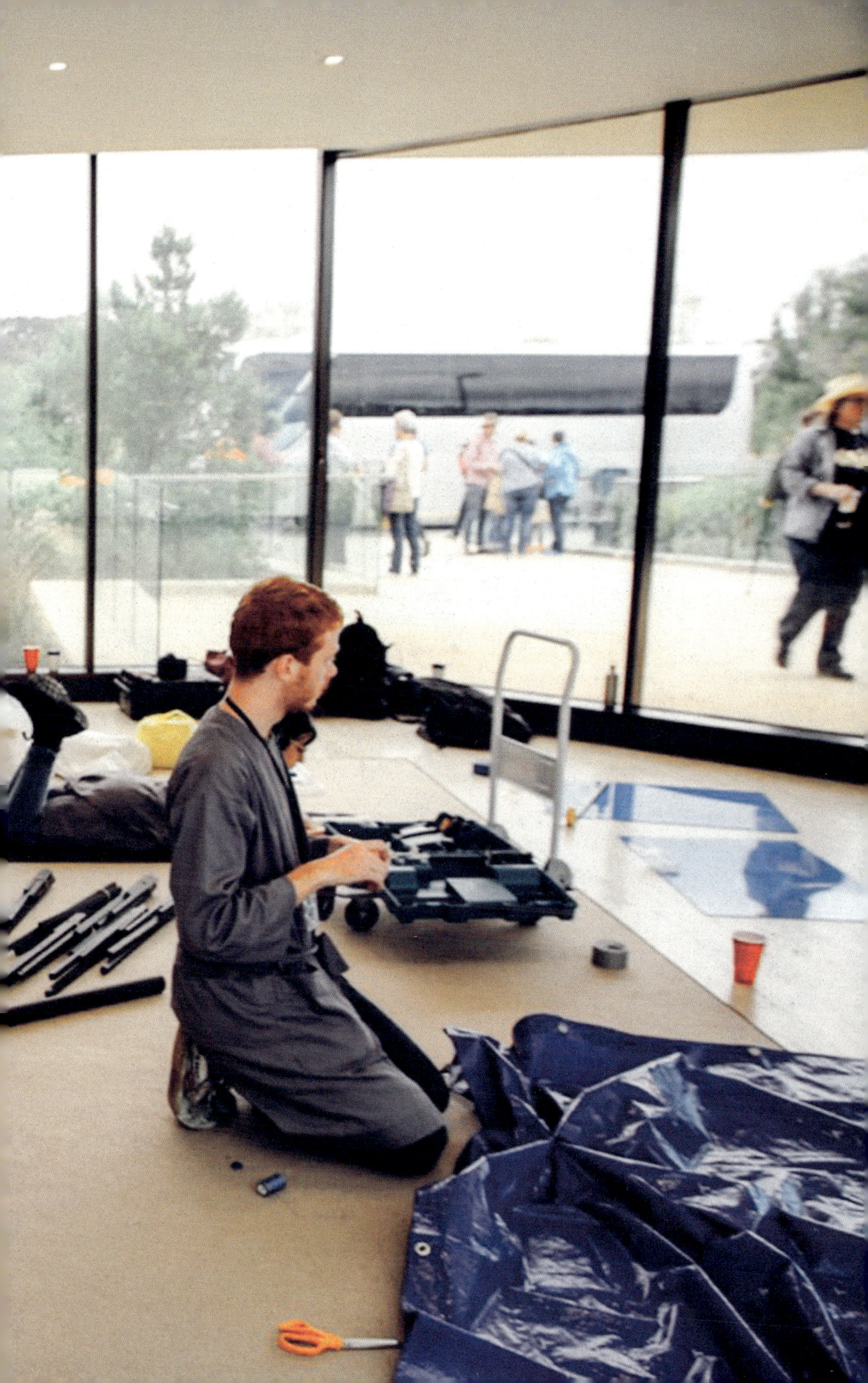

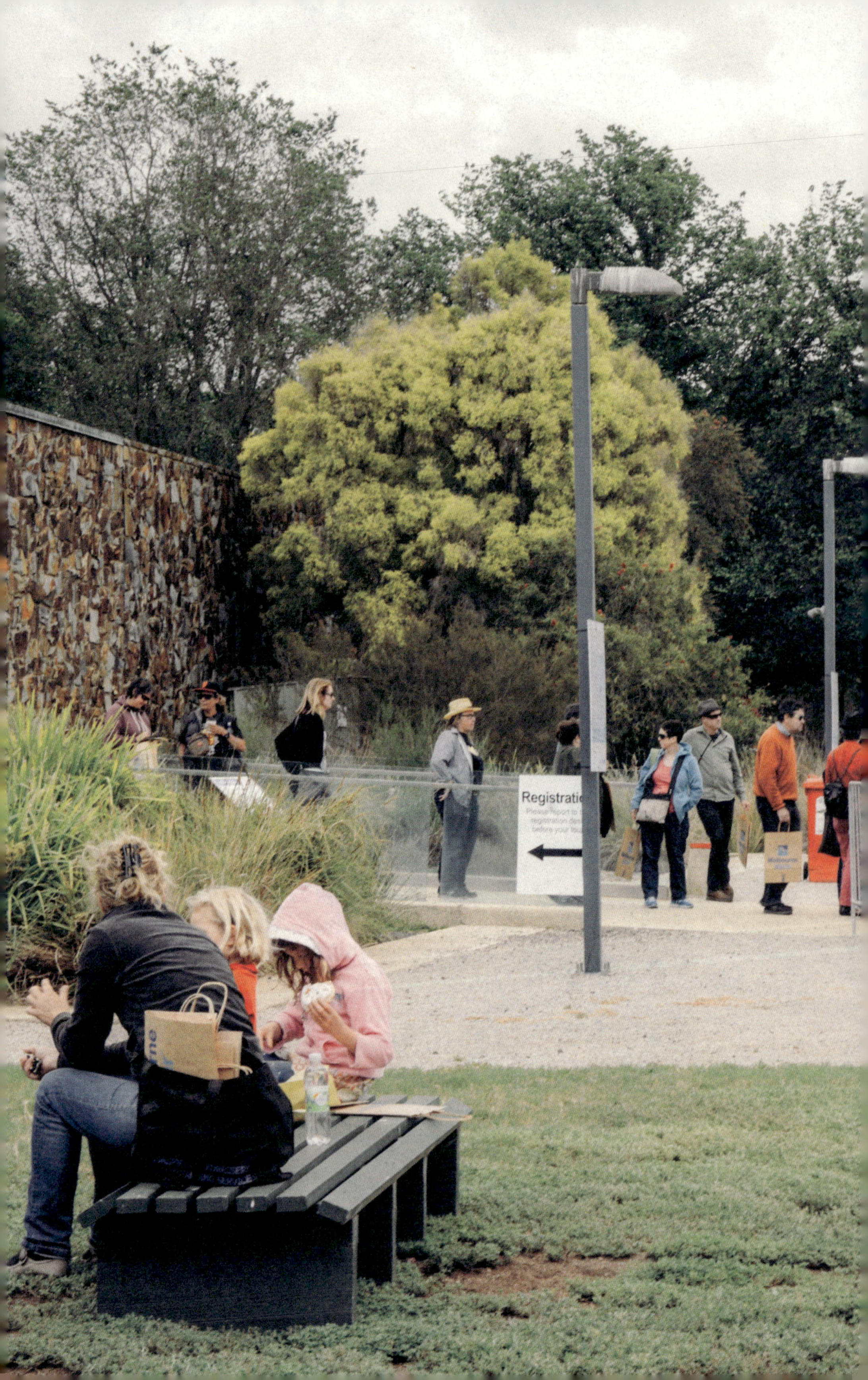

Registratio

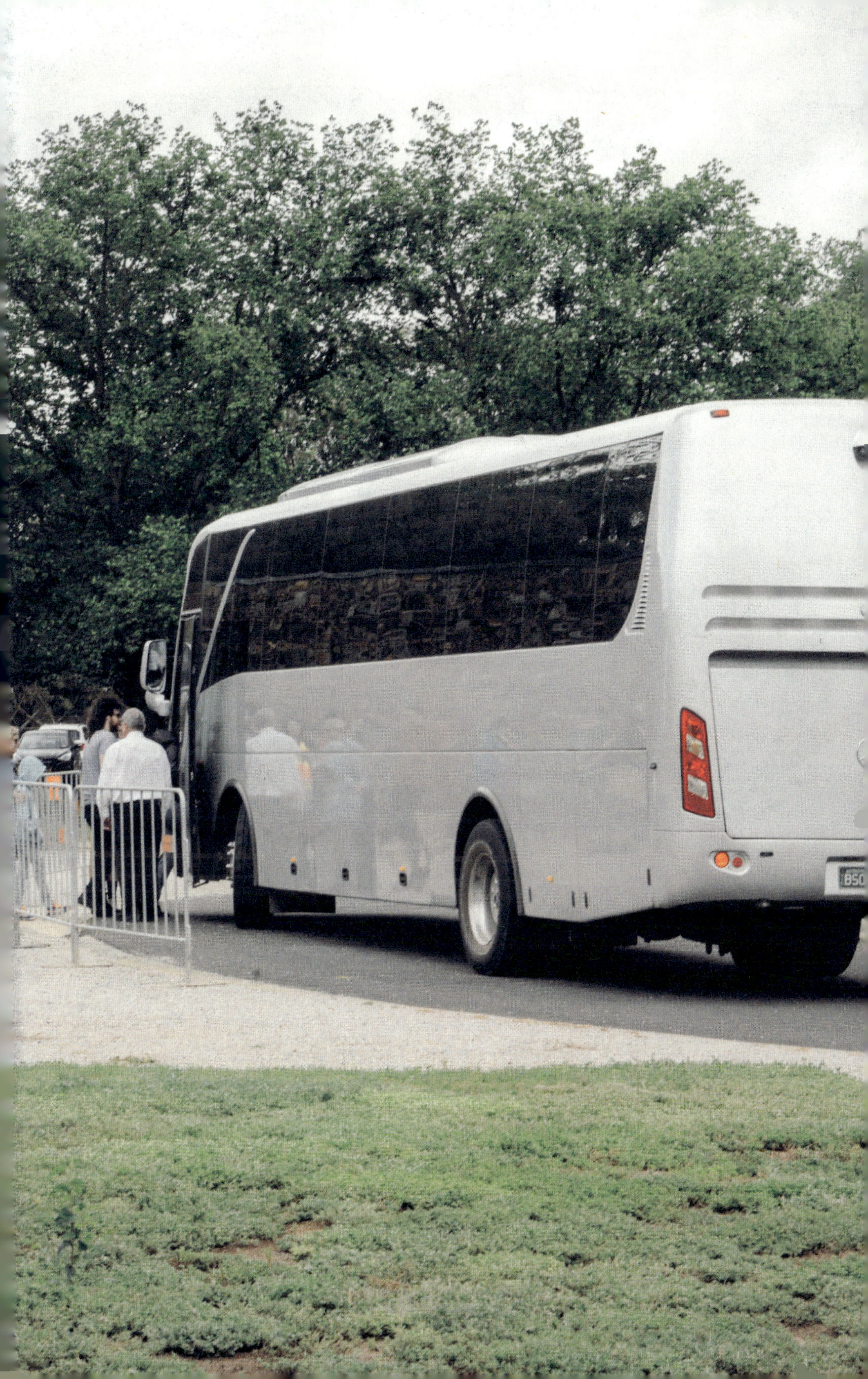

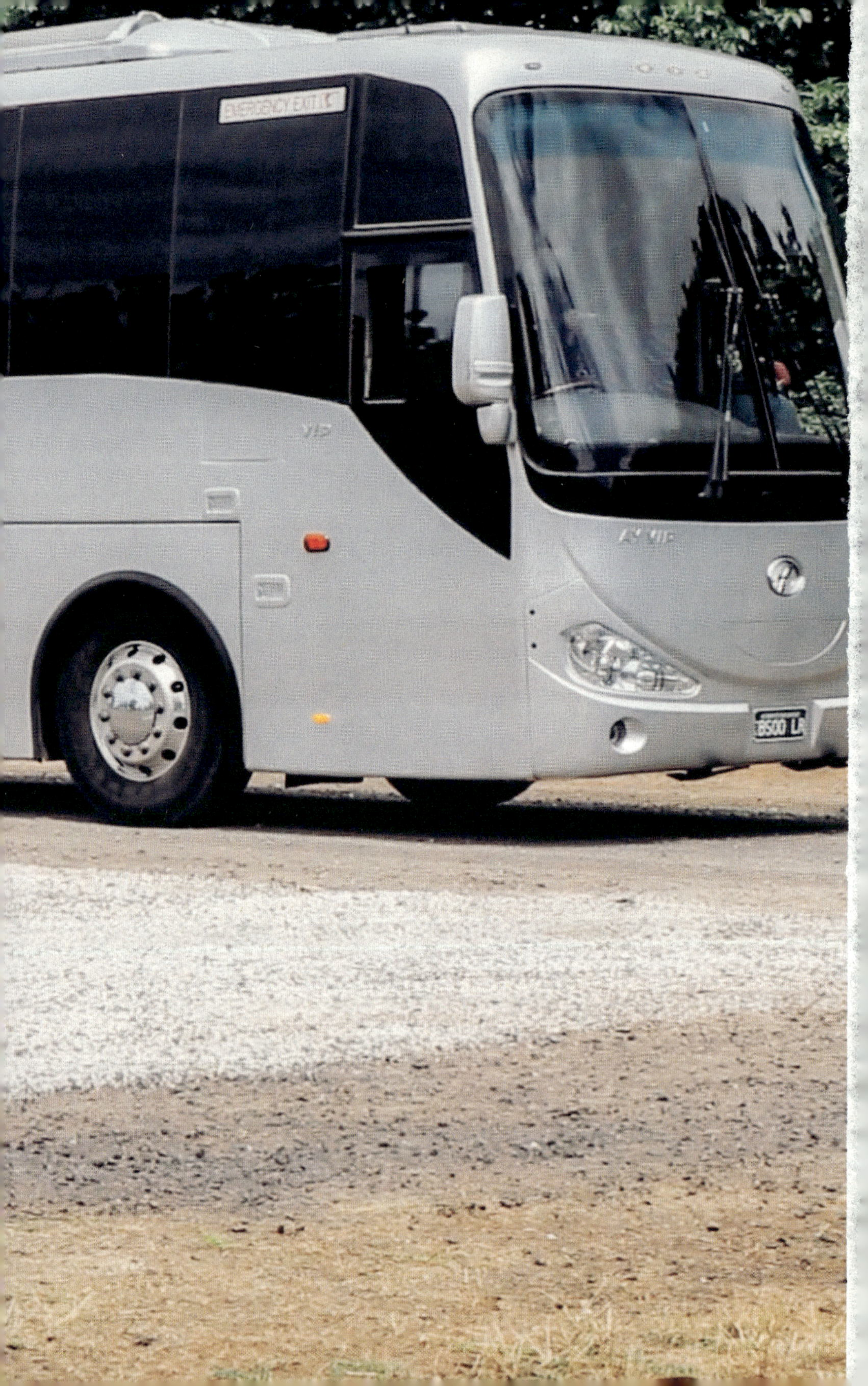
EMERGENCY EXIT

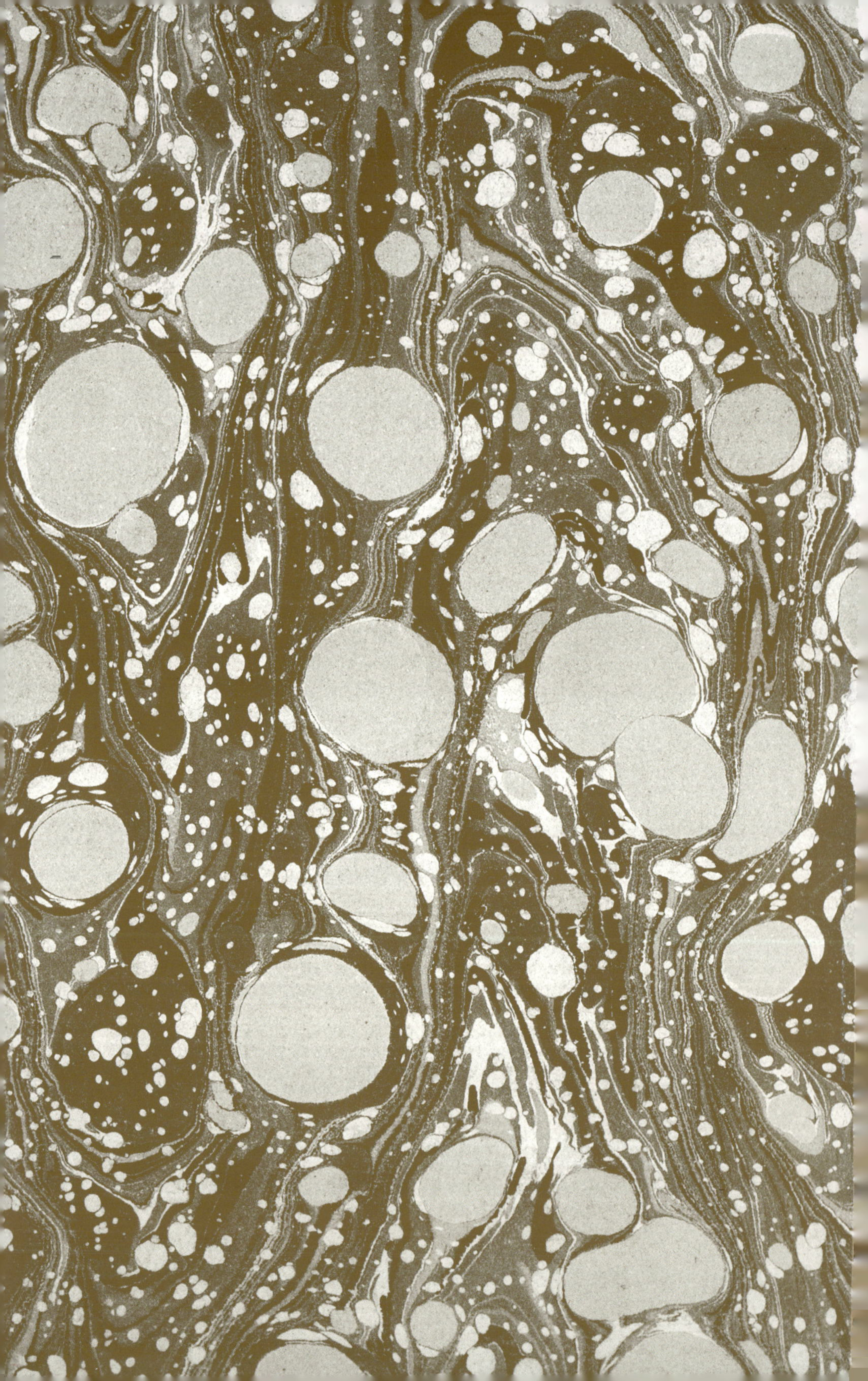